SCHOOL
LEADERSHIP

FOURTH EDITION

Stuart C. Smith • Philip K. Piele

Foreword by Joseph Murphy

SCHOOL LEADERSHIP

Handbook for Excellence in Student Learning

FOURTH EDITION

CORWIN PRESS
A SAGE Publications Company
Thousand Oaks, California

For information:

Corwin Press
A Sage Publications Company
2455 Teller Road
Thousand Oaks, California 91320
www.corwinpress.com

Sage Publications Ltd.
1 Oliver's Yard
55 City Road
London EC1Y 1SP
United Kingdom

Sage Publications India Pvt. Ltd.
B-42, Panchsheel Enclave
Post Box 4109
New Delhi 110 017 India

Printed in the United States of America

Library of Congress Cataloging-in-Publication Data

School leadership : handbook for excellence in student learning / edited by Stuart C. Smith and Philip K. Piele; foreword by Joseph Murphy.—4th ed.
        p. cm.
Includes bibliographical references and index.
ISBN 1-4129-3653-5 (cloth)—ISBN 1-4129-3654-3 (pbk.)
    1. School management and organization—Handbooks, manuals, etc. 2. Educational leadership—Handbooks, manuals, etc. I. Smith, Stuart Carl, 1944- II. Piele, Philip K.
LB2801.A1S34 2006
371.2—dc22   2005037811

This book is printed on acid-free paper.

06   07   08   09   10   10 9 8 7 6 5 4 3 2 1

Acquisitions Editor:	Elizabeth Brenkus
Editorial Assistant:	Desirée Enayati
Production Editor:	Laureen A. Shea
Copy Editor:	Julie Gwin
Typesetter:	C&M Digitals (P) Ltd.
Proofreader:	Caryne Brown
Indexer:	Michael Ferreira
Cover Designer:	Lisa Miller

Contents

PART IV. THE STRUCTURE

PART VI. THE SKILLS

Foreword

For much of the last quarter century, educators, policymakers, and the general citizenry have been engaged in an unbroken quest to understand the school-improvement equation. That is, there have been ongoing efforts, sometimes systematic and often ad hoc, to identify the factors that explain school performance and student achievement and to deepen our understanding of how they work both as individual components and as parts of the system of schooling.

Research over these years has consistently underscored leadership as a critical theme in the school-improvement narrative. Indeed, evidence from nearly every realm of investigation—beginning with effective-school studies through the most recent work on comprehensive school reform—confirms leadership as an explanatory variable in schools where all students meet ambitious achievement targets.

Over that time, our understanding of leadership has deepened and become more complex. We have rediscovered a central truth of leadership: Although leadership is always important, during periods of fundamental transition (for example, to a new system of schooling in which all youngsters are to be well educated) and hardship (for example, nurturing troubled schools into healthy organizations), leadership is even more critical. We have learned about the centrality of instructionally focused leadership and the importance of transformationally anchored leadership work. We have also learned that leadership is as much a property of the school and its culture as it is a dimension of administrative roles. We have greatly expanded the information base on the knowledge and skills that define the various aspects of leadership, such as visionary and cultural leadership.

And it is here, in Smith and Piele's fourth edition of their hallmark volume on *School Leadership*, that these understandings are thoughtfully captured and carefully arrayed for maximum usefulness by school leaders at all levels of the educational system. Although it is impossible to enumerate all the strengths of this landmark analysis, several points merit special notice. The authors devour huge chunks of the knowledge landscape on leadership, in terms of both scientific and practice-based learning. But equally important, they are masters of integration and presentation.

The overall framework for the book works especially well on these issues. The six parts of the book provide excellent scaffolding and warehousing for what we know, and are continuing to learn, about school leadership. In addition, the individual chapters are finely crafted and beautifully written. Difficult concepts and complex ideas are made accessible without trivializing important content. School leaders of all stripes (principals, teacher-leaders, district office staff, staff-development professionals) will resonate to the way this volume is constructed. All will find that it quite nicely accomplishes what handbooks are expected to do, that is, provide a tool that allows readers to regularly return to the knowledge base as information is needed.

Smith and Piele and their colleagues have taken on a massive assignment and pulled it off with considerable success. In so doing, they provide us with the most comprehensive and extensive treatment of the school leadership literature available to date. In the process, they help us tune in to and then stay focused on the most central leadership issues in education today. They provide a research-based platform for leadership for the 21st century. They help us understand that leadership is about both the person and the organization, that it is both an art and a science, that leadership practice is anchored in both knowledge and values, that leadership flows both from the organization and from the consent of others, and that our understanding of leadership is informed by both practice and scientific research.

The authors build our understanding of school leadership outward from student learning. They help us see that the ground or anchor for school leadership today must be the core business of schooling, not only the management, organization, and governance of that business. For all these reasons, and many more, Smith and Piele have provided a great service to the profession. Their *School Leadership* handbook is a gift to all of us in education.

Joseph Murphy
Professor of Education
Department of Leadership, Policy and Organizations
Peabody College
Vanderbilt University

Preface

With this fourth edition, *School Leadership* marks its 25th anniversary. We compiled the first edition of this handbook in 1981, after principals, superintendents, and other administrators told us of their need for practical information that would help them lead more effectively.

School leaders responded with eagerness to that handbook and to the subsequent two editions, confirming the need for a readable synthesis of research findings and best practices. Many administrators have told us they consult the handbook regularly, and the book also has been widely used as a text in the preservice and inservice training of school leaders throughout the country.

This latest edition emphasizes the school leader's role as a champion of student learning. In recent years, school leaders have had to cope with both new licensure standards focused on student learning and new expectations for student achievement in state and federal legislation, especially the No Child Left Behind Act. The book's new subtitle, *Handbook for Excellence in Student Learning,* signals our intent to make this edition a resource for leaders to succeed in this new environment.

Evidence now clearly shows that principals can make a real difference in student learning, and they do not have to return to the classroom for face-to-face interaction with students to make it happen. Their influence on academic learning is indirect yet significant, exerted through a set of key leadership behaviors that create the right kind of conditions in their schools for effective instruction and learning to occur. The benefit of this handbook is that it shows principals how to excel in those behaviors so they can make the most of their impact on students' academic success.

This new and expanded edition draws from the growing knowledge base on educational leadership to help school leaders meet the challenge of making sure all their students learn.

The theme of leadership for learning gave us the rationale to expand the book from its previous 15 chapters to 19. Coverage of instructional leadership, for example, grew from one chapter in previous editions to three in this one, and other new chapters likewise emphasize this theme. As authors revised or completely rewrote preexisting chapters, they gave added attention to how leadership affects student learning.

At the beginning of the book, we added two chapters in a new part, "The State of School Leadership." The first chapter provides an overview of issues surrounding the principalship, and the second summarizes research findings on the effects of leadership.

In addition to the five new chapters on instructional leadership and the state of leadership, six new chapters address topics that have risen in prominence since the previous edition appeared:

- Accountable Leadership
- Distributed Leadership
- Political Leadership
- Engaging the Public
- Managing Data for Decision Making: Creating Knowledge From Information
- Allocating Human, Financial, and Physical Resources

To make room for these new chapters, we were able to carry over only eight chapters from the previous edition, and these have undergone varying degrees of revision, some at the hands of new authors.

HOW THIS BOOK WAS WRITTEN

The purpose of this book is not necessarily to present new views or the authors' views of leadership. The chapter authors are free to express their opinions, but their primary mission is to summarize and explain a large body of literature with which educational leaders want and need to be familiar.

A perusal of the original sources cited in the references makes it apparent that no busy administrator or student has time to read all these books and articles. To make these important works easily accessible, the authors have tried to present the best ideas briefly and succinctly. This technique of distilling the most useful and important ideas is called "information analysis."

The authors of this book are more than mere translators of information and ideas. They also attempt to synthesize information, to show how theories and ideas are connected, and to resolve conflicting views. Several chapters in this edition also benefit from the expertise of academicians and educational practitioners who bring a lifetime of learning and professional wisdom to their topics.

Perhaps the most important kind of information synthesis in this book is the integration of theory and practice. Many books explain leadership theories, and many others are concerned with the "how-to" of leadership practice. Practitioners complain that the theoretical writing is not useful in their everyday work, and researchers and theoreticians look askance at "practical" works whose ideas and suggestions are not empirically validated.

Practitioners perceive that researchers and theoreticians are too isolated from the real problems of schools, that theories validated in laboratory settings may disintegrate in actual classrooms. Researchers and theoreticians argue that recommendations validated by the experience of only one administrator or one school are much too subjective to be useful to others.

Few books try to integrate these two competing views. This book tries to present the most useful aspects of theory along with the most thoughtful recommendations for action.

A synthesis of the two, especially in areas where findings agree, can avoid many of the problems inherent in each method alone. The book also contains ideas from practitioners within the field.

The numerous citations in this book are representative and by no means inclusive of all literature in the field of school leadership. We encourage our readers, as they have time, to conduct their own searches of literature on topics of interest and apply their own analytic skills to the information they find.

INTENDED AUDIENCE

The handbook is written primarily for school-based and central-office educators in administrative and leadership positions at all levels from kindergarten through Grade 12. Principals, assistant principals, teacher-leaders, staff-development personnel, superintendents, and other educators can use the handbook as a reference when particular issues arise. They can also turn to it on a regular basis for knowledge and insight that can help them grow in their leadership skills and effectiveness.

Those who aspire to leadership roles in education will gain knowledge of both the tasks and processes of leadership and the cultural and organizational context of schooling in which they will exercise their leadership.

Instructors in leadership training programs will find that this edition, even more than previous editions, exposes their students to a comprehensive set of leadership issues, dilemmas, challenges, and questions to stimulate their thinking and reflection and to prepare them for effective practice. Students in leadership preparation programs will appreciate not only the handbook's rich content but also its accessible style and structure.

METHOD OF CITATION

To enhance readability, the book adheres to a sparse reference style. We avoid footnotes and try to keep the text uncluttered by parenthetical citation data. When citing a published work in a chapter for the first time, we merely give the author's full name, without a date or page numbers. Subsequent citations to the same work usually mention only the author's last name. To distinguish between multiple publications by a single author, we add dates (sometimes in parentheses) or use other conventions in the text to clearly indicate which title is being cited.

References are listed alphabetically, grouped by chapter at the back of the book in the reference section. For those readers who want to explore a topic further, these ample references are an ideal starting place.

Note that citations in the text include authors' full names, just as they appear in the works cited. This preference is contrary to the use in much of the academic press of only initials for first and middle names, a practice we consider both dehumanizing and impractical in the age of Internet searching. (Try to do a Google search for M. M. Johnson, for example, and compare your results with those for Marlene M. Johnson.)

SCOPE AND ORGANIZATION

This volume looks at school leadership from five perspectives: the person, the values, the structure, the mission, and the skills. In addition, two chapters in Part I, "The State of School Leadership," provide an overview of the position of the principal in today's schools and of what research tells us about the effects of educational leadership. Both chapters in Part I are new in this edition.

Three chapters in Part II, "The Person," provide something of a theoretical background. These chapters answer several key questions: What characteristics do leaders exhibit? Which leadership styles and strategies seem to work best in which circumstances? How are school leaders inducted into their positions, and how do they grow as professionals?

The first two chapters in this part have been updated with new content, and the third chapter (formerly on training and selection of leaders) has been rewritten with a focus on leadership development.

The three chapters in Part III, "The Values," deal with the foundation of ethics, vision, and values that give moral purpose and substance to the practice of school leadership. What are the leader's ethical responsibilities? Why is vision vital to the leader, and how is it grasped? How can the leader help construct a prolearning culture in his or her school?

The first two chapters in this part are revisions, and the third, "Cultural Leadership," replaces the previous edition's chapter with the same title.

Four chapters in Part IV, "The Structure," take a look at the organizational and political systems or support structures that underlie school leadership. These chapters examine the framework of accountability, the balance of authority between the central office and the school site, the distribution of leadership functions among the school staff, and the political context of school leadership.

These chapters, all of which are new or completely rewritten for this edition, concern structures and management systems that can make good educational leadership possible—or impossible.

Because of the heightened interest in leadership for learning, instructional leadership is now the subject of three new chapters, in Part V, "The Mission: Student Learning." These chapters give school leaders an authoritative guide to research-based methods of supporting the learning process, monitoring learners' progress, and cultivating a learning-focused community.

The chapters in Part VI, "The Skills," highlight the abilities needed by administrators to be effective leaders in education today. This part of the volume looks at such essential skills as how to communicate verbally and in writing; how to engage stakeholders in the community for the support of schools and learning; how to display data for decisions about school improvement; and how to allocate human, financial, and physical resources for optimum support of learning.

The chapters on use of data and resource allocation are new in this edition. The chapters on communication and community engagement (formerly "coalition building") were rewritten in entirety.

Finally, after each chapter, we added "Reflections," which are action points or questions to help readers put the ideas into practice. In classroom settings, instructors can use the questions to stimulate discussion about the chapters' major themes.

The book's writing and editorial style aim for clarity and precision. Each chapter is a straightforward exposition of ideas and evidence on the topic, free of jargon and technical data.

This book is called a handbook because it is designed to be used as a reference when particular problems and concerns arise as well as to be read straight through. Readers concerned about vision or political leverage or the advantages of different leadership strategies can turn directly to the appropriate chapters for the information they are seeking without reading the previous chapters. It is a book to be sampled, to be digested slowly, and to be turned to again and again as leaders grow in their skills and effectiveness.

As the lineup of chapters indicates, this handbook distills an increasingly robust body of research on school leadership. In offering this latest edition to you, we are therefore more confident than ever that you will find within these pages the counsel necessary to help your staff, your students, and yourself succeed.

We welcome your comments and suggestions, as well as feedback on how this book has helped you perform and grow as a leader. Contact us at stusmith@uoregon.edu and ppiele@uoregon.edu.

Acknowledgments

M any people deserve credit for bringing this book to fruition, and foremost are the talented and learned chapter authors.

The only author, besides one of the editors, who contributed to both the previous and current editions is Larry Lashway, a senior research analyst for the ERIC Clearinghouse on Educational Management until it closed and now for the Clearinghouse on Educational Policy and Management (CEPM).

Specializing in leadership issues, Larry writes with exceptional clarity and turns in drafts that excel in both substance and style. His many bylines in this edition attest as well to his remarkable productivity and wide range of interests. Larry has earned our deepest gratitude, for this book simply wouldn't exist without his sizable contribution.

Another accomplished research analyst who had worked under contract with the ERIC Clearinghouse wrote three chapters. Wendell Anderson specializes in communication, and his expertise as a communicator is evident to everyone who reads his work. Wendell is a conscientious and productive writer whose attention to detail and ability to meet deadlines earned our heartfelt gratitude.

We were confident this edition would achieve our goal of helping leaders more effectively serve students' academic needs when Dr. Ronald Beghetto accepted our invitation to write an entire part on instructional leadership. Ron's academic background and his applied work with schools ideally qualify him to show principals and other educators how, in practical terms, to support the learning process, monitor students' progress, and establish a learning community. Thanks to Ron and his colleagues Julie Alonzo and Dr. Leanne R. Ketterlin-Geller, readers of this volume now have more detailed and expert guidance in their efforts to lead their schools to instructional excellence.

We are likewise delighted to welcome Dr. Faith Crampton and her coauthor Randall S. Vesely to these pages. Faith's gifts as a scholar and policy analyst first impressed us when she taught at the beginning of her career at the University of Oregon's (UO's) College of Education. Randall's experience as a school administrator adds an evident practical relevance to their chapter. The talents and backgrounds of both these authors are on display in their concise and authoritative presentation of the research on allocation of human, financial, and physical resources.

Three current colleagues of ours at the UO's College of Education wrote what is, in our estimation, the most remarkable chapter in this volume. Our plan for this edition from the beginning included a new chapter on data-based decision making. What we did not expect was the innovative, step-by-step guide to use of graphic displays of students' performance data that came from Dr. Gerald Tindal, Luke Duesbery, and Dr. Leanne R. Ketterlin-Geller. We are indeed grateful to Jerry, whose many accomplishments and expertise in large-scale testing have earned him national recognition, and his coauthors for this chapter showing school leaders how displays of data can inform their decisions about the instructional program.

In addition to these current contributors, credit must go to several writers who labored on past editions. This fourth edition, built as it is on the structure and content of preceding editions, owes much of its conceptual foundation to those who analyzed earlier generations of the research literature. One of the clearinghouse's most accomplished research analysts, who helped pioneer this book as a coeditor of its first edition, is JoAnn Mazzarella, whose name still appears in the byline of Chapter 3, "Portrait of a Leader." Another name in that same byline is Thomas Grundy, who updated that chapter for a previous edition.

We are especially thankful and proud to have another name on this book's cover. Professor Joseph Murphy, who knows the field of school leadership as few others do, graciously wrote the eloquent foreword to this edition, and we hope this book lives up to his kind and generous words.

Matt Bauman, in charge of CEPM's publications sales, provided necessary clerical and logistical support. Credit also is due to Anna Smith, the lead editor's daughter, for her help with citations.

We thank our good friend Tom Koerner, former director of publications for the National Association of Secondary School Principals, for his many kind remarks about this book over the years and for encouraging us to undertake another edition.

Finally, the ERIC Clearinghouse having closed, this book was without a publisher. Our search led eventually to Corwin Press and a warm welcome by Acquisitions Editor Lizzie Brenkus, whose professional wisdom and advice added substantial value to what you now hold. We also thank copy editor Julie Gwin for imparting consistency of style, no easy task for a book this size.

Corwin Press gratefully acknowledges the contributions of the following individuals:

Sara Armstrong, Educational Consultant
Sara Armstrong Consulting
Berkeley, CA

John Casper, Supervisor of Instruction
Nelson County Public Schools
Bardstown, KY

Ginnie Drouin, Principal
Alfred Elementary School
Alfred, ME

John Enloe, Director of Student Services
Sevier County Board of Education
Sevierville, TN

Cynthia Lemmerman, Superintendent
Fostoria Community Schools
Fostoria, OH

Teri Marcos, Director of MA in Educational Leadership/Tier I PASC
Azusa Pacific University
Azusa, CA

Joen Painter, Educational Consultant
Yuma, AZ

Richard Yee, Principal
Oster Elementary School
San Jose, CA

About the Editors

Stuart C. Smith is associate director of the Clearinghouse on Educational Policy and Management, College of Education, University of Oregon. He directed the publications program of the ERIC Clearinghouse on Educational Management from 1967 until its close in 2003 and was editor of the Oregon School Study Council from 1980 to 1997.

Mr. Smith developed the method of information analysis that was used in the ERIC Clearinghouse's numerous books and other publications, several of which won Distinguished Achievement Awards from the Educational Press Association of America and APEX Awards for Publication Excellence.

During his tenure at the ERIC Clearinghouse, Mr. Smith formulated cooperative ventures and relationships with many organizations and agencies to advance the quality of information available through the ERIC system. His publications have focused on educational leadership, school culture, collaborative bargaining, and cooperation among teachers and administrators on school improvement.

Philip K. Piele is professor emeritus and director of the Clearinghouse on Educational Policy and Management and former head of the Department of Educational Leadership, Technology, and Administration in the College of Education at the University of Oregon. He also directed the ERIC Clearinghouse on Educational Management from 1969 to 2003.

A member of the University of Oregon faculty from 1968 to 2005, Professor Piele taught courses on educational law, economics of education, and education information systems. He is the author of numerous books, monographs, and journal articles and has delivered papers on educational information systems at international conferences in several European and Asian countries.

Piele was a visiting scholar at Stanford University; a visiting professor at the Ontario Institute for the Study of Education, University of Toronto; and a visiting lecturer at several major Australian universities. He is the past president of two national professional organizations and is listed in *Who's Who in America* and *Who's Who in the World.*

About the Contributors

Julie Alonzo is earning her PhD in educational leadership with a specialization in learning assessment and systems performance at the University of Oregon. Her primary research interests include teacher professional development and the meaningful inclusion of students with diverse learning needs.

Wendell Anderson is a former community college English and writing instructor. He is now a freelance educational writer and editor, and the owner of NorthStar Writing & Editing in Eugene, Oregon. His work has appeared in a variety of educational, trade, and popular publications.

Ronald A. Beghetto is an assistant professor in the area of teacher education at the University of Oregon. He received his PhD in educational psychology from Indiana University. His research examines the influence of teacher beliefs and practices on student learning, motivation, and creativity. He has authored more than 25 articles, book chapters, and reports. His recent work has appeared in a variety of scholarly journals and edited volumes, including *Journal of Educational Research, Creativity Research Journal, Educational Psychologist, Journal of Creative Behavior,* and *Creativity and Reason in Cognitive Development.*

Faith E. Crampton is associate professor and head of the Department of Educational Organizations and Leadership at the University of Wisconsin–Milwaukee, where she specializes in education finance, policy, and the economics of education. She received her PhD in educational policy and leadership from The Ohio State University. Her primary research focus is state education funding policy. She is the author of numerous refereed journal articles, many of which have appeared in the *Journal of Education Finance,* and of several influential policy analyses, such as *Principles of a Sound State School Finance System.*

Luke Duesbery is a licensed administrator earning his PhD in educational leadership with a specialization in assessment at the University of Oregon. His primary research interests include measurement, data systems, and accommodations in assessment.

Editors' Note: In addition to the authors listed here, one chapter's byline includes two research analysts, JoAnn Mazzarella and Thomas Grundy, who contributed to previous editions. As has been the practice in past editions, whenever a chapter is updated by another writer, all the authors' names appear.

Leanne R. Ketterlin-Geller earned a PhD in learning assessment and systems performance in the area of educational leadership at the University of Oregon. Currently, she serves as a visiting assistant professor and as the director of research projects for Behavioral Research and Teaching at the University of Oregon. Her research focuses on issues related to the measurement of academic achievement.

Larry Lashway resides in Olympia, Washington, where he is a program specialist with the Office of the Superintendent of Public Instruction. A longtime teacher educator, he has also worked for Washington State University and has directed the Teacher Leadership program at Silver Lake College, Manitowoc, Wisconsin.

Gerald Tindal is professor and director of the Behavioral Research and Teaching unit as well as head of the area of educational leadership at the College of Education, University of Oregon. He teaches courses and conducts research on measurement systems for general- and special-education teachers and administrators. His work focuses primarily on large-scale assessment, curriculum-based measurement, and secondary content knowledge. He is the recipient of numerous large research grants and contracts from the U.S. Department of Education and the Oregon Department of Education.

Randall S. Vesely is a doctoral candidate in the Urban Education Doctoral Program at the University of Wisconsin–Milwaukee and a secondary school administrator in Racine, Wisconsin. His areas of specialization are educational leadership and school finance.

Introduction

Leadership for Excellence in Learning

E ach time we begin work on a new edition of this book, our first task is to ascertain the extent to which the theory and practice of school leadership have evolved since we last assessed the field. In the eight or nine years between editions, change is inevitable in a field that seems to be in perpetual reform mode. Of course, school leaders drive much of this reform themselves, because as conscientious professionals who care deeply about their schools, they continually seek to improve their practice.

An assessment of the field's progress during the past decade leaves no doubt that several external forces have been the major drivers of change. Much of the current reform push comes from states and the federal government, whose mandates can suddenly rearrange educators' priorities.

Demographic shifts and economic cycles also leave telltale marks on schools, and leaders must cope with the accompanying challenges. Even new technologies can add to the principal's set of responsibilities, of course with the promise, seemingly never quite fulfilled, that they will make the job in some way easier.

Those factors alone, however, cannot account for the extraordinary degree of change in this field since the previous edition appeared in 1997.

The most significant trend in school leadership over the past decade—and the reason for this book's new subtitle—has been the coalescing of attention on what is now unmistakably the profession's top priority: the need to improve student learning. For all of today's educational leaders, but especially principals, the work centers on enhancing learning opportunities for all children.

THE MISSION IS STUDENT LEARNING

The current emphasis on student learning owes much to the efforts of a variety of stakeholders, acting with a single-mindedness seldom before seen. Perhaps the most significant agent of change has been the standards for principals that the Interstate School Leaders Licensure Consortium (ISLLC) approved at the end of 1996. The theme of the standards is evident in the first of seven ISLLC principles: "Standards should reflect the centrality of student learning" (Council of Chief State School Officers).

The consortium's chair, Joseph Murphy, stated that the "goal has been to generate a critical mass of energy to move school administration out of its 100-year orbit and to reposition the profession around leadership for learning." Through the consortium's partnerships with states, professional associations, universities, private firms, and other groups, the standards have become widely embedded in principal preparation programs, licensure, professional development, and evaluation. According to Murphy:

> The consortium maintains that the Standards for School Leaders—and the intellectual pillars on which they rest—provide the means to shift the metric of school administration from management to educational leadership and from administration to learning while linking management and behavioral science knowledge to the larger goal of student learning.

Another agent of change arose in 2001, when the federal government, following a decade of efforts by states to toughen academic standards, imposed its own blueprint. The No Child Left Behind Act, in the U.S. Department of Education's words:

> embodies four key principles—stronger accountability for results; greater flexibility for states, school districts and schools in the use of federal funds; more choices for parents of children from disadvantaged backgrounds; and an emphasis on teaching methods that have been demonstrated to work.

In a synthesis of research on educational leadership, Kenneth A. Leithwood and Carolyn Riehl note the changed landscape of educational accountability:

> Pressure is on actors at all levels, from students themselves to teachers, principals, and superintendents. In these times of heightened concern for student learning, school leaders are being held accountable for how well teachers teach and how much students learn.

Amid all this daunting pressure, present and prospective school leaders at least can take heart from another development in recent years. While school leaders are performing their jobs in a constantly changing environment, researchers from one end of the country to the other are observing, writing, and publishing what they see. In this way, the knowledge base on school leadership keeps expanding, and school leaders gain progressively more guidance for their mission.

The body of knowledge about school leadership in years past has been known for conflicting theories and gaping holes in evidence to support effective practice. Today, there is still much that we do not know, but research is becoming a more reliable guide for leaders piloting their schools through uncertain skies. (Chapter 2, "The Effects of Leadership," summarizes the conclusions of several syntheses of this growing body of research.)

Additional help has come from professional associations, which have been aggressive in developing more specific leadership standards and other resources to help their members turn their schools into effective learning organizations. For example, the National Association of Elementary School Principals (NAESP), in *Leading Learning Communities: Standards for What Principals Should Know and Be Able To Do,* states, "Student learning must be at the center of what schools are all about and should drive all the decisions school leaders make."

The National Association of Secondary School Principals' (NASSP's) detailed field guide, *Breaking Ranks II: Strategies for Leading High School Reform*, shows its members how, through collaborative leadership, to increase the academic rigor of their schools while at the same time personalizing the learning environment for students.

The dramatic and ongoing changes in the field of school leadership briefly sketched here meant that this book had to change in step with the profession and offer content suitable for the job's many current challenges. Consequently, this edition incorporates much more than the usual revisions. This new and expanded edition draws from the growing knowledge base on educational leadership to give school leaders—and those preparing for the role—insight and wisdom they will need to meet the challenge of helping all their students learn.

WHAT IS LEADERSHIP?

Everyone knows how necessary and important leadership is, but agreement becomes more tenuous when people begin to discuss *what* it is. Literally hundreds of definitions of *leadership* have been offered. Behind each definition, in turn, is a different theory about the source, process, and outcome of leadership. As Malcolm J. Richmon and Derek J. Allison explain, leadership has variously been thought of

> as a process of exercising influence, a way of inducing compliance, a measure of personality, a form of persuasion, an effect of interaction, an instrument of goal achievement, a means for initiating structure, a negotiation of power relationships or a way of behaving.

Linda Skrla and her colleagues note that several words and phrases stand out when defining leadership: "purpose, direction, individuals, groups, culture and values, shared strategic vision, priorities, planning change." These concepts, they say, point to several conclusions:

- If leadership is occurring, someone is following. You can't lead in an empty room.
- Leadership is purposeful and directional. It does not move aimlessly.
- The direction of leadership is always based upon priorities. Even good things must sometimes be set aside in order to pursue what is most important. Choices must be made.
- Significant leadership results in change.
- Effective leadership rests upon the integration of the ideas of the organization's stakeholders. (Skrla and others)

Some definitions differentiate between management and leadership. Carl E. Welte defined *management* as the "mental and physical effort to coordinate diverse activities to achieve desired results" and included in this process "planning, organization, staffing, directing, and controlling." In contrast, he saw leadership as "natural and learned ability, skill, and personal characteristics to conduct interpersonal relations which influence people to take desired actions." John P. Pejza expressed the difference in simpler terms: "You lead people; you manage things."

This emphasis on personal relations occurs in many definitions of leadership. Fred E. Fiedler, Martin M. Chemers, and Linda Mahar noted that leadership includes "the ability to counsel, manage conflict, inspire loyalty, and imbue subordinates with a desire to remain on the job." Speaking more plainly, former President Harry S. Truman said, "My definition of a leader in a free country is a man who can persuade people to do what they don't want to do, or do what they're too lazy to do, and like it."

One of the best definitions of leadership was suggested by George R. Terry, who called it "the activity of influencing people to strive willingly for group goals." A simpler and yet somehow more elegant way of putting the same definition was offered by Scott D. Thomson when he was executive director of the NASSP: "Leadership is best defined as 'getting the job done through people.'" This definition means that two things are necessary for effective leadership: accomplishment (getting the job done) and influencing others (through people). These two are intertwined. An ability to get things done makes leaders more influential.

Studies have shown that teachers are influenced most by principals who have "expert power," a term that simply means competence. Teachers are less influenced by the principal's power to punish, by his or her status or position, or even by the power to reward than by their perception that the principal is an expert, is competent, and can get the job done. One goal of this book is to give school administrators more of this expert power by helping them become more expert at what they do. A theme that recurs in many chapters of this book is that the leader's competence is most clearly manifest in the ability to inspire and empower others.

Competence alone, however, is not a sufficient qualification for leadership. Walter F. Ulmer, former president of the Center for Creative Leadership, advances the notion that leaders are able to gain, through ethical means, the followers' consent to be led:

> Leadership is an activity—an influence process—in which an individual gains the trust and commitment of others and without recourse to formal position or authority moves the group to the accomplishment of one or more tasks. (as cited in Kenneth E. Clark and Miriam B. Clark)

Leaders' influence over others, then, is a product of, in addition to competence, their integrity—or, more broadly, their moral foundation. Thomas J. Sergiovanni defines *moral leadership* as a form of stewardship that motivates people by appealing to their values. Moral leaders do not seek benefit for themselves but instead for the common good.

By their principled behavior, leaders earn trust and inspire loyalty. This is a vital lesson in an age when scandals and broken trust in corporations, financial institutions, and government agencies make daily headlines. Schools, certainly as much as any other institution, deserve ethical leadership.

For one last perspective, we turn to Marshall Sashkin and Molly G. Sashkin, who argued that the kind of leadership that matters transforms organizations and the people who work in them. It does this by instilling self-motivation and confidence in people and empowering them to develop their own competence to lead. Thus, leadership expands throughout the organization and becomes the possession of not just an individual but of the organization as a whole. This transformational leadership, the Sashkins say, drives and sustains high performance.

In our view, a definition of leadership in schools should include the influence, competence, moral, and transformational dimensions. These are the critical processes and values that guide how leadership functions. Still missing is one more element: The definition should state the desired end to which leadership aspires.

Here, then, is the definition of *school leadership* on which this book is based:

> The activity of mobilizing and empowering others to serve the academic and related needs of students with utmost skill and integrity.

This wording may lack the simple elegance of some of the definitions of generic leadership noted previously, but it expresses well the key concepts of this book. Our intent is to lay out the knowledge, values, structure, mission, and skills necessary for a leader to inspire and empower all members of the school community to work together toward the goal of an excellent education for all students.

ASSUMPTIONS ABOUT THE NATURE OF LEADERSHIP

The exercise of leadership involves people: a leader or leaders, a follower or followers, and the interaction of their personalities, knowledge, skills, and moral predispositions. It also involves a place: a group or organization, with its particular structure, culture, resources, and history.

Because so many variables of personality and context go into the workings of leadership, it is not surprising that people have observed and studied leadership from many different perspectives. Theories and models of leadership abound.

So the reader might know what to expect from this book, we set forth here our own assumptions about the nature of leadership in schools. At the same time, consistent with this book's method of information analysis, we cite many others who have written on the subject.

Leadership Expresses Itself in Varied Ways

Good leaders operate out of a clear understanding of their values, goals, and beliefs and also those of their followers. Leaders both influence and are constrained by the organizational context. Leaders may, with good results, use any of a variety of styles and strategies of leadership, including hierarchical, transformational, and shared (or participative), depending on their reading of themselves, their followers, and the organizational context.

Because leadership is multidimensional, affected by variables in both people and environment, it follows that there can be no single recipe for leading any organization, let alone an institution as complex as a school. Leithwood and Riehl stated, "Leadership functions can be carried out in many different ways, depending on the individual leader, the context, and the nature of the goals being pursued."

As Bradley Portin put it, in a report by the Center on Reinventing Public Education, "Individual styles, school-specific challenges, politics, and governance issues all produce different leadership stories in different schools."

For this reason, school districts should not "treat principals as easily interchangeable commodities" (Portin). Different leaders have different skills that suit them for different types of situations. Portin recommends that districts place principals in schools whose needs match the principals' experience and skills:

> A school with a stable staff, but a weak instructional program, may do well with a principal who was an experienced teacher. On the other hand, a school with high teacher turnover and a lack of confidence needs an institution builder who can set direction and motivate people. A school that is misusing its funds or wants to expand its physical plant may need someone who specializes in management.

One conclusion we can draw from the variable nature of leadership—and the needs of different schools for varying kinds of leadership—is that leaders who can draw from a wide repertoire of skills and styles of leadership will be at a premium in their school districts. Flexibility is an important quality in a school leader.

Schools Need to Be Both Managed and Led

If education executives had to choose between being regarded as leaders or as managers, we suspect most would pick the former. They know their schools need high-quality leadership, and they are confident they can supply it. In addition to this very practical reason, the thought may be in some executives' minds that more prestige comes with wearing the mantle of leadership.

Richmon and Allison speculate that leadership is receiving more attention in education today in part because of its positive connotations. Leadership, these authors point out, is seen as a dynamic activity associated with terms such as *honor, charisma, loyalty, respect,* and *greatness.* Administration, in contrast, is commonly thought of as having to do with the perfunctory tasks of running organizations and institutions.

In the press to develop strong leaders for schools, what must not be overlooked is the need for the right balance between good management and competent instructional leadership. A deficit in either one of these clusters of skills will be to the school's detriment. Here is how E. Mark Hanson described the damage that can be done by strong leaders who are weak managers:

> In education we often see this individual generating grand ideas about sweeping reforms or innovative new programs. He or she effectively whips up enthusiastic support on all sides. Unfortunately, ideas and enthusiasm are not enough, and not long after execution of the changes is attempted, the vision begins to crumble. By that time the strong leader, more often than not, has a better job somewhere else and is creating a vision for another audience. Meanwhile, those who were left behind are in deep water.

In actuality, much of what passes for leadership in schools is really management. This should come as no surprise, because school administrators are trained primarily as managers, not leaders. Schools must comply with laws, establish consistent policies and procedures, and operate efficiently and on budget. But schools also need, in the words of Lee G. Bolman and Terrence E. Deal, "purpose, passion, and imagination"—the products of a leader. "Particularly in times of crisis or rapid change," they said, "we look to leaders, not to managers, for hope, inspiration, and a pathway to somewhere more desirable."

Many principals would like to be relieved from some management duties to free time for involvement with instruction, and several alternative organizational arrangements have been proposed to do just that. But principals cannot use their management load to excuse a lack of instructional leadership. In today's climate of accountability, student learning is the number one priority, and true leaders will find a way to get the job done.

As NAESP's report on standards points out, principals must learn how to balance the roles of leader and manager:

> The trick is not to do more, but to rethink how and why you're doing what you're doing. And to keep a simple concept in mind: Everything a principal does in school should be focused on ensuring the learning of both students and adults.

Most school districts do not have the resources to hire for each school one person to manage and another to lead. So, by necessity, those who are trained to manage must also learn to lead.

But is it realistic to expect every school principal to do it all—both manage the school's many operations and lead the instructional program with the proficiency it takes to comply with world-class standards? No, said Vincent L. Ferrandino and Gerald N. Tirrozi, executive directors of NAESP and NASSP, respectively, in one of their paid columns in *Education Week*. They detailed the multiple expectations of school leaders in this era of school reform:

> Yesterday's principal was often a desk-bound, disciplinarian building manager who was more concerned with the buses running on time than academic outcomes. Today's principal must concern herself with not only discipline, school safety, and building management, but also must act as an instructional leader who knows how to use research and testing data to improve teaching methods, student achievement, and classroom management. Today's principal is a visionary leader who spends significant time working with faculty and interacting with students and rarely sees her desk. Today's principal coordinates staff development and community engagement. Today's principal wears far too many hats.

That school leaders continue to perform such varied duties with confidence and composure in these turbulent times should merit our respect. Perhaps they also deserve to be cut some slack. Michael A. Copland, writing about the myth of the "superprincipal," argues it is not reasonable to assume that every principal can live up to "*every* expectation that falls out of our literature-based conceptions":

> As certainly as there are a small number of .350 hitters in baseball, there are undoubtedly a small number of extremely gifted school leaders (or would-be leaders) who possess all the knowledge, skills, abilities, characteristics, and attitudes portrayed in various scholarly conceptions. However, we squander enormous

potential resources by setting the bar so high. Not only are we likely to fail to attract such rare persons, but they will never exist in the numbers necessary to staff the principals' offices of even a small percentage of America's schools. Rather, most of those positions will be filled by mere mortals who will fail periodically, who will recognize that they won't be able to do all, and who shouldn't be expected to do so.

The expansion of this book from the previous edition's 15 chapters to this edition's 19—to address the new skills and knowledge required of today's school leaders—itself testifies to the point Ferrandino, Tirrozi, Copland, and no doubt others are making. Not only do principals, especially those new to the job, deserve to be cut some slack, they deserve consideration by state and federal policymakers, who perhaps could better foresee the consequences of their mandates. And they need ongoing support from school districts, which must give principals resources and training in proportion to the higher expectations of them.

Until a way is found and universally applied to lighten principals' loads, the training must aim to elevate principals' skills as both managers and leaders.

Leadership Makes a Difference

After interviewing 60 corporate and 30 public-sector leaders, Warren Bennis and Burt Nanus concluded, "The factor that empowers the work force and ultimately determines which organizations succeed or fail is the leadership of those organizations."

Sashkin and Sashkin analyzed research from the business, medical care, and education sectors and found "clear evidence that transformational leadership matters." There are no guarantees, they acknowledge, but

> we know roughly how much of a difference transformational leadership makes. In terms of bottom-line measures, our conservative estimate is that transformational leadership accounts for between 5 and 25 percent of performance results.

Every organization wants strong performance, but the value of transformational leadership does not end at the bottom line. An all-important additional benefit, the Sashkins say, is that "such leadership makes a practical, meaningful difference in people's lives." Helping people find meaning in their work lives is the ultimate reason transformational leadership matters.

Also commenting on the human benefits of leadership, Clark and Clark of the Center for Creative Leadership state, "The exercise of leadership accomplishes goals more effectively than the usual management methods of trading rewards for performance." Much of the power of leadership lies in its ability to inspire commitment, capture the imagination, and earn trust.

Summarizing propositions derived from research on leadership in corporate, military, governmental, and educational settings, the Clarks point to a range of effects: "(a) profitability of cost centers, (b) performance of work units, (c) quality of work output, (d) reduction of stress in the workplace, (e) worker satisfaction and morale, (f) reduced absenteeism, and (g) reduced accidents."

The positive impact of principals' leadership gained validation in the 1970s when researchers found that instructionally effective schools were led by principals who set clear goals, participated in the instructional program, and made it clear to teachers and students that they were expected to excel.

One reviewer of the early studies done on effective schools, Ronald Edmonds, found leadership to be a key factor. In his summary of the "indispensable characteristics" of effective schools, Edmonds gave highest priority to "strong administrative leadership without which the disparate elements of good schooling can be neither brought together nor kept together."

As the research database expanded over the years, other reviewers affirmed the finding that effective schools have effective leaders. "Principal leadership can make a difference in student learning," said Philip Hallinger and Ronald H. Heck, who summarized a decade and a half of empirical research. By influencing their schools' policies and norms, teachers' practices, and other school processes, principals indirectly affect student learning. The studies Hallinger and Heck reviewed consistently point to one leadership behavior in particular that is tied to student achievement: "sustaining a schoolwide purpose focusing on student learning."

Leithwood and Riehl's synthesis of research, referred to earlier, led them to conclude, "Leadership has significant effects on student learning, second only to the effects of the quality of curriculum and teachers' instruction." For more evidence that school leaders can make a difference in student achievement, see Chapter 2, "The Effects of Leadership."

Findings such as these provide the logical basis for holding school leaders accountable. After all, if leadership were shown to make no discernible difference in the performance of schools, it would be grossly unfair to sanction leaders when their schools fail to perform.

There is an important corollary to this observation, however. To be justly held accountable, principals must have control over those things that research has shown can make a difference. Portin explains that the type of governance structure school leaders work under can either free or constrain their ability to lead.

Portin's in-depth interviews with principals, vice principals, and teachers in 21 schools led him to conclude, "For principals to succeed, their authority and responsibility have to be inextricably linked." District rules and policies, legal decisions, and collective-bargaining agreements can restrict the ability of school principals in traditional governance structures to exert leadership in critical areas. Said Portin:

> In traditional public schools, principals were sometimes unable to exert much authority over leadership in areas like instruction (because the district drove the curriculum) and human resources (because of centralized recruitment and hiring).

If constraints such as these keep principals from being anything more than a middle manager, they cannot rightly be expected to make a difference, and their schools will be at a loss because of it.

There Are No Substitutes for Leadership

Devolution of authority and responsibility remains a vibrant trend in the nation's school systems as well as in corporations and governments. We expect this trend to continue, as more schools establish site councils and more teachers, parents, and members of the community participate in school decision making. As in past editions, several chapters of this book recommend procedures for site-based management, distributed leadership, and community engagement.

None of these more inclusive governance processes replaces the need for leadership. Granted, the leader's role might change from a directive style to an enabling or facilitating style. But someone in a leadership position, presumably the principal, still must perform several essential tasks. A leader or leaders must be able to set direction, create networks, build teams, develop people's skills and empower them for action, resolve and creatively use conflicts, build consensus on the school's vision, secure resources, and, especially important, focus attention on the goal: student learning.

What about schools where teachers attain a high level of professionalism and form self-renewing learning communities? These teachers initiate their own improvement strategies, reflect on their work, share their insights with one another, and collectively enforce high standards of performance. Such schools, it may be assumed, can operate on autopilot. They don't need a leader, only someone to manage the buses and bells. In actuality, rather than having outgrown the need for leadership, strong professional communities require a commensurately higher caliber of leadership.

Self-renewing schools would appear to prosper with leaders who can "enhance the collective ability of a school to adapt, solve problems, and improve performance," which is the definition David T. Conley and Paul Goldman give for *facilitative leadership.* In addition to performing the tasks noted previously, facilitative leaders possess the abilities to channel teachers' energy toward common goals and stimulate teachers' readiness for change.

Schools going through the process of restructuring seem to require this same kind of facilitative leadership. Paul V. Bredeson interviewed principals of 20 schools where teachers were taking on more responsibility in curriculum decisions, professional development, community outreach, and other school-improvement activities. Many of the principals experienced a transition in their roles from traditional manager-oriented leadership behaviors to group-centered leadership behaviors:

> These adjustments included increasing attention to group needs, relinquishing control and responsibility for task completion to others, becoming consultants and facilitators, providing a climate of support, modeling leadership behaviors, and entrusting group maintenance and process problems to members of the group. (Bredeson)

Worth noting is that this facilitative style fits our definition of a leader as one who mobilizes and empowers people to serve group goals. With shared governance and professional community, the group, not the individual, becomes the primary work unit. Group work places a premium on leadership; it is easier to manage the work of a collection of autonomous individuals than to lead a group.

This observation reinforces the principal's unique role, which we must not minimize or take for granted in the quest for leadership as an organizational function. Principals may not be the only leaders in their building, but they are responsible for orchestrating and focusing the energy of everyone else, including other leaders, on the school's mission.

Leadership Can Be Shared

Once it is understood that shared governance and professional community do not reduce the need for leadership but actually require a purer expression of it than a hierarchically run school does, the question becomes, Who leads?

We find it hard to believe that a school could give birth to a vibrant professional community, self-initiating and self-renewing, without the active participation and encouragement of the principal. If teachers do take the initiative to form such a community, a principal who hasn't bought into the notion of faculty-as-change-agent is more likely than not to use his or her positional authority to sabotage the movement. The principal must actively support the process, either by taking a leadership role or by recruiting and supporting others who take that role.

Skrla and her coauthors put it this way:

One of the principal's primary objectives is to create conditions in which other leaders thrive. A second is to develop the leadership potential of others. The school, as a knowledge-work organization, requires that all its members be integrally involved in the problem solving and information process that drives the school forward. There are leader and follower roles for both principals and teachers in the leadership relationship.

Participants in a forum hosted by the National Institute on Educational Governance, Finance, Policymaking, and Management noted that instructional leadership takes on different forms in different schools. Principals are closely involved with classroom teaching in some schools, whereas in others, they may designate teacher-leaders to work directly with teachers.

Leithwood and Riehl say that because "leadership is a function more than a role," those functions "may be performed by many different persons in different roles throughout the school."

The past decade's school-reform movement has given increased legitimacy to teacher leadership. Teachers engage in action research, perform staff development, serve as lead teachers or chair site councils, and so forth. Their craft knowledge is indispensable in the process of school renewal. When leadership is shared in this way, more might be involved than teachers' simply taking on leadership roles.

Marlene M. Johnson suggests that those who study and observe leadership have too readily assumed it is always the function of an individual. "The possibility of leadership as being a synergistic, interactive process created by numerous individuals within an ever-changing context has remained a 'blind spot.'" Studies of facilitative leaders lend support to the idea that leadership can become an organizational function.

Facilitative leaders beget other facilitative leaders, say Conley and Goldman. Facilitative leadership by the principals they observed induced teacher-leaders likewise to behave in a facilitative manner:

Teachers who took advantage of new leadership opportunities tended to involve others rather than hoard personal power. There was less fear of being excluded from important decisions, or of needing to guard one's resources. The collegiality that occurred when many teachers interacted regularly and took leadership roles both reduced fears and presented many more forums for concerns to be raised. New leadership roles and structures were tools to solve problems, not merely maintain the status quo.

Facilitative leadership in these schools was contagious. Begun as an individual activity, it became collective practice and eventually characterized the manner in which the organization itself functioned.

Power Given Away Is Power Gained

The acquisition and use of power are prerequisites for successful leadership. Leaders rightly seek power, for it is an essential instrument for getting things done. How leaders wield their power, however, can make or break their effectiveness.

There is a paradox about the use of power, Sashkin and Sashkin say, that has three aspects. First, transformational leaders use power to benefit the organization and its members, not themselves. Second, and less obviously, once they gain power, they strive to "give it away." Effective leaders are secure in their own sense of power, which frees them from the desire to control others. Instead, they use power in a prosocial way to empower others, as the Sashkins explain:

> They spread power and influence throughout the organization. In this way, the organization becomes one in which everyone feels more powerful and everyone has a sense of being able to influence what happens. This sense of high control by organization members is characteristic of high-performing organizations.

The third aspect of use of power by transformational leaders is perhaps the most paradoxical, say the Sashkins. In addition to not using power to benefit themselves and instead using it to empower others, these leaders "show others how to use power and influence in ways that benefit the organization." As stewards of power, transformational leaders seek to develop in their followers "the same sense of stewardship, of prosocial use of power and influence, that they have themselves."

By sharing power and perpetuating the same ideal in others, these leaders help move their organizations toward peak productivity. Just as facilitative leaders can increase leadership throughout the organization, as we saw in the previous section, so leaders who empower others can increase the total power of the organization. Power is not a finite quantity allocated to only a few chosen people, but can grow throughout the organization, thus increasing its capacity to perform. A synergy occurs when leaders interact with and inspire other leaders.

In summary, the issue isn't desire for power, but the end to which it is used. The Sashkins quoted Lao Tzu, who wrote the classic *Tao Te Ching* to show China's warlords how to be better leaders: "Great leaders give others opportunities, not orders." "It is not too strong a statement," the Sashkins wrote, "to say that the very core of transformational leadership is based on empowerment."

Motive Matters

Our last assumption touches on a matter of the heart. School leaders must know why they want to lead. "What do I hope to gain from holding this position, indeed, from succeeding in this position?" Most individuals would readily answer, "To make a contribution to kids' learning."

But honest reflection might yield other answers, too, some of which a leader might be reluctant to admit: to enjoy the prestige the principalship affords; to attain all the rewards that come from success, such as the approval of colleagues and possible advancement to a bigger school or the superintendency; and to earn more income than is available to a teacher.

Now, prestige, the esteem that accompanies success, and money (honestly earned) are not venal desires. But they are self-centered when compared with wanting simply that kids learn.

Everyone performs a job for a mixture of selfish and altruistic reasons. In some careers, the motivation can be entirely selfish and probably not affect the quality of the job done. A school leader, however, must set a higher standard by demonstrating a commitment to serve the institution and its members before oneself.

Must leaders check their egos at the schoolhouse door? Not at all. Most successful leaders have a healthy ego that propels their desire to achieve and that followers are quick to admire. What sets successful leaders apart from others is how they employ their egos. Jim Collins, in his book *Good to Great,* describes great companies that owe their success to what he calls Level 5 leadership. Collins reports:

> Level 5 leaders channel their ego needs away from themselves and into the larger goal of building a great company. It's not that Level 5 leaders have no ego or self-interest. Indeed, they are incredibly ambitious—*but their ambition is first and foremost for the institution, not themselves.*

Humility and self-confidence are an attractive mix. In contrast to humble leaders with a healthy, appropriate dose of self-regard are flashy, charismatic individuals who seek leadership positions so they can be admired. The Sashkins refer to them as narcissists: "Their real concern is not for followers or the organization; their only concern is self-concern."

Sergiovanni distinguishes between two dimensions of self-interest. Individual self-interest seeks the greatest gain (or the smallest loss) for oneself. The second dimension—"too often overlooked in management theory and leadership practice"—is self-interest broadly conceived. The individual, realizing that his or her welfare is connected to that of everyone else, concludes his or her long-term interest is to promote the common good.

In other words, to live for the cause and for the advancement of others does not require that the leader adhere to an absolute altruism that denies all self-concern. Rather than subordinate all self-concern to the welfare of the group, the leader realizes that his or her success lies in helping others succeed.

Leadership theorists typically assume that leaders are motivated by their needs for varying amounts of affiliation, power, or achievement. We agree with Rabindra N. Kanungo and Manuel Mendonca, who argue that limiting the focus to these kinds of motivators ignores "the more profound motive of altruism, which is *the* critical ingredient of effective leadership."

The question is not whether leaders are motivated by the needs for affiliation, power, or achievement, but to what higher end? For instance, does a leader seek warm relationships with followers out of a need for their approval, or is the leader's motive to value them as partners in the enterprise—to put their ideas and skills to use in achieving the organization's mission? Does a leader seek power to aggrandize himself or herself or regard it as an instrument to serve the needs of the institution and its members?

These are fundamental questions that pierce to the core of a leader's character. How leaders—and more important, their followers—answer them ultimately governs the success or failure of their exercise of leadership. As Kanungo and Mendonca have said, "Regardless of the need that operates as the motive, the leader's effectiveness will ultimately depend on whether the behavior manifested by that need is a reflection of and is guided by the overarching altruistic need."

Altruism derives its power from the followers' perception that the leader is committed to their welfare. In reciprocal and paradoxical fashion, followers gladly bestow power on leaders who eschew it for themselves but use it to serve others.

Especially in education, where the product is knowledge, skills, and values instilled in young people, it matters a great deal whether the leader of a school or district is after self-advancement or the highest good for children. Dale L. Brubaker collects the life stories of principals who attend his graduate education class at the University of North Carolina, Greensboro. Many of his students express dismay at the increasing politicization of their jobs, as Brubaker explains:

> In the minds of many principals, good ol' boy superintendents as politicians have been replaced by smoother but equally political "sharks" whose self-interest is still more important than student learning and teachers' welfare. Such superintendents, principals argue, set the stage for like-minded principals to behave in similar fashion. These are the principals who always have the media in their schools, have glitzy bulletin boards without substance, and insist on public relations events for parents that often distract students from the learning that should take place in classrooms.
>
> For such principals, test scores are more important than students receiving a solid education. These principals build a system of rewards for "the star teacher," thus passing down to the teachers self-serving norms of behavior.

The proposition that motive matters may be impossible to prove, because self-reports—the only way to establish motive—are of questionable validity. But if we assume a connection between a person's reason for doing something and the extent to which that "something" dominates the individual's thinking, we may be able to infer motive.

Is there any evidence that principals' thinking patterns influence their effectiveness as leaders? We find some support for this notion in the findings of a study reported by Samuel E. Krug. He and two colleagues examined the ways in which principals thought about—reflected on—their activities during five consecutive work days. Five times each day, the principals responded to a pager that activated randomly.

Each time the pager beeped, the principals recorded what they were doing, whether it was relevant to instructional leadership, and what they felt or thought about the activity. Then Krug and his associates, having used another instrument to evaluate each principal's instructional leadership, compared principals' thinking patterns with their performance as leaders.

"One of the most important conclusions of this study," Krug wrote, "was that, while all the principals engaged in very similar kinds of activities, they did not all think about them in the same ways. Principals who are more effective perceive and use these activities as opportunities for exercising instructional leadership."

Moreover, the principals' leadership scores showed a consistent relationship with student learning. "As leadership scores rose, student achievement scores rose; as leadership scores fell, student achievement scores fell."

The following statement by Krug underscores the link between thought and action:

One principal saw a disciplinary meeting with a student as an opportunity to communicate the school's mission, monitor learning progress, and promote the instructional climate. A second principal saw the situation simply as an exercise in the management of discipline.

What is it that explains why these principals thought as they did? Did they think and act differently because their motives differed, one burning with passion to see every child succeed, the other consumed with adult issues of school politics? Or did they actually share the same passion to see their students excel, but one principal was simply quicker than the other to realize that any encounter with a student can serve an instructional purpose?

We cannot definitively answer these kinds of questions from Krug and colleagues' data or, for that matter, from any research study. The answers will come only as these leaders search their own hearts to discern the pulse of their beliefs and commitments.

Finally, to say that motive matters is not to say that motive is all that matters. Individuals must possess an array of technical and organizational skills and knowledge to be considered for a position of school leadership. This point is obvious, but it is worth noting if for no other reason than to highlight the opposite: Candidates' motives matter too little in most hiring decisions. Jim Collins told Carlotta Mast of *The School Administrator* that people with Level 5 leadership potential are everywhere, but too few of them are at the top of our institutions. "We keep giving the keys to the wrong people," he said (as cited in Mast).

CONCLUSION: A PASSION FOR LEARNING

Leadership springs from an internal set of convictions, action following thought in the manner declared by this proverb: "As a man thinks in his heart, so is he." A principal whose thoughts center on bolstering his or her reputation will behave differently than a principal who passionately wants kids to learn and succeed. Outstanding school leaders start with a conviction about what schooling ought to be. This conviction gives birth to a vision, a mental image that guides these effective leaders in their daily routine activities and interactions with teachers, students, and communities.

We offer this book as food for the mind and nourishment for growth of the leader's conviction, passion, vision, and effectiveness.

PART I

The State of School Leadership

1

The Landscape of School Leadership

Larry Lashway

Travelers across America see a landscape that changes, but at variable rates. Board a Seattle-bound train in Chicago, and you'll find a long stretch through North Dakota and eastern Montana where the scenery hardly seems to change at all. The world outside the window is a flat, featureless terrain punctuated only by the occasional small town flashing past. You can doze off for an hour or so and be confident that when you awake, things will still look the same.

The experience is quite different near the end of the journey as the train climbs into the Cascades. Every few minutes brings a different vista: mist-shrouded peaks, tumbling rivers, dense conifer forests, or a small town nestled in a valley. Within an hour, the mountain view is replaced by ocean, and then a final quick run through an increasingly urban landscape.

For anyone journeying in the landscape of school leadership in recent years, the experience has been much more like Washington than North Dakota. The view seems to change almost every time you look up: new standards, new policy mandates, new demands for accountability. Whereas school leadership once changed at a measured pace, it now seems to ricochet from one new goal to another, each of which raises profound (and so far unanswered) questions:

Editors' Note: Portions of Chapter 1 were adapted from Larry Lashway, *Leaders for America's Schools: Training, Recruiting, & Selecting Principals for Success*. Eugene, OR: ERIC Clearinghouse on Educational Management, Electronic Edition, 2003.

- How do we reduce the achievement gap?
- What are some viable strategies for reaching Adequate Yearly Progress?
- In a nation in which the gap between rich and poor is growing, how can we develop a school system that promotes social justice?
- How can school leaders manage the political tensions that surround today's schools?
- What is the proper balance between efficiency (doing things right) and effectiveness (doing the right things)?
- In an increasingly multiethnic and multilingual society, how can schools educate children in a way that celebrates difference yet creates unity?
- How can principals share leadership responsibility to develop a true community of learning?
- How do we prepare and develop leaders who can find answers to these questions?

Efforts to find answers have led to a plethora of policies, experiments, theories, and proposals aimed at improving leadership practice. As the field of ideas competing for attention has become increasingly crowded, so too have other trends added to the complexity of school leadership. Since the previous edition of this handbook, published in 1997, the following developments have occurred:

- The Interstate School Leaders Licensure Consortium (ISLLC) standards, which were brand-new in 1997, have been adopted in the majority of states as the guiding framework for principal preparation and development.
- Accountability, which barely rated a mention in 1997, has become the core challenge for many principals.
- Education has become much more politicized, with disputes over evolution and sex education increasingly common.
- Advocates of collaborative leadership have gone from saying that leaders should share certain decisions to saying that everyone in the school is a leader.
- The federal emphasis on scientifically based research has challenged scholars to prove the common intuition that leaders make a difference and to show how they get results.
- School renewal, which in 1997 was considered a priority for a relatively small number of distressed urban schools, is now a way of life for almost everyone.
- The No Child Left Behind Act has elevated testing to a high-profile annual event that increasingly controls and (some say) distorts normal learning processes.
- Data-based decision making, which wasn't even mentioned in the previous handbook, gets a full chapter in this edition.
- Market-based solutions such as charter schools and vouchers remain hotly contested but are growing in strength.

Other developments could easily be added to this list, but it's clear that the number and complexity of the challenges facing school leaders are growing. Not surprisingly, recent discussions of the principalship have been laced with the word *crisis*. The Institute for Educational Leadership provided a typical example when it said that a lethal combination of escalating job demands and a shrinking pool of candidates meant that "the future of the principalship is in question" and that failing to address the issue could result in "catastrophe."

Although the institute's strong language has been echoed in numerous journals, conferences, and district offices across the country, principals themselves seem more upbeat. A number of recent surveys have revealed a leadership cadre that seems confident it can do the job. Today's principals will admit to being frustrated by the system, pressured by demands for accountability, and busier than ever, but they convey no hint that things are falling apart (James L. Doud and Edward P. Keller; Steve Farkas and colleagues; National Association of Secondary School Principals [NASSP]).

This apparent discrepancy between analysts and practitioners may arise from their different frames of reference. Principals live in a world of very immediate demands and measure their success by how well they handle the tasks before them. Most schools, most of the time, function well, offering safe environments for learning, employing well-qualified teachers, and working hard to meet the needs of an increasingly diverse student population. Whatever their complaints—and they have many—principals take justifiable pride in what they have been able to accomplish under difficult conditions.

The scholars, policymakers, and superintendents who have been sounding the alarm take a longer view and perceive a crisis that may be embryonic but is nonetheless dangerous. Seeing an ever more demanding job description and fewer people interested in filling it, they worry that the leadership pipeline is about to run dry. They also see a problem that goes beyond numbers: Given the increased complexity of today's schools and the relentless demands for deep reform, are traditional definitions of the principal's role adequate, or must the job itself be redesigned?

That question lurks in the shadows of most discussions of the principalship today, and it increases the difficulty of the principal's job exponentially. School leaders are not only expected to reinvent the school system, they are often simultaneously urged to reinvent the way they go about their work. Appreciating the magnitude of this challenge is the key to understanding the topics in the rest of this handbook. For that reason, this chapter examines the status of the principalship and the debates surrounding it.

We begin with a brief snapshot of today's principal, followed by a discussion of the core issues at the heart of the profession's identity, which affects candidates' attraction to the position. The final section, on the principal's role, places the issues in the context of the ISLLC standards.

THE STATE OF THE PRINCIPALSHIP: A SNAPSHOT

Before considering the somewhat theoretical debates over what the principalship should be, we may benefit from a quick look at what it currently is. A number of surveys and reports over the past seven years provide some insights.

Demographics

Susan M. Gates and colleagues, who analyzed 1999–2000 data from the federal Schools and Staffing Survey, found that the 84,000 public-school principals in the United

States had an average age of 49, with 9 years of experience as a principal and 14 years of experience as a teacher. The authors concluded that "overall, the data suggest that principals are an aging population," a matter of some concern because public-sector principals tend not to remain on the job much past 55.

Surveys in the past decade from the National Association of Elementary School Principals ([NAESP] Doud and Keller) and the NASSP support the idea of an aging population. Among high school principals, 28 percent in 2001 reported they had been principals for more than 15 years, compared with 23 percent in 1988. Elementary respondents in 1988 had a median age of 50, 3 years older than in 1988, and the oldest ever reported in an NAESP survey.

The analysis by Gates and colleagues found that more than 43 percent were women—a gain of almost 20 percent over 1987–1988; almost 60 percent of the new principals in 1999–2000 were women. The number of minority principals remained low at 17.8 percent, with some indication that numbers were growing (20 percent of new principals were minorities, compared with 15 percent of new principals in 1987–1988).

Working Conditions

A national survey of salaries and wages in public schools from the Educational Research Service (Alicia R.Williams, Nancy Protheroe, and Michael C. Parks) reported that in 2002–2003, the average annual salary for principals ranged from $75,291 (elementary) to $86,452 (high school). The range for assistant principals was $62,230 to $70,847. Typically, average figures can disguise some rather startling variations, depending on size and geographic region. One survey reported that in 2001, the salaries of Illinois high school principals stretched from $46,071 to an eye-opening $191,650 (Robert F. Hall and Max E. Pierson).

Psychologically, compensation is relative as well as absolute. That is, the size of the salary seems larger or smaller when it is compared with alternative jobs available to jobholders—a key concern at time of shortages. Gates and colleagues analyzed information from 1999–2000 and found that public-school principals made an average of 33 percent more per year than experienced teachers (when adjusted for length of contract). Again, the range was considerable, with some principals earning less than experienced teachers at their school. The Gates team also found that relative compensation for principals and other types of managers had remained stable from 1984 to 1999.

Only 15 percent of elementary principals in NAESP's 1998 survey (Doud and Keller) reported that their salary was based on any form of merit pay, and only a fifth of those said that student achievement was a factor. (More recent data are not available, but anecdotal evidence suggests that the pressures of No Child Left Behind may be pushing these numbers up.) Almost 80 percent had a contract, and a similar percentage had a written job description. The typical elementary principal worked 54 hours a week, up more than 3 hours from 1988 and 9 hours from 1978.

Stresses

Principals responding to these surveys were not shy about identifying their frustrations with the job. Almost unanimously, "time" topped the list. In the NAESP survey,

72 percent of the respondents said that "fragmentation of my time" was a major concern; in the NASSP study, almost 70 percent listed time as a major or somewhat major problem. Principals in a 2001 survey by Public Agenda (Farkas and colleagues) identified "politics and bureaucracy" as a major concern; only 30 percent said the system helped them get things done (48 percent said they could get things done, but only by working around the system).

Principals were particularly frustrated by their limited authority to deal with low-performing teachers. The Farkas and colleagues survey also revealed some ambivalence about testing and accountability. In the words of one principal, "Accountability is great, but schools should not be judged by what students do on one test on one day in March." A plurality (48 percent) thought holding principals accountable for test results was a bad idea, whereas 34 percent said it was a good idea.

Optimism

For all their frustrations, principals seemed engaged with their jobs and confident of having an impact. In the Farkas and colleagues survey, 97 percent of the principals agreed that "behind every great school is a great principal." Fully 90 percent of respondents to the NASSP survey graded the quality of education in their school as an A or B. Less than 1 percent of elementary principals reported that their morale was low; more than 90 percent described it as good or excellent.

A 2004 survey found that 96 percent of principals were either "very" or "somewhat" satisfied with their jobs (MetLife).

This quick overview shows the daily world of the principal to be complex, fragmented, and stressful—but still manageable. School leaders face enormous challenges and at times feel overwhelmed, but so do professionals in many other fields. They still see themselves as leaders (in the sense of having followers) and believe they can have a positive impact on students.

THE SUPPLY AND DEMAND CHALLENGE

What created an aura of crisis around so many recent discussions of school leadership was the prospect that there simply wouldn't be a sufficient number of qualified people to do the job. The concern originated in the late 1990s in anecdotal accounts by superintendents who reported alarming decreases in the number of active candidates for principalships. Undoubtedly, the worry was also fed by then-current predictions that schools would have to replace 2 million teachers over the coming decade.

Despite the gloomy predictions, survey research has painted a more complicated picture, especially if *shortage* is defined as an "absence of warm bodies." A 1998 survey by the Educational Research Service found half the districts reporting a shortage of qualified candidates. The 2001 Farkas and colleagues study painted a more favorable picture. Only 3 percent of superintendents reported a "severe" shortage of principals, and almost 60 percent reported no shortage.

Similarly, a 2003 study by Marguerite Roza and colleagues found little evidence of an immediate crisis. At a minimum, virtually all districts are still able to find an appropriately credentialed candidate to fill the position.

Of course, supply and demand are not evenly distributed. For example, districts in urban or high-growth regions are frequently hard pressed to fill their leadership needs (Farkas and colleagues; Roza and colleagues). For small districts, the margin can be razor thin. Commenting on a survey of Colorado schools, Kathryn Whitaker noted that some rural districts were reporting one to three candidates for secondary principalships.

And even within districts, candidates seem to seek out some schools while going out of their way to avoid others. Schools serving low-income or minority students often have the hardest time attracting candidates (Cynthia Prince; Roza and colleagues).

Demographic projections show a substantial number of principals approaching retirement age (Doud and Keller; Gates and colleagues; NASSP). Eligibility for retirement does not automatically lead to retirement, but it does create a pool of leaders who could walk away on relatively short notice. Any deterioration in work conditions—at the district, state, or even national level—could lead to a sudden exodus of talent.

In some quarters, the apparent shortage has sparked recommendations that schools recruit leaders from nontraditional sources (Frederick Hess; Thomas B. Fordham Foundation). Advocates maintain that when qualified candidates are scarce, the education system cannot afford to overlook any source of talent, and that there are many exceptionally talented leaders who come from noneducational backgrounds. But because most states require administrators to have teaching experience, outsiders find the path blocked. A few innovative programs are opening the door, but alternative routes remain relatively scarce and not well used (C. Emily Feistritzer).

Diminishing Quality?

Beyond the immediate concern with raw numbers, some recent research suggests that the real shortage may be qualitative rather than quantitative. A surprising number of district administrators report misgivings about the ability of today's principal candidates to handle the job. For example, no more than a third of superintendents in one survey pronounced themselves "happy" with principals' ability to communicate a clear vision, use money effectively, make tough decisions, and—most of all—hold teachers accountable for results. Most superintendents said those skills should be "a little better," but 10 to 20 percent saw serious deficiencies (Farkas and colleagues).

The survey did not directly ask whether the perceived problems were greater with new principals, but only a third of superintendents believed that the quality of applicants had improved in recent years, 36 percent said it had stayed the same, and 29 percent said it had gotten worse (Farkas and colleagues).

In another survey, 80 percent of superintendents agreed that finding qualified candidates was either a major or moderate concern (Roza and colleagues).

In that context, a diminishing candidate pool intensifies the quality concerns. One midwestern administrator put it this way: "Four or five years ago, there might be 50–200 applicants for a principalship, then there were 25 to 50—now it's only 15 to 20" (Educational Research Service 1998). The smaller the pool, the less likely a district will find someone with exactly the qualities it is seeking.

Doubts about the quality of new principals usually reanimate long-standing suspicions that university preparation programs are failing to fulfill their mission. Practitioners have long expressed disenchantment with the relevance of their formal training. For example, 80 percent of the superintendents in the Farkas and colleagues survey felt that typical leadership programs were "out of touch with the realities."

A recent study by Arthur Levine cited even more negative views and went on to say that the quality of the majority of programs ranged "from inadequate to appalling." Critics of Levine immediately questioned his method and also noted he failed to recognize a wide range of reforms under way (Michelle D. Young and colleagues). Other sources present a more hopeful picture that suggests many states are making progress in improving the preparation of principals (Southern Regional Education Board).

Because the rapidly changing nature of school leadership implies the need for ongoing training, more attention is also being paid to the often-ignored issue of professional development for principals. Kenneth Leithwood and colleagues acknowledge that "we know little about which experiences are helpful and why." They note, though, that the complexity of the principal's world requires learning opportunities that are authentic and job embedded. (There is little need to present principals with textbook problems when their day is already filled with real problems involving real people.)

Does Anybody Want This Job?

Another question generated by the perceived shrinkage of the candidate pool is whether the principalship is losing its appeal as a career choice. One of the oddities of the shortage is that administrator preparation programs turn out ample numbers of certificated principals, but many never take an administrative position or even apply for a job (Educational Research Service 2000).

A 1999 Minnesota study estimated that whereas some 6,500 licensed school administrators lived in the state, state schools employed only 1,800 principals and superintendents (Timothy D. Sheldon and Lee W. Munnich Jr.). The others fell into the "replacement" group (currently employed as educators but not administrators), the "new" group (recent graduates of preparation programs), and the "hidden" group (status unknown). The clear implication is that some licensed individuals must be consciously declining to throw their hats into the job ring. Why?

Some of the reluctance may have nothing to do with the job. Teachers who enter administration programs may have no intention of becoming administrators, but instead find the program a convenient way to earn a master's degree and move up the salary schedule. Others enter a program undecided and gradually realize that the job simply isn't a good match for their temperament or skills; they may finish the program but never apply for a position.

Many reasons could make well-qualified candidates hesitate. Teachers eyeing an administrative career see long days, substantial stress, and a salary not commensurate with the responsibilities. Many may simply say, "No, thanks" (Van Cooley and Jianping Shen 1999; Diana G. Pounder and Randall J. Merrill).

One obvious concern is salary. When Educational Research Service (1998) asked administrators what discourages principal candidates, 60 percent identified "salary/ compensation not sufficient as compared to responsibilities." The Farkas and colleagues study likewise found 65 percent of principals believing that "improving the pay and prestige of administrators" would be a "very effective" way of upgrading the leadership cadre.

But even apart from salary, the sheer burdens of the job may discourage applicants. Pounder and Merrill cited a promising young assistant principal who was willing to move up to the principalship—but only for 3 to 5 years. He said, "The demands of the job are just too great—the time commitment, the stress, and the difficulty in implementing change due to organizational, political and legal constraints." He liked the idea of making a difference in students' lives, but was not willing to subject his family life to the kind of stress that would be involved.

Some 92 percent of the principals surveyed by Farkas and colleagues believed that the time and responsibilities associated with the job discouraged candidates. When discussing the parts of the job that were most stressful or discouraging, they identified such things as dealing with politics and bureaucracy, handling public criticism, and trying to remove ineffective teachers.

Some researchers have gone directly to potential applicants to find out how they viewed the principalship. Pounder and Merrill interviewed high school assistant principals and middle school principals and found that only 30 percent intended to apply for a high school principal position in the next three to five years. Members in this group, who are probably the most immediate source of principals, were ambivalent about the job. They were drawn by the opportunity to make a difference, help students, and reform schools, and they also found the increased salary to be attractive. But they hesitated because of the hours, job stress, political pressure, teacher grievances, and difficulty of balancing job and family responsibilities.

Paul A. Winter, James S. Rinehart, and Marco A. Munoz surveyed all the holders of principal certificates in a large midwestern city and found that only 10 percent were likely to apply for principalships in the near future. Many were approaching retirement or were simply satisfied with their current positions, but others identified specific disincentives such as long hours, less job security, and time away from family.

An Impossible Job?

When Harry Wolcott published his classic 1973 ethnographic study *The Man in the Principal's Office*, it was widely regarded as a realistic and in-depth portrait of the principal's work life. For an entire year, Wolcott shadowed his subject, "Ed Bell," as he went about the daily business of running an elementary school.

Principals who read this account today will recognize much in Ed Bell's world, particularly the countless unplanned and unscripted encounters that filled each day and the constant demands for attention from teachers, students, and parents. Yet his world clearly belongs to another time, one that from today's perspective seems almost quaint.

Bell's job strikes us as orderly and largely predictable, offering challenges but rarely a major crisis. His concerns about discipline did not include gangs, guns, and lewd T-shirts; parent involvement was channeled into Parent Teacher Association (PTA) discussions about menus at the school fair; and teacher-union militancy was just a distant cloud on the horizon.

Although Bell often talked about change, no one was clamoring for him to reinvent education. In fact, Wolcott noted that Bell devoted most of his efforts to controlling change and maintaining stability. Having inherited a functioning school, he was clear about his mandate: Don't make mistakes.

Almost four decades later, Ed Bell would hardly recognize the world of the school leader. Massive social, demographic, and cultural changes have overtaken schools, upsetting comfortable old assumptions and behaviors. These outside forces have a major impact on the shape of education as well as the recommendations for school renewal (Pedro Reyes, Lonnie H. Wagstaff, and Lance D. Fusarelli). For example:

- Population shifts have greatly increased student diversity, not just in the usual urban pockets but throughout the country. Schools everywhere are confronting unprecedented ethnic, cultural, and linguistic differences that they are ill prepared to deal with.
- A society that expects schools to be positive moral influences has become much less confident in its definitions of right and wrong and much less capable of providing firm guidance to children. A rising divorce rate and the entry of women into the workforce have left many children on their own much of the day, saturated with media images.
- School safety, which once meant not putting the swings on asphalt, now requires metal detectors and SWAT teams.
- Student achievement remains unacceptably low, at least for policymakers, and all 50 states, supported by the federal government, are engaged in a massive effort to overhaul both curricular goals and instructional methods.
- Schools that once were considered a safe haven from the bickering of politics have become heavily politicized, subject to relentless legislation and litigation. Some initiatives offer sweeping changes that would transform education from a public agency to a consumer commodity.

In the face of these challenges, society's expectations for schools keep rising. Legislators continually turn to schools for a cheap fix to vexing social problems. (Perhaps policymakers reason that if they cannot actually solve problems such as AIDS, violence, and drugs, they can at least try to help the next generation gain the proper outlook.) Policymakers have likewise set a high standard for achievement and have decreed that those high standards are for all students, but without providing any kind of road map for getting there.

Just as expectations for schools keep escalating, so do the expectations for school leaders. Descriptions of school leadership for the 21st century are both visionary and ambitious:

The principal—the instructional "artist in residence"—establishes a climate for excellence, puts forth a vision for continuous improvement in student performance, promotes excellence in teaching, and commits to sustained, comprehensive professional development for all staff members. (Gerald N. Tirozzi)

Good principals lead change, inspire students and staff, leverage resources to make improvement happen, and bring community members into the process of change. (National Association of State Boards of Education)

Principals today must also serve as leaders for student learning. They must know academic content and pedagogical techniques. They must work with teachers to strengthen skills. They must collect, analyze and use data in ways that fuel excellence. They must rally students, teachers, parents, local health and family service agencies, youth development groups, local businesses and other community residents and partners around the common goal of raising student performance. And they must have the leadership skills and knowledge to exercise the autonomy and authority to pursue these strategies. (Institute for Educational Leadership)

The new expectations aren't simply replacing the old ones. Van Cooley and Jianping Shen (2003) found that secondary principals were engaged in new roles that had simply been "layered" over the old job. That is, instead of replacing former responsibilities or integrating them into the job, the new duties were simply added to what was already there.

Thus, it isn't surprising that many principals feel overwhelmed or that superintendents report difficulty in finding candidates who can deftly handle the many strands of the job. Already, some observers have suggested that the job may have become impossible for all but a few "superleaders" (Michael DiPaola and Megan Tschannen-Moran; J. Casey Hurley).

This realization has generated calls to redesign the job to make it more manageable, mostly by spreading out the principal's duties across a greater number of people. In some cases, the proposals involve reallocating duties among administrators in a co-principalship or "multi-principalship" (Michael Chirichello; Peter Zeitoun and Rose Mary Newton).

Another body of work urges more far-reaching and complex forms of "distributed" leadership, taking advantage of the leadership capacity of everyone in the organization (Richard F. Elmore; James P. Spillane, Richard Halverson, and John B. Diamond). These efforts raise the possibility that thoughtfully structuring the principalship to fit human capabilities may be more productive than trying to recruit candidates with superhuman attributes.

WHAT IS THE PRINCIPAL'S PROPER ROLE?

All these conditions—the shortage of applicants, questions about quality, escalating expectations—have given new life to a perennial question: What should be the principal's role?

This is a question with deep roots. As Lynn Beck and Joseph Murphy have noted, the principalship since the early 20th century has been "extremely malleable," with each generation molding its image of the principal to fit the needs of the time. During economic depression, principals were expected to be thrifty stewards of limited resources; in time of war, they were expected to mobilize the next generation to defend democracy; amid fears of declining achievement, they were expected to be instructional leaders.

How is school leadership defined today? Kenneth Leithwood and Daniel Duke, having examined all articles on educational leadership published in four major administration journals from 1985 to 1995, identified six distinct conceptions of leadership:

1. instructional (influencing the work of teachers in a way that will improve student achievement)

2. transformational (increasing the commitments and capacities of school staff)

3. moral (influencing others by appealing to notions of right and wrong)

4. participative (involving other members of the school community)

5. managerial (operating the school efficiently)

6. contingent (adapting their behavior to fit the situation)

Without a doubt, the most talked-about role is "instructional leadership," a phrase that echoes throughout current discussions. Hardly anyone would deny that improved student learning should be at the heart of the principal's job. But once one moves beyond the easy consensus that student learning is the ultimate measure of the principal's success, the picture becomes muddier. Exactly what does it mean to be an instructional leader, and how do principals accomplish it?

Today's conceptions of instructional leadership are much more complex than earlier versions. In the 1980s, instruction was often portrayed as a straightforward management problem that could be tamed by communicating high expectations, focusing on curriculum, and increasing time on task. Today, instructional leadership is more often seen as a complicated problem of organizational learning that requires a well-grounded vision, deep knowledge of adult learning, and the ability to connect with the larger community—all under the spotlight of high-stakes accountability.

This conception obviously requires school leaders to have exceptional skills. It shouldn't be surprising, therefore, that many potential candidates might shy away from the job or that superintendents would report that principals are not completely up to the task. But even if we assume that the more ambitious visions of instructional leadership are feasible, questions remain:

- How, exactly, do principals perform the task of instructional leadership?
- What qualifications and training are needed to be an effective instructional leader?
- Does instructional leadership completely define the principal's role, or are there other crucial functions that must be fulfilled?

This section examines current thinking on the role of the principal as expressed in the ISLLC standards and then discusses several areas of ambiguity or tension not fully resolved by the standards.

ISLLC Standards

For many decades, debates over the role of the principal were vigorous, but those discussions took place over extended periods in a variety of forums such as academic journals, practitioner magazines, and professional conferences. Hence, it was difficult to get a clear fix on what ideas were driving professional practice.

Then, beginning in the 1980s, various groups of practitioners, academics, and policymakers began to articulate the specific skills needed by today's school leaders and to crystallize those many role expectations into explicit standards of performance. Unfortunately, each group formulated its standards to serve slightly different needs, so the profession found it necessary to sort through a series of competing documents that were not completely consistent (John Hoyle).

That inconsistency has become less of a problem over the past decade, as the standards of the ISLLC have clearly dominated the discussion. The product of a collaborative effort among university professors, state policymakers, and professional associations, the standards by 2005 had been adopted as a guiding framework in 37 states, were integrated into national accreditation of leadership preparation programs, and provided the foundation for the School Leaders Licensure Assessment used in a number of states as a licensure requirement (Murphy 2003).

The ISLLC standards are by no means universally admired. Murphy (2003), who played a key role in development of the standards, notes that they have been variously criticized as being too vague (or too prescriptive), undermining university autonomy (or strengthening the university monopoly), being too dominant (or teetering on the edge of failure), and favoring left-wing (or right-wing) philosophies. They have also been accused of elevating naive idealism over empirical research. Wryly observing that these criticisms can't all be right, Murphy (2003) defends the standards as a useful tool with a strong rationale.

Whatever the validity of the criticisms, the standards are the logical starting point for any discussion of the principal's role, both because they have been so widely accepted and because they were designed to make a clear statement about what that role should be.

The standards leave little doubt about the essential core of school leadership: improving student learning. Each of the six standards begins with the statement, "A school administrator is a leader who promotes the success of all students by . . ." (Council of Chief State School Officers [CCSSO]). Thus, even the mundane tasks of budgeting and bus scheduling are harnessed to the overriding goal of student success. The second standard focuses specifically on the leader's role in "advocating, nurturing, and sustaining a school culture and instructional program conducive to student learning and staff professional growth."

This language clearly puts instructional leadership at the heart of the profession. But exactly what does that mean? The authors of the standards provided hints with a listing of specific indicators. For example, indicators for Standard 2 include the following:

- Knowledge of student growth and development, learning and motivational theories, principles of effective instruction, and assessment strategies
- Dispositions that commit the leader to student learning as the fundamental purpose of schooling, the proposition that all students can learn, and the variety of ways that students can learn
- Actions that create a culture of high expectations, provide students with multiple opportunities to learn, eliminate barriers to student learning, and treat all individuals with fairness, dignity, and respect

Those examples suggest that the ISLLC's conception of instructional leadership is much broader than the rather hard-edged versions of the 1980s, which envisioned the principal as a highly efficient taskmaster who set high expectations, monitored curriculum and instruction, and assessed outcomes.

Did ISLLC Get It Right?

Although ISLLC's vision of instructional leadership seems to be widely accepted across the profession, it leaves a number of questions unanswered.

Describing the origin of the ISLLC standards, Murphy (2003) notes that the recommendations were broadly responsive to the research on school leadership at that time and have been further validated by more recent research. He also explains that the consortium intended the specific knowledge, skills, and dispositions associated with each standard to be suggestive rather than prescriptive. Also, the developers of the standards believed that desirable leadership skills and strategies could not be completely described and probably are relative to the context. Thus, they did not attempt to provide empirical justification for each indicator.

Taking a different position, Tim Waters and Sally Grubb have argued that principals should focus on specific strategies that research shows are linked to student learning: "When school leaders fail to identify and focus on the classroom practices that are most likely to improve student achievement, their leadership can have a negative impact."

Waters and Grubb, reviewing an extensive body of empirical studies, found complex relationships among leadership, instruction, and organizational change. For example, of 21 strategies correlated with student learning, 8 were linked to deep, sustainable change: flexibility, strong ideals and beliefs, knowledge of curriculum, instruction and assessment, monitoring and evaluation, change agent (actively challenges the status quo), intellectual stimulation (engages faculty in discussion of new ideas), and optimizer (inspires innovations).

At the same time, four leadership characteristics—communication, culture (fosters shared beliefs and a sense of community), input (involves teachers in decisions), and order (establishes regular operating procedures)—were negatively associated with second-order change. In other words, in schools undergoing changes that require new ways of thinking, principals (as perceived by teachers) rank lower on these characteristics.

Waters and Grubb recommend that principals engaged in second-order change should keep one eye on how others perceive their efforts in these four areas. If their analysis is correct, it demonstrates that instructional leadership is a complex process and that we still have much to learn about it.

What Does It Mean to Be an Instructional Expert?

The recent focus on instructional leadership has reaffirmed a long-standing belief by many practitioners that principals should have teaching experience. Despite calls for opening the profession to qualified leaders from other occupations, virtually all states continue to require principals to have teaching experience, and on the rare occasion that states have eliminated the requirement, districts have continued to seek principals with such experience (Jeff Archer).

Some scholars agree. Mary Kay Stein and Barbara S. Nelson found in a case study that administrators acting as instructional leaders drew on their own classroom experience and knowledge of the subject. The authors concluded that school leaders should have in-depth knowledge of at least one subject:

> As we move away from the classroom, knowledge about subject matter does not disappear, and what administrators need to know does not become more generic. The needed knowledge remains anchored in knowledge of the subject and how students learn it.

Stein and Nelson claim that leaders need deep expertise in at least one content area, including knowledge of how children learn that subject. And they also should have

> substantial experiences of some depth in every subject, in which they experience what it is like to be a learner of that subject, in which they study what is known about how children learn that subject and become familiar with the best instructional methods for that particular subject.

That prescription faces some obvious practical difficulties. Where will busy principals find the time to gain the necessary breadth of expertise? Acknowledging that barrier, Stein and Nelson suggest that use of distributed leadership offers an alternative. That is, the principal can rely on the subject expertise of others and lead more through coordination and oversight than by direct decision making.

Similarly, drawing on insights gained from interviews with educators in 21 schools, Bradley Portin and colleagues say that instead of being "one-man bands," principals could function as "orchestra leaders." The leadership of conductors does not depend on playing an instrument but on coordinating the playing of others; the same can be true of instructional leadership. The principal's job is to see that it gets done, not to personally do it.

Whether or not principals require instructional expertise to be effective, research is beginning to show that their expertise (be it minimal or extensive) does make a difference. Jennifer Z. Sherer found that instructional leadership is not generic; the leaders she observed behaved very differently when overseeing literacy instruction than when overseeing math instruction. Sherer concluded: "It is no longer enough to state that leaders lead instruction. They specifically lead instruction differently in different domains."

Beyond Instructional Leadership

The ISLLC's emphasis on instructional leadership is echoed in many other discussions of the principal's role, and there is little doubt that most analysts and practitioners see improved student learning as the ultimate test of a principal's success. Another healthy body of thinking, however, takes a "yes, but . . ." stance. Without denying the importance of instructional leadership, some commentators suggest that it should not overshadow other key dimensions of the principal's job.

In some cases, the caution about instructional leadership may come from a belief that the phrase has become a euphemism for an overreliance on high-stakes testing. In other cases, it seems to spring from the recognition that in a time of major social transformation, defining the job too narrowly would fail to meet the needs of today's children. In particular, three alternative roles stand out as competitors to instructional leadership: the principal as manager, the principal as moral leader, and the principal as entrepreneur.

The Principal as Manager

In their study of how conceptions of the principalship have changed over time, Beck and Murphy found that the job itself—the day-to-day duties—actually remained quite stable over time. Irrespective of scholarly debates, principals stayed focused on the immediate need to build schedules, order textbooks, and maintain discipline.

Larry Cuban sees this tension running like a fault line through the history of school leadership. Even when principals are eager to transform, redesign, and create, they are unable to escape the "managerial imperative" that keeps them anchored to mundane tasks. Even the most visionary principals have to keep the buses running on time.

The leader/manager dichotomy is not absolute. A principal's walk around the school may serve both as an inspection tour to see that everything is functioning well and as a chance to demonstrate concern and support for teachers and learning. Indeed, Terrence E. Deal and Kent D. Peterson have suggested that effective principals have a kind of "bifocal vision" that allows them to invest routine tasks with deeper meaning.

Even with such virtuoso displays of leadership, just dealing with the dozens of administrative tasks that make up each day is often a full-time job. Advocates of a dynamic leadership role for principals have usually not explained where the additional hours will come from. For example, the ISLLC standards list management as just one of six standards—yet management tasks easily take up more than a sixth of the principal's time. Many principals try to fill both roles, and sometimes employers demand it, asking them to be Superman or Wonder Woman (Cuban).

Aside from the time issue, the leadership/management split may create a kind of psychic tension for principals. Most are former teachers, and many still have strong emotional ties to the classroom and to instructional issues; they easily feel guilty over the amount of time they have to spend on managerial concerns (Cuban).

In recent decades, many commentators have been somewhat disdainful of the managerial dimensions of the principalship, fearing that too sharp a focus on those responsibilities will produce unimaginative technocrats rather than real leaders. Some analysts have argued, in contrast, that managerial expertise is "fundamental to organizational stability" (Leithwood and Jantzi).

Philip Hallinger and Kamontip Snidvongs likewise suggest that today's emphasis on planning for school improvement requires principals who can not only formulate an educationally appropriate plan but use business strategies such as knowledge management, enterprise-resource management, and customer-service management.

The Principal as Moral Leader

Although the ISLLC standards clearly place instructional leadership at the center of the principal's world, they also recognize other responsibilities. For example, the school leader must be an ethical leader, must reach out to families and community, and must be responsive to the larger social, cultural, political, and legal environments. These ideas are expressions of a growing belief that the principal must be, in the words of Joseph Murphy (2002), "a moral steward."

The new expectations elevate ethics above the traditional concern with observing professional codes of behavior. Instead, principals' moral responsibility fits into a much broader context of social justice. For example, the ISLLC standards ask leaders to be committed to "the ideal of the common good, the principles in the Bill of Rights, and the right of every student to a free, quality education" (CCSSO). School leaders are expected to recognize the transformative power of education in the lives of children and to act as advocates for all their students, not only protecting their rights, but seeking to extend and improve those rights.

This belief is based on the recognition that schools reflect a society's deepest values and hopes and that administrators today are not just custodians of the school system, but creators of it. Required to spend much of their time defining purpose and choosing directions, they must operate from a strong base of beliefs that are sensitive to issues surrounding social justice, human dignity, and care for others.

A part of this moral responsibility comes from the principal's interpersonal connections with others. Schools are communities, consisting of teachers, students, parents, school boards, and the community at large, and principals must be community builders. This requires that they "lead not from the apex of the organizational pyramid but from a web of interpersonal relationships—with people rather than through them" (Murphy 2002).

As the NAESP put it:

> Schools and communities are inextricably intertwined, and the Principal is the linchpin in creating a learning community that seamlessly integrates the work and expectations of students, teachers, parents, citizens, community and business leaders and policymakers.

Living in simpler times, Ed Bell did not see a great need to cultivate community involvement, and sometimes resented it:

> I get pretty annoyed by the idea expressed that because a person has a child in school he is an expert about education. The learning process is so complex that parents should leave it up to school people and have confidence in them. (Wolcott)

Bell knew that his public generally respected and trusted the schools. Living in a homogeneous community, he also assumed that he knew what citizens needed and wanted. Therefore, except when a school budget was up for approval, good community relations required nothing more than a monthly PTA meeting, periodic open houses, and an occasional speech at a Rotary luncheon.

Today's social landscape is dramatically different. Distrust of government is high, citizens are more inclined to assert their rights, and schools have become a battlefield in the culture wars. As icons of American democracy, schools are inevitably pulled into the debates over public policy and the state of American society, and school leaders must be prepared to engage the public proactively, not just defensively.

And although educators today would agree with Ed Bell that learning is complex, they now take that as a reason parents should be involved. With the benefit of three decades' more experience, they believe that learning is a reflection of the total context of children's lives, not just the formal instruction that takes place during school hours. More conscious of the many styles and pathways to learning, they distrust a one-size-fits-all philosophy that ignores the diversity of today's population.

Thomas J. Sergiovanni has framed the principal's moral and community responsibilities in terms of the "lifeworld": the culture, values, and relationships that form the heart of school life. The lifeworld coexists with the "systemsworld" of rules, schedules, and mandates. Principals have obligations to both dimensions—and both are necessary—but Sergiovanni says the systemsworld keeps trying to assert its supremacy over the lifeworld (and is often successful). Thus, a key part of the principal's role is protecting the lifeworld.

The Principal as Entrepreneur

Historically, principals have functioned as middle managers, one link in a bureaucratic chain that extends from policymakers to students. They apply rules, soothe disputes, and make sure the cafeteria is supervised.

Today's principals operate in a tumultuous environment where schools now compete with market-based approaches such as charter schools and voucher systems. For this reason, some analysts are rethinking the principal's traditional role as middle manager. Robert J. Brown and Jeffrey R. Cornwall have argued that if principals are to succeed in this new environment, they must become entrepreneurial. Entrepreneurial leaders are those who

- view change as an opportunity as well as a threat;
- operate proactively, acting to control their own destiny rather than waiting for events to overtake them;
- understand the difference between a good idea and a great opportunity;
- are ready to exercise creativity and think out of the box; and
- are willing to take risks.

As employees and civil servants, principals will not be entrepreneurs in the classic sense, but they can act entrepreneurially in the district (sometimes called *intrapreneurship*), and they can work to build an entrepreneurial school.

Entrepreneurial leadership among principals has not been well studied, and most descriptions of it are anecdotal (for example, see Thomas B. Fordham Foundation; Bill Triant; Elaine K. McEwan). Such accounts leave the impression that today's principals are more likely to form partnerships, challenge conventional ideas, and assert their autonomy. These behaviors are often associated with charter schools and other schools of choice, with which principals may feel they need to compete.

Entrepreneurial leadership could equally well result from simple desperation. Faced with expectations of rigorous accountability for which conventional strategies are no match, some principals feel they have little choice but to try the unconventional.

Will the pressures of school reform and school choice sustain a sense of entrepreneurialism? One reason this question cannot be answered with certainty is that high-stakes accountability of the type legislated through No Child Left Behind engenders conflicting motivations. It may push some principals to take risks, but it also places a heavy emphasis on bureaucratic compliance.

New Ways to Lead

A role can do more than point out what principals are expected to do; it can also specify how they are to do it. Here, too, things continue to change.

Historically, principals have been seen as authoritarian figures. Their control may have been softened by an affable personality or sense of benevolence, but no one really doubted who was in charge. The early days of the school-reform movement reinforced this image, though with a heroic tinge. Successful principals led with a no-nonsense, take-charge stance that put them at the front of the educational parade.

The recent literature on distributed leadership places much more emphasis on community and shared leadership. For example, Joseph Murphy and Amanda Datnow found that successful principals in comprehensive school reform built "dense leadership organizations" by developing teacher leadership, finding resources to support the growth of professional community, giving teachers the confidence to grow, and managing the leadership agenda systemically. Collaborative approaches are not only viewed as more dynamic and productive, they are sometimes also seen as a solution to the growing demands of the principalship.

Sharing decisions and developing leadership in others can have benefits for any organization, but these behaviors also create ambiguity about authority and accountability. The relentless demands of accountability seem to call for energetic, take-charge strategies. Indeed, success stories typically focus on principals and superintendents who came in and "turned things around."

With a reform agenda that leaves little margin for error, principals may be ambivalent about putting their fate in the hands of others. (Likewise, teachers and others who are invited to take on the mantle of leadership may be ambivalent about accepting responsibility, preferring to leave accountability in the hands of the principal.)

Because society sends so many mixed signals about the nature of leadership, the marriage between accountability and collaboration is sometimes rocky, and there are few well-mapped pathways. Principals thus have to create their leadership styles even as they take on other unaccustomed responsibilities. (See Chapter 11, "Distributed Leadership," for additional discussion.)

Creating a Synthesis

The preceding discussion by no means exhausts the ways that scholars, practitioners, and policy analysts have characterized the principal's role. Other models and images compete for attention: the principal as change agent, the principal as cultural leader, the principal as lead learner, the principal as facilitator—the list seems endless.

Indeed, the proliferation of roles may itself constitute one of the key challenges for the profession. Each role carries a compelling rationale and responds to a real need, but if each is simply added to the to-do list as an equally urgent priority, the job quickly grows beyond human capability.

Hurley, discussing the trend toward ever-more-ambitious job descriptions for principals, asks, "Why are policymakers continuing to define the principal's role in such a way that few people want the job and even fewer can be effective at it? Do they really think it is possible for principals to do more?"

Moreover, the multiplicity of demands creates role conflict. For example, surveys persistently find that principals feel torn between the instructional leadership that almost everyone agrees should be their top priority and the daily management chores that are almost impossible to ignore (Tak Cheung Chan and Harbison Pool; Cooley and Shen 2003; Rebecca H. Goodwin, Michael L. Cunningham, and Ronald Childress; Diane Ricciardi and Joseph Petrosko). Failure to prioritize can lead to unproductive hopscotching from one task to another, or, alternatively, to paralysis.

In the ferment of current thinking about the principalship, is there any hope that a consensus will emerge from continued discussion or research, or must principals resign themselves to a career spent running after the latest set of expectations?

At first glance, prospects for consensus appear dim. As Beck and Murphy have reminded us, expectations for such a visible public position will always be subject to change as the society itself changes. When society changes quickly or deeply, as is currently happening, role expectations can shift even faster. Given all the forces pushing and pulling on today's principal, any kind of national consensus on the role is unlikely anytime soon.

Some analysts, relying on the promise of distributed leadership, paint a more hopeful picture. Portin and colleagues, after listing seven key leadership functions, say the important thing is that the seven functions are carried out, not that the principal is the one who does them. The principal's true role is "master diagnostician," the person who determines what the school needs and how to get it done: "It requires the ability to 'read' a school's goals, commitments, context, and resources. It requires understanding a school's strengths and weaknesses. It means setting priorities, spurring others to act, and thinking long-term."

This view seems consistent with the well-supported research finding that "setting direction" is a key leadership function (Kenneth Leithwood and Carolyn Riehl).

Carrying out this kind of diagnostic function undoubtedly requires a high degree of skill, but principals who do it well may gain the added benefit of relief from "role overload." Instead of trying to be all things to all people, the principal can concentrate on coordinating activities that allow others to step forward and take on various roles.

Another mitigating factor that may relieve role strain is that the context of a particular school may not require the principal to fulfill all roles at the same time with equal vigor. In a school that has endured years of less-than-competent leadership, a new principal may find that emphasizing his or her managerial role will be the healthiest strategy (at least for a while). In a school that has a long history of faculty collegiality and collaboration, the principal will surely find the community-building role easier than in a building where all the teaching was done behind closed doors.

In other words, in some settings, principals can perform their many roles selectively and sequentially rather than concurrently.

Nonetheless, today's principals are pursuing an ambitious agenda. The role that Wolcott's Ed Bell mapped out for himself—serving as a kind of genial shepherd—falls far short of the complexity and intensity of the new standards. Today's principalship is a high-stakes, high-pressure job that requires a high degree of knowledge, skills, and commitment.

CONCLUSION: WHAT'S OVER THE NEXT HILL?

This chapter began with the observation that landscapes sometimes change quickly. School leadership has unquestionably been going through such a period in recent years. Is it likely to continue?

Without the ability to predict what will happen in the social, economic, and political contexts that surround schools, the question is probably unanswerable in any meaningful way. But there seems to be little reason to expect any letup in the pace of change. The stable, self-assured world of Ed Bell is long gone, and many analysts predict that it won't return in the foreseeable future. More than ever, what happens in the smallest school in the remotest part of America is influenced by what happens at the national—and increasingly, the global—level.

Most principals, given the choice, would probably vote for a breathing spell, but the prospect of unending change need not be the cause for despair. In fact, there are reasons to be optimistic and even excited by the changes in the educational system. A time of rapid transformation can present an opportunity for dramatic improvement. In some respects, school leaders today are like the leaders of the American Revolution—they have a chance to invent institutions that give voice to their ideals and shape the course of events for a long time.

And, at least so far, school leaders have exhibited remarkable resilience and resourcefulness. They are undoubtedly under stress, but they are also coping admirably. As these veteran leaders are joined by new principals who come of age in the changed world of schools, we can expect their collective capacity to continue growing.

The editors and authors of this handbook are not in a position to provide school leaders with a detailed road map; principals and others who lead must continue to blaze their own trails. This being said, the remaining chapters can serve as a compass that will provide familiarity with the major landmarks and a general sense of direction.

REFLECTIONS

1. Does the principalship remain an attractive career option in your school district? What dimensions of the job constitute major disincentives?

2. What is it about the principalship that has attracted you to the position or that keeps you going? What dimensions of the job give you second thoughts?

3. Do you see the principalship as being at risk? That is, under current conditions, will schools be able to find and retain principals who can provide the kind of leadership being demanded? If not, how should the job be changed?

4. In your view, how should principals exercise their responsibilities as instructional leaders? Does it require in-depth knowledge and a hands-on approach, or can the principal play more of a coordinating role, as Portin and colleagues suggest? Is it important that principals have teaching experience?

5. In your district, what are the different roles that principals play? Are some more important than others?

6. If you had complete control over your role as principal, what would the job look like? What barriers stand in the way of developing your ideal role? What steps would allow you to move closer to that ideal?

2

The Effects of
Leadership

Larry Lashway

M any principals, pressed for the reason they come to work every day, say simply, "I want to make a difference."

Do they succeed? At the end of the day, when students and teachers have departed, can principals be confident that they've achieved something other than survival? What evidence do we have that school leaders make a difference? And what kind of difference?

From one viewpoint, these are odd questions to ask, since both professionals and the public are virtually unanimous that not only do principals make a difference, they are the key players in school success. Those beliefs are buttressed by numerous anecdotal accounts of inspirational leaders who have turned around troubled schools.

But at a time when expectations for accountability have skyrocketed and policymakers are demanding increasingly rigorous forms of evidence, anecdotes are not enough. Is there credible empirical evidence that principals have a positive impact on schools? And if so, how much impact, and what kind?

This chapter examines the research base on the effects of school leadership. The first section discusses the conceptual and practical difficulties in answering the previous questions, that is, in gathering and weighing the evidence on leadership's effects. The second section introduces three major reviews of research findings on school leadership.

Then, the third section highlights the core leadership behaviors found by these reviews to be associated with student achievement or other positive outcomes. As the final section points out, limitations of the research on school leadership do not allow leaders to put wholehearted trust in the findings as prescriptions for their practice, but the accumulated evidence does give them a defensible starting point as they seek to make a difference in the performance of their faculties and students.

THE SEARCH FOR LEADERSHIP EFFECTS

As with any thoughtful question, the first challenge is to determine exactly what we're looking for. In this case, the answer will be influenced both by our definition of leadership and by our ability to establish a causative link between leadership behaviors and leadership results.

Conceptions of Leadership

Every theory of leadership serves as a lens that puts certain behaviors or traits into sharp focus and sees others only fuzzily, if at all. Thirty years ago, there were no studies linking vision with school success, simply because contemporary leadership theories didn't address vision. Since vision was not considered a part of leadership, it didn't occur to researchers to measure its effects. Today, vision is frequently mentioned as a key leadership attribute. In general, every leadership theory has "blank spots" (unaddressed issues) and "blind spots" (biases) that leave us with an incomplete or distorted picture (Ronald H. Heck and Philip Hallinger).

In much the same way, the theories we hold shape our definition of leadership success. Advocates of instructional leadership in the 1980s measured success by improved test scores, whereas supporters of transformational leadership in the 1990s were more inclined to look at the principal's ability to change school culture.

Heck and Hallinger note that at least half a dozen major theories have competed for attention in the past couple of decades. This diversity of views provides a useful reminder that any study claiming to demonstrate the effects of leadership will reflect the researcher's assumptions and will always provide an incomplete picture.

Discerning Leadership's Effect on Learning

Despite these cautions, it seems likely that most nonresearchers who inquire about the effects of leadership are interested in knowing the principal's impact on student achievement. Student learning has been at the center of school reform for the past decade, and the enactment of No Child Left Behind has elevated that concern to unprecedented heights. In some districts, Adequate Yearly Progress has become the only leadership effect of interest.

Student learning is paramount, but researchers have also been interested in other effects of leadership, such as attendance, student self-concept, positive climate, and teacher perceptions of school effectiveness. Why look at these when the bottom line is academic learning? In some cases, such as student self-concept, the outcome may have inherent value, since academic learning is not the only goal of interest. But there is also growing evidence that the principal's main influence on student achievement is channeled through such intermediate effects. For example, the principal may have a direct impact on the creation of a positive school climate, which in turn allows teachers to more effectively improve student learning.

There is at least some evidence that the principal can play a role in creating a wide range of enabling conditions, including an orderly environment, a strong school vision, high expectations of student learning, positive communication and interaction, feedback to teachers, support of risk taking, and use of data for school improvement (Kathleen Cotton).

Heck and Hallinger concluded: "Continued reliance on narrow standardized measures for assessing the impact of school leadership distorts the meaning of the question, 'Does school leadership make a difference?'"

The evidence cited in this chapter uses a variety of outcomes to measure principal effectiveness, though in most cases, student achievement is the key measure.

Linking Leadership With Results

Research on leadership effects is motivated not just by the usual academic curiosity, but by a search for practical guidance. If we can learn why leaders are successful, then we can hire people with the right traits or help principals engage in the right kind of activities. Ideally, research would determine cause-effect relationships that let us say, "If you engage in action *x*, then you will achieve result *y*."

Unfortunately, trustworthy recommendations of that type are exceedingly rare in educational leadership. To reach unambiguous conclusions, a researcher would have to do the following:

1. Identify and clearly define a leadership behavior of interest.

2. Randomly separate a representative sample of principals into treatment and control groups. Those in the treatment group would agree to use the target behavior, and those in the control group would agree not to use it.

3. Monitor participants to be sure the treatment group was implementing the behavior correctly, whereas the control group was refraining from using it.

4. Identify the target outcome and measure it before and after the treatment.

5. Replicate the study in many other settings.

The obvious practical challenges inherent in such studies have discouraged researchers from doing many of them. Also, it isn't clear that even a large body of experimental studies would yield the kind of concrete guidance that school leaders and policymakers prefer. Experiments tend to focus on one key variable while controlling all others, but effective leadership may actually be multicausal. Organizational experts have long recognized that leadership is highly contextualized; what works in one situation will not always work in another (see Chapter 4, "Leadership Styles and Strategies").

This seems especially true of today's school leadership, which is not only complex but highly dynamic. Ellen Goldring and William Greenfield have pointed out not only that the work of principals is people intensive and morally weighted but also that the school's core activity of learning is unstable and affected by changing demographics, new demands for accountability, growing teacher professionalism, and novel forms of governance.

In such an environment, everything seems connected to everything else, and the effects of a leader's action may depend on three or four other variables. For example, some leaders have turned around schools by implementing a research-based curriculum. But the success of that approach may be influenced by how well the curriculum matches faculty beliefs about teaching and learning, how much professional development is provided, previous staff experiences with school reform, the alignment between the curriculum and state assessments, the degree of parental support, and the current state of labor negotiations in the district. It would take a massive research effort to fully tease out those contextual variables.

An equally difficult obstacle for researchers is the lack of an immediate connection between principal behavior and student learning. Unlike teachers, principals are not in daily classroom contact with students; most of their interactions are with teachers, parents, and other adults. Thus, their influence on students is usually indirect, a conclusion supported by Philip Hallinger and Ronald H. Heck, who found no evidence of a direct impact on student learning.

Some researchers and analysts have begun to search for "through-lines" that will connect the dots. That is, the principal's behavior *A* has an impact *B* on teachers, who in turn have impact *C* on students. That the principal's influence on learning is indirect does not make it any less significant. Anyone who has observed a principal turn around a struggling school can testify to the power of leadership to make a difference in student performance.

Correlational Research

Given the difficulties of experimental research, it is hardly surprising that most quantitative studies of leadership rely on correlations. Correlational research seeks to uncover statistical relationships among variables. If we consistently find that student achievement is high in schools where the principal frequently observes classroom teaching, then it seems reasonable to speculate that there is some kind of relationship between the two variables.

Correlational studies are generally easier to conduct than experimental research, so work of this type has dominated the literature on school leadership since the 1970s, beginning with the well-known school-effectiveness literature. A typical correlational study will compare one or more leadership variables with an outcome measure (typically an achievement test).

An increasingly common form of correlational research is the meta-analysis, which examines a series of studies and produces an average effect size to measure the impact of particular variables. Meta-analysis is useful in detecting and confirming relationships across studies that might otherwise be missed or discounted. It provides a statistically sophisticated way of reconciling a series of studies that may show conflicting results. At the same time, this kind of review requires caution in choosing the studies to include;

high-grade statistical analysis means little if the original research was poorly designed or carelessly conducted. The decision to include or exclude certain studies may have a significant impact on the results.

Although correlational research has added much to our understanding of school leadership, it does have significant limitations. First, as every introductory statistics course emphasizes, correlation is not causation. The fact that A is correlated to B does not mean that A causes B; it is equally possible that B causes A, or that both A and B are caused by C. In the example cited earlier, the fact the principal has time to make frequent observations suggests that the school has ample human and financial resources. The school's affluence may contribute to achievement in many ways, or the higher achievement may simply reflect students' socioeconomic status.

In addition, many correlational studies rely on indirect measures of leadership. Instead of observing leader behaviors, researchers may use a simpler proxy, such as teacher perceptions of leader behavior. Such perceptions have two limitations. First, they rely mainly on what is visible to the teacher; the principal's behind-the-scenes activities may not be reflected in teacher perceptions.

Second, teacher judgments, which are considered to be the independent variable, may to some degree be dependent. That is, perceptions of leadership are often swayed by the "leadership fallacy"—the tendency to assume that because leaders are supposed to be in control, success or failure can be attributed to the leader's actions, irrespective of any tangible evidence. (This effect is well known in the sports world, where managers and coaches with losing records are inevitably fired, even when no one can pinpoint what it is they've done wrong.) In schools, teachers may assume that high test scores mean the principal is doing something right, even if they're not quite sure what it is. Hence, they tend to give the principal high marks on a wide range of survey questions.

Another inherent limitation of correlational studies is the assumption that success can be defined in measurable terms. Any quantitative study defines learning in terms of the measures used. For example, the measures used in many school leadership studies are standardized test scores. Although such scores are fully legitimate indicators (especially in the context of No Child Left Behind), they may not fully capture the range of a leader's influence on learning. It's quite possible that certain leadership behaviors may be associated with high achievement on standardized tests of basic skills, but not on assessments that look for higher-level thinking skills.

Finally, because these studies are often rooted in a quest for school improvement, many have been conducted in troubled, low-achieving schools. Possibly, what works in that kind of environment may not be equally effective in a high-achieving school.

SYNTHESES OF THE EVIDENCE

Leadership research involves so much interpretation and complex statistical analysis that it's possible for scholars to look at the same body of literature and arrive at different conclusions. For this reason, it's far too early to speak of consensus. Recent research, though, does appear to be converging on a credible set of key leadership behaviors that are consistently associated with student achievement and other positive effects.

This section briefly describes three major reviews of research findings on school leadership. The reviews, by leading scholars in the field, differ somewhat in their focus and method, yet collectively, they provide a comprehensive look at research on educational leadership over the past two decades.

Hallinger and Heck reviewed 40 studies that appeared in scholarly journals, peer-reviewed conferences, and dissertations between 1980 and 1995. They chose studies that were explicitly designed to examine leadership behavior, that included an explicit measure of school performance as the dependent variable, and that sampled leadership effects across cultural contexts (11 of the 40 studies were conducted outside the United States).

Kenneth A. Leithwood and Carolyn Riehl conducted a systematic review of the literature for the American Educational Research Association. They did not attempt statistical treatment such as meta-analysis, but they did focus on quantitative studies. Their synthesis identified three major clusters of "core" leadership behaviors that influence school success: setting direction, developing people, and redesigning the organization.

Most recently, Tim Waters, Robert J. Marzano, and Brian McNulty, after reviewing 5,000 leadership studies, chose 70 that met certain criteria of design and rigor and subjected them to a meta-analysis that yielded 21 leadership behaviors correlated with student achievement. The authors noted that leadership theory and professional wisdom to some degree influenced their conclusions, but all 21 of the key behaviors were supported by quantitative evidence. The authors reported that the 70 studies involved 2,894 schools with approximately 1.1 million students and 14,000 teachers.

The three reviews differ somewhat in their methods, and they did not look at exactly the same body of evidence. Nevertheless, collectively they offer the most comprehensive picture available on the effects of leadership. The discussion that follows focuses on the core leadership behaviors found by these reviews to be associated with increased student performance or other positive effects. Table 2.1 ("Core Leadership Behaviors Associated With Student Learning") summarizes these factors, grouping them into clusters of related behaviors.

ESSENTIAL ACTS OF LEADERSHIP

Evidence of the leader's effectiveness centers on behaviors in four major roles: providing direction, developing the capacity of others, pioneering change, and establishing an orderly environment.

Setting Direction

One of the strongest themes to emerge from these studies is the importance of the leader's role in providing focus, direction, and goal orientation. This effect showed up in the first generation of school-effectiveness studies in the 1970s and 1980s. Analysis at that time often had a top-down flavor, implying that the leader provided the direction by formulating ambitious goals, communicating them to the staff, and then monitoring to ensure they were achieved.

Table 2.1   Core Leadership Behaviors Associated With Student Learning

Research Syntheses

Core Behaviors	Leithwood & Riehl	Waters et al.	Hallinger & Heck
Setting direction	1. Identifying and articulating vision 2. Fostering acceptance of group goals 3. Creating high performance expectations	*Culture:* fosters shared beliefs and a sense of community and cooperation *Focus:* establishes clear goals and keeps them at the forefront of the school's attention	Purpose: goal framing and mission building
Developing people	1. Offering intellectual stimulation 2. Providing individualized support 3. Providing an appropriate model	*Intellectual stimulation:* ensures faculty and staff are aware of current theories and practices and makes discussion of these an aspect of the school's culture *Ideals/beliefs:* communicates and operates from strong ideals and beliefs about teaching *Visibility:* has quality interactions with teachers and students *Contingent rewards:* recognizes and rewards individual accomplishments *Communication:* establishes strong lines of communication with teachers and among students *Relationships:* demonstrates an awareness of the personal aspects of teachers and staff *Affirmation:* recognizes and celebrates school accomplishments and acknowledges failures *Input:* involves teachers in the design and implementation of important decisions and policies *Outreach:* is an advocate and spokesperson for the school to all stakeholders	Structure and social networks People Organizational culture
Leading change	1. Redesigning the organization 2. Strengthening school cultures 3. Modifying organizational structures 4. Building collaborative processes	*Optimizer:* inspires and leads new, challenging innovations *Change agent:* is willing to and actively challenges the status quo *Monitors/evaluates:* monitors the effectiveness of school practices and their impact on student learning *Flexibility:* adapts leadership behavior to the needs of the current situation and is comfortable with dissent *Situational awareness:* is aware of the details and undercurrents in the running of the school and uses this information to address current and potential problems *Curriculum, instruction, assessment:* is directly involved in the design and implementation of curriculum, instruction, and assessment practices	
Establishing managerial order		*Order:* establishes a set of operating procedures and routines *Discipline:* protects teachers from issues and influences that would detract from their teaching time or focus *Resources:* provides teachers with materials and professional development necessary for the successful execution of their jobs	

Today, the discussion is more likely to invoke concepts such as vision, learning communities, and distributed leadership, but the core conclusion remains the same: Effective leaders keep the school focused on essential outcomes.

Leithwood and Riehl see three key elements at the heart of setting direction:

1. *Identifying and articulating a vision.* When people can see an attractive picture of the future that embodies their values and believe that it is achievable, it inspires their commitment and focuses their energies. Many educators possessing a strong values orientation nurture individual visions, but collective visions that unify the staff are hard to create and sustain. Schools are pulled in many directions by a diversifying population, conflicting instructional philosophies, multiple levels of governance, and fickle policymakers. Principals who weave those disparate threads into a coherent fabric have taken a crucial first step toward success.

2. *Fostering the acceptance of group goals.* The culture of teaching is notoriously individualistic, with teachers operating autonomously behind closed doors. Leaders who can inspire collaboration and consensus on common goals have the potential to create breakthrough performance.

3. *Creating high-performance expectations.* One of the earliest findings of effective-schools research was the conclusion that when teachers and principals held high expectations for student achievement, students indeed performed better. Policymakers at the time often assumed that low standards resulted from a certain lack of toughness on the part of educators, but continuing experience with school reform suggests that a more fundamental cause is teachers' lack of belief that all children can learn. This is particularly true in schools where large numbers of students arrive with backgrounds, attitudes, and language skills that don't respond well to teachers' instructional repertoires. Vision and acceptance of group goals are important precisely because they offer an avenue for overcoming such doubts.

Leithwood and Riehl also note that leaders' ability to establish direction is enhanced by three other practices: monitoring organizational performance; communicating ideas; and working with those outside the school, such as parents, business leaders, and district personnel.

Developing People

Organizational theorists as well as practitioners point to the importance of human relationships in educational leadership, and the research offers ample support. More than a third of the 21 key behaviors identified by Waters and colleagues involved the leader's interactions with others.

Some of these interactions involve fundamental human affirmation. Teachers cherish recognition for the countless efforts they make on behalf of students, students thrive on any recognition of their individuality, and parents appreciate knowing that their children are well cared for. Effective principals are highly visible and plugged into the various social networks centered on the school. They communicate ceaselessly, both formally (newsletters and speeches) and informally (phone calls and corridor conversations). They actively reach out to others, both in the school and in the larger community.

All this activity is more than routine social lubrication. Effective principals seek to develop the capacity of those they work with, helping them to understand the issues at stake, encouraging growth, and rewarding accomplishments. One of the key behaviors here is intellectual stimulation. Good leaders are continually sharing new ideas with their staff, pointing out strategies that might be worth exploring. They seek out relevant professional development activities and encourage teachers to participate. And they keep asking questions: What do we need to be doing? How could we do it better? What would happen if . . .?

In their efforts to develop others, the best leaders do not forget themselves. They deliberately model the kind of behaviors and attitudes they encourage in their staff.

In discussing the leader's social interactions, Hallinger and Heck characterize them as "transformational" rather than "transactional." That is, they are rooted in values and a vision for improvement, not just maintaining a pleasant environment.

Leading Change

Wouldn't school leadership be greatly simplified if principals merely had to maintain the structure that was already in place? The task then might involve not much more than applying oil to the squeaky parts or, in failing schools, getting out the manual and performing a repair job. The reality is that schools today are in the midst of fundamental change, moving from a comfortable century-old structure to something that is not yet well defined. Principals must not only ensure that things go smoothly each day, they must also find ways to simultaneously develop new ways of doing things.

Research suggests a number of ways leaders pioneer change in their schools. Most obviously, they consciously define themselves as change agents with a willingness to challenge the status quo. They continually monitor the impact of the school's practices on student learning and promote innovations that would improve the school's performance.

Researchers are increasingly distinguishing between two types of change: first order and second order. Waters and colleagues describe first-order change as occurring at the surface level; it tends to be incremental or marginal and stays comfortably within existing norms and paradigms. Second-order change breaks with the past, requiring new knowledge, skills, and beliefs; it tends to challenge fundamental assumptions and alter the deep structures of the school.

For example, a new curriculum may involve first-order change if it just requires teachers to teach new content using familiar methods. If it also demands radically different methods or deep collaboration among teachers, it may constitute second-order change. The distinction is significant because some research suggests that substantial and lasting reform depends on second-order change (Jeffrey T. Fouts).

Creating second-order change is not just a matter of selecting a "difficult" innovation and implementing it. Leaders also have to find a way to manage the human equation. As Waters and colleagues put it:

> To the degree that individuals and/or stakeholder groups in the school or school system hold conflicting values, seek different norms, have different knowledge, or operate with varying models of schooling, a proposed change might represent a first order change for some and a second order change for others. Individuals who see

a proposal as first order change are likely to view it as a solution; those for whom it constitutes second order change are more likely to view it as a problem.

Leaders thus have to be aware of the differing degrees of readiness for change in their building and in their community and must tailor their strategy to the school's ever-changing dynamics. Waters and colleagues note that the key behaviors identified in their meta-analysis have differing implications for first-order or second-order change.

Establishing order and discipline, for example, is generally consistent with first-order change (though it may be a necessary precondition for deeper forms of change). Fostering school culture may involve first-order change if it just focuses on promoting cooperation and a sense of well-being among staff. But if it also includes development of a shared vision of rigorous standards for all children, it probably constitutes second-order change. Thus, promoting lasting change requires choosing the right strategy at the right time, with the right people.

Establishing Managerial Order

The importance of an orderly environment has been a staple of the school-effectiveness literature since the 1970s. The earliest research appeared at a time when schools seemed threatened by disruptive student behavior, so this finding was often interpreted in terms of strict discipline and no-nonsense rules.

Since that time, the importance of an orderly environment has continued to show up in research, but the concept has broadened considerably. First, discipline is now regarded more in terms of establishing a moral order and cultivating responsibility. James J. Scheurich put it this way:

> Discipline, or order, as traditionally construed, is not the focus. The focus is on embedding an understanding of appropriate conduct (conduct that applies fairly and equally, even lovingly, to both adults and children) into the organizational culture of the school itself.

Also, the past decade has drawn attention to the need for school environments to be safe as well as orderly. Safety has both physical and psychological dimensions. The school must not only protect students from drugs, gangs, and random shootings, it must provide a haven from bullying and psychological abuse.

Managerial order, though, goes well beyond quiet hallways and well-behaved students. As described by Waters and colleagues, it involves consistent rules, structures, and procedures for staff as well as students and requires that the principal shield the school from unnecessary distractions or interruptions. In such an environment, teachers and students have the luxury of being able to concentrate on the main order of business—learning.

How Big Are the Effects?

Waters and colleagues reported that the average correlation between the 21 behaviors and student achievement was .25. This may initially seem unimpressive, but the researchers point out that in practice it can make a real difference. They estimate that improvement of one standard deviation in leadership performance could boost average student achievement from the 50th percentile to the 60th percentile. Furthermore, "focusing on the most effective or most needed practices can change a school's passing rate from 50 to 72%." Considering the wide range of factors that contribute to students' performance, including their prior academic history and family background, this is a substantial impact.

Kenneth A. Leithwood and colleagues note that the effects are more likely to occur where they are most needed—in schools that are not performing well. "Indeed," they add, "there are virtually no documented instances of troubled schools being turned around without intervention by a powerful leader."

CONCLUSION: A COMPASS, NOT A ROAD MAP

As noted earlier in the chapter, any conclusions we come to on leadership effects will be influenced by our conceptions of leadership and by the way we choose to measure success. Hallinger and Heck note that their selection criteria eliminated some credible conceptions of leadership. "The predominant paradigm of the 1980s—school effectiveness—drove the review," they say. As a result, views of leadership that depended on nonquantitative research methods were not represented, nor were studies that focused on "process variables" such as academic learning time rather than on outcomes such as test scores. Also, studies that found sources of leadership beyond the principal were not included.

Similarly, Leithwood and Riehl acknowledge that their synthesis tends to overlook qualitative research such as case studies in favor of a rather traditional emphasis on knowledge that can be generalized across contexts. They point out that there are other ways of understanding leadership, such as complexity theory, critical theory, and political theory. Also, facets of school leadership that have not yet been studied much, such as moral and spiritual leadership, naturally get little attention in their analysis.

How significant are these omissions? Certainly, the limitations of these studies should cool the ardor of anyone inclined toward wholesale adoption of their findings. The majority of the research involved is at least a decade old and does not fully reflect recent trends such as distributed leadership, heightened accountability (especially No Child Left Behind), and the spread of educational choice. These developments have undoubtedly changed the landscape significantly, constraining principals' options in some ways but possibly providing alternative pathways to influence student learning.

Leithwood and colleagues have also noted that the state of research knowledge on school leadership does not yet permit detailed prescriptions for practice across varying contexts. There are many unanswered questions about how the key leadership behaviors play out in settings with different school characteristics, different student populations, and different state and local policy environments.

But even if these three syntheses and others like them are incomplete, they are significant. For one thing, they do affirm that the intuition of so many practitioners and policymakers is correct: Principals make a difference. Their influence on student achievement appears to be indirect, which is not surprising, because their job rarely entails face-to-face academic work with students. Rather, their impact comes from creating and sustaining the conditions that enable and encourage teachers and students to do their best work.

Statistically, the overall amount of principals' influence on student learning may appear modest, but the picture looks different to those on the ground. Particularly in schools where conditions are preventing teachers and students from performing to their capabilities, principals are in a position to make a dramatic difference.

Another reason these syntheses have value is that the cumulative research evidence points in particular directions, drawing our attention to key leadership behaviors that appear to be at the heart of school success. The state of our knowledge does not yet allow us to connect all the dots and develop detailed strategies to suit every context; in that sense, the research provides a compass rather than a road map. But those responsible for implementing leadership preparation or professional development programs can be confident that these findings constitute a defensible and productive starting point.

For principals themselves, the research provides clues to finding the leverage points that can best move student learning and school change in a positive direction. The local school context will determine the specific actions that will have maximum impact, but armed with these research findings, principals can take significant steps toward making the kind of difference that drew them into the profession in the first place.

REFLECTIONS

1. To what degree do the empirical findings discussed in this chapter match your prior perceptions of effective leadership? Has the research identified anything you would not have expected to find?

2. Conversely, are there any key leadership behaviors not captured by this research? Does reliance on quantitative data tend to overlook certain traits or behaviors?

3. When you think of especially effective principals you have known, to what degree can you recognize the leadership behaviors discussed in this chapter?

4. To what extent does this research uphold the popular image of the principal as the key person in the school's success? Does it overstate or understate the principal's importance?

5. Is this kind of research really necessary, or are people capable of recognizing good leadership when they see it?

6. What implications does this research hold for you personally? Does anything need to be added to your professional development agenda?

PART II

The Person

3

Portrait of a Leader

Larry Lashway, JoAnn Mazzarella,
and Thomas Grundy

WANTED: Elementary principal for progressive suburban school district. Must have master's degree and relevant state certification, strong leadership qualities.

Ads like this appear thousands of times each year, symbols of every organization's search for leaders. What are these school districts looking for? How will they know when they have found it?

At a minimum, we can be sure they want someone who can carry out a long list of specific duties. The new principal will be expected to arrange class schedules, resolve discipline problems, administer a labor contract, evaluate teachers, and apply the oil of public relations to points of friction with the community. And that's just in the morning.

In short, school leaders must first of all be skillful managers—at worst, getting through the week without major disasters; at best, keeping the school humming with happy activity. Whatever else a district may want from its leaders, managerial skill is essential; without it, no school leader will last long.

But in asking for "strong leadership qualities," this district hints it may be looking for something beyond managerial competence. The search committee might have trouble defining this "something," but they undoubtedly hope to recognize it when they see it: a knack for inspiring trust, perhaps, or a talent for creating enthusiasm, or the ability to provide a sense of direction in a confusing world.

Most of us know people like that; if we're lucky, we work for them. But just what is it that we sense in them? Could we, on hearing a description of an utter stranger, recognize the qualities that make a leader? More to the point, could we work our way through a long list of applicants and be confident of making the right choice?

THE CHARACTERISTICS OF LEADERS

Scholars have been exploring these questions for more than a century, often with the assumption that leadership resides in the person, that certain individuals have some set of inherited or acquired traits that enable them to leave their mark on the world. Thomas Carlyle summed up an early version of this attitude with his claim "The history of the world is but the biography of great men." For many years, this belief led social scientists to concentrate almost solely on the personal traits of leaders. They studied the characteristics of corporate executives, football captains, or Girl Scout leaders and frequently came to different conclusions. Their research produced no shortage of attributes: intelligence, self-assurance, enthusiasm, good health, initiative, sociability—the list is almost endless. In fact, it became too large to be of any use.

Critics of the "trait" approach pointed to the unwieldy nature of the list and to the widely varied characteristics to substantiate their claim that there is no essence of leadership that will hold for all cases. As Warren Bennis (1984) remarked of the leaders he studied, other than demonstrating certain similar abilities, they were "tremendously diverse. They were tall, short, fat, thin. . . . They evinced no common pattern of psychological makeup or background."

Because of this disappointing result, researchers after World War II abandoned trait theories in favor of situational theories of leadership based on the belief there are no inherent leadership traits, just leader styles or behaviors that change from one setting to another. "Contingency theorists" believe that a person who is a leader in one situation may be a follower in another; traits useful in one situation may actually be disastrous in others. Hence, leaders are not born with any particular traits that determine leadership. Contingency theory is less interested in who a leader is than in what he or she does in a given situation.

More recently, some researchers have advanced the view that leadership is *distributed.* By that, they mean not just that it can be shared, but that it is a product of complex relationships that are embedded in the life of the organization. The wry observation that "you aren't a leader unless you have followers" actually reflects a fundamental reality: Leaders work through others. If followers refuse to respond, then you may have someone with the title of leader, but no leadership. Leaders can't do the work, and they can't directly supervise everyone all the time, so they extend their leadership through delegation, rules, and even physical objects. (The traditional time clock in factories is a familiar example.)

In some discussions of distributed leadership, the leader as a person seems to fade from view, leaving only leadership as an attribute of the organization as a whole. (See Chapter 11, "Distributed Leadership," for more discussion of these points.)

A Role for Traits

It may be a bit premature, however, to throw out trait research. Although personal characteristics do not offer a complete explanation of leadership, they certainly play a key role in how leaders pursue their goals. Before taking action, the leader measures the demands of the situation against the resources of his or her personal endowments. What leaders do is always affected by their traits, and no matter how broadly leadership may be distributed throughout an organization, people remain at the heart of it.

Thus, Peter G. Northouse was able to conclude, in a recent review of the literature, that "the trait approach is alive and well." Although researchers today are more skeptical about finding some universal "X-factor" that will explain everything, they continue to see value in knowing about the traits leaders possess.

Even if studies yield modest generalizations, they may still point us in the right direction. One report that leadership correlates with intelligence does not mean much; if 20 studies about 20 different types of leaders indicate a correlation, the findings are more convincing.

Also, continued research may find that certain traits are especially important for certain kinds of leaders. Studies about Girl Scout leaders are quite valuable to Girl Scout leaders—and those of school leaders are most valuable to school leaders. Focusing on these traits can simply make us aware of how a particular leader gets results.

And even if we fail to find any universal generalizations, study of leader characteristics is useful in the same way that the study of history is useful. Anyone who approaches history with the goal of determining the absolute truth about "what really happened" will inevitably be disappointed; new facts keep surfacing, old facts are continually reinterpreted, and historians never reach consensus. The very attempt, though, deepens our understanding and educates our insights about human nature. So, too, with the study of leadership. Daniel L. Duke put it this way: "How people make sense of leadership can tell us a great deal about how they regard themselves, their society, and the future."

This chapter explores the most significant findings of previous trait research as well as more recent research on educational leaders to paint a portrait of an effective leader.

Limitations

As we sort through these findings, we should keep in mind some of the inherent limitations of this kind of research. "Leadership" is a broad abstraction, incorporating everything from Harry Truman's decision to drop the atomic bomb to a quiet parent's volunteering to be a room mother. Researchers can't measure it with any precision unless they make a number of assumptions:

1. Many studies define a leader as anyone occupying a position with formal authority over others. If there is a difference between leadership and managerial competence, these studies may not capture it.

2. Many studies define leadership as whatever leaders do, without distinguishing between effective and ineffective actions.

3. Some studies define leadership by performance on short-term tasks in a laboratory setting (often using college students as participants). But real-world leaders operate in real-world institutions over long periods.

4. Some studies define leadership through peer ratings; that is, a leader is someone whom others perceive to be a leader. Although there is good reason to respect

human judgment, there may be important differences between perceived leadership ability and objective leadership skills. (For example, a number of studies have shown that taller men are more likely to be perceived as leaders. There is no reason to think that height has anything to do with actual leadership skill.)

5. Finally, many generalizations about leadership derive from research conducted when leaders were predominantly white and male: No matter how the leadership portrait commonly was drawn, it seemed to include pale skin and a Y chromosome. That has begun to change, particularly in kindergarten through twelfth-grade education, where the number of female principals has increased dramatically in recent decades. Still, the concepts and assumptions derived from earlier studies remain in circulation and may not be fully reflective of today's reality. In other words, leadership as we have known it does not exhaust the possibilities of leadership as it might be.

It is also important to remember that none of this research reveals any single characteristic that determines leadership. Rather, it suggests there are constellations of qualities that appear to correlate with leadership. Not all leaders have these traits, and not even effective leaders have all of them. Many nonleaders have many of these characteristics, and still more have at least a few. Nonetheless, having many of these traits does appear to give one a better chance at leadership effectiveness.

Finally, it is important to remember the leader does not exist in a vacuum, but in an environment made up of people who are acted on by historical, philosophical, religious, cultural, and social influences, assumptions, and biases that influence their responses. Leadership is not simply the execution of impersonal tasks in a rational way, and even the most rigorously designed scientific study may fail to capture the full leadership experience. For that reason, this chapter supplements the findings of research with the insights of seasoned leaders.

What follows, then, is at best a picture, a still life, a portrait in time of what we now assume to be the qualities that make up a leader in our culture. Readers may want to accompany this chapter with an imaginary checklist to see how they compare with this portrait of an effective leader.

PERSONALITY

Some people assume leadership is an offshoot of *personality,* a rather ill-defined term that usually refers to the distinctive ways people handle tasks, interact with others, and structure their lives. The problem for researchers is the overwhelming number of traits that can be considered a part of personality: enthusiasm, aggressiveness, sociability, self-confidence, emotional balance, sense of humor, emotional expressiveness, empathy, flexibility, and many, many others. (Elliott Jaques claimed to have identified 2,500 adjectives describing different dimensions of personality.)

Researchers have found correlations between leadership and many of these dimensions, yet they have never found anything that could be called a "leadership personality." Leaders come in all flavors, an insight that has been partly responsible for the enthusiasm about "styles." Several traits are so prominent, though, that they merit a closer look.

Energy and Involvement

Edmund Morris tells how the young Theodore Roosevelt approached his daily work as police commissioner of New York City. He would come striding briskly down the street, "goggling his spectacles enthusiastically at everything around, about, and behind him." Arriving at headquarters, he'd fly up the stairs, rush to his office, and, in one motion, sit down, take off his hat, and attack the nearest pile of documents, swiftly making decisions on major policies and minor details. After a day's worth of that, he'd prowl the streets at night, popping up like an apparition before malingering officers and sending them scurrying back to their posts.

Roosevelt was probably in a class by himself, but leadership has often been associated with high levels of energy and involvement. This energy may be physiological (the result of good health or lucky genes), or it may come from a desire to be at the center of things. This latter trait is sometimes called "dominance"; according to researchers such as Harrison G. Gough, it correlates significantly with leadership.

Arthur Blumberg and William Greenfield describe effective principals this way:

> They appear to have a high need to control a situation and a low need to be controlled by others. They rather like being in charge of things, proposing ideas, and initiating action. They strongly dislike it, and tend to reject it, when constraints are put on their prerogatives or when their freedom of action and initiative are restricted in any way. They prefer to find their own solutions to ambiguous situations than to be told how to do it by others, particularly their organizational superiors.

Shirley M. Hord and Gene E. Hall likewise found that in facilitating instructional improvement, the most effective principals were those who were most actively involved. Labeling three styles in order of increasing effectiveness—responder, manager, and initiator—they found that the principal who was most actively involved with teachers was the most effective.

One result is high visibility; involved principals walk the hallways and poke their noses in classrooms rather than sequestering themselves in their office. Arthur Blumberg provides a memorable example of one principal's 5-minute trip to get a sandwich, during which she flushed smokers out of the washroom, asked a teacher how things were going in a particular program, chatted with a cafeteria worker, checked with a teacher about a discipline case, complimented a student on some work he had done, picked up pieces of paper from the floor, and hustled some lingering students off to class. The value of episodes like that is not just in their immediate practical results, but in the aura of leadership they create.

Sociability

Trait research has consistently identified sociability as a key attribute of leaders. Not surprisingly, leaders enjoy the company of others and tend to be friendly, outgoing, and expressive. Bernard M. Bass cited research showing strong correlations between leadership and extroversion—and a negative correlation with shyness.

We should be careful, however, about equating sociability with gregarious, back-slapping camaraderie. Mary H. McCaulley, reporting on a number of investigations using the Myers-Briggs Type Indicator, found sizable numbers of introverts among leaders in a variety of fields. She concluded that "it is wise for leadership research to allow for successful leaders with both the extraverted and introverted orientations." Apparently, one may like and be able to work with people without necessarily wanting to party with them.

Sociability is not always an unalloyed benefit. For some less effective leaders, the need to affiliate with others overshadows the need for accomplishment. They avoid conflict and confrontation, and they are not inclined to assert their will if they believe it will offend others or diminish their own popularity (Richard L. Hughes, Robert C. Ginnett, and Gordon J. Curphy).

It's also worth noting that sociability and interpersonal skills are not completely synonymous. One can enjoy being with people without truly understanding them or using that understanding to forge productive work relationships.

Still, having a genuine interest in others is likely to be a major asset for school leaders. According to one high school principal interviewed by Arthur Blumberg:

> I want to know whom I'm working with, what touches them, what motivates them, why they are in education. I want to know what's going on in their lives because so often things that are affecting their lives outside of school affect their performance in school. I spend a great deal of time trying to figure out my subjects as if they were models on a tapestry. Like each one is a small part of that tapestry, but yet every one of them has to fit together for the total tapestry to be complete.

Charisma

Sometimes the leader's personality is so striking it earns the descriptor *charisma*. Originally, the term was coined to describe leaders whose authority was based on personal characteristics rather than official position. In recent decades, it has come to mean something akin to a magnetic personality.

Bernard M. Bass found that leaders described as charismatic do have some common personal traits. They are emotionally expressive, self-confident, free from inner conflict, independent, insightful, eloquent, and energetic. They present a clear vision for the future and the conviction that it can be fulfilled.

Bass also notes that personality alone does not explain charismatic leadership; followers must be receptive to forming a strong identification with the leader. This identification may occur for psychological reasons (for example, low self-esteem) or for social reasons (a national state of crisis). To cite a classic example, Adolf Hitler had the necessary personal traits, but he also needed a crisis in German society (economic trauma and political instability) to become fully charismatic.

A leader who has charismatic traits but whose followers are not receptive to that kind of relationship may become what Bass calls an "inspirational" leader. Inspirational leaders create excitement and enthusiasm about social or organizational goals, but their followers invest loyalty in the ideas, remaining free to criticize the leaders.

Some thinkers see a darker side to charisma, pointing to emotional imbalance and even irrationality. Marshall Sashkin and Molly G. Sashkin claim that charismatic leaders seek obedience from and control over followers, who then become dependent on the leader. In contrast, transformational leaders empower followers to take independent action and become leaders themselves. Although charismatic leaders promise "a magical process of identification" through which the follower will become like the leader, the typical result, the Sashkins say, is exploitation. James MacGregor Burns (2003) goes further: "At best, charisma is a confusing and undemocratic form of leadership. At worst, it is a type of tyranny."

COMPETENCE

Having an aura of leadership is an obvious asset, but it quickly fades if the leader fails to deliver. People like their leaders to have energy, but they demand competence. Researchers have explored a number of types of competence, of which three stand out: intelligence, technical skill, and thinking skill.

Intelligence

Intelligence is such a fundamental human trait that researchers have often looked for a connection with leadership—and have usually found it. Bass, reviewing work in this area, reported a fairly high correlation (.5) between intelligence and the likelihood of being perceived as a leader. He also cited a number of earlier studies that found positive (but somewhat lower) correlations between intelligence and leadership.

These studies don't show how intelligence facilitates leadership, but we can make some reasonable guesses. Since most IQ tests contain a substantial verbal component, high scorers may have a mastery of the language that allows them to articulate ideas in a persuasive way, aiding in the essential task of communication.

Leadership of complex, dynamic organizations also requires considerable abstract-thinking ability. Jaques, in his extensive studies of executive leadership, says the key variable is "cognitive complexity," the ability to handle many variables at different degrees of abstraction. At the highest level, for example, a leader can deal with multiple streams of information at a high level of abstraction. The higher the level of thinking, the more a leader can step back from the immediate situation and see long-term, large-scale patterns and trends.

The importance of intelligence is undeniable, but its role needs to be qualified in several important ways. First, we may want to reserve judgment on how well the general findings on intelligence and leadership apply to schools—an issue that has not been much studied. Because school leaders have proved themselves capable of earning a master's degree, most of them are likely to have above-average intelligence. As a matter of simple statistics, correlations are likely to be lower when a trait has a narrow range. (It's a bit like examining the relationship between height and basketball success. If we study the whole population, height will obviously have a lot to do with ability to excel on the court; if we study only NBA players, height will be less important in distinguishing superstars from everyday players.)

Second, the literature suggests there may be a point of diminishing returns. Bass notes a number of studies that suggest leaders who are far more intelligent than their followers are less likely to be successful. The reasons aren't clear, though one guess is that highly intelligent leaders use higher-level concepts and vocabulary that may place a barrier between them and their followers.

Technical Knowledge and Skill

Every job requires mastery of certain ideas and processes. Research in a variety of fields indicates that those who master these core technical skills are more likely to be seen as leaders and that subordinates readily accept "expert power" (Bass).

In education, this commonsense notion is embodied in certification requirements that require school leaders to have teaching experience. The assumption is that since principals have to supervise teachers, they will have better capability and more credibility if they themselves have firsthand experience performing that role.

But expertise is a double-edged sword. On one hand, principals need to demonstrate their expertise to gain the respect of their staff, since teachers sometimes nurse a suspicion that administrators have lost touch with classroom realities.

On the other hand, the nature of teaching discourages top-down management. Richard M. Ingersoll notes that "teaching is an inherently ambiguous, unpredictable, and fluid craft" requiring highly individualized decision making. Teachers have a strong sense of responsibility for what happens in their own classrooms and seldom appreciate administrative decisions that limit their flexibility.

The recent emphasis on teacher empowerment and facilitative leadership has sharpened this dilemma. Nona A. Prestine, studying schools engaged in restructuring, found some principals frustrated at having their substantive ideas on curriculum ignored by a newly empowered faculty. Thus, it appears that though knowledge of teaching and learning is a valuable asset for principals, they have to employ this expertise with tact and discretion.

Some observers believe technical expertise is overrated as a leadership trait. They argue that the leader's job is not to do the work but to see that the work gets done, and they point out that executives frequently make the leap from one industry to another. In pursuing this question, Bradley Portin found that schools required seven kinds of leadership: instructional, cultural, managerial, human resource, strategic, external development, and micropolitical. The principal's most crucial role, though, was diagnostician—determining what kind of leadership was needed where. Portin concluded:

> The essence of the principalship lies in ensuring that these seven leadership functions are performed. Whether principals perform or delegate the functions is a secondary consideration.

Cognitive Skill

Leaders confront an endless procession of problems, many of them ill structured (lacking routine solutions). Do they think about these problems differently or more effectively than nonleaders? Some evidence appears to say yes.

Jaques found that cognitive complexity increases with the level of leadership: the higher the leader, the more sophisticated the thinking. He particularly noted a steady increase in breadth of thinking. Top leaders dealt with forests rather than trees, and the scope of their thinking stretched over a longer period (their strategic vision usually looked ahead 2 to 5 years).

Sashkin and Sashkin agree that cognitive capability is what enables effective leaders to comprehend and advance a vision. Their superior ability to think clearly about chains of cause and effect equips them to conceive a relatively long-term plan of action for achieving the vision. Transformational leaders, the Sashkins emphasize, contribute to the success of their organizations by helping to develop the cognitive abilities of their followers.

Leaders cannot afford to look exclusively to the horizon, however. Derek J. Allison and Patricia A. Allison found that effective administrative problem solvers had the flexibility to switch their attention from concrete to abstract and back again, depending on the demands of the problem. Ronald A. Heifetz and Marty Linsky have made the same point. Effective leaders take a "balcony view," stepping back to take a systemic view from a third-person perspective—but then returning to the field of action.

Others, such as Warren Bennis (2003), have suggested that conscious linear-thinking processes may not tell the whole story. Reality is "organic, dynamic, whole, and ambiguous," and effective leaders often make decisions on an intuitive basis. Robert J. Sternberg and Elena L. Grigorenko have made much the same point about "tacit knowledge," which is practical know-how learned informally on the job.

Tacit knowledge includes such things as how to manage oneself (for example, avoiding procrastination), how to manage others (such as motivating), and how to manage tasks (such as communicating ideas clearly). Although much of this knowledge is learned through experience, Sternberg and Grigorenko emphasize that some leaders are simply better than others at acquiring it. Early studies (using simulated problems) have found that tacit knowledge is a better predictor of performance than intelligence.

MASTERY OF SELF

In a world of conflicting values and continuous change, leaders need trustworthy ground on which to stand. For many, the foundation is a deep understanding and firm mastery of self. Bennis (2003) says, "People begin to become leaders at that moment when they decide for themselves how to be." Self-mastery begins with self-awareness and includes other dimensions of psychological health, along with self-assurance.

Emotional Intelligence

Daniel Goleman, Richard Boyatzis, and Annie McKee claim that the foundation of leadership success is "emotional intelligence," a trait that begins with self-awareness. Effective leaders can read their own emotions, know their strengths and weaknesses, and have a strong sense of self-worth. They also manage themselves with discipline, keeping a tight rein on disruptive emotions, acting flexibly when the unexpected occurs, and behaving with integrity.

Goleman and his colleagues have tied emotional intelligence to the physiology of the human brain. This does not mean the trait is fixed; self-awareness can be learned and enhanced. Effective leaders are voracious learners.

Bennis (2003) suggests two components are particularly important in the learning process. One is "an appetite for experience," a willingness to expose oneself to novel situations and ideas, even at the risk of confronting unpleasant truths. The other is reflectiveness, "a means of having a Socratic dialogue with yourself, asking the right questions at the right time, in order to discover the truth of yourself and your life." Bennis notes that the leaders he interviewed mentioned reflection repeatedly, and its importance is underlined in much of the leadership literature.

Psychological Health

Psychological studies of great leaders often show they were driven by forces that border on the pathological. For example, biographers have suggested that Lyndon Johnson's extraordinary will to dominate others was the result of deep-rooted insecurity and that Woodrow Wilson's career was a lifelong attempt to escape his father's shadow. Collectively, accounts like this may create the impression that pathology is a leadership asset.

Though psychological deficits can provide the energy to propel people into leadership roles, it is much less clear that personal flaws and neuroses result in effective leadership. (It's worth recalling that the careers of both Johnson and Wilson ended in disappointment and defeat.) Leaders motivated by such needs may elevate their personal agenda over the needs of others or the good of the organization.

If the leader's inner turmoil expresses itself in bullying or abuse, it can cripple organizational effectiveness. In education, for example, Joseph Blase and Jo Roberts Blase (2003) have documented the devastation caused by abusive principals. Goleman and colleagues point out that leaders set the tone for the organization and that their emotional tactics are likely to echo throughout the organization.

The importance of psychological health was often stressed by psychologist Abraham Maslow, who believed that humans had a built-in drive to become all that they were capable of becoming. People could block this self-actualizing tendency when they had deficits in basic needs such as safety, comfort, love, and self-esteem, but when those needs were satisfied, people lived their lives with more vigor, creativity, flexibility, and compassion for others. Individuals with those traits were more likely to be effective leaders.

One problem (for researchers as well as leaders) is that with some traits, more is not always better. Robert E. Kaplan, for instance, has found that executives' "expansiveness" (highly focused energy and drive) is a valuable leadership trait, but only up to a point. Excessive levels of expansiveness turn the leader into a rigid, domineering tyrant with little sensitivity to others' feelings. Recognizing the dividing line can be difficult, says Kaplan. "Some excess is virtually unavoidable. It is too much to expect high-powered individuals to be finely calibrated at all times." Yet he notes that some executives consistently go over the line, whereas others are able to "throttle back" and keep their drive in balance.

The importance of balance is echoed by Gough, whose work with the California Psychological Inventory has led him to develop a scale for measuring "integration." According to Gough, those who have integrated their traits into a balanced whole are more likely to be seen as leaders—no matter what their basic predilections.

Closer to home is the testimony of a number of Blumberg and Greenfield's principals. Like Kaplan's expansive executives, they had great energy and a strong determination to get things done. Yet they repeatedly mentioned the importance of not pushing too far, too fast. They talked of "planting seeds" and "dangling bait," and freely told stories of how being overeager had gotten them into trouble. For these leaders, patience was not a natural condition, but they had learned its value from experience, and their psychological balance allowed them to make the adjustment.

Self-Assurance

Blumberg and Greenfield found that effective educational leaders are secure; that is, they are not threatened by new ideas or confrontations with others. "Their sense of themselves as people and what it is they are about seems rather highly developed." The authors believe this feeling of security and sureness about themselves fosters a high tolerance for ambiguity. They can survive in a confusing situation where rules are ill defined, and they can live with uncertainty.

Effective leaders are also secure enough to shun the spotlight and let others take the credit. Jim Collins, in his influential study of extraordinarily successful companies, found that their leaders had a "compelling modesty." They downplayed their accomplishments and took responsibility for their failures. Although they had an unwavering resolve, their ambitions were focused on the company, not personal advancement.

None of this means that leaders are free of self-doubts and anxiety. James A. Autry, a successful consultant and publishing executive, told of a lunch conversation with a fellow executive:

> At this lunch, he stopped eating abruptly, put down his knife and fork and asked, "Do you ever get the feeling that one day they are going to come into your office and say, 'Okay, Autry, we found out about you'?" "Yes, yes," I said, almost shouting, "I frequently get that feeling. You, too?" He nodded, and we both began to laugh.

Autry concluded that even the highest leaders are never as self-assured as they seem, because they are always contending with the expectations of others. He suggests that effective leaders define success by their own standards of importance, realizing that

> if you can achieve satisfaction and fulfillment in the very effort of trying, rather than in the accomplishment of *everything* you set out to do, you will have achieved 99 percent of the value of what success really means.

Whatever doubts and insecurities at times plague successful leaders, they do not succumb to indecision. Inability to act is "one of the most important factors that 'derail' otherwise promising leadership careers," according to the Sashkins. They say self-confidence is "the personal characteristic that enables leaders to plan and take action."

INTERPERSONAL COMPETENCE

School leadership is people intensive; principals rarely go more than a few minutes without interacting with someone. Being friendly and outgoing is not enough; forging and maintaining productive relationships requires a formidable combination of sensitivity, skill, and compassion.

Empathy

If self-awareness is the foundation of emotional intelligence, awareness of others is the complementary capability that marks a leader. According to Goleman and colleagues, effective leaders are highly sensitive to the social relationships that surround them. Specifically, they have empathy (the ability to sense the feelings and perspectives of others), organizational awareness (the ability to understand the interplay of human relationships at the organizational level), and a service orientation (the ability to identify the needs of their customers or employees).

Those capabilities also serve as the platform for relationship management: creating consensus on a common goal, resolving conflicts, and building teamwork. Goleman and his associates explain that all this is not just friendliness, but "friendliness with a purpose," designed to move the organization in the right direction.

These relationship skills may be especially important in school settings, where teachers operate as semiautonomous professionals who often resent administrative intrusion into their classrooms and sometimes do not have a strong habit of collaboration with peers. Building social consensus in schools is seldom a matter of logical persuasion; dialogue, support, and encouragement are generally more effective tools. Joseph Blase and Jo Roberts Blase (1994) have documented teachers' positive responses to principals who operate in this way.

Communication

Communication is a persistent theme in the research on leadership, and it would be difficult to find researchers or practitioners who downplay its importance. For example, Blumberg and Greenfield observed "extremely well-developed expressive abilities" among the eight outstanding principals they studied. "All of these principals had very well-developed interpersonal skills and were able to communicate effectively in face-to-face interaction with a diverse range of individuals and groups."

Successful communication depends on finding the appropriate words, words that will convey the essential meaning and provide just the right tone. More than one promising leadership initiative has been smothered beneath a sea of verbal sludge; jargon, clichés, and dry statistics rarely inspire enthusiasm.

Effective Communication

What does work? Bass found evidence that employees tend to remember brief messages that neatly summarize organizational values (for example, "If you're not helping, you're hindering"). Howard Gardner, after examining the lives of great leaders, concluded the prime ingredient is the ability to tell a story that resonates with the deepest ideals and aspirations of followers. For example, Martin Luther King Jr. told a story of ordinary people vanquishing oppression through steadfast, courageous actions.

Leaders who tell such stories—and embody them in their lives—forge a deep bond with their followers. In school leadership, stories that highlight the work and achievements of teachers, students, and parents can send a powerful message (Colleen Armstrong).

But communication is more than a matter of finding the right word; the message has to be delivered in a timely and appropriate way. Peter L. Wright and David S. Taylor argue that effective communication requires leaders to understand the situation (What are the issues?), be able to read people, and tailor the message accordingly. They identify a number of basic communication patterns, such as "tell," "tell and sell," and "problem-solving." Knowing which of these is appropriate is a key skill.

In addition, Bass notes a number of other factors that may be critical: timing, style (formal vs. informal), linguistic form (directive vs. request), nonverbal language, concern for individual differences, and the amount of time spent on communication.

William Foster offers another perspective by arguing that a chief function of the leader is to clear away the distortions that enter language through some people's desire to maintain domination and power. For example, student failure may be casually attributed to "unmotivated students" or "poor home environment," thus blaming the student rather than examining the school's failure to meet that student's needs. Some labels are accurate, but others are not: Leadership is telling the difference.

Some forms of communication are nonverbal. James M. Kouzes and Barry Z. Posner (1987) point out that skillful leaders send distinct messages through the use of symbols, artifacts, and ceremonies. Posters, buttons, and T-shirts can be a tangible way of reinforcing key values. Personal example—practicing what you preach—is another powerful communication tool, one that says, "This is for real!" Even the use of architectural space (for example, reconfiguring the school office to make it more welcoming) is a communication tool.

Listening

Most researchers comment on the good listening skills of effective principals. Blumberg said, "Every time I asked an administrator what was most important for him or her to be able to do well, the response was, 'Listening.'"

Good listening goes beyond hearing the words. Rather, it demands complete attentiveness to the other person. A high school principal interviewed by Blumberg explained his approach this way:

So a stranger, a parent, comes into your office. There are lots of things I pay attention to, 'cause I have to make a judgment about what to do. First, I try to remember if I've seen them in other places, in other settings. I watch how they approach me. I listen to the kinds of things they say, the adjectives they use, their tone of voice. I try to get a sense of whether or not they seem inclined to be even-handed or whether they seem to be exaggerating. And all those things put together helps [sic] me understand the kinds of things I may be able to do in the situation. Whether, for example, we can hold a dialogue with each other or I just have to use my authority to shut them off.

This kind of attentive listening has two advantages. First, it communicates care and consideration, qualities usually associated with employee satisfaction, according to Bass. The principal's "personal touch," said one teacher in a restructuring school, "helps build my sense of empowerment because it establishes a foundation for mutual respect. It helps make you feel comfortable about discussing classroom problems because you feel that she values your feelings and opinions" (Blase and Blase 1994).

Second, careful listening may keep the administrator from making snap decisions based on false assumptions. Principal B. J. Meadows found that it allowed her to find common ground with parents who complained about misbehavior at bus stops. "In the past, I had sometimes proposed a solution before I understood a problem completely. I then became invested in my way of solving the problem and unconsciously set up a power struggle."

(For more advice on how to communicate effectively with the spoken and written word, see Chapter 16, "Communicating.")

CHARACTER

Before social scientists talked about traits, most people judged leaders by their *character*, a word that implies humans are not just bundles of skills but embody a particular outlook on life, a certain integrity of belief and action. Nineteenth-century educators ranked character high in the constellation of leadership virtues—often at the very top. Character was less prominent in 20th-century research (perhaps because it is difficult to measure), but it has recently recaptured the attention of scholars.

Authenticity

Recent thinking places high value on authenticity. An authentic leader is one with integrity, which is a kind of consistency. Robert Evans says, "At the simplest level it means standing for something, having a significant commitment and exemplifying this commitment in your behavior."

What leaders stand for is part of what makes them distinctive—their passion. The commitment shows that they practice what they preach. Modeling the values seals the deal, assuring followers that the leader is a reliable and trustworthy person. Although they do not use the term *authentic,* Sashkin and Sashkin agree that consistency and credibility create trust because they reduce uncertainty and ambiguity.

Moral Strength

What do people value most in their leaders? Is it competence? Warmth? Flexibility? No, the word that shows up most often is *honesty* (James M. Kouzes and Barry Z. Posner 1993; Michael D. Richardson and colleagues).

For a long time, 20th-century images of high-powered leadership did not leave much room for this traditional virtue. It was either taken for granted or ignored by social-science researchers who preferred to deal with more objective and measurable traits. But the 1990s have seen a surge of interest in values and morality. Words like *covenant, stewardship*, and even *spiritual* have been popping up regularly in discussions of leadership.

Empirical research in this area is still limited, but a growing school of thought says the leader's job is inherently moral: It is not just a matter of doing things right, but of doing the right things. Thomas Sergiovanni argues that this responsibility extends beyond personal ethics and that the principal must be dedicated to creating a "moral community" and "virtuous school." Leaders who see themselves as stewards will be able to create school communities that are both collegial and responsive to the needs of community members.

Beliefs

We've seen that the research linking intelligence with leadership indicates success depends on how—and how well—leaders think. But what leaders think may be equally important.

Samuel E. Krug, in arguing for a "constructivist" perspective on leadership, points out that surface behaviors may disguise deep differences in outlook that lead administrators to respond to the same event in very different ways. He gives an example of two principals required to personally supervise the cafeteria. One principal saw the duty as a time drain that interfered with "important" tasks. The other saw it as an opportunity for publicly recognizing student achievements, thereby reinforcing the school's academic mission and building school-parent relationships. In each case, the duty was the same, but one principal's beliefs turned it into something much more meaningful.

Are there particular beliefs that lead to success? The early effective-schools literature identified one: The best schools had principals who sincerely believed students could and would succeed. More recently, researchers interested in restructuring have suggested that school change requires leaders with a specific set of beliefs. Sylvia Mendez-Morse says effective change agents have a distinctive vision, a mental image of what the school is capable of becoming. They believe the contributions of staff members are vital. They also believe schools are for learning and students come first.

Leaders also have certain beliefs about themselves. Bass notes successful leaders have a high degree of "self-efficacy"—they believe they can make a difference, and they have confidence in their actions. Not surprisingly, most studies show leaders to have high self-esteem (though there may be some cases in which leadership is an attempt to overcome low self-esteem).

LEADERSHIP BEHAVIORS

Over the years, skepticism about trait theory has led many researchers to zero in on what leaders do. In their view, leadership is less a matter of qualities within a person and more a matter of how the leader functions in the organizational or political environment. The list of key leadership behaviors is nearly as long as the list of essential leadership traits, but three occupy an especially prominent place in current leadership discussions: building coherence, acting entrepreneurially, and infusing spirit into the organization.

Building Coherence

More than 70 years ago, Mary Parker Follett distilled the essence of leadership thusly: "Out of a welter of facts, experience, desires, aims, the leader must find the unifying thread. He must see a whole, not a mere kaleidoscope of pieces."

Although Follett may have been ahead of her time, vision shows up today on virtually every short list of top leadership traits. It has become virtually axiomatic that school leaders interested in restructuring must generate and share a dynamic vision of the new direction.

Indeed, virtually every current study of leadership makes this point. And when you think about it, it makes perfect sense. To lead means to take somebody someplace. If you don't know where you are going, you can't really be leading someone there—and you won't know when you've arrived. Hence, the ability to visualize goals is a prerequisite for leadership. "Leadership," says Mendez-Morse, "requires vision. It is a force that provides meaning and purpose to the work of an organization. Leaders of change are visionary leaders, and vision is the basis of their work."

Admittedly, the concept of vision suffers from a certain imprecision, and it has at times been the victim of faddishness. But the basics are not mysterious. A vision is an attractive picture of the future—a way of saying, "Here's where we should be going." Visions work because they provide clarity, creating coherence in an otherwise chaotic environment. Moreover, when they are attuned to the values and beliefs of followers, visions inspire passion, commitment, and great effort.

(See Chapter 7, "Visionary Leadership." For a summary of research findings on setting direction, see Chapter 2, "The Effects of Leadership.")

Acting Entrepreneurially

Because principals have often been portrayed as cautious bureaucrats, examination of school leadership has rarely included the entrepreneurial spirit sometimes found in the private sector. But with the arrival of market forces in public education, that may be changing.

Robert J. Brown and Jeffrey R. Cornwall describe entrepreneurial leaders as alert to the opportunities that change brings and willing to take risks. They can operate in the organization as "intrapreneurs," seeking out pathways not contained in the standard job descriptions. More ambitiously, they can work to create an entrepreneurial school that will support the efforts of teachers to think and act outside the box. According to Brown and Cornwall, entrepreneurial educators are relentlessly goal oriented, constantly scan the environment for opportunities, encourage innovation, and act decisively.

The newfound interest in entrepreneurial behavior has not yet been the subject of research, so there is little information on the role it plays in today's schools. But the multiple pressures faced by principals will likely force them to become ever more resourceful.

(Chapter 19, "Allocating Resources," includes a section on educational entrepreneurship that looks at such activities as school and parent fundraising, local education foundations, business-education partnerships, advertising, corporate sponsorship, and merchandising.)

Infusing Spirit

In recent years, leadership discussions have taken an inward, reflective turn, and words like *spirit*, *soul*, *poetry*, and even *jazz* have pervaded the literature. Because these concepts do not readily lend themselves to empirical research, there is little solid evidence for them, but the discussion has struck a chord with many students of leadership.

Spirit is an inherently abstract term, and most definitions seem to center on personal identity and meaningfulness. Individuals with healthy spirit feel connected with something larger than themselves and believe that their life is greater than the sum of their visible behaviors. In the leadership literature, spirit is not specifically a religious construct, though many people, including many educators, are religiously grounded and may see their work as a form of ministry.

Russ S. Moxley puts spirit in the context of human energy. Just as people draw on physical energy, mental energy, and emotional energy, they also need spiritual energy to thrive. When drawing from spiritual energy, people feel "alive" or "in touch" or "fully human." The absence of spirit is not always recognized, but it is felt in the form of apathy, hopelessness, and alienation. In work settings, low spiritual energy is usually described as "low morale."

Leaders can elevate spirit by creating a shared sense of values and collective mission and by establishing conditions that let followers see how their work contributes to that mission. In Moxley's view, strong spirit grows from partnerships characterized by interdependence, mutual respect, and shared power.

In some respects, this account of spirit echoes the themes of transformational leadership articulated by James MacGregor Burns (1978). From his study of political leaders, Burns deduced that the most effective leaders evoked morally purposeful behavior from their followers. These transformational leaders rallied followers into a common cause for worthy goals. In other words, they offered personal and social meaning, not material benefits.

THE GENESIS OF LEADERSHIP

If leaders do have traits and characteristics that separate them from followers, these traits must be acquired somewhere. Some, such as intelligence, come from a poorly understood combination of genetic endowment and early nurturing. Others, such as cooperativeness and ease in groups, are believed to spring chiefly from parental influences. Many specific leadership skills are obviously learned through experience.

Heredity

One of the oldest debates in psychology is how much human behavior can be attributed to heredity. After decades of trying to untangle the threads of nature and nurture, the issue is still unresolved—and probably irresolvable.

It seems likely that some key facets of temperament are either inborn or established in the cradle. For example, some infants seem to be naturally sociable and outgoing—traits that may very well pave the way for a leadership role later in life. Likewise, some infants boldly explore their world at the earliest opportunity, whereas others hang back, cautious or even fearful.

Despite these natural tendencies, most modern researchers stress nurture over nature. For example, in their study of effective leaders, Warren Bennis and Burt Nanus say it is a myth that "leaders are born, not made":

> Biographies of great leaders sometimes read as if they had entered the world with an extraordinary genetic endowment, that somehow their future leadership role was preordained. Don't believe it. The truth is that major capacities and competencies of leadership can be learned, and we are all educable, at least if the basic desire to learn is there and we do not suffer from serious learning disorders. Furthermore, whatever natural endowments we bring to the role of leadership, they can be enhanced; nurture is far more important than nature in determining who becomes a successful leader.

It may well be people are born with certain genetic predispositions to behave in one way or another, but these tendencies are modified and shaped by experience.

Birth Order

Any child with siblings can tell you about the trials and tribulations of being the first-born or the last-born or an in-betweener. In recent decades, popular psychology has made much of the "birth-order factor," but its relation to leadership is ambiguous. Some studies show the oldest child to be more socially maladjusted, more conservative, less aggressive, less self-confident, more introverted, and less inclined toward leadership than other children. To the extent that firstborns acquire these characteristics, it may be because their parents are inexperienced and less secure in their marriage and finances, or because older children must adjust to decreased attention when siblings arrive (Bass).

At the same time, in some families (especially in stable, one-parent households or two-parent households where both parents work), the firstborn may be encouraged to take on leadership roles and thus may well acquire more leadership abilities than the younger siblings. Also, in extended families, where other adults are present to provide support for the new parents, the oldest child may not suffer from the lack of security and parental inexperience that hampers the parents of "nuclear" families.

Bass concluded: "In all, taken by itself, it would seem that birth order may or may not make a difference, depending on other aspects of family life."

Family

When people name the greatest influences on their lives, parents are usually at the top of the list. Therefore, it seems reasonable to ask how family life might affect the development of leadership.

For much of the 20th century, psychoanalytic thinkers looked for the roots of leadership in the psychodrama of family relationships. A number of "psychobiographies" reconstructed the early lives of figures such as Martin Luther, Adolf Hitler, Mohandas Gandhi, and Vladimir Lenin, finding clues in oedipal relationships, traumatic events, and sibling rivalries. As compelling as these biographies were, they seldom led to convincing generalizations. In the end, each life seemed to constitute its own unique world.

More recently, Bass reviewed studies that linked child-rearing practices to traits believed to be valuable in leadership. In one study, children allowed to participate in family decision making were more resourceful, self-reliant, cooperative, and at ease in groups. Another concluded that "sociability and cooperativeness were greater when parents were clear and consistent, explained decisions to their children, offered opportunities for decision making, had rapport with their children, and better understood their children's problems."

Studies of successful leaders also show that their parents instilled high standards, especially a strong work ethic, and provided opportunities to act independently. Leaders often report having at least one strong parent who provided a positive role model.

Such generalizations remain modest, though, and the combination of heredity, family environment, and unique life events make it difficult to predict how a child will respond to even the most careful upbringing. Many children raised under nearly ideal circumstances will go through life without seizing the opportunity for leadership. Others, subjected to an emotionally tumultuous childhood, prove resilient. The path to leadership takes many surprising twists and turns.

Socioeconomic Variables

Many studies over the years have found that those in leadership positions tend to come from higher socioeconomic groups. In spite of the myth that great presidents are born in log cabins, Bass said few have come from lower socioeconomic groups. One study he mentioned found that town leaders tend to be children of town leaders and that 70 percent of the fathers of businessmen are businessmen.

As it happens, determining parental socioeconomic status is notoriously difficult, because the different elements of status (occupation, income, education, and prestige) do not perfectly correlate.

We need to be especially cautious in drawing conclusions about school leaders. Dan C. Lortie, in his landmark study of teachers, observed that teaching (the starting point for most administrators) has long had a reputation as a convenient path for the upwardly mobile. Using figures from the 1960s, he estimated almost a third of the teaching force had parents who were blue-collar workers. C. Emily Feistritzer, examining data from the mid-1980s, found that 20 percent of teachers' fathers had unskilled or semiskilled occupations, whereas another 15 percent were farmers.

Also, keep in mind that those who go on to become administrators may differ from those who remain in the classroom. In any case, it's important to remember socioeconomic status is only associated with reaching a leadership position—not necessarily with distinguished performance. Class and wealth may smooth the way to the top but are less helpful in solving the problems that come with that territory.

Education and Training

If you ask superintendents and principals where they learned to do their job, the universal answer is "on the job." Blumberg agrees. His conversations with principals convinced him school administration is a craft, learned inductively in hundreds of little episodes. School leaders do not operate from scientific principles or rigid rules, but from informal "rules of thumb" that have been tested in the fires of real life.

This is not to suggest it is easy to learn to be a leader. There is no simple formula, no rigorous science, no cookbook that leads inexorably to successful leadership. Instead, it is a deeply human process, full of trial and error, victories and defeats, timing and happenstance, intuition and insight. Learning to lead is somewhat like learning to be a parent or a lover: Your childhood and adolescence provide you with basic values and role models, and books can deepen your understanding, but you can become proficient only by doing it.

Of course, not everybody survives this plunge into the deep end of the pool. Those who do, says Blumberg, are the ones who learn from mistakes, develop and trust their "sixth sense," and encounter both positive and negative role models.

And what of formal preparation programs? Blumberg suggests they play a modest (but useful) role by providing future administrators with a perspective—a way of thinking about their craft. Unlike dentists, who learn and hone their core skills in courses, school leaders get a more philosophical orientation. Although some are frustrated by the lack of explicit skill training, Blumberg believes learning what to do may be more important at the initial stage than learning how to do it.

WHAT WE DON'T KNOW ABOUT LEADERSHIP

We've learned a lot about leadership in the 20th century. Compared with the simplistic beliefs of earlier times, current views seem diverse and sophisticated. But simple fairness demands that we also ask what isn't known about the traits of leaders. Are there major gaps in our understanding? The answer seems to be yes.

No Magic Bullet

The most obvious disappointment with the research is the lack of simple answers. Kenneth E. Clark and Miriam B. Clark, summing up extensive research, say, "Our studies have found no single comprehensive list of leadership qualities. Every investigator who studies dimensions of leader and manager behavior comes up with a slightly different, or substantially different, list."

There is no leadership gene, no ideal incubator for nurturing the kind of leaders we need and want. Who gets to be a leader, remains a leader, and thrives as a leader results from a complex process that eludes easy description.

New Faces, New Approaches

We noted earlier that many current descriptions of leadership rely on research that was conducted when the population of school leaders was predominantly white and male. Will the infusion of women and minorities into leadership positions force us to rethink our conceptions of leadership?

Because women and minorities come to leadership with a different set of experiences, there is reason to think these experiences may give them a unique perspective on the leadership role—a valuable asset at a time when the whole educational enterprise is being rethought. In recent decades, a growing number of case studies and reflective analyses have pointed out possible differences.

For example, Cynthia B. Dillard concluded from studying a female African American high school principal that the principal's actions, a blend of nurturing, toughness, and high expectations, were rooted in her experiences as an African American woman. Similarly, Maenette K. P. Ahnee-Benham and L. A. Napier found that Native American leadership features strong themes of commitment to community, respect for family, respect for cultural heritage and language, and openness to multicultural perspectives.

Catherine Marshall reported that "atypical" administrators (mostly minority or female) use persuasion rather than top-down directives, are strongly sensitive to the needs of children and teachers, and willingly take risks when human needs collide with bureaucratic demands.

Other studies have yielded more ambiguous results, however. For example, Carole Funk and colleagues interviewed a dozen outstanding superintendents and found that males and females were more alike than different in the way they conceived of leadership. Sashkin and Sashkin surveyed 1,500 business leaders and found small differences between males and females that were statistically significant but "trivial, from a practical viewpoint."

Alice H. Eagly, Stephen J. Karau, and Blair T. Johnson did a careful meta-analysis of 117 studies on gender and style among school principals and found mixed results. Overall, female principals did not appear to be more relationship oriented than their male counterparts, but they were more task oriented and used a more democratic style.

Eagly and her colleagues also found evidence that gender differences were greater in more recent studies, as well as in cases where female principals had many female peers. This suggests that as female principals become more numerous, they feel more at liberty to be themselves, rather than imitating the dominant male style.

Sashkin and Sashkin made a similar discovery. When they compared female leaders who owned their own businesses with female executives who were not owners, they found that owners showed significantly stronger transformational leadership behaviors than did their nonowner peers. It may be that the owners felt secure enough to avoid conforming to masculine leadership norms.

Clearly, the relationship between leadership and race or gender is complex. There is little reason to doubt that the different experiences of women and minorities will enrich the ways they define and enact leadership roles. Yet context counts; individual circumstances will lead them to tailor their strategies to the needs of the situation. Thus, it seems the last thing we should expect is stereotypical behavior, whether the stereotypes are old or new.

The Person Behind the Mask

Traditional social-science research gives us a fairly detailed picture of the leader as leader—operating professionally and authoritatively to get the job done. In recent years, a growing number of less formal studies have allowed us to hear the unfiltered voices of principals and superintendents. These voices remind us that every leader remains a human being, bringing to the job an individual history and a full range of passions, frailties, and idiosyncrasies.

We don't know nearly as much as we should about how leaders integrate their work with their personal lives. For example, does parenthood affect leadership? Psychologist

Abraham Maslow once said that a few months of watching his infant convinced him behaviorism could never explain human behavior—thereby changing his philosophy and the course of American psychology (as cited in Frank Goble). Do school leaders rethink their craft for similar reasons?

More generally, we know little about how a person's life journey affects leadership. Charles J. Palus, William Nasby, and Randolph Easton claim that every life is a story that seeks to reconcile "who I was, who I am, and who I might become." Working out that story—finding love, making one's place in the world, coming to terms with parental ghosts—is bound to affect the way people lead, but how?

The answers to these questions may lie more in biography than in correlational studies, but without them, our portrait of the leader will always seem just a little bit hollow.

IMPLICATIONS

We return now to the advertisement that began this chapter. What can we say to the school in search of leadership? As members of the search committee wade through the stack of applications and grill the sweaty-palmed applicants, what clues should they be looking for? Can we offer them a formula for success?

The short answer is no. As we've seen, there is no sure-fire litmus test. The longer answer is more complex, but more hopeful. The portrait we have drawn does suggest some starting points for search committees—and for those who may be contemplating a career in school leadership:

1. *Good leaders are good thinkers, whether they express this skill as intelligence, technical knowledge, or basic beliefs.* Interviewers will want to engage applicants in a vigorous exchange of ideas on a variety of issues. The best candidates will not only have many ideas, they will be able to articulate them clearly.

2. *Good leaders are people oriented.* Measuring such skills is tricky, though a number of instruments can provide a rough-and-ready estimate. The personal interview can be especially helpful in gauging how well job candidates or current administrators communicate and listen, especially if a variety of people and stakeholders pose the questions.

3. *Character is a crucial element in leadership.* Selectors must ask themselves some basic questions about the person before them. Is this someone who can be relied on? Someone who can stand up to the buffeting that every leader must take? Someone who is the kind of human being they would be proud to know?

4. *Since so much of school leadership seems to be self-taught, selectors might want to discover how candidates view their craft.* What mistakes have they made, and what have they learned from them? What are the most important things they know now that they did not when they started? Who was the best (or worst) role model they had? The goal here is to decide whether this is a person who will continue to learn from experience. (Or, to borrow a well-known witticism, is this someone who has had 10 years of experience or 1 year of experience 10 times?)

The literature also offers a few insights into the training of administrators. School leaders often criticize their preparation programs as "impractical" or "too theoretical," and it's now easy to see why. So many of the characteristics of leaders—social orientation, initiative, psychological balance—are not easily taught (nor would most universities feel comfortable in using these traits to select candidates).

Just as important, leadership is highly dependent on context. Effective principals do not just know schools, they know their schools—the history, the personalities, and the sights, sounds, and smells. (Blumberg gives the example of a principal who detected something on the floor above that didn't quite sound right. She couldn't specify just what she was reacting to, and an observer hadn't heard anything unusual, but a quick investigation revealed several students who didn't belong in the school.)

So although training programs might do a better job of teaching specific skills (perhaps through simulations, case studies, or problem-based learning), whatever is learned will not have quite the flavor of the real thing. Any generalized skills will eventually have to be adapted to a highly specific environment.

Current training programs may not be that far off the mark when they provide candidates with an intellectual and philosophical perspective on the school system. As we've seen, leaders are good thinkers, with a particular set of beliefs and a strong sense of purpose. There may be no better time to confront future administrators with difficult questions. What is the purpose of the educational enterprise? Who are schools meant to serve, and how well are they doing it? And what are they, the future leaders, doing here? What can they accomplish as administrators that they can't do as teachers?

There is always a danger such speculations may become sterile, abstract exercises, but it should take no great effort to connect them with the very practical problems school leaders wrestle with every day. Certainly, once administrators get caught up in the maelstrom of a working school, there will be precious little time for leisurely reflection.

CONCLUSION: A SKETCH FOR EACH LEADER TO COMPLETE

A small part of our leadership portrait has been revealed by each of the research studies and reviews mentioned here. Now, like the pieces of a jigsaw puzzle, all the fragments can be assembled to reveal a more coherent (though by no means complete) portrait of an effective educational leader.

This portrait shows leaders are competent both intellectually and socially. They have a high degree of energy and initiative, but have also learned the value of patience. They get along well with people and are skillful communicators. They are psychologically well balanced, and they thus can integrate their diverse traits into a smoothly functioning whole. They have a distinctive set of beliefs and values that they communicate clearly.

As children, they were probably challenged by high standards and the opportunity to exercise responsibility. Much of what they know about leadership has been learned on their own, through practical experience.

As portraits go, this one is rather impressionistic, displaying nebulous shadings of color rather than sharp edges. There is much we don't know, and much of what we think we know may eventually prove to be misleading or just plain wrong.

Moreover, the sketch itself is not of a real leader but only of an imaginary one. The leader whose characteristics are set down here is a pure form, who in actuality does not exist. Like the "typical voter" or the "typical consumer," the "typical leader" is only a composite of common characteristics. No real flesh and blood counterpart exists.

Even if we could find someone with all the traits we've listed, there is no guarantee he or she would be a leader. As Daniel L. Duke has said:

> It is conceivable that there are individuals who manifest all the behaviors associated with leadership, yet fail to embody leadership. . . . Some master all the necessary operations—from planning to decision making—but they do not convey the impression of leadership. Leadership seems to be a gestalt phenomenon, greater than the sum of its behavioral parts.

So what, then, is the point of this incomplete portrait of a nonexistent leader? Simply this: Becoming a leader is ultimately a do-it-yourself project. Examining views of leadership can teach us much about ourselves and our culture, our conceptions and preconceptions. The hope is that leaders, or future leaders, can find in these pages themes that resonate in their own lives and that can help them reflect more deeply on their own journey to leadership.

When things get rough and they are tempted to lock themselves in their offices, such a vision can remind them that human-relations and communication skills are important. When they are coasting along, day by day, not going anywhere in particular, it can remind them that being goal oriented does make a difference. When they are criticized by superiors for breaking unnecessary rules and cautioned not to make waves, it can give them the courage to continue doing things their own way—as long as that way has been successful in accomplishing their highest priorities.

In short, the most important use for this portrait is the function performed by any ideal. It can caution us while at the same time offering us something to strive for.

REFLECTIONS

1. From what you know of school leadership, what are the essential traits or behaviors of effective principals? How does your answer compare with that of your peers? Is there a reasonable consensus?

2. What does your self-portrait as a leader look like? What leadership strengths do you see in yourself? What areas do you worry about?

3. When you compare your self-portrait with the portrait drawn in this chapter, what implications do you see for your professional development as a leader?

4. What light does your own career shed on the development of leadership? Has leadership been a persistent theme throughout your life, or is it a more recent development? What brought you to where you are now?

5. Some leaders are admired as effective; others are remembered as great. What's the difference?

6. In an earlier, perhaps more innocent age, people spoke unhesitatingly about the heroes who had inspired them. Is it still meaningful to talk about personal heroes? If so, what heroes have inspired you, and what leadership qualities did they possess?

7. Take any leader on the national stage during the past several decades, and imagine him or her in the role of school principal. How would the leadership qualities of George W. Bush, Hillary Clinton, or Martin Luther King Jr. (for example) be helpful or harmful in the principalship?

4

Leadership Styles and Strategies

Larry Lashway

S imple observation reveals that different leaders work in different ways. Some are visible and voluble, whirlwinds of loud activity who dominate a room just by walking into it. Others glide quietly through the corridors, observing more than talking, pausing occasionally for brief conferences—a compliment here, a gentle nudge there.

Some are dreamers, painting the future in broad, confident brushstrokes. Others are mechanics, endlessly tinkering with organizational nuts and bolts. Some rush in where angels fear to tread; others wait for research showing which way the angels are headed.

When researchers after World War II turned their attention from leadership traits to leadership behaviors, they soon found distinctive patterns. For example, some leaders were task driven, focused on the technical challenges of reaching organizational goals. Others, more concerned with the human dimensions of the job, concentrated on motivation and communication.

Eventually these findings led to the notion of *style:* the characteristic way in which a leader uses power, makes decisions, and interacts with others. Style quickly gained acceptance as an important element in leadership, partly because it provided an understandable explanation of everyday experience.

Today, researchers are still far from a conclusive account of the many ways that leaders approach their work, much less any answer to the question, What works best? Louise Stoll, Raymond Bolam, and Pat Collarbone summed up a common view when they concluded: "In essence, no single leadership model sufficiently captures the breadth and complexity of contemporary educational leadership."

There is still good reason to explore these issues of style and strategy, because they can enrich our understanding of leadership behavior. The first three sections of this chapter describe some of the major theories about style and their implications for school leaders. Then, several sections explore three basic strategies leaders can choose from to best fulfill their schools' missions.

As this chapter unfolds, the distinction between styles and strategies may admittedly seem somewhat arbitrary. These categories indeed do overlap, but a key difference becomes clear: Leadership behaviors result not just from temperamental differences but from deliberate strategic choices.

For example, some leaders are directive with subordinates because they are inclined to operate that way when faced with any kind of decision. They identify the problem, determine a solution, and aggressively implement it without much consultation from others. In other cases, leaders who don't share those inclinations may nonetheless consciously behave in a directive manner because they believe it will help the organization achieve its goals. The former case would likely be described in terms of style, the latter case in terms of strategy. In the world of everyday practice, however, the distinction might not be apparent to observers.

DIMENSIONS OF LEADERSHIP STYLE

Over the years, researchers have described style in a variety of ways—not all of them compatible. With some oversimplification, we can identify several broad themes in the literature as a way of categorizing leadership styles.

People or Work

One of the oldest and most enduring themes in style research is the contrast between "task orientation" and "relationship orientation." Some leaders are fascinated by the technical challenges of getting things done: setting goals, organizing meetings, and monitoring activities. Other leaders, seemingly more attuned to the people around them, display great skill at communicating and motivating.

Researchers have identified these as critical dimensions of leader behavior, but they disagree on whether the two characteristics are independent (like intelligence and height) or opposite ends of a continuum (like thin and fat). Fred E. Fiedler, one leading style theorist, believed that leaders are able to focus on either tasks or relationships but not both.

Robert R. Blake and Jane S. Mouton, on the other hand, argued that leaders can be high on one dimension, both dimensions, or neither dimension. They devised a "managerial grid" that allows for four basic styles as well as a "middle road." One combination (high task and high relationship) is regarded as especially powerful, whereas another (low task and low relationship) is considered to be "impoverished."

Despite these disagreements, the task/relationship distinction has had a long and vigorous history, and it appears to capture a fundamental difference in the way that different leaders approach their work.

Directive or Participative

Another perspective on style focuses on decision making. Some leaders ("autocratic" or "directive") make decisions by themselves, without asking for input or participation from subordinates. Others ("democratic" or "facilitative") involve subordinates and trust their ability to make good choices.

Unlike the task/relationship distinction, there is little doubt that decision making is a single continuum—leaders cannot simultaneously be directive and participative. Robert Tannenbaum and Warren H. Schmidt, who developed one of the earliest descriptions, saw the range extending from "boss-centered" to "subordinate-centered." At the boss-centered end, leaders make the decision themselves and announce it (sometimes with an explanation). At the other end, leaders give subordinates great freedom within very flexible limits.

Tannenbaum and Schmidt believed that subordinate-centered approaches were good for both the employee and the organization, but they cautioned that subordinates should not be given more freedom than they were ready to handle. Foreshadowing a major theme in style theories, they argued that effective managers accurately analyze each situation and then adopt the appropriate style.

Personality Type

Might each leader's style be a reflection of deeply rooted personal characteristics that show up in every part of life, from making dinner to choosing a career? Yes, according to one popular theory. The Myers-Briggs Type Inventory (MBTI) was developed by Isabel Briggs Myers, based on a personality theory of Carl Jung, and it has been widely used in a variety of settings. In essence, the theory says that human personality is structured along four dimensions, each containing two contrasting possibilities (Isabel Briggs Myers and Peter B. Myers).

1. *Introversion-extraversion.* This dimension has to do with the way people relate to the world around them. Extraverts are outwardly oriented, energized by interacting with many people in a spontaneous way. Introverts are inwardly oriented—not necessarily shy, but uncomfortable sharing their thoughts spontaneously in public. When extraverts have to make a decision, they talk about it to anybody who walks into their office; introverts first figure out what they believe before sharing it with a wider audience.

2. *Sensing-intuition.* This dimension focuses on how people gather information. Some, the sensers, need concrete, down-to-earth data; they need to see, hear, and touch things in the real world. Intuitives use a global perspective, seeing large, abstract patterns and possibilities; they love dealing with hypotheticals and what-ifs.

3. *Thinking-feeling.* This dimension has to do with the kind of data people use to make decisions. Thinkers tend to approach things rationally and objectively, basing decisions more on abstract principles than on specific situations. Feelers tend to use a more personal and subjective approach, paying special attention to how the decision will affect others.

4. *Judging-perceiving.* This dimension has to do with the way people structure their lives. Judgers are methodical and well organized. They like to know what will happen when, and they enjoy checking things off lists. Perceivers prefer to keep their options

open. They like to gather as much data as possible before making decisions, and they're quite comfortable with uncertainty and surprises.

In the Myers-Briggs system, everyone tends to favor one alternative or the other in each of the four dimensions. The result is a total of 16 basic personality types, each with a distinctive flavor and a unique way of approaching life. For example, Myers and Myers described the ESTJ (extraverted/sensing/thinking/judging) types as practical, detail oriented, analytical, and impersonal, with a strong desire to organize the world around them. (Not surprisingly, this is the most common type among executives, including school leaders.)

UNANSWERED QUESTIONS ABOUT STYLE

Style theories have been highly popular and influential. Uncountable handbooks, workshops, seminars, and articles seek to help leaders improve their leadership through style. Experts still disagree, though, on how to describe styles, much less how they affect leadership. We are left with a number of challenging questions.

Can Style Be Changed?

Just what are we looking at here? Are styles a reflection of deeply rooted personality factors—dispositions that are either innate or acquired through early family experiences? Or are they merely behaviors that can be changed at will? Answers vary.

The Myers-Briggs theory seems to give the most fatalistic answer, since it assumes that style is a reflection of personality, something so much a part of us that we don't even notice it. Although most Myers-Briggs specialists agree that people can always modify their behaviors, temperament is unlikely to change quickly or permanently. It's a bit like writing with your opposite hand—you can do it, after a fashion, but it takes a major effort to become fluent. Leaders who become aware of their preferences can behave differently, but they will always tend to drift back to the old way, especially in times of stress.

Opinions about the other style theories vary on this question. Fiedler believed that leaders can alter their styles very little, if at all. He saw task motivation and relationship orientation as a part of personality and thus difficult to change, especially through short-term training. At best, it takes several years of intensive psychotherapy to create lasting changes in personality structure.

Gene Hall and colleagues expressed a similar view based on their work with principals. They claimed that style is so closely tied to personality and history that changes will seldom be permanent. On the other hand, Paul Hersey and Kenneth Blanchard, who developed a popular model based on the task/relationship distinction, insisted that successful leaders can and should adapt their style to meet the needs of the group. But even they hesitate to claim that every leader can become proficient in every style.

Can Style Be Reliably Identified?

The first step for leaders wanting to improve their use of style is to become aware of what their style is. Yet this seemingly simple task turns out to be complicated.

The Myers-Briggs system reminds us how hard it can be to perceive our own style. Traits like introversion, extraversion, thinking, and feeling go to the core of our identities. "The way we are" seems so natural that we fail to recognize it in ourselves or to realize that others see the world differently.

This lack of perception is especially true for leaders immersed in the rapid-fire pressures of organizational life. Hersey and Blanchard point out that awareness of perceived style depends on regular, accurate feedback, which is hard to come by. Employees are often reluctant to be honest with their superiors.

For this reason, many of the style systems use written assessments. The Myers-Briggs inventory, for instance, asks participants a number of forced-choice questions spanning the four major dimensions. Similarly, Fred E. Fiedler, Martin M. Chemers, and Linda Mahar developed a teaching guide that helps leaders identify whether they are task oriented or relationship oriented. The guide asks leaders to rate themselves on a number of specific indicators, rather than asking them to make guesses about overall styles.

Leaders should use such assessments with caution, since any personal assessment has room for error. In looking at the MBTI, for example, David J. Pittenger raised concerns about the validity and reliability of the instrument. His review found a "conspicuous absence of evidence that 16 different types represent distinct and unique affective, behavioral, and cognitive propensities."

A well-written instrument can be more objective, but any self-assessment will reflect the participant's blind spots. For this reason, Hersey and Blanchard provided two instruments, one to be completed by the leader and the other by subordinates.

In any case, leaders should not be too quick to embrace the judgment of any instrument. In particular, they should not make casual judgments about themselves and others, especially when making major decisions such as hiring.

Is There an Ideal Style?

One of the first questions leaders usually ask about style is "Which approach is best? Which way will get the results I'm looking for?" Researchers have asked the same questions, but have reached a variety of conflicting answers. Bernard M. Bass, summing up a variety of studies, concluded that participative styles are generally associated with worker satisfaction and cooperation. He also cited studies showing that some workers may prefer autocratic styles, and even a few studies in which participation was not satisfying for employees. Of more significance, the available research provides no clear evidence that style affects productivity.

Blake and Mouton argued that the ideal leader combines high task orientation with high relationship orientation. Bass agreed there is considerable theoretical and empirical evidence for this position but also noted mixed or negative results in a substantial number of studies. For their part, most Myers-Briggs enthusiasts, such as Robert Benfari, have declined to promote one style over another, saying that each makes special contributions. Instead, they urge leaders to use their knowledge of style to improve mutual understanding and work relationships.

Does this mean that style makes no difference? Most theorists decline to draw that pessimistic conclusion. Rather, they argue that the effectiveness of different styles depends on the situation.

How Does Situation Affect Style?

Sometimes one style will work best; under other circumstances, another style will be more appropriate. Taking over a school in disarray, a principal may well benefit from using a strongly directive style; teachers would likely appreciate the new sense of order. Later, when the school functions more normally, the same directive style might be resented.

What parts of a situation influence the leader's choice of style? Answers come from a number of researchers, including Hersey and Blanchard, Bass, and Victor H. Vroom and Arthur G. Jago:

1. *The nature of the task.* A minor task that is simple and unambiguous may benefit from a directive style. A major issue that is complex and ambiguous will often benefit from a more participative style.

2. *The experience, expertise, and motivation of employees.* Employees with little training or expertise will often benefit from clear, detailed directions or emotional support. Highly capable employees may resent micromanagement from above.

3. *Time.* When circumstances dictate a quick decision, participation may have to be sacrificed for efficiency.

4. *Organizational culture.* Culture has been characterized as "the way we do things around here," and these ingrained patterns of behavior may crimp leadership style. Pressure may come from superiors (for example, a superintendent who demands quick results), it may come from peers who are not eager to have their own comfortable styles challenged by new ways of doing things, or it may come from subordinates who have gotten used to a particular administrative style.

5. *The likelihood that subordinates will accept the leader's decision.* A participative style may soften resistance to new ideas.

6. *The external environment.* Events in the surrounding community or the larger society may affect style. Ten years ago, principals were being urged to use strong top-down leadership; today, they are being encouraged to use participative styles.

THE IMPORTANCE OF STYLE

So where does all this leave school leaders? Should they rush out to take the first style assessment they can lay their hands on? Should they make a point of consciously altering their style for each new situation? Or is style one of those fads that will eventually find its way to the consulting attic?

The early enthusiasm for style has cooled off somewhat in recent years, as leaders and analysts have gradually realized that it offers no reliable formula to guide leaders' behavior. As Peter G. Northouse has observed, "The style approach is not a refined theory that provides a neatly organized set of prescriptions for leadership effectiveness."

Also, some researchers, such as Lee Bolman and Terry Deal (1997), have criticized the superficial methods sometimes used to teach style—what Bolman and Deal call "thin books with thin advice." In particular, they argue that most style systems don't cover the full range of leader behavior. They also point out the paucity of research validating the different style theories. Commenting on the Hersey and Blanchard model, they conclude that there is "considerable reason to believe that the model is wrong and little evidence to suggest that it is right."

On the other hand, Northouse points to considerable evidence upholding the belief that the distinction between task orientation and relationship orientation is both real and important. The two dimensions "form the core of the leadership process."

Northouse says that the style system provides a "conceptual map" that leads to better understanding of leadership. Indeed, self-awareness may be the greatest benefit of considering styles. When we encounter other styles, they may seem mystifying, annoying, or deviant. When "perceivers" run a meeting, they tend to linger over each item, looking at all the options in depth and happily entertaining motions to table items for later discussion, leaving the judgers in the group to fume, "Why can't we ever get anything decided?" Knowledge of styles helps us recognize that such differences are expressions of deeply rooted style rather than ineptitude or contrariness.

For leaders, it is especially important to recognize how they themselves operate and how others are affected. Leaders may or may not be able to flex their style at will, but understanding it will at least allow them to soften its impact on those around them. One of the effective principals interviewed by Arthur Blumberg said this:

> I really do like to control things, but I know that I have to keep that part of me under wraps. In the back of my mind, I frequently keep reminding myself, "Don't appear to be overly in control." Because if they feel everything is set before they even talk about it, then, in fact, it will backfire.

That principal understood his natural style and how it affected others. He couldn't change his personality, but he kept it from dominating his life, using it as a scalpel, not a sword.

LEADERSHIP STRATEGIES

Some style theorists suggest that leaders can at least temporarily adapt their natural tendencies to suit the situation. When they do this, are they just responding to each situation as it arises or are they guided by some broader set of principles? Do they, in other words, use a strategy?

A leadership strategy is a consciously chosen pattern of behavior designed to gain the cooperation of followers in accomplishing organizational goals. Over time, some leaders consistently use a particular strategy that seems to be more than a reflection of their psychological makeup. Despite the pushes and pulls of daily events that require them to be flexible and pragmatic, they have an image of the kind of leader they want to be, an image they can describe and justify—a philosophy, not just a style. School leaders can choose from at least three basic strategies: hierarchical, transformational, and facilitative.

Strategies originate in the minds of leaders as they confront the complexities of running a school. Two kinds of perceptions are especially important: the way leaders view power, and the lens through which they view the situation.

Types of Power

Although power can be viewed in many ways (see Chapter 12, "Political Leadership"), we'll use a definition offered by Hersey and Blanchard: Power is "influence potential—the resource that enables a leader to gain compliance or commitment from others."

Most descriptions of power boil down into two broad categories. One is *coercive*: The leader has the ability to control the environment in a way that will harm or benefit the follower. Coercive power may be based on raw physical force (as in many dictatorships), on legal penalties, or on the ability to offer material rewards for good performance. The leader-follower relationship thus rests on a straightforward contract: Give me compliance, or bad things will happen; give me commitment, and good things will come your way.

The second type of power goes under various names but can be capsulized as *moral* power. The leader's influence comes from followers' respect for his or her personal qualities, expertise, or position. American presidents, for example, might be respected because of their honesty, their ability to handle foreign policy, or the simple fact that they have been democratically elected. With moral power, leaders can have significant influence even when they have no coercive power.

In recent years, some analysts have characterized the difference between coercive and moral power as "power-over" versus "power-through" (Diane Dunlap and Paul Goldman). In power-over, followers are instruments of the leader: The leader decides, and followers execute. By contrast, power-through recognizes the autonomy of the followers, who have wide discretion to pursue organizational goals.

Every organization relies on some degree of coercive power (for example, if workers don't show up, they won't get paid), but organizational excellence is frequently associated with moral power. Coercion may gain outward compliance, but moral power leads to performance above and beyond the call of duty.

No leader can avoid the issue of power. The choice is not whether to use it, but how. The way leaders answer that question will have a lot to do with the strategies they choose.

Analytic Frames

Leadership strategy is also a product of the leader's analysis of the situation. What am I trying to do here—what's the goal? What are the barriers? What will help us? Whom do I have to convince? Bolman and Deal (1992 and 1997) have offered a useful way of thinking about these issues by delineating four domains (or "frames") for analyzing a situation.

The *structural* frame calls attention to the formal system that gives everyone an officially assigned role defined by rules, policies, and contracts. Through this structure, the school formulates goals, makes plans to achieve them, and evaluates progress. Leaders using the structural frame focus on planning, supervising, communicating, and allocating resources. The ultimate goal is coordination and control through rational analysis.

The *human-resource* frame emphasizes the human needs of employees. Leaders using the human-resource frame pay close attention to relationships, feelings, and motivation. The goal is to make the workplace congenial and rewarding.

The *political* frame sees organizational life as an arena for the pursuit of personal agendas. All employees have something they want to get from their relationship with the institution (security, salary, autonomy, job satisfaction). Since these agendas often clash, people continually jockey for power and resources to protect what is important to them. The result is a nonstop process of coalition building, lobbying, bargaining, and compromising (much of it behind the scenes). Leaders using the political frame recognize and accept these tactics as natural. The goal is to resolve the conflicts peacefully and informally.

The *symbolic* frame sees organizations as cultures, not just collections of formal roles and rules. They have myths, heroes, and sacred rituals designed to symbolize and reaffirm the underlying meaning of events. Thinking in the symbolic frame is sensitive to these cultural factors. The principal is able to recognize, for example, that the year-ending faculty get-together, with its satirical slide show, is not just a raucous party but a way of renewing emotional bonds, atoning for the year's sins, and celebrating one more revolution of the wheel. Leaders using the symbolic frame seek to create an organization with a rich culture that everyone in the organization shares and appreciates.

Bolman and Deal (1992) believe that effective leadership requires the use of multiple frames, but they report that only a quarter of the educational leaders they studied used more than two frames and that only one leader in a hundred regularly employed all of them. Each of the strategies examined next relies heavily on one or more of these frames.

HIERARCHICAL LEADERSHIP

In 1958, Robert N. McMurry, reacting to the growing interest in participative strategies, came to the defense of nondemocratic leadership, which he described as follows:

> The benevolent autocrat structures his subordinates' activities for them; he makes the policy decisions which affect them; he keeps them in line and enforces discipline. He is like a good quarterback, who does not ask the line to decide what plays to attempt or what formation to use, but tells them—and woe betide the hapless player who refuses to follow his orders.

Four decades later, McMurry's portrait is still instantly recognizable. Despite recurrent interest in democratic strategies, most organizations continue to rely heavily on leadership that is hierarchical (sometimes called "top down," "directive," or "autocratic").

Hierarchies have been around for thousands of years, but it was only in the 19th century, when commercial and governmental organizations became bureaucratic, that the hierarchical method of administration blossomed into the standard way of doing business. One of the first scholars to recognize this change was the German sociologist Max Weber, whose study of bureaucracy is still useful in understanding today's organizations.

In Weber's view, hierarchy develops when organizations grow large and complex. Needing people with a variety of knowledge and skills, they divide themselves into departments, each having a specific responsibility that allows workers to concentrate on their areas of expertise. This division of labor requires clear lines of accountability designating who is responsible for what decisions and to whom they report, as shown by the familiar pyramidal organization chart.

The leader's power thus derives from the position he or she occupies in the hierarchy, not from any unique personal traits. Policies govern who can make what decisions at what time and in what manner.

For the most part, the leader's power is coercive; failure to follow orders subverts the whole enterprise and will usually lead to discipline or dismissal. (Because leaders are chosen for their expertise, Weber argued that at least some of their power will be moral.)

This view of leadership dominated business management through World War II, and it became prominent in education as well. As Raymond E. Callahan has described, early 20th-century school leaders, eager to be seen as hard-headed decision makers, maintained that well-run schools were no different from well-run factories.

One leading educator argued that school administrators should "keep the workers supplied with detailed instructions as to how the work is to be done, the standards to be reached, the methods to be employed, and the materials and appliances to be used." Metaphorically, management was the head, responsible for making decisions; labor provided the hands to do the actual labor.

In later decades, the extreme versions of this idea were softened by attempts to make schools more democratic, but many of the underlying practices remained the same. As recently as the 1980s, many school-reform plans contained strongly hierarchical assumptions. Likewise, some characterizations of "instructional leadership" portray the principal as a highly directive leader.

The Psychology of Hierarchical Leadership

Hierarchy rests on logic and rationality. It assumes there is one best way of doing things that can be identified through careful analysis by experts. Once the decision has been made, the organization's job is to carry it out as efficiently as possible, each worker doing his or her assigned part.

Although many disdain hierarchical leadership as outmoded, ineffective, or undemocratic, the very nature of organizations makes it unavoidable in some form. No matter how strongly collaboration is valued, every organization needs a way to make and enforce decisions that not everyone may agree with.

Although hierarchical leadership is inherently coercive (failing to follow directives could lead to sanctions), it does not necessarily breed resentment or hostility. One reason is that hierarchical methods have been so dominant for more than a century, they simply seem right or natural. Most employees, however much they might grumble about the wisdom of certain decisions, nonetheless agree that *someone* has to decide.

Hierarchical leadership rests on more than threats. In his classic study of leadership, James MacGregor Burns pointed out the transactional nature of many organizations. That is, leaders could gain compliance through a series of social transactions: In return for supporting organizational goals, employees receive wages, promotions, recognition, and job security. Thus, employees comply with directives out of simple self-interest. Even if they disagree with decisions, there are compensations.

This kind of implicit horse trading may be especially important in schools, where the principal has few opportunities to use direct coercive action (E. Mark Hanson). For one thing, the behaviors principals want from teachers are often subtle and difficult to monitor. Whether a teacher turns in attendance slips on time is easily determined; whether he or she consistently uses best instructional practices requires much more discerning judgment. The most important things that teachers do are done in their own classrooms, often behind closed doors. Richard M. Ingersoll, in his analysis of administrator-teacher relationships, cites a case in which a teacher instructed students to keep the officially prescribed textbook visible on their desks—but never used it.

Another limitation on principals' power is the laws, policies, and rules set by others. Discipline of teachers is carefully controlled by union contracts, and the uniform salary schedule almost eliminates compensation as a means of control. Administrators often report that one of their greatest frustrations is the inability to remove incompetent teachers (Steve Farkas and colleagues). Hanson cites research showing that teachers generally don't believe they will be punished for failing to teach the prescribed curriculum or be rewarded for doing so.

Of course, as Ingersoll points out, principals are not without resources in negotiating everyday transactions. They are able to allocate physical space, determine course or grade-level assignments, assign students to classrooms, assign nonteaching duties, and allocate discretionary parts of the budget (such as funds for professional development). Most of all, teachers depend on principals to back their handling of student misbehavior—a "great source of anxiety and frustration for faculty," according to Ingersoll.

Overall, Ingersoll's research led him to conclude that the actual use of such powers was less important than teachers' perceptions that they could be used: "Teachers considered carefully the costs of non-compliance because of the decidedly widespread sense of their dependence on the goodwill and benign judgment of administrators."

Advantages of Hierarchy

The persistence of hierarchical strategies implies that they meet some important needs. The most obvious advantage is efficiency. The emphasis on logical decision making and worker accountability offers a clear formula for getting things done. Weber was convinced that bureaucratic methods were technically superior, doing for organizations what machines did for manual labor.

Anyone who has worked in the pressure cooker of public education understands the allure of a system that promises quick and decisive action. Every day brings a multitude of decisions that require mastery by an expert, not drawn-out debate.

In addition, the emphasis on rules and accountability increases the likelihood of fair and impartial decisions, which are especially important in publicly accountable systems. Both workers and clients are more likely to accept decisions that have been made logically and even handedly.

Another benefit was noted by McMurry in his tribute to benevolent autocracy: Not all employees have pure motives and cooperative attitudes. Every organization has its share of slackers, goldbricks, and subversives who don't respond to democratic trust. For reasons of both fairness and efficiency, someone has to have the coercive power to deal with these individuals.

The final advantage of hierarchical strategies is that people have what Weber called the "habit of obedience." Most recognize the value of having someone be in charge and are willing to accept leadership from whoever is in that position. Indeed, followers often don't want to be bothered with the responsibility of making decisions.

Limitations of Hierarchy

Despite their widespread use, hierarchical strategies have certain limitations. First, as noted earlier, the same hierarchy that gives power to a leader also restricts it with board policies, union contracts, and state laws.

But even if school leaders had unlimited powers, they might not be able to use them effectively. Teaching is an activity that doesn't march to administrative drums. Joseph B. Shedd and Samuel Bacharach note that teachers' roles are extraordinarily complex, involving instruction, counseling, and supervision of students who are highly variable in their needs and capacities. There is a high degree of unpredictability and little consensus on the best steps to take in any given situation. Detailed directives from the top simply don't make sense; teachers are in the classroom, and principals are not.

Another problem is the school's stubborn refusal to behave in logical ways. Jerry L. Patterson, Stewart C. Purkey, and Jackson V. Parker have pointed out that the "if A, then B" assumption doesn't always work out in practice. People may fail to communicate through the prescribed channels; organizational goals may be ignored or tacked on as an afterthought to justify long-standing routines; decisions may reflect political clout rather than rational analysis. No organizational chart can accurately capture the rich, varied, and occasionally quirky behaviors of human beings.

Another limitation of hierarchical leadership is its affinity for the status quo. It assumes that organizational goals are clear (or easily clarified) and concentrates on the how-to. If changes are needed, they are likely to be small scale and incremental. Major restructuring threatens the rules that define everyone's jobs. Teachers may find the annual evaluation irksome, useless, or mildly threatening, but the contract at least ensures that it will be predictable, staying within parameters they can cope with. Why risk leaving that for something uncertain, even if it sounds rather intriguing?

Finally, as even Weber recognized, the strengths of bureaucracies can turn into weaknesses. Impartiality based on rules can become insensitivity to individual circumstances. Bureaucratic expertise can lead to arrogance and manipulation. Emphasis on order can stifle creativity and imagination.

The Exemplary Hierarchical Leader

For all its limitations, the hierarchical strategy remains dominant in American schools, and even its critics generally concede that it is an essential part of the leader's tool kit. What is the secret to using it well?

Managerial Skill

One obvious skill is keeping the organizational machine well oiled. Teachers cannot teach if the books aren't ordered on time, or the chalk runs low, or the buses don't arrive when they should. In most schools, this is the primary expectation for principals. Failing to do it well will undermine anything else they hope to accomplish.

Effective hierarchical leadership requires looking at the school through a structural frame, seeing the rules, relationships, and resources that will get things from Point A to Point B on schedule.

Doing so requires a delicate touch, however. Teachers expect a smoothly running school, but they want it done painlessly. As Dan Lortie noted years ago, "Teachers want to teach." They are irritated by anything that takes attention away from teaching: stacks of paperwork, long announcements over the public address system, or lengthy meetings on business that could be handled in a one-page memo.

Effective Coordination

Coordination is another essential hierarchical function. Teachers are specialists, preoccupied with doing their own work in their own classrooms. They have little time for learning what others are doing, much less coordinating their mutual efforts. Thus, school leaders must continually pose questions that no one else has time to ask. Does the fifth-grade science curriculum prepare students for the sixth-grade science curriculum? Does teachers' use of different discipline standards send mixed messages to students? Does early dismissal for athletic events create havoc with afternoon classes?

An especially important part of this coordination is establishing and maintaining organizational goals. Schools are subject to a multitude of cultural and political pressures that can easily deflect them from their path. No sooner has one set of goals been adopted than some new social crisis shoves them into the background. The leader's role is to act as the institution's conscience on goals, keeping it on target.

Effective coordination requires the leader to be fully aware of what's happening in the building. Hierarchies are notorious for filtering out bad news as it works its way up the chain of command, and leaders need to be aggressive about staying in touch. Blumberg calls this "having a nose for things," and says it doesn't come just from randomly walking around the school but from making a conscious effort to identify problems. One central-office administrator put it in terms of picking up subtle cues:

> For example, there's a teacher whom I know very well. One day he said, "Our high school principal, he's probably the best you can get." Interpretation: There are some things he screws up on. And my knowing this teacher and him knowing me, he's telling me that there's some communications lag taking place in the school, and there was. (Blumberg)

Enforcement of Rules

Leaders must be ready to use the coercive power at their disposal to enforce policies that are essential to the school's mission. Applying discipline is never a pleasant task—especially in an institution that tends to be filled with tender-hearted idealists—but at times it must be done.

Edwin Bridges, in his study of incompetent teachers, noted that much of the administrative anguish over nonperforming teachers is self-inflicted. Rather than dealing forthrightly with a problem, many administrators deny it, look the other way, or try to pass it on to someone else. When leaders fail to use their power to solve an obvious problem, it not only weakens the institution but also diminishes the leaders' power.

Leaders must use their coercive power sensitively, with recognition of the corrosive effects it can have on relationships and motivation. When acting hierarchically, leaders can ease tension by viewing events through a human-relations frame, a perspective that seems especially important in schools. Lortie found that teachers derived most of their motivation from the psychic reward of reaching their students, and what they most wanted from their principals was support, appreciation, and fairness.

Teachers respond warmly to simple friendliness. Joseph Blase and Jo Roberts Blase recorded one teacher's assessment of her principal: "She has a cheery attitude, almost always smiling, and always considerate and pleasant. This gives me encouragement to ask for help with my problems. She is not forbidding."

Listening is an important part of relationship orientation. Prior to making unilateral decisions, leaders will find that informal consultation with followers is possible and often desirable. The flip side of listening is marketing. Teachers are a well-educated, critical group. Even when making a decision hierarchically, school leaders can't afford to neglect the need to enlist support by explaining the benefits and responding to concerns.

TRANSFORMATIONAL LEADERSHIP

Marcus Foster was principal and superintendent in some of the nation's most beleaguered urban districts during the volatile 1960s and 1970s (David Tyack and Elizabeth Hansot). Against overwhelming odds, he revitalized the schools he was responsible for, reducing truancy, enriching the curriculum, and building bridges to a suspicious community. He had a zestful and highly personal approach, greeting everyone he passed in the hallways with smiles, handshakes, and compliments.

After one contentious meeting with a community group that ran late into the night, one of the participants pulled up next to Foster at a stoplight:

> I looked over and there he was with a smile upon his face, singing at the top of his voice. I can't begin to tell you the impression made upon me, because to me it typified the ebullience, the magnificent joy of life—the joy he took in working with the community. (Tyack and Hansot)

Leaders such as Foster leave an indelible impression on everyone they touch. Weber described them as "charismatic," having authority based on "gifts of body and spirit" that inspire excitement and loyalty. In 1978, Burns picked up this theme and described a form of leadership he called "transformational."

Transformational leaders were those who got results through persuasion, idealism, and intellectual excitement. They motivated their followers not by offering material (transactional) rewards, but by convincing them that their deepest interests and values could be fulfilled through the organization's agenda.

What Burns had in mind was not just glib manipulation, but a genuine elevation of people to higher levels of motivation and morality. Effective leadership, in his view, was never just a matter of technical efficiency—it had to meet the genuine needs of followers. Thus, John Kennedy's inaugural address and Martin Luther King Jr.'s "I Have a Dream" speech were examples of transformational leadership; Adolf Hitler's equally powerful speeches were not.

Burns's work turned leadership research in a new direction by sparking interest in leaders who generate deep commitment among followers. Appearing in the midst of rapid cultural and social change, a theory that promised the power to transform was highly attractive.

Despite the widespread interest in this kind of leadership, precise behavioral definitions are elusive, as Northouse points out. Kenneth Leithwood notes that some definitions are based on the concepts identified by Burns and his followers, whereas others are based on the generic meaning of the word (that is, anything leading to change is considered transformational). Nonetheless, we can easily formulate a composite portrait from a variety of sources.

The Nature of Transformational Leaders

Bernard M. Bass and Bruce J. Avolio characterize transformational leaders by "the Four I's." *Idealized influence* allows the leader to serve as a role model that followers want to emulate. *Inspirational motivation* builds enthusiasm, optimism, and team spirit. *Intellectual stimulation* encourages innovation and creativity by questioning assumptions and supporting problem solving. *Individualized consideration* gives personalized attention to each individual. These strategies, often packaged with a dynamic personality, stimulate employees to a greater awareness of the organizational mission and higher levels of performance.

Marshall Sashkin and Molly G. Sashkin point to four key traits. First, transformational leaders are good communicators, not just in the sense of speaking and writing effectively, but in their use of metaphor that speaks to the deepest concerns of followers. (That is, they must be adept in using the symbolic frame.)

Second, they are credible, a quality that results from behaving consistently over time and doing what they say they will do. Transformational leaders are trusted.

Third, transformational leaders convey a sense of caring, having not just an abstract respect for the welfare of others, but a personal interest in them.

Finally, transformational leaders are willing to take the risk of trusting followers with major responsibility. Sashkin and Sashkin note that the risk is more apparent than real, since they make sure that followers have both the capability and the support to do the job.

Nancy Roberts sums up many of these points:

This type of leadership offers a vision of what could be and gives a sense of purpose and meaning to those who would share that vision. It builds commitment, enthusiasm, and excitement. It creates a hope in the future and a belief that the world is knowable, understandable, and manageable. The collective action that transforming leadership generates, empowers those who participate in the process. There is hope, there is optimism, there is energy. In essence, transforming leadership is a leadership that facilitates the redefinition of a people's mission and vision, a renewal of their commitment, and the restructuring of their systems for goal accomplishment.

Advantages of Transformational Leadership

The most obvious advantage of transformational leadership is its ability to motivate and inspire followers. Leithwood notes that this ability may be especially important in schools because teachers are oriented to intrinsic rewards. Much has been written about the isolation and loneliness of classroom teachers; some of those barriers can be overcome by making staff feel part of a collective effort in a worthy cause.

Much of the motivating power comes from the leader's enthusiasm and self-confidence. Teaching always involves ambiguity, and teachers can never be completely sure how much good they are doing their students. A leader with confidence and energy can dissipate those doubts and convince teachers of the rightness of their work.

At a time of dramatic school restructuring, the vision that transformational leaders bring to education is crucial. Research on principal effectiveness has consistently identified vision as a key leadership quality (Kenneth Leithwood and Carolyn Riehl; Tim Waters, Robert J. Marzano, and Brian McNulty). The ability to help teachers articulate their deepest hopes for the future is an essential step toward creating that future.

Although transformational leadership is not easy to measure, researchers have found evidence that it is associated with higher performance across a variety of organizational settings. Sashkin and Sashkin report that their studies show transformational strategies can account for 10 to 30 percent of variation in performance. Kenneth Leithwood and Daniel L. Duke, summarizing research on transformational leadership in school settings, report modest but positive effects on variables such as student participation, teacher commitment, organizational learning, and school climate.

Limitations of Transformational Leadership

One major limitation of transformational leadership may be the difficulty of attaining it. When Peggy C. Kirby, Louis V. Paradise, and Margaret I. King asked 58 educators to describe some "extraordinary educational leaders" they knew, their descriptions included many of the characteristics associated with transformational leaders, but only 9 said they could easily identify such a person. Another indicator comes from Bolman and Deal (1992), who report that only 5 percent of the leaders they studied use the symbolic frame in devising strategies.

According to Leithwood, transformational leadership requires highly developed intellectual skills. Also, descriptions of transformational leaders often suggest that personal qualities, not just behaviors, may play a role. Traits such as charisma, the ability to inspire others, or the drive for power are often cited. Such qualities are not evenly distributed through the leadership pool, and it may take more than an act of will to become the kind of exceptional leader enshrined in memory. There are many talented basketball players; there are only a few Michael Jordans.

One consequence of the prominence of these personal qualities is that even though transformational leadership calls attention to the needs, capacity, and potential of followers, observers are likely to attribute success to a heroic leader, not to the collective efforts of everyone in the organization.

Another problem is that transformational leaders can use their qualities in less positive ways. Sashkin and Sashkin noted that leaders can use their power in service to the organization or for personal benefit. Jay A. Conger, along with other analysts, has warned about a "dark side" to charisma: Leaders become infatuated with their success, and confidence becomes arrogance. They then fail to exercise care in developing a vision, or use their excellent communication skills to manipulate others, or simply become sloppy about everyday management practices.

Another problem is that transformational leadership may create high expectations that the leaders cannot easily satisfy. Weber observed that charismatic authority is based on demonstrated heroic deeds. Having created enthusiasm and high expectations, the leader must deliver. Failure to do so leads to disillusionment and abandonment by followers. Some followers of Martin Luther King Jr., for example, criticized him for being too timid or too accommodating with the white power structure.

Finally, transformational leadership is associated with change and restructuring. Once a school has achieved a new structure, what happens? Can intellectual excitement be maintained over a long period, or do people reach a plateau where they need to slow down and assimilate the changes? Do transformational leaders then move on to new jobs? Does incremental change again become important? So far, we don't have answers to those questions.

The Exemplary Transformational Leader

Leaders interested in transformational strategies may initially be a bit intimidated when the usual role models are John Kennedy, Martin Luther King Jr., Winston Churchill, and the like. When transformational strategies are analyzed as behaviors, though, most of them appear to be within the reach of mere mortals. Leithwood has identified six basic behaviors of transformational school leaders:

1. Transformational leaders take the leading role in identifying and articulating an organizational vision. This is not just a matter of formulating goals, as hierarchical leaders do, but something much deeper. Terrence E. Deal and Kent D. Peterson say that symbolically aware principals

> listen carefully for the deeper dreams that the school community holds for the future. Every school is a repository of unconscious sentiments, expectations, and hopes that carry the code of the collective dream—the high ground to which they collectively aspire.

Thus, although transformational leaders have strong personal values, the real source of the vision is in the group. The leader is the voice of conscience that keeps whispering, "We aren't yet all that we can be."

2. Transformational leaders foster the acceptance of group goals. That is, they promote cooperation and persuade employees to rally around the common cause. Whereas hierarchical relationships are built on contracts, transformational relationships are built on covenants.

Says executive Max De Pree: "A covenantal relationship rests on shared commitment to ideas, to issues, to values, to goals, and to management processes." A contract has nothing to do with reaching our potential, he argues; covenants fill deep needs and allow work to be meaningful.

Thomas J. Sergiovanni (1992) says that covenants are developed through continual dialogue that invites everyone—leaders and followers—to consider explicitly the values, beliefs, and behaviors that unite the school community. All members must be willing to examine their practices in the light of the covenant and hold themselves accountable to it.

3. Transformational leaders convey high performance expectations. As they communicate the organization's core values, they also make it clear that these values are non-negotiable. Sergiovanni (1992) stresses the importance of visibly taking offense when basic standards are violated. Leaders can direct their outrage at threats from outside the school or within the school. He tells how Principal Madeline Cartwright solved a problem with teacher attendance by personally answering the phone, rather than having a secretary take the sick calls. She told teachers, "You either talk to me or you come to school, simple as that."

4. Transformational leaders provide appropriate models. When administrators stand up and point to an exciting future, battle-scarred teachers are likely to say, "After you." As the most carefully watched people in the school, principals are expected to live out the visions they promote.

Deal and Peterson argue that even routine activities can hold important symbolic weight, especially when used to affirm core values. Principals send important messages by how they use their time, how they arrange and decorate their office, whom they reward, and how they relate to teachers, students, and parents. In the end, vision is as vision does.

5. Transformational leaders provide intellectual stimulation. This initially sounds intimidating, but it often consists of small, low-key actions. One of Blumberg's principals gave an example:

Here's the incoming mail pile here. I'll look through that tonight and there will be a zillion notes to people tomorrow, like "Will you stop in and see me about this or that?" Sometimes it's just that I want them to be aware of new things for the kids that they may want to check out. And I want them to know that I'm aware of what is going on and I want them to stop in and talk about it.

Another administrator described it as just being a matter of dangling a large enough variety of bait on a large enough number of hooks; eventually, someone will bite.

6. Transformational leaders develop a strong school culture, in particular by reinforcing values that emphasize service to students, continuous professional learning, and collaborative problem solving. As described by Deal and Peterson, they must be "anthropological detectives," constantly using the symbolic frame and always looking beneath surface events to understand how others interpret school life.

Again, small acts can have the biggest long-term effect: giving recognition to those who support the school's core values; telling stories that connect the school's past, present, and future; and finding room for the idiosyncratic little rituals and celebrations that bind people together.

FACILITATIVE LEADERSHIP

> The principal always felt we could handle problems and solve them! We, in turn, felt we could solve problems of the school. We felt in control, part of the school. We were always thinking of improving our school. We acted on problems and solved them without concerning the principal. (Blase and Blase)

This teacher, interviewed by Blase and Blase, had experienced a form of leadership that turns hierarchy on its head: facilitation. Researchers have long asked whether democratic strategies can succeed in the workplace, but schools have only recently begun to explore the possibilities. Indeed, facilitative leadership is so new that even the name of the concept is unsettled. In addition to *facilitative leadership,* terms such as *participative leadership, shared leadership,* and *distributed leadership* are commonly used to refer to the same or similar ideas.

The concept behind these terms has emerged from the work on transformational leadership. Both strategies are change oriented, but there is a distinct, if subtle, shift in emphasis. Whereas the transformational leader remains center stage, a dynamic and inescapable presence, the facilitative leader works in the background.

David T. Conley and Paul Goldman define facilitative leadership as "the behaviors that enhance the collective ability of a school to adapt, solve problems, and improve performance." The key word here is *collective*; organizations are believed to work best when employees at all levels are actively engaged in solving problems. The leader's role is to get that involvement.

That much is similar to transformational leadership. The key difference is the view of decision making. Transformational leaders ask followers to freely commit effort and psychic energy to the common cause, but "common cause" does not necessarily imply democratic decision making.

Some transformational leaders operate in a top-down manner, and followers can become energized and excited without expecting formal involvement in decisions. Facilitative leadership, by contrast, relies explicitly on mutuality and synergy, with power flowing in multiple directions. Whereas the transformational leader offers followers a vision that reflects their highest values, the facilitative leader offers a daily partnership in bringing the vision to life.

Leaders still hold formal positions of power, but they use their authority to support a process of professional give and take. Facilitative power is power-through, not power-over.

This kind of power is especially appropriate in schools, according to Dunlap and Goldman, because teaching requires autonomy and discretion, not standardized formulas. Teachers can't produce learning just by subjecting students to certain methods; rather, they have to work indirectly, creating conditions under which students will learn. Principals control learning even less directly; they have to create environments in which teachers can work effectively.

Despite the emphasis on mutuality, facilitative power does not rely on voting or other formal mechanisms. Dunlap and Goldman emphasize that facilitation occurs within the existing structure, meaning that whoever normally has legal authority to ratify decisions continues to do so. Similarly, facilitation is not delegation, where the administrator unilaterally assigns tasks to subordinates. In a facilitative environment, anyone can initiate a task and recruit anyone else to participate. The process thrives on informal negotiation and communication.

Conley and Goldman list half a dozen key strategies used by facilitative leaders: overcoming resource constraints; building teams; providing feedback, coordination, and conflict management; creating communication networks; practicing collaborative politics; and modeling the school's vision. Facilitative leaders inevitably make heavy use of the political frame, seeking to identify the key players, what they are looking for, and how their needs can be reconciled.

Successful facilitation may depend less on any particular set of behaviors, however, than on the underlying belief system. Conley and Goldman emphasize the importance of trust, "a letting go of control and an increasing belief that others can and will function independently and successfully within a common framework of expectations and accountability."

Advantages of Facilitative Leadership

As noted previously, facilitative leadership seems especially suitable for schools, since teachers are already considered semiautonomous professionals, at least in their own classrooms. Facilitative leadership extends this professionalism to the next level: collaborating on schoolwide issues. The results can be exciting:

> Trust just opened teachers up to their fullest potential. They began to get ideas and be creative. They figure, "Okay, we were allowed to do this little-bitty thing, maybe we can do something else." The first thing you know, you have teachers talking with each other, not about what they did last weekend or about the latest little piece of gossip. They're talking about instructional things—workshops they've been to, professional books they've read, ideas that they have. (Joseph Blase and colleagues)

That kind of interaction helps teachers make the transition from friendly congeniality to the shared values and commitment of collegiality (Sergiovanni 1992). Collaborative work is often difficult and frustrating, but that very difficulty provides a crucible for forging the bonds of community. Schools end up not only with a more cohesive program, but with relationships that are strengthened and enriched.

Facilitative strategies also provide the satisfaction of working in an institution whose practices are consistent with the deepest values of society. More than one critic has noted the irony of preparing children for life in a democracy by educating them in a strongly hierarchical system.

The issue is more than symbolic, however. According to Linda McNeil, there is a strong link between administrative leadership strategies and classroom teaching strategies. She found that in high schools where the principal was highly directive and controlling, teachers were more likely to use a constrained lecture-and-quiz method, declining to use more dynamic but less predictable methods.

Lynn Balster Liontos interviewed a teacher who saw a direct relationship between the principal's collaborative approach and what was happening in classrooms:

Students have to learn to use their own minds and be creative and do problem-solving on their own. So what teachers really need to be doing is to show kids how to become learners themselves, so that they can then chart their own paths. And I think essentially what Bob [the principal] is doing is modeling that approach to teachers, who may then pick up on it and use it with students.

Finally, recent studies of school reform have emphasized the role of shared leadership in helping schools navigate the uncharted waters of major organizational change. One series of studies concluded that success was associated with the principal's ability to create "dense leadership" by creating highly collaborative communities of practice (Joseph Murphy and Amanda Datnow).

Limitations of Facilitative Leadership

The radically different assumptions of facilitative leadership may create ambiguity and discomfort. New roles can be difficult for both administrators and teachers. Nona Prestine says that active participation by the principal is crucial, yet it must be a kind of participation that does not dominate. "Sometimes I have ideas," said one principal, "but I have to wait for the right time. I can't just go in and tell them what I think."

Even when principals try to sit back quietly, teachers may still see them as in control, not quite trusting that the new roles can be taken seriously. In other cases, teachers may shy away from responsibilities that may plunge them into schoolwide controversies from which they are normally buffered, or they may resent the frequent committee meetings that pull them away from their top priority—teaching.

Another serious issue is the blurring of accountability. Facilitative leadership creates a landscape of constantly shifting responsibilities and relationships, yet the formal system continues to hold one person responsible for results. Leaders may wonder about the wisdom of entrusting so much to those who will not share the accountability (Conley and Goldman; Prestine).

Not everyone agrees that all decisions should be shared. Edwin A. Locke argues that certain issues, especially those involving core values and the organizational vision, require one person to have the final say. "It simply does not work for a ship to have two—or more—captains." Getting input is one thing, says Locke, but someone has to take charge.

Advocates of facilitative leadership often argue that skillful administrators can reconcile this dilemma by building consensus, but the slow pace of developing such broad agreement runs into another difficulty: limited time. Principals are always being pressured to act immediately on a host of issues. For example, a proposal to replace basal readers with a whole-language approach is likely to generate a wide-ranging debate that deserves a full airing, yet looming over the process is an arbitrary requisition deadline. Some days, the principal must allow the issues to play themselves out; other days, he or she needs to say, "It's time to move on."

Like transformational leadership, facilitation may create great excitement and high expectations, unleashing multiple initiatives that stretch resources, drain energy, and fragment the collective vision. Somehow, the principal must keep a hand on the reins without discouraging the innovators.

At the same time, the risky business of change will intensify teachers' traditional demands for emotional support and protection from bureaucratic demands. The facilitative leader must know when to provide this support and when to challenge the comfortable status quo (Conley and Goldman).

The Exemplary Facilitative Leader

Although facilitative leadership is still in its infancy, we have a sufficient number of accounts to piece together a picture of the facilitative leader at work (Blase and Blase; Blase and colleagues; Conley and Goldman; Shirley M. Hord).

Facilitative leaders create an atmosphere of and a culture for change. This dimension covers a lot of ground, and includes such things as supporting risk-taking activities even while acknowledging that mistakes are inevitable; cutting through red tape; ceaselessly talking, debating, and negotiating with teachers; facing conflict openly; selecting staff members who are in tune with the vision; and nurturing rituals and traditions that express the school's values.

In carrying out these diverse activities, leaders must take on many roles: mediator, ambassador, knowledgeable resource, negotiator, cheerleader, skillful manager, and supportive colleague. Above all, they must strike just the right balance between aggressive action and watchful waiting. All the evidence so far suggests that facilitation is not a laissez-faire stance; a principal who simply delegates a task and walks away will be perceived as unsupportive or uninterested. At the same time, facilitators must communicate in word and deed that their involvement is not intended to dominate but to support collegial decision making.

Like transformational leaders, facilitative leaders are keepers of the vision. But whereas transformational strategies credit the leader with an almost mystical ability to articulate the needs of the organization, facilitation explicitly sees vision as a creation of the entire school community, something evolved through dozens of daily encounters. Leaders contribute their values to this discussion, but may have to swallow their preferred images of the future. Their main role is to keep the conversation alive.

They provide resources. Facilitative leaders put money behind the rhetoric. They understand the importance of tangible support for change and use resource allocation as a way of communicating priorities and affirming values. In particular, they free up time for faculty members to do what needs to be done.

Because they understand that change and collaboration require deep personal changes for teachers, they make training and development a major priority. This task goes far beyond hiring an occasional consultant; effective facilitators seek out qualified people in their own schools to serve as ongoing role models.

They monitor and check progress. Hord notes that nothing goes exactly as planned, requiring leaders to shift gears, adapt, redeploy, and change direction. The need to keep in touch requires them to be out and about on a daily basis. Facilitative leaders will seldom be found sitting in their office.

They take the long view. They know that real change doesn't come overnight, and they don't let their attention flit to new plans with every shift of the winds. Because they recognize that there are ups and downs in any change process, facilitative leaders help staff members get through the low spots. They encourage teachers to recognize the progress being made and celebrate major achievements.

Most of all, they know that change is a process, not an event. Individuals must change before the institution can, and they do so in different ways and at different rates. Facilitators must adapt their strategies to these individual variations.

IS THERE A BEST STRATEGY?

Clearly, leaders have broad strategic options that will lead them down very different paths. Is there a best strategy? This is an obvious question with a fuzzy answer. In the first place, the question itself may be unfair, since no one seems to be arguing that leaders should use one strategy all the time. Rather, it is a question of emphasis.

Much of the current literature seems to favor transformational and facilitative strategies, but wise administrators will try to distinguish enthusiastic advocacy from objective evidence. Lynn G. Beck and Joseph Murphy point out that metaphors for school leadership come and go. Just since 1960, principals have been asked to be efficient bureaucrats, scientific managers, humanistic educators, instructional leaders, and now transformational or facilitative leaders. Beck and Murphy note that prevailing images may say more about the preoccupations of society than the inherent needs of schools.

Although it's too early to expect conclusive evidence from empirical studies, advocates of transformational and facilitative strategies can cite research support (Blase and colleagues; Leithwood). In particular, a number of qualitative studies have provided rich, compelling accounts of schools that are reinventing themselves and of teachers who see themselves, their schools, and their students in a dramatically new light. Clearly, the promises of transformational and facilitative leadership are not just idle fantasies.

A reality check is in order, though. Most recent studies of transformational and facilitative leaders have been of schools that were consciously trying to restructure themselves. These schools may have had a predisposition for change, an itch that could only be scratched with major reform. Would the effects be the same in a complacent school? If the hallways are quiet, and teachers are competently teaching as they have always taught, and parents believe all the children are above average, will a school have the heart to take on the aggravation of reform?

In other words, are transformational and facilitative strategies a realistic option for all school leaders? So far, we don't know.

Also, we should look carefully at what the research is actually saying. For instance, many studies measure perceptions rather than actual behavior. In such studies, principals and teachers are asked to agree or disagree with statements about the principal's leadership strategies. Although there is reason to respect these judgments, they may contain biases.

(An earlier generation of research showed that teacher satisfaction correlated with more hierarchical leader behaviors. Perhaps there is a kind of halo effect, in which satisfied teachers rate principals higher on whatever scale the studies use.)

We can predict that definitive conclusions about effects of transformational and facilitative leadership on learning will be elusive, for as teachers and administrators rethink what it means to teach and learn effectively, their definitions of success will also change. The kinds of easy correlations with standardized test scores that drove the instructional-leadership movement are unlikely to satisfy educators who work in transformational and facilitative environments.

The bottom line? As always, the resolution of these matters rests in the hearts and minds of school leaders. The strategic choices they make will reflect their deepest values and their assessment of the school's needs.

CHOOSING A STRATEGY

In talking of transformational leaders, or facilitative leaders, or hierarchical leaders, we do not mean to imply that these are either-or choices. On any given day, leaders may shift gears from one hour to the next, at 1:00, cautioning an employee about excessive absences; at 2:00, chatting with a teacher about a promising new Internet resource; and at 3:00, sitting quietly in a technology committee meeting as teachers decide how to spend next year's state grant.

Although leaders may differ in the emphasis they give to each strategy, nothing requires use of any one exclusively. If leaders can operate from episode to episode in all three strategies, how do they make their strategic choices?

We have little direct evidence so far, but we can assume that style plays a role. A principal who is a "judger" on the Myers-Briggs inventory will probably gravitate toward hierarchical strategies; the ambiguous nature of facilitation will always be somewhat stressful for this leader.

Certain strategic choices are unavoidable. Every leader with a formal position—principal, superintendent, curriculum coordinator—must use some hierarchical methods. The position is part of the hierarchy, and the job description calls for making certain judgments. Even if officeholders want to be completely democratic, no one else will forget that they hold coercive power.

Leaders will undoubtedly make some choices as a matter of philosophy. Many advocates of transformational and facilitative leadership believe that institutions in a democracy should operate according to democratic principles. Likewise, many affirm that every organization has a responsibility to nurture the talents and aspirations of its employees (Blase and colleagues).

But for most administrators, the choices will probably be more pragmatic. Just as leaders can, at least to some degree, choose leadership styles to fit the situation, so can they select among strategies. Four principles guide the matching of situation and strategy:

1. Sergiovanni (1994) has suggested that organizations, like people, exist at different developmental levels. A school that has traditionally operated with strong top-down administrators may not be ready to jump into a full-blown facilitative environment. One principal reflected on her first year:

> I don't know that it was a real good idea to come in as a democratic leader the very first year before I got a reading of the staff. There was a perception that I didn't want to make decisions, that I couldn't make decisions, that I didn't want to accept the responsibility for decisions. (Blase and colleagues)

Other schools may have a strong tradition of faculty involvement so that even seemingly routine decisions should involve subordinates.

2. Not all decisions are equal. Many involve trivial or noninstructional issues that can be disposed of in a hierarchical way with the full approval of the staff. Issues with direct impact on teachers' core work usually call for more participative strategies.

Ronald A. Heifetz notes that some problems are well defined and the solution is clear; the decision is technical in nature and can be made by anyone with appropriate expertise. In other cases, the problem may be transparent, but no solution is obvious. Here Heifetz would suggest a more participative approach, if only because the leader doesn't have the answer.

In still other cases, the problem itself may be poorly understood. For example, a faculty becomes concerned over an increasingly negative tone in student attitudes. In such cases, says Heifetz, organizations will have to collectively "learn their way forward."

3. Strategic choices also have to strike the proper balance between product and process. Leaders have a dual obligation: to achieve the goals of the organization and to nurture the people responsible for fulfilling them. At times, those obligations clash. No matter how much principals may want to empower their teachers, there are times when school goals take precedence.

One principal expressed it to Blase and colleagues this way: "My responsibility as a principal really is to the children, and if I see areas that are ineffective, I've got to say that we're not effective here and that we have got to change."

At times, the choice between process and product (or means and end) will reflect philosophical positions. For example, Blase and colleagues take the position that it is inherently good for schools to run democratically. On the other hand, Conley and Goldman argue that the goal is not workplace democracy, but enhancing student learning.

4. Leaders should be alert to the possibility that the same action can serve more than one strategy. Deal and Peterson, who believe that a balanced strategy is essential, urge principals to develop the kind of "bifocal vision" that makes the most of any opportunity. Supervising bus arrivals, for example, serves an obvious hierarchical function, but it also presents an opportunity for greeting students, establishing visibility, assessing the social climate, and reinforcing key school values.

For additional help in choosing among the three leadership strategies described in this chapter, see Table 4.1 ("Comparison of Three Leadership Strategies"), which shows how they vary according to such dimensions as task/relationship and autocratic/democratic, and the different ways they view power, teaching, and change.

CONCLUSION: THE NEED FOR CLARITY OF PURPOSE

To be a leader is to act, and this chapter has reminded us of the enormous differences in the ways leaders act. These differences owe in part to leaders' psychological makeup (styles) and in part to the conscious choices they make in pursuit of organizational goals (strategies). It's a delicate balancing act at times, as school leaders try to take the pushes in one direction and the pulls from the opposite direction and hope the result isn't a stalemate.

Table 4.1   Comparison of Three Leadership Strategies

Dimensions	Hierarchical	Transformational	Facilitative
Task/ relationship	Primarily task, but may be supplemented by relationship	Relationship	Relationship
Autocratic/ democratic	Autocratic	Ambiguous; leader invites emotional participation but may or may not share decisions	Democratic
Myers-Briggs	Thinking, judging, sensing will be especially useful	Intuitive will be especially important	Perceiving will be especially useful
Bolman and Deal's Four Frames	Primarily structural; may be supplemented by human resource (often with emphasis on material needs)	Symbolic; human resource (with focus on psychological needs)	Political and symbolic
View of power	Mainly coercive, with elements of moral	Moral; leader's authority rests on core values shared with followers	Moral
View of teaching	A technical activity, capable of being standardized	Diverse and individualized activity, but bound together by common ethos	Professional activity; dynamic and unpredictable; autonomy required
View of change	Rationally planned and incremental; future is predictable and controllable	Aims at wholesale transformation and paradigm shift; is driven by common vision	Is continuous and unpredictable; evolves toward shared vision through dialogue
Advantages	Technically efficient; clear accountability; emphasis on rational policies, not individual whims	Inspires and motivates followers; provides affirmation of core values and vision for the future	Affirms autonomy of teachers; creates collegiality and community; sets positive tone for school climate
Limitations	Oriented to status quo; emphasis on rules may reduce leader's flexibility; fails to recognize nonrational behavior; may lead to bureaucratic insensitivity	May require exceptional traits; is difficult to sustain over time; may create unrealistic expectations and overreliance on leader	Requires participants to learn new roles; has unclear accountability; is time consuming

What gives coherence to this act of leadership is the leader's sense of purpose. Blumberg tells the story of the sculptor who explains that the statue is already somewhere in the block of stone. His job is to chip away the parts that don't belong. Blumberg says the same applies to education: "It's as though for every school building, there's a beautiful school in there somewhere and, if you keep on chipping away, you'll find it. But you have to know what you're looking for."

REFLECTIONS

1. How would you describe your leadership style? In what ways is this style an advantage? What disadvantages does it have?

2. Think of an especially effective educational leader you have known. How would you describe his or her leadership style? To what degree did this leader's style account for his or her effectiveness?

3. Do you agree with Edwin Locke that there are certain decisions that can never be effectively shared or delegated? If so, what kinds of decisions are in that category?

4. Looking back on your experience in schools, can you recall cases in which leaders failed because they adopted the wrong strategy? Why did their strategy prove ineffective?

5. Again drawing on your experience in schools, does transformational leadership seem to be as rare as some researchers suggest? If so, why? What are the barriers to becoming a transformational leader?

6. Identify a major issue in your school. What leadership strategy (or combination of strategies) would be most appropriate to resolve the issue?

5

Developing
School Leaders

Larry Lashway

N ext year, thousands of individuals will walk through the doors of schools as new principals. Those individuals may be male or female, white or black, tall or short. Their training may have been at a major research university or a small private college. Their school may be a tiny rural outpost, a well-worn urban bastion, or a sprawling suburban campus. Yet for all their differences, these principals will share one common mission: to steer a highly complex organization to unprecedented levels of student learning.

How they fare matters not only to them but to the schools and students they serve. The principalship is such a pivotal position that failure can demoralize the faculty, polarize the community, and cause long, painful legal action. Even worse is "failure to thrive," with the principal not really succeeding but not failing so badly that anyone is willing to endure the pain of correcting the mistake. A school can spend years mired in mediocrity when that happens.

Districts are aware of this, of course, and work hard to find candidates who can do the job. The problem comes if that is all the district does—hire excellent leaders and then stand back as they exercise their inherent skills. In reality, of course, principals' leadership abilities do not attain full capability at the end of their preparation program. Instead, their learning curve extends throughout their careers.

Career-long learning has always been the case for school leaders, with each new day inevitably bringing new experiences and new challenges. Traditionally, most principals have been able to adapt smoothly without much opportunity for structured learning and reflection. Those days may now be over. At a time of wholesale change, when the entire paradigm of schooling is shifting, thoughtful, well-designed professional development for leaders is essential.

This chapter examines the development and learning needs of principals through four phases of their careers: recruitment into the profession, preparation, induction, and career growth. The first section discusses two processes woven throughout the growth of leaders: development and socialization. Then follows a description of principals' learning needs in four stages of their careers. The chapter concludes with a review of some tools that can help principals better understand their learning needs.

A DEVELOPMENTAL PERSPECTIVE

Modern psychologists, from Freud to Piaget to Erikson, have firmly established the principle of human development. That is, people don't just change over time, they change in "patterned, orderly, and sequential" ways, as L. Nan Restine put it, as they deal with distinctive sets of challenges at different points in life. For example, in Erikson's account of the human life cycle, newborns face the crucial task of developing a basic sense of trust, whereas adolescents must establish a basic sense of personal identity. These stages are not biologically determined, but result from the individual's need to integrate a variety of physical, social, and cultural influences.

Although developmental changes are most dramatic in childhood, they continue throughout the life span. Over time, new experiences and new challenges lead to new understanding. (For most of us, thinking back to our first year on the job will produce at least mild embarrassment over how simplistic our thinking was.) At certain points, a person's behaviors and thought processes will be so distinctive they can be characterized as a stage.

Career Ladder or Continuous Slope?

In this framework, some researchers have found evidence that an individual's career may move through distinct stages (Forrest W. Parkay, Gaylon G. Currie, and John W. Rhodes). If so, principals' learning needs will differ over time. What first-year principals need to know may differ qualitatively, not just quantitatively, from what a 10-year veteran needs to learn.

Historically, professional development for principals has not acknowledged a developmental perspective. The administrative career is often visualized in terms of "ladders," suggesting a climb from one elevation to another. People accept a position, work diligently, and gain a promotion to the next plateau. Not surprisingly, attention often focuses on the rise from one level to the next, not on the individual's growing mastery of his or her existing role.

But all career ladders narrow at the top, and thus only a minority of principals can move up to the superintendency. Some may switch to staff roles such as reading or curriculum specialist, whereas others return to teaching or leave education altogether. But most will remain as principals.

For such career principals, today's dynamic work environment will challenge and reshape their goals and beliefs. Several decades ago, newly minted principals could assume that by the completion of their induction, they would have a skill set that would adequately serve them through the remainder of their careers. There were always new things to be learned and skills that could be strengthened, but there was no expectation that they might have to master a whole new paradigm. Not so today. For that reason, it makes sense to view principal development less as a series of scrambles up a ladder than as a steady trek up a continuous slope.

Socialization

Preparation and development for an occupation are often framed in terms of *socialization*, the process by which aspirants acquire the knowledge, skills, and values needed to thrive in that line of work. Although socialization is often viewed as something that is done to newcomers, L. Joseph Matthews and Gary M. Crow have pointed out that the process is reciprocal. Would-be principals engage not only in role taking (adapting to the expectations that society holds for principals) but role making (helping reshape the profession with their particular skills and values).

In the early stages of the career, the emphasis is probably more on role taking, but as principals gain skill, perspective, and confidence, they are more likely to engage in role making.

In fact, socialization is best viewed not as an end point, but as a career-long phenomenon in which principals continually engage in a silent "debate" over their proper role. At times, they adapt to society's ever-changing expectations, accepting new responsibilities and learning new skills (as many have done in recent years by taking a more aggressive role in instructional leadership). At other times, their values and actions help change society's expectations of what the principalship is or could be. For example, some observers have suggested that the growing number of women in leadership may help create an "ethic of care" not often associated with leaders.

Matthews and Crow distinguish among three types of socialization. *Professional* socialization deals with the knowledge, skills, and values society expects principals to have. *Organizational* socialization involves the way a particular school or district defines leadership. *Personal* socialization comes from the ways friends and family may either reinforce or resist the changes that a prospective principal is going through. For example, how a new principal responds to the time demands of the job depends in part on the needs and understanding of his or her family.

In addition, socialization has a time dimension:

- *Anticipatory* socialization occurs in the early stages of entry to the profession. Even before people become principals, they form expectations for the job from observation, from conversations with other teachers, or even from the mass media.
- The *encounter* period occurs after entry. People in this stage are performing the role, but often with feelings of uncertainty and anxiety that things are not quite under control.
- *Adjustment* comes as principals master their craft, expand their influence, and achieve the status of insider.

Outcomes of socialization can vary, particularly in the balance between role taking and role making. Some principals may become conformists, narrowly adhering to the role handed down to them; less commonly, they may reject the traditional expectations and attempt to reinvent the role. Or they may land in the middle, accepting the broad expectations for the role but refining it through what Matthews and Crow call "creative individualism." As noted previously, this balance may change over time.

Finally, socialization is not a purely cognitive or behavioral process, but may evoke complex emotions. Adopting new roles and expectations often requires leaving behind former roles and beliefs, and, to some degree, adopting a new identity. Letting go of the old self can create a sense of sadness and loss; for example, new principals frequently regret the loss of direct contact with students.

THE PHASES OF PRINCIPALS' CAREERS

This section examines the development of principals throughout their careers, from recruitment into the profession to preparation, induction, and career growth. The discussion seeks to identify principals' needs at each stage and to highlight programs and strategies for addressing those needs.

Phase 1: Recruitment Into the Profession

Why do teachers choose to become principals? In most cases, it is not simply the realization of a longtime dream. As Catherine Marshall and Katherine L. Kasten note, "Few 6-year-olds say, 'When I grow up I want to be a principal.'" Most principals start their careers in education as teachers; becoming a principal thus represents a shift in thinking that occurs while they are teaching.

What turns their attention to administration? We know distressingly little about the process by which they make that decision but can infer that they go through a form of anticipatory socialization. That is, they form impressions and create expectations about the job while they are relative outsiders. As they observe school leaders in action, they make certain judgments about the life of a principal and their own ability to fill the role.

Closeted in their classrooms for most of the day, teachers necessarily get a limited picture of the principal's job. What they see and hear in faculty meetings, casual hallway encounters, and faculty lounge gossip doesn't give a well-rounded view. Also, these impressions are colored by their status as teachers. They may define "good leadership" by what principals do to support the work of teachers, rather than by the full sweep of the principal's duties.

This "apprenticeship of observation" may result in a somewhat one-sided and simplistic view of role expectations that can have two undesirable consequences. First, teachers who like what they see of administration may decide to enter the field even though it is not a good match for their personal capabilities. Second, teachers who see only the "three Ps"—pressure, paperwork, and politics—may conclude that they can best fulfill their desire to help children in the classroom.

Thus, one crucial developmental step at this stage is forming an accurate picture of what the job requires. In part, this requires exposure to a candid portrayal of the challenges of today's principalship, but it also means that aspiring principals should understand the transformative potential of the job.

Many teachers are in the classroom because they have a strong commitment to the welfare of children, and the same appears to be true of administrators. Diana G. Pounder and Randall J. Merrill found that when assistant principals were asked to consider the desirability of a high school principalship, they gave the most weight to psychological benefits, particularly the opportunity to influence education. The ability to earn a higher salary exerted a modest influence, whereas disincentives included time demands and the complexity of the role. If prospective principals see only an unholy blend of paper pushing and crisis management, they will have little motivation to take up the challenge.

District Programs

Some districts, faced with a shortage of qualified leaders, have begun formal programs to provide prospective principals with accurate insight into the nature of the job. For example, one recent program (Leadership Academy: An Urban Network for Chicago) seeks to introduce aspiring administrators to the realities of the job by focusing on topics such as instructional leadership, school management, interpersonal effectiveness, and school climate. The program uses a variety of methods, including presentations, simulations, case studies, small-group problem solving, and reflective writing (Kent D. Peterson).

Similarly, the First Ring Leadership Academy connects Cleveland State University with 13 area districts in a program that identifies highly qualified candidates and provides an accelerated pathway to the principalship. Participants are given release time from teaching to complete a series of two-and-a-half-day training modules over a 15-month period. Between modules, which cover topics ranging from social justice to the use of technology for improving instruction, candidates engage in site-based leadership projects such as designing teacher development projects or working with parent groups. As a supplement to the coursework and activities, participants have frequent opportunities for reflection and discussion with other cohort members (U.S. Department of Education).

Even in districts that do not have the resources for such efforts, principals can informally provide promising teacher leaders with insights into the nature of leadership as they collectively work together on school-improvement projects. Simply thinking aloud about certain leadership dilemmas is one way principals can help teachers understand the way leaders think about issues. Would this proposal fit our school vision? How do we gain acceptance for this idea? How do we get the community more involved? Articulating questions of that type not only helps groups solve the problems at hand, it gives teachers a chance to reflect on the tasks of leadership.

Confidence to Choose

As teachers begin to learn about the challenges of leadership, it is also important for them to have an opportunity to measure themselves against the demands of the job. The principalship is not for everyone; helping teachers make appropriate career choices benefits both them and the schools for which they work. Not surprisingly, research has shown that teachers who believe they can be successful as principals are more likely to choose that pathway (Pounder and Merrill; Paul A. Winter, James S. Rinehart, and Marco A. Munoz).

One obvious strategy for building self-confidence is to encourage teacher leadership. Teachers who get involved with the change process do many of the tasks that principals do: reflect on the school's vision, examine data, formulate strategies, motivate others, and evaluate outcomes. As they build skills in these areas, they are better able to persuade themselves that they could succeed in the principal's office.

Teachers' sense of efficacy can also grow as a result of simply being told by a credible source that they have the potential to do well as a principal. Such a "tap on the shoulder" is not only flattering, it often sparks a self-examination that ultimately leads to a new career. Teachers with nascent leadership skills do not necessary recognize that they have those skills or that they would be especially successful in the principalship. This has been especially true for women and minorities, who have not traditionally had an abundance of role models to point the way. Mary E. Gardiner, Ernestine Enomoto, and Margaret Grogan cited one female administrator who benefited from this kind of invitation:

> I can remember my thinking, "Why would you want me to do that?" [Women] don't see themselves in that [leadership] role. So until you ask them to go there, they won't, because they won't seek it out themselves.

More generally, current principals should be careful about overemphasizing the difficulty of the job. In an environment that constantly hammers home the impossibility of the principal's job, teachers may perceive too large a gap between the magnitude of the challenge and the depth of their personal capability. The implication for districts is that they need to help teachers acquire a sense of optimism about the possibilities of leadership.

Phase 2: Preparation

Entry into a university preparation program typically marks the beginning of the formal socialization process, a period in which candidates are expected to learn what it means to be a principal and to acquire the knowledge and technical skills needed to perform effectively. Historically, policymakers have front-loaded principal development under the assumption that the necessary knowledge, skills, and values for the profession can be conveyed in university classrooms prior to any on-the-job experience. Not surprisingly, policymakers (and the candidates themselves) have often been disappointed in the results.

This section considers developmental and socialization needs during formal preparation and examines how programs can meet those needs.

The Developmental Challenge of Preparation

Candidates in preparation programs occupy an ambiguous position. Their entry into the program publicly marks them as future administrators, but they are still on the outside looking in. Some may not be completely convinced that they want to be principals or may be unsure that they are up to the challenge. Also, their coursework requires them to begin thinking like principals even as they continue to serve as classroom teachers.

Tricia Browne-Ferrigno found that *role-identity transformation*—acquiring a new mind-set—was "a critical step in the professional development process" among the leadership candidates she studied. One prospective principal said, "I feel like I have a split image . . . no, I don't think of myself as a teacher as much anymore. But, you know, there's a part of me saying goodbye to that. And that's a little bit sad."

Shifting roles in this way is never easy. Michèle Schmidt found that teachers considering administrative careers had a range of emotions: satisfaction at the thought of a more influential role, frustration with the negative aspects of the principalship, regret at leaving teaching, anxiety about their ability to live up to expectations, and many others. Peter Gronn and Kathy Lacey have described the importance of providing "positioning space," a kind of temporary psychological haven that allows candidates to manage those feelings.

A more obvious component of socialization in this period is the acquisition of formal knowledge about the principalship. In university classrooms, candidates are exposed to a wide range of information about curriculum, supervision, finance, research, school law, the nature of leadership, and organizational theory. At first glance, much of this material seems relevant, but candidates often complain that it is abstract and not easily applicable to the school setting.

Surveys of principals consistently find skepticism about the value of university coursework (James L. Doud and Edward P. Keller; Steve Farkas and colleagues; Arthur Levine). The most frequent complaint is that programs "are out of touch with the realities of what it takes to run today's school district" (Farkas and colleagues). Although there are hints in the literature that recent graduates view their preparation more favorably (Bradley Portin and colleagues), the overall findings are discouraging.

The difficulty may not be with the course content itself, but with the nature of academic study, which is quite different from thinking on the job. Abstract textbook knowledge is the currency of higher education, and most programs place a high value on theory, research, and critical analysis. By contrast, the principalship, like most jobs, requires a high degree of "practical intelligence," which practitioners employ to solve problems that are highly contextualized (Robert J. Sternberg and Elena L. Grigorenko).

Even when professors want to incorporate more applied thinking, they find it difficult to do in a university classroom. Without a real-world context, there are so many variables that trying to provide a comprehensive set of strategies is virtually impossible. At any given moment, the answer to the question "What's the best course of action?" is "It depends."

Finally, unlike students preparing for most occupations, would-be principals usually have a job that they can seldom afford to leave for full-time study. Inevitably, balancing job, family, and study creates significant strains. Tricia Browne-Ferrigno and Rodney Muth recorded the comment of one principal candidate:

> We should NOT have to teach while we're doing this. If the school districts really want to train excellent leaders, they need to help fund the program and provide *time* away from other jobs so that we can get the experience we need. We also need more time for *study*, mulling [over issues], and discussion during the week. Growth takes *time* and emotional energy.

Is Leadership Preparation Up to the Task?

Preparation programs are a perennial source of dissatisfaction among school reformers. One recent study concluded that "the majority of programs range from inadequate to appalling" (Levine).

Analysts have compiled a list of concerns: little targeted recruitment, lax admission standards, an ill-defined knowledge base, little academic rigor, fragmented curriculum, lack of connection to the world of practice, uninspired instructional methods, mediocre faculty, scheduling based on student convenience rather than program integrity, lack of diversity in students and faculty, use of an academic rather than a professional model, and a part-time student body (Carolyn Kelley and Kent D. Peterson; Levine; Joseph Murphy).

Nonetheless, few people seem inclined to do away with formal training. Although outside critics have proposed quick-entry pathways for capable people from other occupations, few states have acted on the recommendation (C. Emily Feistritzer). This may be so for several reasons:

1. A period of formal preparation, whatever the content, is a crucial socialization tool. It forces future leaders to consciously confront the issues they will face as principals. University classes provide the opportunity for focused reflection on leadership dilemmas. Once on the job, leaders will find reflective opportunities to be much rarer.

2. In today's frenetic educational climate, on-the-job training is a luxury. There may have been a time when a district could install promising candidates and patiently wait for them to get up to speed. With the pressures of No Child Left Behind, rapidly changing demographics, and limited resources, that kind of grace period no longer exists.

3. People who choose to enter training programs may have illusions about the nature of the job. A well-designed program will confront them with some hard realities, allowing them to rethink their plans before they take a job, not in the middle of it.

4. Formal preparation exposes prospective principals to state-of-the-art ideas, critical perspectives, and new paradigms. On-the-job training is more likely to teach people how to cope with the job as it exists, not how to transform it into something better.

In summary, it appears that university preparation programs will remain the chief entry path for the overwhelming majority of principals for the foreseeable future. The key question is whether universities will be able to reinvent their programs to meet the needs of prospective principals.

Promising Reforms

Given the widespread agreement on the inadequacy of initial preparation programs, many universities have responded by overhauling their admission standards, curriculum, methods, field experiences, and delivery systems. This section briefly reviews a number of these innovations:

1. *Admission standards.* Historically, entry into administrator programs has been based on self-selection: Teachers decide they want to be principals, provide evidence that they meet the minimum admission requirements, and write a tuition check. Thereafter, they need only keep passing their courses to reach the principalship. Not only does academic quality of candidates appear to be low (Educational Testing Service), but admission

procedures seldom include an evaluation of the applicant's leadership potential (Theodore Creighton and Gary Jones).

In response, some programs are beginning to toughen screening procedures. For example, the First Ring Leadership Academy, a collaborative program between Cleveland State University and 13 area school districts, requires that candidates be formally nominated by a superintendent. Applicants must also submit a personal theory of action about school leadership and be screened by a committee that includes local superintendents.

Similarly, the New Leaders for New Schools program uses a nationwide recruitment and nomination process, followed by submission of a 14-page application, an initial hour-and-a-half interview, analysis of a case study, and a final day-long interview that includes more case studies, role playing, and a presentation. In 2004, the program admitted 56 candidates from the initial pool of 1,100 (U.S. Department of Education).

2. *New standards.* The introduction of standards from the Interstate School Leaders Licensure Consortium (ISLLC) has dramatically changed the assumptions underlying the typical preparation curriculum. The ISLLC standards distill school leadership into just six focus areas: vision, school culture, effective management, community collaboration, ethical action, and social engagement. All six explicitly aim to attain one goal: producing an "educational leader who promotes the success of all students." A majority of states recognize the standards and often require preparation programs to align their curriculum accordingly.

Although the standards are not universally admired, they are widely respected and are the driving force in many states' reform efforts. Because of their focus on student learning, they align well with the current emphasis on standards-based accountability.

3. *Curricular changes.* Partly because of the impact of ISLLC standards, preparation curricula are shifting from an abstract, social-science paradigm to a model that makes room for more personal and humanistic perspectives. Theory and research today are more likely to involve personal perspectives and questions of meaning and to use qualitative rather than quantitative methods. In addition, ethics and values are playing a new role, not just as a set of rules that can be covered in one course, but as a foundational way of looking at leadership (Robert J. Starratt).

4. *New methods.* Along with new curricular content, many programs are reinventing teaching strategies, particularly in an effort to better connect course content with the world of practice. For example, case studies can provide rich descriptions and contextual details of lifelike situations. They provide a kind of "cognitive apprenticeship" that allows instructors to articulate the tacit knowledge relevant to real-world problems (Nona A. Prestine).

Problem-based learning (PBL) goes beyond case studies to provide interactive simulations of a real-world task. For example, one PBL exercise asks students to serve on a teacher-selection committee with the goal of hiring a fourth-grade teacher. As background, students are given information about the school and its teacher-evaluation process, as well as readings on related topics such as recruitment, selection, and school law.

The students' task is to design and implement a selection process, during which they interview candidates and observe demonstration lessons. After deliberating, the committee must prepare a report to the personnel director making and justifying its recommendation. The students then receive feedback from a faculty member and the teachers they interviewed (Edwin M. Bridges and Philip Hallinger). PBL seems especially well suited to dealing with the "messiness" of real leadership problems, where multiple issues may be embedded in a single decision.

5. *Connecting to the world of practice.* By all accounts, the biggest struggle preparation programs face is helping candidates apply course knowledge to real-world contexts. Academic knowledge comes neatly packaged in separate courses, whereas actual school leadership lacks clear boundaries; everything seems connected to everything else.

Efforts to bridge this gap cover a range of strategies. Some programs provide course assignments that center on real-world activities. Candidates may be asked to bring about a change in some aspect of a school's structures, norms, or traditional procedures by working directly with the school's personnel. Examples include improving a school's attendance procedure, developing a volunteer recognition program, and conducting a cost-benefit analysis of a school-improvement plan.

Such practicum experiences offer a number of benefits. Candidates work on authentic contextualized problems, not abstract textbook exercises. Not only are the skills they learn more likely to be useful, they have the satisfaction of knowing that their efforts have made a difference. Accomplishing the work of a principal may help them feel like a principal. Because the experience is still part of a university course, professors can offer them advice and feedback.

Although practicum experiences offer a taste of the real world, they fail to replicate the intensity of being a principal. For that reason, the recent trend has been to propose extended internships. The National Association of State Boards of Education spoke for many reformers when it said, "Carefully designed and closely supervised internships are a critically necessary component of any high-quality principal preparation program."

Ideally, an internship is a full-time, semester-long (or even yearlong) assignment that immerses principal candidates in the realities of school leadership. In practice, most internships fall short of this goal. The Southern Regional Education Board (2005), after a survey of internship practices in 16 southern states, concluded that "in far too many principal preparation programs, the internship 'vessel' is leaky, rudderless, or still in dry dock."

One major obstacle to adequate internships is financial. Many candidates hold full-time jobs as teachers and cannot afford to trade their regular income for an unpaid internship. The alternative is for their districts to grant them paid release time, an expense most district budgets will not permit. As a result, candidates have to grab internship hours as their schedule allows, rather than arranging a coherent schedule of meaningful activities.

Too often, a student is assigned a hodgepodge of low-level tasks and loose ends that the regular administrator hasn't gotten around to. As a result, people are being prepared to serve as instructional leaders by spending 5 to 10 hours per week supervising bus loadings, calling the homes of truant students, filling out forms for the central office, or devising new student handbooks. These tasks are relevant to the job but are far removed from the core leadership issues principals face. The survey by the Southern Regional Education Board (2005) found that a minority of university programs required candidates to engage in activities centered on student learning or school improvement.

Ronald L. Capasso and John C. Daresh say a good internship has three characteristics:

1. It provides the candidate with significant leadership activities that require problem solving and decision making.

2. It helps candidates understand the scope of the principal's job.

3. It provides the candidate with meaningful tasks that make a contribution to the cooperating district.

Mike Milstein, summarizing the experiences of Danforth institutions, adds three other conditions:

1. The internship should be spread over multiple settings so the candidate can experience a variety of settings and styles.

2. The internship should be closely supervised and evaluated, and the respective roles of mentor and supervisor should be made clear.

3. Opportunities for reflection should be provided on a weekly or biweekly basis.

The last point is easy to overlook, since many participants assume that one learns from experience simply by experiencing. But unreflective experience leads to little except imitation; genuine learning requires the student to connect events with some framework of knowledge. Anne Weaver Hart notes, "What has been tacit becomes increasingly explicit and, therefore, more deliberate and amenable to modification." Expertise comes when principals can move from theory to practice and back again (Ronald Williamson and Martha Hudson).

6. *Program delivery*. Preparation programs have traditionally delivered their courses cafeteria style. From the offered menu of courses, students could pick whatever selections suited them at that time. In the past decade, this pattern has been challenged by two developments: the use of cohorts and the emergence of virtual learning.

Cohorts comprise groups of students who take the same courses at the same time and thus remain together through the preparation sequence. Initially, cohorts merely simplified program management, but many university faculty members have found that they have educational benefits as well.

The most widely reported advantage of cohorts is the development of a learning community (Cynthia J. Norris and colleagues). As members of the group pursue a common purpose under common conditions, they typically form strong bonds with their peers. Group members offer strong mutual support and build solidarity; many use the concept of family to describe the group. In a climate of trust, students are more comfortable expressing their ideas. Students also become interdependent and develop collaborative skills that facilitate the formation of a learning community.

In general, faculty members and students speak highly of this social learning (Bruce G. Barnett and colleagues). The academic impact of cohorts is less clear, however. Jay Paredes Scribner and Joe F. Donaldson found that the social dynamics of the cohort sometimes overpowered the actual learning opportunities. For example, the desire to avoid conflict and reduce tension sometimes led students to back away from contentious issues that would have benefited from further debate. In addition, the high degree of collaboration sometimes allowed students to avoid working on skills that needed strengthening.

Distance learning is a fast-growing delivery method that offers some obvious attractions to busy professionals, who would rather learn in the comfort of their homes than battle heavy traffic in questionable weather. Electronic programs are a special boon to learners in rural areas, who normally have to drive long distances to get to classes. Online courses are also asynchronous, allowing students to work at their own convenience rather than having to dedicate a specific block of time to the class.

Virtual learning poses some formidable challenges for principal preparation, particularly the lack of face-to-face interactivity so characteristic of the principal's work. Joellen Killion notes:

> Effective leaders must listen fully to messages delivered not only in words, but also in voice tone and gestures. They use a full range of critical analysis skills, communication skills, and human interaction skills to respond and to participate in discussion, dialogue, or team meetings.

She adds that such skills are unlikely to be developed online.

7. *Partnerships*. Although most preparation programs remain in the university orbit, school districts are becoming more active players in the preparation process. As noted earlier, programs such as New Leaders for New Schools and the First Ring Leadership Academy are strongly field based. Thus, they provide a meaningful context for the theory and research that candidates are studying.

Such programs do not challenge the existing licensure system, as they operate through arrangements with accredited universities. They considerably enhance the developmental process by providing candidates with authentic opportunities for the practice of leadership, along with mentoring, coaching, and other forms of support.

Phase 3: Induction

By all accounts, the most intensive period of professional development in a principal's career comes in the first couple of years on the job. Suddenly, after years of living with a teacher's relatively predictable agenda, the newcomer is plunged into a nonstop whirl of activity often summed up as "reality shock." One of the principals interviewed by Parkay and colleagues expressed it vividly: "I am so spent that all I want to do is crawl upstairs and lie in the bed in a fetal position and say, 'That's it! That's it! That's it!'"

Principals face such an astonishing range of challenges that no preparation program can be expected to acquaint candidates with every issue they will face. The principalship has many of the characteristics of a craft (Roland S. Barth; Arthur Blumberg). To cite one notable example, the position requires practical wisdom or "street smarts" that can be learned only on the job. Some challenges seem laughably trivial, but they loom large at the time. Daniel L. Duke mentions one principal's recollection:

> Standing in the office on Labor Day looking at the clock and wondering, "How in the hell do you ring the bell?" is perhaps my most vivid memory. It also sums

up many of the things I encountered that were simple but were things I had not done before.

More broadly, research on new principals has shown that they face a range of surprises, frustrations, and problems, including a sense of isolation; struggles with time management; lack of feedback; and the need to hone technical skills, learn the unwritten rules, and develop a sense of efficacy (Mark Anderson; Parkay and colleagues).

This section examines the nature of the challenges that newcomers face and describes some ways school districts have responded.

Developmental Needs of New Principals

New principals are no longer outsiders: They have responsibility for a school and are expected to lead. Yet they may still feel like outsiders: Their mastery of many routine tasks is less than complete; they need to learn a large number of names and faces; they have to learn the politics of the district; and if the job is in a new community, they are still finding their way around town. Having made a major investment in a new career direction, they have a need to succeed, for emotional as well as practical reasons.

The first thing they learn is that textbooks won't be of much help (except this one, of course!), not because the content is irrelevant, but because so much of leadership depends on tacit knowledge acquired from experience. New principals are not only performing a variety of tasks, they are simultaneously learning how to perform those tasks. Unfortunately, the relentless pace of the job allows little time to reflect on what they are learning.

Induction is obviously a critical period for professional socialization. This is when new principals learn—at a gut level—what it means to be a leader. Much of their learning involves technical skills, but there are also emotional issues. The separation from teaching that began in preparation programs is now official; however much they may miss the classroom, they are now on the other side of the divide.

Organizational socialization is also crucial. Beginning principals must learn not only what it means to be a principal, but what it means to be a principal in this particular school (Parkay and colleagues). Every school has a unique history and culture that influence the kinds of decisions that can be made. Anderson, in his study of new principals, noted that many of these local expectations are tacit, requiring the rookies to ferret out the unwritten rules.

The change in leadership is itself unsettling for any school. When a new principal walks into a school, teachers know that comfortable routines may change, new priorities may push aside the established agenda, and alliances may shift, rearranging the lines of power and influence. The new leader will come under intense scrutiny, and even minor missteps may have disproportionate impact.

Not surprisingly, newcomers are under considerable personal as well as professional stress. The new job with its new schedules and responsibilities may affect family life, particularly for women. If the job requires moving to a new community, there will be the stress of moving as well as acclimation to a new living environment.

Parkay and colleagues, while observing principals during their first 3 years, identified distinct stages in the socialization process, moving from *survival* (the initial period of feeling dazed, disoriented, and inadequate) to *professional actualization* (collaborating with teachers to advance a long-term agenda for change).

This observation suggests that professional development for newcomers must accomplish two distinct goals. First, it must provide immediate technical support. New principals have to assert control; they must sort through the barrage of demands on their time, set priorities, and execute the necessary tasks. At the same time, they must keep their eyes on the vision and keep the school moving in a positive direction—not just surviving.

These two needs may conflict. Parkay and his associates described the early stages as somewhat defensive, focused on coping rather than trying to transform the school. The danger is that the initial focus on survival may lead to behaviors and relationships that inhibit the potential for transformational change. One third-year principal noted, "I am finding [that] the more comfortable the faculty and I get, the more difficult it appears to effect change with 'em."

This same study found that most third-year principals believed they had entered with unrealistic visions and inadequate skills for facilitating change. Although some new principals are able to adapt their visions to reality and keep their schools working toward improvement, others may conclude that significant change is not possible and settle for a more custodial role.

Realizing that new principals have often been left to sink or swim, policymakers and practitioners have recently begun to put significant resources into the induction period.

Learning From Others

Induction for principals has become almost inseparable from the topic of mentoring. Many schools have seized on the idea as a helpful, easily implemented solution for the problems of the entry period. The rationale is obvious: The availability of an experienced and presumably wiser peer can provide newcomers with practical problem-solving tips and can ease the "lonely at the top" syndrome. Indeed, informal mentoring has always been a part of the scene; many principals can point to people who provided crucial advice and support along the way.

In the business world, mentoring carries connotations of "sponsorship," with a senior executive effectively "adopting" a promising newcomer and not only sharing knowledge and wise counsel, but paving the way for promotion. This kind of sponsorship is not unknown in school leadership. In their in-depth study of administrator recruitment practices, Catherine Baltzell and Robert A. Dentler noted something akin to a good old boys' network, in which existing leaders picked out potential candidates in their own image and eased the candidates' way into power. As described by Baltzell and Dentler, this process operated through quiet winks and nods, more a case of anointing than developing.

Gary M. Crow and L. Joseph Matthews have suggested that the sponsorship function is less important in educational leadership because career ladders are truncated; there simply are not very many upper-level positions available for advancement.

John Daresh (2004) points out that although sponsorship may provide a career boost to newcomers, it does not necessarily provide the kind of immediate help that new principals need. For that reason, recent developments in mentoring have emphasized intentional and formal programs. Perhaps the most accurate summary is that mentoring for educational leaders covers a wide spectrum of possibilities, from spontaneous one-to-one buddy relationships to formal, mandated programs required for continuing certification.

Benefits of Mentoring

Mentoring in school leadership serves several functions. Perhaps most obviously, it constitutes a kind of professional development, as mentors share knowledge, values, and technical skills. Daresh (2004) notes that this is not just a matter of picking up practical tips not covered in university courses, but it is a way of translating textbook theory into real-world practice:

> Having a mentor and guide who already speaks the language of school adminis-tration . . . allows the novice to begin to understand subtle relationships between what was learned in books with what must now be learned through daily interactions with parents, teachers, staff, and students.

Second, mentoring promotes reflection and self-analysis. Having a knowledgeable veteran comment on one's practice provides an objective, outside perspective that can help new leaders balance the strong subjective feelings they experience.

Finally, mentoring provides psychosocial support. Having the ear of a trusted confi-dant helps the novice sort out the personal stresses that come with the job. Lisa C. Ehrich, Brian Hansford, and Lee Tennent, in a review of mentoring in educational settings, found that participants most frequently cited support, empathy, and encouragement as benefits. Crow and Matthews note that protégés may gain greater visibility, avoid potential land mines, take on more challenges, and show more confidence.

Mentors themselves may benefit as they gain renewed enthusiasm, new insights, and validation of their skills (Daresh 2004). Of course, the school as a whole also gains from new principal's accelerated development.

Crow and Matthews observe that mentoring can go awry, particularly if the mentor does not give priority to the protégé's development. Some mentors see the relationship as a chance to clone themselves or to advance a particular leadership strategy that works well for them but may not be as effective for the protégé. Some mentoring relationships create dependency, as protégés come to rely on the mentor rather than doing their own problem solving.

Guidelines for Mentoring

Despite its almost universal appeal, mentoring has not often been the subject of rig-orous research, and it does not have a well-developed theoretical foundation (Richard Ackerman, Laura Ventimiglia, and Melissa Juchniewicz). Nor does the literature reveal clear trends in the nature of mentoring programs. Many programs apparently go no fur-ther than pairing a new principal with an experienced peer and letting the two work out their own relationship. Most analysts, though, recommend the establishment of formal programs. Crow and Matthews observe that "all principals need mentors, not just those who are in the right place at the right time."

Crow and Matthews describe five components that a thoughtful program should address:

1. *Organizational planning.* Numerous structural and logistical questions must be answered. Who will plan the program? How will mentors be selected and trained? How will mentors and protégés be matched? How will the program be evaluated? Failure to address these questions up front may undermine success.

2. *Mentor selection.* Mentors should be highly skilled leaders and exemplary role models, and they should be able to engage others in learning. Excellent leadership does not automatically equate to effective mentoring. Mentors have to be genuinely interested in helping others and be willing to commit the necessary time and energy to the relationship.

3. *Mentor training.* Helpfulness comes naturally to many principals, but mentoring requires specific skills. Mentors must exercise tact, encourage reflection, and understand adult learning. Crow and Matthews suggest that experienced principal mentors are best suited to conduct the training.

4. *Matching mentors and protégés.* Mentoring is like any other relationship: Sometimes participants immediately connect, finding themselves on the same wavelength, whereas other partnerships never get off the ground. Some evidence suggests that mentoring works better when partners can choose each other freely, but this is not always possible. Program coordinators should attempt to pair principals who share similar philosophies or styles.

5. *Evaluation.* As with any program, evaluation and analysis of results are critical. How much mentoring (and what type) has actually occurred? How helpful was it? How can mentor training be improved? Answers to those questions will help the district refine and improve the program over time.

Laura F. Dukess offers similar recommendations, saying that the best programs include careful matching of mentors and protégés, clear expectations and guidelines for participants, adequate time for mentors, and selection of mentors who have a record of success and who are "reflective, compassionate, good listeners, good communicators, and able to speak the hard truth."

Most analysts have also identified some common pitfalls in programs. Frequently mentioned problems are inadequate training, poorly matched mentors and protégés, lack of resources, insufficient time, and inequitable implementation (Crow and Matthews; Daresh 2004; Ehrich and colleagues). Daresh (2004) notes that mentoring will be ineffective if it just reproduces current leadership strategies.

Other Induction Strategies

Although mentoring is the most intuitive response to the needs of newcomers, districts can structure professional development in a variety of ways, including portfolios, professional development plans, study groups, leadership academies, focus groups, peer coaching, workshops, and retreats (Peterson).

Districts are not the only providers of professional development. Some states sponsor school leadership academies with workshops, mentoring, and other forms of guidance for new principals (Southern Regional Education Board 2003).

A number of states have realigned their certification requirements to better support the developmental needs of leaders (Southern Regional Education Board 2002). Some have developed two-tiered licensure systems in which full certification comes only after successful experience as an administrator, aided by structured mentoring, focused coursework, and other forms of assistance. All these measures lead to full-fledged certification after a successful first year. Programs such as these provide a useful framework districts can use to support their new leaders.

Professional associations also offer a variety of resources. The National Association of Elementary School Principals (NAESP) conducts workshops, assessments, and training opportunities. NAESP also partners with Nova Southeastern University to offer intensive mentor training and certification. The National Association of Secondary School Principals has long been a leader in using assessment centers to promote principal development.

Universities offer still another source of support. For example, the New Teacher Center at the University of California, Santa Cruz, provides trained coaches to give individualized guidance to new administrators. Participants meet every 2 weeks and also maintain contact by e-mail and phone. Services include observation and coaching in authentic work dilemmas (Gary Bloom).

Direct empirical evidence is scarce, but some researchers have suggested that formal induction programs improve retention. Linda M. Morford, after interviewing 10 new rural principals who had no access to any kind of induction program, found 2 years later that 9 of them had either moved on to other positions or returned to teaching. If nothing else, reports from new administrators (Anderson; Gary N. Hartzell, Richard C. Williams, and Kathleen T. Nelson) make it abundantly clear that they will regard any help extended during the first few years as a cherished lifeline.

Elaine Fink and Lauren B. Resnick have described the comprehensive approach to professional development used by Community School District 2 in New York City. Professional development is not just an add-on activity but rather is embedded in the everyday work of the principal. District 2's strategy involves an extensive menu of development activities:

- Monthly daylong principal conferences that focus on a variety of instructional issues common to schools in the district
- Periodic institutes providing an in-depth treatment of specific instructional concerns
- Support groups for new principals (led by the deputy superintendent) that provide discussion of topics such as assessing student performance, evaluating teachers, and managing staff development
- Visits to other schools to see how principals there have handled certain instructional issues
- Informal mentoring or buddy groups
- Individualized coaching on establishing budgets, determining objectives, and other technical skills

The district also conducts periodic supervisory walkthroughs, in which the deputy superintendent spends a morning visiting a school. The visit includes a discussion of the school's goals, a review of student learning data, and observations in every classroom. It culminates in an evaluation conference that establishes professional development goals for the principal.

This ambitious model is not possible for every district, but it does illustrate the range of activities available for professional development. Thoughtfully chosen, induction strategies can fulfill Judith Aiken's recommendation that they "support principals through paradox, help to demystify leadership practice, and provide opportunities for collaborative and reflective learning."

Phase 4: Lifelong Professional Development

Whereas the need to support new principals is now widely accepted, veteran principals are frequently treated like gifted children: left to their own devices because everyone assumes they can get by without much help. The current pressure on schools to show yearly progress in student learning is putting new attention on lifelong development of school leaders' skills. With today's accelerating pace of change, even the most experienced leader faces a steep learning curve that can benefit from structured opportunities for professional development.

Accordingly, the induction activities described in the preceding section are equally appropriate for principals at all levels of experience. Even mentoring, often viewed as a service for newcomers, can be beneficial for principals throughout their careers, say Crow and Matthews.

Unlike traditional professional development, which has often been driven by a scattershot combination of convenience, cost, and curiosity, today's efforts increasingly respond to the need to align principal learning with the demands of school improvement. In many cases, the necessary structure is provided by some body of standards representing the collective wisdom of the profession or the findings of research.

For example, the NAESP has outlined a curriculum for instructional leadership with its 2001 publication *Leading Learning Communities: Standards for What Principals Should Know and Be Able to Do.* Districts could easily use the standards as a reference in setting up developmental experiences.

The ISLLC standards, which already guide principal preparation in many states, can easily be extended to induction and professional development. The six standards are both broad enough and deep enough to present a challenge to veterans and newcomers alike. A recent publication from West Ed has shown how the standards can be benchmarked at different levels of expertise, allowing principals to progressively move closer to exemplary practice.

Another way of structuring professional development is to link it directly to the school's improvement efforts. Analysis of student test scores and other school performance data will invariably reveal areas needing improvement. For needs that are sufficiently serious, developmental activities can be planned to address the issue. For example, persistently low math scores might trigger attendance at a math workshop, visits to schools with successful math programs, or participation in study groups aimed at raising math achievement.

Perhaps the most important guidepost for professional development is that it be embedded in the culture of the district, clearly conveying the expectation that learning and leadership are virtually synonymous (Richard F. Elmore and Deanna Burney). But, at a minimum, districts should be prepared to take at least four steps:

1. Orient beginning principals to the district, including operational procedures, community characteristics, district philosophy, and any special challenges associated with the assigned school.

2. Provide some form of mentoring, even if it is informal. Novices should not have to face the stress and turmoil of the first year without some kind of human support system.

3. Give beginning principals feedback on their performance, both formally and informally. Newcomers often have difficulty determining the adequacy of their performance and welcome this kind of guidance.

4. Develop a plan for professional growth. To help beginning principals continue to develop leadership skills and grow professionally, devise a growth plan that includes specific learning objectives, activities to help in the development process, an implementation timeline, and an evaluation plan.

Developmental Needs of Experienced Principals

If the learning needs of experienced principals are often overlooked, it is because the needs are not easily visible. Principals with 5 or 6 years' experience appear to have scaled the formidable learning curve of the first few years. They have polished their technical skills, they have established productive relationships throughout the school and the community, and they are enacting their vision in strategic and politically savvy ways. From most angles, they seem confident and in control.

Current discussions of leadership suggest three themes may be especially important in the development of veteran principals:

1. *Career development.* For many, stepping into a principalship represents the achievement of their career goals, and they may give little thought to the question "What's next?" For them, the principalship appears to be a featureless career plateau stretching 15 or 20 years into the future.

In reality, the principalship encompasses a variety of career possibilities that unfold over time. Some principals may continue on an upward trajectory, gravitating toward central-office positions. Alternatively, they may choose to remain principals, but seek advancement in the form of larger schools, higher salaries, or more desirable communities. Or, they may define career success in terms of meeting formidable challenges (such as reducing the achievement gap), irrespective of the school setting.

Less positively, leaders may stagnate. Having achieved a manageable equilibrium in a particular school, they may be content to put their energies into maintaining the status quo.

In short, career development is best viewed not as a matter of changing positions but as a process of accepting and mastering a series of challenges that may or may not involve switching jobs.

Unfortunately, we know little about how experienced principals view their careers, and there is virtually no evidence that they have many structured opportunities to reflect on the path they are following.

2. *Continual learning.* No one questions the need for principals to engage in continual learning. Fast-paced change is an inescapable feature of today's environment: On every side, leaders confront shifting community expectations, new curricula, and rapidly changing regulations and laws.

Consequently, the principal's learning agenda cannot be satisfied simply by absorbing new information at workshops or through journal articles. That is, school leaders are being asked not just to fine-tune the existing system but to transform it into something else. (For example, just in the past decade, principals have been called on to implement standards-based reform and to share decision making throughout the school community.) Such challenges may require major shifts in perspective, including the need to unlearn as well as to learn. Thus, professional development for leaders can act as a conservative force that supports the status quo or as a transformational force that can help change the system.

In addition, Neil Dempster has pointed out that professional development can be driven by the needs and interests of individual leaders or by the needs of the system. Districts may use very different philosophies in supporting leaders' learning. Many simply provide a set amount of funding that principals can use as they see fit; others require principals to engage in activities that closely align with district priorities. Dempster sees merit in both orientations and suggests that a balance of district-initiated and principal-initiated development will yield the most productive results.

3. *The human side of leadership.* Traditionally, professional development for leaders has provided knowledge and skills closely linked to the daily demands of the job. Principals generally attend a workshop to improve their communication skills or to learn how to use data for making decisions.

Yet there are deeper dimensions to leadership that in the long run may be even more important to long-term success. All leaders, even the most powerful or most revered, never stop being people, subject to all the doubts, frailties, and miscalculations that go with being human. In the pungent words of satirist E. Y. Harburg:

> *No matter how high or great the throne,*
> *What sits on it is the same as your own.*

In recent years, scholars of leadership have begun to explore the connections between the professional and the personal, and they have generally concluded that the two cannot be separated. Russ S. Moxley, in his exploration of the spiritual side of leadership, says, "We must know ourselves and be our true and whole selves if we are to successfully and effectively engage in the activity of leadership."

Being a leader does not just challenge our technical skills, it stretches our ability to maintain positive relationships, poses ethical dilemmas, and tests our belief in our own abilities. Remaining optimistic and open to others is not always easy. Ronald A. Heifetz and Marty Linsky claim that "the most difficult work of leadership involves learning to experience distress without numbing yourself."

To grow as professionals with integrity, school executives know they must deal also with the dark side of leadership. Heifetz and Linsky say it is important for leaders to "manage their hungers," resisting the temptations that come from the enjoyment of power or self-importance. Recognizing and coping with such vulnerabilities is essential.

Similarly, Parker Palmer has identified five "shadow-casting monsters" that bedevil leaders: (a) insecurity about one's identify and worth, (b) a belief that the universe is a battleground and that enemies are everywhere, (c) the conviction that responsibility for everything rests with us, (d) fear of the natural chaos of life, and (e) the denial of death itself—sometimes we have to let go.

Failure to recognize these tendencies may lead to the delusion that our actions are benign and that the problem rests with others.

Principals, like most leaders, do not often have access to forums in which such issues can be articulated and shared with empathetic listeners, and there are few established models to draw on. What may be needed more than anything are small "communities of practice" in which leaders are willing to engage in sustained conversations about the issues they wrestle with.

Karen F. Osterman and Robert B. Kottkamp have provided a detailed description of one such community, in which administrators in the same district periodically met for unstructured discussion of the issues they confronted. Over time, the meetings evolved into a trusting, supportive, sometimes moving experience that allowed participants to voice ideas that had no other forum. Whatever the forum, successfully dealing with these issues can make the difference between thriving and merely surviving as a leader.

THE SPECIAL CASE OF THE ASSISTANT PRINCIPAL

Many school leaders actually begin their careers as assistant principals. Because assistants' job responsibilities often differ from those of the principal, their developmental needs may also differ.

Assistants occupy a unique rung on the leadership ladder. They have authority, but it is seldom final authority, and it tends to be concentrated in a few areas. They are often managerial specialists, assigned to mete out discipline, schedule athletic events, and supervise the lunchroom. Even more troubling, the job may lack coherence. The assistant's daily agenda may be dictated by a job description that says "such other duties as may be assigned by the principal" (Daresh 2002).

Such a job profile creates a developmental dilemma. L. David Weller and Sylvia J. Weller put it this way: "In no other position does one walk such a fine line between the maintenance and survival needs of the school and the needs and demands of the students, teachers, and principal." The key challenge for the assistant, they wrote, is making the transition from manager to leader.

For new assistant principals, survival depends on the ability to execute well a rather narrow series of technical tasks requiring organization and efficiency. If they fail to do these jobs well, they cannot hope to move into the principalship. Yet if they focus all their energies on such tasks, they may fail to develop the broader leadership skills that principals exercise.

If they are too successful in doing the work of an assistant, they may become "typecast" as a managerial specialist rather than as a leader (Daresh 2002).

Research by T. C. Chan, Linda Webb, and Charles Bowen found that assistant principals were aware of the importance of broad leadership skills such as developing a vision, and they assigned high importance to instructional support and curriculum development. Most of their time, though, went to tasks such as discipline and cafeteria supervision. Thus, the assistants expressed concern that their current job profile was not allowing them to develop the broader skills needed to advance to the principalship.

For such reasons, career development has a special prominence for assistant principals. Daresh (2002) notes that some assistants are upwardly mobile (on a fast track to the principalship), some find their ambitions satisfied by an assistantship, and still others are "plateaued" (aspiring to a principalship but making no progress). Assistants in each of these categories may need different kinds of mentoring and developmental experiences.

Some districts have begun to design formal developmental opportunities for assistants. Daresh (2001) has described the Assistant Principal Academy of the Socorro, Texas, school district, which provides participants with the skills needed to advance to the principalship. Monthly meetings over a 2-year period offer a range of ISLLC-based leadership topics, as well as mentoring on interviewing skills. For many participants, the greatest value of the sessions is the chance "to get together and talk about our unique concerns."

Ultimately, meeting the career-development needs of assistant principals may depend on districts' ability to redesign the role of assistant principal in a way that elicits the development of the full spectrum of leadership skills.

ASSESSMENT TOOLS FOR DEVELOPING LEADERSHIP

A quick stroll through any bookstore will confirm that self-improvement is a major industry, and leadership is no exception. Not only do hundreds of books profess to share leadership secrets, but several dozen assessment tools offer structured reflection and feedback for leaders who wish to know more about their strengths and weaknesses.

As noted previously, professional development for school leaders is gradually becoming more systematic and focused, but many principals still find themselves in districts where development opportunities are limited. Formal assessments may offer an efficient, cost-effective way of gaining insights into one's general leadership skills and styles. Assessment tools have several advantages:

- They tend to be objective.
- They have usually been tested for reliability and validity.
- Results are quantified, which gives leaders some sense of how they compare with others.
- They tend to be comprehensive, systematically probing a range of skills.

Kenneth E. Clark and Miriam B. Clark argue that information collected systematically and combined objectively provides better predictors of performance than observer judgments—even when the observer is highly qualified and knows the candidate well.

Self-assessment (the most common form of assessment for professional development) is also notoriously susceptible to bias and blind spots.

Although a well-designed assessment tool is a valuable resource, formal testing is not foolproof. Not all tests are well designed, nor are they always used appropriately. Test scores should be an invitation to reflect and use human judgment—not replace it.

What Do Leadership Tests Measure?

Making a leadership assessment can be a deceptively simple process. Sitting at a desk for half an hour, a leader responds to a series of short questions, and in a short time (often just minutes), receives an impressively detailed profile showing his or her strengths as a leader.

But this seemingly straightforward process masks considerable ambiguity. Measuring leadership is not like measuring temperature; we can expect that any well-made thermometer will give us pretty much the same result. Each leadership test makes its own assumptions about what leadership is and how it can be recognized, and each test uses its own language, format, and measurement strategies.

Some tests seek to identify heroic leadership qualities such as vision and motivation, whereas others zero in on more mundane managerial dimensions such as delegating, mastering technical knowledge, and solving problems. Some focus on beliefs, others on styles.

The most common measures are paper-and-pencil instruments. These typically ask participants to agree or disagree with statements about their behaviors or beliefs, often using a Likert-type scale (for example, 1 means *always* and 5 means *never*).

In some cases, a similar instrument is given to superiors or subordinates, asking them to rate the leader on the same criteria. Such tests do not directly measure leadership performance; instead, their validity rests on studies that have shown a relationship between test scores and on-the-job performance.

Sometimes the test must be sent to the publisher for scoring; sometimes it can be scored by anyone who has received special training or certification; sometimes it can be scored locally.

Although almost any assessment can offer something of value to leaders, some choices will be more productive than others. Before selecting any test, potential users should determine whether it will suit their purposes. What is the assessment's stated purpose? Who is the intended audience? Does the content address the user's main areas of concern?

For information on available tests, consult the test-locator Web site operated by Educational Testing Service (www.ets.org/testcoll/index.html). A description of many tests is available in a 1999 publication from the former ERIC Clearinghouse on Educational Management (Larry Lashway).

Using Leadership Tests Effectively

If the goal is professional development, simply taking a test and generating a score will offer relatively little help. A well-chosen instrument will provide a structure for self-analysis, reflection, and focused activity:

1. *Analysis.* Most instruments are based on theory or research that implies certain leadership behaviors are more effective than others. Nevertheless, assessments will almost never end up with a simplistic judgment of "good leader" or "poor leader." Instead, the results will show a combination of strengths and weaknesses. Some of them are critical issues for the leaders to address, whereas others have only a marginal impact on success.

Participants need to sort through the available data with some care, neither rejecting the findings out of hand nor embracing them uncritically. Data are simply data; they require human judgment to determine their significance.

2. *Reflection.* The leader will benefit only to the extent he or she thoughtfully applies the somewhat abstract judgments provided by the test to the leader's work. If the test has identified communication as a potential area of concern, can the leader identify situations in which that was the case?

3. *Planning.* Ultimately, leadership assessments are more than an intellectual exercise. Weaknesses should be addressed; strengths should be exploited. For that reason, participants in assessment should be encouraged to develop an action plan as soon as possible. Richard Lepsinger and Antoinette D. Lucia say, "If participants do not take meaningful steps to translate their feedback into action within two weeks of leaving the work session, they will probably never do so."

An action agenda should be couched in specific behavioral terms; that is, What must the leader do to build leadership capacity? (Banal generalities such as "be more decisive" and "improve communication" are rarely helpful.) Craig Chappelow suggests three questions that may be helpful in choosing a goal: "Does the goal motivate and energize me? Will achieving this goal help me be more effective in my current position? Will my organization benefit from this goal?"

Lepsinger and Lucia emphasize the importance of putting the development plan into tangible form. An effective written plan will include a clear statement of the goal, the standards for measuring success, the change strategies, the related action steps, and key resource people.

The plan should be reviewed periodically, at which time the leader can identify difficulties, celebrate successes, and modify strategies where appropriate.

CONCLUSION: A PATHWAY UNCERTAIN YET SURE

As professionals keenly attuned to the developmental needs of their clients, educators have been surprisingly slow to recognize that they, too, face different challenges at different stages in their careers. For most school administrators, leadership does not arise from a sudden epiphany that illuminates a clearly marked highway to success. Rather, the pathway is often shrouded in uncertainty, filled with bone-jarring potholes, and marked by what seems to be painfully slow progress. In a time of intensive change that makes lifelong learning more than a slogan, professional development for principals should be systemic, comprehensive, and continuous.

REFLECTIONS

1. What has been the biggest mental adjustment you've had to make in becoming a principal? In what way do principals see the world differently than teachers?

2. Levine claims that administrator preparation programs range in quality from "inadequate to appalling." Does that statement seem supportable? Does it match your experience in a preparation program? Based on your experience, what are the most important changes that should be made in programs for preparing principals?

3. How would you describe your career goals in terms of the future positions you will seek? In terms of the things you hope to accomplish before you're done?

4. What role has mentoring played in your career? Was it a beneficial experience? Would you support a proposal to make mentoring available for all new principals?

5. If you are an experienced principal, what was the most difficult challenge during your first year? Based on that experience, how would you design a mentoring program for first-year principals?

PART III

The Values

6

Ethical Leadership

Larry Lashway

A principal on the verge of initiating dismissal proceedings against an incompetent teacher receives a call from an administrator in a neighboring district, asking for a recommendation on the teacher, who is applying for a position there. An honest answer will probably result in the teacher not being hired.

In the face of severe budget restrictions, the superintendent tells a principal to shift funds from a successful afterschool program for English-language learners to a program for gifted children that has been demanded by some of the school's more affluent parents.

A parent complains to a high school principal about the football coach, saying that his high-pressure, verbally abusive approach damages the self-esteem of adolescents, especially those who are not stars. The principal shares the concerns, but the coach is a popular, almost legendary figure in the community, and his teams are always in contention.

To be a school leader is to live with ethical dilemmas. Not just a few times a year, not just weekly, but every day. The dilemmas come in various forms. Sometimes they announce themselves like flashing neon signs; sometimes they try to slip past disguised as mere technical problems; and sometimes they just lurk in the background, throbbing like a toothache that won't quite go away.

How do administrators meet these ethical challenges? Unfortunately, we know less than we'd like, because researchers for many years preferred to view administration as an objective science, thereby downplaying the role of values, as Lynn G. Beck and Joseph Murphy point out. But we do know that school leaders are keenly aware of the ethical issues surrounding their work (Carol Campbell, Anne Gold, and Ingrid Lunt; Neil Dempster and Pat Mahony; Alan Flintham). Moreover, scholars of educational leadership have increasingly viewed it through a lens that highlights moral and ethical issues.

Christopher Hodgkinson, for example, asserts that education connects with the whole range of human values and that administrators must be aware of "the deep roots of purpose" that underlie their schools. For Hodgkinson, and many others, educational leadership is "the moral art." This view is also reflected in the Interstate School Leaders Licensure Consortium (ISLLC) standards, which not only call for leaders to act "with integrity, fairness, and in an ethical manner," but ask them to influence the political, social, economic, and legal environment on behalf of students (Council of Chief State School Officers [CCSSO]).

This new emphasis on ethical responsibility actually reflects a return to the profession's roots. David Tyack and Elizabeth Hansot note that 19th-century educators regarded themselves as an "aristocracy of character" with a profoundly moral mission. Their energy and self-assurance came from an unshakable conviction that what they were doing was simply right. In turn, the institution they served often exuded an uplifting sense of moral purpose.

But by the middle of the 20th century, according to Tyack and Hansot, school leaders were basing their authority on science rather than morality. Instead of relying on character, leaders now sought expertise; instead of fighting evils, they now solved problems. What happened?

First, public education in the early 20th century became infatuated with the efficiency movement, which sought to reduce costs by stripping human labor to the bare essentials. Searching for ways to increase public confidence in their institutions, school leaders were quick to hop on the bandwagon. One turn-of-the-century superintendent exemplified the new attitude in his comparison of the cost of different subjects:

> I am convinced . . . that when the obligations of the present year expire, we ought to purchase no more Greek instruction at the rate of 5.9 pupil recitations for a dollar. The price must go down, or we shall invest in something else. (Raymond E. Callahan)

Seeing efficiency as a convenient, defensible, and culturally approved standard for running their schools, administrators became increasingly preoccupied with questions of fire insurance, plumbing, and janitor service, while they began to equate learning with industrial output.

Second, after World War II, the training of administrators became dominated by the belief that administration was a science to be understood through objective analysis of cause-effect relationships and determining how things worked (Beck and Murphy). Determining how things should work was another issue; value questions were beyond the reach of science. Thus, two generations of school leaders received training that minimized ethical issues.

A third influence has been the splintering of moral consensus in American culture as a consequence of several ongoing trends. Lingering traces of the school's religious heritage have been gradually eliminated by court decisions, creating widespread resentment. The emergence of ethnic consciousness has challenged the school's traditional melting-pot rhetoric. And a rapidly changing moral climate has undermined trust in the school's ability to defend traditional values. The result is a seemingly unmanageable pluralism.

Yet public schools remain one of the major unifying elements in American life. David E. Purpel and Svi Shapiro have argued for a "moral and spiritual language that addresses questions of meaning and purpose and that recognizes the importance of community." Principals have both an opportunity and a responsibility to create communities in which questions of right and wrong are taken seriously and in which ethical behavior is a priority.

Ethical leadership is a complex phenomenon not easily captured by conventional research, and scholars disagree about the nature and role of values in educational leadership (Malcom J. Richmon).

Accordingly, this chapter provides a multifaceted view of the leader's ethical responsibilities. First, we consider the ethical behavior required of school leaders and follow that with a discussion of ethical decision making and reasoning. The final section deals with the principal's responsibility to be an advocate for students and for learning.

THE VIRTUOUS LEADER

Students of ethics are unanimous on one point: Moral leadership begins with moral leaders. In that respect, morality is unlike technical expertise. One can effectively lead a high school without being able to teach all subjects, and one can coach a sport without having the refined skill of an athlete, but no one can create an ethical institution without being ethical. Howard Gardner says of great leaders that they embody the message they advocate; they teach, not just through words but through actions.

Whereas modern philosophers have tended to emphasize ethical reasoning, a much older tradition is concerned with the art of being the kind of person one should be. In this tradition, dating back to the Greeks, character is more important than cognition; the key question is not "How do I solve this particular dilemma?" but "How do I live a worthy life?" (David Norton). This section explores some ways school leaders can answer this universal question.

Essential Virtues

Leaders are people first; in every moral leader is a moral human being. Virtue comes from consciously trying to live one's life in a certain way, striving to do the right thing even when tempted to do otherwise. As Aristotle observed long ago, virtue is less an act of reason than it is a disposition to live well, cultivated in a hundred daily acts, not just in moments of crisis.

Any list of cardinal virtues is arbitrary, since it is difficult to imagine any virtue that wouldn't help leaders. But the following have obvious importance.

Honesty

Honesty may be the fundamental virtue. As Hugh Sockett observes, it would be impossible to carry on a meaningful social life without being able to assume that most people are telling the truth most of the time. This is why James M. Kouzes and Barry Z. Posner (1995), after surveying 20,000 business people, found that honesty was the trait most valued in leaders. In the words of Kouzes and Posner, "Credibility is the foundation of leadership."

In both personal and professional life, temptations to be dishonest are legion. To avoid confrontations, soothe feelings, or simply get through the day with sanity intact, it seems so easy to lie, shade the truth, omit crucial information, or just let people believe what one knows to be untrue. In fact, outright lying may be the least common offense. But anything that keeps us from saying what needs saying is deceitful:

- Employing euphemisms that whitewash an ugly reality with soothing words
- Managing meeting agendas to choke off important but painful topics
- Ignoring a difficult situation in the hope that it will go away on its own
- Failing to challenge others who are spreading misinformation
- Answering questions like an attorney, dealing in technicalities rather than responding to the human need behind the questions

The worst thing about these evasions is that they seldom fool anyone for very long. Instead, they just put the institutional stamp of approval on denial as a way of life. Eventually, the illusion will be destroyed when some previously avoidable problem erupts into crisis.

Loyalty

Whenever we commit ourselves to work with others in a common enterprise, we have an obligation to maintain that commitment over time, even in the face of obstacles, disappointments, and distractions. "Placing our loyalty somewhere is an important act of identity," says Ira Chaleff:

We can place it in ourselves and often this is important to help us stay a difficult course. But if we place no loyalty outside ourselves we become a kind of brigand, justifying any action regardless of its cost to others.

School leaders can be especially torn because they are responsible to so many people. They are expected to support and protect subordinates, especially teachers; at the same time, they owe loyalty to superiors and the governing board. Most important, according to Chaleff, they also have a commitment to the mission of the institution they serve.

These conflicts can pose painful choices, but Chaleff argues that loyalty to institutional purpose is the priority. When others threaten to undermine the common goal toward which we are working, the time has come to challenge or even to disobey. When life or health are at risk, when common decency is violated, when laws are violated, or when the interests of the many are sacrificed to serve the interests of the privileged few— these are times when blind loyalty is a vice rather than a virtue.

One major threat to loyalty is self-interest. Many districts can tell stories of dynamic new leaders who won the community's heart with eloquently stated visions and who stirred teachers and parents to accept the risks of wholesale change, only to jump ship when the first attractive job offer came their way, leaving behind a wounded and disheartened community.

Courage

School leadership requires courage. In the course of a typical year, a principal may have to

- publicly take the blame for someone else's mistake;
- make a decision for the greater good that is hurtful to an individual;
- approve a highly visible innovation that has no guarantee of success;
- disappoint esteemed friends and allies by compromising on an emotional issue; and
- tackle a messy, complicated issue that might be ignored for a while longer.

M. Donald Thomas defines *courage* as "congruence between one's actions and one's principles," adding that it is "the ability to practice what one preaches, to stand on principle if the need arises, and to accept the consequences of one's actions without excuse or attempt to circumvent them."

Chaleff notes that courage requires an unnatural act—embracing risk rather than reducing it or running from it. For some, the source of courage is religious values or personal philosophy, some draw inspiration from personal heroes, some are deeply conscious of their commitment to others, and some act in response to previous experiences that have affected them deeply.

A perverted form of courage is martyrdom. Some leaders say (justifiably) that leadership is not a popularity contest but then use that as a rationalization for acting arbitrarily or refusing to consider the views of others. These leaders collect criticisms and complaints as trophies that prove their courage and justify dominating others.

Respect

Kenneth A. Strike, Emil J. Haller, and Jonas F. Soltis equate the principle of respect with the Golden Rule, saying, "It requires that we regard human beings as having intrinsic worth and treat them accordingly." This means that we cannot treat them as objects or as means to advance our own ends and that we must respect their freedom of choice.

Thomas J. Sergiovanni (2005) links respect to the related virtues of piety and civility. *Piety,* which he defines as the exercise of respect, loyalty, and affection in tightly knit groups, helps create a sense of community. *Civility* allows cooperation even when groups are diverse or disunited. Together, piety and civility enable schools to form learning communities.

Respect must be shown concretely—by soliciting feedback, being accessible, promoting constructive debate, and listening carefully (James M. Kouzes and Barry Z. Posner 1993). Experience in school settings suggests that similar behaviors are crucial in empowering teachers to accept the risks of significant change (Joseph Blase and colleagues).

Respect can be easily undermined by professional arrogance, such as when educators are too quick to discount the views of lay people. One newspaper columnist who complained about educational fads reported numerous responses from educators asking the same indignant questions: "'Who are you? What is your expertise? What is your advanced college degree in and where did you get it?'" (Maggie Gallagher).

Respect is also easy to forget when working with children. Educators find it all too easy to treat students as objects or as tactical problems to be solved. But immature or not, children have a deep sense of dignity. As one sixth-grader confided, "'You know, kids really like to learn; we just don't like being pushed around'" (as cited in John Holt).

Justice

Justice asks this fundamental moral question: What do we owe to whom? In a world with scarce resources, how do we allocate goods in an equitable way? In a world where every life is unique, how do we determine what is fair? Philosophers have debated such questions for millennia. Thomas J. Sergiovanni (1992) suggests using John Rawls's "veil of ignorance," which asks that we make decisions as if we didn't know our personal interests in the case.

For example, in handling a parental complaint about a teacher, we should act as though we are somehow unaware whether we are the parent, the teacher, the student, or the principal. Under those conditions, we would have much more incentive to be fair minded and consider the interests of everyone. Self-interest is always a danger for administrators, simply because almost everything that happens in a school affects their interests.

But there are other difficulties as well. Most standards of fairness involve some notion of treating everyone the same, yet people are so different that the same treatment may have very different effects. For example, a $500 fine is far more burdensome for a poor person than a rich person. So one danger is administering justice too abstractly, forgetting the individuals involved and how they will be affected. The other danger is being so swayed by individual circumstances that we lose sight of the larger principles involved.

Grace

Unlike the other virtues on this list, grace is not instantly familiar (perhaps because it is less common than it used to be). Kenn C. Rishel and Suzanne Tingley define the term to include elements of "elegance, dignity, stature, bearing, and ease of movement." As they describe it, it involves forbearance—not giving in to displays of temper and pettiness that might be fully justified.

Rishel and Tingley give the example of a superintendent who had been continually badgered by a woman who came to every board meeting with a highly critical attitude. When the woman's failing eyesight made it impossible to continue driving, the superintendent made a point of personally driving her to each board meeting. He explained that her opposition was just honest disagreement, and he refused to take it personally.

Grace of this kind is rare, perhaps because no one would blame a leader for not showing it. Everyone would understand a leader's sigh of relief when an annoying adversary disappears. Yet it is precisely the refusal to indulge themselves that allows some leaders to gain the enduring confidence of their followers.

Ethical Codes

The unique responsibilities of school leaders are sometimes recognized in professional codes of conduct. C. J. B. Macmillan said that such a code has several essential characteristics:

- It is formulated and enforced by autonomous practitioners.
- It goes beyond the general moral code of society to articulate the special responsibilities of those who belong to the profession.
- It provides a mechanism for clients or members of the public to seek redress when the code has been violated, with meaningful sanctions for violators.

School administrators formulated a code in the 1970s as a cooperative effort of the National Association of Secondary School Principals, the American Association of School Administrators, and several other administrator associations (Arthur E. Smith, Paul D. Travers, and George J. Yard). According to this code, the school administrator

- makes the well-being of students the fundamental value in all decision making and actions;
- fulfills professional responsibilities with honesty and integrity;
- supports the principle of due process and protects the civil and human rights of all individuals;
- obeys local, state, and national laws;
- implements the governing board of education's policies and administrative rules and regulations;
- pursues appropriate measures to correct those laws, policies, and regulations that are not consistent with sound educational goals;
- avoids using positions for personal gain through political, social, religious, economic, or other influence;
- accepts academic degrees or professional certification only from duly accredited institutions;
- maintains the standards and seeks to improve the effectiveness of the profession through research and continuing professional development; and
- honors all contracts until fulfillment or release.

This code has provisions for enforcement but is seldom invoked. Nor is it easy to tell when a violation has occurred; "the well-being of students" and "sound educational goals" are broad abstractions that could mean almost anything.

In addition, despite the claim that student well-being is the ultimate guiding principle, the code contains pointed reminders that administrators are accountable to rightful authorities. School leaders are likely to hit the ethical wall when the governing powers ask them to do something that might hurt the well-being of particular students (such as identifying and reporting illegal immigrants).

On the whole, there is little evidence that national codes have had a significant impact on educational practice, leading some critics to suggest the development of local codes. Sockett, for example, argues that moral accountability must be based on trust, which is best gained through repeated face-to-face encounters; therefore, small interactive communities offer the best chance of providing the conditions for meaningful accountability.

Sockett offers guidelines for developing such a local code:

1. The code should be in the form of guidelines rather than specific prohibited acts, broad enough to cover many situations, but specific enough to provide real guidance.

2. Public and parental input is essential so educators can understand the perspectives of other stakeholders. To avoid role blindness, professionals should adopt the "what-if-it-were-my-kid" test.

3. The code should be publicly promoted "until it becomes a living thing in the minds of the public to whom it is owed." Parents must know what to do when they believe an educator to be violating the code.

4. The code should contain meaningful sanctions. Sockett notes that sanctions may be threatening or offensive, but he points out that rules without sanctions do not inspire trust among the public.

Betty A. Sichel has suggested the use of ethics committees similar to those found in many hospitals. Such committees would raise awareness of ethical issues, formulate ethical codes, and advise educators grappling with ethical dilemmas. Sichel emphasizes that the committee would not rule on specific cases; the goal is not to make decisions for educators but to create a climate in which they can make decisions with help from a supportive community of peers.

Living a Virtuous Life

Where does virtuous behavior come from? How can it be nurtured? Although some preparation programs are now adding courses in ethics, Robert J. Starratt (1994) says that a leader's moral force comes from something much deeper:

> It will be found in the narrative of that person's life—in the influences of parents, role models, and heroes; in the lessons learned from a multitude of positive as well as painful experiences; from reflection on the commentaries of historians, poets, and novelists. Such moral force comes from a lifetime's search for meaning and purpose in human existence.

As Starratt (1994) hints, it would be a mistake to see this search as a solitary quest. Alasdair MacIntyre suggests that virtues are nurtured in communities having shared traditions and shared standards of excellence, such as families, churches, and professions. As members of such communities, we learn virtues from the words and actions of others, and we discipline ourselves to behave virtuously through our sense of social obligation. The key, according to MacIntyre, is to have a sense of commitment to the community and to its standards.

For school leaders, mustering this commitment requires them to come to grips with the use of power, since even their routine decisions can affect the lives of others in significant ways. School is a place where teachers and students spend almost half their waking hours, a place that can be a source of productive enterprise and deep satisfaction, or, in Arthur G. Wirth's phrase, a place that makes them crazy.

The danger in power is that it becomes a convenient substitute for virtues such as caring, respect, and justice. Karl Hostetler uses the example of agenda control, in which a principal structures an upcoming faculty meeting in a way that leaves no time for teacher complaints about the new duty roster. Such behavior fails to treat teachers as thinking beings and instead tries to manipulate them.

The antidote to overreliance on power is *stewardship,* which Peter Block (1993) defines as "the willingness to be accountable for the well-being of the larger organization by operating in service, rather than in control, of those around us." It means accepting responsibility for outcomes without trying to impose control on others.

Rabindra N. Kanungo and Manuel Mendonca speak of a similar outlook they call altruism:

> Our thesis is that organizational leaders are truly effective only when they are motivated by a concern for others, when their actions are invariably guided primarily by the criteria of the benefit to others even if it results in some cost to self.

Robert K. Greenleaf calls this behavior *servant leadership.* The servant leader is a servant first and only gradually chooses to lead. The true servant leader puts others first: "Do those served grow as persons? Do they, while being served, become healthier, wiser, freer, more autonomous, more likely themselves to become servants?"

The notions of stewardship, altruism, and servant leadership present leaders with a formidable challenge, since they clash with conventional images of leadership. Here we have a leader, vested with power and status and expected to act with authority, who is contrarily asked to adopt the demeanor of the humblest member of the organization. Can it be done?

Greenleaf said the secret is to develop the disposition to listen first so others will recognize us as servants. Block (1993) said we must be scrupulous about our own accountability before worrying about that of others.

Finally, we can add some 2,000-year-old advice from Aristotle: Virtue is a habit. Just as musicians develop musical ability by playing an instrument, people become virtuous by practicing virtue. As Chaleff notes, "Our 'courage muscle' will develop to the degree we exercise it. If we exercise it when the risks are small, it will be strong enough to meet the challenge when the risks are large."

MAKING ETHICAL DECISIONS

Many discussions of ethics in leadership focus on the kind of dilemmas that opened this chapter. An imminent decision requires an answer to the question, "What is the morally right thing to do?" Rushworth M. Kidder notes that such issues occupy the domain between freedom and law. That is, we can make certain decisions without restraint, based purely on our own preferences; other decisions are regulated by society through a system of laws. Leaving a tip is a matter of freedom; leaving the restaurant without paying is not.

Ethical questions arise when people believe a certain behavior is highly desirable but the law is silent. For example, no law requires us to notify a neighbor that he or she has left his or her headlights on, but most people would agree that this is something we should do. Similarly, an administrator may be able to resolve a problem by lying or blaming an innocent party, but most people would agree that this is not desirable behavior. Kidder cites Lord Moulton's comment that ethics is "obedience to the unenforceable."

Ambiguity and Uncertainty

Ethical issues are inherently ambiguous. The absence of formal laws forces us to consult beliefs, which are seldom unanimous. Even if there is consensus (for example, that lying is wrong), the principles are stated so abstractly that we still have to determine how (or if) they apply to a particular situation. (Is it wrong to lie to spare someone's feelings?)

This ambiguity means that before we can do the right thing, we have to determine the right thing. This may be especially difficult for school leaders, who work in a complex public arena in a morally conflicted society. William D. Greenfield Jr. said:

> It often is not clear what is right or wrong, or what one ought to do, or which perspective is right in moral terms. Or, it may be clear what one ought to do, in moral terms, but circumstances may not permit that course of action.

This sort of uncertainty constitutes an ethical dilemma. A decision must be made; there are at least two possible choices, each of which will affect other people for better or for worse; and each choice can be plausibly supported by citing various moral principles.

Kidder argues that a true dilemma forces us to choose between two competing goods (or between the lesser of two evils). If we hesitate over a choice between right and wrong, we are facing a moral temptation, not an ethical dilemma. The thought of lying to cover up a mistake constitutes a temptation; the prospect of lying to evade a harmful bureaucratic regulation is a dilemma.

School leaders experience ethical dilemmas on a daily basis. Some of their dilemmas are universal in nature; that is, they involve the fundamental moral rules that all humans grapple with—telling the truth, respecting others, being fair.

Other dilemmas arise from the special challenges of the education profession. Should schools distribute condoms? Should parents be informed if a counselor learns that their daughter is considering an abortion? Should corporal punishment ever be used? Educators are often divided on what is in the best interests of the child.

Another type of dilemma comes from the principal's status as middle manager. School leaders have a responsibility to higher authority, but they have a simultaneous obligation to the teachers and students in their school. When the bureaucratic demands clash with student needs, principals must make a choice. Arthur Blumberg and William Greenfield recorded one principal's doubts:

> He ended up serving detention last night. It was a real conflict. I really don't think he threw it. So here I am penalizing him for something I really don't think he did. But I believe in the concept that I have to support my staff, whether it's a teacher,

a custodian, a cafeteria worker who's involved. I don't feel good about it. I wrestle with it.

School leaders constantly face the need to keep the school moving forward while fending off a host of disruptive forces. In this case, the principal decided that the disruptive potential of not backing a teacher outweighed the possible injustice to one student. Some studies have suggested that this kind of trade-off is common (Katherine L. Kasten and Carl R. Ashbaugh; Peggy C. Kirby, Louis V. Pardise, and Russell Protti) and that principals often defer to superiors or take refuge in official policies. Kasten and Ashbaugh concluded that "administrators are a cautious group."

In summary, then, school leaders cannot avoid ethical uncertainty. The only question is whether they can find a way to resolve the dilemmas.

Ethical Reasoning

No matter how thoughtful and comprehensive the ethical code, it will never eliminate the need to deliberate on moral issues. A code provides a guideline, a reminder of core principles. Each practitioner must examine the case at hand to determine how the principles apply.

Moreover, reliance on a code may not fulfill a leader's ethical responsibility. Barry L. Bull and Martha M. McCarthy dispute the common assumption that behavior can be separated into distinct zones of "ethical" and "unethical." In this view, once a person has determined which behaviors are impermissible, everything else is a matter of personal and professional discretion. In reality, Bull and McCarthy argue, ethical principles touch almost everything administrators do.

Thus, professionals must be capable of skillful ethical decision making. Confronted with a decision, they must be able to recognize its ethical dimensions and determine their responsibility. Given the painful choices that are often involved, how do they choose what is fair, ethical, and wise?

One school of thought says that moral reasoning is not a matter of deep abstract thinking, but simply the willingness to respect the moral impulses that we all have. James Q. Wilson, Robert C. Solomon, and other scholars have argued that humans by nature have an intuitive moral understanding. Solomon said:

Justice is to be found, if it is to be found anywhere, in us, in our sense that there are wrongs in the world to be righted. You don't need an all-embracing sense of justice to recognize the presence of injustice, often right in front of your nose.

Similarly, Anne Colby and William Damon, studying exemplary moral lives, found that their participants had a strong, self-assured grasp of what was right:

Among our exemplars, we saw no "eking out" of moral acts through intricate, tortuous cognitive processing. Instead, we saw an unhesitating will to act, a disavowal of fear and doubt, and a simplicity of moral response. Risks were ignored and consequences went unweighed.

Is moral decision making, then, just a matter of listening to our hearts? Strike and colleagues disagree, saying that not all moral intuitions stand up against further examination. (A common moral intuition of 19th-century Americans, for example, was that "inferior" people were not entitled to the same consideration as were "civilized" nations.) Rather, intuitions are just the initial raw material for the decision-making process. We must also consider factual evidence and reflect on the principles behind our intuitions.

Moral Reasoning

Ethical decisions are not made in a vacuum; like legal decisions, they involve specific people in particular circumstances. Change the circumstances and the decision may change, even though our guiding beliefs remain the same.

Thus, faced with an apparently ineffective teacher, a principal must first ask some basic questions about the case. What is the evidence of ineffectiveness? Has the teacher tried to improve his or her performance? In what ways are students being put at risk? Is the teacher demonstrably less effective than colleagues? How long has the teacher been with the district? What will be the financial and psychological costs of dismissing the teacher? What impact would a dismissal have on the morale of other teachers? What will happen to the dismissed teacher? The answers to these questions will strongly influence the decision simply because they help shape our view of what is at stake ethically.

Strike and colleagues note that even with sensitivity to our moral intuitions and a clear knowledge of the facts, we still may be in doubt because basic beliefs are in conflict. The case of the ineffective teacher may lead us to a brutal conclusion: We can impair the education of a large number of students or ruin a teacher's career. Two evils—how do we choose the lesser?

One of the best-known frameworks for moral reasoning came from Lawrence Kohlberg (as cited in Dawn E. Schrader), who saw moral reasoning as a developmental progression from amoral, egocentric thinking to abstract, principled thinking. At one end is the young child, defining "right" by immediate personal consequences; at the other end is the thoughtful adult, reasoning from universal principles with full awareness of obligations to others (Schrader).

Moral Principles

The Kohlberg system is process oriented, seemingly more concerned with the quality of reasoning than with the outcome. In real life, however, we are more likely to be preoccupied by the particular standards that allow us to tell right from wrong.

Some standards, of course, are the same ones we were told to follow in childhood: Always tell the truth, share with others, keep your word, be fair, and do unto others as you would have them do unto you. Other principles are more abstract. Strike and colleagues list several that are likely to be important for school leaders:

- *Intellectual liberty:* People have the right to hold and freely express their views.
- *Personal liberty:* People have the right to conduct their lives as they see fit, except as their behavior infringes on the rights of others.

- *Equality:* Each person should be treated the same or at least be provided equal opportunities.
- *Due process:* People in apparent violation of rules and laws should be given a fair chance to defend themselves before any penalty is applied.
- *Democracy:* Members of a community should have an equal opportunity to participate and have an influence in making decisions that will affect them.

Most of these principles are rooted in the American democratic tradition, and they have an inherent rightness to anyone raised in that tradition. They are also rather abstract, leading some critics to look for principles that reflect the rich emotional interactions that characterize classroom life.

The most frequent nominee is caring. Lynn G. Beck says that caring is best defined by its goals (promoting human development and responding to human needs) and by the behaviors it implies: appreciating the perspective of another person, responding appropriately to this understanding, and remaining in the caring relationship for as long as required. Whereas many moral principles seem intellectual in origin, caring has emotional roots and is personal in nature. We don't just care in general; we care about particular people.

The Difficulty of Deciding

Even armed with these principles, school leaders will find it difficult to resolve many ethical dilemmas. For example, Strike and colleagues present a hypothetical situation in which a superintendent must choose between two new programs, one to benefit children of migrant workers, the other to benefit gifted and talented students (there is not enough money for both programs).

In this dilemma, the relevant principle is equality, but what exactly does that mean? Does equality require treating everyone the same, or does it mean making sure that all parties get what they need? Is it important to look at who has the greater need? Should we consider what would benefit society the most?

In this predicament, as in most worthy dilemmas, a clear-cut answer does not leap to the forefront. We can easily imagine different leaders (of equal goodwill and moral sensitivity) making different decisions. Does moral reasoning eventually reach a dead end? Must we ultimately take refuge in relativism, declaring that moral claims are irreconcilable and making decisions purely on practical grounds?

Strike and colleagues strongly disagree, noting that befuddlement is not necessarily permanent. If nothing else, we can make progress: "If the process of moral deliberation is not always decisive or clear, or completely objective, it is also rarely fruitless. Moral reasoning and debate always gets us somewhere, and as moral agents we are obligated to participate in it."

Guidelines for Moral Reasoning

Although there are no easy recipes for moral reasoning, we can find guidelines:

1. *Seeing what is important in a situation.* Moral reasoning occurs in specific cases that come attached with names and facts. Some of those facts have a legitimate bearing

on our decisions; others are irrelevant. For example, in the case of the two competing programs, does it matter that most of the migrant students will probably move out of the district by next year? That the school is in a region attracting numerous high-tech industries? That the gifted students will probably be able to make satisfactory progress even without the program?

How can we learn to recognize what is important? The best strategy may be to open ourselves to the perspectives of others, particularly those whose experiences and backgrounds differ from our own. Colby and Damon found that their moral exemplars showed a lifelong pattern of engaging in dialogue with others, attentively considering alternative views, and gradually assimilating other perspectives into their own moral framework.

2. *Reflecting.* Strike and colleagues say that moral intuitions are never sufficient, if only because they tend to be unexamined. In a school community that brings together so many different viewpoints, leaders have the responsibility of subjecting their intuitions to conscious reflection and evaluation. Failing to reflect on how one lives, Strike and coauthors say, "is to refuse to be responsible for one's self. In a fundamental way, it is to refuse to be a person."

Reflection is often thought of as a solitary activity. Kanungo and Mendonca claim that it is only in silence that leaders can hear the "inner whisperings" that will point them to the right path. They seem to be suggesting that ethical problem solving is very different from the kind of hard-driving, action-oriented posture that leaders need to get through their day.

Moral decision making can also be effective when carried out in communities of like-minded individuals who raise provocative questions, challenge each other's assumptions, and provide emotional and intellectual support. Such communities need not be large, as long as they share intellectual honesty and a commitment to search for moral truth.

Karen F. Osterman and Robert B. Kottkamp provide a detailed description of one such community, in which a number of administrators in the same district periodically met for unstructured discussion of the issues they confronted. Over time, the meetings evolved into a trusting, supportive, sometimes moving experience that allowed participants to voice ideas that had no other forum.

3. *Searching for alternatives.* Moral dilemmas are agonizing because either choice is painful. Kidder says we can sometimes avoid that pain by challenging the assumption there are only two choices. Some dilemmas are actually "trilemmas," offering a third path that avoids the negative consequences of the first two. For example, faced with a parent who objects to a particular homework assignment on religious grounds, many principals have been able to negotiate an alternative assignment, thereby preserving academic integrity without trampling on parental rights.

4. *Weighing the choices.* School leaders are not philosophers, but they can benefit from using standards that philosophers have employed for centuries. Kidder suggests three.

First, we can examine the consequences of each choice and attempt to identify which will lead to the most positive outcome. This requires determining who will be affected and in what ways. Historically, this principle has been characterized as "the greatest good for the greatest number." The idea of maximizing happiness has great appeal, but Kidder notes that it requires more than counting heads. Sometimes a small benefit for many people will be outweighed by a great harm to only one person. Moreover, it isn't always easy to determine how people will be affected by an action.

Second, we can invoke moral rules. Rules are based on the belief that the world would be a better place if people always behaved in a certain way. Rules ask us not to make exceptions to allow for individual circumstances, because every exception nibbles away at an important value.

One school district illustrated this belief when it suspended a junior high school student whose mother accidentally packed a beer instead of a soda in her lunchbox. Despite criticism for punishing an apparently innocent student, the district reasoned that making an exception would erode its zero-tolerance alcohol policy.

Rule-based approaches can make people uncomfortable because they seem impossibly strict, sometimes snaring the innocent. Moreover, rules often conflict, leaving us in doubt about which one should have priority.

Third, we can examine a dilemma from a perspective of caring. Kidder sums up this principle with the Golden Rule: How would we like to be treated under similar circumstances? He argues, "Ethics is not a blind impartiality, doling out right and wrong according to some stone-cold canon of ancient and immutable law. It is a warm and supremely human activity that cares enough for others to want right to prevail."

Caring is an appealing stance because of its apparent compassion, but it has important limitations. For one thing, decisions affect different people in different ways. Whom should we care for the most? There is also the practical reality that people would often like to be treated in ways that benefit their self-interest rather than the greater good.

Kidder suggests that each of these perspectives throws a different light on a dilemma, highlighting certain features and obscuring others. Using all three as filters will provide a much firmer foundation for making an informed decision.

LEADERS AS ADVOCATES

At the height of the Great Depression, progressive educator George S. Counts published a slim book with a bold title: *Dare the School Build a New Social Order?* His question rested on the premise that educators should work to transform society, not just support it. Writing at a moment of national despair, when many thought the American democratic experiment was at risk, Counts underscored the social and economic injustices that were built into the system.

Although his call to arms electrified many of those who read it, it had almost no impact on the profession. Most educators at the time were clinging desperately to their jobs, often at reduced wages (or no wages at all), and remained securely under the control of school boards that assumed the purpose of schooling was to preserve a great civilization, not create a new one. Few principals or teachers were in a position to challenge entrenched American institutions.

Seven decades later, Counts's manifesto seems like a brief quixotic impulse that was purely a product of the times. Yet his call to action remains relevant today, reminding us of one of the enduring tensions in American education. On the one hand, schools are highly conservative institutions, aimed at preserving and passing on the best features of

American life. On the other hand, Americans since the time of Horace Mann have also seen education as a tool for social improvement. (Today, for example, schools are being asked to fight bias, eliminate bullying, and stamp out obesity.)

The ISLLC standards, by asserting that school leaders must influence "the larger political, social, economic, legal, and cultural contexts of schooling," seem to call for advocacy (CCSSO). Admittedly, most discussions of the standard have not envisioned the kind of social activism that Counts endorsed. Indeed, some ISLLC critics have complained that the standards favor the status quo (Fenwick English). Nonetheless, ISLLC standards clearly expect that school leaders will be players on a much larger stage than their own school.

As John I. Goodlad, Corrine Mantle-Bromley, and Stephen John Goodlad have noted, "Schools do not exist in vacuums. They are embedded in a vast and complex social, political, and economic surround. Schools affect their context and their context in turn affects them."

But on whatever scale, leadership that is rooted in a sense of ethics and morality will inevitably result in a call to advocacy. Every principal has to confront the question whether his or her sense of values compels action to challenge the system.

Leadership and Advocacy

L. Joseph Matthews and Gary M. Crow define *advocacy* as "supporting, maintaining, and defending moral, legal, and thoughtful educational principles and practices for children and youth." Most school leaders would probably see this as an accurate description of their behavior, and anyone familiar with schools can cite examples of principals serving as advocates:

- Seeing a group of at-risk students who are failing to thrive, a principal works with teachers to establish an alternative program.
- Faced with a student who has been persistently disruptive and disrespectful, an assistant principal nonetheless goes out of her way to ensure that the student is accorded all due-process rights.
- Noticing that a few veteran teachers have repeatedly voiced the sentiment that "some children just can't be expected to reach the standards," an elementary principal provides some discreet mentoring on alternative instructional methods.

Although this kind of advocacy seems to be an integral part of today's school leadership, principals seem less inclined to take their advocacy outside the immediate school setting. Matthews and Crow claim that principals have traditionally shunned public advocacy altogether or attempted to serve as a buffer between the school and the outside world.

For example, Janice R. Fauske and Bob L. Johnson Jr. found that principals were keenly aware of the larger environment and were constantly scanning it for threats, but their stance seemed almost wholly defensive. Their primary goal was to deflect threats from outsiders, and they showed little inclination to try to change the world outside their doors.

Nonetheless, school leadership has a long history of advocacy, ranging back to the 19th-century school administrators who saw education as "the great lever, to be employed under Providence, for the political and moral regeneration of the world" (Tyack and

Hansot). Goodlad and colleagues describe the moral dimensions of schooling as "inescapable." The call to advocacy is likewise unavoidable.

The Roots of Advocacy

Given the constraints on principals' time, why should they invest their energy in attempts to influence the world beyond the school? Michael Fullan points out one reason when he notes that meaningful, sustained change almost always requires a change in the context. Schools do not become dysfunctional because people want them to be that way; rather, a host of environmental forces push them in that direction. "Change the context," says Fullan, "and you change behavior."

Robert J. Starratt (2004) sees the motivating force as a confluence among three elements: responsibility, authenticity, and presence.

Responsibility exists in many forms. School leaders have responsibility as humans, citizens, and administrators; they have responsibility to students, teachers, parents, districts, and others; and they have responsibility for creating environments that enable quality learning, healthy working relationships, and civic virtue. Moreover, these wide-ranging responsibilities extend beyond the precept "do no harm" to the proactive obligation to do good. That is, at the end of the day, principals should be able to point to ways in which they actively advanced the school's moral agenda.

Authenticity is the inner sense of integrity that allows leaders to navigate their complicated ethical environment. Authenticity is the voice that speaks out loud and clear when something is amiss: "That isn't right!" The voice is saying not just that a situation is wrong but that it is intolerable—"I cannot accept it and still be true to the person I am." This kind of authenticity is similar to the concept of "leading by outrage" advanced by Sergiovanni (1992).

Presence is the state of awareness that allows us to recognize both our responsibility and our authenticity, and the connection between them. Starratt (2004) says:

> Being fully present means being wide awake to what's in front of you. It could be another person, a passage in a book, a memorandum you are composing to the staff, a flower on your desk. . . . Being present means taking the other inside of yourself, looking at the other really closely, listening to the tone of the other, the body language of the other.

Being present allows the leader to sense both the pain and the potential of others and to better understand how administrative decisions will impact the people in the school. By being fully present, as Starratt (2004) says, "I can begin to discern what the situation or event asks of me." The fuller the presence, the greater the moral awareness.

The Goals of Advocacy

Given the scope of the school's mission, the call to advocacy can occur almost anytime in any situation. But several issues seem to draw out the most impassioned responses.

Learning

The centrality of learning in today's schools frequently raises moral issues. If there is too little funding or if schools are threatened by disorder, learning will suffer. Likewise, if students come to school hungry or have inadequate access to health care, their progress will be undermined. Professional associations such as the National Association of Elementary School Principals and the National Association of Secondary School Principals have a long history of pursuing legislative remedies to those concerns.

But there are other issues as well. What if, as Starratt (2004) claims, the learning achieved by students is "inauthentic learning, superficial learning, fake learning, make-believe learning, rather than something that intrinsically adds values to students' lives and prepares them for responsible citizenship?" Wouldn't the principal have a responsibility to do something about that?

Because American education lacks a universally accepted definition of learning, the content and methods of schooling must be continually renegotiated. For example, American educators have struggled for a century to resolve the tensions between two competing visions of learning. One vision sees learning as imitative, aimed at having students acquire the knowledge and skills valued by society. The other vision sees learning as an act of creation, aimed at having students reshape existing knowledge and skills in the context of their own lives, thereby transforming their understanding of the world (Philip W. Jackson).

American schools have swung between these two poles for decades, sometimes veering wildly in one direction or the other, but more often borrowing elements of both. Occasionally the tension breaks out into open cultural warfare, as in the phonics versus whole language debate.

For leaders, simply avoiding or resolving conflicts in this area is not enough; they also have a responsibility to see that school learning fully meets the current and future needs of students as well as the society at large.

Social Justice

In many discussions of American democracy, the school is the gateway to opportunity that can erase inequalities in the larger society. No matter what one's social or economic starting point, access to a free public education provides a level playing field that allows anyone to climb the ladder of success.

In recent decades, however, critics have challenged this interpretation, arguing that schools are more likely to perpetuate than alleviate social injustice. Although these critics lace their analysis with abstract concepts such as hegemonic discourse, their argument rests on a disarmingly simple premise: People who hold social and economic advantages will work hard to maintain their privileged position. Because school governance is dominated by social and economic elites, the education system reproduces and reinforces the existing social order (Michael Apple).

Not everyone endorses this analysis, but many educators have no trouble listing the tangible indicators of injustice:

- Low-income children are less likely to be taught by fully qualified teachers (Craig D. Jeald).

- Schools with high proportions of low-income children get less funding than schools with high-income children (Kevin Carey).
- Students belonging to racial minorities receive proportionately higher rates of suspension and expulsion (René A. Rocha).
- Most troubling, the achievement of low-income and minority students continues to lag behind that of others (Paul E. Barton).

Budgetary cuts have led parents in some districts to launch fundraising efforts to keep class sizes down. In some districts, school officials have announced that they will accept such funds only if the money will be shared equally among schools in the district. Without this stipulation, children in schools serving affluent neighborhoods—already having many natural advantages—would gain an added edge.

When such issues arise, Carolyn M. Shields suggests that leaders can keep social justice in the forefront by asking several questions:

- Who benefits; who is disadvantaged?
- Who is included; who is excluded?
- Who is marginalized; who is privileged?
- Who is legitimated; who is devalued?
- How do we know; to whom are we listening?
- What data are we using for our decision making?

Advocacy for social justice can be risky because it generates controversy. Many people accept and even applaud advocacy for social justice when it is carried out under the rhetorical banner of fairness, but they may resist changes that appear to threaten their own privilege. Jonathan Kozol, in his searing indictment of school funding *Savage Inequalities,* notes that inequities persist because those who currently benefit from the system fear that increased funding for poor schools will result in reduced spending for affluent districts.

Caring

Children arrive at school with a full range of human needs: needs for food, safety, friendship, love, and intellectual stimulation. Increasingly, schools have accepted responsibility for seeing that those needs are satisfied, and there are many reasons for doing so (Beck; Nel Noddings 1992). Nel Noddings (2002) summed up one of the most compelling reasons when she said:

Every human being, at every stage of life, hopes for some form of positive response from other human beings. No one wants to be harmed by others or to live in fear of them. Everyone hopes for a helping hand in time of danger or more trouble than he or she can handle alone. Everyone wants enough respect to maintain at least minimal human dignity.

As defined by Beck, caring is more than simply providing services to those in need. Rather, it requires empathizing with others, responding to their needs, and making a long-term commitment. Noddings (1992) said, "When I care, I really hear, see, or feel what the other tries to convey. . . . I receive what the other conveys, and I want to respond in a way that furthers the other's purpose or project."

An ethic of care frequently leads administrators to go beyond existing rules and policies. For example, caring principals are likely to raise questions about high-stakes testing because of potential negative effects on student development and motivation, dropout rates, and teacher demoralization (Kenneth A. Sirotnik). In general, a caring attitude is likely to focus attention on the dimensions of schooling that restrict rather than enhance human potential.

Caring can be a powerful motivator for advocacy because it puts a human face on otherwise abstract issues. It is one thing to reach an intellectual judgment that the academic achievement gap constitutes a social injustice. It is quite another to personally witness the human potential of vibrant young lives being squandered. Indeed, the firsthand experience of being in a caring relationship ("caring for") may provide the foundation for the development of social justice ("caring about").

Democratic Community

From the time of Jefferson, Americans have recognized an intimate link between schooling and democracy (David Tyack). When successful governance depends on the ability of citizens to weigh all sides of the issues and arrive at intelligent, informed decisions, schools can make an obvious contribution to knowledge, literacy, and critical thinking.

But schools make an even more critical contribution to democracy, as Benjamin R. Barber explains: "Public schools are not merely schools *for* the public, but schools of publicness: institutions where we learn what it means to *be* a public and start down the road toward common national and civic identity."

That is, schools are the setting in which society most clearly articulates the core values of the culture—the knowledge, skills, and beliefs most worthy of being handed down to the next generation. Carl D. Glickman put it this way:

> What should we be doing in our schools, our curriculum, our placement, our scheduling of students, our allocation of resources, and in our teaching that gives each child his or her inalienable rights to life, liberty, and pursuit of happiness?

For that reason, educational decisions are never merely technical (What reading method should we use?); they are also deeply moral (What kind of people should our children become?). In a pluralistic and increasingly polarized society, such questions can be highly contentious; the very use of the term *democracy* triggers ambivalence in groups that have experienced oppression while living in an ostensibly democratic society (Glickman).

But the responsibility for democratic community goes beyond academic instruction. As one of the primary institutions of American society, the school must also be a democratic community. A school that fails to operate democratically cannot teach democracy to students or gain the confidence of citizens (Amy Gutmann; Theodore R. Sizer and Nancy Faust Sizer).

In many respects, the history of American education is a struggle to reconcile the needs of the individual against the need for a cohesive society. As Tyack observes, "The *unum* and the *pluribus* have been in inescapable tension, constantly evolving as Americans struggled to find common ground and respect their differences." School leaders are at ground zero in that debate.

Speaking Out

The research on advocacy among school leaders is sparse. We know that they work for change through their professional associations, frequently lobbying for caring, social justice, and democratic community. On an individual level, however, we are limited to sporadic case studies or anecdotal accounts of heroic leaders who combine passionate moral vision with the willingness to confront the larger environment. Yet precisely because these principals are regarded as heroic, they may not be typical.

Still, it seems likely that most administrators treat advocacy the same way most people treat religion: They weave it into the fabric of their lives in ways large and small, acting on their beliefs to differing degrees, but seldom discussing it explicitly. Overt statements of moral vision are mostly confined to formulaic statements such as "assuring that all students learn."

Catherine Marshall and Michael Ward, after interviewing 10 national-level educational leaders, characterized their stance toward social justice as "yes, but." Yes, social justice is a moral imperative, but the system does not really support advocacy by school leaders: Injustice is too deeply embedded in the system, the goals of social justice are controversial, and leaders are not trained to take on this role.

Constraints

Indeed, the barriers are many. For one thing, principals are agents of the school district and are naturally expected to implement a policy agenda that has been set by others. Setting an independent course can lead to clashes with superiors and even jeopardize job security when the wrong toes are stepped on.

Moreover, in their official capacity, principals represent the entire school community, which is rarely in complete agreement on any issue. When principals speak out, they may appear to give official weight to opinions that are actually an expression of personal values. The boundary between official responsibility and First Amendment freedom is not always easy to locate.

Finally, time-stressed administrators may see advocacy as simply too big a task to wrap their arms around. Running a school is a challenge; changing society seems like a fantasy. Even those with the ambition often have not been provided with the training (Cynthia J. Reed and colleagues).

Nonetheless, in today's principalship, advocacy is probably inevitable. The old structure, in which principals could comfortably operate as enlightened bureaucrats, has been irrevocably changed by stringent demands for accountability, a highly politicized environment, and growing recognition of the failures and injustices of the system. If, as many commentators insist, principals must be change agents, then they must also be advocates.

Guidelines

Fulfilling the advocate role is both difficult and risky, but several guidelines may be useful:

Articulate a moral vision. Most educators are driven by a deep yearning to make a difference, somehow, somewhere. However strong this desire, inarticulate feelings provide too narrow a foundation for effective advocacy.

Thus, leaders must be able to identify the specific practices and conditions that create neglect, failure, and injustice. Where does the school fall short of its ideals? Where are children being hurt? How? Whose needs are being neglected? What provokes righteous anger? What changes would make a difference? Asked persistently, such questions will lead to an action agenda.

Start small. Activists in other fields often adopt the slogan, "Think globally, act locally." That is, recognize and reflect on the big issues confronting society, but then take appropriate action close to home, changing the parts of the world over which you have some influence. Such local action will not solve the problems for society as a whole, but it will at least be a small step in the right direction, offering a model (and hope) to others.

For example, principals cannot single-handedly eliminate the influence of popular culture on children, but they can sponsor a television withdrawal campaign in which children and their families agree to live without television for a week.

Form communities of like-minded people. Parker Palmer, noting that the urge to be an advocate is "a frail reed," susceptible to second thoughts and self-doubt, counsels educators to form "communities of congruence." Coming together with those who share your outlook provides moral reassurance, eases the loneliness that often accompanies advocacy, and builds a common language that helps communicate the driving vision.

Find the balance between courage and caution. Inevitably, advocating for change—especially when it upsets powerful interests—leads to a moment of truth when the principal must decide to either back off or stay the course. Peter Block (1987) says that in those moments, leaders must consider the trade-off between their values and their practical realities. Sometimes it's important to choose courage over caution, but it's also important to distinguish between courage and suicide.

Block (1987) suggests that it makes sense to play it safe when the leader is new to the environment, when the organization has just come through a period of risk and expansion, when organizational survival is at stake, or when the environment is characterized by zero trust.

On the other hand, there may come a moment when personal integrity demands action, regardless of risks. Palmer speaks of the decision to "live with an undivided heart," refusing to accept and cooperate with destructive policies and practices. Palmer calls this the "Rosa Parks decision."

Ultimately, advocacy is inseparable from leadership. Schools today still face the moral imperative set down by John Dewey more than a hundred years ago: "What the best and wisest parent wants for his own child, that must the community want for all of its children."

Principals are leaders in the truest sense when they help the school community determine what that means and how to accomplish it.

CONCLUSION: A QUESTION OF DESTINY

To be an ethical school leader, then, is not a matter of following a few simple rules. The leader's responsibility is rooted less in technical expertise than in simple human integrity. Leadership stretches that integrity, pitting it against a host of pressures and demands that threaten to deflect us from our purpose. Negotiating the turbulence requires a leader who thinks carefully and reflectively yet acts decisively, who cares about others but has the courage to confront them, and who has a sense of history but also sees the world as it might be.

Most of all, it requires leaders who are fully aware of their own humanity, with all its faults and virtues.

It sounds overwhelming, but William Bridges has provided some career advice that may help. "Most of what has been worth doing since the beginning of time has been accomplished by people who were (like you and me, most of the time), tired, self-doubting, ambivalent, and more than a little discouraged." Rather than chasing after some illusory image of perfection, we should simply concentrate on becoming the kind of people we are capable of being. Bridges reminds us of the words of Rabbi Zusya: "In the world to come, I shall not be asked, 'Why were you not Moses?' I shall be asked, 'Why were you not Zusya?'"

REFLECTIONS

1. Thomas Sergiovanni (1992) advocates "leading by outrage." What are the issues in your school that trigger your sense of outrage?

2. Can you identify an administrator in your experience who exemplified ethical leadership? What virtues did he or she demonstrate? Conversely, can you identify an administrator who did not show ethical leadership? What virtues was he or she lacking?

3. Using an ethical dilemma you have faced in the past year, identify the elements that made it difficult to resolve.

4. Can you recall a time when your responsibility to the district conflicted with your responsibility to students? How was the conflict resolved? If you had to do it again, would you respond the same way?

5. What examples of advocacy by teachers or administrators have you seen in your school? What visible effects have their efforts had?

6. Considering the needs of your students, identify one change in policy, practice, or environment that would have a significant, positive impact. As principal, what steps could you take to advocate this change? What barriers would you face?

7

Visionary Leadership

Larry Lashway

When [the common school] shall be fully developed, when it shall be trained to wield its mighty energies for the protection of society against the giant vices which now invade and torment it;—against intemperance, avarice, war, slavery, bigotry, the woes of want and the wickedness of waste,—then, there will not be a height to which these enemies of the race can escape.

—Horace Mann, [1848] 1957

At a time when school leaders are being urged to create new paradigms for the 21st century, it is worth remembering that the present school system grew out of one of the most successful visions in American history.

Although no one would claim that public schools have accomplished everything Mann envisioned, most Americans still accept the mission that he and his generation laid out. Many no longer have an unquestioning faith that the school system can deliver on its promises, however. Critics frequently describe today's schools as "19th-century bureaucratic dinosaurs" that are "beyond repair" or "dysfunctional." Even observers who are less critical become uneasy when measuring so-so performance against high expectations and routinely talk about the need to reinvent schooling.

For their part, school leaders don't need outsiders to tell them that business as usual is a feeble response to expanded expectations, limited resources, a rapidly changing society, and a skeptical public.

The irony is that Mann's original vision has been so successful for so long that it takes a determined act of imagination to visualize other possibilities. Virtually everyone has

153

attended school and has absorbed the same unspoken assumptions about what school is supposed to be like. Those with alternative visions have struggled to make a lasting dent in the existing system. Reform efforts have typically been local, incremental, and short lived, as David Tyack and Larry Cuban point out.

After two decades of talk about "visions for the 21st century," school leaders find themselves squarely in the 21st century but still uncertain about the guiding vision. Many principals can list things they'd like to change or can even envision a different kind of school altogether. Much of their time, however, goes into trying to make sense of the conflicting mandates that reflect the vision of policymakers. Advice is plentiful but often vague; leaders are urged to have vision without being told what a good vision looks like or where it comes from.

As David T. Conley, Diane M. Dunlap, and Paul Goldman note, vision in school settings simply hasn't been studied much. We don't yet have an extensive literature on how school leaders establish a vision or what current educational visions look like, much less the best way to establish one. Vision building is still more of an art than an applied technical skill.

At the same time, it would be a mistake to consider vision a mystical process reserved for a few high-powered leaders. Increasingly, vision building is regarded as a core leadership task that can and must be mastered by all leaders. This chapter provides school leaders with a practical guide for developing and implementing both a personal vision and a vision for their institutions. First, we must distinguish between what vision is and is not and explore what it accomplishes.

THE NATURE OF VISION

Burt Nanus defines *vision* as

> a realistic, credible, attractive future for your organization. It is your articulation of a destination toward which your organization should aim, a future that in important ways is better, more successful, or more desirable for your organization than is the present.

James M. Kouzes and Barry Z. Posner say that vision is a kind of "seeing"; it creates images of what the future might hold. A principal interviewed by Linda Tinelli Sheive and Marian Beauchamp Schoenheit exhibited this ability when he said:

> I believe you need to carry around dreams. You begin to see scenarios in your head. We're going to combine our two high schools some day, and I can already see the first assembly when all the kids come together. I can already see the parade through town when we celebrate it.

Arthur Blumberg and William Greenfield identify vision with "moral imagination," a quality of character that gives someone "the ability to see that the world need not remain as it is—that it is possible for it to be otherwise, and to be better." In their view, vision is thus more than a technical task; it reflects the leader's values and is the source of his or her moral authority.

Some extend the definition of vision to cover not only the ultimate goal but the process of getting there. Michael Fullan says that skill in bringing about change is as important as the content of the vision, which must be continually revised in "a dynamic and fluid relationship."

What Vision Is Not

Definitions of vision are still loose and unsettled, and many educators associate the concept with "mission" and "strategic planning." However, some argue that there are important distinctions among these ideas.

Nanus, for example, asserts that mission concerns *purpose*, a statement of core principles; it answers the question "Why are we here?" Vision, in turn, imagines how that mission will be fulfilled in the future.

Thus, a typical mission statement might look like this: "Asimov Elementary School exists to provide a positive environment in which all children can actualize their potential." For Nanus, this would not be a vision because it does not spell out a future state that is noticeably different from the present.

The mission is linked to the vision, since mission points to the kinds of changes that are needed. If teachers at Asimov Elementary come to the conclusion that not all students are actualizing their potential or that societal changes will make current methods inadequate, they must visualize a future in which the mission is fulfilled: "Asimov students will become skillful, self-directed learners by participating in a linguistically enriched, integrated curriculum, with portfolio-based assessment and a strong emphasis on self-evaluation." Another school with the same mission might arrive at a very different vision. As Kouzes and Posner note, each organization is unique, and there are many ways to achieve the same results.

Another related term is *strategic planning*, which has received considerable attention in the past decade. Like visions, strategic plans imagine a future state that is different. Unlike visions, plans offer a systematic, sequential strategy for getting to the future. The entire plan is mapped out at the beginning with specific, quantifiable objectives, in enough detail that the entire process can be captured on flowcharts (Roger Kaufman).

Visions likewise are goal directed, but they don't always map out a clear pathway, especially if the goal is something that has never been attained. Most descriptions of vision seem to suggest a looser, more improvisational process. For example, Conley and colleagues note that in some of the schools they studied, the vision emerged only after several years of experimenting with alternative strategies. Apparently, teachers and administrators had to see some ideas in action before they were ready to articulate a vision they could commit to. Karen Louis and Matthew Miles found the same thing in urban high schools they studied.

In theory, the tools of strategic planning could be used for implementing visions; indeed, Kaufman portrays planning as a means of achieving a school's "ideal vision." The two processes differ, however. Plans are road maps, offering a predictable itinerary; visions are more like compasses, pointing out the right direction, but leaving a lot to interpretation.

Robert H. Beach and Ron Lindahl have suggested that the rational and systematic nature of strategic planning is not a good fit for the dynamic and nonrational environment of public education.

What Vision Does

Vision is one facet of direction setting or coherence building—the crucial act of leadership that helps members of an organization make sense of an often-chaotic environment. As publicly accountable institutions, schools are constantly pulled in one direction and then another by the conflicting demands of policymakers and local constituents. As mass institutions in a rapidly changing society, schools are among the first to feel the impact of demographic shifts and cultural conflicts. As institutions of learning, they are confronted with dozens of vendors, consultants, and experts who claim that their particular instructional method is better than another. Without a clear set of priorities, schools will respond to whatever demand is most pressing at that moment, solving the immediate problem but making little progress in the long run.

Robert Evans says that leaders provide coherence by ensuring clarity, focus, and continuity. *Clarity* is the shared understanding of organizational goals: "Here is where we are headed, not there." *Focus* is mobilizing organizational resources on the goals that are most important, rather than trying to be all things to all people. *Continuity* is bridging the gap between new and old, assuring employees that the necessary changes are not an abandonment of all they hold dear.

A strong vision can aid in these tasks by unambiguously expressing what it means to work in a particular school and providing a shared standard by which teachers can gauge their own efforts. According to one teacher in a school that had recently developed a vision, "People are speaking the same language, they have the same kinds of informal expectations for one another, more common ground" (Conley and colleagues).

In addition, the right vision has powerful motivational effects, energizing people and building commitment. Warren Bennis, Jagdish Parikh, and Ronnie Lessem note that when workers believe their efforts contribute to a larger purpose, they are more likely to bring vigor and enthusiasm to their tasks.

THE IMPACT OF VISION

Both theory and research point to vision as a key element in organizational effectiveness. Kenneth Leithwood, Doris Jantzi, and Rosanne Steinbach say that "setting directions" is a common theme that cuts across many otherwise differing theories of leadership. In an extensive literature review, Kenneth A. Leithwood and Carolyn Riehl note that many motivational theories emphasize the importance of goal setting, particularly when the goal is challenging but achievable. Such goals help structure people's lives and give them meaning.

Leithwood and Riehl describe creation of a vision as a central part of direction setting. Value-based visions increase commitment and spark professional development, as well as encourage staff to accept and work toward group goals. Leithwood and Riehl also suggest that visions are more effective when leaders monitor the organization's performance, communicate skillfully, and interact effectively with a variety of constituents.

Philip Hallinger and Ronald H. Heck, who have extensively studied the effects of principal leadership, call attention to the role that vision plays in helping organizations accomplish the necessary step of implementing specific achievable and measurable goals. Goal setting in schools is often bureaucratic, fragmented, or uninspiring; connecting goals to an inspiring vision can build enthusiasm and commitment to act.

Joseph W. Licata and Gerald W. Harper found that teachers' perceptions of organizational health correlate with their perceptions of a robust school vision. That is, when they reported the existence of a clear, compelling vision, they also tended to describe their workplace as open, collegial, supportive, and trusting.

Perhaps most important, Tim Waters, Robert J. Marzano, and Brian McNulty found evidence that vision correlates with increased student learning. A number of leader behaviors related to vision, such as articulating purpose, fostering shared beliefs, expressing well-formed beliefs on education, and establishing clear goals, were also associated with improved student learning. Like most research on leadership, this study was correlational, so we cannot yet conclude that vision caused the improved learning. But the results support the beliefs of many leadership experts that vision building is essential to success.

THE PROBLEM WITH VISION

Despite the near-unanimity that vision is crucial, practitioners seldom list it as a major priority, and even scholars who emphasize its importance disparage the clumsy way that it is often implemented. Evans, noting the buzzword status of vision, says, "One need only say to an audience of educators, 'Let's talk about vision' to start a small epidemic of sighing, coughing, fidgeting and eye rolling." He points to educational vision statements that are overly long, fragmented, impractical, or simply clichéd. For all the labor that goes into them, formal vision statements are seldom memorable; once written, they tend to fade from sight.

Moreover, the written document is only a by-product of a much broader process. Robert J. Starratt points out that the vision must be translated into organizational reality. Leaders must allocate resources, formulate workable policies, and negotiate permission with higher authorities.

A second problem with many vision-building attempts is the assumption that it is a linear, logical process. The idealized notion in many accounts is that the vision is created through a careful reflective process, is communicated clearly to everyone in the organization, and thereafter guides everyone's decision making. In reality, says Michael Fullan, visions tend to emerge from a continual process of debate, trial and error, and reflection. Visions, rather than being created, are discovered.

Finally, the association of "vision" with "visionary" often leads to the assumption that it is a product of an extraordinary leader. In this conception, a brilliant, far-seeing, and imaginative executive studies the environment, intuits what the organization needs, crafts an eloquent statement, and communicates it persuasively. In reality, most students of vision see it as the expression of the collective beliefs of everyone in the organization. The leader has a personal vision that influences others, but he or she may have to let go of some parts of it for the common good (David T. Conley and Paul Goldman).

THE LEADER'S ROLE

Even with the recent emphasis on distributed leadership, analysts continue to see formal leaders as the main catalysts of vision. Bennis and colleagues wrote:

> If there is a spark of genius in the extraordinary manager at all, it must lie in this transcending ability, a kind of magic, to assemble—out of all the variety of images, signals, forecasts and alternatives—a clearly articulated vision of the future that is at once simple, easily understood, clearly desirable, and energizing.

Thus, although development of a vision can be a highly collaborative process, the leader plays a unique role that requires special insight into the goals of the organization and the motivations of followers. Howard Gardner describes it as the ability to relate a story that provides meaning to the lives of followers, a story in which the leader and followers are main characters. "Together," Gardner says, "they have embarked on a journey in pursuit of certain goals, and along the way and into the future, they can expect to encounter certain obstacles or resistances that can be overcome."

No matter who formulates the words, the leader is the "keeper of the vision," the person responsible for posing the questions that focus attention in the right places, for marshalling resources to support the vision, and for protecting it from outside forces.

Perhaps most important, the leader embodies the vision in thought, word, and deed. Visionaries do not just communicate their dreams in so many words, says Gardner; "They convey their stories by the kinds of lives they themselves lead and, through example, seek to inspire in their followers." Clearly, leaders remain the key people in the process even if they are not the sole authors of the vision.

Despite wide agreement that vision is a key leadership function, leaders can turn to few detailed descriptions of how vision develops in school settings. At times, the process seems straightforward and logical; at other times, it seems intuitive and mysterious. Sometimes it is elevating and exhilarating, reawakening dormant idealism and recharging low batteries; sometimes it is frustrating and baffling, seemingly an act of creating something out of nothing.

Despite these contradictions and uncertainties, we can outline at least three dimensions of the visioning process:

1. First, the leader must have vision; that is, he or she must be able to unite moral purpose with a capacity to see beyond the world as it is.

2. Second, the leader, in concert with others, must develop a vision that projects a better future for a particular school and that becomes the collective property of the entire school, open to growth and enrichment from the lessons of experience.

3. Finally, the leader aligns rules, structures, and resources to support the vision, thereby institutionalizing it.

The remainder of this chapter examines each of these dimensions.

DEVELOPING PERSONAL VISION

For principals who sit in the shadow of in-baskets stacked high with mundane tasks, vision can seem abstract and nebulous. Leaders tend to see themselves as doers, not dreamers. They take pride in managing real-world complexities rather than speculating on hypothetical possibilities. Is it realistic to expect them to engage in what seems to be a very creative process? The answer is clearly yes.

We can take a cue from fiction writers, exasperated when fans ask, "Where do you get your ideas?" Writers find the question difficult to answer. On the one hand, they certainly don't pull down an Idea Encyclopedia and pick a plot; on the other hand, they don't sit around in a trance-like state waiting for inspiration to strike. Rather, the best writers fully engage life, their eyes open for the dramas, characters, and oddities that make up human existence. At some point, inspiration bubbles to the surface, but it would be wrong to say it comes out of nowhere.

Kouzes and Posner, arguing that intuition is "the wellspring of vision," claim there is nothing mystical about it. An idea may seem to come out of nowhere, they say, but "it's the years of direct contact with a variety of problems and situations that equip the leader with unique insight. Listening, reading, smelling, feeling, and tasting the business—these tasks improve our vision." Thus, the foundations of vision lie in everyday experience.

Stephen R. Covey connects vision with *voice,* which he defines as the intersection of talent, need, passion, and conscience:

> When you engage in work that taps your talent and fuels your passion—that rises out of a great need in the world that you feel drawn by conscience to meet—therein lies your voice, your calling, your soul's code.

For Covey, vision is simply the part of voice that imagines the possibilities of following our calling.

Similarly, Robert E. Quinn speaks of "the fundamental state of leadership," in which people are purpose centered, internally directed, focused on meeting the needs of others, and open to moving outside their comfort zone. Leaders who operate in this way are more likely to form a vision that can transform an organization.

Small Beginnings

Kouzes and Posner point out that in the beginning the grandest vision is only a glimmer of an idea, "a vague desire to do something that would challenge yourself and others." At this stage, the operative word is *possibility*, not *probability*. What counts is that it could happen, not that it is probable.

Roland S. Barth is convinced every school leader has a vision. He concedes, however, that practitioners' visions are usually "deeply submerged, sometimes fragmentary, and seldom articulated." Too often, he suggests, people begin their educational careers with a strong sense of idealism and "a 20/20 personal vision," only to have it collide with bureaucratic procedures and mandates. Most people learn to keep their visions in the closet to avoid the painful discrepancy between real and ideal.

Barth suggests that the vision begins to reemerge when leaders allow themselves to complete open-ended statements such as:

- "When I leave this school I would like to be remembered for . . ."
- "The kind of school I would like my children to attend . . ."
- "The kind of school I would like to teach in . . ."
- "I want my place to be a school where . . ."

Similarly, Edward W. Chance and Marilyn L. Grady suggest that vision may originate in the principal's answer to these questions:

- "What are my five greatest strengths?"
- "What are my five greatest weaknesses?"
- "What are three things I value most in my professional life?"
- "With which leadership style am I most comfortable?"
- "What do I want to prove as a leader?"

Peter M. Senge and his colleagues suggest that the vision does not emerge fully formed in a single session but requires refining over time. They note that the initial vision can be subjected to further reflection and questioning. In particular, they recommend asking two questions:

1. "If I could have this now, would I take it?" Some dreams are driven by what we think we should want, not necessarily by what we do want, or they may be super-ficially appealing until we consider what they really entail.

2. "Assume that you have your vision now. What does it bring you?" This question enriches the vision and deepens our understanding of what it means.

All these authors believe that the seed of vision is in everyone; it merely needs to be cultivated.

Vision and Values

In his groundbreaking analysis of transformational leadership, James MacGregor Burns observed that figures such as Adolf Hitler have charisma and persuasive power but do not exercise true leadership. Genuinely effective leaders elevate followers to higher levels of morality. In Abraham Lincoln's phrase, they "summon the better angels of our nature."
Starratt notes that vision always springs from

> assumptions and beliefs about the nature of learning, about the essence of being human, about the nature of human society, about the purpose of schooling. The leader dwells inside these beliefs and meanings, and calls attention to them   .
> through a vision statement.

Leaders with vision are the ones who struggle to bring these buried beliefs and assumptions to the surface, where they can be critically examined and either reaffirmed or abandoned. This kind of searching is at the heart of vision. Gardner says leaders are distinguished by how well or to what extent they search for these buried meanings. Ordinary leaders tell the culture's traditional stories, innovative leaders take neglected stories and give them a fresh twist, and visionary leaders actually create new stories.

Sheive and Schoenheit found that the administrators they studied invariably linked their visions with their sense of values. At some point in their careers, those values collided with organizational realities. Something good came from their frustration, however, as these leaders were able to clarify and strengthen their visions. One superintendent put it this way: "It happens when you are deeply committed and it appears that outside forces constrict you. It is an irritant. Just like with an oyster, you create a pearl around the grain of irritation."

Developing vision, then, is an act with fundamentally moral implications, which makes it all the more important for school leaders. Schools, invested with a "public trust," carry the hopes and aspirations of an entire community.

Cultivating vision thus requires posing some thorny questions:

- What gives life meaning?
- Is there hope for the future?
- Under what conditions do children learn best?
- What are the greatest needs that children bring to school?
- Under what conditions do teachers teach best?
- What would best help children prepare for their future?

These are not small issues, nor is it easy to articulate answers. But those with vision make an effort, however fumbling, to do so.

An Eye to the Future

One obstacle to developing worthwhile visions is the natural tendency to assume that the near future (5 to 10 years) will be much like the present. But the environment is always changing, and a vision that fails to anticipate change is a vision that won't have much impact. (Imagine a buggy-whip company in 1905 that sets a 10-year vision of making the world's best buggy whip.) Marshall Sashkin and Molly G. Sashkin identify thinking about the future as a key trait of transformational leaders. The Sashkins note that top executives routinely think a decade or more beyond the present.

John R. Hoyle points out that the future is not something that simply shows up unannounced a few years down the road; instead, it is created by the actions we take today:

We must assume that we can change our course as a captain would steer a boat to the harbor or down a rapidly moving river. The swifter the stream and the larger the boat, the sooner the steering must begin for the ship to arrive safely at its mooring. We must begin now to avoid running a ground [sic].

"Future sight" seems especially important now, at a time of unprecedented social change. Management expert Peter F. Drucker has put it bluntly, saying that work, society, and government in developed economies are qualitatively and quantitatively different not only from what they were in the first years of this century but also from what has existed at any other time in history: in their configurations, in their processes, in their problems, in their structures.

So a reasonable person would anticipate that schools in 10 years will find themselves in an environment that differs noticeably from today's world. But what will the changes be? Does vision require predicting the future?

Peter Schwartz, an expert in long-range planning, says prediction is not the point. No one can know the future with certainty; instead, the goal is to increase awareness of possibilities. Having considered what might happen, a leader is better prepared for what does happen.

Imagine, for a moment, the following scenarios:

- A dramatic increase in voucher systems places schools in a highly competitive market.
- The number of high-risk students grows dramatically.
- The number of students enrolling through the Internet in virtual schools multiplies tenfold.
- The federal government imposes a common achievement test in all 50 states.
- The town's major employer closes down.
- A major high-tech company establishes an office that will attract thousands of well-educated workers to the community.
- Increased demand for adult education leads schools to remain open 15 hours a day for all kinds of courses.

Obviously, no one knows which (if any) of these scenarios will actually unfold, yet any of them could. Exploring the possibilities serves several purposes. First, some important trends may become obvious once we take the trouble to look for them. The enrollment decline of the 1970s and 1980s was perfectly predictable, yet many schools were caught unaware, forcing them to lay off teachers and close schools in a crisis atmosphere. Current demographic projections show a continuing increase in student diversity, especially in populations that schools have been least successful with.

Second, even those possibilities that never come to pass may stimulate useful thinking. For example, the prospect of a high-tech boom is wishful thinking for most communities, but simply asking the question generates some interesting thoughts. Aside from the obvious issue of facilities, the influx of well-educated workers into the community might raise some curricular questions. Would the newcomers demand more academically challenging classes and a stronger college-preparation program? Where is our curriculum? Whose needs are we meeting? Even if the high-tech company never comes here, our children will be growing up in a high-tech world—will they be ready for it?

Looking to the future takes us out of the here and now, reminding us that our best efforts today may fall far short tomorrow.

Reflective Practice

What's clear from the previous discussion is that visionary leaders are reflective; they not only act, they think about the significance of their actions, now and in the future. This does not imply abstract theorizing. Starratt says that leaders' thinking "is not something that they are consciously aware of; it is something habitually beneath the surface of their decisions and responses." He adds, however, that at times, this stream of thought needs to be brought to the surface, preferably through dialogue with members of the school community.

What sort of reflection? Starratt gives three examples.

1. *Problem naming* is a conscious effort to diagnose a problem rather than just categorize it by its most obvious features. Thus, a high rate of teacher absenteeism might quickly be blamed on lack of responsibility, whereas a closer look would show it to be the result of low morale or a sense of futility. How the problem is defined determines how we will act.

2. *An educational platform* is one's philosophy of education—the basic beliefs and assumptions that provide the foundation for vision. Starratt notes that the platforms of leaders tend to be visible more in their actions than in any formal statement. Nevertheless, brief written exercises can be helpful. For example, leaders can complete short open-ended statements such as "Students learn best when . . . " or "Classroom learning ought to emphasize . . . "Leaders can use such statements to assess their own leadership ("Does my school live up to these beliefs?") as well as to generate dialogue with others.

3. *Double-loop learning.* Citing the work of management expert Chris Argyris, Starratt says that much administrative thinking involves *single-loop learning*, that is, problems are treated as separate entities. Leaders assess the situation, pick a strategy, evaluate the results, and move on (or try again).

By contrast, *double-loop learning* deals with the immediate problem while simultaneously seeing it as part of the larger context of institutional dynamics. For example, a poorly performing teacher presents not only the surface problem of finding a way to improve instruction, but also affects relations with the union, the teacher's career, the reputation of the principal, and the learning of the students.

Creative Thinking

Perhaps the greatest challenge in reflection is to escape the bonds of the mental models that direct our thinking along well-worn paths. Senge and colleagues observe, "In any new experience, most people are drawn to take in and remember only the information that reinforces their existing mental models." W. Patrick Dolan adds that when a system is dysfunctional, early attempts at improvement "will generally be a magnification of its pathology." In other words, leaders will attempt to do the same things at a more intensive level.

Bennis and colleagues suggest that less analytical kinds of thinking may be helpful. Logical reflection tends to keep us in a mental world that is realistic, constrained by our experience with things as they are. The most exciting visions imagine things that have never been.

Bennis and his coauthors urge leaders to cultivate intuitive thinking that breaks conventional mind-sets. They suggest that such thinking is best done in relaxed, receptive states of mind and that it relies more on visual images than abstract language. For example, principals could take a mental walk through their ideal school. Strolling through the corridors, what will they see? What are students working on? How are they working? What is on the walls?

Vision sees, and in the seeing, it becomes real. Reflective thinking may lead us to what we think works best; intuitive thinking leads us to what we most desire. Together, they form a powerful visionary tool.

Blocks to Vision

Sometimes, of course, the ideas don't come. Bennis and colleagues suggest a number of causes:

- Being too focused on daily routines. (The concreteness of the daily routine tempts one away from the more ambiguous challenge of developing a vision.)
- Wanting to be just one of the crowd. (A bold vision is risky; it calls attention to oneself and creates new expectations.)
- Flitting from one thing to the other. (Some people are overwhelmed by possibilities; in trying to cover everything, they end up without a clear focus on anything.)
- Reckless risk taking. (Some leaders enjoy a high-wire act in which they are the stars.)
- Clinging to established principles to avoid ambiguity. (Creating a new future is filled with uncertainty; some leaders just tinker around the margins.)
- Being too open minded. (Some leaders find it difficult to choose.)
- Believing you have all the answers. (In their hearts, some leaders simply do not believe that major change is needed.)

TAILORING THE VISION TO THE SCHOOL

Just as leaders must know their own beliefs and values, they must know their schools—the strengths, the weaknesses, and the climate and personality. Nanus recommends a series of questions that can point the way:

1. *What values and beliefs guide decision making in this organization?* Prevailing norms often determine attitudes toward the vision. For example, a faculty might be guided by these values (often unstated):

- Academic proficiency is the highest goal.
- Teachers never criticize other teachers' methods.
- Go along to get along.
- Above all, students should learn to believe in themselves.
- Parents should be an integral part of the school.
- Some students just can't learn.

Leaders must develop the insight to be able to recognize the faculty's norms; indeed, the vision process includes helping everyone in the school bring these assumptions to the surface and examine them. Once the norms are identified, leaders should not be fatalistic about accepting them.

2. *What are the organization's strengths and weaknesses?* Visions are easier to fulfill if they can build on the school's strengths or avoid its weaknesses. For example, an analysis may show that the school has strong relationships with parents and community; a diminished tax base that threatens finances; a rapidly changing population bringing more students who need individual attention, remedial work, and access to social services; a capable, veteran staff that works hard to meet students' needs and is comfortable with the status quo; aging buildings; and a cohesive written curriculum for all grade levels. All these factors will affect the vision.

3. *What strategy is the school following to fulfill the current mission? Is it working?* Unlike the private sector, where competition forces companies to think strategically, schools may see themselves as steady-state service providers whose main responsibility is to provide a protective, supportive environment for teaching and learning. A true strategy explicitly links activities and programs to the mission. For example, recently added programs (such as drug education) often represent a conscious strategy; the role of more traditional offerings (such as science) may be taken for granted.

4. *Does the organization currently have a clearly stated vision? If so, what is it?* If a vision already exists, the leader's task changes. Reviewing and renewing a vision requires a somewhat different approach than creating a vision for the first time.

5. *If the organization stays on the current path, where will it be heading in the next decade? Is that good?* Here is where leaders must try to determine how the environment may change in coming years and how the changes will affect the school.

6. *Do key people in the organization know where it is headed and agree on that direction?* This is an important reality check. The mere existence of a formal vision statement does not guarantee it a significant role in the school's culture. Do people accept the official plan? Is it part of their everyday professional vocabulary? Do they judge actions by their effect on the vision? Or do they give only lip service to the statement?

7. *Does the system—structures, processes, resources—support the current direction?* For example, if the vision calls for technological literacy, does the budget provide sufficient technological resources? If the vision calls for a significant shift of direction, do teachers have the appropriate training or the time to collaborate on necessary changes?

Developing a Shared Vision

For organizational leaders, vision brings with it an uncomfortable paradox. To be authentic, the vision must tap into their deepest values and their passions, and it must clearly express their unique voice. Yet to make it come alive, they must be prepared to let go of it.

Earlier conceptions of vision portrayed a heroic, charismatic leader single-handedly articulating a vision and then persuading everyone to accept it. A dynamic combination of brilliant thinking, persuasive power, and high energy—all possessions of the leader—would get the organization moving in the right direction.

Today, the prevailing belief is that the vision must be shared. Although the leader is still the prime catalyst, the vision itself is a creation of many people throughout the organization. This kind of sharing goes far beyond passive acceptance or buy-in. As Peter M. Senge expresses it, "A vision is truly shared when you and I have a similar picture and are committed to one another having it, not just to each of us, individually, having it."

This notion can be unsettling for a number of reasons. First, when the principal articulates and models an appealing vision, it can have a positive impact. Most teachers recognize and appreciate when school leaders have a clear sense of direction, and most will work cheerfully to help implement it. Even if they don't completely agree with this vision, its existence provides reassurance that there is a plan. Since everyone seems content with the arrangement, leaders have little incentive to move beyond it.

Second, the very idea of shared vision seems contradictory. If the ideal vision expresses a leader's true voice—his or her deepest values, talents, and passions—it will be unique, since no two people are completely alike. If many people share a vision, won't it lose some of the very characteristics that make it so energizing in the first place?

Finally, the task of creating consensus around educational purpose is formidable. Americans as a group have yet to achieve that kind of agreement, and most public school communities reflect the diversity and divisions of the larger society. How can a principal bridge those differences? How, when, and to what extent should others become involved?

Notwithstanding these doubts, many leaders have succeeded in creating a truly shared vision that drives the organization forward. Although their examples provide no easy formula, this section describes some principles that may be helpful.

Charting the Landscape

Despite the idealistic aura that often surrounds the topic of vision, school leaders must work in an environment characterized by entrenched interests, limited resources, and swirling political currents that have little to do with learning. Vision does not demand passive acceptance of those forces, but it does require leaders to recognize them.

Schools differ in their readiness to develop a shared vision. Ironically, as David K. Hurst points out, organizations in crisis may be the ripest for change. When employees are bombarded with daily evidence that things just aren't working, when they can see the organization's failure in their own experience, they are more likely to listen to someone who says there is a better way.

Leaders new to their school may also have certain temporary advantages. New principals don't carry the weight of long-established routines and relationships. Teachers recognize this blank slate and are usually anxious to know what the new agenda will be. Often, there is a honeymoon period in which the staff, recognizing the principal's need to make a mark, will good-naturedly accept some new initiatives. At this stage, even small actions by a leader can have a major impact on the school's future direction.

Now consider the opposite scenario: an established principal in a good school with competent and committed teachers, adequate resources, and a satisfied community. This principal may face the biggest challenge. People who are content with the present have little motivation to go looking for the future.

Beyond the issue of staff receptivity, every school is part of a larger system, subject to rules and regulations that may limit the school's freedom to innovate. The leader must thus determine: How free are we to reinvent ourselves? Are certain changes off limits? (Could we, for example, decide to operate our school from 10 A.M. until 5 P.M., or is the district's bus schedule sacred?) Will resources be available to put our ideas into effect? Is the union receptive to changes in teachers' work roles?

Leaders who charge ahead without considering those questions may unleash powerful forces that threaten the existing order and make people aware of uncomfortable facts or philosophical disagreements. Unwary leaders may find themselves with a boiling pot and no way to turn down the flames.

Dolan argues that vision development is unlikely to succeed without "deep buy-in" from the board, superintendent, union, and anyone with effective veto power over the school's vision. Getting public, formal approval from these groups diminishes skepticism that "the system" won't permit real change.

Such explicit approval is not always available, of course. Those responsible for managing a whole system are not always eager to encourage mavericks who may disrupt the bureaucratic machinery by seeking special treatment. In this case, the principal may have to quietly negotiate informal understandings that will provide a sense of the political and economic limits.

But he or she must also make some careful risk calculations. Leaders are usually urged to "dream no small dreams," since incremental change rarely stirs excitement. Peter Block counsels, however, that under certain conditions, caution may be advisable: during the first 6 months on the job, at moments when organizational survival is in doubt, following periods of expansion and adventurous change, and in a zero-trust environment. Vision requires boldness, Block says, but the goal is "nonsuicidal courage."

Opening a Dialogue

The mention of shared vision sometimes evokes images of an unwieldy committee ponderously trying to edit a vision statement into existence. But developing shared vision is not a formal governance process, and not everyone has to vote on every decision. Senge and colleagues wrote:

> It doesn't mean taking people's input, selecting some of it, and discarding the rest. It means establishing a series of forums where people work together to forge the future direction of the school. None of the participants (including the superintendent) will get all of the outcomes in the exact form desired; but all will get outcomes they respect and can make a commitment to.

The forums can be any place in which the leader interacts with others in the school community: faculty meetings, PTA meetings, booster club events, or even spontaneous corridor conversations. These discussions need not—and usually do not—have vision as the overt topic. Rather, they focus on the myriad mundane issues that arise in any school: textbook adoption, discipline policy, grading practices, curriculum development, and dozens of others. What turns them into vision discussions is the leader's persistent probing of the larger implications. Why is this issue important? What would an ideal solution look like? What would we need to do to make it happen?

Over time, leaders can develop a sense of the beliefs, values, and hopes that provide the foundation for a common vision. Covey suggests that leaders must understand "four realities" before they can meld a common vision:

1. What do people in the organization see as the major challenges, constraints, and resources that affect their work?

2. What are the unique strengths of people in the organization—what do they do best?

3. What are the needs of the customers or clients the organization serves?

4. What values drive people in this organization?

One way to get answers to these questions is to organize formal meetings or structured activities. Tony Wagner describes how 14 school districts around the country formed teams of parents, educators, community members, and older students to conduct focus groups and interviews with constituent groups in the community. The result was a thoughtful dialogue that helped each group see how its concerns connected with others', and that provided a solid foundation for developing a vision for change.

Hoyle suggests sessions in which participants design their ideal school or imagine what it would take to be a world-class school in, say, 10 years. He also recommends "scenario-building," activities that speculate on alternative futures the school may face.

Another strategy is to use data to spur discussion and self-examination. Schools today are awash in data generated by state and federal accountability policies. This information is useful for more than reporting to policymakers.

Edie L. Holcomb notes that a school's sense of mission often needs anchoring to something concrete. She suggests challenging the school community's perceptions by comparing "what we say" with "the evidence we have." Teachers can sometimes be brought up short by objective evidence that contradicts staff beliefs about what is happening. A common example is the discovery by a high-performing school that its overall high scores disguise a distinct achievement gap among certain groups of students.

Knowing how members of the school community perceive these issues is the first step to forming a shared vision. Such conversations have other benefits as well. Just as the principal learns what is important to others in the school, teachers, parents, and other stakeholders begin to understand the principal's vision. In addition, the principal is signaling that the undeniable pressures of daily school life do not dictate a narrow focus on the here and now and that it is important to talk openly about what we are trying to do and how we might do it better.

The Vision Emerges

Personal dreams take tangible shape when we realize others share them. As leaders talk with teachers, they should be listening for the common ground, looking for the signs that say, "This is what this school is about!" Kouzes and Posner say:

Leaders find the common thread that weaves the fabric of human needs into a colorful tapestry. They develop a deep understanding of the collective yearnings; they seek out the brewing consensus among those they would lead. They listen carefully for quiet whisperings in dark corners and attend to subtle cues. They get a sense of what people want, what they value, what they dream about.

Those signs are out there, in words, stories, body language, and most of all, actions. Leaders can find them if they look, if they devote enough time to roaming the hallways and talking to teachers, students, and parents.

As leaders begin to sense the areas of consensus, they can feed their impressions back to the faculty. Through this dialogue, leaders can confirm vague impressions and spark further reflection and discussion.

In all this process, the leader must strike a delicate balance between openness to new ideas and insistence on establishing a consistent direction. The early stages of the vision building process can be exciting, since people are feeling empowered to voice their hopes for the future. However, as Douglas B. Reeves points out, "There is an inherent tension between the need of the leader to be open-minded toward a variety of points of view and the need for focus." The value of a shared vision is that it expresses a coherent, unifying sense of direction; consequently, it requires the discipline to say no to attractive ideas that are not at the core of the collective vision.

Nor is the leader just a neutral facilitator. Teachers are keenly interested in what the principal values and the course he or she is trying to steer. At the same time, they appreciate the opportunity to have their views listened to respectfully and incorporated into the emerging school vision.

Testing the Vision

At some point, the ongoing dialogue must be expressed in concrete form so it can be examined and evaluated. One way is to articulate it in writing.

Committing the vision to writing gets it out in the open so it can be evaluated more objectively. As any writer can testify, what seems so marvelously clear in one's mind becomes impossibly murky when first set down on paper. Seeing the words in black and white will raise questions, doubts, and calls for revision. Through many iterations of the document, the school's thinking about the vision will become sharper.

There is no need to produce the statement according to any particular schedule. Nanus suggests allowing time for ideas to simmer. Slowly start to sketch out possibilities; at some point, begin to draw up alternative visions, write them out, and share them with others.

How does one know the statement is ready? Here again, there is no textbook answer, just a need for finely tuned professional judgment. Nanus suggests some possible criteria when he says the vision should be future oriented, utopian (leading to a better future), appropriate for the organization, reflective of high ideals and excellence, indicative of the organization's direction, capable of inspiring enthusiasm, reflective of the organization's uniqueness, and ambitious.

Another key test is putting the words into practice. For example, the emerging vision may imply that collaboratively examining student work would help create a desirable learning community. A few experiments with that activity would not only help fine-tune the strategy, it would raise questions about the vision. Is this the kind of activity that furthers our core beliefs? Is this really what we want to be doing? Does it feel right? In the long run, visions become real only when they are enacted.

Ultimately, the best sign of a ripe vision may be in the emotions it arouses. Bennis and colleagues quoted Kevin Kingsland:

When you have found your vision you do not ask yourself whether you have one. You inform the world about it. If you're wondering whether you have a vision, then you haven't got one.

When you've discovered your vision you abound with inspiration. Your eyes sparkle. You can see it in the atmosphere. It is pulsing with life.

Providing Inspiration

Throughout the process, there will be hesitations, doubts, and moments of discouragement. Teachers, having seen all too many grand initiatives that slowly faded away, may be inclined to retreat quietly rather than suffer yet another disappointment. Principals can encourage, support, and inspire the school community through the inevitable ups and downs by attending to four things:

1. *Keeping a positive, uplifting focus.* The power of a vision is its ability to help people feel they are part of something special, part of an effort that is not just going to make improvements but transform their work. William G. Cunningham and Donn W. Gresso argue that developing a vision is not just a matter of solving problems:

> Problem-solving creates a group dynamic of defensiveness, protectionism, power struggle, mistrust, and an ultimately adversarial relationship. Applied to the improvement of schooling, the model usually results in feelings of failure, incompetence, and depression. . . . A sense of inadequacy develops within the culture.

A visionary approach, they say, puts aside the need to justify failures and instead asks, "Where do we go from here?" Bennis and colleagues characterize it as the difference between saying, "I am cutting stone" and saying, "I am building a cathedral."

Even simple language habits may make a difference. Kouzes and Posner urge leaders to say "will" rather than "try." They say this does not require being naive or unrealistic about the difficulties, which should be openly recognized. It is more a matter of projecting an attitude that says, "I'm confident we'll work through all the difficulties and reach the goal."

Starratt, too, points to the importance of language. He notes that vision statements often employ vivid imagery that hits home. Metaphors that liken school to "gardening," "family," "symphonies," and "journeys" will touch the heart as well as the mind.

2. *Empowering people to act.* Talking about vision is one thing; following through is another. The principal can signal, through innumerable small actions, that acting on personal vision is not only permitted but encouraged. Teachers get the message, as in this example reported by Joseph Blase and Jo Roberts Blase:

> The principal is very receptive to new ideas and ways of doing things. She values the opinions of all her staff members.
>
> She realizes that our school and our students are unique and welcomes suggestions and ideas for improving instruction. We have an instructional task force

that continually teaches new methods of instruction and we are encouraged to try new techniques.

Blase and Blase emphasize it's important for teachers to be able to carry out this experimentation in a nonthreatening environment, without fear of criticism when ideas don't work.

3. *Inspiring others.* Kouzes and Posner note that most people, even though they don't consider themselves inspiring, can have inspirational effects by being emotionally expressive:

> Expressiveness comes naturally to people talking about deep desires for the future. They lean forward in their chairs, they move their arms about, their eyes light up, their voices sing with emotion, and a smile appears on their faces. In these circumstances, people are enthusiastic, articulate, optimistic, and uplifting.

In part, then, inspiration is a matter of expressive style. Words and gestures that convey enthusiasm and excitement are likely to be contagious. Of course, the leader's convictions must be genuine to be convincing.

4. *Dramatizing core beliefs.* As the vision begins to emerge, it will initially seem tentative and shaky. The leader's role is to dramatize it. As abstract statements of principles, visions may seem distant and unreachable; connected to the drama of human life, they take on deep meaning.

Terry Deal argues that organizational improvement takes on life when portrayed through metaphor, poetry, drama, stories, and rituals. For example, one thing that inspires teachers is the occasional classroom encounter that makes a better future seem possible. Encouraging teachers to tell stories about these exciting moments is a good way to spread the excitement and make the vision seem reachable.

Something as simple as meeting off-site can lend drama and significance to the effort. One experienced teacher, veteran of many a reform, observed that just once it would be nice to launch a change with a nice meal at a carpeted conference center instead of with stale doughnuts in a drafty cafeteria.

Living the Vision

Although it would probably be misleading to consider vision development as ever complete, there does come a time when it seems well established: People can articulate it, it forms the basis for many conversations, and it is generating action. But the leader's work is far from done.

One major error in vision building is to confuse the statement with the vision. In their work with businesses, Michael Hammer and Steven A. Stanton have observed that the official statement usually receives a major publicity blitz—in memos, posters, and wallet-sized laminated cards (not to mention key rings, buttons, and notebook covers). Unfortunately, they said this effort is often wasted on empty slogans or feel-good words like "excellence," "integrity," or "teamwork." The problem is not that the visions are somehow wrong, but that they never become more than glittering generalities trapped under the plastic.

Likewise, Nanus observed, "A vision is little more than an empty dream until it is widely shared and accepted. Only then does it acquire the force necessary to change an organization and move it in the intended direction." A complete discussion of change processes is beyond the scope of this chapter, but several issues are especially pertinent to vision.

Gaining Acceptance

If the vision came into being through a collaborative process and is truly responsive to the beliefs of the staff, acceptance is likely. Yet there is no such thing as 100 percent acceptance. There will always be those who lack enthusiasm and commitment to the vision. Dolan estimated that for most major changes, 10 percent of the teachers will be flatly opposed, 20 to 25 percent will be in favor, and the rest will be skeptical but willing to be convinced.

Resistance occurs for a variety of reasons. Some teachers have seen too many clashes between vision and bureaucracy or too many grand schemes that went nowhere. Some objections may come from an unwillingness to change comfortable routines and lesson plans that have taken years to develop. Enacting a new vision is both time consuming and risky.

Other resistance is political, rooted in the challenge to existing patterns of influence and status. For example, a high school department chair may fear that collaborative decision making will diminish his or her influence on curriculum decisions. Leslie Santee Siskin, studying the vision-building efforts of three high school principals, found that strong, autonomous academic departments could make development of shared vision more difficult.

Sometimes resistance is a matter of honest philosophical disagreement. Some teachers on every staff gravitate toward child-centered, open-ended environments, whereas others believe in highly structured, academically oriented approaches. Ironically, those who care the most about what they do may be the strongest opponents of the new vision.

Finally, some resistance is simply good sense. As Andrew Gitlin and Frank Margonis point out, when a proposed change imposes extra burdens on teachers without providing additional resources, resistance is just a way of saying, "This is unrealistic."

It is also worth noting that what we call resistance is often just a normal human response to change, one that everyone (including the leader) is likely to experience. Management consultant William Bridges points out that any major change requires a significant psychological transition. He outlines three stages:

1. First, every new beginning is actually an *ending* that requires letting go of the old order, sometimes even inducing a grieving process.

2. Second is a *neutral zone* that represents a kind of limbo in which the old way is gone and the new isn't yet comfortable.

3. Finally comes the actual new *beginning*, in which the new way begins to seem natural and normal.

Bridges argues that all three stages are necessary and ultimately healthful; they need to be properly managed, not avoided.

Whatever the cause of resistance, Hammer and Stanton caution leaders against looking for logical reasons. "Ultimately, it is how people feel about a new situation that determines how they will respond to it. If they feel frightened, or threatened, or uncomfortable, or uncertain, then their reaction is likely to be a negative one."

Responding to Resistance

Hammer and Stanton point out that resistance is actually a positive sign, an indicator that something significant is happening. It is a natural human response, not a sign that the vision is somehow deficient.

Yet resistance presents leaders with a sensitive human-relations dilemma. On one hand, the vision embodies the core values of the school and demands allegiance from everyone who chooses to work there. Although the vision should allow teachers reasonable autonomy and flexibility, it also makes certain nonnegotiable demands. Thomas J. Sergiovanni says, "It is the leader's responsibility to be outraged when empowerment is abused and when purposes are ignored."

When teachers conspicuously fail to honor those purposes, or continually disparage and demean the vision, or even settle for passive resistance, they can spread a contagious dampening cloud over the whole project.

On the other hand, directly confronting the resisters doesn't always work. For one thing, direct confrontations sometimes escalate into dramatic showdowns that tenured teachers seldom lose. Moreover, such drastic action may, in the long run, be counterproductive. Even teachers who support the vision may be unnerved by the idea that there is a politically correct view that affects job security.

Bridges does not attribute resistance to animosity or stubbornness, but to normal human psychology (even among those who support the change). He suggests a number of strategies that may be helpful to people in the midst of a transition:

1. *Identify what the resisters may have lost.* It may be a position of influence or status; it may be a philosophical allegiance (for example, a teacher who has long prided herself on teaching the basics may feel that effort is being abandoned as the school moves toward a whole-language approach).

2. *Honor what is being lost.* The old ways may no longer be appropriate for the new century, but in their day, they may have served many children well. The need for new directions does not mean that those using the old ways have wasted their lives.

3. *Mark the endings.* People often cope with change through ceremonies (funerals, birthdays, graduations) that dramatically and publicly announce the new order.

4. *Emphasize the continuity in the new vision.* As noted earlier, a good vision will build on the organization's past. The vision may be a shift in course, but it's still the same ship.

5. *Publicly recognize the inner turmoil that everyone is experiencing.* People are often reluctant to talk about confusion and negative feelings, thereby denying themselves the comfort and counsel of others. Leaders must set the tone by being open and honest about their own confusions and uncertainties as well as being sensitive to the uncertainties of others.

6. *Make sure that everyone has a part to play.* This means that people not only understand what changes the vision requires of them but have an opportunity to take part in the vision process. As people invest time and effort in a goal, they begin to acquire a psychological stake in its success.

7. *Be consistent.* The vision calls for certain new behaviors and attitudes, which should be implemented and rewarded. Principals can be sure that teachers will be watching closely. Failing to act consistently with the vision may be taken as a sign of wavering or even hypocrisy.

8. *Strive for early successes, even small ones.* In the early stages of implementation, when not everyone is fully convinced, even minor results have an impact out of proportion to their actual importance. By highlighting certain low-risk tasks or arranging for some long-sought concession or resource from higher authorities, leaders can score important points when it matters most. Bridges says, "Quick successes reassure the believers, convince the doubters, and confound the critics."

INSTITUTIONALIZING THE VISION

As the previous section suggests, the leader must continue to be chief cheerleader and communicator for the vision, working to make it real in the hearts and minds of the school community and to weave it into the fabric of the school's culture. In addition, leaders must use their administrative skills to create the policies, resources, and structures needed to implement the vision.

Aligning Organizational Elements

Starratt visualizes the school as an onion. At the core are the beliefs, assumptions, goals, and myths that are the source of vision. The outer layers are composed of policies (the basic rules governing organizational behavior), programs (the division of the school's work into departments, grade levels, and offices), organization (the distribution of resources through budgets, schedules, and staffing), and operations (the visible work of classroom teaching and learning).

Unless the outer layers are infused with the spirit and implications of the core values and are aligned with the goals, the vision is unlikely to last or have an impact on student learning. For example, if a middle school seeks to develop a team approach, it must adjust the schedule so teachers on the same team have common planning time. Likewise, a commitment to technological literacy will require acquisition of considerable hardware, and the desire to move to a whole-language program will be undermined if the school continues to emphasize achievement tests closely linked to basal readers. In short, the vision must be institutionalized if it is to survive.

As Starratt describes it, integrating the vision and the organization seems to require ambidextrous principals. With one hand, they administer, managing materials and resources to get the job done; with the other, they lead, nurturing the organization's soul.

At times, implementing the vision will seem prosaic and technical, as in the action plan recommended by Jerry J. Herman:

Step 1:   Identify all tasks that must be accomplished without regard to the order in which they are to be completed.

Step 2:   Place a sequential number beside each task that has been identified.

Step 3:   Identify the person or people who are responsible for completing each task.

Step 4:   Identify the resources necessary to accomplish the objective.

Step 5:   State the measurement that will be used to determine whether the objective has been achieved.

At other times, the way will be unclear and the vision will appear nebulous or even unrealistic. At those moments, the principal must turn again to the leadership skills that nurtured the vision in the first place.

Maintaining Emotional Balance

Inevitably, implementing a vision takes the school through an arduous emotional journey, from the exhilaration of previously unimaginable success to the despair of fond hopes being dashed. Pursuing vision is simply hard work. When those efforts are carried out in an environment of escalating external accountability, overload and burnout are possible.

Leithwood and colleagues advise leaders to pay attention to three issues—depersonalization, personal accomplishment, and personal exhaustion:

1. Depersonalization is what happens when teachers perceive that school goals are incompatible with their professional goals. Principals may need to coach these teachers to find links between their goals and the shared vision.

2. A strong, shared vision can raise expectations dramatically. Even when teachers have a deep commitment to the new direction, living up to it is not easy, and their sense of accomplishment and self-efficacy may diminish. Leaders may need to provide coaching, positive reinforcement, and other forms of support.

3. Although people often associate burnout with disengagement, it can result from sustained excitement and unremitting effort. As principals monitor the pace of implementation, they can watch for signs of emotional exhaustion, help teachers stay focused on the most critical goals, and provide feedback that points out the short-term successes.

BEYOND VISION: THE LEARNING ORGANIZATION

James C. Collins and Jerry I. Porras, in their study of visionary companies, found that "a charismatic visionary leader is absolutely not required for a visionary company and, in fact, can be detrimental to a company's long-term prospects." Rather, effective leaders concentrated on building an *organization* that was visionary. As the authors put it, "They sought to be clock builders, not time tellers."

Collins and Porras compared George Westinghouse, the visionary leader who created the alternating-current power system, with Charles Coffin, the first president of General Electric. Coffin never invented anything, but he did create the General Electric Research Lab, which came up with a multitude of inventions and improvements.

According to Collins and Porras, visionary companies share several characteristics:

- They have strong organizational ideologies ("cult-like cultures").
- They have towering ambitions ("big hairy audacious goals").
- They ceaselessly experiment ("try a lot of stuff and keep what works").
- They develop their own leaders ("home grown management").
- They keep trying to top themselves ("good enough never is").

In short, visionary companies are learning organizations that see change not as a threat but as a spur to become even better. In education, as elsewhere, the pace of change—and the need for learning—shows no sign of slackening. Visions push leaders and teachers into a learning mode. As Quinn put it, "When we commit to a vision to do something that has never been done before, there is no way to know how to get there. We simply have to build the bridge as we walk on it."

CONCLUSION: CHANGE AS A DRIVING FORCE FOR EXCELLENCE

The traditional view of organizational change has been described as "unfreeze, change, freeze." That is, change was seen as a temporary process to get from one status quo to the next. Organizational excellence was a matter of developing the best system possible and maintaining it as long as possible.

Today, change is regarded as a permanent process, and the best organizations are those that have found a way not only to cope with change but to use it as a driving force for excellence. Learning organizations are a lot like surfers: They can't control the wave they're riding, but they can continually adapt to it, using its energies to get them where they want to go.

In this process, vision is crucial, not because it marks a beginning or an ending, but simply because it reminds us where we want to go. We may never arrive quite where we think we're headed, but visioning assures us that the journey will be worthwhile. Along the way, it provides an uplifting and ennobling spirit in a job that threatens to swamp practitioners in trivia and daily crises. As Peter Senge quoted George Bernard Shaw:

> This is the true joy in life, the being used for a purpose recognized by yourself as a mighty one . . . being a force of nature instead of a feverish, selfish little clod of ailments and grievances complaining that the world will not devote itself to making you happy.

REFLECTIONS

1. In a few sentences, describe your personal educational vision. If someone were to observe you over a period of a week, what outward indicators of your vision would they see?

2. To what degree does your school have a shared vision? Briefly describe it. What outward indicators of this vision would a visitor to your school see?

3. Does shared vision play an important role in the life of your school? Is it frequently discussed or used as a standard in making decisions?

4. To what degree is your school's vision a result of leadership? How influential has the principal been in creating or sustaining the vision? What leadership behaviors have had an impact on vision?

5. How closely does your personal vision match the school vision?

8

Cultural Leadership

Stuart C. Smith

Neither culture nor leadership, when one examines each closely, can really be understood by itself. In fact, one could argue that the only thing of real importance that leaders do is to create and manage culture and that the unique talent of leaders is their ability to understand and work with culture.

—Edgar H. Schein (1992)

Broadly speaking, this entire book is about how the school leader creates and manages a culture that facilitates student learning. The leader's character and competence, styles and strategies of leadership, ethics, vision, values and beliefs, methods of decision making, political savvy, instructional leadership, communication skills, community outreach, and allocation of resources all vector in on culture formation, which is at the core of the leader's role.

Despite this broad spectrum of matters involved in cultural leadership, it would be wrong to say that everything the leader does helps form culture. There are effective and ineffective ways to construct culture, just as some cultures support the school's mission and others impede it. Good intentions are of little value in this effort; the leader must enter the fray knowing what works and what doesn't. Helping school leaders to distinguish between the two is the purpose of this chapter.

According to Schein (1992), an organizational psychologist who has written two authoritative books on the subject, culture formation is the unique function of leadership that distinguishes it from administration and management: "Leaders create and change cultures, while managers and administrators live within them."

THE POWER OF A STRONG CULTURE

The culture of the local school is one of several "potentially powerful determinants of student learning" for which strong evidence exists, say Kenneth Leithwood, Karen Seashore Louis, Stephen Anderson, and Kyla Wahlstrom, who advise school leaders to take their cues from this evidence.

Culture affects every part of the school's operation. Its influence ranges "from what faculty talk about in the lunchroom, to the type of instruction that is valued, to the way professional development is viewed, to the importance of learning for all students," say Terrence E. Deal and Kent D. Peterson. To underscore the power of a strong collaborative culture, Deal and Peterson point to these effects:

- Culture fosters school effectiveness and productivity.
- Culture improves collegial and collaborative activities that foster better communication and problem-solving practices.
- Culture fosters successful change and improvement efforts.
- Culture builds commitment and identification of staff, students, and administrators.
- Culture amplifies the energy, motivation, and vitality of a school's staff, students, and community.
- Culture increases the focus of daily behavior and attention on what is important and valued.

For all those reasons, culture is well worth every school leader's attention. The importance of the task is obvious to all, yet not everyone agrees on how to do it, and for good reason. Culture is a complex and multifaceted subject not easily grasped, and our quest in the pages that follow—to understand its nexus with a similarly elusive subject, leadership—compounds the complexity. Our first task, therefore, is to choose the direction this chapter will take.

THE PERSPECTIVE OF THIS CHAPTER

This chapter comes at the subject of cultural leadership from a different perspective than much of the literature written for school leaders. That literature takes mainly a pragmatic stance, telling principals and other leaders how to improve school culture by opening up more shared decision making, forming work teams, sharing vision, establishing a caring environment, interacting more with parents, praising staff and students for their efforts, and even making sure to fill bathroom soap dispensers, to mention just a few techniques.

These commonsense recommendations do have merit, and some have research evidence to back them up. Also, they correctly assume that culture influences (and is influenced by) every part of the school—its mission and structure, the interactions of those who work and study there, even its physical facilities.

Because other chapters of this book address most of the topics that fit this pragmatic strategy, this chapter doesn't have to revisit those subjects. There is also another, deeper reason to go a different direction.

The problem is that once we understand what culture is, we'll realize that surface changes of the type commonly proposed don't have much chance of altering it. That's the warning sounded by Schein, whose insights, along with those of Marshall Sashkin and Molly G. Sashkin, guide this chapter's conception of culture. School leaders need to know what they are up against when trying to enliven an ailing culture.

We'll explore the meaning of culture and plumb Schein's wisdom about both the intransigent nature of culture and some of the principles that govern the transformation of culture. The Sashkins then serve as our guide to how leaders construct culture. Finally, because academic learning is this book's focal point, we'll explore one of the chief yet often overlooked influences on students' learning: the world of their peer subculture.

What this chapter can't do is discuss in meaningful depth the complicated processes of assessing your school's culture and, if it is found to be dysfunctional, transforming it. For sure-footed guidance on those matters, both of Schein's books—especially his more accessible *The Corporate Culture Survival Guide* (1999)—and the Sashkins' *Leadership That Matters,* one of the best recent syntheses on the theory and practice of leadership, are highly recommended.

As the chapter unfolds, we'll see that the aspects of culture that really matter—those that control the organization's performance—are difficult to discern. Because our focus is on cultural leadership, it makes sense to begin by inquiring into the hidden motives of the leader's own heart.

THE HEART OF THE MATTER

The Introduction to this book, in a section titled "Motive Matters," asks school leaders to examine why they want to lead. Nowhere is this question more important than in formation of a school's culture, because cultural leadership starts with commitments made in the leader's heart.

Cultural leaders must be imbued with what Michael Fullan calls *moral purpose,* by which he means an acute sense of responsibility to others: "School leaders with moral purpose seek to make a difference in the lives of students."

Concern for the advancement of others is at the center of Fullan's description of "the principal of the future—the Cultural Change Principal." Student learning is this principal's paramount concern, and not just in his or her own school. Fullan argues that "principals should be nearly as concerned about the success of other schools in the district as they are about their own school," because sustained improvement requires the whole system to keep moving forward. These principals forgo competition against their colleagues for recognition and advancement because they identify their own success with the system's success.

When combined with essential leadership skills, concern for others is a prerequisite for leaders who want to create for their schools a strong culture that supports student learning.

The National Association of Secondary School Principals (NASSP), in *Breaking Ranks II,* its impressive guide to reform of high schools, asks why a principal would want to undertake such reform. One stated reason expresses this motive well: "Realizing the educator's dream means realizing each student's dream." A chief way of helping all students realize that dream, the guide states, is to promote a culture of continuous improvement that gives each student the opportunity to achieve at high levels.

Jim Collins examined reasons for the "enduring greatness" of 11 highly successful businesses. In his book *Good to Great,* Collins points to two paradoxical characteristics shared by their executives: They "blend extreme personal humility with intense professional will." The great companies were led by people who exhibited what Collins calls Level 5 leadership. "The essence of a Level 5 is someone who is ambitious first and foremost for the cause or the organization, not for themselves, and has the stoic will to make good on that ambition."

Whatever labels we apply—moral purpose, humility, altruism, putting the cause first, servant leadership—they all describe an essential attribute of those who would lead their schools to excellence. For convenience's sake, we'll call it the *prosocial motive*, borrowing this term from the Sashkins, who use it to describe the use of power to achieve a positive benefit for the organization.

This concept has much in common with Thomas J. Sergiovanni's call, in his book *Moral Leadership,* to base the practice of leadership on moral authority. The school leader is motivated to subordinate personal self-interest to the common good of the school out of a sense of duty that derives from shared values, ideas, and ideals.

The bottom line: Principals who seek their own interests over those of their staff and students will breed a culture of cynicism and selfishness. Following the leader's example, staff members will put in just enough effort to take home their paychecks. In contrast, principals who find their own fulfillment in the empowerment of others and in the accomplishment of group goals will inspire others to do the same.

NASSP's *Breaking Ranks II* argues that the core beliefs of the school must be "anchored in improving students and practice for students (not focused on the needs and wants of the teachers)." The principal who eschews his or her personal interests can legitimately call on faculty members to subordinate their own welfare to the mission of the school. As Sergiovanni (1992) stated, "When leadership practice is based on moral authority, teachers can be expected to respond to shared commitments and felt interdependence." Thus, the organization as a whole dedicates itself to serving students and the community.

Although the role of the prosocial motive needs to be qualified in several ways as discussed in this book's Introduction, its importance is undeniable. This theme of empowering others and serving the common good echoes through the pages that follow, in sometimes surprising ways.

We're now in a position to explore the meaning of culture and highlight some of the contemporary and historical factors that influence the culture of the school.

THE MEANING OF CULTURE

Culture refers to the social context of a particular grouping of people who share a common history. As Schein (1999) points out, "Wherever a group has enough common experience, a culture begins to form." The group's culture then takes on a power of its own that influences the behavior of the group and its members. Culture, in Schein's words, "is a powerful, latent, and often unconscious set of forces that determine both our individual and collective behavior, ways of perceiving, thought patterns, and values."

Anthropologists apply the term to distinct communities of people who have developed their own ways of life. In a complex society such as our own, culture exists at many different levels. In addition to being part of the broad American culture, each person identifies with the cultures of his or her region, neighborhood, ethnic group, religion, profession or trade, and workgroup.

Influence of External Cultures

Schooling, too, has many different levels of culture. John I. Goodlad (interviewed by Lynn Olson) distinguished between what he called the "culture of schooling" (he meant business principles by which schools are run) and the culture of the local school, which is highly personal and varies, so that what works in one school doesn't necessarily work in another.

The culture of each school is influenced by numerous external cultures, most notably the culture of the community and school district of which it is a part. Deborah E. Stine observed the formation of the culture of a new high school and was struck by the close connection between the school and its external community. So interdependent are they that the school's culture can be regarded as a mirror to the community.

"The culture of the school," Stine said, "was established through the complex interaction of the external environment and the groups within the school, forming a network with specific goals." Conflicts among some cultures and special-interest groups inside and outside the school led to compromises and agreements that helped define the school's values and beliefs.

The broader societal culture dramatically affects the culture of the local school; violence, homelessness, media, drug use, racism, as well as popular attitudes that disparage cultivation of the intellect are but a few of the influences that intrude on the learning process.

There is also what Goodlad called the "culture of school reform," which embraces a set of expectations imposed by state and federal policymakers, all having their own cultures (as cited in Olson). Likewise, the cultures of institutions that train educators and of scholars who carry out education research in turn influence the culture of the local school. Educators in middle schools and high schools must contend, in addition, with a strong student peer culture that can have pernicious effects on learning.

The Mark of History

Clearly, the school is not an island free of outside cultural influences. But even if a school could be found that was free of these external influences, it still would not be a blank slate waiting for a leader with the vision and acumen to imprint on it a strong and vital culture of learning.

Perhaps the main reason no school is a blank cultural slate is that the history of schooling in this country has written on each school, in large, bold letters, its own beliefs and expectations about what schooling ought to be. Each school is a product not only of its own past but of American education as well. Today's schools may not look at all like the one-room schoolhouses of pioneer times, but Carl D. Glickman, Stephen P. Gordon, and Jovita M. Ross-Gordon see a clear connection: "Discussing the present work environment of schools without discussing the one-room schoolhouses would be comparable to talking about issues in Western democracies without acknowledging the Magna Carta."

Glickman and colleagues traced common beliefs and expectations today's teachers hold about their work to the age when a single teacher in one room was solely responsible for the curriculum and the instruction of all students. Glickman and his colleagues wrote:

> This legacy of independence, isolation, and privatization of teaching remains alive and well in many schools today. Instead of having physically separated one-room schoolhouses, we often see the one-room schoolhouses repeated every few yards down a school corridor. Each teacher sees his or her students, within the four walls, as his or her own school.

To what extent the work environment of today's schools is a product of history or of a natural human preference for working independently can be debated. The point for our purposes is that school leaders who want to create in their schools strong learning cultures will encounter a complex array of cultural forces, internal and external, some positive and some negative, that will test their will, discernment, and patience.

In the next section, we probe deeper into the meaning of culture by examining three levels of organizational culture outlined by Schein (1992, 1999).

THREE LEVELS OF CULTURE

Culture plays a dominant role in organizational life. To define it is one thing; to perceive how it influences performance is quite another. Culture is as complex as human behavior itself. Part of it is visible and understandable; other elements are hidden and obscure. Schein argues that the best way to think about organizational culture is to conceive of it as existing at three levels: artifacts, espoused values, and shared tacit assumptions.

Tangible Artifacts

The artifacts level, the most visible of the three, is perhaps the level most closely associated with what we think of as school *climate*—how people perceive the school. A school's artifacts include its structures and processes, architecture, rituals, and icons that are most conspicuous to the casual observer. Teachers' mode of dress, roll call in class, the bell for first period, and the smell of a long hallway represent elements of the artifacts level of culture.

The initial feel of the school emanates from this tangible level of experience. Thus, people who appear at the school for the first time are most likely to recognize this level of culture. They may experience it as a mood or feeling, a certain style, or a physical presence.

If we want to trace the complex pattern of school culture, we should begin at the artifacts level, but identification of culture at this level only scratches the surface of understanding, offering but a glimpse of the complete picture. As Schein emphasizes, what an observer cannot tell from the artifacts is what they mean, that is, why the principal, staff, and students behave as they do and why the school operates as it does. The second level of culture provides deeper insight into the ideas that guide the school's sense of its mission.

Espoused Values

A truism about educators is that, as people of letters, they value the expression of what they value. School mission statements abound with affirmations of high expectations for student achievement, responsiveness to students' diverse learning styles, and mobilization of resources for the goal of improving student learning.

Educators expect that a list of such values, having been discussed, agreed on, and publicized, will guide the school's operation. The National LEADership Network Study Group on Restructuring Schools expressed this expectation as follows: "Through shared values and beliefs, members of the organization develop a sense of direction that guides their day-to-day behavior" (Joan Burnham and Shirley Hord). If the school has designated respect as an important value, for example, people are expected to treat others with consideration and respect.

Values and beliefs are an important part of an organization's culture. This is true both of values corporately espoused and of those held by individuals. Practitioners bring with them a particular set of principles that form their philosophy of education. For example, a teacher's belief in the value of experiential learning becomes an expression of culture as reflected in his or her actions.

Sashkin and Sashkin distinguish among the following terms:

- *Values* tell us what is right and wrong.
- *Beliefs* are summaries of cause and effect; that is, they remind us what is likely to happen when we act in certain ways.
- *Norms* simply state expected standards of overt behavior.

Values are not necessarily supportive of a school's mission. As the Sashkins explain, "Shared values and beliefs can support increased organizational effectiveness but they can also impair effectiveness. When everyone holds to the same flawed beliefs, their combined efforts may lead to disaster."

Also, values and beliefs are not, as Schein points out, a reliable guide to an organization's culture. For one thing, they are not always explicitly stated. Nor are they always consistent with observed behavior.

One other problem with relying on the values promulgated by an institution is that its members may or may not agree with those values where it really matters, in practice. For example, a school's mission statement may declare that all children can and are expected to succeed, but one or more teachers, when pressed for their own views, may confide that some students simply can't meet the conditions for succeeding in school. In such a case, teachers' tacit values, much more than any official statement displayed in the school's hallway or discussed in faculty meetings, govern their actual behavior.

This hidden realm of what staff members actually believe—consciously or unconsciously—is what school leaders who want to set their school's culture in a positive direction must penetrate. And this brings us to Schein's third level, which recognizes the hidden aspects of culture, those cultural patterns that truly influence the organization's performance.

Underlying Assumptions

An organization's culture manifests itself in tangible artifacts and espoused values and beliefs. But the essence of the culture lies hidden in what Schein (1999) calls "shared tacit assumptions." Although this level of culture is difficult to recognize, it is more powerful than the first two levels because these underlying assumptions, though largely invisible, shape the behavior of the organization's members. "As a responsible leader," Schein (1999) warns, "you must be aware of these assumptions and manage them, or they will manage you."

Shared tacit assumptions are powerful because, as Schein notes, they influence all aspects of an organization's functioning: "Mission; strategy; means used; measurement systems; correction systems; language; group norms of inclusion and exclusion; status and reward systems; and concepts of time, space, work, and human nature are all reflected in the culture" (1999).

Note that culture at this third level does not exist alongside or independently of these elements; rather, Schein insists that it pervades and shapes them. Using the analogy of a human body, we could say that culture is not just an arm or a leg but rather the mind and personality that govern all the members. Too often, culture is assumed to be simply one component of an organization that can be controlled and fine-tuned at will by an astute leader.

A further source of the power of these tacit assumptions is that they operate undetected below the radar screen, ready to trip up unsuspecting leaders who too quickly think they have correctly analyzed their organization's culture but have only identified its superficial elements. Warns Schein (1999), "If you are serious about managing culture in your organization, the biggest danger you face is that you do not fully appreciate the depth and power of culture." Now we are ready to explore some implications of Schein's robust conception of culture. The first ought to be obvious: Deciphering your school's culture is no simple task.

Identifying Your School's Culture

Surveys and questionnaires cannot measure culture, says Schein. They can tell you how individuals perceive the work climate (whether they feel involved in decisions, like or dislike the way supervisors communicate, and so forth) or how well people understand the organization's espoused values. But there's little chance a survey will uncover tacit assumptions, which constitute the actual culture.

Another reason Schein says surveys don't work is that culture is a group phenomenon. Expecting individuals to be able to report shared assumptions on a questionnaire is a poor strategy. "It is far easier to elicit information in groups by asking broad questions about different areas of organizational functioning and seeing where there is obvious consensus among the members of the group" (1999).

Schein lays out in his *The Corporate Culture Survival Guide* a 4-hour group process by which an organization, with the help of a facilitator, can decipher its culture. The language and examples come from the business world, but educators can readily apply the process to schools.

PRINCIPLES FOR SHAPING SCHOOL CULTURE

Schein makes several assertions about culture that have important implications for the possibility and process of cultural transformation. Three of his insights are explored in this section with consideration for their application to the shaping of school culture.

What's Your Goal?

Always have a particular reason for wanting to transform your school's culture, Schein advises. Focus on a specific problem area, he says, because if you set out with the vague goal of changing the entire culture, you will be overwhelmed. Culture is too broad for you to decipher all of it, and it is difficult to change.

The problem need not be a breakdown in performance. It could be a new strategy such as a schoolwide improvement program. Whatever the issue, you'll need to discover whether the solution or strategy will meet resistance in the culture. This requires trying to identify the shared assumptions that could either help or hinder you in solving the specific problem.

Focus first on identifying the assumptions that can aid you. "Try to see your culture as a positive force to be used rather than a constraint to be overcome," he says (1999). Then employ positive assumptions in your strategy to change the negative ones. Here is how this process might work in a school:

Problem to be solved: Teachers experience similar kinds of challenges with classroom management, but they don't get together to share their successful strategies.

Positive assumption: Department heads are respected by administrators and staff for their expertise and leadership skills.

Hindering assumption: Teamwork, though espoused as a core value, is not rewarded or encouraged in practice.

Solution: Department heads develop and administer suitable incentives and make time available for teachers to collaborate on classroom management.

Nothing Succeeds Like Success

Your school's present culture came about because of what happened in its past, but not everything an organization experiences has the power to form a culture. Schein refers to culture as the "residue of success." He notes that "culture is stable and difficult to change because it represents the accumulated learning of a group—the ways of thinking, feeling, and perceiving the world that have made the group successful" (1999).

Schein's insight—we'll call it the "principle of success"—is useful in analyzing both how your school's culture came to be and how to improve it. The principle applies not only to the school level but to changes in the general culture of schooling over time.

Contending With the "Residue of Success"

A couple of historical examples illustrate how the principle of success operates at the macro level of culture. The one-room schoolhouse succeeded in the 1800s in accomplishing the objectives of its originators—to deliver basic instruction in the three Rs to sparsely populated areas. Consequently, a strong culture arose in support of its structure and individualistic staffing pattern.

Now skip ahead to the mid-20th century, when centralized command-and-control structures were put in place in an attempt to make schools run as efficiently as factories. For the sake of argument, we can say those schools likewise succeeded in accomplishing their designers' intent. Consequently, schools' predominant culture over time shifted to support the new design while still having to accommodate the residual assumptions of the one-room schoolhouse era.

Today's educators generally reject some of the values and assumptions that once undergirded the one-room schoolhouse (privatism, isolation, autonomy) and the factory model (bureaucratic rules; top-down, authoritarian decision making; impersonalization). But to implement their preferred vision of schooling today, educators must still contend with the residue of success from previous eras.

Further complicating matters is lack of unity on the particulars of an ideal vision of schooling. Policymakers and educators continue to apply different measuring rods to schools to gauge their success. Most policymakers and many educators agree with the goals and methods of the No Child Left Behind Act, for instance, whereas some other policymakers and many other educators do not.

Both historically and at present, conflict over vision, goals, and means of education has prevented a common, consistent definition of success. This lack, in turn, has impeded formation of a common, consistent school culture.

Shifting attention to the micro level, the same is also true of the typical school. Not only have these kinds of broad disagreements left their mark on each school's culture. So have previous administrations and faculties, whose definitions of success may have been different from those of the current regime.

If you are a leader of an elementary, middle, or high school, the principle of success explains the origins of parts of your school's culture and why you may struggle trying to improve it. Like education at the national level, your school, unless it is new, has its own history. Previous principals and faculties have, over time, succeeded in implementing their own visions, missions, and strategies. The culture you are experiencing is the product of their success. If your vision and that of your faculty harmonize with what came before you, chances are good you will feel at home in the existing culture. But if not, you may need to better understand the existing culture before proceeding with your own agenda.

Of course, leaders, staff, students, and entire schools can "succeed" in ways that run counter to effective learning. Principals can succeed in avoiding the risk of failure; teachers can succeed in avoiding scrutiny of their instructional practices; students, as we will see in a later section, can succeed by thwarting the success of others. These kinds of successes breed and perpetuate their own facilitating cultures that school leaders must decipher and transform into prolearning cultures.

Insight for Cultural Renewal

Being mindful of the principle of success can help you in two ways as a cultural leader. First, it can help you analyze how dysfunctional assumptions derive their power. Those assumptions persist because they succeed in meeting people's needs at some level. Second, the principle underscores a critical prerequisite for cultural renewal: Whatever strategies you employ, make sure you succeed.

If, for example, half of your staff members are in favor of implementing a particular comprehensive school reform and the other half are indifferent or opposed, the principle warns you not to proceed. The residue may not be a stronger culture but a failed program and, perhaps worse, a bitterly divided school. So you must find some other program, strategy, or method more likely to accomplish the school's mission, with the expectation that a stronger culture will emerge from the school's success.

Anita Woolfolk Hoy and Wayne Kolter Hoy, who acknowledge Schein's influence on their thinking, address the question of how shared values develop in schools:

> There is no easy or simple answer. Leadership can help. If a principal, for example, can convince teachers to act based on trust and collegiality and if such actions are perceived as successful, then the perceived value that trust and collegiality are "good" gradually starts a process of cognitive transformation. Over time this transformation can lead to a common set of shared values or beliefs, but the process will proceed only if the actions continue to work well.

If you identify an element of the culture that impedes the school's performance, a strategy Schein recommends is the establishment of a parallel structure. You can bypass the undesirable element of the culture by forming a task force, a committee, or some other structure to carry out the desired function. This strategy also works to neutralize an influential faculty member (such as department head) who opposes reform; you can appoint someone else whose values accord with the desired culture. Just make sure to give the new structure or work group or individual the resources to succeed.

The Sashkins note that when transformational leaders seek to empower followers by assigning them greater responsibility, they make sure to design the situation for success:

> Leaders' sense of self-confidence allows them to feel in control, instead of at risk, when empowering followers. Transformational leaders don't handle risk by trying to maintain personal control. Instead, they reduce risk by making sure that the followers they have empowered can achieve the goal.

Is Culture Relative to Mission?

In Schein's view, there is no right or wrong culture in an absolute sense. A culture can be judged only in regard to how well it helps the organization achieve its mission and goals. A culture becomes dysfunctional when it impedes the organization's mission. This can happen, for example, when the organization changes its mission and strategy and the culture does not change to support the new direction. In such a case, the organization may fail unless it addresses those aspects of its culture that are no longer supportive.

Many educators would disagree with Schein, arguing that for schools, there is a right culture. Schools live in a different environment from the competitive corporate world where Schein's experience lies, educators might point out. Also, despite the disagreement over schools' visions, missions, and strategies discussed earlier in this section, overall, those missions are more similar, from school to school, than are those of businesses, whose missions and strategies vary greatly from one sector of the economy to another.

Despite these possible shortcomings, Schein's analysis offers a useful lesson for educators. The organizational context of schools does vary sufficiently to warrant use of different forms of instruction, teaching practices, and styles of leadership. To succeed in inner-city schools, for example, principals "often find it necessary to engage in more direct and top-down forms of leadership than do successful principals in suburban settings," note Leithwood and his colleagues. Successful principals in small schools, they point out, typically model desirable forms of instruction, whereas those in large schools employ less direct ways to influence teachers, such as planning professional development.

The lesson to be learned from these differences isn't just that a school's instructional programs must fit its context or that principals must adapt their leadership styles to the situation. Of course, both of these assertions are true (though sometimes ignored). The more important lesson is that the school's culture (not just its espoused values but staff members' latent assumptions) must support the entire mix of programs, instructional methods, teaching practices, and leadership styles.

Consider the example of a failing inner-city school where a new principal has been assigned for the purpose of turning it around through strong, assertive leadership. What if it is staffed with teachers who, because of their training and previous experience, prefer and expect a consensus-building style of leadership? Conflict over how decisions are made could worsen the school's performance.

The principles discussed in this section guide cultural leaders in a general direction:

1. If you believe your school's culture needs to improve, have a specific reason for reshaping it, identify the particular elements of the culture that need to improve, and focus on changing only them.

2. Use the principle of success—culture forms as a result of people seeing that things work well—to your advantage by making sure your strategies succeed.

3. Understand that a strong, positive culture for your school will not necessarily be like that of other schools, but it must support your school's unique mission, strategies, and practices.

The next section turns to more specific ways by which leaders construct culture. Keep two points in mind as you consider both the previous general principles and the more specific recommendations that follow. First, do not assume that you correctly understand your school's culture. And second, understand that culture transformation is not a matter of tips and techniques, but of heart, accurate discernment, and informed strategy.

HOW LEADERS CONSTRUCT CULTURE

Have you found it difficult to relate to some of the language commonly used in the literature on culture building? Is it hard to see yourself as a shaman or priest (or priestess), manipulator of symbols, inventor of rituals, storyteller, dramatist, or master of ceremonies?

If these roles seem a little obscure or outside your realm of experience and expertise, perhaps you have responded by losing interest in the idea of culture building altogether, thinking it's just not relevant to your job. You'd rather stick to what you know best: dealing with the realities of the daily routine of overseeing and monitoring programs, practices, and personnel in your school. The truth is, you may be more of a culture builder than you thought you were.

Leaders have been misled by many management consultants into believing that the way to construct culture is to develop rituals and ceremonies, tell stories, and promote organizational heroes. This is the assessment of Schein. Agreeing with him, the Sashkins say in their insightful book *Leadership That Matters,* "Some see these methods as dramatic and inspiring, but we think of them as heavy-handed efforts to impose culture." These methods may help reinforce an existing culture, say the Sashkins, but they don't construct culture.

Constructing culture, according to the Sashkins, is foremost about defining values and beliefs and bringing them to life in the actions of everyone in the organization. People live out the organization's values and beliefs through the everyday routines of implementing policies and following practices that are known to work.

There are three basic ways, say the Sashkins, that leaders construct culture:

1. First, leaders (with the involvement of others) define an explicit *organizational philosophy,* a clear, brief statement of values and beliefs.

2. Next, leaders work with others to determine *policies,* develop *programs* and institute *procedures* that put the philosophy into action.

3. Finally, leaders *model* values and beliefs by their moment-to-moment *actions* and their consistent *practices.*

In their synthesis of research on effective school leadership, Kenneth A. Leithwood and Carolyn Riehl describe the role successful school leaders have played in strengthening school culture:

> Effective school leaders helped develop school cultures that embody shared norms, values, beliefs, and attitudes and that promote mutual caring and trust among all members. School culture sets a tone and context within which work is undertaken and goals are pursued.

These concepts are similar to the first two steps advocated by the Sashkins. Values and beliefs establish the context for goals and how work is done, that is, through policies, programs, and procedures.

The remainder of this section explores the Sashkins' model with a view to its application in schools. The discussion is necessarily limited to a brief overview of key concepts and some options for action by school leaders.

Collaboratively Define Organizational Philosophy

The Sashkins state, "Transformational leaders don't simply impose the values that define an organization's culture. They derive values collaboratively, with followers, and with recognition of the organizational context."

It would be an overstatement to say that educators have attained consensus on the primary values and norms that should guide education. As has been pointed out previously in this chapter, lack of such consensus remains an impediment to culture formation in many of the nation's schools. And when the sample widens to include policymakers, agreement is even more elusive.

Despite lingering areas of disagreement, the vast majority of educators affirm several values, beliefs, and norms as desirable foundations of a strong school culture. If not yet fully put into practice in many schools, they are at least worthy of aspiration. Some of these core values are as follows:

- Creation of a learning community that emphasizes faculty collaboration and continuous improvement toward the goal of high student achievement
- Insistence on high standards and personal accountability for results
- Relationships that foster trust, respect, and caring
- Establishment of a safe, supportive environment for students that addresses their developmental needs and affirms cultural diversity
- Behavior and instruction that advocate and model the core values of a democratic and civil society
- For students, a sense of belonging and a sense of ownership over the direction of their learning

Each school's administrators, teachers, and students, in concert with parents and community members, can begin with a list such as this in defining their own core values.

A school that stays focused on its core educational values can withstand setbacks such as a budget cut, a staff member being charged with improper sexual behavior, or a decline in parental support. This is the message of Jerry Patterson, Janice Patterson, and Loucrecia Collins, who advise principals that agreement on values is vital to enabling the school to overcome adversity. Principals who lead their staffs in identifying the school's core values can, when adverse circumstances arise, then guide the staff in not wavering from those values.

Core values, say Patterson and his colleagues, "become the philosophical basis for clarifying why you and your school do what you do." The writers list these sample values that pertain to teaching and learning:

- We value organizing our teaching strategies around the most current research and best practices.

- We value a school environment that holds all adults accountable for all students achieving at the highest level possible.
- We value creating a teaching and learning environment that emphasizes to everyone that we believe in you, you can do it, and we won't give up on you.

Once values such as these are set in place to guide the school's practice, the principal can use several strategies suggested by Patterson and coauthors to keep the school on course: (a) Resist the temptation to add new programs or initiatives unless they conform to the values; (b) buffer teachers from anything that might sidetrack them from attention to student learning, such as paperwork, public address system announcements, or other intrusions; and (c) model the values on a daily basis.

In addition to all other core values any organization may select to define its philosophy, the Sashkins point to one overarching cultural value for which any transformational leader must gain widespread acceptance: "That value states, in essence, that values are not debatable or individual; they are 'ours,' shared by all who want to be a part of the organization."

Collaboratively Establish Policies and Procedures

As noted previously, Schein holds that shared tacit assumptions influence all aspects of an organization's functioning, including mission, strategy, means used, measurement systems, correction systems, and status and reward systems, among other organizational elements. If culture at the level of tacit assumptions pervades and shapes these functions, is the influence reciprocal? Can changes in the way the organization operates reconstruct the culture?

The answer is a resounding yes. Sashkin and Sashkin explain:

Policies, programs, and organizational systems that carry out "standard operating procedures" are what really build organizational cultures. These traditional aspects of organizational operations may not be very exciting. They are, however, absolutely crucial for constructing culture.

As NASSP's *Breaking Ranks II* points out, "Changing structures can change beliefs." The guide cites heterogeneous grouping as an example. Many teachers will not believe such grouping will work until they get involved. Likewise, the guide notes, teachers who get involved with teams never look back to departmental structures.

Conversely, *Breaking Ranks II* names several structures in high schools that are "absolutely guaranteed to impede change and limit students": tracking students, department-head structures, traditional grading practices, scheduling with short learning periods, and teachers working in isolation.

Structure affects culture, but culture also has a lot to say about which structures can succeed. A principal wanting to change one aspect of a school's structure faces a situation like that of a doctor who must decide whether an ailing patient is a good candidate for an organ transplant. The doctor knows the patient needs a new organ but also realizes the patient's condition could worsen if the body rejects the new organ. For the principal, this calculation is especially critical if the goal in part is to improve an ailing culture through the structural change.

To make sure the new structure succeeds—and guard against its rejection by your school's existing culture—you may need to deal first with some negative elements of the culture.

Principles for Organizing Schools

Thomas J. Sergiovanni has been a strong advocate for a theory of management for the principalship that is based on what he considers to be the realities of teaching and learning. The management systems he proposes in *The Principalship: A Reflective Practice Perspective* are generally consistent with the examples of values listed previously. He stated, "A new theory of management for the principalship must give primary attention to professional socialization, shared values, and collegiality and interdependence as control strategies because they match the complexity of teaching and learning at its best."

Sergiovanni (2001) advances six basic principles (summarized in the following list) to guide the way schools should be organized to facilitate good teaching and learning. When administrative structures, practices, and coordinating mechanisms conform to these principles, Sergiovanni believes schools will respond better to their problems, principals will lead more effectively, teaching will be enhanced, and learning will increase:

1. The principle of *cooperation*: Organizational structures enhance cooperation among teachers, thus counteracting teachers' isolation.

2. The principle of *empowerment*: Organizational structures enhance empowerment among teachers, giving them a sense of ownership and increasing their commitment and motivation to work.

3. The principle of *responsibility*: When teachers and other school professionals are provided with more responsibility, they perceive their work to be more significant and important, and their success is more easily recognized.

4. The principle of *accountability*: Teachers participate in setting local standards and norms and then are held accountable for their decisions and achievements.

5. The principle of *meaningfulness*: When teachers find meaning in their work, they feel intense intrinsic satisfaction.

6. The principle of *ability-authority*: Authority to act is delegated—formally and informally—to those having the ability to act effectively. Organizational structures promote authority based on ability.

Sergiovanni (2001) argues that when these principles are manifested in organizational structures, and the underlying values are emphasized, they function as substitutes for leadership. "Leadership is much less intense and much more informal as issues of control and coordination take care of themselves naturally."

Shared values make all the difference in easing the task of gaining compliance, as Sashkin and Sashkin explain: "Transformational leaders don't have to tell followers what actions are 'right' and 'wrong' or 'correct' and 'incorrect.' They work with followers to develop clear shared values. It is those values that guide behavior, not the leader's orders."

Organize the School Day

Scheduling may seem like a small factor in determining school culture, but in practice, it may be one of the biggest. Consider that the scheduling of the school day affects almost all school activities. It determines how students are grouped, how they use their free time, and what choices they make. The same conditions apply to teachers. Scheduling affects how teachers plan lessons, what they do with their free time, and where they see themselves in the organization. In fact, say Martin L. Maehr and Rachel M. Buck, "Action in these areas is critical to determining and transforming the culture of the school and is an important way in which the learning and motivation of students is influenced."

Maehr and Buck use the 40- to 50-minute class period as an example. They suggest that this type of class is well suited for more rigid didactic instruction. Schools interested in project-centered instruction would probably want to consider a longer class period. This would allow for instruction beyond the school walls and would help students and teachers develop and understand projects more fully.

Each school will adopt a schedule that best fits its values. This is a choice for each principal to make, in collaboration with staff and the school's community.

Select Compatible Staff

One of the principal's toughest yet most vital tasks is selecting staff members who share his or her values and beliefs about education. Nothing is more counterproductive to a healthy school culture than for the faculty and principal to hold incompatible convictions about what schooling should be. A principal who is mindful of culture building seeks faculty members who are not only technically qualified but whose values are consistent with the school's vision.

Effective school leaders go to great lengths to build a cohesive faculty, using the processes of recruitment, selection, and induction to shape their schools' culture. They carefully recruit and select new faculty, and they help teachers who do not share their values find positions at other schools. They use the selection interview as an opportunity to clearly communicate the school's core values to each candidate. And after they hire a teacher, they socialize the new faculty member into the values of the school.

Underperforming teachers test principals' resolve to adhere to publicized values of high expectations for both staff and students. Patterson and his colleagues commend the nonnegotiable stance taken by a middle school's principal and staff. The principal told those authors:

> The only time I see a problem with morale is when a teacher comes here and is not carrying his or her own weight. Other teachers know that they are giving 110 percent and they can't carry any more. They will come to me and say, "He either needs to get with the program or get out."

Model Values and Beliefs

The Sashkins quote Albert Schweitzer: "Example is not the main thing in influencing others. . . . It is the *only* thing." A primary way leaders inculcate values and beliefs is through their own personal practices, say the Sashkins. "They model organizational values and beliefs by living by them, constantly and consistently." In the case of school leaders, a living example can only proceed from a heart motivated to serve the students.

You may be a persuasive advocate for your school's purpose and vision. You may set high expectations for students and staff and speak with passion about your commitment to children. But to make an impact on the work lives of your staff and the success of your students, you've got to walk the talk.

As Patterson and his colleagues put it, "Your passion had better be genuine, because staff and community can see through phony passion in a heartbeat."

Modeling sets an example. A principal who acts with care and concern for others will encourage like-minded behavior. A principal who has little time for staff or students will participate in creating a self-centered culture. The principal who leads by action makes beliefs and values of the institution highly visible and inspires others to follow his or her example.

Our attention now shifts to an important yet often overlooked aspect of culture, particularly in middle schools and high schools. Consider this question: Who are the cultural leaders in your school? If your answer did not include students, you may need to reassess your assumptions. The dominant peer group in your school could be an obstacle on the path to a prolearning culture.

Visiting this topic also affords an opportunity to illustrate how school leaders can apply the principles and strategies of culture formation to a particular subculture of the school.

SHAPING THE STUDENT SUBCULTURE

Helping students with diverse racial and ethnic backgrounds achieve at higher levels has long been a favored goal of educators and policymakers. Other efforts have focused on creating a sense of community for students. These are vitally important aspects of culture, each with an extensive body of literature.

Less attention has been paid to the norms students themselves establish that govern how they behave and interact. Yet peer culture can have a significant effect on students' motivation to learn.

This section suggests strategies for shaping students' norms in regard to academic learning. The final section discusses students' sense of being cared for and connected to the school.

The Influence of Peer Culture on Learning

John H. Bishop led a team of researchers who sought to understand how peer culture in middle schools and high schools exerts influence on students' attitudes and behavior concerning academics. The team analyzed survey questionnaires completed by nearly 100,000 middle school and high school students from 1998 to 2001. The Educational

Excellence Alliance collected the survey data from more than 400 schools located in predominantly white, upper-middle-class neighborhoods in the Northeast.

"Popular students are role models and exemplars of cool," said Bishop and his colleagues. Because popular students enjoy the respect of many of their more numerous peers, "their example influences the dress, attitudes, and behavior of other students much more than the wishes and examples of parents, teachers, and school administrators."

The ability of popular students or another dominant crowd to influence schoolwide norms doesn't end with the power of their example. In many schools, they enforce their norms through harassment and bullying of students who act outside the favored norms. At one high school, for instance, to stop an unpopular girl from asking questions in class, some popular boys humiliated her by standing up in the classroom and shouting, "You're a loser, just shut up and get out of this class." This incident, Bishop and his colleagues noted, sent an unmistakable message: "Populars get to talk in class, not geeks."

Most peer cultures do not directly oppose an academic focus, but many do set an upward limit on learning by pressuring students to spend their time on other things, such as socializing and participating in extracurricular activities. "Peers encourage each other to hang out and reward those who do with popularity," said Bishop and colleagues. Unless students can study and hang out at the same time, they will inevitably spend less time studying and learning.

"The traits that are most often associated with being popular reflect services—telling jokes, being entertaining, going out for sports—that the popular students are providing for their classmates," Bishop and colleagues said.

The observation that students earn popularity by providing services to their classmates goes to the heart of an economic (cost-benefit) model Bishop's team developed to explain the origins of the anti-nerd culture in schools. Nerds are vulnerable to harassment precisely because their lack of the most desired traits—social skills, athleticism, and good looks—prevents them from benefiting their classmates. Students who possess these traits, on the other hand, can be studious and still be accepted by their peers.

Nerd harassment, in this perspective, is a rational, albeit reprehensible, response by the other students, who resort to harassment as the result of a cost-benefit analysis. Harassment is all the more to be expected, the researchers theorized, if schooling is set up as a competitive ranking system, with students being graded on a curve and a finite number of good grades being allotted. Nerds, by hoarding the good grades, impose a cost on the other students, who would rather spend their time socializing or engaging in other fun activities. Because nerds impose a cost without supplying a compensating benefit, they become a rational target for abuse.

Recalling Schein's assertion that culture is a set of learned values and behaviors that persist because they work (the principle of success), we can see that the cost-benefit model developed by Bishop and colleagues is actually just another way of saying the same thing. Armed with this insight, school leaders have a clearer sense of what action to take in regard to redirecting a negative peer culture toward prolearning values.

Strategies for Promoting a Prolearning Student Culture

If you work in a middle school or a high school, research evidence of the type gathered by Bishop's team provides an excellent starting point for an assessment of your school's peer culture. The team's interviews, which sought to elicit students' perceptions, approximate the facilitator-led process recommended by Schein as the best way to decipher culture. Of course, the evidence came from only one study and pertains to only one aspect of the school's culture. Also, the authors present their cost-benefit model as a hypothesis needing further investigation.

With these limitations understood, the following recommendations assume that the study's findings and the authors' model for explaining those findings accurately represent the peer culture of many secondary schools. The recommendations, many of which were advanced by Bishop and his colleagues, are organized according to several of this chapter's main themes.

Know Your Purpose

You want students to reinforce one another's commitment to learning and to study hard. In opposition to this prolearning value, the most powerful crowd of students may instead value fun, socializing, sports, and other extracurricular activities over learning. They may, in addition, harass students whose studying threatens to consume a limited supply of good grades. Your goal is to influence the student culture so that it coexists in harmony with the school's prolearning culture.

Promote the School's Prolearning Philosophy

Bishop and his colleagues encourage administrators and teachers to push hard for their own values and beliefs. If the adults in the school do not aggressively take charge of the culture, students will determine its norms by default. "The incidence of harassment was lower in schools with demanding and motivating teachers," Bishop and his research team reported. Also, "students studied together more frequently, were more engaged in class, and did their homework more regularly."

One strategy the researchers suggested is to enlist student leaders' support for a commitment to academic achievement. For example, try to persuade them to set high goals for themselves, such as admission to a prestigious university. In two high schools the researchers studied, student leaders' commitment to academics helped to set a norm of studying hard for the entire school.

If the strategy of co-opting students fails, you can confront negative values head-on and forcefully insist on positive ones. In straightforward dialogue with student leaders, specifically state what you perceive to be the negative values on which they are basing their actions and explain the consequences their actions have for other students, the school, and themselves. Praise their leadership abilities as an asset that can be put to use for the benefit of the school.

As principal, your bully pulpit has power to persuade and advocate your values, both to student leaders and the entire student body.

Implement Prolearning Policies and Procedures

Bishop and colleagues' cost-benefit model helps explain the motivations of the powerful crowd for harassing nerds. By consuming a limited supply of good grades, nerds impose a cost on popular students. By not being sociable or entertaining, nerds contribute no benefit to other students.

In terms of Schein's analysis, particularly the principle that culture forms because values and behaviors succeed in meeting needs, we can readily see that for the powerful crowd, this peer culture works. Harassment of nerds enables popular students to spend their time socializing and still obtain acceptable grades. The culture formed and persists because it helps the popular crowd achieve its goals.

Policies appropriate to address the situation must go to the heart of the popular students' motivation. The strategy should be twofold: (a) Take away the popular students' perceived need to harass nerds, and (b) make it possible for students to meet their social needs in a way that aligns with learning goals. Bishop and colleagues recommended several policies and instructional practices that accomplish these very things:

Abandon grading on a curve. You should remove one of the major reasons for the pressure against studying: students' perception that learning is a zero-sum game. As Bishop and his colleagues put it, peer norms are more likely to devalue learning when students perceive that academic classrooms "pick winners and losers but cannot make everyone better off." This perception is also the driving force for harassment of those who do study hard. To avoid these negative outcomes, school leaders can follow the researchers' advice:

> The academic enterprise should be and should be perceived to be a positive-sum game in which everyone can be successful. Teachers should not grade on a curve. Grades should be based on student effort (for example, completing homework assignments) and absolute achievement (results of quizzes and tests). The school should not publish or call attention to class rank.

Capitalize on students' fondness for socializing. Let students, as much as possible, socialize while they work on academic tasks. For instance, the researchers suggested that teachers assign group projects students can work on after school hours and that teachers encourage students to form study groups.

This is the same method Anna M. Sullivan observed a teacher of a Catholic primary school in Australia implement in her classroom. The teacher realized that students will create a peer culture of some kind in the classroom and that they especially liked to interact with peers, so she spent a few weeks at the beginning of the school year teaching social and collaborative skills with the goal that the class would work together productively. She sometimes structured her lessons so that students had to collaborate with one another.

Group projects carry the risk, Bishop and colleagues acknowledged, that some students will ride free on the efforts of others and that some groups will not engage the assignment.

For middle school students, a fun activity such as a pizza party may be a suitable reward for hard work. In high schools, the researchers suggest promoting "extracurricular activities with an academic focus such as debate club and interscholastic academic competitions." Plan some time at each event for students to have fun socializing.

Discipline policies also can use students' socializing to the advantage of learning. If students don't study hard or complete assignments, they may forfeit being able to participate in specified social activities.

Institute no pass–no play policies. Athletes, among the most popular students in most schools, will have to meet minimum standards for academic achievement or face dismissal from the team. Once dropped from the team, they will no longer be part of the popular crowd. In this way, said Bishop and colleagues, no pass–no play policies can alter the composition of the popular crowd and redirect the crowd's norms in alignment with academic learning. The researchers recommend that this policy also apply to cheerleaders and participants in other extracurricular activities held in prestige by students.

Model Care and Compassion for Others

Harassment—the debasement of another human being to advance one's own interests—is a brutally selfish act. If the researchers' cost-benefit model is correct, popular students view harassment of nerds as a rational option for attaining their goals. The previous policies are designed to convince the popular students that learning—and encouraging others to learn—is the more rational choice.

These policies will have more force if you and the other adults in the school exhibit and promote prosocial motives. Students would not consider harassment of their peers an option if they began to think of their own interests as being linked to the common good of the entire school community. Since laboring for the benefit of your students—for their academic and social advancement—is your passion, let them see it in your words and actions. Let them feel your passion, and communicate to them that these are the values you want to see manifested in them and all members of the school community.

FOSTERING A SENSE OF COMMUNITY

Many would say the chief task of cultural leadership in schools is to form a community that features collegial interactions among staff members and a feeling of connectedness to the school among students. In the case of students in particular, feeling cared for by adults and having a sense of belonging and engagement with the goals of the school may go a long way toward overcoming the negative influence of peer culture described in the previous section.

Mark A. Royal and Robert J. Rossi say their research suggests that students with a higher sense of community are "less likely to report class cutting behavior or thoughts of dropping out of school and more likely to report feeling bad when unprepared for classes." They also found that such students "less often feel burned out at school."

Similarly, Leithwood and Riehl, in a synthesis of research about successful school leadership, note the connection between a sense of community and student learning: "A strong sense of affiliation and caring among all students and adults in a school is crucial to engaging and motivating students to learn. This is especially true in school settings where trust and cohesion have been low."

Royal and Rossi summarize the elements of community in schools:

In our view, in a school community, communication is open, participation is wide-spread, teamwork is prevalent, and diversity is incorporated. Staff members and students share a vision for the future of the school, a common sense of purpose, and a common set of values. They care about, trust, and respect each other, and they recognize each other's efforts and accomplishments.

A school's size can influence the ease with which these elements of community form in a school. Leithwood and Riehl note that smaller schools, schools within a school, or other personalized learning environments can help in establishing communal cultures and a sense of community among both adults and students.

NASSP's *Breaking Ranks II* lists several strategies for personalizing the school environment:

- Creating structures so that students cannot remain anonymous for four years
- Establishing schedules and priorities that allow teachers to develop an appreciation for each student's abilities
- Creating structures in which the aspirations, strengths, weaknesses, interests, and level of progress of each student are known well by at least one adult
- Providing opportunities for students to learn about the values associated with life in a civil and democratic society, their responsibilities within that society, and the ability to exercise those values within the school
- Offering parents, families, and community members opportunities for involvement in students' education
- Ensuring that the physical and mental health needs of students are addressed
- Providing students with opportunities to demonstrate their academic, athletic, musical, dramatic, and other accomplishments in a variety of ways

The guide notes that implementation of these structural changes provides the shell that facilitates productive relationships to occur in a systematic way in the school.

Breaking Ranks II also lists several strategies to banish anonymity in larger schools. For example, schools can promote opportunities for student voice; hold conferences and meetings in which students take the lead; implement looping (students keep the same teachers rather than changing teachers each year); and place students with the same group of peers, rather than an entirely different set of class-mates for each course.

CONCLUSION: HAVING THE HEART TO PERSEVERE

Cultural leadership embraces a complex set of tasks and requires a refined gift of insight. Thus, this chapter has visited a wide range of topics, principles, challenges, and recommendations. To assist your recall, the main themes of this chapter are listed in capsule form as follows:

- Culture formation is the school leader's most important function.
- Outstanding leaders put the cause and the interests of their followers above their own personal interests. You, as school leader, have a moral duty to advance student learning.
- Each school's culture is a product of its own history and the influences of numerous external cultural forces.
- Some parts of culture are visible and easily understandable; the most powerful elements are hidden and obscure.
- Stated values and beliefs are not a reliable guide to a school's actual culture.
- Shared tacit assumptions, which give the culture its real power, influence all aspects of the functioning of the school, from mission and goals to strategies and day-to-day practices.
- Because culture is too broad and too difficult to transform at once in its entirety, your best strategy is to transform a school's culture piecemeal, targeting the most crucial elements one at a time.
- Schein refers to culture as the residue of success to convey the idea that culture represents the accumulated learning of a group that has enabled it to succeed. You can use this principle to your advantage by making sure that the methods you use to change the culture succeed in accomplishing your school's mission.
- A positive culture for your school will not be identical to cultures of other schools, because each school's culture must be supportive of its particular blend of mission, strategies, and practices.
- Leaders construct culture by leading the school community in the definition of an explicit philosophy, developing policies and programs that put the philosophy into practice, and modeling values and beliefs in their daily actions.
- Structural changes can transform the culture if they succeed in improving the school, but you may need to address first any negative elements of the existing culture that would impede the new structure.
- In many schools, the dominant peer crowd has the power to impose its norms on other students. If those norms run counter to learning, you and the staff will need to aggressively confront the negative peer culture in your school. You can do this by promoting your school's prolearning philosophy and implementing appropriate prolearning policies and procedures.
- Another step toward a constructive student peer culture is to foster a sense of community so that students feel connected to the school and cared for by adults.

Transforming a school's culture is a challenging task. To navigate the complexity, leaders must be committed for the long haul. In an interview by Carlotta Mast, Jim Collins said that being a Level 5 leader "is demanding and requires sacrifice." To persevere through adversity, the leader must care sufficiently about the cause and about the people whose interests the leader is entrusted to serve. These matters of the heart are where culture formation begins and has its fulfillment.

REFLECTIONS

1. Have other leaders you know exemplified the prosocial motive described at the beginning of this chapter, and to what extent has your desire to serve as a school leader been inspired by their example?

2. How might humility, which characterizes the outstanding (Level 5) leaders Jim Collins observed in his book *Good to Great*, influence how the leader might try to assess and transform a school's culture?

3. Thinking about the school (or other organization) in which you now work, can you identify some of its espoused values? Shared, taken-for-granted assumptions?

4. Which of these assumptions facilitate accomplishment of your school's mission? Which ones don't?

5. Identify one or two dysfunctional assumptions held by personnel in your school. Recalling that cultural elements persist because they succeed in meeting people's needs at some level, can you analyze how those dysfunctional assumptions continue to derive their power?

6. In what ways do you consistently model for others what you stand for?

7. How would you characterize your school's student peer culture in regard to its influence on learning? Can you see evidence that students in your school may behave in the manner predicted by Bishop and colleagues' cost-benefit model?

PART IV

The Structure

9

Accountable Leadership

Larry Lashway

S chool leaders have always felt the heavy hand of accountability in the same way that all leaders do. When things go wrong at school, all eyes turn toward the principal's office.

But in the past decade, demands for accountability have reshaped the very nature of the job. Today's principals are not just called to task when things go wrong, they are expected, on almost a daily basis, to provide a highly public accounting of exactly how well things are going. In many states, parents and citizens can log onto a Web site to see the local school's test scores or dropout rates, or they can even find their child's score on the latest math quiz.

Moreover, student progress is not just the subject of casual discussion. It also carries explicit expectations for annual improvement, with the possibility of significant penalties when the school's Adequate Yearly Progress (AYP) fails to measure up.

Nor have these expectations led to a slackening of other legislative and policy mandates. Leaders must improve student performance while simultaneously ensuring that special-education students fulfill their individualized educational programs, teachers have adequate knowledge of their subjects, and students are shielded from calorie-laden snacks.

Finally, school leaders strive to maintain an internal accountability to the values and visions that drew them to education in the first place. Within these values, test scores do not necessarily equate with learning, and children have many needs beyond the mastery of academic content.

Editors' Note: Portions of Chapter 9 were adapted from Larry Lashway, 2001, *The New Standards and Accountability: Will Rewards and Sanctions Motivate America's Schools to Peak Performance?* Eugene, OR: ERIC Clearinghouse on Educational Management, University of Oregon.

All these pressures have forced many principals to reconsider their leadership strategies—and sometimes their future in administration. This chapter examines the impact of standards-based accountability on the principal's role. The first section looks at the nature of today's accountability, and a discussion of the challenges it presents to principals follows. The final section discusses ways principals can meet the challenge.

THE MANY FACES OF ACCOUNTABILITY

Robert B. Wagner has described accountability as literally an "accounting," a way of explaining one's actions to those who have a right to such an explanation. But to whom do school leaders owe such an explanation? And for what?

As employees, principals don't dispute that they have responsibilities to superintendents, school boards, and the public at large. As professionals, they certainly feel responsible to students, teachers, and parents. But having responsibilities is not quite the same as having to justify publicly one's actions and provide objective evidence of success. School leaders today are not just being held responsible, they are being held responsible in unaccustomed ways.

Types of Accountability

Linda Darling-Hammond has identified at least five varieties of accountability that currently influence policy:

1. *Bureaucratic accountability* comprises the web of district, state, and federal rules that either mandate or prohibit a wide range of actions. This type of accountability has a long history in American schools, and most successful administrators become proficient at dealing with such rules. Bureaucratic accountability is ever present, constituting a pre-existing structure that channels decision making in certain directions, helping define the possibilities for change. However, some enterprising principals find ways to co-opt, subvert, or simply ignore rules that block productive change.

2. *Legal accountability* grows out of the complex structure of legislation that simultaneously empowers and restricts schools. This kind of accountability is often routine, as when administrators check to see that teachers have the required certification. It can also have profound effects on school life, as with the federal No Child Left Behind Act (NCLB).

3. *Political accountability* reflects the reality that schools are public institutions in a democracy, which means they must not only answer to elected policymakers but must do so in a very public way. Not only are test results easily accessible, many of the district's decision-making processes are carried out in the public spotlight to a degree that businesses would find intolerable.

Political accountability is often formalized in the laws and rules that make up legal and bureaucratic accountability, but it also takes more dynamic forms that directly influence daily decision making. As experienced principals know all too well, any of the school's multiple constituencies can spontaneously rise up at any time to object to a policy or practice.

Administrators learn to respect the sacred cows and tiptoe around the land mines that have the potential for setting off such eruptions.

4. *Market accountability* is the discipline that results when schools have to compete for students. Market accountability has been a very limited force in American educational history. Private schools have always existed side by side with public schools, but as adjuncts rather than as competitors. When parents wanted something that public schools couldn't provide, such as a religious education or the prestige of an exclusive college preparatory program, they could turn to private schools. All that has changed dramatically in recent years.

More than 40 states now authorize the creation of charter schools, and others have experimented with the use of vouchers. Although some of these efforts seek simply to diversify the kind of educational experiences available to students, most types of school choice spring from an explicit belief that competition will encourage regular schools to focus more on results.

5. *Professional accountability* reflects the belief that there are certain best practices (learned through research and reflective experience) that will lead to positive results. But because students are so diverse, these practices must be modified and attuned to the needs of individual students, something that is only possible at the classroom level. Hence, professional accountability offers considerable autonomy to educators, allowing them to make many instructional decisions.

Under professional accountability, educators, like doctors, are responsible for adhering to recognized professional standards, not necessarily for results. (Poor results may lead to careful scrutiny of the professional's practice, but doctors who use widely accepted procedures are not criticized when the patient dies.) Although professional accountability involves a certain amount of bureaucratic verification (for example, accreditation visits and classroom observations), it relies on trust to a much greater extent than do other forms of accountability.

Although recent state and federal policy has not paid much attention to professional accountability, it has been a part of the educational scene since early in the 20th century, when reformers worked to insulate education from partisan politics. Their success led to an implicit bargain in which lay board members agreed to defer to the judgment of educators on issues of curriculum and instruction. Even today, most board members would profess to trust the judgment of educators on purely instructional issues.

In addition to the five varieties identified by Darling-Hammond, some analysts have recently added moral accountability to the list (Jacob E. Adams Jr. and Michael W. Kirst; William A. Firestone and Dorothy Shipps). *Moral accountability* reflects the obligation of practitioners to serve and protect the children entrusted to their care. Although sometimes explicitly stated in ethical codes, moral accountability more commonly resides in the tacit norms valued by practitioners.

Unlike the other forms of accountability, moral accountability is mostly internal, a matter of conscience rather than a duty imposed by some third party. For example, many teachers feel compelled to spend extra time working with students, even when no authority is requiring them to do so.

Clearly, the accountability environment is highly complex. Although usually expressed as a singular noun, *accountability* actually represents a plurality of contentious and contradictory forces that do not all flow in the same direction. For example, high-stakes testing currently enjoys strong bureaucratic support, but it often encounters political pushback from parents concerned that their children may be negatively affected. At the same time, some teachers claim that standardized testing violates their sense of professional accountability by elevating narrow academic goals above other needs of children. Likewise, some educators object to certain forms of testing out of a sense of moral accountability that sees some racial and ethnic groups being unfairly treated.

Being accountable thus requires serving more than one master. As Firestone and Shipps put it, principals must manage "multiple accountabilities."

Accountability as an Instrument of Change

At the most basic level, accountability obligates someone to explain and justify his or her actions to some other person or group. Money managers are accountable to their clients for making wise investments; coaches are accountable to team owners for producing a winning record; politicians are accountable to voters for delivering on their promises. Implicit in this kind of relationship is the expectation that failure to provide an adequate accounting will lead to some kind of sanction, such as loss of employment.

The demand for accountability is especially high in the public sector, because public employees expend scarce resources that belong to everyone. Public-sector accountability is further complicated (and subject to more controversy) by the fact not everyone necessarily has authorized how those scarce resources are allocated. Stockholders can express their unhappiness by dumping their stock and terminating the relationship; taxpayers cannot simply reclaim their money and walk away.

Despite the importance of accountability in public life, public employees are often perceived as being somehow immune from consequences when they fail to deliver. In education, for example, the image of an obtuse union stubbornly protecting incompetent teachers is a staple of many policy debates. This sort of image, combined with alarm over a perceived decline in educational quality, has led policymakers across the nation to demand better results, with sanctions for those who fail to deliver.

In the past decade, however, accountability has transcended the simple demand for results to become a theory of change. That is, policymakers have come to believe that a carefully crafted accountability policy will not just communicate results but will improve results.

How? There are actually several answers to that question, depending on which accountability strategy one prefers. The following discussion compares bureaucratic, standards-based, and market accountability as strategies for reforming schools.

Bureaucratic Accountability

Traditional bureaucratic accountability is deeply established in school governance. Dating to the 19th century, it provides a way for central authorities to maintain consistency and quality among far-flung local entities. Central policymakers not only determine system goals but also specify operating procedures. Some decisions may be delegated to local officials, but their freedom of action is always exercised within the broad framework of rules. Failure to operate within the rules usually leads to some kind of sanction, such as fines, withheld resources, or loss of unemployment.

Bureaucratic accountability is based on the assumption that there is one best way of doing things that can be reliably determined by policymakers and controlled from a distance. Its success depends on two primary factors.

First, it promises a system based on rationality and consistency, not individual whim or political manipulation. Experts can determine the appropriate pathway and establish rules to ensure that everyone follows it.

Second, bureaucracy provides clear lines of authority—and blame. When disputes occur, they can be resolved by consulting the rules or referring them to the appropriate office. When things go awry, the blame can be traced back along the decision-making channels to find the guilty party. Overall then, bureaucratic accountability provides a sense of credibility and legitimacy to a complex enterprise.

To a 21st-century audience, the very term *bureaucratic* evokes a host of negative images, so it is easy to forget that many of the achievements of American public education came at a time when bureaucratic accountability was predominant. Many a recalcitrant local district has been pushed to adopt reforms, however grudgingly, by the steady pressure of state authority.

Nonetheless, over the decades, the limits of bureaucratic accountability have become increasingly clear. For one thing, control is not easy to achieve. The annals of American education are filled with skirmishes between state and local authorities; local boards often won these conflicts by quietly ignoring state dictates. The state education agency has limited capability to monitor events in thousands of schools in geographically remote regions. (And even within districts, the central office often does not know what happens behind closed classroom doors.) The bureaucratic reach never extends as far as policymakers would like.

Second, despite its claims to rationality and responsibility, bureaucracy often produces rules that are ineffective, overly restrictive, counterproductive, or simply senseless. In addition, officials have often been adept at evading responsibility through ambiguity, jargon, and endless referrals to committee. James Boren once summed up the bureaucratic credo this way: "When in doubt, mumble."

Finally, bureaucratic accountability is compliance oriented, making it most suitable for situations in which there is wide agreement on best practices. At a time when policymakers, citizens, and educators themselves are calling for reinvention of public education, there is lack of consensus on what a reinvented school would look like and what steps will get it there. For that reason, policymakers in the 1990s began moving toward standards-based accountability.

Standards-Based Accountability

Although schools continue to be subject to traditional bureaucratic rules, policymakers have dramatically redesigned the accountability system in the past decade. Instead of just being held responsible for following procedural rules, schools are now being held accountable for results.

Although technically a form of bureaucratic accountability, the redesigned system is distinctive enough to be considered a new category. In particular, four features of the new system stand in sharp contrast to the traditional method:

1. *Identification of explicit standards.* Despite long-standing rhetoric about rigorous standards, the first wave of school reform was not very specific about the desired outcomes. But policymakers in the 1990s reasoned that making learning outcomes explicit would bring greater clarity and focus to reform efforts.

The result was an unprecedented explosion of learning standards in all subjects at both the state and national levels. Robert J. Marzano and John S. Kendall, after a review of national kindergarten through twelfth-grade subject-area standards, estimated that students might be able to achieve all of them if they stayed in school until Grade 22.

2. *Focus on results.* Traditional accountability is oriented to inputs, assuming that if schools hire qualified teachers, offer 180 days of instruction, and follow state-of-the-art curricula, learning will follow. Repeated disappointment with that approach has led to a new accountability contract: Schools will be held responsible not for the procedures they follow but for the results they get. In fact, some early discussions of standards-based accountability held out an explicit promise that schools would be granted considerable authority over the *how* as long as they achieved the *what.*

With the passage of NCLB, the focus on performance has intensified. The act requires states to set specific annual benchmarks in pursuit of the highly ambitious goal of bringing all children up to standard by 2014.

3. *Emphasis on assessment data.* Results can be measured in many ways, but the logic of standards-based reform has inevitably led to large-scale, high-stakes testing as the predominant assessment tool. Since standards are now the benchmark of progress, it only makes sense to measure progress by tests aligned with those standards.

4. *Rewards and sanctions.* Traditional bureaucratic accountability always implied that noncompliance would bring consequences, but significant penalties were rare. Barring overt malfeasance, local officials were unlikely to lose their jobs, face fines, or have their schools taken over by the state. But consistent with the new focus, policymakers believed that results should have consequences.

For the first time, states considered performance bonuses for educators in schools that exceeded expectations and penalties for schools that failed to measure up. For example, persistent low performance might lead to a school's being reconstituted, with its existing staff being transferred elsewhere and a new staff assigned. Although rewards and sanctions have not been everyday occurrences, they have at least created the expectation that performance should carry consequences. Again, NCLB has raised the stakes with an escalating series of sanctions for schools that fail to meet their learning targets.

The current push for accountability is driven in part by a tacit belief of many policymakers that low performance is largely a failure of will. That is, if educators would simply focus their energies properly and apply themselves steadily, student learning would improve. Amid these assumptions, the role of standards is to set a clear target, and the role of rewards and sanctions is to provide motivation. Unlike its bureaucratic cousin, standards-based accountability makes no claim that particular instructional or curricular strategies are the preferred pathway to improvement. Rather, it assumes that properly motivated educators will create the necessary strategies.

These assumptions have not yet been fully tested. Analysts generally agree that standards-based accountability has succeeded in getting the attention of teachers and administrators (Larry Lashway); in most schools, the year's efforts build to a crescendo during test week. Although many schools have made gains, they have yet to show whether they can sustain progress over the long term.

Market Accountability

Market accountability draws from classical economic theory, which argues that in a free-market economy, competition spurs innovation and improvement. As producers compete for the patronage of consumers, they work tirelessly to give them what they want. Some school reformers have argued that the same logic works equally well in education. John E. Chubb, a longtime advocate of school choice, has put it this way:

> Schools subject to market pressures tend to develop clear missions (parents know what the school stands for), focus on academics (parents want to see their children learn), encourage strong site-based leadership (great schools are headed by principals who take charge of student achievement), and build collaborative faculties (great schools make achievement a team effort).

The major avenues for adding choice to the system are charter schools or vouchers. Charter schools, which provide a publicly funded alternative to traditional schools, are authorized in more than 40 states. Typically, state laws allow charter schools some degree of exemption from normal regulations, such as the content of the curriculum, length of the school day, and teacher qualifications. Voucher programs—more controversial than charter schools—offer public funds to parents, who may use them to enroll their children in private schools, including religious schools.

More recently, NCLB has injected a market element into accountability systems through use of public-school choice. Low-income children in low-performing schools gain the right under the law to transfer to higher-performing schools. In addition, schools that fail to meet their learning targets must use some of their federal funding to offer students tutoring from outside vendors. For schools that persistently fail to meet their targets, the law envisions the possibility of a takeover by a private corporation.

The debate over school choice has become highly politicized. Opponents have argued that market psychology may not be as powerful in education as it is in consumer commodities. Switching schools is much more burdensome than switching breakfast cereals. In addition, the theory behind school choice assumes that parents are highly motivated to choose high-performing schools and have accurate knowledge of how schools compare—conditions that do not always prevail.

Research on market alternatives is in its infancy, and the picture is still murky. There are conflicting data on the relative performance of children in charter schools and regular schools, and there is mixed evidence on whether the existence of choice actually spurs public schools to compete (Caroline Hendrie).

In the initial implementation of NCLB, relatively few parents have chosen to transfer their children out of low-performing schools (Duke Helfand and Joel Rubin).

Will the Mix of Strategies Succeed?

Today's accountability, then, is based on several competing theories of change. The system is predominantly standards based, a path forged by many states in the 1990s and now buttressed by federal law. (In particular, the timetable for improvement and sanctions for low performance have become much more emphatic.) At the same time, bureaucratic mandates remain, sometimes distracting schools from the core tasks of instructional improvement. And market accountability is growing, forcing school leaders to develop strategies for attracting and retaining students.

As the current driving force in accountability, NCLB has complicated the picture considerably. The law was designed to build on existing state accountability systems, not replace them; states can continue to set their own standards and choose their own tests. However, NCLB clearly added major new elements: a strict system for determining annual progress, annual testing, accountability for performance of designated subgroups of students, explicit sanctions for low performance, requirements for teacher qualifications, mandated public reporting, and, of course, the ultimate goal that all students would be performing at standard by 2014.

Even though the U.S. Department of Education gradually began offering greater flexibility in some areas, many states struggled to integrate federal requirements with their own systems.

Moreover, NCLB actually incorporates features from all three strategies. Testing, AYP, and sanctions for low performance are key elements of standards-based accountability. The requirement for highly qualified teachers is a form of traditional bureaucratic accountability. And the school transfer and outside tutoring provisions are an effort to build choice into the system.

This layering of different strategies in the same system obviously gives school leaders a heftier agenda. But it also may complicate the task in unexpected ways, since it is not yet clear that such divergent strategies will align smoothly. For example, encouraging students to jump from school to school may create instability, making it difficult for a school to chart a steady course toward improvement. The demand that all teachers demonstrate strong knowledge of content may distract teachers and administrators from the core task of instructional improvement. Despite the clarity of goals in NCLB, it throws educators into an uncharted landscape, with no reliable maps at hand.

THE LEADERSHIP CHALLENGE

Principals, by definition, are middle managers, poised between directives from the top and the daily life of the school. When federal, state, and district officials order rigorous accountability measures, they expect principals to be strong advocates and skillful implementers. Teachers, on the other hand, want leaders to buffer them from the worst excesses of the mandates.

In satisfying both demands, school leaders must become what Linda Skrla calls "policy mediators." At times, they engage in what Eddy A. Haynes and Joseph Licata term "creative insubordination," reshaping or selectively enforcing unpalatable mandates to preserve the underlying goals. Simultaneously, they must patiently work with faculty to develop understanding and support for the policy as well as find ways to integrate it into the life of the school.

They must do this within a system that does not completely support the ultimate goal. Fiscal resources are limited; technology for data analysis is still in its infancy; proven instructional strategies are in short supply.

Moreover, the political rumbling that always accompanies public education can erupt at any time. Although standards-based accountability continues to enjoy broad public support, specific features of the accountability system may elicit opposition. For example, parents can be uneasy about high-stakes testing that directly affects their children, and some have taken to the streets in protest. Navigating this complex new landscape poses a number of major challenges for school leaders.

Developing a Coherent Response

To the casual observer, there is frequently nothing on the surface that distinguishes failing schools from their more successful cousins. Richard F. Elmore notes that in many of these schools, teachers work hard, students are engaged, and the environment is orderly—yet test scores are stagnating. Why?

Elmore's research indicates that the struggling schools lack coherence in their expectations for student learning as well as in their beliefs about desirable instructional practices. The accountability system has successfully gotten their attention, but it has not provided any guidance other than "get better."

Forging a consensus is inherently difficult in public schools, which must answer to a citizenry that has a lengthy to-do list for the educational system. As John Goodlad observed many years ago, when it comes to educational goals, "We want it all." Add these multiple, sometimes-conflicting goals and expectations to the push and pull of multiple accountabilities, and it is easy to understand why schools can quickly become rudderless.

Pressure for quick results leads to scattershot activity that dissipates energy and slows progress. Not surprisingly, recent research on school leadership has clearly and consistently identified vision and goal setting as major factors in principals' effectiveness (see the syntheses by Keith A. Leithwood and Carolyn Riehl and by Tim Waters, Robert J. Marzano, and Brian McNulty; both are summarized in Chapter 2, "The Effects of Leadership").

One of the lessons emerging from research on accountability is that schools are more likely to make progress when leaders focus the school's attention on a few key goals. Robin J. Lake and colleagues (1999) found that schools used test data to determine weak points and zeroed in on those areas. Although this required discipline—teachers had to redesign some of their favorite units—the payoff was more learning.

Robert Evans characterizes the challenge in three words: clarity, focus, and continuity. *Clarity* requires unambiguous communication about goals and priorities. *Focus* means taking one thing at a time and dealing with it thoroughly, rather than jumping from one change to another. *Continuity* is helping staff see that change involves building on what has already been achieved, not totally abandoning it for something new. Leaders who can create these conditions have provided an essential foundation for improvement.

Complying With Proliferating Rules

The early promise of standards-based accountability—greater flexibility in exchange for better results—has never been fully realized. Policymakers have generally reserved that kind of trade-off for charter schools. In most public schools, bureaucratic accountability is as pervasive as ever.

Explicit mandates challenge principals in three ways. First, and most obviously, they limit freedom of action. A state test may conflict with a school's beliefs about the nature of meaningful learning, but it still must be given.

Second, in an era of rapid change, the rules keep getting revised, and leaders must invest considerable time in simply keeping up with changes and determining the implications for their school. Identifying highly qualified teachers sounds simple on the surface, but many teachers do not fit neatly into the standard boxes. Does a shop teacher have to be highly qualified in math if he or she is teaching an applied-math course? Determining the answer may require reading voluminous policy guidelines, talking to other administrators, or tracking down a state official who can give an authoritative answer.

Third, rules generated by a variety of policymakers do not always align and sometimes work at cross-purposes. Under NCLB, sanctions begin with just a few years of low performance and escalate quickly. Schools subject to corrective action must continually respond to each new sanction, creating instability and diverting energy from the core task of instructional improvement.

Maintaining Morale

For teachers, accountability means change, not only in classroom instruction, but in the way they define success. With change comes emotion, much of it negative. Andy Hargreaves, in interviews with 50 Canadian teachers, found two kinds of reactions to change. Change that was imposed on teachers by policymakers was associated with anger, despair, and frustration; self-initiated change was viewed more positively.

For professionals with a strong sense of internal accountability, the imposition of strong external accountability can be demoralizing. The implicit message, no matter how tactfully stated, is, "We don't trust you." When combined with perceptions of unfairness and the lack of a clear road map, the impact on staff morale can be devastating.

Although not publicly quarreling with the need for accountability, many teachers find the current system troubling for a number of reasons. First, results-oriented accountability tends to clash with the kind of internal accountability that drives most teachers. Teachers measure their contributions by effort; if they work long hours and refuse to give up on any student, they are fulfilling their responsibility (Charles Abelmann and Richard Elmore). By contrast, standards-based accountability uses a bottom-line ethic: Irrespective of effort, if you fail to reach the goal, you have not fulfilled your responsibility.

What makes that perspective especially troubling for teachers is their conviction that they are not the only ones responsible for student learning. They argue that even excellent teaching has little impact when children arrive at school lacking fundamental social and language skills, when parents fail to support school goals, and when students themselves decline to make an effort. The idea that teachers can be held accountable for results they do not fully control strikes them as fundamentally unfair.

Another source of dismay is the use of high-stakes standardized testing to measure progress. Some teachers argue that the unrelenting pressure to improve test performance places students under enormous pressure, and they offer abundant anecdotal reports of children dissolving into tears or falling ill from stress as test day approaches.

In addition, some teachers believe that standardized tests represent an impoverished view of achievement that cannot begin to capture the richness and complexity of human learning. They worry that narrow test-preparation activities will crowd out reflective thinking and creativity; even recess is seen as at risk.

Some teachers are also convinced that no matter how enticing the slogan, some children will be left behind, especially those who are already on the wrong side of the achievement gap.

Finally, the sanctions built into NCLB create fear, especially in those schools that consistently fail to make AYP. Even if the school has been improving or if the majority of students have met the target, it may ultimately face extinction. At some point, a whole new staff may be brought in, or the school may be put under the management of a private company.

Turning Data Into Wise Action

One of the assumptions behind standards-based accountability is that assessment is not just a way of judging success, but a tool for inquiry. By reviewing, interpreting, and reflecting on test results, educators can adjust and redirect their instructional efforts to address areas of deficiency.

Unfortunately, theory remains ahead of established practice. High-stakes state tests are not always geared to formative assessment. Diagnostic feedback may be limited, and the results are usually returned months later (sometimes after the start of the next school year). Even with the information in hand, its usefulness may be limited.

Relatively few tests report value-added results (that is, the gain made by a specific group of children). Instead, this year's third graders are compared with last year's third graders, meaning that the apparent gain or decline may actually reflect the differing characteristics and capabilities of the two groups. In addition, annual tests provide only the broadest kind of feedback: Yes, scores went up, but which strategies (out of the many attempted) account for the success?

Finally, information is just that: information. It does not become knowledge—much less wisdom—without extensive discussion, reflection, and collaborative work. (Teachers and administrators can find more detailed guidance on making judgments based on student performance data in Chapter 18, "Managing Data for Decision Making: Creating Knowledge From Information.")

Making Headway

The ultimate challenge, of course, is to improve student learning, which would be a formidable task even without the looming shadow of accountability. Twenty years after *A Nation at Risk* (National Commission on Excellence in Education), educators remain far from consensus on what strategies will do the job. Debates still rage over the relative effectiveness of direct instruction versus constructivism, a variety of whole-school designs compete for reformers' attention, and some reformers argue that simply increasing teacher content knowledge will accomplish far more than new instructional strategies.

Increasingly, researchers and analysts suggest that significant and lasting improvement depends not just on reshuffling the instructional deck but on creating second-order change that reaches deep into the life of the school. First-order change skims the surface of organizational culture by intensifying current strategies or substituting new strategies that can be implemented without major adjustments in structure or belief systems.

Second-order change, by contrast, is transformative. It challenges prevailing beliefs and requires deep changes in values, relationships, or organizational structures (Jeffrey T. Fouts; Tim Waters and colleagues).

Fouts uses the example of class size to illustrate the difference. Reducing class size is an appealing and easily understandable reform, but if the only change is fewer students per class, it is unlikely to have a big payoff in performance. A breakthrough toward second-order change will occur only if teachers use the opportunity to rethink their instructional strategies (for example, moving from lecturing to more individualized approaches).

Unfortunately, the pressure for immediate results that often comes with accountability may push leaders to focus on the "low-hanging fruit," the easily achieved quick fixes that temporarily improve performance. When those initial gains level off, principals seek other solutions that can be put into place quickly. Jumping from one initiative to the next often results in a loss of focus and reform burnout.

Substantive school improvement is a long-term process with an erratic rhythm. Elmore has discerned as many as eight possible phases that do not unfold at a uniform pace. Typically, schools begin with quick fixes, encounter a stagnant period, turn to outside help, experience a crisis of confidence, and then break through to real change.

The leadership challenge is to keep moving forward through the inevitable false starts and wrong turns without being pressured into decisions that have short-term appeal but are sterile in the long run. Implementing second-order change is a matter of developing capacity, requiring leaders to focus not just on the change but on the staff's ability to execute it. Unfortunately, genuine gains in capacity do not always register immediately on test scores, creating the temptation to try something else.

Accountability in the era of NCLB overlooks the uneven rhythms of reform by requiring states to set an explicit timetable, gauge success primarily by one measure of performance, and establish severe consequences for schools that do not make the grade. Moreover, schools now carry out their work in the glare of unrelenting publicity. In the face of these pressures, adhering to a philosophy of "slow and steady wins the race" requires considerable discipline and not a little courage.

USING ACCOUNTABILITY TO IMPROVE LEARNING

Several years ago, Thomas J. Sergiovanni drew a contrast between two competing forces in school leadership. The *systemsworld* consists of the policies, rules, and laws that provide structure and rationality to the educational system; it has to do with achieving efficiency, outcomes, and productivity. The *lifeworld* consists of the school's culture—the needs, values, beliefs, desires, and purposes that give human meaning to education.

Both the systemsworld and the lifeworld are necessary, but they exist in uneasy tension. Sergiovanni wrote that the systemsworld has a tendency to "colonize" the lifeworld, putting the system above the needs of people. (Illustration of this process can be seen in the application of zero-tolerance policies. Well intentioned, they sometimes lead to decisions that violate common sense—such as when a grade-schooler who absent-mindedly brings a pair of scissors to school is suspended for a weapons violation.)

The clash between lifeworld and systemsworld is at the heart of the principal's dilemma. The system, in the form of high-stakes testing, rigid goals, and harsh sanctions for low performance, has the potential to crush many of the goals, hopes, and passions that students, teachers, and parents bring to the school experience.

Viewed in this light, the accountability challenge lies in finding ways to respect the demands of the system while honoring and advancing the lifeworld of the school. In recent years, a number of scholars and educators have begun to identify some perspectives and strategies that can help school leaders accomplish this task. The remainder of this chapter reviews the possibilities.

Accepting the Challenge

When school critics glibly promote a "No excuses!" attitude in schools, it's easy for principals to be cynical. In a way, the slogan is emblematic of the whole accountability movement, which sets very high standards and assures everyone that the goals can be met, but offers no reliable road map for getting there. In truth, most principals would have no trouble identifying half a dozen valid reasons why school improvement is difficult.

Nonetheless, early evidence indicates that improving schools have leaders who have resolved to focus their energies on what can be done rather than enumerating the many reasons it cannot be done. As one principal put it, "We may not like everything about the game, but this is the game that we're in, and so if we're going to play it, let's play it well and let's play to win" (Robin Lake and colleagues 2000).

As used by such leaders, "no excuses" does not concede that educators alone are responsible for student learning or that school improvement requires only a strong back and a cheerful heart. Rather, it recognizes that improvement is needed, that educators must take the lead, and that continual harping on the unfairness of it all is an unproductive distraction.

A no-excuses attitude also does not prevent leaders from quietly educating policymakers and the public about how difficult the journey will be or how it may endanger the welfare of certain students. There are abundant reasons to criticize features of the current accountability systems. But such criticism usually carries more credibility when expressed by those who are making a good-faith effort to implement the policy.

Surveying the Landscape

Given the complex, multilayered nature of accountability, each school operates in a unique context, one that differs at least slightly from others in the district and that may differ dramatically from schools in other states or other communities. NCLB tends to level the playing field somewhat, but even if the rules are the same, the dynamic interplay of policies, values, and environmental pressures will lead to differing sets of priorities.

In one district, failure to make AYP may put a principal's job at risk; in another, the board may be satisfied with a good-faith effort. Similarly, different constituencies may interpret accountability in different ways. The local business community may focus solely on bottom-line performance, whereas parents may temper their support with concerns about the effects on children. For example, parents in Tacoma, Washington, urged the school board to mandate daily recess periods rather than leave it to the discretion of principals; they were worried that testing might put children under undue stress (Debby Abe).

An effective accountability effort grows from a thorough understanding of who is demanding what, as well as knowledge of the resources available. The following questions can generate essential information:

- How is performance being measured? What particular knowledge and skills must students acquire?
- How well is the school's curriculum aligned with the expectations?
- How has the school performed in the past? What are the areas of strength and weakness?
- What targets must be met to demonstrate AYP?
- What improvement efforts have already been made? What initiatives have been successful or unsuccessful? How have they been viewed by faculty?
- How do various constituencies view accountability? Are board members, central office staff, parents, and community members overtly enthusiastic about accountability or just responding to federal and state mandates? What community partnerships have been established or could be established?
- What resources have been allocated to improve performance? What additional resources are needed?

Building a Local Accountability System

Given the profusion of state and federal mandates, development of a local accountability system may seem entirely superfluous. Why add expectations to an already overburdened system? The reason goes to the heart of Sergiovanni's distinction between the lifeworld and the systemsworld.

When outside authorities impose requirements that appear irrelevant or hostile to the beliefs and values of teachers, the result is stress, frustration, and resistance. Hargreaves found that teachers were much more comfortable with change when it was self-initiated rather than imposed. However, even mandates were well-received if they allowed teachers to continue to act on the goals and values they brought to the classroom. The implication is that when external mandates are integrated into a local framework, they are more likely to be accepted.

Eric W. Crane, Stanley Rabinowitz, and Joy Zimmerman note that accountability policies are most effective when they "grow out of local needs, establish reachable goals, inform school reform, and reward outcomes that are prized locally."

Admittedly, some conflicts may be irreconcilable. If teachers are committed to the development of critical-thinking skills and the state test focuses on narrow factual knowledge, they are unlikely to see the test as anything other than a necessary evil. But if the state test is portrayed as only one part of the local accountability effort, its impact on morale is likely to be less severe. If the district also tracks and publicizes advances in critical thinking, teachers are more likely to believe that those goals are still valued.

Federal and state accountability typically focuses on academic achievement as measured by large-scale tests. Ken Jones has suggested that a locally designed accountability system can provide balance to one-dimensional mandates by addressing the physical and emotional well-being of students, the degree to which teacher learning is supported, equity and access to learning opportunities for all students, and the extent to which schools are involved in continual improvement efforts.

Douglas Reeves, advocating "holistic accountability systems," likewise points to districts that measure such diverse factors as the percentage of students scoring proficient or higher on school-based assessments, the percentage of assessments that require use of technology, the percentage of students involved in community service, and the percentage of students involved in visual or performing arts.

By creating their own system, schools can showcase their strengths and demonstrate progress on a wide array of indicators. Those measures may not impress state and federal policymakers, but they will create better understanding within the district.

Keeping Assessment in Perspective

Without question, assessment is the most salient feature of today's accountability systems, the component that grabs attention, makes headlines, and casts its shadow over the entire school year. And sometimes schools make it that way, as they implement a schoolwide countdown to test day, put other activities aside to drill for the test, and hold pep assemblies to squeeze the last bit of motivation from students.

But more frequently, teachers and principals are ambivalent about testing. They recognize the potential value of the data but fear the side effects of overemphasizing one measure of learning. They worry that tests will narrow the curriculum, that students already at risk will be further imperiled, that students will suffer unhealthy stress because of test pressures, and that the tests will fail to capture the wide range of their efforts during the year. And most of all, they fear failure.

Nor are they alone in their concerns. Many test experts also believe that large-scale, high-stakes tests do not bring the promised benefits, such as increased motivation and accurate information about performance. Rick Stiggins says little research indicates that large-scale tests positively influence student learning. He cites the observation of Lorrie Shepard:

> Under intense political pressure, testing scores are likely to go up without a corresponding increase in student learning. In fact, distortions in what and how students are taught may actually decrease students' conceptual understanding.

Nonetheless, state-mandated tests are not going away soon, and managing them effectively is a key leadership task. Two perspectives provide a solid foundation for these efforts:

1. *View assessment broadly.* The annual state-mandated test is not an assessment program. Although important to policymakers, it actually offers limited data. It samples a selected set of outcomes using a particular instrument on one occasion. Results may not be available for months, limiting their diagnostic value.

Stiggins argues that the most meaningful kind of assessment—the kind useful for improving learning—is found in classrooms throughout the year. Classroom-based assessment is tuned to local needs, provides quick feedback, and can be personalized to meet the learning needs of students. He cites research showing that thoughtful use of classroom assessment has a positive effect on achievement scores.

2. *Use test results to promote learning.* State-mandated tests are usually regarded as summative, that is, they measure the results of a year's effort and form the basis for judging success. If anyone misses the point, state report cards and rankings drive the message home.

Any test also can be used formatively, however, to improve the school's instructional processes. State tests vary in the usefulness of their diagnostic feedback, but even the process of analyzing the results and developing a response demystifies the test and provides some sense of control.

Moreover, state tests are useful in working with students. Paul Black and colleagues suggest that teachers can help students understand their test performance and use it to guide their improvement. Stiggins adds that for students, test results are deeply personal, the basis by which they determine how (or whether) they fit into the world. Leaving a student to silently ponder a failing score on a high-stakes test is to miss a learning opportunity—and possibly to lose a student.

In short, leaders can continually articulate and reinforce the perspective voiced by Ruth Mitchell: "Assessment is information." Assessment is a tool that provides the necessary data to monitor progress and suggest avenues for improvement.

Incentives

Part of the theory behind standards-based reform is that people will perform better if they have some incentive—either a reward for a job well done or sanctions for failure to perform. This seemingly commonsense view looks much more complicated in the field, however. For example, Carolyn Kelley, Herbert Heneman III, and Anthony Milanowski found that the motivational effect of performance-based monetary awards was sometimes muted because teachers did not actually believe that policymakers would deliver on their promises.

At first glance, principals have little control over the accountability incentive system. Rewards for performance are determined at the district or state level (and are actually rather scarce), whereas the major sanctions are set at the state and federal levels. Yet principals must find a way to manage the impact of the incentive system, which is not always positive.

For many principals, the primary challenge is to deal with fear of sanctions. NCLB, with its high expectations and stringent sanctions, puts many schools at risk of failure. Although teachers face no immediate risk of losing their jobs, the ultimate corrective action of reconstitution or outsourcing to the private sector casts a troublesome shadow over current efforts. Even more important is the embarrassment of being publicly labeled a failing school.

In the short term, such fears, though unpleasant, may have a motivational effect. Researchers and analysts generally agree that standards-based accountability, especially NCLB, has captured educators' attention. In virtually all American schools, bringing up test scores is the number one topic.

In the long run, however, sanctions will have a positive motivational effect only as long as teachers can see improvement or at least hold out hope that solutions can be found. Many motivational theorists point out that incentives work only as long as people believe they have the capacity to reach the desired goal. No matter how alluring the reward or how drastic the sanction, individuals who are convinced they lack the capacity will not persist in trying for very long.

For that reason, helping faculty remain hopeful about improvement is a key leadership responsibility. One way to instill confidence is to maintain a broad-based local assessment system. If the state-mandated test is not the only indicator of progress, schools have a much better opportunity for demonstrating improvement across a broad range of indicators.

In addition, leaders can serve as advocates in the community, helping local citizens understand the meaning of assessment results and pointing out the progress being made.

But defusing anxiety over the test does not constitute a motivational program. To bring about the kind of difficult transformational change that accountability demands, leaders also have to encourage positive incentives. How do principals manage this task?

One possibility is to work toward a compensation system that rewards improvement. Allan Odden and Marc Wallace note that some districts are experimenting with salary schedules that reflect the needs of accountability. One approach, knowledge- and skills-based compensation, rewards teachers for demonstrating the capabilities associated with school improvement—mastering new curricula, achieving National Board status, taking on leadership responsibilities, and so forth. A second approach, school-based performance awards, provides bonuses to the whole faculty when student performance improves.

Odden and Wallace concede that not all these experiments have gone smoothly, either because of teacher opposition or because funding dried up when the economy hit a downturn. They point out, however, that districts need not do a radical makeover, but can take an incremental approach.

Nonetheless, for most principals, the primary rewards they have to offer are psychological: recognition, support, appreciation, and the conviction that teachers' efforts will lead to a better future for their students.

Remaining Morally Accountable

Standards-based accountability has strong support among policymakers and much of the public. As publicly employed administrators, principals have an unquestioned obligation to lead the implementation.

However, that responsibility does not erase the demands of moral accountability. Legislation as complex as NCLB will always have unintended consequences and will affect individuals in ways that no one anticipated. When the impact is harmful, principals have a responsibility to alleviate the harm or at least to speak out.

The early implementation of NCLB has revealed a number of morally weighted issues:

Equity. NCLB puts a spotlight on the achievement gap by requiring learning gains across subgroups. Schools can no longer succeed by posting adequate overall results; the gains must be shared by whites, African Americans, Asian Americans/Pacific Islanders, Native Americans, Hispanics, limited-English-proficiency students, special-education students, and economically disadvantaged students. Although this requirement promises welcome attention to the academic needs of those students, it also does little to address the underlying social inequalities that create the achievement gap. Imposing rigorous high-stakes standards without a comprehensive strategy for improvement may just end up punishing the victims, as Stan Karp warns.

Impoverished views of learning. Assessment tends to gravitate toward those things that are most easily measured. Standardized, machine-scored tests are inexpensive, efficient, and easily understood. Unfortunately, many worthy learning goals—some would argue, the most important goals—do not easily fit into that format. Moreover, pressure to boost scores may create myopic behavior that shunts aside content and learning activities that will not appear on the test. In the face of those pressures, principals must be advocates for a more expansive view of learning.

Honesty. Advocates of accountability want results, but when they get results that are too good, too quickly, they get suspicious. Although some of these cases may reflect true breakthrough performance, others are what they appear to be: the result of teacher or principal dishonesty. There are plentiful opportunities. Educators familiar with the test content can coach students beforehand; during the test, they can signal correct answers; after the test, they can change incorrect student answers. More subtly, they can arrange to exclude marginal students from testing or work to keep the number of students in a low-achieving subgroup below the minimum number that triggers the reporting requirement.

The extent of such cheating is not clear, though a study by Brian A. Jacob and Steven D. Levitt in Chicago found a rate of 1 to 2 percent. The number is small, but educator dishonesty gets wide publicity, undermining the efforts and credibility of those who have achieved genuine high performance. Worse, it deprives students of the honest feedback needed to promote academic growth.

Avoiding this sort of dishonesty involves two steps. First, principals should avoid sending messages (explicit or otherwise) that add to the sense of threat that teachers already feel. In addition, they should quietly monitor test results for anomalous patterns and investigate where necessary.

CONCLUSION: A CORE LEADERSHIP RESPONSIBILITY

Long experience with school reform leads many educators to the hope that the current focus on accountability will fade away, as so many other reforms have done. Although the policy wheel will continue to revolve, and specific measures like NCLB will eventually be amended or even abandoned, accountability will remain. Policymakers may move on to other improvement strategies, but principals will always have the responsibility of defining goals, examining the results, and taking appropriate corrective action. In that sense, accountability is at the core of what leaders do.

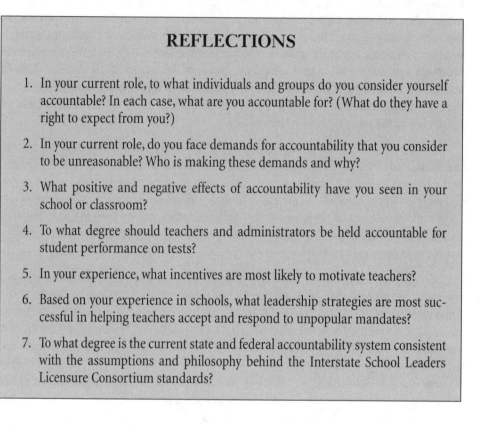

REFLECTIONS

1. In your current role, to what individuals and groups do you consider yourself accountable? In each case, what are you accountable for? (What do they have a right to expect from you?)

2. In your current role, do you face demands for accountability that you consider to be unreasonable? Who is making these demands and why?

3. What positive and negative effects of accountability have you seen in your school or classroom?

4. To what degree should teachers and administrators be held accountable for student performance on tests?

5. In your experience, what incentives are most likely to motivate teachers?

6. Based on your experience in schools, what leadership strategies are most successful in helping teachers accept and respond to unpopular mandates?

7. To what degree is the current state and federal accountability system consistent with the assumptions and philosophy behind the Interstate School Leaders Licensure Consortium standards?

10

Site-Based Management

Wendell Anderson

In the emerging site-based management school, the principal becomes the lightning rod for every change and program that is implemented at the school and assumes a much more important role in the scheme of things.

—I. Carl Candoli

Site-based management (SBM) is a widespread education-reform strategy that goes under various names—*school-based management, school-based leadership, school-based decision making, site-based decision making, shared decision making, school-based improvement, school improvement*, and *decentralization*. These terms may vary slightly in meaning, but for clarity and consistency, this chapter uses *SBM* throughout.

Simply stated, *SBM* is the shifting of decision-making authority from the district office to individual schools. Instead of school boards (government bodies) mandating policy and procedure, constituents (teachers, parents, community members) decide how their schools will operate. Proponents contend that SBM, with its independent decision-making structure, increases school effectiveness and creates a more involved school community.

The basic principle of SBM is this: The closer a decision is made to the student, the better that decision is likely to serve the student.

The fundamental purpose of SBM is to improve student performance by bringing together administrators, teachers, staff members, parents, interested community members, and, in high schools, students and empowering them with the administrative authority to govern their schools. Other stated goals of SBM include:

- decreasing the size and authority of state and local governments,
- increasing local control of social institutions,
- building learning communities,
- enabling teachers to become more professional and effective,
- allowing schools to make decisions based on the needs of students, and
- holding schools more accountable for children's education.

Other objectives notwithstanding, the foremost goal of SBM, and all other education-reform strategies, is to improve student performance.

Whatever it is called and whatever its purpose, SBM demands substantial contributions from school principals, district superintendents, and central-office administrators. It also requires a change from the traditional roles of the administrator as director and manager to one of leader and advocate.

This chapter examines SBM and the roles the practice requires of school leaders, district executives, and school board members. It begins with an overview that includes a short history of the SBM movement, descriptions of various SBM models, and a listing of the components necessary for SBM to work. It continues with a brief discussion of research into SBM's effects on academic achievement.

The remainder of the chapter describes the roles and responsibilities of principals, superintendents, and other central-office administrators, including mention of the vital role of school board members. Also in view are the various skills these individuals must exercise to design, implement, guide, support, and evaluate SBM for it to succeed.

HISTORY AND STRUCTURE OF SBM

For many years, centralization of authority over schools was the norm throughout the United States. The power was concentrated in the district's central office. Figure 10.1 represents the traditional district organizational structure. The movement to decentralize authority in public education began as a response to calls for school desegregation and busing, and it advanced further during the social and political changes of the 1960s and 1970s.

SBM is a natural outgrowth of trends in educational priorities over the past 100 years, as displayed in Table 10.1.

By the 1980s, demands for decentralization in all areas of public life were common, thanks in no small part to the Reagan Administration. Education reformers became increasingly critical of centralized authority. They argued that the real needs of students varied from district to district and even from school to school. SBM, as we know it today, is one of the most popular strategies to come out of the 1980s school-reform movement.

Now, in the early years of the 21st century, SBM, if not the norm, is certainly common. A possible explanation for its widespread acceptance, say Robert Brown and G. Robb Cooper, is its adaptability to different settings and situations.

Figure 10.1 Sample of a Traditional Organizational Chart

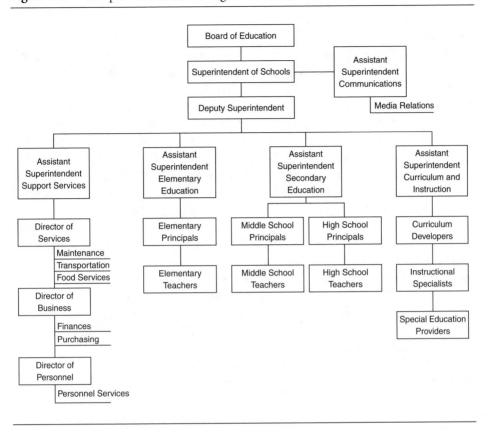

Table 10.1 Shifting Priorities in Education

First Half of the 20th Century The four Bs:	*Since the 1980s* The four As:
1. Bonds 2. Budgets 3. Buses 4. Buildings	1. Academic standards 2. Accountability 3. Autonomy 4. Ambiguity
1960s and 1970s The four Rs:	The five Cs:
1. Race 2. Resources 3. Relationships 4. Rules	1. Collaboration 2. Communication 3. Connection 4. Child advocacy 5. Community building

Source: Institute for Educational Leadership, Inc. 2001. *Leadership for Student Learning: Restructuring School District Leadership.* Washington, DC: Author.

Adaptable Models

SBM assumes a number of different forms, depending on where the decision-making power lies. In an SBM system, Lori Jo Oswald reports, authority for decision making can transfer from the state government to school boards, from school boards to superintendents, from superintendents to principals, or from principals to teachers and parents, or it can have some combination of these arrangements.

States vary greatly in their policies on school district governance. Some have mandated the decentralization of decision making to the local level, whereas others have retained most of the decision-making authority. In this state-driven model, the state government makes most of the decisions on policy and allows districts and schools to carry out that policy according to local needs, circumstances, and culture. Darrel W. Drury sees this practice as an obstacle to effective SBM. Legislation and state regulations may restrict the distribution of authority, teacher-initiated programs, and decision making at the school level.

When the decision-making authority moves to the district, another form of SBM emerges. In this district-driven model, as described by Candoli, learning goals for the entire district are set by the board of education in the form of a strategic plan for the district. Each school in the district develops a campus-improvement plan based on the district's strategic plan. The central office then approves each school's improvement plan and establishes benchmarks and timelines for each school in meeting district goals. The central office continues to provide support but does not dictate how to deliver the educational services outlined in the strategic plan.

Drury points out some of the obstacles to effective SBM in the district-driven model. The central office may limit the authority it accords to individual schools because of concerns over compliance with legal requirements such as due process, employment guidelines, negotiated union contracts, educational equity, and economies of scale based on the size of the district.

In the eyes of most reformers, the truest and most effective form of SBM places the decision-making authority in the hands of the local school community. The earliest design for this model was developed in New York City and Buffalo, New York, in the 1960s, when inner-city parents called for community control of schools. Since then, this basic model of SBM has evolved into some form of a joint community/school decision-making body.

That body, generally called a *site council,* comprises administrators, teachers, professional and nonprofessional staff, parents, interested community members, and, in high schools, students. Figure 10.2 shows a sample organizational structure under this model of SBM.

More Variations

Theodore Kowalski views SBM as a broad construct rather than a specific program. His model has five variables that identify differences in implementation among schools:

1. *Structure:* how decision-making authority is realigned

2. *Flexibility:* the ability to change easily and quickly

3. *Accountability:* the responsibility for the decisions made

Figure 10.2   Sample of an Organizational Chart Under SBM

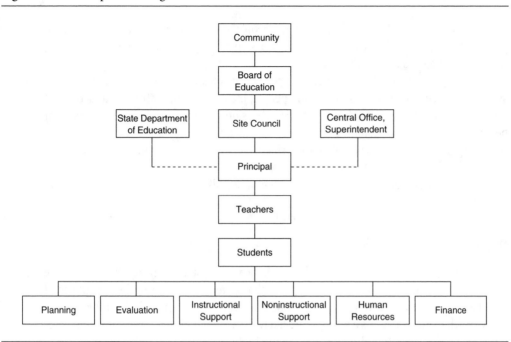

4. *Productivity:* the quality of decisions affecting student outcomes

5. *Change:* how much the concept transforms the school's organization, politics, culture, and teaching practices

Drury proposes yet another model, which he calls *school-based improvement.* School-based improvement (a) stresses student achievement over decision making, (b) emphasizes districtwide change, (c) demands the participation of teachers and parents, and (d) encourages continuous improvement through data-driven decision making.

Principles of SBM

Regardless of the model, according to Kowalski, the basic principles of SBM derive from three assumptions about school improvement: (a) Meaningful change is most likely to happen at the school level rather than at the district or state level; (b) for change to happen, individual schools must be free to implement broad policies and goals; and (c) shared decision making creates a sense of community and commitment to change.

Kowalski adds to this foundation the following general principles of SBM: (a) Educational improvement must be the key component and driving force of every SBM program, (b) a long-term commitment by all participants is required to ensure the effectiveness of an SBM program, (c) participants are more committed to decisions they were involved in than to decisions handed down to them, and (d) those closest to students have the best information about students' needs and capabilities and are most committed to their academic accomplishments.

PARTICIPANTS

The success of any SBM program relies on the people involved. The principal, in particular, plays a crucial part in SBM. (More detailed discussion of the principal's and other administrators' roles appears later in the chapter.)

For all participants, SBM demands a change in roles prescribed by the traditional system. Such change is difficult for some people, including administrators, to accept. At the school level, Deanna Woods says, sharing decision making means stakeholders must be willing to share responsibilities as well, which means not only assuming but also surrendering responsibilities. One job of the principal is to help participants ease into, thrive in, and contribute in their new roles.

The next sections discuss the stakeholders in an SBM program and their potential contributions to the process.

Parents

Parents are, perhaps, the stakeholders with the most vested interest in the school. The Institute for Educational Leadership reports that parents seem to be better informed about and less satisfied with public education than are other community members, especially in urban areas. Parents are also more likely than other community members to voice opinions on decisions that directly affect their children.

Parents have much to contribute to the educational effort overall and SBM in particular through a number of support activities, Candoli points out. These activities include volunteering at the school, helping teachers in the classroom, evaluating programs, serving on site councils and advisory committees, and providing general support for the school.

Community Members

Candoli points out that the community really owns the schools and that community members have a participatory right to be a part of the schools' governance and decision-making structures. Before a serious effort toward SBM is attempted, says Candoli, the community should be informed of the process and invited to participate in the final definition of SBM for its district and individual schools.

Many community members might agree with these expectations, even if they have no children in the schools. Business leaders, in particular, are demanding more from schools and becoming more involved with public education.

As "critical friends," at-large community members contribute to the school in a number of ways. They provide expertise on topics in which they have special knowledge, help inform curriculum, supply resources, and participate in external advisory groups and site councils.

State Department of Education

In some states, the department of education initiates the movement toward SBM because state law requires it. Involvement may be heavy or light, depending on the state's philosophy and policies.

State involvement can be an obstacle to effective SBM, according to some of its advocates. Although certain laws and rules are necessary to protect students, some, by their statutory nature, may restrict the implementation of SBM at the school level.

A light touch, on the other hand, can bolster the SBM process. State departments of education can encourage and assist local districts and schools by providing resources and support for planning, evaluating, and staff development.

Candoli asserts that for SBM to succeed, the state department of education must, at times, overlook deviations from state mandates that may be irrelevant to a particular school's practice of SBM. If a school were to respond to a situation in a way not strictly in accordance with state policy, the state department could veto that school's decisions and conceivably suppress its SBM effort. Candoli believes the school needs the flexibility to react to certain circumstances without consulting the state manual of policies and procedures.

Board of Education

The local board of education does not become obsolete in the movement toward SBM. On the contrary, the board can be extremely useful in many ways in supporting SBM. In Drury's model, for instance, board members:

- create the district's vision of a successful learning environment;
- provide structures, programs, and resources to sustain quality decision making and continuous improvement;
- demand accountability from schools;
- determine ways to measure success and establish a system of rewards and consequences;
- serve as advocates for the schools in political and business arenas; and
- serve as a bridge between the school and the community.

Drury also notes that boards can impede SBM efforts. Some board members may limit school-level decision making because they view the SBM approach as contrary to their philosophy of educational management or perceive it as a threat to their authority.

School Support Staff

Support staff members, both professional and nonprofessional, are integral to the success of SBM. In an SBM environment, professionals and paraprofessionals who provide career guidance, academic counseling, tutoring, health care, and other instructional and noninstructional services are part of the team that develops programs to meet students' learning needs. Classroom aides, secretaries, and maintenance workers support the learning environment through their daily tasks and often have insights into student behavior and needs.

Teachers

One of the basic principles of SBM is that those closest to students possess the best information about them and are most committed to their academic success. Teachers, who know more than anyone else about students' achievement, should be considered full partners in the shared decision-making process and be heavily represented on the site council. Among the teachers should be a representative from the teachers' union.

Teachers stand to gain or lose the most professionally and personally in the SBM process. Candoli points out that the move from a traditional school organization to SBM forces a change in the traditional role of the teacher. The teacher shifts from being a purveyor of facts to a manager of a learning system. The teacher's new duties include diagnosing the learning style of each student in the class and developing an instructional approach that meets the learning styles of the entire class.

In addition, the teacher must contribute to the creation of the school-improvement plan and assist the principal and community in the development of the policies that will direct the SBM efforts.

Students

Whenever possible, students should participate in the shared decision-making process. Generally, only high schools include students in the governance process, for obvious reasons. Select students can represent the entire student body and actively participate in the work of the school's site council.

SITE COUNCILS

In the basic SBM model, the mechanism that allows participants to contribute is the site council. Virtually all SBM programs operate through some form of site council. This is not a Parent Teacher Association type of activity, nor is it quite the same as an advisory committee. Serving on a site council requires commitment and active involvement from all participants.

The function of the council and the role of members are often divisive issues. R. Craig Wood and colleagues found three areas of contention: (a) composition of the council, (b) matters the council should consider, and (c) who has final decision-making authority. Resolving these issues is another task for the principal.

Council Membership

The makeup and size of a site council, like other elements of an SBM program, vary and depend on the needs and resources of each school. In one model, the council comprises 50 percent community members and 50 percent teachers and school staff, with the principal representing the tiebreaker. In other models, the majority may favor teachers or community members. Some states decree the size and membership of the council.

Research findings by Peter J. Robertson and Kerri L. Briggs suggest that schools with the independence to create their own structure fitting their particular needs, culture, and participants have a better chance of developing effective decision-making processes. External influences on the composition of the council can adversely affect decision making and thus the potential for schools to create meaningful change.

Robertson and Briggs recommend holding principals accountable for all members' satisfaction with their opportunities to participate in decision making. Such accountability, the researchers say, induces principals to initiate ways to invite and involve a broad constituency on a council.

Wood and colleagues found in their research that the composition of the council itself plays a small role in the success of a school's implementation of SBM. More important are the relationships among the members and how the schools exercise their new power.

Council Business

What business the site council conducts and what decisions it makes, again, depend on the needs and circumstances of the school. An active site council may be involved in drafting budgets, hiring and developing staff, approving curriculum, determining teaching assignments, establishing discipline policy, allocating financial and human resources, engaging the community, or evaluating its own performance. On the other hand, the council's decisions may be limited to such matters as planning school-community events or selecting instructional materials. Other councils may merely advise the principal on such items.

Wood and colleagues report that many school districts, because of either established policy or collective-bargaining agreements, limit the authority of site councils. If the site council is charged with establishing the educational goals of a school, the principal may have to decide what role the site council should have in instruction and school operations.

Council Authority

Benjamin F. Wyman found that as varieties of the basic SBM model have been implemented, common issues have emerged. The most common, and contentious, issue is who should have decision-making authority over what.

Wood and colleagues identified three general models of site-based authority. One is dominated by teachers, one by community members, and one by principals.

In the principal-dominated model, the school principal is the ultimate authority, responsible and accountable for all decisions. Principals applying this form of SBM typically rely on site councils to advise them. In this model, principals benefit by receiving input from the other stakeholders and by having a workable mechanism for gaining consent on important decisions. Also, because the council makes principals aware of the concerns of teachers, students, and parents, principals are freer to research new ideas and address problems before they get out of control.

Robertson and Briggs found three problems that hindered effective decision making. One was autocratic behavior, when principals failed to include other stakeholders in the decision-making process. In some instances, principals actually believed they were acting in a participative manner, but the other stakeholders felt their input was being ignored. Another problem was the emergence of distinct factions in the school: departments competing for resources or groups supporting or opposing change.

A third problem was apathy on the part of staff members. Although most did not actively resist the decisions made, their indifference posed an obstacle. These staff members stood aloof from the process, just wanted to be left alone, and put no energy into improving themselves or the school.

Council Detractors

As important as site councils are to a successful SBM effort, they do have their detractors. Some administrators and teachers resent sharing power with nonprofessionals, especially when decisions involve academics.

In a study of decision-making councils in Kentucky, Patsy E. Johnson and Joyce Logan found that the councils were more effective and productive in noninstructional areas than in areas that directly affected student achievement. This finding reinforces some teachers' concerns about parents' and community members' lack of understanding of educational issues in general and issues affecting specific students in particular.

The flip side of the coin is that not all parents and other members of the community are eager or willing to contribute to school reforms. Some members of the community—particularly those who detect political agendas in educational policies, practices, and curricula—are reluctant to serve on educational committees. There are, no doubt, many site councils in which the community is underrepresented because of mistrust or apathy. Some parents, particularly those who may not have had much academic success when they were students, feel intimidated by the school.

In such cases, the principal has to step up by reaching out to the community, inviting people's participation, and communicating the school's vision (see Chapter 17, "Engaging the Public"). No matter what opposition or indifference may exist, the principal is ultimately responsible for making the site council function effectively and for guiding it toward its goal of improving student performance.

In summary, to operate successfully, a site council should have the following elements:

1. *Focus on students.* Even though administrators, staff, and the community may be the most active members, students remain the focal point. A site council must be committed to learning.

2. *Diverse membership.* All segments of the learning community should be represented on the council: district administrators, site administrators, teachers, paraprofessionals, nonprofessional staff, parents, interested community members, and students.

3. *Training.* As necessary, training should be provided to all council members on consensus building, leadership, goal setting, budgeting, planning, teamwork, and communications.

4. *Careful organization.* Successful councils are built around a model of a learning community. The roles of all members, especially parents, should be clearly defined. Principals are active participants but, for the most part, should not chair councils. External consultants can assist in the early stages of organization.

5. *Operational guidelines.* Each council needs to develop its own guidelines and bylaws. Because shared decision making will be the process, complicated procedures consistent with *Robert's Rules of Order* are ineffectual. A committee should be assigned to

deal with policy issues. Minutes of each meeting should be taken, distributed to all stake-holders, and made available to the public.

6. Decision-making model. Councils that design their own methods for shared decision making—always keeping in mind the needs and culture of the school and students—are the most effective.

7. Accountability and recognition. Means to assess whether the council's efforts and decisions are having a positive effect on student learning should be developed. Ceremonies should be created to celebrate and reward group successes and individual accomplishments.

SBM AND ACADEMIC ACHIEVEMENT

This section addresses the central questions of the chapter: Does SBM lead to improvements in academic achievement? Is it an effective reform? The short answer, as with so many contextual factors in education when researchers try to find a measurable effect on learning, is "It depends."

The Goals

Before examining the research, we need a working definition of *academic achievement.* Most definitions rely on success in standardized tests. Taking an expanded view of academic achievement, Richard H. Goodman and William G. Zimmerman Jr. report on innovative forms of school district governance that enable school boards and superintendents to work together in raising students' performance. Academic achievement, they argue, goes beyond performance on standardized tests to include these multifaceted goals:

- Higher order thinking skills, intellectual curiosity, and creativity
- Vocational preparation
- Citizenship, including community service and abiding by the laws
- Appreciation of the arts
- Character development, including an understanding of the diversity of our society
- Physical development and health

The Research

In general, researchers have found either no discernible correlation between SBM and students' academic performance, or they have identified a small but statistically significant improvement in student learning when the implementation of SBM meets certain conditions. Hence, the research begs us to inquire into those conditions on which SBM's success depends.

Patricia Wohlstetter reported the results of one notable study, by the Center on Educational Governance, in 1995. The center examined how 44 schools in 13 school districts in three countries had implemented SBM. The researchers did find an improvement in student performance in schools that successfully implemented SBM. But there was an important additional criterion these schools met. At the same time they implemented SBM, they also restructured their curriculum and instruction.

In schools where SBM failed, Wohlstetter said administrators and teachers viewed SBM as an end in itself rather than as a way to improve teaching and learning. In the worst cases, SBM ignited a political struggle to decide who would gain power to make decisions for the school.

Wohlstetter noted the difficulty of identifying a causal link between SBM and student performance. The presumption that a governance reform can by itself have an effect on academic achievement may itself be unrealistic.

Other studies have arrived at similar conclusions. They have found either no effect on student performance or some indirect effects, particularly when SBM is part of a larger effort to improve the school's learning outcomes.

Leanna Stiefel and her colleagues reported on an impact study of New York City schools that implemented Performance Driven Budgeting (PDB), a 1997 initiative of then-chancellor Rudolph Crew. PDB explicitly linked school-level budgeting and school planning. Schools aligned their decisions about resources with their instructional improvement plans. The study found that PDB had a positive effect on student achievement.

Christina Warden, writing about the same PDB initiative, stated that its successful implementation requires instructional leadership from all levels of the system, along with good planning and a culture that supports collaboration. In such a culture, principals, teachers, parents, and community members are free to link resources to teaching and learning.

Frank Brown observed that even when studies find no relationship between SBM and academic achievement, they can provide useful information that can help schools improve their practice of shared decision making.

When Lynn G. Beck and Joseph Murphy reviewed the research literature, they found that SBM received mixed reviews as a reform strategy. Only a few researchers observed clear changes in student achievement as result of site-level autonomy and shared decision making. At the same time, most researchers noted a link between SBM and positive changes in the school culture or parent or teacher satisfaction with the school.

When schools devote their efforts to matters other than student learning, the results are predictable. In a New Zealand study of SBM cited by Neil Dempster, school boards were expected to focus on learning but instead spent most of their time on property and finance. No effect on learning was found.

Studies of school effectiveness in Australia, Dempster reported, found differences in performance among schools that practiced SBM. The most productive schools were those with the resources to support reform efforts, with motivated and committed site councils, and with a focus on participative management.

Dempster concluded that, on the surface, the research does not support the notion that SBM leads to improved learning. He did note that elements of SBM associated with planning and communication may indirectly influence classroom practices.

Wood and colleagues reported that in many districts, teachers have not been the ones to decide on changes to curriculum.

In a study of site councils in Chicago public schools, Raja S. Krishnamoorthi found "only correlation, not causation" between council performance and student performance.

He acknowledged the difficulty of proving or even describing how some council actions contribute to student achievement more than others do. Nevertheless, he concluded, a council free to accomplish its purpose appears to have a positive effect on student achievement.

The Conclusion

In summary, the following factors may lead to improved learning outcomes in a well-designed and -managed SBM program:

- A school culture that encourages collaborative structures, particularly shared decision making
- Active involvement of parents and other community members in student learning and management of the school
- An active and committed site council focused on student learning and unencumbered by external authorities
- Teachers fully involved in decisions affecting curriculum and classroom practices
- Student-centered rather than teacher-driven instruction
- Adequate resources managed at the site level
- Strong instructional leadership from the school principal

ROLE OF THE PRINCIPAL IN SBM

By all accounts, the principal is the star of an SBM production. The leadership abilities, personal characteristics, and attitudes of the principal can be the difference between a hit and a flop. SBM, compared with a more hierarchical organizational structure, heaps a completely new set of demands on the principal. These new demands, especially of time and accountability, have helped to restructure the principalship.

This section addresses the principal's role in SBM. A general discussion of the skills principals must exercise for SBM to work is followed by a more detailed examination of the principal's role in three areas under SBM: accountability, student learning, and staff development.

Prerequisite Skills

The principal is the most important figure in an SBM effort. Candoli says the principal must be flexible, cooperative, and accommodating; operate from a set of personal values; and maintain the determination to serve all the students of the school.

Candoli and other observers note that achieving success as a principal in an SBM environment is much more demanding than in the traditional organization, in which the principal consults the district's policies and procedures manual before making major decisions. In areas the manual does not cover, the principal has the central office to fall back on for guidance.

Under SBM, the principal, not always the manual, decides what is best for the individual student and the entire learning community. Even though decisions may involve other school personnel and members of the community, the principal is ultimately responsible. This level of responsibility and autonomy requires self-confidence and courage. Drury cites the principal's fear of increased responsibility and accountability as one of the obstacles to effective SBM.

The principal's attitude toward shared decision making often determines the success of the process, Wyman concluded. If the principal is not an active and visible participant and advocate, teachers and parents may not take the SBM process seriously.

According to a study of Kentucky's implementation of SBM (described by Wyman), what overcame teachers' resistance to changes in the decision-making process was the principal's resolve to see the process work. Principals believed much more strongly than did teachers and counselors that SBM would improve the quality of local decision making, and principals' confidence in the reform made the difference between success and failure.

Wyman summarizes the findings of a survey on SBM in Tennessee that describes the ideal principal when part of a site council. This principal:

- understands clearly what needs to be done to improve the school,
- seeks input from other council members,
- accepts and promotes other council members' points of view, and
- believes that others on the council are capable of making sound choices.

Principals, like all leaders, are always more effective when they approach their work from a positive point of view. The most successful leaders remove rather than create barriers, build on others' and their own strengths rather than weaknesses, and plan according to what went right rather than what went wrong.

In her guide for school improvement, Woods notes characteristics of principals who lead schools where students succeed. The following characteristics from her list apply particularly to principals operating in an SBM environment:

- The ability to involve others, including students, in setting standards for student behavior
- Active participation in shared decision making and staff empowerment
- Collaborative practices that help establish an environment in which they and their staff learn, plan, and work together to improve their schools
- A sense of self-efficacy about working through others to achieve school success
- The active search for, and support of, community involvement in both instruction and governance
- A continuous push for improvement that is a permanent part of school life
- Involvement in decisions about curriculum and instruction with staff, both as facilitator and as participant
- Respect for their teachers' skills and judgment, allowing them considerable autonomy in organizing and managing their classrooms, and protecting them from excessive intrusion by forces outside the school
- Support for risk taking to improve their school, including encouraging teachers to take risks

Principal Accountability

Teachers may take on more responsibility and parents may increase their involvement with the school under SBM, but principals remain ultimately accountable for meeting the program's goals. Under SBM, Oswald reports, principals must take on increased responsibility for creating and managing school programs and curricula, personnel decisions, and student and program success. Principals, like other successful leaders, must act in ways that acknowledge the "accountability-oriented policy context" in which they work, say Kenneth A. Leithwood and Carolyn Riehl.

Principals should not be expected to take on these added responsibilities without being also given added authority. As mentioned earlier in the discussion of SBM's influence on academic achievement, when principals are given the authority and flexibility, not merely the responsibility, to determine how to meet standards, student performance improves.

David Grissmer and Ann Flanagan, in a study of rapid gains in student achievement in North Carolina and Texas, found that greater flexibility for administrators and teachers led to the improved test scores. They concluded that the test-score gains could be attributed in part to changes in state education policy. In addition to holding schools accountable for improvement in all students' performance, policymakers in both states realized that educators could not be held accountable unless they were given the authority and flexibility at the site level to decide how to meet the standards. As a result, administrators and teachers were free to use a wide range of instructional practices, which appears to have helped raise the scores.

Student Learning

A major component of most SBM programs is the individual education plan (IEP), which personalizes the student's learning experience. The National Association of Secondary School Principals (NASSP) explains that personalized learning helps the student to understand himself or herself better, decide what adult roles are appropriate, and find productive ways to realize academic and personal goals.

One model of an IEP proposed by the NASSP—called the *personalized learning plan*—begins around Grade 7 or 8. The model features independent study designs, personal learning projects, portfolio exhibits, standards-based assessments, and standards-based transcripts.

Computer technologies and the SBM organizational structure make it possible for local schools to develop an IEP for each student. Teachers and staff members who provide professional support are invaluable contributors to this undertaking. Candoli suggests that principals and teachers wanting to learn how to develop an IEP work with and ask questions of special-education teachers, who have long been producing IEPs for their students.

The development and use of IEPs will move the teacher from the role of dispenser of facts to that of manager of learning systems. The principal, as the leader of the learning community, is aware of the technologies and data available to the school and can share this knowledge with staff and interested community members. Under the principal's informed leadership, SBM schools can create focused educational plans designed to meet the academic needs of each student, thus leading to improved performance.

Staff Development

SBM requires the development of new skills and techniques by all staff members, professional as well as nonprofessional. Joseph Blase and Jo Blase, in a study of teachers' perspectives on principals, found that teachers ranked promoting professional growth as a major task of principals.

Effective professional development encourages continuous improvement of both individual and organizational capacities. As such, professional development becomes part of the school's long-term campus-improvement plan, and its design emerges from the organizational needs of the school and the individual needs of staff members.

In the SBM environment, design of training activities is a cooperative task led by the principal but involving all staff members who will receive the training. Site council members may benefit from training in communication, conduct of meetings, problem analysis, interpretation and use of data, conflict management, and other skills useful for effective operation of the council. The chapters in Part VI, "The Skills," address several of these issues.

Summary of Leadership Responsibilities

The principal's foremost responsibility is to ensure that SBM does not become a political football but remains a means to an end: student learning, and not just in the narrow sense of higher test scores, but in the development of students' creativity, character, artistic ability, citizenship, and vocational readiness.

SBM can make the school a more interesting and personally fulfilling place for the professionals who work there, and no one can disagree that a more professionally satisfying work environment is a desirable goal in itself. Yet the benefit for adults must remain secondary to the school's fundamental purpose of serving students' needs.

To maintain the school's focus on student learning, the principal orchestrates the strengths and efforts of teachers, other staff members, and community members toward the development of the school's vision, mission, and goals. This process leads to the design and implementation of a strategic plan for school improvement.

Once the plan is in place, the principal secures resources necessary for the plan to succeed, serves as a persistent advocate for students, and makes sure that all programs and activities at the school serve students.

At the same time, the principal, through formal and informal activities and relationships with all participants, fosters a culture that supports shared decision making, collegiality, and caring. Thus, the principal creates participatory structures, encourages the involvement of others in decision making, and communicates regularly with all participants and school constituents.

Communication, indeed, is the oil that keeps the process running smoothly. The principal becomes a broker of information, sharing appropriate knowledge with all members of the school community. He or she also acts as a liaison between the school and parents, community members, the central office, the school board, and the department of education.

Another vital responsibility is to organize and facilitate site council meetings. The principal authorizes and encourages teacher participation in site councils, makes sure training is provided for council members, motivates members through ceremonies and rewards that acknowledge their efforts, and monitors and evaluates the performance of the site council.

ROLE OF THE SUPERINTENDENT AND OTHER ADMINISTRATORS

The installation of an SBM program at the district level does not signal the dismissal of the superintendent and other central-office administrators. As it does with principals and teachers, SBM requires changes in the duties and mind-sets of central-office administrators and staff.

This section begins with an overview of the role of central-office personnel in SBM and the general tenets that guide district leadership. It continues with a look at specific responsibilities of the superintendent and other central-office administrators under SBM.

Business Not as Usual

In a district with a traditional structure, the superintendent manages all functions and aspects of system operations. In smaller districts, the superintendent may operate like the president of a small firm. This executive/administrator may be personally in charge of budgeting, purchasing, community relations, long-term planning, transportation, hiring, and curriculum development, among a long inventory of other responsibilities related to district business, human relations, and student learning.

In larger districts, the superintendent functions like the chief executive officer (CEO) of a large company. He or she is responsible for carrying out board policy, implementing federal and state mandates, and providing leadership to the organization. The CEO/superintendent is aided by a staff of vice-presidents and midlevel administrators.

As do vice-presidents in business, central-office staff members specialize in the many domains that compose the organization of the district. Highly trained and experienced, these specialists are rightfully proud of their expertise and contributions to the system.

When a district operating under a traditional form of governance decentralizes and reorganizes, the superintendent and other central-office administrators suddenly find themselves as part of larger cast. Now, instead of appearing in a starring role, they must make the transition to a supporting role. A shift to SBM may mean a shift in job function, which, for many administrators, requires a shift in self-concept, attitude, and career goals.

It appears, Candoli says, that members of the central-office staff have much to lose from the implementation of the SBM organizational structure. The new structure may require some specialists to become generalists, to relinquish authority over their area of expertise, to support rather than direct operations, to work as team members rather than as freelancers, and to give up certain perquisites. For some administrators, this amounts to a loss of power and status in the system.

SBM requires the active cooperation and participation of the central office. Wood and colleagues found that central-office staff members who see themselves in positions of support rather than control and who regard the schools as clients rather than subordinates more willingly accept decentralized decision making.

Central-office staff members must become accomplished planners, evaluators, and support personnel, Candoli insists. If central-office administrators do not or cannot accept their new roles, SBM cannot succeed. Willingly or unwillingly, the central staff can undermine the entire process.

The Superintendent's Role

As the principal provides necessary leadership for SBM to succeed in the school, so the superintendent must provide appropriate leadership for SBM to succeed in the entire district. This requires that the superintendent assume several diverse roles. Goodman and Zimmerman suggest that the title "superintendent of schools" be changed to "superintendent of education," because SBM calls for broad community support for all children, not only the management of schools.

Chief Supporter

As Angela M. Sewal pointed out, effective leaders provide vision, direction, and support. For the school superintendent, this means accommodating the board of education, principals, and the community in developing the district's instructional goals. It is up to the superintendent to ensure that the entire learning community focuses on student achievement. Through words and actions, the superintendent must convey the importance of high-quality teaching, adequate resources, and parental involvement.

Change Agent

The superintendent facilitates change in the district, which includes prodding those not open to change. The superintendent's primary task, Candoli says, is to prepare the central-office staff and the board of education for the changes that SBM brings. Members of these two bodies will have to welcome new responsibilities and behaviors.

Central-office staff's responsibilities change from directing the system and programs to supporting schools as they develop and implement their plans to meet the needs of their students. Candoli believes that helping staff make this transition is the most important and difficult task the superintendent faces when the district commits to SBM.

With the superintendent's input, the school board develops policies that make the development and implementation of SBM a smooth process. The superintendent can also help board members understand the changes they will need to make in their practices and expectations so that SBM can proceed.

Communicator

In this era of accountability, the superintendent must communicate the district's goals, public business, successes, and failures to a wide audience. The organizational principles of SBM make it even more imperative for superintendents to maintain open two-way communication with their staff, the principals in their charge, the board, and the larger community. Superintendents do not withhold information to build their power but share appropriate information with those who are responsible for the operation of schools and programs in the district.

Nor do superintendents avoid their constituents. They allow principals, in particular, direct access at all times. They welcome dialogue, create opportunities and forums for sharing ideas, and ensure the central-office staff are also open to communication.

Team Player

SBM thrives on the team concept, culminating in the practice of shared governance. Nowhere is the idea of shared governance more prominent than in the superintendent's relationship with the school board. For SBM to succeed across the district, the board and superintendent must become a leadership team with a shared purpose and commitment to student success.

Goodman and Zimmerman list five areas in which the superintendent and board work together as a team to implement SBM in the district:

1. *Unity*: The team leads the district to the fulfillment of its educational goals.

2. *Vision*: The team encourages the community and school staffs to create and continually develop a shared vision for all students.

3. *Structure*: The team establishes policy, builds a management plan, and provides the financial resources to sustain the vision.

4. *Accountability*: The team devises measures to evaluate the SBM program and reports on progress to the public.

5. *Advocacy*: The team becomes a champion for students by fighting for the resources to maintain quality education and by celebrating the accomplishments of principals, teachers, and students.

Planner

Under SBM, the superintendent's role as a planner is even more important than it is in a traditional system, Candoli says. Under SBM, the central office develops plans to direct, advise, or assist individual schools in implementing the district's strategic goals and educational objectives. As individual schools develop their improvement plans, the superintendent, along with central-office staff, interprets and evaluates those plans to make sure they align with the district's master plan. This process requires superior planning skills.

Information Broker

The central office, with the superintendent's guidance, provides district schools with the latest information on teaching, learning, child development, educational technology, health and wellness, and other subjects that can affect student performance. In larger districts, research analysts and writers in the central office keep principals and teachers apprised of current research findings and best practices.

Data technologies have become an essential asset for district and school improvement processes. The superintendent and staff can provide, through reports and the district Web site, a steady flow of information about each school's work and its outcomes. School personnel can use data to track student achievement, guide professional development, link interventions to results, create school-improvement plans, and decide on resource allocations.

Mediator

The shared-governance aspect of SBM means that a lot of people are involved in the planning, evaluating, and decision-making processes. When people work together, differences in opinions and styles can escalate into disputes. Under SBM, the central office becomes the court of appeals, the mediator of disagreements.

Central-office staff must be able to help people avoid misunderstandings, work through conflicts, and settle disputes. The superintendent and staff can model and teach such skills as listening with an open mind, being able to see the big picture, and having the courage to make and stand by one's judgments.

Development Coordinator

The role of the central office in personnel matters has traditionally been that of hiring, firing, and evaluating staff. Under SBM, many of those functions shift to the school. The district's human-resource office still has an important function: providing professional development, particularly for principals and central-office administrators.

Training for administrators should emphasize the instructional needs of students and secondarily address the career aspirations of administrators. It is the superintendent's job to assess the training needs of administrators and supply the training. (See Chapter 5, "Developing School Leaders," for more information about the forms this training can take.)

Summary of the Superintendent's Leadership Responsibilities

The Institute for Educational Leadership describes three related and complementary types of district leadership: organizational, public, and instructional. The following list of some of the primary responsibilities of superintendents under those three types of leadership incorporates the recommendations of various researchers and analysts:

Organizational Leadership

- Provide vision, direction, and support to the school board and to principals.
- Build organizational systems to support student learning.
- Maintain a professional climate.
- Prepare central-office staff and the board of education for change.
- Develop programs of communitywide collaborative leadership.
- Authorize the transfer of budget and personnel decisions to individual schools.

- Create an accounting system that provides revenue and expenditure information to individual schools.
- Serve as CEO to the board of education.
- Form and maintain a working team composed of the superintendent and the board.
- Build and maintain solid working relationships with the board of education and principals.
- With the board, create policies for the district.
- Design and advocate a districtwide plan for academic improvement.
- Evaluate campus-improvement plans and assist schools as they design and implement their plans in accordance with the districtwide plan.
- Hold central-office staff accountable for satisfying their responsibilities to the schools.

Public Leadership

- Maintain good relationships with local and regional media.
- Communicate policy and progress to the community.
- Be available to the board, principals, and the community as a whole.
- Create opportunities for dialogue with constituents.
- Represent the educational community in civic, political, and business arenas.
- Participate in community events.
- Join and participate in local civic, business, and fraternal associations.

Instructional Leadership

- Ensure that the entire learning community maintains its focus on student improvement.
- Ensure that schools invest in ongoing professional development and training for administrators, teachers, and other staff members.
- Provide data on student demographics and progress to the schools.
- Stay informed of educational policy and trends in teaching, learning, and child development; share this information with principals and teachers.
- Follow through in a timely manner on every promise made to schools.
- Work with central-office staff, principals, and teachers to plan curriculum.
- Create, maintain, and monitor a safe, friendly, and inclusive learning environment for all students.
- Develop a structure of awards and compensation for administrators, teachers, and other staff members.

CONCLUSION: LEADERS' COMMITMENT DRIVES CHANGE

Born of the social changes of the 1960s and 1970s, SBM is now a widespread school-reform measure. From all indications, SBM, in all its variations, will be an important part of the American public education system for years to come. Its adaptability is one of its strengths. Innovative administrators can shape the basic model of SBM to fit the unique circumstances and culture of their district or school.

As popular as SBM may be, it still has not conclusively proved itself an effective tool for improving academic achievement. Research results are mixed. Although some evidence points to improved test scores in districts and schools that have implemented SBM as part of an overall plan to elevate student learning, there is no way to establish cause and effect. SBM may have an indirect, beneficial, but small effect on student performance. Districts whose schools can focus on academic achievement and have the autonomy to determine their own academic goals and manage their own resources are most likely to see improvement.

One fact of SBM is quite clear: Administrators are the key to a successful program. Principals, superintendents, and central-office administrators who are creative, who are willing to take on responsibility, and who believe in and practice participative management drive the process. The role of the administrator in an SBM environment, compared with his or her role in a traditional structure, changes from that of manager to leader, director to supporter.

Change is the central concept that school and district leaders must grasp, actuate, defend, and evaluate under SBM. The leader becomes the chief change agent for the district or school. At the same time, SBM has had a profound influence on the very nature of the job of educational leader. SBM's demands for time, multifarious leadership skills, and increased responsibilities have helped shape the modern principalship and superintendency.

REFLECTIONS

1. Why or why not does shared decision making seem to you be an effective form of governance for a school district? For a school?

2. What are the vulnerabilities and weaknesses of an SBM system? Are these weaknesses inherent? How would you try to overcome them?

3. As a school principal, how willing would you be to trust and accept judgments on instructional issues from members of the community who are not educators?

4. How would you deal with teachers and other school staff members who refuse to participate in SBM or any school-improvement program?

5. What school-level noninstructional structures, policies, and practices might enhance student performance?

6. What personal and professional knowledge and skills do you think you should add to your own repertoire to better equip you to serve as an effective leader in an SBM environment?

11

Distributed Leadership

Larry Lashway

Principals face a wide range of expectations that can change rapidly and are not always mutually consistent. In the past decade, for example, school leaders have been at the center of the drive for accountability. Policymakers want schools to show results, and principals are expected to step up, take charge, and lead the school to success.

At the same time, a growing body of opinion wants principals to be collaborative and share their power. For some, this is counterintuitive: Stricter accountability seems to call for tighter control. Yet many scholars of leadership agree with Warren Bennis that organizations operate at half speed because they continue to believe that leadership must be heroic:

> We cling to the myth of the Lone Ranger that great things are accomplished by a larger-than-life individual shouting commands, giving direction, inspiring the troops, sounding the tocsin, decreeing the compelling vision, leading the way and changing paradigms with brio and shimmer.

Bennis and many others now argue that 21st-century leadership must come from everyone in the organization and that formal leaders must adopt very different ways of operating. This new conception of leadership goes by many names, but most recent discussions have used the label "distributed leadership."

With few proven models and little empirical research for guidance, many school leaders are cautious about venturing into uncharted waters. Yet if distributed leadership challenges conventional ideas, it also offers hope of alleviating the impossible job of the principal. At a time when principals are experiencing unprecedented stress, the idea of spreading the burden of leadership across the organization has enormous appeal.

This chapter outlines current thinking and research on distributed leadership, examines the forms that it can take, and offers suggestions for principals who want to expand their school's leadership capacity. The final section takes a close look at the use of work teams in a school environment.

WHO WAS THAT MASKED MAN, ANYWAY?

American thinking on leadership has often been dominated by heroic images. In a nation that extols rugged individualism and the self-made person, it isn't surprising that we would cast our leaders in the same mold: people who can take charge and get the job done.

Television and movies have often reinforced this brand of thinking. In some ways, the Lone Ranger is a prototype of the ideal leader: He appears at just the right moment, he carries silver bullets, and he leaves town as soon as the crisis is over.

This kind of thinking has often surrounded the principalship as well. It frequently surfaces in Hollywood films, such as *The Principal* and *Lean on Me*, that portray school leaders heroically imposing discipline on chaotic schools with one hand while battling complacent bureaucrats with the other.

But even analyses of school leadership that are more reality based often assume the answer to improved schools is recruitment of take-charge individuals. For example, a recent manifesto on school leadership by the Thomas B. Fordham Institute and The Broad Foundation listed the traits needed for success: leadership, focus, political savvy, a sense of urgency, managerial competence, resourcefulness, effective use of data, energy, resilience, and dedication. Although conceding that some form of shared leadership might be necessary, the authors clearly preferred to place their bets on a wider search for talented individuals possessing these heroic qualities. The manifesto was accompanied by inspirational profiles of principals who appeared to have all the necessary traits to shake up the system.

Rodney T. Ogawa and Steven T. Bossert link such conceptions of heroic leadership with the dominant "technical-rational" theories of leadership. These theories hold that organizations are designed to accomplish certain predetermined goals in a logical, systematic way and that certain appointed individuals are responsible for influencing followers to accomplish the goals.

This kind of leadership is based on authority of position; the only true leaders are those who have been designated as such. They are the actors, and followers are acted upon. Leadership is thus a one-way relationship; both success and failure are attributed to the leader's actions. When failure occurs, the problem is fixed by replacing the leader. In short, leadership is "an aria sung by one prima donna" (James O'Toole, Jay Galbraith, and Edward E. Lawler III).

AN ALTERNATIVE CONCEPTION: DISTRIBUTED LEADERSHIP

Although the technical-rational view matches our intuitive beliefs about leadership, a growing number of theorists have pointed out that it is a less-than-perfect description of reality. For one thing, even the most dominant leaders don't have total control over events;

rather, they exercise influence with whatever tools are at their disposal. Because influence in an organization flows in many directions, not just from the top down, formal leaders' efforts to control events are often countered by others.

A formal leader can give orders, but followers can choose among a range of responses, from enthusiastic acceptance to open resistance. Over time, followers can have a strong influence on leaders' behavior. For example, a principal may hesitate to change the bus-duty schedule out of fear that teachers' unhappiness over the change may spill over to an important curricular reform. In short, if leadership is defined as influence, then everyone in an organization has at least some.

The other challenge to technical-rational assumptions comes from the reality that formal leaders, no matter how insightful or skilled, cannot single-handedly accomplish the goals of the organization. They necessarily work through others. The principal may possess deep knowledge about curriculum and instruction, skillfully articulate a compelling vision for change, and focus resources on key areas—but it is still teachers who must teach.

In schools, this reality constitutes more than a simple division of labor in which leaders set the direction and followers carry out the plan. Unlike factories, where managers have the technical knowledge to specify what is to be done and how to do it, schools require professional decisions that can only be made at the classroom level. Children and adolescents are not identical, inert materials moving down an assembly line at exactly the same pace. They are unique human beings who take initiative and put their own stamp on the world, and each child responds somewhat differently to learning materials and classroom activities.

The principal can identify a preferred instructional strategy, but it remains the teacher who must adapt and apply it to the particular characteristics and needs of each child in the classroom. At best, instructional reform can only be guided, not controlled, as Richard F. Elmore points out.

Elmore notes that each person in the school community has a role that he or she is uniquely suited to play. Policymakers set standards and provide incentives; superintendents recruit, evaluate, and provide professional development for principals; principals recruit, evaluate, and provide professional development for teachers; and teachers design instruction, evaluate student work, and participate in professional development. As Elmore states, this is not an industrial-age division of labor, but a distribution of expertise aimed at a common goal.

Along the same lines, James P. Spillane, Richard Halverson, and John B. Diamond have likened distributed leadership to distributed cognition, in which an intellectual task is accomplished through the use of socially embedded resources. For example, a homeowner preparing to paint a room may determine the square footage using a calculator, may rely on a written formula to determine the necessary amount of paint, and may consult a chart to decide on a pleasing combination of colors. Even though the task appears to be carried out by an individual, he or she actually depends heavily on the thinking of others—the creators of the calculator, the formula, and the chart.

The situation is much the same for leadership tasks. Even a leader who seems to be orchestrating the whole show must rely on the initiative and leadership actions of people throughout the organization. For example, the success of a principal's decision to implement a new approach to math instruction depends on central-office administrators to provide the necessary resources and on the willingness of teachers to undertake the necessary professional development and use their creativity in adapting the strategy to meet the needs of the students in their classroom.

From this perspective, theorists of distributed leadership are not just saying that it is a strategy school leaders should use, but that it more accurately describes how every organization, especially one as complex as a school, in fact operates. In other words, leaders do not choose to "do" distributed leadership; rather, they must respond to the reality of its existence and do their best to capitalize on its strengths (and navigate around its liabilities) in pursuit of the school's mission of helping students learn.

From another perspective, however, as we shall see in the following sections, leaders and their staffs can enhance the distribution of leadership in their schools by implementing a variety of structural reforms that encourage shared decision making and give teachers more opportunities for leadership. School leaders can benefit by viewing the function of leadership in their schools from both perspectives.

THE CONTINUUM OF LEADERSHIP

Although some distribution of leadership is an inherent part of organizational life, leaders differ in the degree to which they embrace collaboration and strive to increase shared decision making.

Wilfred H. Drath places leaders along a continuum. At one end of the scale are those leaders who seek to fit the heroic mold, who make all the decisions and accept all the responsibility for success or failure. Further along the continuum are leaders who operate through interpersonal negotiation, recognizing the value of other perspectives and incorporating them into their decision making. Despite their more collaborative style, leaders of this type are still responsible for coordinating the varied views of others and are still regarded as much more influential than others in the organization.

At the far end of the continuum is leadership built on intensive dialogue and "sense making" aimed at helping members of the organization understand the complex environment in which they work and determine a sense of direction for the organization. At this end of the continuum, there are still formal leaders who have certain duties, but leadership is seen as everyone's responsibility, because each person holds a piece of the puzzle.

Depending on the organization's environment, there are times when each point on the continuum may offer the possibility of success. Joe Clark, the authoritarian principal portrayed in *Lean on Me,* was initially successful because teachers welcomed any attempt to impose order on a chaotic environment. Once order was restored, however, teachers began to chafe under Clark's top-down leadership.

Drath argues that heroic leadership works best in a simple environment in which there is general agreement on the organization's direction. As the environment becomes more complex—less certainty and more diversity—it becomes more likely some form of distributed leadership will be required. Under those conditions, there is a need for deep dialogue across roles, and the key role of formal leaders is to ensure that such discussion occurs.

If Drath is correct, schools today constitute fertile ground for this last kind of leadership. There is a growing consensus that the existing educational structure no longer meets our needs, but little agreement on exactly what kind of change is required. Critics call for systemic change, the nature and needs of the student population are changing rapidly, and old certainties are now in doubt. Under these conditions, leadership is needed from everyone in the organization.

DISTRIBUTED LEADERSHIP IN SCHOOLS

Distributed leadership is a popular topic in recent discussions of school leadership, but it has not yet been subject to a great deal of empirical research. Nor does the concept seem to have a widely accepted definition. Despite the careful theoretical formulations of scholars such as Spillane and his colleagues, as well as Elmore, current usage encompasses a wide range of possibilities.

In some cases, the term may be little more than a convenient catchphrase, used to express vague beliefs that have not been fully articulated (such as "collaboration is good"). Spillane and Jennifer Z. Sherer, in their 2004 paper for the American Educational Research Association, noted that "distributed leadership," "shared leadership," and "democratic leadership" are often used interchangeably, suggesting that in some cases, people may just be slapping a new label on an old concept.

Jennifer York-Barr and Karen Duke found that concepts such as "teacher leadership," "participative leadership," "leadership as an organizational quality," and "parallel leadership" share with "distributed leadership" the belief that "leadership is not vested in one person who is high up in the hierarchy and assigned to a formal position of power and authority." Instead, this kind of leadership is viewed as a process of mutual influence that cuts across roles.

In practice, the term does not seem to be tied to any one form of organizational structure. Sometimes distributing leadership involves a realignment of formal leadership positions, as when a district creates a co-principalship. More commonly, it seeks to broaden involvement in decision making. As such, it encompasses a variety of organizational arrangements: work teams, site councils, teachers on special assignment, and many others. Occasionally, it consists of little more than an optimistic hope that "everybody acts as leader without appointment simply because they are motivated to do so by feelings of personal responsibility" (J. Barrett as cited by Anne Storey).

Peter Gronn distinguishes between *additive* and *holistic* distribution. Additive distribution is accomplished simply by spreading leadership tasks across the organization and involving more people. Whereas additive sharing may involve little more than performing delegated tasks individually, holistic distribution pays more attention to the interactions and interdependencies among people at all levels of the organization. Holistic distributed leadership generally assumes that the whole is greater than the sum of the parts and that sharing leadership in teams will create synergy that takes the organization to new levels of functioning.

The surge of interest in distributed leadership in schools stems from a number of sources:

- Since the mid-1980s, school reformers have promoted the professionalization of teaching, emphasizing the potential for teacher leadership.
- School reformers have been humbled by the difficulty and complexity of their task, leading many to doubt that a few leaders at the top—no matter how talented and dynamic—can single-handedly bring about the kind of change needed.

- The principalship is increasingly viewed as an "impossible" job that places unrealistic demands on school leaders; dispersing the workload may make it more manageable.
- The idea that everyone can be a leader appeals to our beliefs about equality and democracy (Storey).

Advocates claim many benefits come from distributing leadership. Of most immediate interest to principals is the possibility of reallocating their workload to make the job more manageable. At a time when the school leader is seemingly responsible for everything, the notion of farming out some tasks to others holds enormous appeal, especially if it allows principals to focus their energies on core issues. Jonathan A. Supowitz wrote that one benefit of distributed leadership is that "it will free up time for principals to become true instructional leaders."

According to some accounts, distributing leadership may also benefit others in the school community. Reviewing the literature on teacher leadership, Joseph Murphy noted three primary claims:

1. Teacher leadership increases teacher professionalism, which in turn positively affects teacher learning.

2. It improves organizational health and climate, in particular making the school more of a learning organization.

3. It results in improved student learning.

Thus far, research has been too sparse to uphold these claims. Murphy, after assessing the evidence base for teacher leadership, concluded: "In the era of the most stringent accountability in the history of education, the near absence of attention to accountability issues in the teacher leadership literature is difficult to justify."

Perhaps the most tangible benefits have been to the morale of teachers (York-Barr and Duke).

These limited results suggest that distributing leadership does not offer simple or immediate solutions to the dilemmas of school leadership. Nonetheless, the growing complexity of the school environment suggests that it offers a promising avenue to explore.

VARIETIES OF DISTRIBUTED LEADERSHIP

Districts seeking to distribute leadership more broadly can use a variety of strategies, but most examples from the literature seem to fall into two categories. The most literal type of distribution parcels out formal leadership responsibilities over a larger number of individuals. For example, some districts have experimented with a co-principalship that invests two or more leaders with coequal authority over a school.

A second pathway is more diffuse, leaving formal job descriptions unchanged, but re-visioning the principal's role as a leader of leaders whose job is to create a culture in which the entire school community is involved in decision making. This pathway grows out of the extensive theory and practice of teacher leadership.

Each strategy offers a different vision of what it means to distribute leadership, each springs from different motivations, and each has certain advantages and disadvantages.

The Shared Principalship

If the job is more than one person can handle, why not give it to more than one? Principals who have often wished they could clone themselves may find the idea simultaneously appealing and troubling. The attraction, obviously, is having someone to share the burden and act as a confidante. The discomfort grows from the deep-rooted assumption that every organization needs clear lines of authority and that there has to be one person who ultimately has the final word.

Shared principalships can take multiple forms (Marian Court; Katherine S. Cushing, Judith A. Kerrins, and Thomas Johnstone). One version essentially puts two schools at one site, with one leader for, say, kindergarten through third grade and another for fourth through sixth grade. Another asks each co-principal to take responsibility for certain functions; for example, one handles curriculum and instruction, whereas the other does discipline and scheduling. A third possibility simply has each leader responsible for all aspects of the role: When parents or teachers raise an issue, their concern could be handled by either principal. Still another variation is job sharing, where two part-time individuals fill a full-time position.

What all these variations share is the presumption of equality between the co-principals. These are not new versions of the standard principal/assistant principal configuration. Each has equal authority and equal salary.

Advocates cite a number of benefits (National College for School Leadership). For the leaders, there is reduced stress, less isolation, and greater professional stimulation. For the school, there is expanded leadership expertise, especially if the two occupants have complementary skills and styles. When leaders look at issues through different lenses, the result should be better decision making. The arrangement also provides backup capacity—if one leader is out of town, decisions do not have to wait for his or her return (Peter Gronn and Andrew Hamilton).

Some practitioners also believe that co-leadership will contribute to more democratic schools by demonstrating that leadership need not be hierarchical (Court).

At the same time, a co-principalship raises several concerns about accountability, efficiency, and effectiveness (National College for School Leadership):

- Will it undermine accountability? If the school fails to progress, who will be held responsible?
- If the two co-principals are equal, what happens when they disagree? Will they be able to send a consistent message to the community? Who has the final say?
- Will teachers and parents know whom to approach when they have concerns or questions?

Although co-principalships have not been extensively studied, some qualitative evidence suggests that "co-leadership is not only possible, it can be a very successful strategy" (Court). The school district in Long Beach, California, for example, has used co-principals for more than a decade and has found the practice to be largely effective

(Duke Helfand). A principal in another district reports that parents and teachers who were initially wary have been won over, mostly because of increased accessibility: "If I can't get one of you I can get the other" (Cushing and colleagues).

Nevertheless, co-leadership requires leaders to think and act in new ways, and careful planning and forethought are essential. Analysts have identified the following issues that need careful consideration:

1. *Match co-principals wisely.* One co-principal has described the relationship as "a professional marriage" (Helfand). As in any marriage, not every pairing works out; the successful ones result from the partners' finding common ground and negotiating the differences. Although the literature offers little guidance on what makes good chemistry, many of the participants talk about how their different styles complement each other; each has strengths that balance out the other's weaknesses.

2. *Commit strong district support.* A co-principalship undermines conventional notions of leadership, and skeptics will be numerous. Districts must be prepared to demonstrate strong commitment to the concept and be willing to devote the necessary resources to it. With two principals instead of a principal and an assistant principal, salary costs will be higher. Districts also must be willing to find ways around bureaucratic rules not written with co-leadership in mind. In one case, regulations required a district to officially identify one person as the principal; the district did so, but did not publicly report the designation to keep from undermining the concept of co-leadership.

3. *Establish mutually agreed-on ground rules.* Although disagreements on various issues are inevitable—and even healthy—co-principals should be willing to operate within a common core of operational principles. The details will vary from team to team, but are likely to include answers to the following questions:

- What will be our shared vision for the school? What should our focus and priorities be?
- How can we divide responsibilities in a way that lets us make the most of our respective strengths? Does it make sense to have each of us be the lead person on certain issues, or will we be equally involved in all issues?
- What policies and practices will guide school operations? When we disagree, how will we work out our differences?
- How will we maintain regular communication to ensure consistency in the messages we send?

4. *Cultivate openness and trust.* Except for arrangements where principals simply divvy up the responsibilities and then operate independently, co-principalships require a high capacity for interdependence. Participants have to accept certain limitations on their freedom of action. They cannot simply act on a good idea; they must first talk it over with their partner. Also, principals operate in a challenging environment where stakes are high, missteps are common, and accountability is strong. Co-principals have to be willing to link their fate with peers and have trust in the capabilities of their partners. Open communication, candid discussion, and a willingness to let go of tight control are essential to success.

Despite the recent surge of interest in co-principalships, operational examples remain rare, and it will be some years before researchers can paint a full portrait of how they work and how successful they are. The current literature makes it clear that partnerships of this type are feasible, at least when the partners have the skills and temperament to work in tandem. Whether such arrangements can move beyond occasional experiments with enthused volunteers is less certain. But given the growing pressures on the principalship and the evident benefits of collaboration, co-principalships are likely to remain on the scene for the foreseeable future.

Teacher Leadership

The plausibility of distributing leadership in schools has been strengthened by two decades of discussion, experimentation, and research on teacher leadership. Since the mid-1980s, school reformers have argued that encouraging autonomy and initiative among teachers is essential to transform schools.

Strengthening teacher leadership is perceived to have many benefits, including improved morale, commitment, and professional growth (York-Barr and Duke), but the primary rationale is that teachers have the instructional expertise needed to move the school forward: "The most reliable, useful, proximate, and professional help resides under the roof of the schoolhouse with the teaching staff itself" (Roland Barth).

At least in principle, the concept of teacher leadership has been widely accepted, though educators have not agreed on a common definition (Murphy). York-Barr and Duke note that early attempts tended simply to put teachers in formal leadership roles (for example, department chairs), where they often became surrogates for principals. More recently, teacher leadership has broadened to envision teachers at the heart of an organizational culture focused on teaching and learning. In these conceptions, giving teachers formal authority is less important than ensuring that their expertise, creativity, and initiative infuse school-improvement efforts.

Teacher leaders can perform a variety of tasks, including mentoring, developing curriculum, doing action research, leading workshops, participating in decision making, and working with parents and community organizations. York-Barr and Duke note some research suggesting that practice may not always live up to the claims made for teacher leadership, but there is little doubt that teachers today are much more engaged in school-wide activities and decision making than in 1980.

An advocate of teacher leadership, Linda Lambert (1998), claims it can have a transformative effect: "Teachers become fully alive when their schools and districts provide them with opportunities for skillful participation, inquiry, dialogue, and reflection. . . . It is no surprise that teacher leadership is at the heart of the high capacity school."

Thus far, empirical research is limited and not completely consistent (Murphy; York-Barr and Duke). Some evidence suggests that the greatest effects of teacher leadership are on teacher leaders themselves, as they gain leadership skills, improve instructional practices, and become more fully engaged in their work. There may also be negative effects, including stress, conflict with colleagues, and time away from their own classroom responsibilities. Some evidence suggests that teachers who assert informal leadership are more likely to be accepted by peers than those who serve in formal leadership roles (Patricia A. Wasley).

Most important, there is thus far little evidence that teacher leadership is associated with improved student learning (Murphy; York-Barr and Duke). In part, this may reflect the difficulties of measuring a concept with such elusive definitions. York-Barr and Duke suggest that the apparent lack of effects may be an artifact of method. They conclude that "it is no easy task to investigate the effects of teacher leadership—given all of its incarnations—on students, teachers, classroom practice, and school communities." Still, the lack of empirical confirmation should provide a reminder that there is often a large gap between a promising practice and a panacea.

MAKING DISTRIBUTED LEADERSHIP WORK

From a theoretical standpoint, distributed leadership is present in every organization, even when the person at the top tries to micromanage everything and everybody. Leaders have influence, not control, and they always rely to some degree on the influence of others. In that sense, leaders don't decide to distribute leadership; it already is distributed.

Leaders still can make conscious choices that create an environment in which others feel free to develop and exercise their capacity for leadership, using it in the service of common goals. In such an environment, there are still formal leaders, but it is taken for granted that at any given moment, it could be someone else who steps forward to take the initiative. This section describes steps principals can take to achieve this kind of environment.

The Leadership Challenge

Distributed leadership holds out the promise of leadership from everyone in the organization, but the irony is that it seldom gets off the ground without the active support and encouragement of formal leaders. Because the traditional leadership paradigm remains strong, people are likely to be skeptical about how effectively leadership can be shared—or even whether it should be. Without a thoughtful, informed, and carefully crafted strategy, principals will have limited success.

The first step is to recognize that sharing leadership creates certain inherent dilemmas for principals.

Challenge 1: Implementing a new paradigm while satisfying the expectations of traditional models. In the early days of the school-reform movement, a Carnegie Corporation task force issued a report (*A Nation Prepared*) that not only supported teacher leadership but envisioned a school of the future that was run entirely by teachers, with administrators doing little more than routine clerical work. Not surprisingly, that vision died a quick death. However much people may agree that collaboration is good, they find it hard to abandon the notion that someone in the organization is the leader, able to set directions, referee disputes, and take responsibility for results.

Employees may appreciate being consulted and being granted a certain amount of autonomy, but few of them would argue for a completely nonhierarchical organization. If principals appear too eager to share decisions, or if the shared decision-making process appears too time consuming and laborious, teachers may regard the principal as weak or indecisive.

Challenge 2: Sharing leadership without giving it away. Distributed leadership does not envision the end of formal leadership. Every organization holds specific individuals accountable for accomplishing certain crucial tasks. In schools, principals are almost always the ones expected to ensure that the schedule is compiled, the curriculum is implemented, and federal, state, and district regulations are followed. In their efforts to distribute leadership functions, principals must preserve their ability to execute essential tasks.

Some theorists, such as Edwin A. Locke, caution that vision, goal setting, and motivation are at the heart of leadership and that these essential leadership functions can never be broadly distributed without undermining organizational effectiveness. Delegating vision is like having "seven oarsmen in a boat, each rowing in a different direction." Locke agrees that others in the organization could contribute to the vision, but says that it would be a mistake to treat everyone as having equal influence in this area.

Many advocates of distributed leadership would argue that these core leadership functions can be carried out in a highly collaborative way, but Locke's position serves as a useful reminder that collaboration does not imply that anything goes. Leaders are guardians of the organization's core values, and some things are nonnegotiable, as Thomas J. Sergiovanni states.

Challenge 3: Using hierarchical leadership to establish a collaborative system. Building a collaborative culture does not always go smoothly. Teachers may be reluctant to participate and may openly resist the changes, or they may behave in ways that violate the norms that underlie collaboration. At times, principals may have to send a firm message that the old paradigm is no longer viable. Both theorists and practitioners have commented on the apparent irony of using positional leadership to promote or enforce shared leadership (Joyce K. Fletcher and Katrin Käufer; Joseph Murphy and Amanda Datnow). The message that sometimes comes across is "We will share decision making. And that's an order."

Challenge 4: Learning new ways of leading. Principals may be intellectually committed to distributed leadership, but they will discover that leading collaboratively requires very different forms of behavior. Gary M. Crow notes that collaboration is built on influence, which in turn requires both parity and reciprocity. *Parity* means there is some degree of equality among participants, not in terms of formal leadership status, but in terms of the power resources they can bring to bear. If one party has all the power, then no matter how many decisions are shared, the relationship will not be collaborative.

Similarly, influence requires *reciprocity*—participants must feel that their collaboration is resulting in a mutual exchange of benefits. Without a sense of reciprocity, the relationship again becomes one-way.

The implication for principals is as follows: Irrespective of their formal leadership status, distributing leadership requires a political process that entails continual negotiation.

This situation is not unique to distributed leadership. As noted earlier, some degree of shared influence is inevitable in any organization; teachers with no formal power still have the ability to resist change in a variety of ways. Any attempt to consciously expand distributed leadership will bring the power of participants into strong relief. Crow notes that some research shows principals are reluctant to let go of their formal authority and resentful of having to negotiate.

Challenge 5: Confronting fear. Even principals who are philosophically committed to the concept of distributed leadership may hesitate to relinquish control over tangible decisions. Despite all the positive rhetoric about collaboration and shared decision making, they know that if things go awry at school, the finger will still point at them.

There is also the fear of appearing indecisive. Many teachers and parents are still conditioned to the image of heroic leadership that permeates the culture. Failing to find it, will they deem the principal to be weak?

Teachers have their own fears when it comes to distributed leadership. Accustomed to working in the thousand square feet of their own classroom, and lacking specific training in leadership, they may feel discomfort in taking the lead on schoolwide issues. And in a professional culture that has always been egalitarian, stepping forward to take the lead may seem presumptuous, setting them apart from their peers.

For all participants, there is simple fear of the unknown. Murphy wrote, "For most educators, the current organizational system is the only one they have known. It is difficult to move to the unknown even when one can glimpse its contours."

At moments of difficulty, there is a strong temptation to move back to the comfortable familiarity of the traditional.

Challenge 6: Living with ambiguity and ambivalence. As the first five challenges illustrate, moving toward distributed leadership creates certain tensions that are not easily resolved. At times, lines of authority will blur, creating confusion over who has the right to make a decision, which in turn may create frustration or anxiety.

Carol Weiss, who has extensively studied shared decision making, says it may be 4 or 5 years before participants are comfortable with their new roles and relationships. In the schools she studied, she did not see "linear progression." "Everywhere there were ups and downs, movement and relapse, optimism and disenchantment . . . [shared decision making] is not a process that, once introduced, necessarily matures and flowers."

Thus, an apparent era of good feelings may turn sour when previously hidden conflicts bubble to the surface. Teachers who were enthused about making decisions may begin to yearn for the simpler days when a benevolent principal listened to teachers and then made the decision.

Principals likewise may feel ambivalent, because others may not recognize their efforts to distribute leadership as leadership. Fletcher and Käufer have noted that in many organizations, people still get rewarded for heroic leadership, whereas shared-leadership practices seem so mundane they may not be recognized as leadership.

Structural Barriers

Aside from the challenges outlined previously, schools present a number of structural barriers to distributed leadership. Typically, schools are organized hierarchically, with rules, procedures, and structures that facilitate certain kinds of leadership and inhibit others.

An oft-cited example is the school's traditional "cellular" structure that requires teachers to spend the majority of their workday isolated from their peers. Consulting with another teacher is limited to the few times during the day when they are not supervising students. Even such free times are already heavily used for calling parents, filling out paperwork, and doing a multitude of other chores.

Another structural problem is the sharp divide created by the past four decades of labor relations in schools (Murphy). Master contracts spell out in meticulous detail the respective roles of teachers and administrators, and the contracts lay down clear-cut boundaries between those roles. When the lines are blurred (as when a teacher appears to do work normally assigned to principals), it can create discomfort or lead to initiation of a grievance. Also, contracts often support the principle that extra duty requires extra compensation, forcing districts to do careful calculations on when, how, and with whom leadership will be shared.

An increasing problem in a reform-intensive environment is stimulus overload (Bob L. Johnson Jr.). Every new initiative takes up time that is already in scarce supply and diverts mental energy from the multitude of tasks already on the to-do list. Lacking clear templates for distributed leadership, teachers and principals are likely to devote considerable time just to puzzling out the new roles and relationships that it requires.

A final barrier is more cultural than structural, but nonetheless can impose formidable obstacles. The teaching profession has historically developed strong norms centered on autonomy and equality. Teachers have often operated with a live-and-let-live philosophy that accepts noninterference with the practices of colleagues in return for their own classroom independence. This stance is easy to maintain as long as teachers deflect responsibility for schoolwide issues onto the principal.

Shared leadership, by contrast, requires a willingness to examine publicly the teaching practices of oneself and others, with the implication that they may need to be adjusted to fit organizational goals.

Similarly, teachers have long viewed their profession in egalitarian terms and have resisted practices and policies that appear to elevate some teachers over others. (Even teacher-of-the-year awards have been known to create resentment toward the recipients.) Although there are signs that recent initiatives such as the National Board for Professional Teaching Standards may be slowly eroding this attitude, teachers sometimes still hesitate to step forward to claim a leadership role out of fear that someone in the back of the room will mutter, "Who put you in charge?"

Building Leadership Capacity

Given the many obstacles to distributed leadership and the fact that teachers' preparation programs seldom include an emphasis on leadership development, attention to leadership capacity is a crucial first step.

Linda Lambert (1998) defined a school's leadership capacity in terms of two dimensions: breadth and skillfulness. *Breadth* is the number of people—administrators, teachers, parents, students, and others—who are engaged in the work of leadership. *Skillfulness* is the degree to which they exercise leadership effectively. The two dimensions can be combined on a matrix that portrays the range of capacity that can be found in schools.

Low participation and low skillfulness are found in schools where leadership opportunities are absent if not actively discouraged. Often, these schools have autocratic principals who cultivate compliance rather than creativity among the teaching staff.

High participation and low skillfulness are often found in schools with individualistic cultures. The principal may operate with a laissez-faire philosophy or may simply lack skill; as a result, some teachers learn to be resourceful in making decisions and getting things done. Still, there is little collaboration, and the overall level of leadership skill is uneven.

Low participation and high skillfulness are found in schools where some teachers are effectively engaged in leadership roles. These individuals have often received special training and have been tapped to fill designated leadership slots. They are few in number, though, and most members of the school community continue to play traditional roles. In some cases, the staff is polarized, with some teachers strongly resisting the leadership of others.

High participation and high skillfulness are found in schools where the principal has exercised collaborative leadership by encouraging and supporting the involvement of the entire staff in decision making. A majority of the teachers effectively play some type of leadership role, and staff members view themselves as part of a learning community.

Lambert (1998) cautions that these four types are only benchmarks designed to show the range of school leadership capacity. In practice, capacity is a continuum with many variations, and not all schools fit cleanly into one of the four categories.

How do principals build capacity? Lambert's (2003) analysis suggests a two-pronged approach that seeks to expand leadership opportunities throughout the school while providing formal and informal training.

Broadening Participation

Actively recruiting people to join committees or work teams is a logical starting point but may have limited impact at first. The ones who initially answer the call are likely to be those with strong interests in a particular issue or may just be joiners. Others, even when interested, may hold back for a variety of reasons: They lack confidence in their leadership skills, they don't believe the principal is sincere about sharing decision making, or they simply don't have the time.

Principals can use a variety of strategies to draw in these individuals. One is to offer different degrees of leadership responsibility. Lambert (2003) describes the "ZCI" process used at Maple Ridge School in Calgary, Canada. Teachers who are authorized to assume major responsibility for an issue are designated with a Z. Those who want to be consulted are identified with a C, and those who want to be informed are identified with an I. Teachers who might hesitate to take major responsibility can opt for a lower level of involvement; over time, they may be drawn into more active roles.

Most people who are willing to accept leadership responsibilities are not interested in leadership per se. Rather, they get involved because they have a strong interest in a particular issue. Thus, generating discussion and dialogue on a provocative issue can be an effective way of drawing people to leadership roles. Using faculty meetings for reflective conversations on significant issues offers one avenue for doing this.

Lambert (2003) notes that inquiry-based activities can offer powerful motivation for involvement in leadership. Confronting teachers with data about student performance can trigger curiosity or create enough dissonance to prompt them to actively pursue the question further.

As noted earlier, traditional structures and assumptions can inhibit the development of shared leadership. Lambert (2003) suggests that principals can take steps to break long-established patterns of dependency. For example, when a teacher approaches a principal with a request, the traditional pattern is for the principal to promptly satisfy the teacher by providing an immediate answer. Instead, the principal could defer an immediate answer by asking the teacher to elaborate on the idea, identify possible advantages and disadvantages, or seek the opinion of others first.

Finally, principals can establish and enforce norms that contribute to collaboration in two critical ways: (a) by articulating the values and expectations of collaboration and, (b) even more powerfully, by modeling them consistently. If the norm is respectful listening, the principal can explicitly state it as an expectation for all faculty meetings, can call to task those who fail to observe the norm, and can listen respectfully to all members of the school community.

Developing Skills

Although willingness to participate is the first requirement for collaborative leadership, the ability to participate effectively is required for long-term success. Without skillfulness, collaboration will breed frustration and cynicism. Because many teachers and other stakeholders enter the process without much formal leadership training, principals need to develop strategies for ensuring that participants have every opportunity to develop collaborative skills.

For that matter, the skills required for collaborative leadership are not necessarily taught in all principal-preparation programs either. Lambert (2003) highlights the essential role of reflection, inquiry, and dialogue, calling them "the primary dynamic of professional practice." These skills, which call for social sensitivity and hard cognitive work, are probably best learned through observation and participation. For this reason, Lambert (2003) emphasizes the importance of job-embedded professional development.

Murphy notes that teacher leadership calls for "a bushel of competencies," many of them involving "social lubrication." Formal training programs exist (York-Barr and Duke), but Murphy suggests there is little reason to think that traditional methods of professional development—"free standing, short term, nonsystematic, and infrequent"—can effectively build collaborative skills. Rather, any formal training should be linked to participants' work, lead quickly to opportunities to apply the skills, and provide opportunities for feedback and reflection.

Supporting the Process

Enlisting participation and developing leadership skills are essential first steps in building collaborative leadership, but continuing support will be necessary. Murphy has described some of the methods, summarized as follows, that principals can employ to facilitate the process:

1. *Link shared leadership to the school's mission, vision, and core goals.* To the extent that teachers and other stakeholders see collaborative leadership as a path to the school's most cherished goals, they are likely to embrace it.

2. *Publicly discuss, promote, and support shared leadership.* By virtue of their positions, principals can play a powerful role in legitimizing a new idea. When principals

visibly pay attention to an idea or practice, teachers are more likely to view it as important (or at least worthy of their own attention).

3. *Identify potential teacher leaders and actively recruit them into the process.* Every staff has teachers with leadership potential. Sometimes they need only be asked; other times they may need to be gradually persuaded. Although the goal is ultimately to encourage leadership from everyone, getting the support of natural leaders is an effective way of priming the pump.

4. *Build relationships with teachers.* A strong, positive relationship with the principal is a major contributor to teachers' willingness to take on leadership roles.

5. *Build a supportive infrastructure.* As noted earlier, schools as they exist put up many barriers to collaborative leadership. Principals can provide critical support by making sure collaborative efforts get the resources they need and by finding a way around the many policies and practices that discourage collaboration.

6. *Rethink power relationships.* For the principal, shared leadership brings to the surface deeply rooted assumptions about what it means to lead. Even leaders who are committed to collaboration may find it difficult to put their formal authority aside and engage in the messy negotiations that characterize distributed leadership.

7. *Keep the focus on instruction.* Early experience with shared decision making showed that some initiatives went astray by focusing teacher energies on rather trivial managerial issues such as parking or bus-duty assignment. The real expertise of teachers—and the real need of students—is teaching and learning, and that is the area where their leadership can make the most difference.

EXPANDING LEADERSHIP THROUGH WORK TEAMS

The call for distributed leadership has often been couched in general terms, fed by the belief that education "can be greatly improved by simply strengthening the connections among people who work at all levels within the organization" (William F. Cunningham and Donn W. Gresso). But spreading leadership across the school depends on more than goodwill—it requires practical strategies that can cut through the organizational and psychological barriers that inhibit distributed leadership.

In the past decade, educational leaders have borrowed a technique used heavily in business: the work team. Originating in the work of W. Edwards Deming, the founder of total quality management, work teams are a deliberate attempt to break down barriers among the different parts of an organization. With their highly compartmentalized structures—operations, marketing, sales, communications—businesses had an obvious need for tools that can cut across departmental lines.

The compartments are not as visible in schools, but they exist. In elementary schools, the primary unit may carry out its work without much communication with the intermediate unit; in high schools, academic departments often function as semiautonomous units that carry out their work in relative isolation from other departments.

When put into practice at schools, Deming's philosophy is said to reduce competition among individuals and departments and increase the energy available for creating environments more conducive to learning (Yvonne Siu-Runyan and Sally Joy Heart).

Elements of Team Success

Experience with teams in many organizations makes it clear that creating a team requires more than simply forming a committee with a diverse membership. Jon R. Katzenbach and Douglas K. Smith emphasize that "teams do not become teams just because we call them teams or send them to team-building workshops." In their book *The Wisdom of Teams,* Katzenbach and Smith say the key is adhering to several "team basics":

1. *Small numbers.* As anyone with committee experience knows all too well, group efficiency tends to be inversely related to group size. Katzenbach and Smith say that teams of more than 20 or so seldom achieve much because there is too little opportunity to form social bonds that can overcome hierarchy, rules, and standard operating procedures. In school settings, logistical issues (such as finding a common meeting time that works for everyone) also work against larger teams.

2. *Complementary skills.* One of the bedrock assumptions of teams is the belief that the whole is greater than the sum of the parts. That is, the collective skill set of a group far surpasses the skills of its most talented member. Where one person is weak, another is strong; where one has great technical expertise, another has well-honed negotiating skills; where one is a practical, hardheaded realist, another is a visionary.

Complex change requires a range of skills, and a smoothly functioning team is well-positioned to supply them. (Katzenbach and Smith warn, however, that at the time of selection of the team's members, the tendency is to overemphasize skills; they observe that participating on the team accelerates development of members' skills.)

3. *Common purpose.* Teams, unlike many standing committees, are highly task specific, focused on a concrete mission. (For example, rather than "reviewing curriculum," a team may be responsible for "aligning the 4–6 math curriculum with state standards.") Purpose is the glue that holds together a diverse group of individuals whose job duties and professional commitments are always pulling them in many directions. Although the initial purpose is often set by formal leaders, team members continually refine their understanding of it as they periodically refer to it and gradually make it their own.

4. *Clear performance goals.* Having a broad sense of purpose is not sufficient; teams must be able to visualize what the specific outcome will be. Clarity about the desired results fuels motivation and provides a way to measure progress.

5. *Commitment to a common strategy.* The team must agree on and adhere to a work plan to guide their efforts. If members continue to rely on individual effort (perhaps by delegating tasks to individual members or by asking one or two members to do the bulk of the work), the group will not become a true team. By continually discussing the nature and progress of their work, team members will develop a "social contract," say Katzenbach and Smith, that strengthens commitment to the team and the work they are doing.

6. *Mutual accountability.* Having identified clear goals, teams hold themselves accountable for achieving the goals. This means not just that they follow through on their individual assignments but that they take responsibility for the success of the team as a whole. This requires the willingness to assess team progress honestly, discuss issues candidly, and, if necessary, confront teammates who are not doing their part.

Types of Teams

Today's reform-driven school environment creates fertile ground for a variety of work teams. Karolyn J. Snyder and Robert H. Anderson cite two major categories:

1. *Permanent teams* specialize in a broad ongoing function such as curricular or age-level instruction. A team consisting of all kindergarten through third-grade teachers or of all members of the high school English department would be examples, as would a district's inservice committee. (Teams can be permanent even if members rotate in or out over time.)

2. *Temporary teams* are "organized for a particular short-term purpose and are dissolved when the task is completed." Examples include a task force for kindergarten through sixth-grade math curricula and a work team that oversees development of a gifted program for a high school.

There is need for both types of groups, though permanent teams may find it more difficult to achieve the cohesiveness and sharp focus on specific goals described by Katzenbach and Smith.

Within these two categories, teams can pursue a range of activities:

Management or leadership teams are responsible for considering schoolwide issues and responding with appropriate decisions and policies. Typically, they consist of the principal, other administrators, teachers, and, in some cases, parents. Site-based councils mandated in some districts are an example.

Subject-area or grade-level teams bring together teachers responsible for instruction in those areas. They may discuss curriculum, testing, scheduling, classroom management, or any other topics that affect the group.

Broad specialty teams take responsibility for certain issues affecting the school as a whole. Examples include professional development, curriculum, assessment, and social functions.

Study groups read and discuss articles or books that challenge their members' thinking, seeking insights that lead to teaching that is more effective.

Action-research teams engage in focused inquiry on a topic directly relevant to the school's improvement efforts.

Task forces take on special topics of schoolwide significance and then disband when they complete their work. Such teams might focus on issues such as aligning a middle school's math curriculum with the high school curriculum, preparing for a school boundary change, or improving the school's capacity for helping English-language learners.

Vertical teams are made up of individuals from different levels of an organization who join together to accomplish a task requiring communication, alignment, or continuity among all grade levels or subunits. In a district, a vertical team might consist of administrators from high schools, middle schools, and elementary schools, whereas in a single school, it might include a superintendent, principal, teachers, support staff, parents, and students.

Because of the greater diversity of perspectives, vertical teams can be more challenging but also more rewarding. Participants cite benefits such as improved communication, respect, and collegiality; increased understanding of other team members' problems and needs; more confidence and trust in others; and ability to see the big picture (Cunningham and Gresso).

Multifunctional teams (also referred to as multidisciplinary teams, cross-functional teams, or cross-disciplinary teams) are groups that deliberately bring together individuals who play different roles or represent different areas. Multifunctional teams are designed to increase communication and collaboration across the usual organizational boundaries. Vertical teams, for example, are multifunctional.

The Principal's Role

Principals often serve as members of work teams, but their most important role is to initiate the team and establish the conditions for success. The first step is to articulate a clear purpose that will help the group stay on course and provide a basic framework for group accountability.

The purpose should point toward some tangible outcome or product that will signal that the group has accomplished its task. Defining a purpose is easiest to do for a short-term task force that has been formed with a particular purpose in mind.

In regard to permanent teams that define their purpose in terms of broad functions (such as "monitoring curriculum"), the principal may be able to sharpen the focus by engaging in some priority setting at the beginning of the year. What are the curricular issues that are most urgent, and what are some steps that would constitute progress? Formulating a clear, action-oriented agenda will signal that the team will not be just another debating society.

The makeup of the team is the second priority. Katzenbach and Smith advise leaders not to worry about the specific skills of team members, who will expand their capabilities as a result of working with the team. Principals should pay attention, however, to the different perspectives that will be represented on the team. The goal is a mix of roles and viewpoints that will force team members to think beyond their own specialty areas and take a schoolwide perspective. In the case of permanent teams, whose membership is often set by school policy or union contract, the principal may have less direct control, but he or she can still informally recruit members to the position.

Finally, the principal must make sure that the team has the resources it needs to get the job done. This includes not only the obvious needs, such as meeting space, but adequate information to make good decisions.

Overcoming Obstacles

No matter how enthused and well motivated, any team can go off the tracks when it encounters obstacles. When that happens, members lose energy, turn cynical, or launch personal attacks. Meetings become extended debates over trivial issues, and candor gives way to caution or political posturing.

Common responses to such roadblocks include changing the makeup of the group, providing a dollop of team building, bringing in a facilitator, and disbanding the team altogether. Katzenbach and Smith say the more effective solution is to keep the team focused on its performance goals. They offer five strategies for accomplishing this:

1. *Revisit the basics.* Reexamining the team's mission, performance goals, and strategy can uncover unspoken assumptions that are causing the problem.

2. *Go for small wins.* Sometimes the obstacle is a goal that for the moment is too big or complex for the team to handle. Redirecting efforts to a different (but still relevant) goal or breaking a big goal into smaller pieces can reenergize a stuck team. Progress creates more progress.

3. *Inject new information and approaches.* Sometimes additional information can provide a fresh perspective. In school settings, such information might come from student performance data, journal articles, or visits to other schools.

4. *Bring in an experienced facilitator or provide additional training.* Teams can become ingrown, replaying the same old debates without seeing how counterproductive they are. A skillful facilitator can bring in an objective, outside viewpoint that helps team members clarify what has been happening. Similarly, carefully selected training can provide new insights and energy. The school leader should monitor the work of the facilitator and trainers to make sure the group's attention stays on performance.

5. *Change the team's membership.* Sometimes adding a new member can bring in a fresh perspective or can change the dynamics of group interactions.

CONCLUSION: WHY THE EFFORT IS WORTHWHILE

In many ways, distributing leadership is an unnatural act. As middle managers hemmed in by federal, state, and district rules and trying to do an exceedingly difficult job, principals frequently feel they have all too little ability to control events. Sharing their limited decision-making power with others does not come easily, especially when the stern finger of accountability is pointed directly at the principal. Sharing power also requires a profound faith in the ability of human beings to govern themselves.

Also, distributing leadership may threaten the tacit assumptions of others, leading to confusion or resistance. And distributing leadership takes considerably more time than simply making decisions oneself.

So why make the effort? In part, distributing leadership is an expression of the belief that, in the long run, organizational effectiveness will increase when leadership is seen as everyone's responsibility. (In the words of the aphorism, "All of us are smarter than any of us.") And for some leaders, distributing leadership lies at the heart of their mission.

Stephen R. Covey, who defines *leadership* as "communicating to people their worth and potential so clearly that they come to see it in themselves," says that sharing leadership, rather than giving up control, transforms it into self-control. Empowering others unleashes their passions, energy, and drive—all the things that create both satisfaction and success.

REFLECTIONS

1. Considering the range of decisions that principals frequently make (scheduling classes, choosing textbooks, arranging professional development for teachers, and so forth), which ones would you be willing to share with others? For which ones would you want to keep your decision-making authority? Why?

2. Think back on the most successful and least successful committees and teams on which you have been a participant. What were the biggest barriers to success? What helped the others be successful? How much did the leader have to do with it?

3. To what extent do you agree with the statement "Everyone can be a leader"? Is this just feel-good rhetoric or a realistic principle? Does it apply to others in the school community besides teachers (for example, parents and students)?

4. In schools in which you've worked, what encouraged teachers to take a leadership role? What discouraged them?

5. To what degree do you consider the leadership in your own school to be distributed? What steps could be taken to broaden the distribution? Would that make the school more effective?

12

Political Leadership

Larry Lashway

T he philosopher Immanuel Kant once claimed that the two most difficult human arts were government and education. Unfortunately for today's school leaders, their job combines both.

Undoubtedly, many educators would prefer a school system devoid of politics. Decisions would be made on the basis of professional judgment informed by the best available research, guided by the developmental needs of children rather than the self-interest of adults. While attractive, this vision is misleading, perhaps even delusional, in describing a condition that has never existed and may be impossible to achieve. As Thomas J. Sergiovanni and colleagues say, the apolitical school is "a myth."

Politics is inevitable because every social group, whether it is a club, organization, or nation, requires a way of reaching decisions that its members will accept. Groups are never completely cohesive and single-minded, and members may disagree on goals or strategies. Individuals also bring purely personal agendas (pursuit of power, wealth, or ideological goals) that don't necessarily coincide with aims of the larger group.

When these differing interests jockey for position in the same organizational arena, the resulting conflicts lead to political behavior, as participants vote, bargain, and form alliances to accomplish their agendas (Gareth Morgan; Peter Block; Lee G. Bolman and Terrence E. Deal). Such behavior isn't selfish, just practical, as Bolman and Deal point out.

The goal of any political system is to produce decisions that are accepted by the group. "Accepted" does not necessarily mean "satisfied" or "happy about"; it means only that people are willing to live with the decision. Without this minimal level of acceptability, the group flies apart or people attempt to impose decisions by physical force. The Civil War began when Lincoln's election was so unacceptable to southern states that they seceded from the Union, an act that was so unacceptable to northern states that they went to war.

Principals can turn a blind eye to the political dimensions of the job, or they can decline to act in ways that seem overtly political, but the political system will continue to function nonetheless. The only meaningful question for school leaders is *how* they will conduct themselves in the political arena. This chapter describes the political dimensions of the principalship and discusses strategies for effectively navigating those challenges.

THE TWO WORLDS OF SCHOOL POLITICS

The political challenge for principals is twofold. First, every school has its own *micropolitical* system that results from the collision of agendas when administrators, teachers, students, parents, and community members come together in a common educational enterprise. Principals experience this system as an unending series of day-to-day efforts to satisfy the interests of various stakeholders while keeping the focus on student learning:

- Lobbying the central office for additional professional development funding
- Persuading teachers to adopt a new reading series that is better aligned with state learning goals
- Easing a parent's concerns about a course grade without undermining the integrity of the grading process
- Defusing a controversy over a star athlete's suspension for drinking
- Resolving concerns of nearby homeowners over trash left by loitering students

All these tasks require a judicious mix of power and persuasion, requiring leaders to soothe, bargain, do favors, assert power, and form coalitions.

This micropolitical challenge is complicated by the fact the school is only a small part of a much larger *macropolitical* system that can support, undermine, or confuse the school's agenda. This larger system comprises the constitutions, laws, elections, political parties, and government agencies that authorize, support, and influence education.

The macropolitical system surrounding U.S. schools is unusually complex because it distributes control across local, state, and national levels, and there is never a completely clear answer to the question "Who's in charge here?" States, which have the ultimate constitutional authority over education, have traditionally delegated much of their control to local school boards (at least until recently). The federal government was only a shadowy presence until the 1960s, but has become increasingly aggressive about intervening at the school level. And local districts, which habitually complain about excessive regulation, still manage to preserve considerable freedom of action. For good reason, American education has been described as "loosely coupled": All the parts are connected, but not in a linear or predictable way (Arthur E. Wise).

Also, educational decision making is subjected to a special set of constraints because schools are public institutions. For example:

1. Practitioners are expected to use their professional expertise, but are always subject to the approval of lay policymakers.

2. School business is public business; decisions must be made openly, and records are always available for public scrutiny.

3. As government agencies, schools are required to observe constitutional protections such as freedom of expression and due process.

4. Education policy is strongly influenced by election cycles; perceived shifts in public opinion can lead to sudden 180-degree turns in policy or, more commonly, gradual loss of interest. Reforms frequently peter out when policymakers move on to other issues.

Principals often do their best to buffer their schools from decisions made in the larger arena (Ellen B. Goldring), but the outside world can thrust itself into school life with little warning, creating unexpected and unwanted issues. (For example, few principals worried much about "highly qualified teachers" until No Child Left Behind forced the issue.)

Political Challenges

The combination of micropolitical and macropolitical issues creates a unique political landscape for each principal. Several issues, though, are pervasive, requiring the attention of every principal.

First, the principal's political world is multilayered. Local, state, and federal policymakers are not always in agreement with one another, leaving school leaders to determine, first, what the expectations are, and second, how to steer a course through (or around) the rules that will preserve reasonable freedom of action. And even when leaders manage to carve out zones of autonomy for their schools, their decisions are further constrained by micropolitical realities. Teachers, parents, and students have their own agendas, and they frequently try to influence the decision-making process.

Second, the political system never stands still for very long, and it has been especially volatile in recent years. Among the trends:

1. *Increased centralization.* While the United States has one of the most decentralized education systems in the world (Richard M. Ingersoll), the balance of power is clearly shifting. Between the late 1940s and the early '90s, the number of school districts in the U.S. dropped from 89,000 to fewer than 16,000 (Michael Kirst). Even more significantly, state and federal officials have been asserting more control over education policy, mandating standards, tightening rules, and demanding accountability. David T. Conley calls this power shift "a revolution."

2. *Greater parental choice.* Since the 1960s, policymakers and critics have increasingly affirmed the notion that parents have both a moral and a legal right to make key decisions about their children's schooling. Special-education laws have given parents a veto power over certain decisions; federally funded programs routinely require a parental advisory committee; and charter schools have affirmed the right of parents to choose their children's school. Many principals have learned to think like entrepreneurs, using the language of customer service.

3. *Growth of interest groups.* Parents aren't the only non-educators to seek influence over schooling. Businesses, testing companies, private foundations, and political parties exercise a potent if unofficial impact on schooling (Joel Spring).

4. *Increased politicization of education.* Since the early twentieth century, Americans generally observed a tacit consensus that education was too important to be sullied by partisan politics (Kirst). Although school affairs remained a legitimate subject of debate in school board elections, positions were seldom cast as "Democratic" or "Republican," and education played almost no role in political debate at the federal level. In recent years, however, the growing polarization of American culture has surfaced in partisan debate, and political parties have found vote-getting power in educational issues (Conley; Spring). A vivid example of this politicization comes from Diane Ravitch, who has documented the way that political pressures affect the language used in textbooks and on tests (see Table 12.1).

These changes will undoubtedly force principals into unfamiliar roles. Conley sees principals increasingly having to act as local interpreters of state and federal policy; networking to gain critical knowledge and resources; adapting state policy to local context; managing data; and eliciting support from teachers.

A third political challenge for principals is to reconcile conflicting governance models. On paper, education is controlled by elected policymakers who establish basic goals and requirements, and then implement their decisions through bureaucratic rules—a seemingly hierarchical and rational system. Observations in schools reveal a much more complex picture, however. After a study of two elementary schools, E. Mark Hanson noted,

Table 12.1 Prohibited Terms for Textbooks or Tests

Prohibited term	Reason	Preferred term
bookworm	offensive	intellectual
bubbler	regional bias	water fountain
Cassandra	sexist	pessimist
Chief Sitting Bull	relic of colonialism	Totanka Intanka
coed	sexist	student
Devil	not given	_____
fraternity	sexist	community, solidarity
gay	suggests homosexual	happy, light-hearted
master plan	not given	comprehensive plan
Mother Russia	sexist	Russia, vast land of rich harvests
Navajo	inauthentic	Diné
polo	elitist	_____
senility	demeaning	dementia
snow cone	regional bias	flavored ice

Foods to avoid mentioning: alcoholic drinks, bacon, cake, candy, coffee, French fries, pickles, potato chips, salad oil
Acceptable food: fish, poultry (unfried), eggs, cheese, enriched and whole-grain rice, fruits, vegetables, pizzas, tacos
Topics to avoid on tests (unless directly relevant to subject being tested) because they might be upsetting or distracting: alternative lifestyles, birthday celebrations, blizzards, brand-name products, criticism of democracy or capitalism, dancing, dinosaurs [implies evolution], disobedient children, fossils, genetic engineering, hunting, junk bonds, masks, parapsychology, pumpkins, rap music, unemployment, yachting

Source: Diane Ravitch, *The Language Police*, copyright © 2003, 2004 by Diane Ravitch. Used by permission of Alfred A. Knopf, a division of Random House, Inc.

Rather than finding a rationally planned and logically executed process of organization and administration controlled from the top of the hierarchy, we found a mixed bag of structured and unstructured activities, formal and informal procedures, and controlled and autonomous behaviors.

The reason for this complexity is that teaching, the main work of schools, does not easily lend itself to standardized bureaucratic solutions. Classroom life is fluid and highly unpredictable. Students are not pliable raw materials: They require individualized attention, and they have a way of resisting control. Not surprisingly, teachers also resist control when it inhibits their ability to respond to classroom needs, and they are often successful in rejecting, ignoring, subverting, or simply outlasting rules and reforms.

Principals find themselves squarely in the middle of this conflict, forced to act as mediators between the demands of the system and the needs of the classroom. Sergiovanni characterizes this tension as a struggle between the "systemsworld" of rules and regulations and the "lifeworld" of values, visions, and human relationships.

School leaders, then, find themselves serving many masters in a complex and highly volatile political environment. As Larry Cuban (1988) puts it, "Principals are sandwiched between what state and district policymakers intend, what the superintendent directs, what parents expect, what teachers need, and what students want." What strategies do they use to get out front and avoid being smothered in the middle?

Macropolitical Strategies

Serving as mediator between schools and community has traditionally been the role of superintendents. Today's principals also interact with a wide range of "outsiders," including parents, social-service workers, elected officials, state officials, law-enforcement officers, and news media. As classic middle managers, they are "boundary spanners" who strive to maintain the school's autonomy while satisfying the people on whom the school depends (Goldring).

Goldring identifies three key strategies that principals use to manage their contacts with the macropolitical environment:

1. *Reducing dependency.* Since schools are highly dependent on the larger environment, principals often seek to increase their ability to set an independent course. For example, they may actively seek grants or other sources of outside funding that buffer the school from budget cuts, or they may create a reservoir of goodwill by publicizing the school's positive activities and achievements.

2. *Adapting to the environment.* Sometimes schools modify their practices to defuse or deflect pressures from the outside. A complaint about a textbook leads to the establishment of a review committee with community representatives. A parental objection to a child's class assignment results in a quiet change in schedule. A state curriculum mandate creates a flurry of professional development activities and adoption of a new textbook.

3. *Changing the environment.* Sometimes principals attempt to reshape the environment. For example, when a principal's commitment to renovate an aging school faces a hostile financing environment, he or she may establish a citizen committee to help

educate the community on the need for a renovation. Or, faced with an unpalatable board policy, the principal may present the case for changing the policy.

In weighing these options, school leaders have to consider many variables, and their strategies may vary from case to case. Boundary-spanning can be seen in a study of a high school principal's interactions with parents. Naftaly Glasman and Mike Couch say that with each contact, the principal had to judge the nature of the parent's request, determine the appropriate response, and take action. The principal was very conscious of the importance of these meetings, both for the school ("public education as a whole is at stake here . . . we need them as allies") and for himself ("my job is constantly on the line"). While he was eager to keep parents satisfied, he also had to defend the school by determining when a request was unreasonable or intrusive.

Cuban (1975) has described such work as "crowded, messy, and unpredictable," noting that the large cast of characters includes some "cranky and fired up individuals." He also points out that "many of these participants enter, make noise and exit at different points in time, with varying volume and energy invested."

The principal's task in this tumultuous environment is to patrol the boundaries in a way that allows the school to accomplish its mission while accommodating the demands of the outside world. Too much protectiveness may isolate the school from the community it serves; too much accommodation may undermine the mission.

Micropolitical Strategies

Engaging the outside world can be challenging, but principals probably expend more political energy within the school. Administrators and teachers do not necessarily share the same goals, nor do all teachers think alike, so the school's daily life is usually enlivened (and occasionally dominated) by a political buzz. How principals manage this continual maneuvering is determined by their answers to two strategic questions.

1. *How will I exercise my power?* Principals sometimes complain about their lack of power. Organizationally, they can be described as "mid-level bureaucrats in a public service endeavor" (Philip A. Cusick), hemmed in by union contracts, district policies, and state mandates.

But for all their frustration, principals do have power, beginning with their formal authority as appointed leaders. The system defines them as leaders and grants them the right to make certain decisions. Teachers may not always respect the people who occupy the office, but they do recognize, and sometimes fear, the power they hold. For that reason, the principal's governance strategies have a critical effect on school politics.

Joseph Blase and Gary Anderson portray these strategies as a matrix with two key dimensions. The leadership *style* can be either "closed" (direct top-down decision-making) or "open" (indirect, negotiable decision making). The leadership *goals* are either "transactional" (oriented to the status quo) or "transformative" (activist and visionary). Together, these two dimensions yield four basic approaches to governance:

1. Closed transactional (authoritarian), which embraces the status quo and exercises power directly (for example, the principal makes a decision and communicates it to teachers)

2. Closed transformative (adversarial), which promotes the leader's vision but subjects it to public discussion (for example, the principal makes a decision and tries to persuade teachers to make a commitment)

3. Open transactional (facilitative), which favors pre-established goals but uses power less directly (for example, the principal makes a broad decision but delegates some of the details to a committee of teachers)

4. Open transformative (democratic, empowering), which works to establish a common vision based on collaborative decision making (for example, the principal identifies an issue and works with teachers to arrive at a solution)

Blase and Anderson join many others in openly advocating democratic leadership, but the best choice may depend on the specific situation. A low-performing school with a demoralized staff may welcome a take-charge authoritarian who can restore order and purpose. Once the school turns around, however, more open forms of leadership may become appropriate.

2. *Where will I set the boundaries between my work and teachers' work?* Not all decisions have equal political weight. Teachers may readily accept a principal's unilateral decision about bus supervision (even if they don't agree with it), but bitterly protest a mandate to use a new instructional method.

The most contentious issues center on the classroom, which is where teachers spend most of their workday. Maintaining order among twenty-five squirmy first-graders or boisterous eighth-graders is difficult enough; helping them reach challenging academic goals is a complex, unpredictable, and often frustrating enterprise. To be successful, teachers must adapt their instruction to the needs of each student, using whatever tools, resources, and teaching skills they have. Anything that restricts their flexibility (such as scripted lessons, narrow curriculum, rigid rules) is unwelcome. Anything that pulls them away from their core work (such as bus duty, unproductive meetings, or paperwork) is resented.

Traditionally, this tension has been papered over with an uneasy compromise of "zones of influence." Decisions requiring schoolwide coordination, such as scheduling, choice of textbook series, and supervision, have been in the domain of administrators. Day-to-day instruction and interaction with students (what goes on behind classroom doors) has been left to the teacher (Ingersoll; Hanson).

The recent escalation of state and federal accountability demands has threatened this long-standing arrangement. When Adequate Yearly Progress is on the line, *all* decisions have schoolwide implications. School leaders thus need to find ways to bridge the usual "spheres of influence" so they can have a real impact on what happens in the classroom.

Accordingly, principals may need to be more assertive about teachers' responsibilities to schoolwide needs. One Washington principal reported:

So we had to talk a little bit about for instance some pet projects that people like to do because they're nice, warm, fuzzy things and they've always done them. We really had to ask the question, "Well, does it get us where we need to go? Is time better used maybe in some other project?" (Robin Lake and colleagues)

Asserting such a responsibility does not imply heavy-handed mandates about specific decisions. Michael Aaron Copland noted that principals in one reform project were moving away from use of formal authority and were promoting instructional change by asking questions and exploring data. More generally, using an open, collaborative leadership style appears to offer promise in promoting instructional change (Blase and Anderson).

Principals can create an environment that continues to allow teachers instructional autonomy, but the autonomy is experienced collectively rather than individually. Newer leadership strategies of this kind do not yet offer a well-mapped route, yet when implemented thoughtfully, they can provide a strong instructional role for the principal without setting off political land mines.

ACTING POLITICALLY

If school leaders are sometimes slow to embrace their political role, part of the reason may be that political behavior is rarely openly acknowledged. Peter Block observes:

> Politics in organizations is like sex was in the 1950s—we knew it was going on, but nobody would really tell us about it.... In fact, the first rule of politics is that nobody will tell you the rules.

The rules can never be reduced to simple formulas, but we know enough about organizational politics to suggest some basic strategies that can help leaders navigate the challenges. These strategies are based on an understanding of two key political concepts: *interests* and *power*.

Interests

Politically, an interest is simply a stake in the outcome of a decision. People lobby for or against a proposal because they believe it will make their lives better or worse.

Although interests are often equated with selfishness or material gain, they actually run the gamut of human motivation—wants, needs, ambitions, goals, values, and beliefs. Some of the fiercest political fights (over abortion, gay rights, and the environment, for example) are fueled almost entirely by values and ideology.

Since interests are as complex as a person's motivational structure, they can be hard to categorize. Nevertheless, Gareth Morgan suggests that within the context of organizational politics we can see at least three clusters of interests. *Task* interests relate to a person's specific job. Teachers, for example, have an interest in maintaining enough autonomy to teach the way they prefer; principals have an interest in seeing that the school makes AYP.

Career interests reflect an employee's desire to have a satisfying and productive career. For example, principals have an interest in maintaining good relationships with people who can help them get ahead (or, in more volatile situations, retain their job).

Extramural interests are the motivations that people bring from their lives outside of work. No matter how engaged they may be with a task, or how ambitious to move up the ladder, workers also want to have time and money to support a family and leisure life.

We could use other terminology (for example, extrinsic vs. intrinsic), but the bottom line is that any individual is a bundle of interests, some selfish, others altruistic; some passionately felt, others evoking little emotion. Not all these interests are compatible, resulting in political stances that are ambivalent, inarticulate, or inconsistent.

Predicting how people will pursue their interests is not a well-developed science, and the uncertainty multiplies when we consider people in groups. As glibly as we talk about "interest groups," implying monolithic blocs, no group is driven by exactly the same motives.

Still, we can venture one plausible generalization about educators at the K–12 level: They tend to be driven by what Dan Lortie has called "psychic rewards." That is, they characterize their greatest source of satisfaction as "making a difference" or "seeing the light bulb go on" in students, and they are less likely to be motivated by money, status, or power. They are not purely altruistic, of course, but the same teacher who doggedly fights for an extra $500 on the salary schedule may then go out and spend the raise on supplies for his or her classroom.

A corollary of this value system is that teachers have a keen interest in conditions that will allow them to succeed with their students. They want an orderly school environment, autonomy in their classrooms, and moral support during the difficult moments (Hanson). Understanding these interests is a critical element in principals' use of power.

Power

Power both attracts and repels. Most leaders have at some point entertained a fantasy about having real power—being able to analyze a problem, determine the solution, and tell the staff, "Make it so."

But power also has a darker aura, an unsavory association with coercion and manipulation that seems out of place in a democratic society. Recent history has supplied all too many examples of the horrors associated with unrestrained power, and popular advice to power-seekers often sounds like a cynical game: "Get others to play with the cards you deal." "Pose as a friend, work as a spy." "Learn to keep people dependent on you." "Crush your enemy totally" (Robert Greene).

Yet power is the currency of leadership, an essential commodity for accomplishing anything. James MacGregor Burns has said, "Power is ubiquitous; it permeates human relationships. It exists whether or not it is quested for. It is the glory and the burden of most of humanity."

In itself, power is morally neutral, capable of being used for good or evil. Block distinguishes between *bureaucratic politics,* centered on manipulative tactics and "myopic self-interest," and *entrepreneurial politics,* centered on authentic tactics and enlightened self-interest. The first leads to dependency, the second to autonomy. Leaders have the ability to choose which path they follow.

Most political scientists and organizational theorists define *power* as the ability to get people to do what they don't want to do (Morgan). Despite its simplicity, this definition encompasses a wide range of behaviors. One of the classic descriptions of power (John P. R. French Jr. and Bertram H. Raven) identified five distinct types, summarized as follows:

1. *Legitimate* power is based on formal authority and position. People expect and want their organizations to have someone officially in charge. Even when formal leaders are not respected as individuals, others will tend to defer to them simply because the organization has granted them the right to make certain decisions.

2. *Reward* power comes from the ability to provide others with material or psychic benefits. It relies on a simple economic transaction: If you do *x*, your reward will be *y*.

3. *Referent* power is built on personal regard. People often go along with leaders they perceive as trustworthy.

4. *Expert* power is built on knowledge and skill. The leader gets others to go along because he or she is perceived as highly competent or in possession of special knowledge about an issue.

5. *Coercive* power is the flip side of reward power: If you fail to do *x*, your punishment will be *y*.

Burns, in his highly influential analysis of leadership, saw power as the reflection of a mutual *relationship* between two parties. It is never just a case of *A* imposing a decision on *B*. Even when the relationship is coercive, as when *A* threatens *B* with dire consequences for noncompliance, *B* retains the power to respond in a variety of ways: total compliance, surface compliance with covert resistance, foot-dragging, or open resistance. In other words, *A* has power only to the extent that *B* accepts the decision.

Some power relationships are limited to a simple exchange: *A* offers some incentive for *B* to support a particular decision. Burns labeled these exchanges *transactional,* as each party gains something it values. Another kind of power grows out of a deeper relationship in which "leaders and followers raise each other to higher levels of motivation and morality." This kind of *transformational* leadership unites leaders and followers in pursuit of a common vision.

In schools, the principal's power can be based on any of the five factors identified by French and Raven, or either of the two relationships described by Burns. Most theorists, however, see schools as being primarily "normative," with power depending less on threats and rewards than on the power of persuasion or an appeal to common values (Amitai Etzioni).

What Power Do Principals Have?

Some theorists characterize principals as having relatively weak power (Hanson), and principals themselves often complain they lack the authority to do the job properly (Steve Farkas and colleagues).

Principals are not alone in this sentiment. Even corporate CEOs and American presidents sometimes feel powerless to accomplish what they want. Harry Truman, on the eve of turning over the presidency to General Dwight Eisenhower, sympathized with his successor:

> He'll sit here, and he'll say, "Do this! Do that!" And nothing will happen. Poor Ike—it won't be a bit like the Army. He'll find it very frustrating. (Richard E. Neustadt)

Peter Block points out that any leader's power is hemmed in by two hard realities. First, others in the organization (including subordinates) have their own sources of power they can use to oppose the leader. (For example, teachers frequently turn to unions.) Second, structural forces and broad social trends that are beyond anyone's control may work against a leader. (For example, principals trying to cultivate civility and decorum among students have to contend with the power of television to create a popular culture that is shallow, flippant, and disrespectful of authority.)

Despite these inevitable limits, principals have enough power to make an impact on teachers, students, and parents. That power begins with position: He or she *is* the principal, possessing the requisite credentials and having been legally appointed by established authorities. This provides legitimacy and creates the expectation that this person is entitled to make certain decisions.

Compared with some private-sector leaders, principals' powers may initially appear somewhat anemic. They have no control over salaries, cannot easily fire teachers, and have relatively little discretion in budgeting. In other domains (such as discipline policy, scheduling, and hiring), a majority of principals report having reasonable autonomy, but even here significant percentages say the central office or school board exercises the most control (Ingersoll).

Still, a principal's position provides some significant advantages:

- They typically have the power to evaluate teachers, which provides them a structured opportunity for addressing instructional issues.
- They are in regular contact with central administration and the school board, giving them inside knowledge about the direction of school policy.
- They are not tied to a classroom, but can move about the building or even leave the building to network with others.
- They can call faculty meetings and determine the agenda, deciding both the topics and the process.
- They have visibility in the community and are treated as ambassadors who are entitled to speak on behalf of the school.

In short, they have an enviable platform from which to influence others.

School leaders can also draw on the natural power that comes from expertise; people are more inclined to listen to those with deep knowledge or well-practiced skill. Credentials notwithstanding, expertise does not automatically come with the position; it has to be demonstrated in the heat of action.

Principals can employ at least two kinds of expertise: skill at being a principal (managing the school) and knowledge of curriculum and instruction. Teachers expect principals to keep things running smoothly, maintain discipline, mediate disputes, prevent unreasonable interference from the outside, and fight for the resources and support that the school needs. Principals who do this effectively are more likely to be given the benefit of the doubt when teachers are uncertain about the wisdom of a particular policy.

Expertise in curriculum and instruction is a more complicated challenge for principals. In the first place, it may be hard to come by. No matter how experienced or well-schooled principals are in this area, it remains difficult for one person to completely grasp the nuances of instruction across the span of grade levels and content areas. Also, each classroom is a unique setting with its own cast of characters, requiring individualized knowledge of the players. Principals simply can't spend enough time in each classroom to develop this knowledge.

For those reasons, principals may face initial skepticism from teachers who are protective of their classroom autonomy. A low-key approach that emphasizes thoughtful questions, careful listening, and empathy for the problems of teaching may be the best way for principals to gain credibility in this area.

Mapping the Political Landscape

Given the dense, multilayered political nature of most schools, how can principals formulate political strategies that will allow them not only to survive but to advance the school's mission? As in so much of leadership, formulas are scarce, but a good starting point is a thorough understanding of the school's political environment. Who are the key players? What interests do they hold in the decision? What specific sources of power can the principal use for leverage?

1. *Who are the players?* A decision can potentially affect everyone in the school, but not everyone will take part in the decision. The first step in developing a political strategy is thus to determine the cast of characters, who typically fall into one of the following categories:

- *Power players.* These are the individuals or groups who have a formal voice in the decision, who either must be persuaded to give their assent or who must be outvoted. For example, scheduling early dismissal days for professional development may require a change in the master contract, meaning that a majority of teachers, or at least the union negotiating team, must be convinced.
- *Shadow players.* Some individuals have no formal role in the decision (or have only one vote among many), yet they have a disproportionate influence on the opinions of others. For example, teachers may turn for advice to a veteran colleague who is well regarded, or they may take their cues from the local union president.
- *Bystanders.* These are individuals or groups who potentially have some formal or informal influence on the decision, but who for the moment are abstaining from direct involvement, either because the issue doesn't seem to affect their interests, or because they haven't decided how they feel about it. Although seemingly not involved, bystanders must be factored into any political strategy, because they can choose to enter the game at any time.
- *Nonplayers.* These are individuals or groups who either have no interest in the decision or have no power or influence over it.

2. *What interests do the players have in the decision?* Knowing what people want is a key element in the political game, and leaders who are well plugged into the school's social networks have an obvious advantage (Hanson). Judging other people's interests is not always easy, however. First, the motives that people publicly espouse do not necessarily represent their true interest. In contract disputes, for example, teachers find it awkward to

say, "This is about money," so they are more likely to frame their position in the language of "fairness" or "the need to attract high-quality teachers." (Conversely, a bitter dispute over a seemingly small amount of money may actually reflect teachers' belief that their work is not respected.)

Second, people do not always adopt positions on the basis of deep reflection and critical thinking. They may respond to an issue reflexively, based on past experience or the opinions of a few peers. If presented with full information, and given candid, thoughtful responses to their questions, they may well decide that their original position was not in their best interests.

Finally, people seldom have simple motivational structures. Teachers, for example, have responsibilities to their students, their families, their union, and their philosophical beliefs. A particular decision may benefit their interests in one area, but simultaneously hurt them in another. As a result, they may be ambivalent or uncertain about where their loyalty lies.

Block argues that our evaluation of other players should not be limited to whether they agree with us. An equally important question is whether they are trustworthy. Some may support our position, but only because they see some personal advantage to be gained. Or they may be perfectly sincere but politically inept, alienating others with personal insults or inaccurate statements.

Block suggests that those with whom we agree and whom we trust are "allies," with whom we can work closely together and share strategy. Those who agree with us but are not trustworthy are "bedfellows," whose support we can acknowledge while being cautious about how we work with them. Those who disagree but are trustworthy are "opponents," with whom we can share our views, learn more about their views, and attempt to develop a mutually acceptable position. Finally, those who disagree with us and are not trustworthy constitute "adversaries," with whom we can share our views, but without expecting too much.

3. *What kinds of power are held by the players?* One of the realities of organizational politics is that the leader is never the only person with power. Every employee has some ability to block the leader's decisions (if only through passive resistance). Analyzing the power dynamics of the situation allows the principal to anticipate threats to his or her agenda and develop proactive strategies to deal with them.

Mapping the political environment in this way will provide leaders with answers to some of the key issues they face. Whom do I need to be talking to? What should I be emphasizing when I talk with them? How will adversaries apply their power, and how can I neutralize their actions?

Strategies

Politics is sometimes likened to a game in which players make a series of moves designed to achieve their goals while blocking opponents. Although the analogy can be carried too far (political rules are seldom as well defined as game rules), leaders who can skillfully execute a few basic political moves are more likely to be successful.

1. *Agenda setting.* If politics is a game, schools are arenas in which multiple overlapping games are being played simultaneously. The first political challenge for principals is making sure that everyone is playing *their* game.

Principals have some real advantages in setting the organizational agenda. As appointed leaders, they are *expected* to identify and resolve problems; no one will question their right to, say, appoint a committee to look into an issue. As boundary spanners, principals are also well positioned to interpret the policy environment and to share "inside" information with teachers: "Here's an issue we need to look at because the board and community are concerned about it." Finally, many principals today have learned to use data to capture the staff's attention.

More broadly, agenda setting is done through creating a common vision. In the short term, principals have little trouble keeping their priorities front and center; in the long run, people embrace an agenda only to the extent that it helps them accomplish their own. A collective agenda can be established over time (see Chapter 7, "Visionary Leadership").

2. *Networking and building coalitions.* Principals can seldom achieve their goals as a solo act. Political success invariably depends on creating relationships, building networks, and forming alliances.

The political mapping process described earlier lays out the leader's agenda:

- Who can be counted on for support? How can we work together?
- Who's on the fence, and what might bring them over to my side?
- Who's the opposition? Why? Is there anything I can offer that would sway them?
- How much power does the opposition have? How can it be countered?

With allies, leaders can share strategy and get emotional support; fence-sitters can be gently lobbied; and opponents can be engaged in dialogue that can at least clarify their concerns if not change their minds. With every social interaction, the principal learns more about what is driving the conflict and how it might be resolved.

3. *Bargaining and negotiation.* Negotiation begins when opponents realize neither side has the power to impose a unilateral decision on the other. This is often the case in schools, particularly in disagreements over curriculum and instruction. Administrators, acting on behalf of policymakers, have the authority to mandate decisions, but teachers have the option of quietly closing their doors and ignoring or subverting the decision.

Bolman and Deal argue that most bargaining can be characterized as either "value-creating" (win-win) or "value-claiming" (win-lose). Win-win negotiation emphasizes relationships and focuses on satisfying interests rather than quibbling over positions. That is, the solution may not be choosing either A or B but instead finding a third position that will satisfy each party's underlying interests.

Win-lose bargaining, by contrast, assumes the two positions are incompatible; if the two sides can't meet in the middle, then one will eventually prevail. To maximize their chances of winning, bargainers are more likely to make use of threats, tough language, and assorted forms of psychological warfare.

Bolman and Deal claim that both strategies are a legitimate part of bargaining, but that the choice will be determined by a number of variables, including the plausibility of a win-win scenario, the trade-off between gaining short-term wins and preserving long-term relationships, and the negotiator's own sense of ethics (which may rebel against the confrontational tactics in win-lose bargaining).

4. *Persuading.* In the political arena, disagreements over specific decisions frequently become absorbed into much wider partisan or ideological struggles. Position *A* is associated with one group; position *B* is claimed by the other side. When this happens, issues will seldom be decided on their merits. Still, there are many times in schools when people can be influenced by the power of persuasion.

Why do people change their minds? Cognitive psychologist Howard Gardner has suggested some possible strategies.

An appeal to *reason* and *research* can be productive when participants have not yet developed entrenched positions. Educators, who are trying to teach their students about the value of rational, well-informed thinking, may be open to modeling it in their own decision making. (Even when people are not completely convinced by logic, it offers them a publicly credible reason for supporting a proposal.)

How decisions are *represented* can strongly influence decisions, particularly when the interests of participants vary greatly. That is, there is more than one way to describe the benefits of a decision, and different descriptions may appeal to different people. For example, a decision that is explained by saying, "The board wants it," will not gain much traction among teachers. But if the principal can point out that the new policy provides an opportunity to increase funding or get a desired new textbook series, the decision becomes much more palatable.

Resonance adds emotional weight to an argument. Persuasion is never completely a cognitive process. The use of certain images, examples, stories, and cultural icons will enlist the values and subconscious emotions of the audience. Ronald Reagan was a master at simplifying a complex issue with a compelling image, phrase, or story. Opponents accused him of oversimplification, but the technique was undeniably effective.

Because teachers (and others) are value-driven in regard to their concern for children, resonance can be an important tool. A simple anecdote about a former student can lead teachers to recall their own anecdotes, and thus put a human face on the issue.

CONCLUSION: BEING POLITICAL, REMAINING ETHICAL

In the final analysis, politics is simply the means by which people in a group make decisions when opinions differ. It serves a constructive purpose by channeling organizational conflict into solution-oriented behavior. People who engage in politics have the opportunity to sell their ideas to others; in the process, proposals are strengthened, new options are created, and minds are changed.

Despite this fundamentally healthy function, politics can go astray, leading participants into unproductive quibbling, dishonest communication, and manipulative behavior, causing the organization to slowly bog down. Political action carries with it some ethical obligations, especially for school leaders.

First, power can have a corrupting effect. Ronald A. Heifetz and Marty Linsky observe, "We all have our hungers, which are expressions of our normal human needs. But sometimes those hungers disrupt our capacity to act wisely or purposefully."

Power can become an end in itself, offering leaders the satisfaction of feeling in control of a chaotic world.

There is little question that some principals abuse their power. Joseph Blase and Jo Blase have cited numerous examples of this abuse, ranging from unfair criticism to favoritism to sexual harassment. They have also documented the negative impact this behavior can have on teachers: loss of confidence, depression, physical ailments, fear, anger, and isolation.

Second, leaders have to determine which political tactics do not meet their standards for ethical behavior. In the midst of confrontations with adversaries, principals may find it politically expedient to talk tough, withhold information, or make threats. These behaviors, however, may conflict with their usual standards for behavior, forcing them to weigh the desirability of the goal against their commitment to a certain set of values. Is the behavior consistent with their deepest commitments? What kind of a model is their behavior setting, and how does it affect others? Are there viable alternative tactics? These are not trivial questions, and each principal has to work out the answers for himself or herself.

Finally, politics, as the means to an end, must remain harnessed to moral purposes. Even a noble end does not justify every means. Principals who keep asking, "How do students benefit?" are more likely to elevate politics from game-playing to an act of leadership.

REFLECTIONS

1. To what extent is your daily work affected or controlled by district policy? State rules? Federal regulations? What rule or policy would you most like to eliminate? Why? What district, state, or federal rules help you accomplish your work?

2. In your school, what decisions (such as curriculum, instruction, discipline, professional development) are considered to be in the principal's sphere of interest? What decisions are in the teacher's domain? What decisions are in a contested zone?

3. Choose a current or recent issue in your school and use the political mapping exercise described in this chapter to describe the key players, their interests, and their power. Given this mapping, what strategy would you advise the principal to use?

4. In your current position, what sources of power do you have to influence school decisions? In what situations have you used that power? What was the outcome?

5. Are you comfortable with the exercise of political leadership, or would you prefer to restrict your attention to the nuts and bolts of the school's instructional program? How might you advance students' academic learning through political leadership?

PART V

The Mission

Student Learning

13

Instructional Leadership

Supporting the Learning Process

Ronald A. Beghetto and Julie Alonzo

I magine yourself embarking on a trek through the Himalayas. Being a savvy traveler, you prepare well in advance. You study maps, research weather conditions, and pick up key phrases in the regional dialects. You assemble your gear and prepare yourself physically and psychologically for the challenge. By the time you begin the ascent of your first mountain trail, you have established your goals for the climb and have developed strategies for ensuring success.

Supporting the learning process has several things in common with preparing to climb a mountain. There is a destination, careful preparation is essential, and certain strategies will increase the chances of success. Everyone in the school, especially teachers and students, must understand the final destination and be equipped with the necessary strategies. The challenge for instructional leaders is to support teachers and students as they gain that understanding and help them employ the strategies that lead to attainment of student learning goals.

In the context of this chapter, *instructional leaders* include principals, lead teachers, and anyone else who provides leadership and guidance in the area of school-based teaching and learning.

The purpose of this chapter is to discuss the importance of clarifying student learning goals and offer considerations for selecting strategies that promote the attainment of those goals. Equipped with this knowledge, instructional leaders will be in a better position to fulfill the primary goal of schooling: supporting student learning.

We begin the chapter with a brief discussion of what learning means and highlight various perspectives of learning. We then explain the nature of school learning and discuss how instructional leaders can support teachers in promoting the learning process. Next, we clarify three types of learning goals: cognitive, behavioral, and motivational. We close the chapter by offering considerations for selecting research-based instructional strategies to ensure the successful attainment of student learning goals.

WHAT IS LEARNING?

Learning theorists conceptualize learning in various ways. Some hold a behavioral view of learning, others hold more of a cognitive information-processing view, and still others see learning as an individual or social construction of knowledge. Although it is beyond the scope of this chapter to provide a detailed discussion of these perspectives, key assumptions for five learning theories are summarized in Table 13.1 ("Perspectives of the Various Learning Theories"). (Interested readers can turn to Marcy Driscoll's *Psychology of Learning for Instruction* or Margaret E. Gredler's *Learning and Instruction: Theory Into Practice* for a comprehensive overview of these theories.)

These various perspectives have developed over time. Behaviorism has declined in favor, and now the majority of theorists adhere to cognitive or constructivist views.

Each of these views represents a different set of assumptions regarding the process of learning, the role of teachers, and the role of learners. Although there are purists who confine themselves to one particular view, most educators take a much more eclectic perspective—drawing insights from various views so as to best accomplish their particular learning goals.

Common to all views of learning is the recognition that learning involves change. The types of change that accompany learning fit in three broad categories (with examples in parentheses):

1. A change in cognition (developing the capacity to monitor one's own reading comprehension)

2. A change in behavior (learning how to interact with others in a group)

3. A change in motivational beliefs (developing the will to understand mathematics)

Of course, the change could be some combination of the three (for example, understanding the scientific method, using particular laboratory equipment to conduct the experiment, and developing a self-recognition of the capability to successfully carry out scientific experiments).

Within the context of schooling, this change is intentional. Teachers and students act purposefully to attain specific learning goals (for example, learn when, why, and how to divide fractions).

Table 13.1 Perspectives of the Various Learning Theories

Theory	Behaviorism	Social-Cognitive Learning	Cognitive Information Processing	Individual Constructivism	Social Constructivism
What is learning?	Learning is a change in behavior.	Learning is the acquisition of symbolic representations that guide future behavior.	Learning is a transformation of information into knowledge and memory.	Learning is the active restructuring of prior knowledge structures (schemes).	Learning is internalization, mastery, and use of signs and symbols of the culture.
How learning occurs	Learning occurs through reinforcement of correct behaviors or repetition.	Learning occurs through observing others and personal experience.	Learning occurs through connecting new information to what is already known.	Learning occurs through individual experience and restructuring what is known.	Learning occurs through social interactions with skilled others and sociocultural tools (books, symbols, computers).
What is teaching?	Teaching is reinforcing correct responses and correcting mistakes.	Teaching is providing models of competent performance and supporting learners' efficacy beliefs.	Teaching is organizing information into manageable chunks.	Teaching is creating learning environments for students to restructure their own knowledge.	Teaching is creating social interactions and support just beyond learner's ability.
Role of teacher	Teacher provides (reinforcing) stimuli.	Teacher is the model (or provides models) to be imitated.	Teacher is the primary source of knowledge and organizer of knowledge.	Teacher is the creator of opportunities for interacting with meaningful ideas, materials, others.	Teacher is a skilled other who assists learners in developing just beyond their current ability.

Theory	Behaviorism	Social-Cognitive Learning	Cognitive Information Processing	Individual Constructivism	Social Constructivism
Role of student	Student responds to external stimuli.	Student is a thinking imitator of skilled others.	Student receives information and makes meaning.	Student is an active constructor of personal knowledge.	Student is co-constructor of knowledge with others.
Role of peers	Peers may reinforce behaviors.	Peers can be good models for "to be learned" behavior.	Peers are a potential source of information.	Peers are helpful for testing/checking what is known.	Peers are essential for individual learning and creating shared knowledge.
Necessary conditions	Reinforcing correct behaviors; eliminating counter-reinforcers.	Observation and experiences that support positive self-judgments of ability.	Reducing distractions and making information personally relevant.	Allowing individual students to actively test/develop their understanding.	Allowing students to interact with skilled others and sociocultural tools.

Sources: Driscoll, Marcy. 2004. *Psychology of Learning for Instruction*, 3rd ed. Boston: Allyn & Bacon; and Gredler, Margaret E. 2001. *Learning and Instruction: Theory Into Practice*, 4th ed. New York: Prentice Hall.

Supporting Purposeful Learning

What does support for purposeful learning entail? Paul Black and Dylan William explain that, for learning to occur, students must possess "recognition of the *desired goal,* evidence about *present position,* and some understanding of a *way to close the gap* between the two." These elements—in conjunction with *progress monitoring* (see Chapter 15)—represent the core features of purposeful learning. Thus, purposeful learning can be represented in four overlapping elements that instructional leaders can use as a guiding framework for supporting student learning. Those four elements are illustrated in Figure 13.1 ("Cyclical Process for Supporting Student Learning").

Clarifying Goals

As illustrated in the figure, supporting student learning is a cyclical process that starts with clarifying learning goals. Learning goals help focus students on what is to be learned. As Richard J. Stiggins notes, learning goals represent targets that serve as a way for teachers and students to monitor progress and render judgments of success.

Without clear learning goals, student learning becomes more a matter of chance than a purposeful effort. Consider a lesson being taught without clear learning goals. Such a lesson is akin to a frustrating game of intellectual hide-and-seek. As a result, some students might correctly guess what the teacher has in mind while many others are left in the dark.

By clarifying learning goals, teachers help demystify the learning process. And in doing so, they create a more transparent learning environment. In this way, all students have an opportunity to recognize the purpose of the lesson as well as understand the criteria for success. (Specific considerations for how instructional leaders can assist teachers in clarifying learning goals for students are presented later in the chapter.)

Figure 13.1   Cyclical Process for Supporting Student Learning

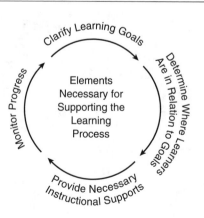

Determining Students' Present Position

Once learning goals have been clarified and communicated to students, the next element in supporting student learning involves determining where students are in relation to those goals. Given that learning involves change, learning can occur only if instructional support is provided to move students beyond their current position. Therefore, teachers and students must have a clear understanding of where students are in relation to the particular learning goals.

Also, determining a student's current position allows teachers to recalibrate learning goals to accommodate the varying and developing abilities of students. This process of determining where learners are in relation to goals helps teachers (and students) recognize what steps are necessary to support the attainment of learning goals.

Closing the Gap

Once a student's current standing has been determined, teachers can focus on the next phase of supporting the learning process: selecting and providing appropriate instructional supports.

Instructional supports represent the various strategies teachers use to promote student learning. The selection of these strategies aims to close the gap between the particular learning goals and students' current position in relation to those goals. As such, the selection of strategies is a purposeful endeavor and, therefore, should be guided by both the immediate context and evidence that the strategy has worked in similar contexts with similar students.

Considerations for selecting instructional strategies are offered later in this chapter.

Monitoring Progress

Finally, progress monitoring must occur throughout the entire learning process. In this way, teachers can determine whether their current efforts are successful, make timely adjustments, and ultimately increase the chances that they are supporting the attainment of learning goals for all students (see Chapter 15). Similarly, the continual monitoring and communication of progress help students be involved in and own the process of learning. And, as Stiggins notes, the more students become active partners in the learning process, the greater the likelihood they will find success both in and outside the classroom.

In summary, learning involves change. The nature of that change depends on the particular view of learning one holds. Within schools, that change often represents a combination of behavior, cognition, and motivation. In addition, the change is typically viewed as purposeful and goal directed. Therefore, support for student learning consists of four overlapping elements:

1. Clarifying the learning goals

2. Determining where students are in relation to those goals

3. Providing necessary instructional supports

4. Continually monitoring progress

Armed with this understanding, instructional leaders can be more strategic and focused in their efforts to support teachers in promoting student learning.

CLARIFYING THE GOALS OF PURPOSEFUL LEARNING

For many experienced climbers, reaching the summit of Mount Everest, the tallest peak in the world, is a lifelong goal. To succeed in cresting the summit requires a passionate commitment of time and energy to prepare and extensively train.

Perhaps the most critical step toward reaching the top of the mountain, however, occurs long before the climber sets foot in the Himalayas: establishing the goals of the climb. Without clear goals, the chances that a climber will find himself or herself on an ice-covered peak overlooking Nepal to the north and India to the south are understandably quite slim. Moreover, as the climber ascends the mountain into ever more hazardous conditions, unerring focus on the goals of the climb increases in importance. Should we take any less seriously the need to identify and maintain unerring focus on learning goals in our schools?

Although multiple learning goals might surface in any given learning initiative, most of these goals fit under three major headings: cognitive, behavioral, and motivational. These three goals are interrelated and work in conjunction with one another. For instance, learning how to become an effective public speaker involves a combination of being able to understand and organize the content of the speech, to develop certain public-speaking behaviors, and to acquire motivational beliefs necessary to actually deliver speeches. Although these goals often work together, for the sake of clarity, each is discussed independently.

Cognitive Goals

To prepare for an ascent of Everest, a climber must learn many foundational concepts of climbing (how to move safely over ice, how to use ropes to negotiate sheer cliffs, how to recognize the warning signs of altitude sickness, and so forth). This understanding is requisite for a successful climb. Likewise, the academic skills and knowledge represented in the cognitive goals of learning serve as the foundation for academic success.

Cognitive learning goals include the academic skills and knowledge most often associated with formal schooling. For example, the cognitive learning goals for ninth-grade students might include an expectation for students to develop competence and mastery of the particular facts, concepts, principles, and strategies of their academic courses. In particular, a ninth-grade science student might be expected not only to know what procedure to use to conduct a scientific experiment, but also to understand how, why, and when to apply that procedure.

Cognitive learning goals represent what it means to be competent in a particular discipline. Increasingly, organizations representing various academic disciplines are developing and publishing cognitive goals for their respective disciplines. Contact information for several of these organizations is displayed in Table 13.2 ("Organizations That Have Developed Cognitive Learning Goals").

Table 13.2   Organizations That Have Developed Cognitive Learning Goals

Organization	Contact	Comments
National Council of Teachers of Mathematics	www.nctm.org	Provides math content goals for Grades PreK–12
National Council of Teachers of English	www.ncte.org	Provides English content goals for Grades K–12
National Academy of Sciences (National Academies Press)	www.nap.edu	Provides science content goals for Grades K–12
National Council for the Social Studies	www.ncss.org	Provides social studies content goals for Grades K–12
American Council on the Teaching of Foreign Languages	www.actfl.org	Provides foreign language content goals endorsed by this organization
Reading First	www.ed.gov/programs/ readingfirst/index.html	Provides suggestions for early literacy goals and instructional programs

Cognitive learning goals can also be found in district, state, and national learning standards. Instructional leaders can help teachers establish cognitive learning goals for their classrooms by encouraging teachers to become aware of and familiar with the discipline-specific learning standards as well as local content standards. In most cases, teachers can easily access content standards via state department of education Web sites. With this increased accessibility, teachers can more readily consult standards when establishing cognitive learning goals for their classrooms.

Once teachers have started to identify cognitive goals for their students to pursue, the next step will be to align their instructional strategies and assessments with these goals. Indeed, teachers are increasingly expected to align local learning goals with state standards. However, as Bradley Portin and his colleagues maintain, consideration should also be paid to the unique local needs of classrooms and schools. Therefore, instructional leaders should encourage teachers to pursue cognitive learning goals that not only represent the key skills and knowledge of the various academic disciplines but also reflect the unique learning needs of students in their school and classrooms.

Following selection of cognitive goals, teachers will need time to clarify their understanding of the content of those goals and determine how to incorporate that content into their instructional activities and classroom assessments. Encouraging teachers to use analytic tools such as updated versions of Bloom's Taxonomy of Educational Objectives can facilitate this process.

Revision of Bloom's Taxonomy

Lorin W. Anderson and her colleagues have recently revised Bloom's taxonomy in an effort to help teachers clarify the content of cognitive learning goals and align their classroom instruction and assessments to those goals. A detailed overview of the taxonomy and method for alignment is presented in their text *A Taxonomy for Learning, Teaching, and Assessing: A Revision of Bloom's Taxonomy of Educational Objectives.*

The revised taxonomy includes a combination of six cognitive processes and four types of knowledge. The six cognitive processes are remember, understand, apply, analyze, evaluate, and create. These cognitive processes help teachers clarify what they are asking students to do cognitively. For instance, a cognitive goal might require students to use the cognitive process *remember*. The natural question that follows from this is, Remember what? The *what* represents the type of knowledge specified in the content of the learning goal. The various types of knowledge include facts, concepts, procedures, and metacognitive knowledge.

Facts can be thought of as specific, discrete forms of knowledge, whereas *concepts* represent a more expansive and general type of knowledge. For example, the concept of war includes a variety of attributes (such as a violent conflict between entities) that can be used to describe specific instances of war.

Concepts are clarified by considering examples and non-examples that represent the various defining attributes. Facts, on the other hand, are situated within specific examples of some larger concept or principle. For instance, a given war has specific facts associated with it (such as dates, locations, who was involved, and so forth).

Procedures represent a form of knowledge that provides specific steps for completing some tasks or solving a type of problem (for example, the scientific method).

Finally, *metacognitive knowledge* represents strategic and self-knowledge that enables awareness and monitoring of one's own thinking. For example, when reading a text, students use metacognitive knowledge to monitor whether they understand what they are reading, to help organize and remember key aspects, and at a later date, to recall and use important aspects of what they read.

To support teachers in clarifying the content of cognitive learning goals, instructional leaders can help them develop their capacity to identify the cognitive processes and types of knowledge that make up those goals. Tools like the taxonomy offered by Anderson and her colleagues can serve as a very useful resource in this clarification process.

Once teachers become facile with the identification of cognitive processes and knowledge types, they will be in a better position to align their classroom instruction and assessments with cognitive goals found in state and national learning standards. Admittedly, this process of alignment is challenging. But with continued effort, teachers can make great strides in aligning their instructional strategies and assessments with student learning goals.

Example of Cognitive Learning in Fifth-Grade Science

Consider a teacher who wants to develop a cognitive learning goal in her fifth-grade science class. First, she identifies a local fifth-grade science standard. Assume the standard has the following wording: "Fifth-grade students are expected to **understand** and **use** the *scientific method* to **conduct** a *scientific experiment.*" Using the taxonomy developed by Anderson and her colleagues, the teacher (ideally in collaboration with her fifth-grade colleagues) could then identify the cognitive processes and knowledge types found in the standard. In this statement of the standard, the bold-printed verbs represent cognitive processes, and the italicized nouns represent the knowledge types.

The teacher might recognize that the scientific method is a particular type of knowledge called a "procedure." Because it is a procedure, it has a set of specific steps that could be taught to students. Next, the teacher might recognize that the verbs *understand* and *use* represent two different cognitive processes.

Starting with the cognitive process "understand," the teacher could develop a rubric defining what is meant by "understand" and later share this rubric with students. This could be accomplished by delineating different levels of performance that represent varying degrees of understanding, for example:

Level 1: Not Yet Understanding

Level 2: Partial Understanding

Level 3: Full Understanding

For each level, the teacher could develop specific criteria and clear examples. For instance, the description for Level 3: Full Understanding might explain that this level of performance requires that students accurately recall each step of the scientific method and provide an example that illustrates how to use each step in an actual experiment. The teacher could then move on to discuss what the cognitive process "use" means and delineate the various levels of competent use. This would continue for each cognitive process and type of knowledge represented in the various cognitive learning goals.

In summary, by taking the time to identify and clarify the content of cognitive learning goals, teachers put themselves in a better position to promote student learning. Instructional leaders can support this process by ensuring that teachers are aware of learning standards for the various disciplines. In addition, instructional leaders should encourage their teachers to clarify the content of those learning goals by using tools like the taxonomy developed by Anderson and her colleagues. As a result of these efforts, teachers will be more likely to incorporate cognitive learning goals into classroom instruction and assessment.

Behavioral Goals

Simply having an understanding (content knowledge) of mountaineering is not sufficient for a climber to ascend and safely descend from the tallest peak in the world. Specific behaviors play a key role in a successful climb to the summit. Similarly, in the classroom, it is not sufficient to focus solely on cognitive learning goals. Success in and out of school requires that students develop a variety of prosocial behaviors.

These behaviors include everything from learning the routines of the classroom, to cooperating with others in small groups, to resolving interpersonal conflicts. Instructional leaders play an important role in helping define the types of behaviors that will be expected of students within the classroom and throughout the entire school environment. In addition, they assist teachers and other instructional staff in identifying and promoting students' attainment of these goals.

On one hand, schools represent a microcosm of the larger society. On the other hand, schools are a somewhat strange and artificial environment. As a result, educators have a responsibility to help socialize students to schooling.

Clearly, this socialization process is more pronounced during the early elementary years of schooling. For example, an entering kindergarten student may be surprised to find that he cannot take a nap, eat a snack, or draw a picture with his new box of 128 crayons anytime he wishes. Most kindergarten teachers are sensitive to this and, through patient instruction, are able to teach incoming kindergarten students the routines and expectations of the school day. However, this socialization does not end in kindergarten.

Effective teachers, at all levels, recognize that the goal is to teach students how and why to follow routines rather than coerce them to comply. In this way, students can internalize prosocial behaviors and develop the skills, understanding, and disposition necessary for managing their own behavior.

As students progress through elementary, middle, and high school, complex and subtle behaviors are required of them—everything from cooperating with one another in small learning groups, to solving interpersonal conflicts, to engaging in structured debates and subject-related discourse. Teachers, therefore, have a responsibility to review, teach, and re-teach the behaviors necessary for students to participate successfully in the learning community.

Setting Schoolwide Expectations

Researchers have found that school-level programs can be a very effective way to support teachers in this responsibility of helping students internalize prosocial behaviors. By communicating and reinforcing behavioral expectations at the school level, instructional leaders help the entire learning community become what Thomas L. Good and Jere E. Brophy described as being "bonded" by shared values. Conversely, when behavioral expectations are unclear or inconsistent across classrooms and throughout the school, students are more likely to cause disruptions and demonstrate other maladaptive behaviors.

Instructional leaders have a responsibility to ensure that the school system operates under a clearly communicated framework of behavioral expectations that all members of the learning community understand and agree on. In doing so, they can see to it that students are treated in a more equitable fashion and that teachers feel supported and part of a larger system of beliefs and practices.

It is beyond the scope of this chapter to provide a detailed overview of schoolwide behavior-management systems. For specific guidance in this area, instructional leaders can consult a variety of resources that will support their efforts to create a prosocial schooling environment. For example, an issue of the *Informed Educator* published by the Educational Research Service (ERS) is dedicated to the topic of schoolwide approaches to discipline. In that issue, Stephanie Porch reports on the characteristics of schoolwide approaches to discipline that foster a culture of safety, support, shared responsibility, and student learning.

ERS also offers a series of Info-files (available at www.ers.org) on topics related to schoolwide discipline; these Info-files combine information from professional journals, summaries of research studies, related sources, and annotated bibliographies.

Components of Successful Schoolwide Systems

Most successful schoolwide management systems have in common several components. Good and Brophy summarized several of these components:

1. *Prepare a philosophy statement.* A philosophy statement should be created, with input from all relevant stakeholders (e.g., students, teachers, parents), that focuses on the importance of problem solving, learning, and healthy relationships within the learning community.

2. *Set school rules.* Developmentally appropriate expectations are established and clearly communicated to students (e.g., "be safe, fair, kind" at the elementary level; "respect the property, rights, and needs of others" at the secondary level).

3. *Establish schoolwide procedures.* Expectations are developed and taught concerning procedures to follow (e.g., cafeteria, playground, and hallway behavior; tardiness and attendance).

4. *Clarify the roles and responsibilities of all parties involved in managing student behavior.* Clear roles and responsibilities are taught to students (and staff). This includes what behaviors are expected of students and how and by whom certain actions will be handled (e.g., what behaviors students, teachers, and administrators are expected to handle, and what actions warrant involving parents, counselors, and other community agencies).

5. *Plan methods for creating a positive school climate and reinforcing students for desired behavior.* The focus is on methods for promoting student involvement and goal setting. This may include using positive reinforcements for students meeting behavioral expectations.

6. *Adopt a problem-solving model and teach it to staff and students.* All staff and students should be taught a general problem-solving model that will be used in resolving conflicts. The problem-solving model should help students understand how their behavior influences others, allow students to help define the problem, involve them in developing a plan to address the problem, and ultimately help students develop the skills to proactively resolve problems and become self-managers of their own behavior.

7. *Adopt a format for developing positive behavior-change plans for students who present ongoing or serious behavior problems.* There should be a plan for addressing serious or persistent behaviors that require immediate intervention. This should be used in conjunction with the school's problem-solving model.

8. *Develop forms for communicating among teachers, administrators, and parents.* A record keeping system that generates reports should be established and used for problem solving. This system can also be used to communicate information to parents, students, teachers, and related educators.

9. *Establish a schoolwide student-management committee and clarify its role.* This group of individuals would work to ensure that the schoolwide management system is working effectively. Roles of the committee might include reviewing school-level student

behavior data (e.g., attendance, behavioral referrals), establishing methods for disseminating information, evaluating policies and procedures, and making any necessary changes to the management system.

Strategies to Combat Specific Problems: Bullying

In addition to a general schoolwide management system, instructional leaders may want to establish strategies for preventing and addressing specific problems, such as bullying. Good and Brophy explain that anti-bullying strategies, such as those modeled after Dan Olweus's program, provide instructional leaders with techniques for cultivating environmental conditions that prevent and successfully address the problem of bullying.

These strategies include use of questionnaires to assess the nature of bullying within the school and enlistment of the entire school community to monitor and address incidents of bullying. In this way, the school system can establish a healthy balance between a school environment that is supportive of students yet quickly and appropriately addresses unacceptable behaviors.

Bullying is a serious and complex problem, and to succeed in stopping it, educators must acquire a deep understanding of how to maintain a positive school environment. School leaders have a responsibility to develop and continually monitor strategies for addressing this unique and important schoolwide challenge.

A variety of resources and general strategies are available to school leaders for both prevention of and response to bullying. For instance, the Committee for Children has developed a three-phase training program, "Steps to Respect: A Bullying Prevention Program." The three phases include getting the whole school onboard; training staff and parents to handle bullying; and teaching students to recognize, refuse, and report bullying. The program helps educators develop the schoolwide capacity to prevent bullying.

Besides training programs, numerous print resources can help leaders develop a proactive strategy. For instance, school leaders may find Walter B. Roberts Jr.'s *Bullying From Both Sides* useful in understanding and developing a plan for working with bullies and victims. Leaders who work in kindergarten through eighth-grade settings may gain insights and strategies from Marie-Nathalie Beaudoin and Maureen Taylor's *Breaking the Culture of Bullying and Disrespect, Grades K-8: Best Practices and Successful Strategies.* Leaders who work in secondary settings can turn to Keith Sullivan, Mark Cleary, and Ginny Sullivan's *Bullying in Secondary Schools: What It Looks Like and How to Manage It.*

Ultimately, for students to successfully navigate the demands of schooling, they must be able to work together, resolve conflicts, and regulate their own learning and behavior within the classroom and broader school community. By ensuring that behavioral goals are clearly communicated, understood, and shared by all members of the learning community, instructional leaders will create a learning environment in which all students can thrive.

Motivational Goals

Returning to the metaphor of mountain climbing, the relationship between a successful climb and the climber's will to succeed is critically important. Likewise, in attempting to understand and support student success, educators cannot afford to overlook the role of students' motivational beliefs.

Paul R. Pintrich, Ronald W. Marx, and Robert A. Boyle describe motivational beliefs as the reason students engage in or avoid achievement behavior. These beliefs influence whether students will pay attention, challenge themselves, take academic risks, sustain high levels of effort, learn from mistakes, and ultimately succeed in their academic endeavors. Therefore, when establishing schoolwide and classroom learning goals, instructional leaders should include goals that focus on cultivation of healthy, adaptive motivational beliefs in students.

Unfortunately, people rarely consider motivational goals when establishing learning goals or when rendering judgments of students' success in attaining those goals. For example, many policymakers, stakeholders, and educators base their judgments of success largely (if not entirely) on test scores. Although test scores provide useful information, most tests measure a far too narrow range of learning outcomes.

The Problem of Measuring Motivational Beliefs

Test scores may accurately show gains in knowledge or skills but fail to reveal whether students are experiencing parallel gains (or declines) in their achievement motivation. Consider, for example, a teacher who promotes students' computational abilities by relying heavily on the use of timed, skill-and-drill mathematics worksheets. As a result of this instructional method, students' scores in math rise. Yet what if students who once enjoyed math now see little value in it, because they associate it with timed, comparative worksheets?

In rendering a judgment on whether instruction was a success, the increase in test scores would need to be weighed against the decline in students' motivational beliefs about math.

Conversely, consider the student who, as a result of a series of positive learning experiences, has—for the first time in her academic career—come to value science. Because of her positive experience learning about science through an instructional method that engaged and challenged her, she looks forward to learning more. To improve her understanding, she decides to take more science classes and do her own independent reading and study. Few would disagree that such an outcome is a sign of successful learning.

Because motivational goals are rarely considered, the initial process of establishing schoolwide and classroom motivational goals can be quite overwhelming. Instructional leaders can anticipate difficult questions to surface early in the process. For example, what motivational beliefs are most important? How can such beliefs be identified and monitored?

Although there are no easy answers to these questions, educational researchers have been busily working to develop insights, suggestions, and considerations for establishing motivational goals.

Types of Motivational Beliefs

Over the past 20 years, relatively consistent findings have enabled scholars to start identifying motivational beliefs that seem most related to positive student outcomes. For example, Pintrich and his colleagues have organized key motivational beliefs along two major dimensions: *value beliefs* and *expectancy beliefs*.

Value beliefs pertain to the reasons students choose to learn. These reasons include personal interest, perceived importance, and achievement goals. Researchers have found that the most adaptive value beliefs include (a) gaining interest in what is being learned, (b) finding personal value in the topic, and (c) holding achievement goals that focus on learning, creativity, and understanding.

Expectancy beliefs pertain to self-judgments of competence. Pintrich and his colleagues explain that these beliefs involve students' perceptions of how much control they have over learning and the extent to which they feel capable of success. Researchers have found a positive association between expectancy beliefs and academic outcomes. Improved academic outcomes have been linked with students' belief that they are in control of their own learning and that they can be successful.

Chapter 14 provides considerations and resources for assessing and monitoring students' motivational goals. In addition, instructional leaders can develop a deeper understanding of student motivation by turning to sources written specifically for educators regarding the cultivation of student motivation.

For example, Paul R. Pintrich and Dale H. Schunk provide a comprehensive overview of applied theories and practical considerations for promoting student motivation in their text *Motivation in Education: Theory, Research, and Applications.* Similarly, Deborah Stipek offers practical guidance and insights in her text *Motivation to Learn: From Theory to Practice.* Both texts provide a thorough survey of the research on motivation as applied to education and will serve as useful resources for developing schoolwide and classroom motivational goals.

SELECTING INSTRUCTIONAL STRATEGIES

After setting the goals of a climb, the successful climber establishes a strategy for accomplishing that goal. The strategy must be flexible enough to accommodate changing weather conditions and obstacles that may be faced on the trail. Yet the strategy must be one that has succeeded on previous ascents (by the climber or others before), and it must be tailored to the strengths, ability, and personal goals of the individual climber.

Similarly, once the learning goals have been established, the next step is to select instructional strategies that will ensure the successful attainment of those goals. An instructional strategy can be thought of as a systematic approach used to promote the attainment of student learning goals. In this view, instructional strategies can take the form of schoolwide literacy programs, an anti-bullying program, or a particular instructional technique for teaching reading (such as phonics or whole language).

Increasingly, instructional leaders are expected to ensure that teachers are using evidence-based instructional strategies to promote student learning. This is particularly the case for instructional leaders who rely on federal funding. For example, the No Child Left Behind Act of 2001 stipulates that federally funded instructional programs must have a basis in "scientifically based research." This legislation defines scientifically based research as "research that involves the application of rigorous, systematic, and objective procedures to obtain reliable and valid knowledge relevant to educational activities and programs" (No Child Left Behind Act of 2001, Pub. I, No. 107-110, 115 Stat. 1425 2002).

The notion of scientifically based research is somewhat contentious. On one hand, scholars worry that such a definition will result in the exclusion of certain viable research traditions, particularly qualitative research. On the other hand, proponents, such as Grover J. Whitehurst, believe that current educational practices rely too much on unsystematic, "hit or miss" techniques. To attain the goal of promoting student learning for all students, educational practice must move toward scientific research, he contends.

Both positions raise important issues and offer compelling arguments. Common to both views is the recognition that practice can and should be supported by educational research.

When selecting instructional strategies, most educators realize that there are no magic bullets or sure-fire prescriptions for success. The outcomes of any given strategy will vary as a function of the context, the students, the teachers, and other relevant conditions in which it is used. Yet selection of relevant instructional strategies that have a basis in research will increase the likelihood the students will attain their particular learning goals. Myriam Met (as cited in Gordon Cawelti) explains:

> Research cannot and does not identify the right or best way to teach, nor does it suggest certain instructional practices should always or should never be used. But research *can* illuminate which instructional practices are most likely to achieve desired results, with which kinds of learners, and under what conditions.

Instructional leaders should help their teachers recognize that research methods cannot account for all possible variations in school contexts, needs, and values, so no conclusions of research are ever foolproof, especially when applied to a particular school culture. Nevertheless, leaders should still stress to their staffs the importance of selecting evidence-based instructional practices. To the extent possible, such strategies should have a solid track record of consistently demonstrated effectiveness in similar learning contexts.

Ultimately, instructional leaders will need to rely on their own and their teachers' professional judgment and expertise in selecting and employing instructional strategies. James Shaver (as cited in Cawelti) elaborates on this point:

> Sound instructional decisions must be based on the educational values of the teacher, the school, the school district, and the community, as well as on district and state guidelines and requirements. Skilled, thoughtful, and motivated teachers must adapt and implement techniques or approaches suggested by research findings to achieve desired student outcomes. . . . The experiences and practical knowledge of the individual teacher and his or her colleagues are crucial in deciding upon applications.

Several resources present summaries of evidence-based practices that can assist teachers in the process of selecting techniques and strategies aimed at promoting the attainment of student learning goals. For example, Cawelti (2004) edited the *Handbook of Research on Improving Student Achievement* (3rd ed.), which provides a well-organized, accessible summary of research on techniques for promoting student learning. Topics in the handbook include everything from a synthesis of research on high-performing school systems to effective techniques across the various content areas, and even summaries of research on staff development.

Similarly, the What Works Clearinghouse summarizes research findings on a variety of educational practices, strategies, and reform initiatives. Established by the U.S. Department of Education, the clearinghouse's resources are accessible at www.w-w-c.org. It plans to provide reports on a variety of topics, including peer-assisted learning, middle-level mathematics, behavior, character education, dropout prevention, English-language learning, and reading. Instructional leaders should be aware that the clearinghouse has critics who argue that the selection criteria may be too restrictive and thus deny access to potentially useful educational research.

Rather than get mired in this debate, instructional leaders can still benefit from sources such as the clearinghouse by viewing their summaries and evaluations of research as potentially useful information for making decisions. This is a message they can share with their teachers. Of course, educators should make decisions about instructional strategies only after consulting multiple sources and exercising their own professional judgment. In this manner, instructional leaders can better support their teachers' efforts to promote student learning.

CONCLUSION: COLLABORATION IS THE ROUTE TO SUCCESS

In this chapter, we have presented an overview of considerations for how instructional leaders can support the learning process. Instructional leaders' responsibilities for supporting the learning process are summarized as follows:

- Think critically about the nature of learning and become familiar with various perspectives of human learning (behaviorism, social learning theory, cognitive information processing, individual constructivism, and social constructivism).
- Recognize that all learning involves change.
- Recognize that school learning involves purposeful, goal-directed change.
- Support teachers' efforts to promote the learning process by focusing on the four interrelated elements of clarifying learning goals, determining where students are in relation to those goals, providing necessary instructional support, and continually monitoring progress.
- Recognize the three basic goals of purposeful learning (cognitive goals, behavioral goals, and motivational goals) and consider how better to support teachers in identifying and clarifying the content of those goals.
- Acquire and use information resources for consideration in selecting research-based strategies to ensure the attainment of student learning goals.

We recognize that supporting the learning process is a challenging task. However difficult this task may seem, instructional leaders who take up the challenge and faithfully perform these responsibilities will see positive results. The likelihood of success increases as leaders collaborate with their teachers—drawing from their collective insights—and use the knowledge provided by the professional research community. All these efforts will result in student success across a wide range of learning goals.

REFLECTIONS

1. What is your own view of how students learn? Does your view align with a particular formal learning theory or aspects of various learning theories? How does your view of the learning process influence your instructional and leadership decisions?

2. How might you take the lead in clarifying student learning goals for students and teachers? What learning goals seem the most ill defined in your building (motivational, academic, or behavioral)? How might you communicate to students, teachers, and parents the importance of clarifying and monitoring all three types of learning goals?

3. How does your school currently select and use instructional strategies? How effective are these strategies for ensuring that all learners successfully attain learning goals? How might you take the lead in considering, selecting, and monitoring appropriate instructional strategies?

4. How might you take the lead in starting conversations with teachers and students about the learning process? And how might you work collaboratively with teachers and students in clarifying learning goals, determining where learners are in relation to those goals, developing strategies for attaining those goals, and monitoring progress?

5. How might you continue to develop your understanding of the learning process? For example, challenge yourself to identify some aspect of the learning process you would like to know more about. Next, develop an action plan to increase and share your understanding. Finally, consider how you might implement your new insights into your instructional and leadership decisions.

14

Instructional Leadership

Progress Monitoring

Ronald A. Beghetto and
Leanne R. Ketterlin-Geller

P rogress monitoring is at the heart of all successful learning initiatives. Regardless of whether the learning initiative is a third-grade math unit or schoolwide literacy reform, students, teachers, principals, and other stakeholders need to have a clear sense of whether their efforts are leading to success. Progress monitoring is a process that provides learners and related stakeholders with the information necessary for continual improvement. Instructional leaders have a responsibility to cultivate a community of practice that uses such information to ensure systemwide success.

In this chapter, we provide an overview of progress monitoring and offer considerations for how to manage this process. The first two sections define *progress monitoring* and highlight the importance of using multiple sources of information. We then discuss how instructional leaders can improve the interpretation and use of information generated by this process. We also comment on the importance of communicating progress. The final section provides an example of a school district that used progress monitoring to help meet learning goals.

WHAT IS PROGRESS MONITORING?

Progress monitoring is a form of evaluative decision making, and it has many of the characteristics of formative assessment. Paul Black and Dylan William explain that the primary purpose of formative assessment is to support student learning. Progress monitoring involves a variety of judgments aimed at promoting student learning, including the following:

- How to define and communicate learning goals
- Whether learners have requisite skills and resources
- Whether learners are making satisfactory progress
- Whether instructional supports and resources need to be adjusted
- How successes can be sustained

Progress monitoring is a never-ending process, but at three major points, instructional leaders must collect information and make improvement-based decisions:

1. Prior to commencing the initiative

2. During the initiative

3. Following the initiative

Prior to Commencing the Initiative

Successful progress monitoring starts with careful planning and preparation. This involves clearly defining and communicating learning goals. Without clear goals, it is difficult, if not impossible, to monitor whether learners are making progress toward those goals. And from the perspective of a learner, if you don't know where you are going, you have little investment in getting there.

To stimulate careful planning, Table 14.1 ("Decisions Prior to Commencing a Learning Initiative") lists the kinds of questions leaders need to consider before launching an instructional initiative.

One responsibility of instructional leaders is to help teachers recognize the importance, prior to starting an instructional lesson, of clearly defining and communicating to students the criteria for success. In doing so, teachers will increase the likelihood that students take ownership of the learning process. Angela, a teacher who came to this realization, told Black and William:

> I have thought carefully about students taking *ownership* of their learning. I have now thought more about letting students know what the intention of the lesson is and what they need to do to *achieve* it. This way they have to think about what they know and take more *responsibility* for their own learning.

Regardless of the scope of the learning initiative, instructional leaders should promote the development of clear and appropriate learning goals. Chapter 13 ("Instructional Leadership: Supporting the Learning Process") explains how to establish and communicate learning goals.

Once learning goals have been clearly defined, the next step involves determining the learners' starting point (or baseline). Unless you know where learners are in relation to the learning goals before they begin, it is impossible to make accurate determinations of progress. Taking the time to assess students' prior knowledge also provides useful insights

Table 14.1   Decisions Prior to Commencing a Learning Initiative

Questions to Consider

What are the goals of the initiative?

- What academic goals do we have for learners (e.g., remembering, identifying, applying, comparing, creating)?
- What behavioral goals do we have for learners (e.g., working independently, collaborating with peers, demonstrating respect)?
- What motivational goals do we have for learners (e.g., high levels of interest and engagement, belief in their ability to be successful)?
- Why are these goals important? What data are we basing this on?
- Are there more important goals?

What strategies will we use to support learning?

- Why are we using these strategies? What strategies might be more effective? What research evidence supports these strategies?
- How will we establish, monitor, and maintain learner engagement?

What will success look like?

- How will we know success when we see it?
- How will we ensure that learners recognize success (e.g., model, demonstrate, provide examples)?

How will we determine whether learners are successful?

- How will we monitor learner success? What are the criteria for success?
- How often and when will we monitor progress?

What prior knowledge and skills do learners need to be successful?

- Do all learners have a realistic opportunity to experience success?
- What will we do if learners do not have the prerequisite skills?

What do learners already know?

- How will we determine what they already know?
- How do we intend to build on what they already know?
- What are learners' attitudes toward this topic?
- How are we ensuring that learners focus on mastery?
- How might we tailor the lessons to learner needs?

What are learners' judgments of their ability to be successful?

- How will we ensure that learners develop or maintain positive self-judgments of their ability?

What are some challenges we expect to encounter?

- What special circumstances or learner needs do we need to be aware of?
- How do we intend to address those circumstances or needs?
- How might these special circumstances impede our ability to monitor progress?

regarding the appropriateness of the learning goals. As Black and William point out, this prior assessment also reveals "any gaps or misconceptions in that knowledge, so that [the initiative] can address the learners' real needs."

Finally, prior to commencing the learning initiative, instructional leaders should take the time to anticipate special circumstances or learner needs that might pose challenges to the success of the initiative. By anticipating challenges early on, instructional leaders will increase the likelihood that they can respond to these challenges.

For example, prior to an initiative to reform math instruction, planners may discover that several students have limited English proficiency. To gain an accurate assessment of these students' mathematical reasoning using story problems, leaders would need to ensure that the prompts are written in the students' primary language. In this way, the results are more likely to reflect their mathematical reasoning rather than their inability to understand the English language.

During the Initiative

By continually monitoring progress, instructional leaders have the opportunity to adjust and fine-tune the goals, instructional supports, and feedback to learners. In this way, success is engineered into the process. Waiting until the end of a learning initiative to determine whether the goals were appropriate or whether instructional supports should have been adjusted is too late. Table 14.2 ("Decisions During a Learning Initiative") provides sample questions to help instructional leaders consider how to improve progress monitoring while a learning initiative is under way.

Instructional reform efforts have a long legacy of initiatives failing and then, after it was too late, leaders discovering that the goals of the reform were never clearly understood or the type of instructional support was not specified for the particular needs of teachers and students. The sooner instructional leaders can identify potential problems, the more likely they can intervene and make necessary adjustments. Therefore, when monitoring progress, they need to ensure that timely feedback is available to learners, teachers, and relevant instructional decision makers. Not only will this information guide necessary modifications to learning and instruction, it will also promote a shared responsibility for monitoring progress.

Given the multitude of responsibilities and limited time of instructional leaders, schoolwide progress monitoring is not feasible without the assistance of computerized data-storage systems. Instructional leaders can use a variety of software products to manage the information necessary for monitoring progress. Michelle Mengeling, a contributor to the *Research Review for School Leaders,* provides an overview of classroom-based products in her chapter "Computer Software Products for Classroom Assessment Purposes."

Victoria Bernhardt has a series of practical data-management tools and materials (for example, *Data Analysis for Continuous School Improvement)* for collecting, managing, and using data to monitor schoolwide progress. Finally, Chapter 18 ("Managing Data for Decision Making: Creating Knowledge From Information") demonstrates how to display data for decision making.

Ultimately, administrators, teachers, and students will only realize the benefits of progress monitoring if they actually use the information it generates to make adjustments to their teaching and learning. To increase the usefulness of this information, it should be

Table 14.2   Decisions During a Learning Initiative

Questions to Consider

How are we doing?

- Do learners understand the goal? How do we know?
- Do learners understand what they need to do to be successful? How do we know?
- Are we meeting our intended goals?
- What can we do to get a better sense of how we are doing?

How are learners doing?

- Do they understand what we are doing?
- Are they engaged in learning? How do we know?
- Are they making meaningful connections to what they already know?
- Where are learners in relation to where they need to be to be successful?
- Are we providing sufficient feedback to learners regarding where they are in relation to where they need to be?
- Are we giving learners an opportunity to demonstrate what they know, what they can do, and their attitudes toward the goals of this initiative?
- Are learners frustrated? Bored? How do we know?
- What are learners' attitudes and beliefs about what we are doing? Are these attitudes and beliefs healthy?

What is happening unexpectedly?

- Why might this be happening? How might we have anticipated this?
- Do we need to adjust our learning goals? What other adjustments might we need to make?
- Do we need to adjust or refine our criteria for success?
- Do we need to abandon our plan and try something new?
- What might we be missing?

---

timely and accessible. Also, this information should both describe learners' current standing and provide specific insights for making necessary adjustments so learners reach their goals.

Following the Initiative

Some learning initiatives have natural ending points (a high school science unit on photosynthesis, for example). Other learning initiatives are ongoing (such as a schoolwide literacy reform) but have natural break points at the end of the academic year. At the end points of an initiative, it is important to make a summative appraisal of how well the initiative has met its goals.

Table 14.3 ("Decisions Following a Learning Initiative") lists sample questions instructional leaders can consider when an initiative ends or reaches a break point. It is important to keep in mind that even though summative judgments should be made (such as "Did we successfully meet our goals?"), the primary purpose of these appraisals is to plan for upcoming and continuing learning initiatives.

Table 14.3   Decisions Following a Learning Initiative

Questions to Consider

How did we do?

- Did we effectively communicate our expectations and the criteria for success? How do we know?
- Did we accomplish our intended goals? How do we know?
- Did we make necessary modifications?
- What other information might we need to collect to determine how well we did?

How did learners do?

- How successful were learners in meeting the intended goals?
- Did learners perform in a way that was consistent with other forms of evidence (e.g., prior performance, external measures of achievement, our expectations)? Why might this be the case?
- Did all the information we collected portray a consistent picture of learner performance?
- How do learners judge their own success of this initiative?
- How did participating in this initiative influence learners' perceptions of their ability to be successful in the future?
- Did something interfere with learners' ability to represent what they know, can do, and believe?
- To the extent that this initiative is successful, how might we sustain this success?

What happened unexpectedly?

- What positive, unintended outcomes resulted from this initiative?
- What challenges occurred unexpectedly?
- Given what happened unexpectedly, can we consider this initiative a success?
- Do we need to revisit aspects of this initiative?
- How will the results of this initiative influence initiatives we undertake in the future?
- What would we have done differently?
- What did we learn from engaging in this initiative?

Summative assessments, such as tests at the end of units, are for teachers a useful tool to guide students toward improved learning. For example, teachers can have students reflect on the results of their tests, try to learn from the process by clarifying misunderstandings, and help students view test results as information regarding what they did well and where they need to continue to focus their efforts. Belinda, a teacher who used summative assessments in the support of ongoing learning, explained her process to Black and William:

> After each end of the term test, the class is grouped now to learn from each other. Clare has interviewed them on this experience and they are very positive about the effects. Some of their comments show that they are starting to value the learning process more highly and they appreciate the fact that misunderstandings are given time to be resolved, either in groups or by me. They feel that the pressure to succeed in tests is being replaced by the need to understand the work that has been covered and the test is just an assessment along the way of what needs more work and what seems to be.

Instructional leaders have a responsibility to help teachers, students, parents, and related stakeholders see summative assessments as yet another form of information to serve the purpose of promoting student learning. In this way, they can help ensure that such information is not viewed as threatening and adversarial, but as feedback that can actually support continued learning.

USING MULTIPLE SOURCES OF INFORMATION TO MONITOR PROGRESS

In every phase of a learning initiative (prior, during, after), instructional leaders should use a variety of tools to monitor progress. Use of multiple assessments lets leaders base their judgments of progress on consistent and comprehensive information. Instructional leaders, therefore, should make it a priority to become aware of a wide variety of assessment methods, so they can be more creative and skillful in how they use this information to render decisions. At the classroom level, leaders also have a responsibility to ensure that teachers are aware of assessment methods and their appropriate uses.

This section briefly highlights familiar and newer assessment sources that instructional leaders and teachers can use to monitor progress on a variety of learning goals.

Richard Stiggins provides an overview of these methods in his 2001 book on assessment. Among the assessment methods he describes are the following:

1. Selected response assessments (that is, assessments made up of multiple choice, matching, true/false, fill-in-the-blank, and short answer items)

2. Essay assessments (that is, open-ended questions requiring an original written response)

3. Performance assessments (that is, requiring students to perform or carry out some specific behavior or activity, for example, conduct a scientific experiment or sing a song)

4. Personal communication assessments (that is, conversing with, questioning, or observing students speaking about their knowledge and understanding of some topic of interest)

In addition, many schools use student portfolios as a way to document student progress. Portfolios are helpful for organizing collections of student work, including performance on tests, class exercises, and homework tasks designed to demonstrate proficiency in a broad domain. To the extent schools determine that portfolios are a useful method for monitoring progress, instructional leaders have a responsibility to provide training opportunities and curricular support for teachers so they can incorporate the portfolios into the school's overall assessment system. Unless portfolios are clearly connected and integrated into systemwide progress monitoring, they can become a time-consuming and meaningless dumping bin of student work.

For monitoring progress on behavioral and motivational goals, it is important to use methods best suited for assessing these goals. Ronald A. Beghetto provided classroom teachers with considerations for assessing students' motivational beliefs. Blaine R. Worthen, James R. Sanders, and Jody L. Fitzpatrick outline several of these methods, as follows:

1. Questionnaires and surveys (used to measure beliefs, attitudes, opinions, and dispositions, for example, surveying students' attitudes toward math)

2. Interviews and focus groups (that is, asking students about their perceptions and experiences of instruction and following up on responses for clarification)

3. Observation (observing behavior, reactions, and interactions of students, for example, looking for engagement, frustration, and so forth)

4. Review of existing documents and records (such as samples of student work, assessment data, classroom grades, and achievement and other standardized test data)

Instructional leaders are responsible for helping teachers understand how to match learning goals with appropriate assessment methods. For example, a multiple-choice test cannot assess a student's ability to perform a scientific procedure, but it can assess the student's understanding of the steps of the procedure and relevant background information. In this case, a science teacher might use, in conjunction with a performance assessment, a multiple-choice test to determine the student's understanding of relevant information related to the particular experiment (such as safety precautions, the sequence of steps necessary for conducting the experiment, the underlying purpose of the experiment).

Likewise, for measuring a student's motivation to learn math facts, a teacher-based observation may be less effective than a brief questionnaire or a one-on-one interview. For help in matching types of learning goals with specific assessment methods, several excellent, practical resources are available. Stiggins's (2001) book on assessment, mentioned earlier, is a particularly useful resource, as is Norman E. Gronlund's *Assessment of Student Achievement.*

For help in schoolwide progress monitoring, instructional leaders can turn to resources such as Mike Schmoker's *The Results Fieldbook* for an overview of practical strategies and best practices from successful school districts. Resources such as this will expose instructional leaders to assessment procedures that allow them to monitor and generate summaries of progress for individual learners, classrooms, schools, and even the entire district.

For example, a well-coordinated progress-monitoring system should be able to provide classroom teachers with information on how well each student is progressing on a learning goal (for example, Joey has met 25 percent of his academic reading goals), and also provide a classroom summary of how all students are progressing (for example, 60 percent of the class has met the academic reading goals). That same system can then aggregate performance data to the school level, so the principal can see how individual classrooms are progressing as well as how well the entire school is doing.

Similarly, district-level instructional leaders can further aggregate that information to determine how well particular schools and the entire district are progressing.

In summary, when instructional leaders help teachers become aware of and use a combination of assessment methods, they help build what Stiggins (2001) refers to as the "assessment literacy" of the school. This capability in turn ensures that student learning is more effectively and efficiently monitored. A robust assessment system, which frequently uses multiple assessment methods, allows instructional leaders at the classroom, school, and district levels to get a more comprehensive picture of how learning initiatives are progressing.

IMPROVING THE INTERPRETATION AND USE OF INFORMATION

Progress monitoring has the primary purpose of providing information that administrators, teachers, and students can act on to improve teaching and learning. Instructional leaders must ensure that this information is interpreted accurately and used appropriately. Improving the interpretation and use of such information starts with an understanding of the concepts of *reliability* and *validity*.

Reliability and validity are technical terms used by test developers, researchers, and other measurement experts. Although teachers and other decision makers do not need to know the technical aspects of these terms, instructional leaders should ensure that anyone who uses assessment information to make decisions has at least a working understanding of reliability and validity.

Reliability

Reliability is about consistency. The Joint Committee on Standards for Educational Evaluation defines *reliability* as "consistency of the scores or information obtained from an information-gathering process." To be reliable, an assessment tool should provide the same or very similar results regardless of when the test was administered and by whom it was given and scored. For example, Sam's results on a test of oral reading fluency should be the same when it is administered and scored by Mr. Chen in the morning and by Ms. Sanchez in the afternoon.

In addition, there should be no mystery in how judgments of progress are derived. The use of rubrics and checklists can be helpful in demystifying the criteria for success. Effective rubrics provide a road map of success by documenting the criteria for different levels of competence. Instructional leaders can refer teachers to practical guides for constructing and incorporating rubrics into their instructional routines. Such guides can be retrieved from the free, peer-reviewed, electronic journal *Practical Assessment, Research and Evaluation* (available at www.PAREonline.net) by conducting a keyword search for *rubrics*.

Also, instructional leaders may want their leadership team to provide a "reliability check" of the information they are using to monitor progress. This is particularly true for important decisions such as those involving funding or student placement. In such cases, instructional leaders could work with a team to develop scoring guides and then conduct independent, multiple assessments to rate progress of a particular learning initiative. If the resulting independent ratings are essentially the same, the results could be considered reliable.

Ultimately, when decision makers base their judgments on reliable information, they are improving the trustworthiness and accuracy of those judgments. Important as reliable information is for making accurate judgments, it is not sufficient. Just because the information is reliable does not ensure the accuracy of judgments based on that information. The accuracy of judgments is related to but different from reliability; accuracy of judgments is a validity issue.

Validity

Validity pertains to the trustworthiness and accuracy of the interpretation and uses of assessment results. Elaborating on this view, the Joint Committee on Standards for Educational Evaluation explains that *validity* is "the degree to which inferences drawn about a student's knowledge, skills, attitudes, and behaviors from the results of assessment methods used are correct, trustworthy, and appropriate for making decisions about students."

As this definition implies, care must be taken in making decisions about student progress based on assessment results. Basing decisions on inaccurate information can do more harm than good. For example, unfounded decisions can misrepresent what students know and can do, diminish student motivation, and unnecessarily limit student potential. This is why James W. Popham describes validity as the single most important consideration for instructional leaders when assessing and evaluating students.

Several forms of evidence about validity can be gathered and evaluated prior to making important decisions based on assessment results. For example, it is important to have a rationale for why an assessment was created and how it will, in fact, measure the intended skills or knowledge. Also, the content of the assessment should match what was taught. To determine how closely they do match, the instructional leader can compare the content of the assessment with the standards or expectations for the particular learning goal.

Results from different assessments of the same content can also be compared to see if the results are consistent and if performance on one assessment predicts performance on another. For example, performance on a multiple-choice math test can be compared with performance on a test requiring students to write out their answers. If the performance is similar across tests, then it can be concluded that the test is measuring the same content.

Finally, information collected from any assessment method is meaningless on its own. To draw meaning from the information for their decision making, instructional leaders must compare it with something: a frame of reference. The most common frames of reference used to interpret assessment information are norm and criterion.

As Gronlund explains, norm-referenced judgments compare the performance of a learner with the performance of others who represent typical performance. Norms provide insight into an "individual's performance in terms of how it compares to the performance of others."

Criterion-referenced judgments, on the other hand, compare performance with a standard of performance (for example, learners' prior standing or state benchmarks). The Joint Committee on Standards for Educational Evaluation states that information about student performance can be compared with a criterion to provide insights into how well a learner performed in relation to specified standards, aptitude or anticipated growth, amount of improvement, or amount learned.

COMMUNICATING PROGRESS

Successful attainment of learning goals depends on frequent communication of progress to learners. Stiggins (2001) recommends that this communication include informative feedback regarding the criteria necessary for meeting learning goals and where learners are in relation to those goals. When instructional leaders, students, parents, and other stakeholders have a clear sense of the learning outcomes and an understanding of the criteria for success, they are more likely to understand what is necessary for continued progress. For this to happen, Black and William explain, "it must be possible to break down the path from the current position to the goal, into a series of steps that the learner can take."

Ideally, the feedback provided to students will teach them how to break down goals into clear steps for themselves. Until students can do this on their own, teachers have the responsibility to provide this information to students in the form of frequent feedback. Unfortunately, Black and William have found that many teachers do not have a clear sense of this progression, nor do they know how to communicate it to students. The candid comments of a teacher they worked with are illustrative: "I know he's a level 4, but I don't know what to do to get him to level 5."

A key responsibility of instructional leaders is to help teachers develop the comfort to reflect honestly on their capacity to support the progress of learning. And when teachers are not ready to guide their students to success, leaders must develop environments that provide the supervision and professional development necessary to build this capacity in their teachers.

In an article published in 2000, Richard J. Stiggins outlined the responsibilities of educational leaders in regard to assessment. Before teachers can effectively communicate the successful progression of learning to their students, they must first understand it themselves, and assessment-savvy administrators can help teachers gain the understanding they need.

Instructional leaders can be confident that effective communication is occurring when students take ownership of their own learning and develop the skills for assessing their own progress. Stiggins (2001) warns, though, that students can only take ownership of the process if they are meaningfully involved. Ultimately, every member of the learning community must be aware of the school's learning goals, know the criteria for success, and be capable of articulating what they are doing to ensure the successful attainment of those goals.

For students, this level of understanding is especially critical. There are few instances of communication about learning as powerful as when students themselves are able to explain to parents, teachers, administrators, and others their learning goals, where they are in relation to those goals, the progress they have made, and the steps they intend to take to continue to make progress in reaching their goals.

AN EXAMPLE: PROGRESS MONITORING IN A SCHOOL DISTRICT

Thus far, we have provided an overview of considerations for monitoring and evaluating progress toward achieving learning goals. To help bring this process to life, we present an example of an actual school district that used progress monitoring to meet its learning goals.

Northwest School District is a suburban district in the Pacific Northwest. (All school and district names have been changed for confidentiality.) The district operates five elementary schools, two middle schools, two kindergarten through eighth-grade schools, and two high schools. Of the district's 4,000 students, 12 percent received special-education services, 45 percent received free or reduced lunches, and approximately 2 percent were served in English as a Second Language programs. Eighty percent of the elementary schools were identified as Title I. The majority of students (88 percent) were white.

The district was faced with the challenge of lacking a comprehensive, well-established reading program. The existing reading program lacked continuity among classrooms and schools within the district. Without a districtwide curriculum, the reading program had evolved over the years into a site-based design permitting teachers to utilize various independent reading programs. This variation eroded the curricular cohesion between grade levels and across the district.

Externally, the district also experienced demographic changes. There was a surge in the number of referrals to the Special-Education Program and a significant number of students within the Title 1 Program. Many of these students had been identified for these programs based on poor reading abilities. Faced with this situation, the leadership at Northwest School District implemented a systemic instructional reform initiative in conjunction with a process for monitoring progress.

Prior to the Learning Initiative

The Northwest School District identified the lack of a comprehensive reading program as the underlying cause of a variety of systems-level as well as individual-level concerns. Upon identifying the root problem, the school district formed a K–3 Reading Committee to establish common goals. During the regularly scheduled meetings, the committee evaluated current practices in reading instruction by reviewing demographic information, student assessment data, and instructional techniques.

The committee also mapped assessment data onto research statistics from the Institute for Development of Educational Achievement to estimate the efficacy of existing reading programs. From the previous year's data, the team identified 15 percent of end-of-the-year first graders as nonreaders.

By synthesizing this information, the K–3 reading committee established a mutual understanding about the condition of the reading program at the school district. The data also provided information about the extent of the problem and highlighted special populations of students who might need more intensive instructional support.

The school district leadership created a sense of power sharing by structuring the committee to include individuals from diverse faculty groups and levels of school administration. Coral Mitchell and Larry Sackney have identified this type of structure as essential to effective communication. By specifying a preference for organizational practices linked with continuous improvement, such as those discussed by Kenneth Leithwood, Doris Jantzi, and Rosanne Steinbach, district leadership established a clear sense of direction for the committee. In so doing, the leadership also created an environment where ideas could be candidly expressed, information discussed in a nonaccusatory manner, conflicts peacefully resolved, and a vision explicitly articulated. Eventually, a learning goal was established: All children will be reading at grade level by Grade 3.

The school district began experimenting with new practices in an effort to realize the learning goal. Persuaded by promising research findings, the school district selected *Open Court* as the core curriculum to begin the K–3 Reading Initiative. They also employed a multitude of supplemental materials to strengthen the primary program and offer a variety of curricular components that would address the diverse needs of their students.

Although this situation may be specific to Northwest School District, the process that district followed to begin its learning initiative can be applied to a variety of contexts. A key to Northwest School District's success was the initial attention to assessing what students already knew and were capable of doing—prior to enacting a learning initiative. From this initial step, they were able to develop a shared understanding of the current situation as well as clearly communicate a common goal. Once the learning goal was communicated and accepted across the system, the district's personnel researched possible solutions and devised a learning initiative that was relevant to their goals and appropriate to their situation.

Monitoring Progress During the Learning Initiative

Once the learning goals were established and an implementation plan was in place, the district enacted the reform initiative and collected relevant data for progress monitoring. First, all classroom teachers and support staff were provided with professional development to prepare them to teach and monitor student progress in attaining the learning goals of the reading program.

All members of the educational team were included in the training and staff development, and this broad participation strengthened professional relationships and commitment to the program. Site administrators participated in staff-development programs, modeled collaborative behavior, and fostered a sense of common understanding necessary to what Leithwood and colleagues have found to be associated with high-achieving organizations.

With the K–3 Reading Initiative under way, the school district began evaluating the effectiveness of the program by collecting data and monitoring assessment results. Information was gathered from a variety of assessment methods administered by the educational team three times during the school year. Performance criteria were established to identify students who needed intensive remediation, strategic interventions, or grade-level instruction to meet the instructional goal. Instructional strategies and progress-monitoring schedules varied due to the intensity of the intervention. For students who were in jeopardy of missing the criteria for meeting the instructional goal, progress was monitored rigorously.

In accordance with sound principles of assessment as outlined by Stiggins in his 2001 book, district leaders ensured that multiple assessments were used to measure student learning. Performance-based indicators of early literacy skills and measures of reading fluency were administered to each student. All measures were considered to be reliable and accurate predictors of subsequent reading achievement, thereby allowing the school district to make appropriate and trustworthy decisions from the assessment results.

As assessment results were compiled, district officials and school-based leaders facilitated the communication of this information to relevant district and community stakeholders. Northwest's instructional leaders recognized that assessments have multiple users (students, parents, teachers, administrators, policymakers), and they sought to communicate that information to each group in a timely and informative fashion. In doing so, they were able to promote a culture of open and honest communication—encouraging all participants to become partners in accomplishing the learning goals.

This open communication also allowed members of the instructional leadership team to critically examine and develop a shared perception of the K–3 Reading Initiative, thereby enabling future learning within the organization to occur.

Monitoring Progress Following the Learning Initiative

Informed by the perspectives of the classroom educational team and the assessment results, Northwest School District's instructional leaders regularly reviewed the effectiveness of the K–3 Reading Initiative. At the beginning of the learning initiative, 32 percent of the kindergarteners required intensive remediation to reach the learning goals. Approximately three months after the initial implementation, this number was reduced to 7 percent.

The same trend continued through the following school year. By the end of the second year of implementation, nearly all students were meeting or exceeding the learning goal. The greatest success for the district was the reduction—from 15 percent to 6 percent—of the number of students at the end of first grade who were classified as nonreaders. A causal relationship cannot be inferred from the data, but the growth of the students over time warranted continued support for these instructional initiatives.

Throughout the process of implementing the learning initiative, the classroom teachers and support staff regularly met with school administrators to discuss current issues and brainstorm intervention options. Because teachers had frequent opportunities to evaluate their instruction and receive relevant feedback, their teaching became more directed at supporting students in attaining their learning goals. The positive results of this evaluation and feedback are consistent with what Leithwood and colleagues have found.

For those students who remained in jeopardy of not reaching the learning goal, teachers and members of the K–3 Reading Committee reviewed the practices and procedures used to provide the instruction. They looked for any external problems that may have influenced the effectiveness of the initiative, such as excessive absences, frequency of progress-monitoring activities, and fidelity of implementation. Where these kinds of problems were found, the educational staff readministered the same intervention. For students who were not responding to the learning initiative for other reasons, the staff reconceptualized and intensified the instructional intervention. The success of these students is an ongoing concern for Northwest School District and other districts across the country.

The instructional leaders worked hard to involve instructional staff in the monitoring of progress. Stiggins (2000) notes that honest and open discussion of assessment data can create a great deal of anxiety and reluctance on the part of teachers. It is therefore important that instructional leaders minimize the threat of criticism and sanction when discussing assessment results. Because the district's instructional leaders fostered an environment free of criticism and judgment, they were able to promote honest and insightful discussions of learning progress.

Instructional leaders also invited various teachers and staff not involved in the K–3 Reading Initiative to participate in group discussions. Their inclusion created a collaborative setting where the contributions of all staff members were valued and their questions and concerns were addressed. The discussions focused on continually identifying, assessing, and redefining common goals. This frequent and honest assessment-based dialogue allowed for ongoing refinement and improvement of their K–3 Reading Initiative and ultimately resulted in students making significant progress toward the district's learning goals.

Although this example is specific to a district-level reading program, it contains lessons that have broad application. All systems that are monitoring progress toward accomplishing a learning goal can benefit from implementing an iterative process to monitor the successes and possible sources of difficulty throughout the learning initiative. Only by reflectively considering these aspects of a learning initiative can the system grow.

CONCLUSION: A CAREER-LONG PRACTICE

Throughout this discussion, we've noted various responsibilities instructional leaders have for monitoring students' instructional progress. Those responsibilities are now summarized as follows:

- Understand the nature of progress monitoring and the types of decisions instructional leaders need to make at each phase of a learning initiative.
- Recognize the importance of using multiple sources of information in monitoring progress and be aware of various methods that can be used to assess academic, behavioral, and motivational learning goals.
- Ensure that progress-monitoring information is interpreted accurately and used appropriately.
- Ensure that there is frequent, meaningful communication of progress to learners— such that all stakeholders develop a clear sense of the learning goals, where students are in relation to those goals, and what learners need to do to make progress toward attaining those goals.

In the second part of the chapter, we provided an example to illustrate how progress monitoring has been implemented in an actual school district. Even though the example was specific to reading, every classroom, school, and district will face similar situations when attempting to realize learning goals.

Because monitoring progress is an ongoing, career-long endeavor, instructional leaders can make great strides by incorporating these considerations into what they are already doing. As a result, they will be in a better position to make accurate evaluative judgments and ensure that they are supporting the success of all their students on a broad range of student outcomes.

REFLECTIONS

1. If you are a practitioner, what assessment methods does your school or district use to gather information about student learning? What additional assessment methods might help instructional decision making at the classroom, building, and district levels?

2. What strategies and systems does your school use to monitor student-learning goals? What learning goals (academic, behavioral, motivational) are in need of better monitoring? How might you take the lead to ensure the effective monitoring of students' progress before, during, and after a learning initiative?

3. What type of information is being used in your building and district to render judgments about student learning? Is this information necessary and sufficient? What might be missing from this information (for example, impact of instructional techniques on student motivation)? And how might you ensure that assessment information used in making instructional decisions is interpreted accurately and used appropriately?

4. How is progress currently communicated to learners and related stakeholders? Is the information meaningful and actionable? What happens to the information? Is it used to make instructional decisions and help students take ownership of the learning process? How might students be more meaningfully involved in the process?

5. How might you continue to develop your own understanding of progress-monitoring techniques, tools, and considerations so as to better support the learning of all students? For instance, challenge yourself to critically reflect on the progress-monitoring techniques and tools used to generate student-learning data. Do these techniques and tools yield information that is accurate and non-biased? Are there better ways to assess student learning? Where can you find out about better tools and techniques? Are there individuals in your building or district who would be willing to share their progress-monitoring expertise with others so as to build the individual capacity and assessment literacy of all instructional decision makers?

15

Instructional Leadership

Cultivating a Learning–Focused Community in Schools

Ronald A. Beghetto

F ew would disagree that the primary responsibility of instructional leaders is to promote student learning. This responsibility is best fulfilled when the entire school community shares in carrying it out.

Unfortunately, keeping the school community focused on student learning can be quite challenging. Schools are often expected to address a variety of student, parental, and societal needs—some of which are only marginally related to student learning. In addition, the challenge of supporting student learning is compounded when students seem withdrawn from the learning process.

Although it is true that several of these challenges result from factors beyond the control of the school community, much can be done within schools to cultivate a learning-focused identity in students, teachers, and staff.

The purpose of this chapter is to provide insight into how instructional leaders can meet the challenge of cultivating and sustaining a learning-focused school community. The chapter starts with a definition of *learning-focused communities* and highlights challenges inherent in cultivating these communities. The next section addresses the question of why students engage in or avoid achievement-directed behavior. Then follows a discussion of how the school community influences student and teacher outcomes. The chapter closes with considerations for cultivating a schoolwide focus on student learning.

WHAT IS A LEARNING-FOCUSED COMMUNITY?

A *learning-focused community* is one type of a "community of practice"—one that focuses on promoting and cultivating student learning. Jean Lave and Etienne Wenger formulated the concept of communities of practice to explain how individuals develop a sense of identity through legitimate participation in a shared, sustained endeavor.

According to Etienne Wenger, Richard McDermott, and William M. Snyder, *communities of practice* are "groups of people who share a concern, a set of problems, or a passion about a topic, and who deepen their knowledge and expertise in this area by interacting on an ongoing basis."

Communities of practice can take many forms, to name just a few:

- A group of poets who read their poetry at a local coffee shop and discuss their poems and the struggles associated with the writing process
- Graduate students who take classes together, study together, and gather at the local pub to discuss the challenges and rewards of surviving graduate school
- Architects who work together in a design studio, share designs for peer review, and turn to each other for innovative solutions

Common to all these groups is the development of a community that was "created over time by the sustained pursuit of a shared enterprise" (Etienne Wenger). For schools, that shared enterprise is student learning.

Martin Maehr and Carol Midgley have observed that schools are often expected to, and to some extent do, play the role of a "full service school"—meeting students' (and parents') nutritional, judicial, psychological, medical, and various other important needs. As schools are increasingly expected to assume these roles, Maehr and Midgley caution that these caretaking responsibilities can only be partially fulfilled. Arguing that schools should not overextend their role, they point out that schools are primarily for and about student learning:

> School must be considered an institution designed to meet basic human needs: to learn, to grow, and to master within a context in which relatedness as well as individuality are stressed. Schools are and must be concerned with self within community. . . . In sum, school is and has to be a very special place revolving around two key concepts: learning and community. In fact, schooling is learning *in* community.

Instructional leaders have a responsibility to support the development of learning in community. This task involves cultivating a learning-focused identity in the community itself and in all the individuals who make up that community. Because faculty, students, and staff help shape the identity of the school community, instructional leaders must ensure that these members stay focused on student learning.

For example, instructional leaders can remind teachers and staff to communicate a commitment to student learning in newsletters, meeting agendas, and hallway decorations. In addition, all that happens in faculty, student council, and parent and community group meetings, and discussions about policies and procedures, should be driven by one overriding question: How does this influence student learning?

Keeping a focus on learning is particularly important when new staff, faculty, and students join the school community. Wenger explains that newcomers enter a community of practice at the periphery and develop an identity as full participants through involvement in the activities of that community. As such, existing members have a responsibility to help newcomers recognize that the primary aim of those activities is to promote student learning. In this way, new staff, faculty, and students can develop their own learning-focused identity and help sustain the broader learning-focused identity of the community itself.

Even with committed faculty and staff, cultivating a school community focused on learning is challenging. There will inevitably be some students who do not share in a learning-focused identity. As Revathy Kumar, Margaret H. Gheen, and Avi Kaplan note, some students have a very negative experience with schooling. These students feel alienated from the community, are skeptical about the value of school, and disengage from or attempt to disrupt the schooling process. Cultivating a community that promotes a learning-focused identity in all students starts with an understanding of why some students engage in achievement-directed behaviors whereas others avoid it.

WHY DO STUDENTS ENGAGE IN OR AVOID ACHIEVEMENT-DIRECTED BEHAVIOR?

Over the past two decades, researchers working in the tradition of achievement goal theory have made great strides in addressing the question of why students demonstrate different patterns of achievement-directed behavior. For a detailed overview of this work, read *Goals, Goal Structures, and Patterns of Adaptive Learning*, edited by Carol Midgley. Summaries appear in most general texts on educational motivation, such as Paul R. Pintrich and Dale H. Schunk's *Motivation in Education: Theory, Research, and Applications*.

(The following overview of achievement goal theory is informed by summaries and findings presented in a 2004 article by Ronald A. Beghetto, in the volume edited by Midgley, and in Pintrich and Schunk's text.)

According to achievement goal theory, students hold varying patterns of goal orientations that serve as their own personal reasons for engaging in or avoiding achievement-directed behavior. These goal orientations also serve as the basis for how students define their own competence. Students' goal orientations are context sensitive and can be influenced by school and classroom procedures, practices, and policies.

Goal orientations are typically classified using the following labels: *mastery goals* and *performance goals*. Recently, researchers and theorists have made further distinctions within these categories by adding *approach* and *avoidance* components. The three configurations of goal orientations that have received the most attention in the research literature include *mastery-approach goals, performance-avoid goals,* and *performance-approach goals.*

Mastery-Approach Goals

Mastery-approach goals represent a learning-focused orientation. Students who hold mastery-approach goals engage in achievement-directed behaviors with the purpose of mastering tasks, learning, and developing deep levels of understanding. They define their competence in terms of self-improvement, creativity, and progress.

Students who hold mastery-approach goals have been found to demonstrate a variety of desirable achievement outcomes: more positive attitudes toward schooling, enhanced interest in learning, choice of more challenging tasks, viewing of errors as informational, attribution of failure to lack of effort, high levels of academic engagement, perseverance in the face of challenges, more risk taking, and asking for assistance when needed.

Performance-Avoid Goals

On the other hand, *performance-avoid goals* represent a learning-avoidant focus. Students who hold performance-avoid goals are focused on avoiding the appearance of being dumb, incompetent, or less able than other students. Rather than being concerned with learning and understanding, students holding performance-avoid goals are focused on protecting their self-worth at all costs. Consequently, they are more likely to avoid learning opportunities and even engage in self-sabotaging behaviors, such as cheating, avoiding help when they need it, and withdrawing effort.

Performance-avoid goals are linked with a host of undesirable outcomes. For example, students who have performance-avoid goals are less interested in learning, experience high levels of anxiety, place less value on tasks, exert less effort, view errors as indicating a lack of ability, give up in the face of difficulty, and ultimately demonstrate lower levels of achievement.

Performance-Approach Goals

Finally, students who hold *performance-approach goals* focus on outperforming others. These students are driven to demonstrate their ability in relation to others, seek superiority, and want recognition. Students with a performance-approach orientation define competence in relation to how well they perform in comparison to others (Did I get the highest grade? Am I the top student in my class?). The primary drive for approaching learning opportunities is to best others and demonstrate their ability to teachers and peers.

Unlike the outcomes associated with mastery-approach and performance-avoid goals, the research surrounding the outcomes and desirability of performance-approach goals is less than clear. For example, performance-approach goals have been linked with undesirable outcomes such as anxiety during evaluations and not asking for help when needed but also favorable outcomes such as higher grades.

Some researchers have interpreted these mixed outcomes as indicating that performance-approach goals may be adaptive for particular students in particular contexts. Depending on the demands of a given learning environment, some combination of mastery-approach and performance-approach goals may be most adaptive. Until more research can be conducted, however, definitive statements linking performance-approach goals with positive student outcomes are not yet warranted.

In summary, research over the past 20 years has led to important insights into why students engage in or avoid achievement-directed behaviors. Although much work is still to be done, it is safe to say that a mastery-approach orientation represents a learning-focused identity and generally leads to desirable achievement outcomes, whereas a performance-avoid goal orientation represents a learning-avoidant identity and is linked with maladaptive beliefs and outcomes.

Armed with a better understanding of why some students develop a learning-focused identity whereas others develop a learning-avoidant identity, instructional leaders can then turn their attention toward understanding how their learning community might support or impede the development of a learning-focused identity.

HOW DO LEARNING COMMUNITIES INFLUENCE STUDENTS' ACHIEVEMENT BEHAVIOR?

Learning communities emerge from and are shaped by the structure, policies, and practices of schools. According to achievement goal theory, these features of schooling send messages to faculty, students, and staff regarding the achievement goals that are valued within that school's learning community. Depending on how these messages are perceived and adopted, students will be more or less likely to adopt achievement goal orientations associated with a learning-focused identity.

An Example: Math Cars

A classroom example will help illustrate how features of the achievement setting can send salient messages about the achievement goals valued in that setting. Consider a third-grade teacher who, in an attempt to engage and motivate her students, has them personalize paper cutouts of race cars. These race cars will then serve as markers of progress during math class. Each student is asked to put his or her name on the car, color it, and hang it on the wall in front of the classroom for everyone to see.

Then the teacher hands students a math worksheet. She announces that for each student who correctly completes the worksheet in the allotted time, his or her math car will move one step toward the finish line.

The structure of this activity can send a variety of undesirable messages to students, including: Quick completion is more important than taking the time to understand the problem, mistakes should be avoided, and only the smartest and quickest students' cars will move. Although the teacher intends to engage and motivate all students to successfully complete the worksheets, some students undoubtedly will have difficulty completing the worksheet in the allotted time.

For those students whose cars have not yet moved, they are reminded in a very public way that they are not as smart, quick, or capable as their peers. And it is not inconceivable to think that otherwise-capable students facing this highly visible public evaluation would start doubting their ability to succeed in math. This, in turn, could lead to their adoption of a learning-avoidant orientation toward math. To avoid looking incompetent in math, they might become disruptive during class, withdraw effort, cheat, and avoid challenging and more advanced math coursework.

Goal Structures

An experience such as the math car activity can send powerful motivational messages to students and shape their subsequent achievement behavior in math. Avi Kaplan and his colleagues refer to the achievement goal messages stressed in classrooms and schools as "goal structures." They explain that these goal structures are related to and, in many cases, influence the personal achievement goal orientations that individuals adopt and pursue in those settings.

As with personal goal orientations (discussed earlier), researchers have distinguished two types of classroom- and school-level goal structures: a *performance goal structure* and a *mastery goal structure*.

Kaplan and his colleagues explain that performance goal structures are evident in environments that stress differences in student ability. In such environments, the importance of getting the right answer, avoiding mistakes, and doing better than others is stressed over individual improvement and learning from mistakes.

According to achievement goal theory, a performance goal structure is represented in classroom and school practices in which students' academic rankings are posted for everyone to see, and only the best work is displayed and rewarded. A *mastery goal structure*, on the other hand, stresses the importance of learning and improvement by recognizing student effort and encouraging students to challenge themselves, learn from mistakes, try hard, and work toward understanding.

Kaplan and his colleagues explain that a school's or a classroom's goal structure is primarily a subjective perception. The goal orientation students adopt depends more on that student's perceptions of the environment than on the objective reality of the policies, practices, and activities in that environment. These researchers explain that two students may perceive a rank-ordered list of test scores in two different ways. One student may perceive the list as stressing the importance of besting others and social comparison. The other student may perceive the list as providing information regarding whether he or she has improved in comparison to prior performance.

Although these researchers recognize that particular individuals can (and often do) perceive the goal structures of the same learning environment in different ways, they stress that, in general, the performance and mastery features of a learning environment encourage the adoption of parallel goal orientations in individuals within that environment.

Benefits of an Emphasis on Mastery

Kumar and her colleagues have examined the relationship between goal structures in the learning environment and the disengagement of students from learning and schooling. These researchers provide evidence suggesting that an environment focused on social comparison and besting others is linked with a variety of negative emotions and behaviors (for example, a sense of alienation, disruptive behaviors). This type of environment, in turn, seems to put students at risk for disengagement from learning and disaffection with schooling.

Conversely, Kumar and her colleagues report that a mastery-oriented environment generally leads to positive emotions, increased engagement, and resilience in students. Students experiencing mastery environments are more likely to put forth sustained effort, feel successful and positive about their schooling experience, and engage in schooling.

In offering suggestions for teachers and school leaders, Kumar and her associates recommend that schools strengthen the mastery goal structure in the learning environment and, to the extent possible, deemphasize performance goals. They maintain that this strategy is particularly important for students who are low achieving or already disaffected with school and point out that high-stakes testing may further exacerbate this situation.

The implications of what Kumar and her colleagues describe place instructional leaders in a challenging position: How to stress a mastery orientation in a culture of performance? The challenge becomes more manageable when instructional leaders recognize that the goal is not necessarily to eliminate the performance-goal features of a learning environment, but rather to place a greater schoolwide emphasis on mastery goals. Leaders can accomplish this by working in collaboration with teachers to monitor how students perceive the school and classroom environment. Fortunately, leaders can choose from a variety of methods for monitoring these perceptions, including surveys, observations, and interviews.

An overview of techniques and considerations for monitoring motivational beliefs can be gleaned from Chapter 14 of this volume and from a recent article, "Toward a More Complete Picture of Student Learning: Assessing Students' Motivational Beliefs," by Ronald A. Beghetto (2004).

We have seen how the school and classroom environments influence whether students adopt a learning-focused identity and subsequently engage in achievement-directed behavior. In addition, instructional leaders should consider how the school environment influences the learning-focused identity and pedagogy of teachers.

HOW DOES THE LEARNING ENVIRONMENT INFLUENCE TEACHERS?

It only makes sense that the achievement goal structures stressed by policies and practices of a school would influence the learning-focused identity and pedagogy of teachers. Robert W. Roeser, Roxana Marachi, and Hunter Gehlbach provide evidence suggesting a connection among teachers' professional identities, their pedagogical practices, and the social and organizational features of their work environment. These authors explain that school-level practices create a goal orientation that supports or undermines the strategies and efforts of teachers. Summarizing research on the influence of the school environment on teachers, they note several important findings:

> Teachers at both the elementary and middle school level who were more performance oriented in their approach to classroom instruction also worked in schools where principals reported greater use of performance-oriented practices and policies, and where there was greater competition among staff and inequitable treatment of teachers by the administration (school performance goal structure for teachers). Similarly, teachers who reported a greater mastery orientation in their approach to instruction also perceived a greater emphasis on innovation and improvement for teachers among the staff and administration and, at the middle school level, had principals who reported slightly more use of mastery-oriented practices and policies.

According to findings cited by Roeser and his colleagues, the school-level environment influences not only teachers' achievement goals, but also their efficacy beliefs (for instance, judgments of their ability to influence student learning). More specifically, teachers were more likely to report higher levels of efficacy if they worked in mastery-focused school environments (focused on innovation and improvement) rather than in performance-focused environments (emphasizing competition and social comparison).

We mustn't overstate these findings, but neither should we overlook the insights these findings provide regarding how the schooling environment influences (and is influenced by) the achievement behaviors of teachers and students. Instructional leaders, armed with these insights, can be more purposeful in cultivating a learning-focused identity in students, staff, faculty, and themselves. As Roeser and his colleagues explain:

> In the end, if we are ever to create learning environments in which students take risks, seek creative solutions to problems, attempt challenging tasks, come to love learning, and help each other in the process, then what we have presented . . . suggests the importance of helping educational leaders and teachers to create environments that nurture these same habits of heart and mind among and within themselves.

Although it is helpful to know that a schoolwide mastery orientation is necessary for fostering a learning-focused identity in teachers and students, instructional leaders still face the difficult task of creating such an environment. The final section of this chapter provides insights into how instructional leaders can cultivate a community with a school-wide focus on learning.

CULTIVATING A FOCUS ON LEARNING IN THE SCHOOL COMMUNITY

In recent years, researchers such as Maehr and Midgley have come to realize that, in addition to teachers' stressing a mastery orientation in their classrooms, these messages should also permeate the entire school community. Although there are no sure-fire prescriptions for creating a schoolwide community focused on learning, scholars have developed a variety of considerations that may guide instructional leaders as they attempt to cultivate such a community.

Drawing from a synthesis of more than two decades of theory and research, Pintrich and Schunk discuss eight overlapping features of schools that may assist instructional leaders in creating a community focused on learning. The first two features are (a) norms, values, and shared beliefs and (b) school climate. The remaining six features derive from research conducted by Carole Ames (see also Carole Ames and Jennifer Archer). Ames developed the TARGET acronym to identify the following aspects of the classroom and school environment thought to promote a mastery focus:

Task and work structures

Authority and management structures

Recognition and reward structures

Grouping practices

Evaluation practices

Time use

These six TARGET features, in conjunction with the norms, values, shared beliefs, and climate of a school, can serve to promote or impede the development of a learning-focused school community. The sections that follow offer suggestions for cultivating a schoolwide focus on learning in each of these eight interrelated features of the school community.

Cultivating Adaptive Norms, Values, and Shared Beliefs

It should come as no surprise to instructional leaders that the norms, values, and shared beliefs of a school will influence whether a learning-focused identity emerges in the schoolwide community. Pintrich and Schunk explain that four general beliefs are particularly important:

1. Nature of students

2. Malleability of learning and ability

3. Norms and beliefs about teaching

4. Shared goals and purposes of the school

Pintrich and Schunk explain that teachers' beliefs about the nature of students and about the malleability of students' ability will likely influence classroom and school practices and, in turn, influence whether students adopt a learning-focused identity. These authors note that how teachers view students influences the structure of the learning environment. Are students basically bad, unmotivated, and needing controls, or basically good, self-motivated, and interested in learning? Similarly, if teaching can influence learning and ability, it only makes sense that school and classroom practices would focus more on promoting the learning of all students rather than a select few.

According to Pintrich and Schunk, a school's norms and beliefs influence teaching and learning on two levels. At one level, school norms may influence whether teachers use or avoid certain instructional practices. For example, if a teacher's colleagues are skeptical about constructivist views of learning, that teacher may limit the use of such instructional approaches in his or her classroom. At a deeper level, a school's norms and beliefs about teaching can affect whether teachers believe they can influence student learning or believe their efforts are futile.

Pintrich and Schunk explain that these beliefs pertain to both teachers' collective ability to influence students ("collective efficacy") and to each teacher's belief he or she can positively influence students ("individual efficacy"). Both individual and collective efficacy have been linked with student motivation and achievement, Pintrich and Schunk report. Therefore, instructional leaders should try to cultivate adaptive teacher beliefs about students and help teachers recognize that their instructional efforts can have a positive influence on student learning.

Finally, Pintrich and Schunk describe how the shared goals and purposes of a school can influence student and teacher outcomes. Consistent with one of the main points in Chapter 13 ("Instructional Leadership: Supporting the Learning Process"), these scholars note the importance of identifying and articulating a clear set of schoolwide learning goals. Indeed, identifying, communicating, and establishing consensus around learning goals is a key function of instructional leadership. Equally important, according to Pintrich and Schunk, is an awareness of the content of these goals and how students, faculty, and staff perceive that content. Because the shared goals and purposes of schooling can shape the achievement goals that students and teachers adopt, instructional leaders must lead the charge in ensuring that the content of the school's learning goals reflects a learning-focused orientation.

Promoting a Positive School Climate

As stated throughout this chapter, teachers' and students' experience of schooling influences whether and to what extent they develop a learning-focused identity. In turn, the school's climate influences how teachers and students experience schooling. A recent report by the National Conference of State Legislatures on improving student achievement identifies a supportive school climate as one of the primary characteristics of high-achieving schools. Although a variety of aspects make up a supportive school climate, Pintrich and Schunk identify the following three aspects as particularly important for cultivating a learning-focused orientation in teachers and students: (a) a sense of community and belonging, (b) warmth and civility in personal relations, and (c) feelings of safety and security.

The more students and teachers feel a sense of belonging to the school community, the more likely they will remain engaged in and actively pursue the learning goals of that community. Conversely, as Pintrich and Schunk report, when a sense of relatedness and mutual concern are absent, students and faculty are more likely to disengage and even drop out of that environment. This sense of mutual concern and relatedness are fostered by warm and civil interpersonal relationships.

In addition, an environment that offers positive, collegial relationships can help combat a sense of isolation and cultivate instead a sense of common purpose aimed at promoting student learning. For example, Michael Fullan reports on research indicating that when the climate of a school is collaborative and collegial, teachers will focus their individual and collective efforts on student learning rather than work at odds with each other:

> What happens in these schools is that teachers as a group and as subgroups examine together how well students are doing (i.e. they study student work and assessment data), they relate this to how they are teaching (i.e. to instructional practice), and they make continuous refinements individually and with each other (i.e. as a professional community). By contrast, in individualistic or balkanized cultures, teachers either leave each other alone or are at loggerheads—disagreeing without any inclination or process to solve differences.

When civility and warmth permeate the entire school community, it seems more likely all members of the learning community will have a positive, affirming experience and be inclined to develop a learning-focused identity.

The last dimension of a positive school climate Pintrich and Schunk identified is a feeling of safety and security. They explain that safety and security can refer to both a sense of feeling free to express one's ideas and opinions as well as a sense of physical and emotional safety. Pintrich and Schunk report on research that demonstrates the link between student achievement and safe environments—a link, they explain, that is particularly pronounced for minority students. And they note that unless safety needs are being met, individuals within the school community will find it difficult to concern themselves with learning-related goals.

Given these findings, instructional leaders will do well to ensure that students, faculty, and staff feel physically and psychologically safe, respected, and meaningfully involved in the school community. If these conditions are being met, instructional leaders can help members of the school community focus on promoting individual and school-wide learning and improvement.

Meaningful Tasks and Work Structures

Tasks and work structures (the first feature represented in Ames's TARGET acronym) pertain to the curricular activities and organization of the classroom and school. As discussed earlier in the chapter, tasks and work structures communicate messages about what the school emphasizes and values. Recalling the math car example, we see how a learning task might actually undermine the development of a learning-focused identity in some students. Consequently, instructional leaders will want to monitor how tasks and work structures are influencing the learning-focused identity of students and teachers.

In addition, as Pintrich and Schunk note, when teachers and students understand why tasks are important and worthwhile, they are more likely to engage in and expend effort on such tasks. High levels of effort and engagement are consistent with a learning-focused identity. Therefore, the assignment of meaningful tasks should become a school-wide emphasis. Instructional leaders can stress this emphasis in the tasks they assign to teachers, and they can encourage teachers to do the same with students.

Participation in Authority and Management Structures

Participating in the authority and management structures of schooling (the second feature of TARGET) is important to both teachers and students. For teachers, involvement in decision making fosters connectedness and individual responsibility. Fullan (citing a report on Chicago school reform by Anthony Bryk and colleagues) explains the benefits of this involvement:

> As teachers develop a broader say in school decision making, they may also begin to experiment with new roles, including working collaboratively. This restructuring of teachers' work signifies a broadening professional community where

teachers feel more comfortable exchanging ideas, and where a collective sense of responsibility for student development is likely to emerge.

In addition to developing a collective sense of responsibility for student learning, teachers' involvement in decision making leads to what M. Bruce King and his colleagues call "shared power." They report that this sense of shared power is linked, in turn, with teachers' use of instructional practices that represent a focus on teaching for understanding.

The benefits of participation in the authority and management structures also extend to students. According to Pintrich and Schunk, students are more likely to invest themselves in classroom and school activities if they feel they have some say in the learning process. This does not mean that teachers should abnegate authority, but rather that they should appropriately involve and empower students in the learning process. For example, students could be given a range of choices regarding what specific topics they pursue in writing a research paper. Also, as Richard J. Stiggins argues, students can be more meaningfully involved in the assessment process—learning how to monitor their own progress in conjunction with the assessment feedback they receive from teachers.

This type of involvement in the authority and work structures of learning enables students to develop a meaningful sense of belonging. This is an important outcome because, as Kumar and her colleagues have found, students who sense that they belong also tend to hold a learning-focused identity. By creating space for students and teachers to be meaningfully involved in the authority and management structures of schooling, instructional leaders can help cultivate a genuine sense of what Maehr and Midgley refer to as "learning *in* community."

Inclusive Recognition and Reward Structures

The way in which student effort and competence are recognized can influence the types of achievement goals students adopt and ultimately whether they develop a learning-focused identity. For example, Pintrich and Schunk explain that well-intended programs such as honor rolls can result in students' focusing on getting the best grade rather than understanding what is taught. Because of this, instructional leaders will want to help their teachers carefully consider how students are interpreting classroom and schoolwide recognition and rewards.

This is not to say that practices such as honor rolls should be altogether eliminated. Rather, teachers and instructional leaders should find ways also to recognize and reward individual improvement and effort. For example, Pintrich and Schunk suggest that teachers recognize a wide range of achievements, including extracurricular accomplishments, artistic and creative accomplishments, and accomplishments in the area of social and community service.

When social comparison and besting others are the only basis for reward and recognition, some students may develop a learning-avoidant identity. These students will focus more on trying to avoid looking dumb or incapable than on their ability to learn and improve. Conversely, when students are recognized for individual learning accomplishments, they are more likely to develop positive self-judgments of their capacity to be successful and may come to see themselves as valued members of the school's learning community.

Effective Grouping Practices

Within classrooms, teachers often arrange students in small and cooperative learning groups (the fourth feature of TARGET). At the school level, middle and high school students may be grouped into classes with varying emphasis on teaching for understanding. According to achievement goal theory, these classroom and schoolwide grouping practices can influence whether and to what extent students will develop a learning-focused identity.

Pintrich and Schunk characterize grouping practices as classroom- and school-level structures that allow or impede social interaction and the development of social skills. Within the classroom, such configurations include small groups and cooperative learning groups. If these groups are used properly, Pintrich and Schunk report, they can be quite beneficial. Unfortunately, if students are thrown into groups with little care for individual and group improvement or as a way to pit students against each other, such groups may result in frustrating and potentially demoralizing experiences.

Instructional leaders will want to ensure that teachers use grouping practices to promote positive social interactions as well as individual and group learning. In this way, teachers can create the social conditions necessary for the development of a learning-focused identity. Jeanne E. Ormrod provides the following research-based guidelines for developing and implementing learning-focused cooperative groups:

- Form groups based on which students are likely to work effectively with one another.
- Give group members one or more common goals toward which to work.
- Provide clear guidelines about how to behave.
- Structure tasks so that group members must depend on one another for their success.
- Serve more as a resource and monitor than as a "director."
- Make students individually accountable for their achievement, but also reinforce them for group success.
- At the end of an activity, have the groups evaluate their effectiveness.
- Consider forming long-term cooperative groups.

Working from guidelines such as those listed by Ormrod, instructional leaders can help their teachers ensure that the use of groups in the classroom serves as a powerful learning opportunity for all students. The effective use of small and cooperative classroom groups can offer all students a legitimate opportunity to learn, understand, and improve.

Similarly, at the school level, all students should have access to courses that focus on learning, deep levels of understanding, and self-improvement. Unfortunately, as Pintrich and Schunk report, courses focused on teaching for understanding are typically limited to upper-level courses—courses to which only some students have access. Instructional leaders, working in collaboration with their teachers, can strive to develop a schoolwide curriculum that focuses on teaching for understanding in all courses. In this way, the classroom and school grouping structures will promote student learning and improvement.

Evaluation Practices That Support Individual Improvement

Evaluation and assessment structures send powerful messages regarding the focus and aim of learning. For example, Pintrich and Schunk explain that standardized assessments that focus primarily on assessing factual knowledge can send messages to teachers that memorizing and recalling facts is more important than deeper conceptual understanding. These scholars note that when this is the case, it should come as no surprise that teachers focus on teaching fact-based information rather than teaching for conceptual understanding. Such assessments can also cause teachers and students to value social comparison over their own learning and improvement.

Instructional leaders' hands are tied with respect to the types of assessments mandated at the district and state level, but they can still make an effort to help teachers be aware of and attempt to counterbalance the messages sent by overly narrow, socially comparative assessments. For example, teachers can be encouraged to use information yielded from such assessments to support individual improvement. Moreover, they can use standardized assessment information in conjunction with other assessment information to help students recognize strengths and build on weaknesses.

Portfolios, for instance, may offer a way to organize assessment information such that students focus on self-improvement and learning from mistakes. Pintrich and Schunk note that although portfolios are time consuming and suffer from problems with reliability and validity, they do offer one way to foster a mastery orientation in students. Perhaps it is safest to say that educators should not rely on portfolios, or any other assessment technique, as the sole means for assessing and communicating assessment results. When used in conjunction with other practices, however, portfolios seem to represent evaluative structures that reinforce students' effort, understanding, and improvement (Pintrich and Schunk).

Instructional leaders recognize that developing assessment and evaluative structures to support learning requires time, creativity, and thoughtful consideration by the entire learning community. For further guidance in using assessments to support learning, readers can consult Chapter 14 ("Instructional Leadership: Progress Monitoring") and sources such as *Assessment FOR Learning: An Action Guide for School Leaders,* by Steve Chappuis and his colleagues from the Assessment Training Institute.

Creative and Effective Time Use

Time is the final feature in Ames's TARGET acronym denoting the elements necessary for promoting a mastery focus in students and the broader school community. How teachers and students experience time is crucial for building a learning-focused school community. Teachers need a lot of time to collaborate, plan, reflect, and restructure the learning environment of their school and classrooms. Indeed, finding the time for such activities may be one of the most daunting challenges facing instructional leaders.

Finding ways for teachers to work together within the constraints of available time will require a great deal of creativity and flexibility. Innovative uses of technology not only can help teachers stay connected to their colleagues but also can facilitate communication with parents and external members of the community. For example, listservs, threaded discussions, and other electronic tools may serve as viable avenues for collaboration, discussion, and reflection. (See Ronald A. Beghetto 2001 for an overview of ways to use such tools to create a virtual community.)

Students, too, can benefit from more effective time management. Pintrich and Schunk explain that teachers can help students develop a sense of control and the capacity to manage their learning time by

- being somewhat flexible about when students do their work so students increase their sense of control and responsibility;
- teaching students how to better manage time;
- providing opportunities to set short-term and long-term work goals; and
- helping students take more responsibility for monitoring their own progress toward attaining goals.

When students are unable to manage their time and feel pressed to finish a task, it only makes sense that they would learn at a much more superficial level. Conversely, helping students develop the capacity to manage time would seem to support their engagement with and ownership of the learning process. Moreover, when students become effective time managers, they can afford themselves the opportunity to learn and understand at a much deeper level. When this happens, students may come to realize that learning has little to do with luck and much more to do with a sustained, purposeful effort. This realization is at the heart of a learning-focused identity.

CONCLUSION: THE NEED FOR CREATIVITY AND RESOLVE

A recurring theme throughout this chapter is the importance of and challenges inherent in cultivating a learning-focused community in schools. Instructional leaders can help cultivate such a community in classrooms, schools, and districts by embracing the following responsibilities:

- Ensure that the content of classroom, school, and district goals reflects a learning-focused orientation.
- Ensure that students, teachers, and staff feel physically and psychologically safe, respected, and meaningfully involved in the school community.
- Help students and teachers recognize the importance and value of assigned tasks.
- Create space for students and teachers to be meaningfully involved in the authority and management structures of schooling.
- Focus recognition and rewards on self-improvement rather than solely on besting others.
- Ensure that the use of classroom grouping practices serves to promote positive social interactions as well as individual and group learning.
- Ensure that all students have opportunities to experience courses that focus on learning, deep levels of understanding, and self-improvement.
- Identify, develop, and use assessment and evaluation structures that support student learning by reinforcing student effort, understanding, and improvement.
- Be innovative in developing avenues such as listservs and electronic discussion boards teachers can use to collaborate, plan, reflect, and develop a learning-focused community in their classrooms and school.

- Collaborate with teachers to help students develop the capacity to manage their learning time and thereby take ownership of the learning process.

Cultivating a community of practice that makes student learning the number one priority will require every bit of intelligence, creativity, and effort of the community's members. Along the way, instructional leaders can expect setbacks and disappointments. Great is the reward for those who persevere, because the cultivation of such a community will yield profound individual and schoolwide learning and improvement. Working in collaboration with teachers, staff members, and parents, instructional leaders can make noteworthy progress in supporting the development of a learning community in which all students feel engaged, valued, and focused on learning.

REFLECTIONS

1. How would you describe the learning climate in your classrooms, school, and district?

2. How would you characterize the motivational experience of teachers and students within classrooms and the school overall? What types of motivational messages does the learning climate communicate to teachers and students?

3. Take some time to observe the messages sent to students and teachers. As you walk into the building, what messages are being communicated? Consider these elements:
   - How are hallways and classrooms decorated? What do those decorations communicate?
   - To what extent do the decorations reinforce a sense of physical and psychological safety, respect, and meaningful involvement of all inhabitants within the school?
   - To what extent do the messages focus on self-improvement, effort, and understanding?

4. How might you take the lead to ensure that classroom, school, and district goals reflect a learning focus?

5. Do all teachers and students have access to opportunities to be meaningfully involved in learning and improvement?

6. To what extent are the importance and value of assigned tasks made clear to teachers and students?

7. How are teachers and students evaluated? Is the focus on quick completion and besting others or on meaningful engagement?

8. To what extent do teachers and students have the opportunity to be meaningfully involved in the decision-making and management structures of schooling? How might you take the lead to make way for such involvement?

PART VI

The Skills

16

Communicating

Wendell Anderson

If I had to cite one proficiency as being the most important to the success of a principal, it would be the skill of communicating.

—Randall B. Parsons

Whether outlining rules to 19th-century schoolchildren in a one-room schoolhouse or explaining site-based management to 21st-century parents in a packed auditorium, school administrators have always needed to be effective communicators.

Leaders in government and business have long known the value of effective communication. The ability of a manager in business to communicate effectively increases productivity in both individuals and organizations, say Courtland L. Bovée and John Thill.

Skilled communicators anticipate problems, make decisions, coordinate projects, teach others, and develop relationships. Through effective communication, they fashion the impressions they make on others. And they are able to perceive and respond to the needs of all stakeholders. It is widely believed in business that communication skills determine a person's success. The same measure applies to educational leadership.

Effective communication is one of the keys to effective leadership. Doreen S. Geddes has found that 66 percent to 78 percent of a leader's time is spent communicating. And, generally, the higher the position, the more time a leader spends communicating. Some jobs consist almost entirely of communicating, those of a director of institutional advancement, for instance.

Stephen H. Davis asked California superintendents to rank the top five reasons why principals lost their jobs. Of 21 behaviors that put leaders at risk, the most frequently cited was failure to communicate in ways that build positive relationships. To avoid a premature end to their careers, principals should evaluate and refine their interpersonal skills, Davis advises.

This chapter offers insights to principals who want to learn how to communicate more effectively with the people within their school. The information will also be useful to superintendents and central-office administrators and, of course, to anyone training for a career in educational leadership. (The next chapter focuses on communicating with people outside the school, office, or district.)

The first three sections concentrate on theory. They discuss basic principles of communication for leaders of all types of organizations and schools, in particular, the link between the school leader's communication skills and student performance, and the communication process. The fourth section is more practical, providing concrete steps leaders can take to improve their listening and nonverbal communication skills. A section on administrative writing skills concludes the chapter.

(For more about effective communication skills for leaders, see Chapter 3, "Portrait of a Leader.")

PRINCIPLES OF ORGANIZATIONAL COMMUNICATION

Communication is an essential function of any organization, the glue that holds an organization together. Without effective communication, information could not be gathered, processed, interpreted, and used.

A school, as an organization, depends on the cooperation and collaboration of its members to meet its developmental and educational goals. Communication plays a major role in meeting those goals. In fact, as Patti L. Chance and Edward W. Chance remind us, if we think about it, the primary function of a school is communication. Learning is essentially gathering, processing, interpreting, and using information.

Communication can also help shape the culture of a school. To a great extent, the culture of a school, or any other organization, is defined by its communication structures. Goals, values, beliefs, and standards are transmitted and interpreted through the process of communication.

Leadership With the Human Touch

Because of the principal's key role in influencing the human-relations atmosphere of a school, it is crucial that he or she communicate effectively. When viewing communication from a personal perspective, the evidence is compelling that communication is a major element in determining the effective practice of a school administrator, notes Theodore J. Kowalski.

Most administrative work, after all, centers on human interactions. Teachers, staff, and even students can easily spot a principal with poor communication skills. Furthermore, the application of knowledge always involves some form of communication.

Kowalski points to a number of studies that have identified weak communication skills as a primary reason for dismissal of principals and strong communication skills as a primary reason for their success.

Communicators as Change Agents

Effective communication skills have become more important as the role of school leader has changed. The principal is no longer a controlling headmaster in command of a closed, authoritarian system. Because of changes in society and, in no small part, calls for comprehensive school reform, the principal is more likely to be a guiding facilitator who manages programs and shepherds constituents in a more open, collaborative system. The principal works primarily through and with other people—most notably teachers—and, therefore, must have strong communication skills.

Christine J. Villani and Linda L. Lyman discuss a study that concluded communicating and listening skills are important characteristics for those who lead school change. These skills, they say, are the basis of principals' "ability to articulate a vision, develop a shared vision, express their belief that schools are for students' learning, and demonstrate that they value the human resources of their peers and subordinates."

Principles of Communication

Ronald W. Rebore has set down 12 principles of communication that apply to leaders of educational organizations. Of these principles, the following are particularly noteworthy for readers of this book:

1. An educational administrator will grow and develop as an individual and as a professional through the communication process.

2. There is a consequence to every communication transmitted by an educational administrator.

3. The development of communication strategies is one of the most important dimensions of being an educational administrator.

4. It is the professional advantage of educational administrators to remember that the content of their communications sets the tone for how others perceive their competence.

5. A significant strategy of effective communication for an educational administrator is choosing the most appropriate medium to transmit a change.

6. Engaging people in dialogue is an important strategy for an educational administrator who is learning how to communicate effectively.

7. Public education is predicated on a social covenant between educators and members of the community, which is strengthened by ongoing two-way communication.

COMMUNICATION AND STUDENT LEARNING

Communication is an essential tool the principal wields to build a positive learning climate. The principal's openness, accessibility, appearance, and language and listening skills all play important roles in building a positive climate for learning.

Phyllis A. Hensley and LaVern Burmeister believe that a principal's effective use of language can create an environment in which teachers, staff, and students can succeed. Effective administrators understand the importance and power of positive language. They know they influence others through what they say—how they communicate who they are, what they believe in, and what they value in themselves and in others.

Viewed in this light, leaders' language helps determine their own success or failure, as well as the success or failure of their teachers, staff, and students. Effective principals say good things about their school, their teachers and staff, their students, their parents, and their community. They encourage cooperation and collaboration. They focus on the positive. They turn weaknesses into successes. And they celebrate the successes of their faculty, staff, and students. They also communicate their school's vision, perhaps their most important role.

Communicating the Vision

One of the leader's main tasks is to develop the school's or district's vision, in collaboration with others, and then to declare, clarify, and promote—in other words, communicate—the vision.

Kenneth A. Leithwood and Carolyn Riehl, in a paper summarizing research-based conclusions about educational leadership, note that effective instructional leaders develop goals for student learning and inspire others with a vision of the school's or district's future. Successful school leaders employ several methods to set direction, Leithwood and Riehl stated.

Identifying and articulating the vision. Effective educational leaders help their schools or districts create and support a shared vision that embraces current best thinking about teaching and learning. They inspire teachers, staff, and students to reach for higher goals.

Creating high performance expectations. Effective leaders proclaim their expectations for high-quality teaching and student achievement. By expressing high expectations, an administrator motivates members of the school community and helps them realize that what is expected can be achieved.

Promoting school or district goals. New models of professional learning communities stress shared goals and efforts. Effective educational leaders encourage cooperation and help the entire school community work together toward meeting shared goals.

Communicating. Skilled leaders focus on the key elements of the school's or district's vision and communicate the vision clearly and frequently. They invite feedback and the exchange of ideas with teachers, staff, and students through an open communication system. They frame issues in ways that will lead to productive discussion and shared decision making.

Language, of course, is the tool for communicating the vision. A principal's spoken language, written language, and body language can serve as motivating forces that shape a positive school culture.

Social Capital

Social capital consists of the social relations, social networks, and norms—particularly of trust and reciprocity—that strengthen organizational life (Helen Marks).

Social capital has become especially important in education, as the socialization of children has come to take place not only in the family but also in the school. In reciprocal fashion, students contribute social capital to the school in the form of their knowledge, values, preferences, attitudes, and behavior.

According to Valerie E. Lee and Robert G. Croninger's research, a school's effectiveness is to some degree a function of how well family bonds extend into the school and how many supportive social relationships form among members of the school community.

Variations in school effectiveness and student performance owe in part to differences in the social capital that educators and students can access to meet educational and developmental goals. Leithwood and Riehl found that expanding the proportion of students' social capital valued by the schools is one of the core dimensions of leadership practice.

A Case Study in Effective Communication

M. Cecilia Martinez reports on an exploratory case study of one elementary school principal who developed the school's capacity through the improvement of social capital. Martinez defines *human capital* as "the leaders' and teachers' knowledge, skills, and dispositions" and describes *social capital* as "the network of vital connections to trustworthy sources of knowledge outside the district and norms of collegiality and trust as well as a functioning network within the district."

For Martinez, internal social capital includes the professional networks formed in the school or district that make it easier for individuals within the network to access resources and services. Social capital works productively for individuals and groups, enabling them to achieve their desired goals.

Maya Angelou Elementary School is in a small New Jersey city with a high percentage of people of low socioeconomic status. The school is in a district characterized by poverty and educational inadequacies. Maya Angelou was required by the state to implement a whole-school reform model that called for the restructuring of curricula, instructional practices, classroom environments, and school management.

The reform efforts have resulted in substantial improvements in learning and teaching. In mathematics, students are exploring problems in depth through a variety of strategies and expressing their mathematical thinking in an effort to move away from textbooks. In the language arts, students have received the highest test scores in the district. They are asked to read 25 books a year of their own choosing and encouraged to write every day. Teachers are helping students to develop metacognitive strategies and are implementing portfolios to track individual student improvement.

Educational consultants working with the school say it has developed high social capital consistent with the promotion of "authentic pedagogy." Through observations and interviews with teachers and the principal, Martinez concluded that the principal, through constant communication of the school's vision and goals, the promotion of a learning culture, and regular monitoring of the curriculum, has developed internal social capital.

The changes at Maya Angelou began with the principal, an experienced and energetic administrator. One of the principal's main tools for implementing change has been communication. She communicates daily with her teachers about the school's problems and ways they can be solved. She constantly seeks feedback from teachers. Teachers report that she is very honest and "up front" about letting people know what is working well and what is not.

At weekly staff meetings and monthly grade-level meetings, she reiterates the school's goals and shares her and staff members' concerns. In one-on-one meetings with teachers, which she schedules with at least one teacher a day, she discusses instructional issues. In these personal meetings, she provides the teacher an outline, based on the principal's classroom observations, of what the teacher needs to do to improve instruction.

"If everybody is meeting the standard, then there is no reason to change, but everybody is not meeting the standard," the principal said. "So what I have to get them to understand is there is room for this much success and you are only getting this much." By establishing that there is room for more success, she hopes to raise teachers' expectations about students' achievement.

A weekly school bulletin includes the principal's reminders about grade-level meetings with her and descriptions of the agendas for weekly staff meetings. She writes words of support and recognizes teachers who have participated in extra school events. She shares information about workshops being held at the school or district. Once a week, she prints the district's vision statement: "The [district name] Public Schools in partnership with its community shall do whatever it takes for every student to achieve high academic standards. No alibis! No excuses! No exceptions!"

THE COMMUNICATION PROCESS

It is a challenge to truly understand how we communicate with one another. Whether a person is speaking and listening to only one other person, writing to a large audience, or reading alone, communication is more than a single act. It is a dynamic, transactional process.

The Classical Theory

Communication theorists have created a number of theories to explain the complex process of human communication. The well-known *classical theory* has six steps. According to the classical theory, a message is interpreted correctly when the receiver assigns to it the same meaning as the sender intended and then responds in the desired way:

Step 1   The sender has an idea, a feeling, or information to share.

Step 2   The idea becomes a message. This is called *encoding* and involves deciding on the form, length, organization, style, and tone of the message. The form of the message depends on the audience the sender wants to reach, the idea the sender wants to convey, and the sender's purpose and personal style.

Step 3   The message is transmitted. The transmission can be accomplished through a number of different media or channels. The channel chosen depends on the size and location of the audience, the formality of the message, and whether there is a need for speed.

Step 4   The receiver receives the message and begins to *decode*, or interpret, it. Decoding involves both physical reception—hearing or seeing—and mental processing.

Step 5   The receiver reacts and provides feedback. Feedback can be either a response or no response. Feedback enables the sender to evaluate the effectiveness of the message.

Step 6   The feedback triggers a new cycle of sending, receiving, and responding.

Chance and Chance stress the importance of understanding communication theory. Knowing the dynamics of human communication will help school leaders to

- comprehend the effects of communication on organizational structure,
- use formal channels of communication more effectively,
- identify key individuals who may hinder or help communication,
- facilitate communication so that the receiver's perception is congruent with the intent of the message,
- understand that organizational communication is ongoing and dynamic, and
- prevent information overload that can inhibit the effectiveness of the school organization.

From Theory to Model

E. Mark Hanson has taken the classical theory and combined it with two other theories, the social-system theory and the open-system theory, to create what he calls the "S-M-C-R (sender, message, channel, receiver) communication model." Hanson assigned the classical theory to Level 1 of his model.

The *social-system theory,* Level 2 of the model, can be traced to the emergence of the human-relations movement in the 1930s. At that time, communication theorists were concerned with the less visible and informal aspects of the classical model and sought to understand why distortions and gaps frequently existed between the messages sent and those received. They studied the motivation and perspectives of senders and receivers, along with nonverbal cues and stereotypes, and the way these informal characteristics influenced the behavior of senders and receivers.

The social-system theory viewed communication as a transactional exchange between two or more individuals. *Communication* Hanson defined as "the exchange of meaning." The words exchanged are actually symbols that stand for something else. To communicate, the sender must create a mental picture of something, name it, and form a feeling about it. The receiver must grasp that name, concept, and feeling for the communication process to be effective. The exchange requires that the sociopsychological makeup of both the sender and receiver be known.

The *open-system theory* comprises Level 3 of Hanson's S-M-C-R communication model. Systems theory, which arose in the 1960s, involves the interconnectedness and functioning of subsystems within the organization. In open systems, Hanson says, *communication* can be defined as "the exchange of messages and meanings between an organization and its environment as well as between its network of interdependent subsystems." In this context, communication can be understood only in relation to the social system in which it occurs. "Communication," Hanson explains, "is in us, not in the words."

Communication Barriers

Communication barriers exist between individuals and within organizations. To understand each other, sender and receiver must agree on the meanings of words, gestures, tones of voice, and other symbols. Following are some of the communication barriers between people:

Differences in perception and language. Senders choose the details that seem important to them, a process known as *selective perception.* But sometimes the perception of the receiver is not the same as the sender's. Language is an arbitrary code of agreed-on symbols. Even though speakers of a common language may think they agree on the definition of a word, sometimes their definitions differ dramatically. The missing of each other's meaning is sometimes called *bypassing.*

Poor listening. People let their minds wander, particularly when they are forced to listen to information that is difficult to understand, as every classroom teacher knows. When people are tired or concerned about other matters, they also may lose interest.

Emotional interference. The old adage, "Don't shoot the messenger," applies here. Communication can be impeded when feelings get in the way of the sender's or receiver's objectivity.

Physical distractions. Noise of all kinds, including poor connections, sloppy appearances, and typos, may not completely block communication, but it certainly reduces the receiver's concentration.

Cultural differences. Communicating with someone from another country who speaks another language is the most extreme example of how different backgrounds may hamper communication. In our ever-diversifying society and school environment, principals may have problems recognizing the communication styles of teachers and students from different cultures. Some linguists and sociologists maintain that women and men within a larger culture come from different subcultures and have different communication styles.

Communication barriers can also exist within organizations:

Information overload. Administrators and teachers, like other professionals, are bombarded with information. Too many directives, policy changes, emotional pleas, and other messages can cause a communication system to falter.

Incorrect filtering. Filtering is screening out or abbreviating a message before it is passed on to someone. The filters between a principal and teachers, for instance, may be an assistant principal, a secretary, or an answering machine. Information theory holds that every relay doubles the noise and cuts the message in half. Filtering works most often from the bottom up. Many times, the gatekeepers are reluctant to pass on bad news to administrators. Consequently, principals may think everything is just fine because they do not hear all the bad news from assistant principals or teacher leaders.

Closed communication climate. A management style that is authoritarian and directive blocks the free and open exchange of information that is the cornerstone of effective communication.

Removing the Barriers

Faulty communication between principals and teachers robs a school of its effectiveness, say Patricia F. First and David S. Carr. Communication barriers can deplete team energy and isolate individuals, who may then proceed on the basis of faulty assumptions regarding personalities or goals. In this type of situation, trust between principal and faculty—as well as overall morale—can be seriously inhibited.

Increased contact, then, would seem to be a logical way to remove such barriers. First and Carr suggest that teachers be involved early in any decision and be kept up to date about whatever is going on. Meetings and various in-house communiqués are often used for this purpose. Private discussions provide the kind of frankness and openness needed to clear the air and remove barriers between people before they become larger problems. Such meetings can also be the occasion for praise and compliments for good work, say First and Carr. In short, a principal should make use of every opportunity and every available medium to let teachers, staff, and students know what is going on in the school.

COMMUNICATION SKILLS

A variety of communication skills are necessary for success as a leader. This section discusses three: listening, giving feedback, and speaking.

Active Listening

A principal needs to gather information to help identify and understand the needs and wants of faculty, staff, and students. One of the surest ways to gather such information is to listen to the members of the school community. The ability to listen well is one of the keys to success in educational leadership.

"Good listening," wrote Mary Ellen Guffey, "means maintaining a positive attitude, being open to new ideas, getting involved in the listening process, and working to retain information."

Communication experts tell us that in most organizations, the percentage of communication time that employees spend on listening is 45 percent to 50 percent. That percentage rises to 60 percent to 70 percent for managers. Unfortunately, managers, including school principals, are notoriously poor listeners because they are more accustomed to being listened to than to listening. According to MetLife's 2003 *MetLife Survey of the American Teacher,* fewer than a third of teachers described their principals as good listeners, whereas more than half of principals rated themselves as good listeners. Fortunately, most people can learn to become skillful listeners.

The Three Types of Listening

Different situations call for different listening skills, explain Bovée and Thill. Communication experts have identified three types of listening that differ in function, purpose, and the amount of feedback that may occur. Skillful listeners vary the way they listen to fit the situation:

1. *Content listening* helps you understand and retain the speaker's message. It does not matter whether you agree or disagree with or approve or disapprove of what the speaker is saying. What matters is only that you understand. When the state superintendent of education delivers an address on the state of education at the annual principals' conference, you listen mainly for content. You want to understand policy.

2. *Critical listening* enables you to evaluate the information you are receiving. The goal is to both understand and evaluate the speaker's message at several levels, including the speaker's intentions, the logic of the argument, the strength of the evidence, the validity of the conclusions, and the implications. When the superintendent presents funding projections for the next school year, you listen while critically evaluating whether the estimates are valid and what the implications are for your school. Critical listening may also involve interaction (feedback) of some kind.

3. *Active, or empathic, listening* helps you understand the speaker's feelings, needs, or wants, regardless of whether you share the perspective. When a teacher complains about the lack of materials, and you know the budget constraints, you listen empathically. In this case, you avoid the temptation to give advice or make excuses and just let the teacher talk.

Listening Inefficiency

Communication experts tell us that we listen at only 25-percent efficiency. That means we ignore, forget, or confuse 75 percent of what we hear. Several factors contribute to such listening inefficiency, Guffey says. Lack of training is one factor. Universities teach pedagogical practices, management methods, and even language arts such as writing and speaking. But apart from some tips on note taking, few courses provide in-depth training in listening.

The sheer volume of noise surrounding us also diminishes listening efficiency. In our noisy world, a great many sounds and sights compete for our attention.

Finally, Guffey says, we are inadequate listeners because of the slowness of speech. Most speakers talk at about 150 words per minute; listeners process speech at about 400 words per minute. This "lag time" leads to daydreaming and tuning out, which greatly reduces listening efficiency.

The Listening Process and Its Barriers

Listening takes place in four stages, says Guffey. And like communication in general, barriers can impede listening:

1. *Perception.* The listening process begins when we hear the sounds around us and concentrate on them. The conscious act of listening begins when we focus on particular

sounds, selecting those we choose to consider. Impaired hearing, noise, inattention, and *pseudolistening* diminish perception. Pseudolistening is the act of pretending to listen when one's mind wanders far from the speaker's words.

2. *Interpretation.* When we have focused our attention on a sound or message, we begin to decode it. Our educational, cultural, and social frames of reference influence our interpretation of the message. Thus, the receiver's interpretation of the sender's meaning may be quite different from what the sender intended.

3. *Evaluation.* Evaluation involves judging messages objectively and separating opinion from fact. A closed mind and dogmatic attitude are major barriers to listening.

4. *Action.* A response to a message requires an action. The response may be to store the message in the memory for future use; to react physically with a guffaw or hug, for example; or to furnish feedback through verbal or nonverbal cues. Listener feedback is essential because it lets the speaker know if the message is getting through clearly. Barriers to action may be a closed communication system in which a teacher, for instance, may be reluctant to supply feedback to an autocratic principal.

Guffey offers a three-step plan for improving your listening skills:

Step 1   Identify your personal bad listening habits. Do you feign listening? Do you tune out difficult or unpleasant topics? Are you more eager to refute than to learn? To exercise your authority than to gather facts?

Step 2   Select techniques to begin working on immediately. Choose at least two suggestions from the checklist in Table 16.1 that you feel you could put to work as soon as possible.

Step 3   Create opportunities for practice. During your next all-staff meeting, write at the top of your notepad, "Today I'm here to listen and learn." Then concentrate on doing just that.

For more tips on becoming a better listener, see Table 16.1 ("Checklist for Improving Listening").

Giving Feedback

Feedback is a way to share understanding about behavior, feelings, and motivations. When giving feedback, say Charles Jung and associates, it is useful to describe observed behaviors, as well as the reactions they caused. Bear in mind these points:

- The receiver should be ready to receive feedback.
- Comments should describe, rather than interpret, action.
- Feedback should focus on recent events or actions.
- Feedback should focus on things that can be changed.

Table 16.1   Checklist for Improving Listening

1. Stop talking.

    - Wait for your turn.
    - Find a quiet place for personal discussions, away from others.

2. Ask questions.

    - Strive for clarification and understanding.
    - Paraphrase the speaker's ideas.

3. Put the speaker at ease.

    - Invite the speaker to tell his or her story.
    - Use nonverbal cues such as smiling and nodding your head.

4. Show you want to listen.

    - Let the speaker be the expert.
    - Be careful of pseudolistening, or pretending to listen.

5. Remove distractions.

    - Don't doodle, shuffle papers, or talk on the phone.
    - Stay involved with the speaker and the whole process of listening.

6. Empathize with the speaker.

    - Try to see the speaker's point of view.
    - Find common ground and common experience.

7. Be patient.

    - Don't interrupt; allow the speaker plenty of time.
    - Look and act interested.

8. Avoid argument and criticism, including internal criticism.

    - Set aside your prejudices about the way the speaker looks or talks.
    - Focus on the content of the message, not the delivery.

9. Hold your temper.

    - Don't shoot the messenger.
    - If you must oppose the speaker, wait for the opportune moment.

10. Stop talking.

    - Expect to learn something.
    - Don't assume all speakers want immediate feedback.

- Feedback should not be used to try to force people to change.
- Feedback should be offered out of a sincere interest and concern for the other person.

When you want feedback, state what you want feedback about, and then check what you have heard, and share your reactions. One especially important kind of feedback for administrators is letting staff members know how well they are doing on their jobs. In

Susan R. Glaser and Anna Eblen's study, the managers who were most valued by high-level business executives gave their employees plenty of timely, positive feedback about their work.

In contrast, ineffective managers stressed poor performance and rarely gave positive reinforcement. "These managers were not there to compliment, but were usually there if something went wrong," the researchers say. Effective managers gave negative feedback privately, without anger or personal attack. They accepted criticism without becoming defensive and used negative feedback about their own performance to learn and change.

Powerful Speaking

Much help is available to administrators who want to improve their speaking skills. Books, personal coaches, and organizations such as Toastmasters International all can provide help. In the meantime, here are a few basic tips from Guffey for making presentations and speeches to small or large audiences:

- Focus on four main areas: preparation, organization, visual aids, and delivery.
- Know your purpose. Determine what you want to accomplish in every presentation or speech.
- Know your audience. Decide how your topic will appeal to the audience, how you can relate information to the audience's needs, how you can earn the audience's respect so they will accept your message, how to effectively make your point, and how to ensure the audience will remember your main points.
- Practice your presentation. Videotape or record yourself. When practicing, remember to time yourself.
- During your presentation, maintain eye contact; speak in moderated tones; eliminate vocal tics such as "uh," "um," and "you know"; move your hands and body naturally; and summarize your main points.
- After your presentation, encourage questions, reinforce your main points, keep control, and end with a summary or remarks of appreciation.
- Adhere to the long-practiced rubric: Tell them what you're going to say, say it, and then tell them what you've said.

THE SILENT LANGUAGE

Another key communication skill is actually a set of skills under the category "nonverbal communication." Combined with words or on their own, vocal characteristics, body movements, hand gestures, and facial expressions send powerful messages to your audience. The barely concealed smirk, the trudging walk, the turned back, the pointing finger, and a swarm of other signals speak volumes.

Modeling Behavior

"Actions speak louder than words," as the old adage goes. Principals can have a profound influence on student achievement by communicating nonverbally through their actions. Leithwood and Riehl found that one of the key dimensions of leadership practice is providing an appropriate model. The effective school leader sets an example for staff and students through actions consistent with the school's values and goals. By modeling desired attitudes and actions, principals enhance others' beliefs about their own potential and their enthusiasm for change.

Being Accessible

One important action is showing up. One of the most important things a principal can do to improve relations within the school community is to be open and accessible. Show people you are available, and welcome personal contact with them. Spend time with various faculty members over lunch, during coffee breaks, in the faculty lounge, or at informal teacher hangouts. Ask people about their families, and call them by their first names. In the 1980s, this practice became known as "management by walking around." An administrator who takes the time to get to know faculty and staff members will be able to identify, develop, and make best use of each member's capabilities.

Common Nonverbal Cues

Ways to communicate nonverbally are many, varied, and culturally determined. The smile, communication experts tell us, is the only universally understood and accepted facial gesture. Following are some of the more common nonverbal cues used in business and social situations in North America.

Body language. Body movements and positions express both specific and general messages. Many movements or gestures, a wave of the hand for example, have a specific and intentional meaning. Leaning slightly toward a person emphasizes interest. Tightly crossed arms and legs say you are closed to others' ideas. Hands on hips can signify impatience. Standing up signals the end of a meeting. Other types of body movement are unintentional and express a more general message. Movements such as putting a hand over your month, slouching, fidgeting, and walking briskly are unconscious signals that reveal your feelings.

Use of space. How a principal's office looks tells a lot. Is there a desk or a table, for instance? Staying behind your desk when someone comes to visit gives the impression that you are unapproachable. Several chairs around a table show you are accessible. Use of space sends other signals as well. Taking up space communicates dominance. Notice how students spread out in the lunchroom to mark their territories.

Space also determines how comfortable people are when talking with each other. North Americans have definite boundaries when it comes to personal space. Between 4 and 12 feet is considered an agreeable and acceptable business comfort zone.

Eye contact. Maintaining eye contact 40 percent to 70 percent of the time conveys openness, receptivity, sincerity, and honesty. A principal who avoids eye contact may give the impression of feeling superior or of hiding something. But 100-percent eye contact is intimidating.

Facial expressions. The human face is capable of expressing a huge range of feelings. A genuine smile projects warmth and interest; a frown, disapproval or deep thought;

a smirk, disbelief; narrowing eyelids, suspicion; raised eyebrows and widely opened eyes, a friendly greeting; a wrinkled nose, unpleasantness; a wink of the eye, a secret or playfulness; and so forth.

Gestures. Appropriate gestures add strength to your message and project self-confidence. Others can be distracting, such as fussing with your hair, tapping your fingers on the table, or picking lint off your jacket. Gestures, especially hand gestures, are highly culturally specific.

Personal appearance. Clothes, posture, and grooming—usually the first things people notice about you—send messages about your status, attitudes, and how you feel about yourself and others.

Voice. The human voice is a remarkable instrument. Through tone of voice, we can communicate warmth, coldness, interest, boredom, confidence, uncertainty, openness, sadness, happiness, superiority, playfulness, and other attitudes. Speaking softly may be seen as a lack of confidence. Speaking loudly may be perceived as aggressive or offensive. Speaking quickly may give the impression of curtness. The high voice of some women, especially when they are speaking fast, is often misinterpreted by men as hysteria.

Use of time. When we make time for others, we communicate openness and respect. Time can also be used to assert authority. Making others wait for you can communicate power or disrespect.

Touching. Touch conveys warmth, comfort, and reassurance. Even the most casual contact can create positive feelings. Bovée and Thill reported on an experiment in which librarians alternately touched and avoided the hands of students while students were returning their library cards. Although the contact lasted only half a second, the students who had been touched reported far more positive feelings about themselves and the library, even though many of them did not even remember being touched. Perhaps because it implies intimacy, touching behavior is governed by strict customs that establish who can touch whom and how. By now, most principals, especially male principals, are keenly aware of the touching taboos in North American schools.

Mastering Nonverbal Communication Skills

Mastering nonverbal communication skills is vital for an administrator. Nonverbal communication is the most basic form of communication. It conveys information quickly and efficiently. Nonverbal communication has more impact than verbal communication and is often considered a more accurate and reliable indicator of meaning than words are. Studies have shown that in face-to-face conversations, only about 7 percent of meaning is conveyed through words, whereas 38 percent is conveyed through tone of voice and 55 percent through body language.

People are more likely to believe nonverbal cues. To test this hypothesis, try this experiment. When answering a question with a spoken yes, shake your head no. Or when answering a question with a spoken no, nod your head yes. See if your questioner responds more to your words or your actions.

Nonverbal communication is generally less structured and more spontaneous than verbal communication; consequently, it is more difficult to control than words. No matter how sophisticated we may be, we cannot control a blush when we are embarrassed or a stammer when we are confused.

Sometimes gestures even determine our feelings. Numerous studies have shown that by simply smiling, we improve our mood. Skilled communicators deploy this maneuver when, for instance, making a speech. The next time you deliver an address to a small or large group and are feeling a bit nervous, try this technique. Just before approaching the podium, take two slow breaths and grin wide enough to feel the corners of your mouth turn up and the corners of your eyes crease. Now you are better prepared to speak.

Because nonverbal communication cues are often involuntary, we may find ourselves unconsciously matching another's gestures or actions. This behavior is known as *isopraxism*. When used properly, isopraxism can be an effective communication tool. Whereas obviously mimicking another person's actions can be insulting, subtly matching those actions can build trust and enhance communication. For example, when meeting with a disgruntled teacher, monitor his or her movements. When the teacher frowns, you frown; when he or she smiles, you smile. When the teacher leans forward or back, slowly, unobtrusively match those actions. Notice if the communication becomes more open and the teacher more relaxed.

Nonverbal cues are many and culturally determined. For instance, the hand gesture of touching the tips of the thumb and forefinger to create a circle means "OK" in the United States and "zero" in southern France. In some parts of South America, the same gesture refers to a part of the female anatomy and is highly insulting. Being aware of such culturally determined meanings can help a principal communicate more effectively with a diverse faculty and student population.

Within a larger culture, subcultures communicate differently. Deborah Tannen and other linguists and anthropologists maintain that men and women are from separate subcultures and approach the communication process in different ways. Generally speaking (and we must avoid stereotyping), men focus on processes, and women focus on relationships. This knowledge can be useful to skilled communicators. Let us say a principal is called on to settle a dispute between a female and a male faculty member. The principal's first step may be to meet individually with each combatant to hear each side of the story. The principal will aid the communication process by sitting face to face with the female teacher and beside the male teacher.

Here are some additional pointers to improve your nonverbal communication skills:

- Do not rely on gestures to convey the entire meaning; use gestures to reinforce your words.
- Pay more attention to nonverbal cues from other people.
- Be careful that you aren't sending out conflicting signals; be sure what you say is consistent with what you do.
- Try to be as honest as possible in communicating your feelings.
- Learn the different ways members of different cultures in your school communicate nonverbally.
- Maintain eye contact; your status allows it.
- Adopt a forceful handshake, and always be the first one to extend your hand.

ADMINISTRATIVE WRITING

Another key communication skill for school leaders—worthy of consideration separately from speaking and listening—is writing. With the ubiquity of the personal computer and subsequent disappearance of the Dictaphone, managers in all fields now do more of their own writing and editing than ever before. Even though they may have had considerable writing experience in their undergraduate and graduate course work, school leaders generally have had little training in the specific kinds of writing needed in administrative work.

Administrative writing, Arthur E. Lehr (2003) states, serves a wide range of purposes: to inform, instruct, interest, persuade, and report. Principals are frequently required to offer concise, detailed information that effectively tells the story of their schools. Because principals serve in leadership roles, their written communications are closely scrutinized both inside and outside the school organization. People judge principals—and all other managers for that matter—on the strength of their writing ability.

Rebore believes that the effectiveness of the administrative infrastructure of a school or district is directly related to its written documents. Mission statements, policy documents, curriculum guides, operating and procedures manuals, and other materials, the author says, give purpose to the many activities of individuals in the school or office.

As we have noted, the principal is recognized as a behavioral model. For the principal, an important payoff for good writing is the influence it may have on student academic outcomes. As an instructional leader, the principal has the opportunity to model and to teach the power of the written word.

As Rebore points out, the principal who regularly communicates in writing with faculty and staff empowers them with information and knowledge. Through writing, the principal demonstrates how to organize and convey thoughts, feelings, and information, and sets a standard for high-quality communication.

"Because the written word may leave an indelible mark on its audience," Lehr (2003) says, "school leaders do not have the luxury of treating casually any writing that they do. Words outlive actions."

There is no space in this forum for a complete lesson in administrative writing, but there is space for some basic tips that can help any school leader to write more effectively.

The Writing Process

Most instructors of business or administrative writing teach some form of a three-step process: planning, composing, and revising.

Step 1: Planning

The first step in the writing process begins as soon as you have an idea or assignment. This prewriting stage involves brainstorming to establish a purpose, gather information, consider the audience, and choose the medium. The most important step is to identify who will read what you write. Everything in written communication stems from knowing as much as possible about your audience. When writing any message, always keep the reader in mind. Visualize your ideal reader, and write directly to that person.

One way of brainstorming is to use the journalistic technique of asking the five "W" and one "H" questions. When communicating a change in instructional policy, for example, you might ask yourself the following questions:

1. *Who* is the primary reader? . . . is the secondary reader? . . . are you to the reader? . . . should perform the desired actions?

2. *What* do you hope to accomplish? . . . is fact? . . . is opinion? . . . is your solution or conclusion? . . . are the alternatives? . . . might the reader ask? . . . does the reader know about the subject? . . . is in it for the reader?

3. *Why* are you writing this? . . . are you writing this now? . . . are you writing to a particular person or group?

4. *Where* does this communication lead? . . . are the reader's blind spots, biases? . . . are the reader's points of resistance?

5. *When* will you deliver this message? . . . will actions and events occur? . . . are the deadlines? . . . will additional information be available?

6. *How* will the reader react? . . . much time do you have to create the message? . . . will you deliver the message?

How you will deliver the message is another key point. The medium affects the style, length, and complexity of the message. Each form of written communication—letter, memo, e-mail, report, newsletter, fax—has its own image, format, level of formality, and delivery challenges.

Step 2: Composing

The second stage of the writing process, composing or drafting, occurs when you put finger to keyboard and apply written language to express your feelings or convey your information. When we speak, we employ a number of extra nonverbal cues to convey exact meaning. When we write, we don't have such help, except for punctuation. Therefore, every word must tell. Following are some simple suggestions for clear messaging.

Use words the reader understands. It's fine to use professional jargon when writing internal memos or letters to other educators. The purpose of writing, nevertheless, is to communicate, not to impress with a large or specialized vocabulary. Keep your reader in mind, and adapt your writing to the reader's level of understanding.

Eliminate word clutter. Conciseness is a virtue in writing. Everyone is busy; few people have time to read all the messages thrown at them. Redundant words tossed into a sentence without contributing to meaning muddle up the message. You can improve the readability of your message simply by eliminating the verbose expressions in the left column of Table 16.2 ("Examples of Concise Writing") and replacing them with the simpler terms in the right column.

Table 16.2   Examples of Concise Writing

Instead of writing	Write
due to the fact of	because
in order to	to
until such time	until
in case of	if
at this point in time	now
inasmuch as	since
in the event that	if
for the reason that	because
as opposed to	instead
I would request	please
thanking you in advance	thank you
It would seem to me	I think
I am in agreement	I agree
you are to be congratulated	congratulations
in the neighborhood of	about
by means of	by
in conjunction with	with
the method by which	how
despite the fact that	although
the majority of	most
a large number of	many
at a later date	later
give consideration	consider
be unable to	can't
be in need of	need
it is our recommendation that	we recommend
until such time as	until
it has come to my attention that	I learned
at the present time	now
your immediate attention to this matter would be greatly appreciated	please respond by
we wish to extend our thanks	thank you
some time next week	next Tuesday at 3:00
approximately 40 staff members	25 teachers, 15 support staff
a gain in test scores	a 14-percent jump in test scores
our school	Kennedy High School
thank you for your good work	thank you for administering our successful reading program

Prefer the specific to the generic. As much as possible, be specific with your readers; do not leave them guessing (see Table 16.2).

Apply current practices. Writing is a social act. Writing styles reflect current thinking. The current trend in business and administrative writing is toward more natural, less formal diction. Occasional contractions ("won't," "couldn't," "didn't"), first-person pronouns ("I" instead of "the writer"), and more conversational constructions ("this paper" instead of "the current study") are acceptable in all but the most formal educational reports. A less formal style is certainly acceptable, and even expected, in internal documents such as memos and e-mails. The aim is to sound professional yet maintain a personal touch.

Use good sentence construction. The English sentence remains the cornerstone of good written communication. Creating complete sentences makes your writing forceful. The key to good sentence construction is emphasizing important ideas. Guffey suggested three ways: (a) Place the important idea at the beginning of a sentence, (b) make the important idea function as the subject of the sentence, and (c) place important ideas in short sentences.

Varying the type (simple, complex, compound, and so forth) and length of sentences makes your writing more vigorous and interesting to the reader. Generally, it is best to keep sentences short, from 17 to 26 words, or about 20 on average. Studies have shown that as sentences expand, reader comprehension contracts. For example, according to Guffey, comprehension drops from 100 percent for an 8-word sentence to 50 percent for a 28-word sentence.

Step 3: Editing

The third step in the writing process is editing, sometimes called revising. This is an important, but often overlooked, step in the process. Editing includes proofreading and fact checking every item, including phone numbers, URLs, totals of columns of numbers, percentages (making sure they add up to 100), spellings of names, and dates.

It is always preferable to have someone else edit, or at least proofread, your work, but when that isn't possible, follow this three-step editing process:

1. *Edit for content and organization.* Check for emphasis on important points, order and flow of ideas, balance among points, mix of general and specific, quality and quantity of evidence, and irrelevant information. Pay particular attention to the quality of the introduction and the conclusion. Readers remember best what they read first and second best what they read last.

2. *Edit for style and readability.* Check for consistent tone, interest level, clarity and understanding, order and flow of ideas, sentence structure, paragraph construction, and transitions.

3. *Edit for mechanics and format.* Check for grammar, spelling, punctuation, typos, usage (includes jargon), consistency of usage, appearance of text, and consistency of format.

Routine Messages

Although the job of a school leader requires the writing of a variety of messages, the most common are routine day-to-day internal messages to faculty, staff, and students. These generally take the form of memos and e-mails, and the topics vary from congratulatory notes, to information on new policy, to staff layoffs. (The next chapter discusses writing messages to people outside the school or office.) Although routine, these messages require an administrator's careful attention.

Effective memos and e-mails are brief, concise, and personal. Their primary function is to convey an idea so clearly that no further explanation is necessary. They employ a conversational yet professional tone, and they focus on a single topic. For readability, they contain a quick summary in the heading. The body is augmented by graphic highlighting (bullets, indents, subheads). The message, or body, of the memo is built on a three-part pattern: (a) the opening: a statement that announces the purpose; (b) the body: details that explain the purpose; and (c) the closing: a request for action or a courteous conclusion.

Follow these additional guidelines for effective e-mail communications:

- Design the format for readability.
- Avoid all-capital letters in the body.
- Do not assume your e-mail is private.
- Be careful of inappropriate material such as jokes, gossip, or angry denouncements.
- Maintain standards of grammatical correctness.
- Include a complimentary close; at least close with your name.
- Do not use e-mail to avoid personal contact.
- Check your e-mail regularly, at least once a day.
- Respond to incoming e-mails as soon as possible, even if the response is only, "Thanks for your e-mail. I'll get back to you soon."

Message Patterns

Administrative messages usually fall into one of two patterns: the direct or indirect pattern. As described by Guffey, the *direct pattern* presents the main idea first followed by supporting evidence. It opens with a summary, a conclusion, or recommendations. This method works for a receptive audience and is useful for both short and long messages, especially those conveying good news. The direct pattern also has these advantages: It conveys confidence, saves the reader time, sets a proper frame of mind, prevents reader frustration, and is easy for the reader to skim.

Example of the direct pattern: "I believe we should implement this program because (a) it saves money, (b) it saves time, and (c) it saves labor."

The *indirect pattern,* on the other hand, presents the evidence first followed by a summary, a conclusion, or recommendations. According to Guffey, this method works well for a resistant audience, is good for persuasive messages, respects the feelings of the audience, ensures a fair hearing, minimizes negative reaction, and conveys an impression of objectivity. In long messages, however, it can be difficult to follow.

Example of the indirect pattern: "This program (a) saves money, (b) saves time, and (c) saves labor. . . . Therefore, I believe we should implement this program."

Delivering Bad News

One type of routine message warrants special consideration. The bad-news message is one of the hardest for administrators to write. No administrator likes to tell students that a favored program has been cut or let instructional aides know their contracts will not be renewed. Writing about bad news requires deliberation and a delicate touch.

Use the indirect pattern to deliver bad news. In the opening, begin with a neutral or positive statement known as the *buffer*. The buffer could be an expression of appreciation, a compliment to the reader, or an assurance of your understanding of a situation. The point of the buffer is to set the stage for the bad news to come.

Deliver the bad news in the body of the message. State it clearly and concisely, and explain the reasons briefly and unemotionally. Avoid apologies; they weaken your explanation or position. Try to embed the bad news in a supporting, not the topical, sentence of a paragraph. Furthermore, try to embed it in a subordinate clause of a sentence. The purpose is not to conceal the bad news, but to soften its impact.

Close the memo or e-mail on a positive, friendly, or helpful note. Do not repeat the bad news, and resist offering advice to the reader. The reader does not need or want a lecture at this point. You might offer alternatives or suggest actions the reader might take, however. Maintain a positive outlook for the future.

CONCLUSION: PERSEVERANCE PAYS OFF

Communicating can be a complex, difficult, and occasionally frustrating business. Yet for the school leader who perseveres in understanding and communicating with teachers, staff, and students, there is a rich payoff. Effective communication with these groups (and other groups, as we will see in the next chapter) can produce a positive school climate that leads to high-quality teaching and student achievement.

REFLECTIONS

1. How would you rate yourself as a communicator? Has anyone ever told you that you are a good listener or an excellent writer? Has anyone ever told you that you are difficult to talk to?

2. How do you feel when someone else edits or proofreads your written communications? Are you grateful for the "extra pair of eyes"? Or do you resent someone else pointing out mistakes or improving your text?

3. How accessible are you to colleagues or those who report to you? Is your office door always closed? Is the answering machine on your phone always engaged? Do you check your e-mail at least once a day?

4. How do you greet and treat visitors to your office? Do you stand up, smile, and come out from behind your desk when they enter? Or do you continue working or talking on the phone, making your visitors wait for you?

5. At the next staff meeting you attend, pay special attention to people's body language. Watch for involuntary actions or reactions such as blushing, perspiring, or stammering. Notice if people's actions agree with what they say. Do your actions agree with what you say?

6. Do you have any communication tics? For instance, do you always frown when hearing bad news? Do you interrupt people to get your point across? Do you pepper your speech repeatedly with words or phrases such as "do you know what I mean?" "you know," "guess what?" or "like"? Ask someone you trust to point out such tics.

17

Engaging the Public

Wendell Anderson

*Perhaps the most important goal of public engagement should be the development
of a community-based strategic plan for raising student achievement.*

—Michael A. Resnick

To paraphrase a concept of the 1990s: "It takes a community to educate a child."
Schools today cannot fulfill their mission in isolation from other community organizations and resources. Perhaps no other institution faces such high and steadily growing
expectations, and it's clear that school leaders alone can't meet those expectations.

One way school leaders can make a difference is to look beyond the school and seek
appropriate help from the community. More schools and districts across the country are
engaging the communities they serve to advance the educational achievement of children.

Widespread community participation benefits students, educators, and community
members alike. Educators frustrated by the troubles students experience at home may see
these problems decrease when social-service agencies collaborate with them on a plan for
the entire family. High schools plagued by truancy, high dropout rates, and apathy may be
energized by coalitions with local businesses that make the curriculum more interesting
and relevant to students' vocational needs. Parents may throw their support behind
restructuring efforts or serve as tutors or mentors to lagging or troubled students.

Public engagement also includes the offer of help to the community, such as parent
education programs, and the invitation of community members to participate in design
of the academic program. Through two-way communication, school leaders reach out in

a concerted effort to make student learning the mission not only of the schools but also of the community.

Communicating with parents and communities is more than sound practice; it's a legal requirement. The No Child Left Behind Act (NCLB) requires school districts to publish school report cards and identify schools in need of improvement. Each district must be able to explain the performance data and build public support for actions the schools may have to take to improve weak areas. An effective plan for public engagement will go beyond mere compliance with NCLB requirements, which address performance in language and math, to seek broad understanding and support for learning throughout the curriculum.

This chapter provides school leaders with practical tips on working and communicating effectively with people outside the school. The information will be useful to principals, superintendents, and school board members.

The chapter begins with a discussion of the importance of community engagement and continues with the leader's role in the process. The next section discusses the beginning steps of a plan for connecting with the community: creation of a governing board, identification of the key players, and assessment of needs.

Then, attention turns to the benefits and key elements of a plan for engaging the public, followed by a description of channels for delivering the message to the community. The chapter also includes detailed guidelines for working with the media. A section on evaluating the program concludes the chapter.

A NEW WAY OF DOING BUSINESS

Society has changed the way it does business, and schools must follow suit. Social institutions are, more than ever, interdependent but, at the same time, more competitive. Schools, fire stations, food banks, and a host of other social services all seek funding and support from the same public. Funding and support do not come automatically to the school as they once did. The school has to work for its support; it has to engage the public.

The Importance of Public Engagement

"By involving parents, members of the business sector, and others in identifying academic goals, standards, resources, and measures of progress, public engagement can be a powerful engine for raising student achievement," Resnick says. "And given the demands of the Information Age, such engagement can also bring valuable outside thinking, expertise, and relevance into a school district's thinking."

Public engagement is a two-way street that benefits both the school and the community. In the case of families, for instance, Kenneth A. Leithwood and Carolyn Riehl found that school leaders can influence family attitudes toward education by engaging in activities that promote trust and communication between families and schools, by providing resources to families, and by educating and supporting families in matters of parenting and schooling. The result is enhanced student learning.

A yearlong research project conducted by the National Conference of State Legislatures arrived at six characteristics of high-achieving schools. Characteristic 6 is family-school-community involvement. The report recommends that school leaders encourage students, families, and communities to share responsibility for school and student performance by forming partnerships to improve student achievement.

A school's involvement of its neighborhood can affect the personal attitudes and educational attainment of students, say Patricia W. Davis and P. J. Karr-Kidwell. Claiming that school-community partnerships are an important strategy for school reform, Davis and Karr-Kidwell believe that strong leadership from the administrative staff is critical to the success of a school-community partnership.

The Role of Leaders

Effective educational leaders, according to Leithwood and Riehl, encourage public engagement. They focus attention on key aspects of the school's vision and communicate that vision clearly and convincingly. They invite the exchange of ideas with multiple stakeholders. They frame issues in ways that lead to productive discourse and decision making. Skillful leaders work with representatives from the community to foster shared meanings, gather resources and support, and establish productive interorganizational relationships.

"To effectively position their schools within their environments, and to respond to legitimate concerns from parents and others, educational leaders are client-oriented, proactive, and focused," Leithwood and Riehl say.

Standard 6 of the National Association of Elementary School Principals' *Standards for What Principals Should Know and Be Able to Do* states: "Effective principals actively engage the community to create shared responsibility for student and school success." The standard involves several interrelated tasks:

- Engaging the community to build greater ownership for the work of the school
- Sharing leadership and decision making
- Encouraging parents to become involved in the school and in their own children's learning
- Ensuring that students and families are connected to the health, human, and social services they need to stay focused on learning

Realizing that it takes a community to educate a child, the perceptive school leader strives to build external social capital, the school's connections with the community. M. Cecilia Martinez explains that social capital has the potential to influence the capacity of schools, urban schools in particular. Urban schools that connect with community organizations and public agencies have the potential to bring resources and expertise to the school.

Douglas J. Fiore has outlined the roles of the principal and the superintendent in a community-relations program. The following summarizes some of the principal's key responsibilities, according to Fiore:

- sets a positive, friendly, and open tone for the school;
- assesses school and community perceptions of needs and resources;
- provides parent education on topics of interest to parents and family members;
- appoints qualified staff to coordinate the school's community-relations program;
- creates professional development activities to assist staff in developing strong communication skills;
- communicates regularly with all key players, soliciting their input formally and informally;
- keeps the superintendent informed of successes and failures in the school's community-relations efforts;
- recognizes and celebrates the accomplishment of all members of the school community; and
- maintains school publications that inform internal and external groups about the school.

The superintendent's role, again summarized from Fiore, is to

- build collaborative relationships with the school board;
- keep the school board and the public informed about the district's progress;
- assist the community-relations governing board by establishing liaisons with public officials, arranging meetings, and providing needed data and information;
- develop and champion the basic school district policy for creating relationships with the community;
- speak to groups within the community;
- ensure a climate of open communication within the school district (internal) and between the district and the public (external);
- recommend additional policies or policy revisions related to community relations; and
- present budget recommendations needed to support community-relations programs and collaborative efforts and initiatives.

When reading lists of duties such as these, school and district leaders might want to consider how other people may rate their performance. Often, we perform better in our own estimation than in the eyes of others. For example, MetLife's 2003 *MetLife Survey of the American Teacher* examined parents' perceptions about kindergarten through twelfth-grade (K–12) school principals. Nearly 90 percent of principals said they interact frequently with parents, but only 53 percent of parents said the same of their children's principals. Not even half of parents considered their relationship with the principal supportive, mutually respectful, friendly, or collaborative.

With these survey results in mind, some of the strategies in the remainder of this chapter for reaching out to parents and other members of the community may take on more meaning, and perhaps more urgency.

The next section examines three prerequisites for launching a community-engagement program: (a) formation of a governing board and clarification of the roles of its members, (b) identification of the key players who will be invited to take part in the program, and (c) assessment of the schools' and the community's needs.

CONNECTING WITH THE COMMUNITY

There are no foolproof recipes for connecting with the community. Each school's or district's set of circumstances warrants its own customized strategy. Most experts agree that it is vital to involve a cross-section of the community. So the first step is to consider who might be involved in a school's community-relations program—who will lead it, what their roles will be, and which key players of the community will be invited to participate. Then attention can be given to assessing the community's needs.

Formation of a Governing Board

Development of a community-relations program begins with formation of a leadership team or governing board. The first step in forming a governing board is to identify the key communicators from diverse community groups. Local conditions will dictate the board's composition and leadership. Principals and superintendents could serve as active directors, as advisors, or simply as advocates.

When recruiting members for a governing board, it is important to look for skills, not names. Milan Wall and Vicki Luther advise officials to recruit representatives from nearly all major segments of the community.

The board's first meeting should be devoted to developing the purpose of the board and an organizational framework, Wall and Luther say. At subsequent meetings, the board can plan activities for the year and begin a marketing plan to keep the larger community informed.

Once key stakeholders are onboard, here are a few simple rules to keep them involved: Keep everyone's self-interests in mind, make the larger perspective obvious, define the tasks, make good use of everyone's time, share the credit for results, and remain flexible.

The Role of the Governing Board

Boards commonly form committees to oversee projects. This serves to divide the work into manageable parts and to enlist participation from additional people. Projects will be determined by the goals of the community-relations program. Generally, a governing board can expect to provide policy, goals, a management plan, and financial support if appropriate. After creating and revising, when necessary, the community-relations plan, the board receives regular reports on the implementation of the plan and evaluates the plan's effectiveness. Above all, the board serves as an advocate for students.

According to Wall and Luther, board members should seek to understand the effects of change on the school and the community. Board members, say the authors, are also in a good position to ask community and business leaders what they think today's graduates must know to be successful in the future. Likewise, the board can help assess local attitudes about schools and determine what information the community needs and does not yet have. One way the board can assist in meeting those needs is to get people from the community meaningfully involved.

Wall and Luther point further to the board's responsibility to monitor the process continually.

The Key Players

A significant task for the board is to decide whom to include in the public-engagement process. For this decision, the board will want to locate key sources of expertise in the community. The broader the community base, the stronger the community-relations program. A wide range of groups merit inclusion.

Parents. Parents are undoubtedly the group most affected by schools and the group most likely to lend their support to them. Chris Cunningham believes that involving families, with a clear focus on improving student achievement, is perhaps the most critical activity schools can undertake to engage the community. Involved families can effectively serve as advocates for schools with the general public. Informed parents are among the best supporters when it comes time for the community to vote on bond issues.

Business leaders. Although the school-business connection is sometimes controversial, schools should collaborate with local businesses. Joining in such coalitions is in the best interest of businesses, which rely on schools to equip students with basic skills that will be needed on the job. Effective schools help develop better employees.

Business participation in school-improvement efforts can also bring benefits to the school. One particular benefit, L. Joan Brown points out, is support for technology. Some schools have found it necessary to engage businesses in the struggle to introduce and maintain upgraded technology for instruction. The business community can contribute to the school in other ways as well, for example, by providing venues for internships and offering expertise and technical assistance for specialized school projects.

Chamber of commerce. Chambers of commerce have a stake in their communities and strong connections to business, government, and education. The local chamber can be a strong ally in a community-relations program.

School representatives. These include local school superintendents, principals, teachers, school support staff, and central-office staff. These people, of course, have first-hand knowledge of what it takes to make a school successful.

Professional organizations. School leaders can gain from membership in regional, state, and national groups of peers. These organizations help administrators keep current with ideas and practices. They provide opportunities to learn from the successes and failures of other schools and programs.

Preschool and day care providers. People involved in early education can spot trends in young children that can help improve school readiness, children's attitudes toward school, curriculum, and parent involvement.

Universities and community colleges. Higher institutions of learning are invaluable partners in K–12 improvement efforts. As Resnick notes, universities and colleges can help articulate the academic standards needed for success at the university level, assist in designing K–12 curricula and programs, provide research data on successful programs and practices, help design research for a specific school or distinct, and enrich student learning through guest lecturers and cooperative programs.

Students. Students can function as a "reality check" to administrators and the governing board by providing frontline knowledge of what goes on in a school.

School boards. School leaders naturally want to build goodwill between the board and the school. Board members, as elected representatives, have their own followings and, if conscientious, are aware of their constituents' views. Administrators can use the board to sound out public opinion and to serve as a conduit for presenting school needs to particular segments of the community. School boards can communicate effectively with other governing bodies. For example, a board of education could meet occasionally with the city council and the county board of commissioners to coordinate policies and increase community involvement in the schools.

Lisa Bartusek and Resnick separately have written on the important role of school board members. The following list combines and summarizes their recommendations. Board members, these authors say, should

- commit their time and talents to community relations;
- support the community-relations program in policy and structure;
- use each board meeting as a community-relations opportunity;
- be visible, accessible, supportive, and positive;
- work with the media;
- listen to the community and school leaders;
- use the informal grapevine to communicate with local opinion leaders;
- build collaborative relationships with political and business leaders to develop a consensus for student success;
- communicate regularly with federal and state officials about student achievement; and
- model behavior that emphasizes trust, teamwork, and shared accountability.

Social-service agencies. Schools and social-service agencies are natural partners. In any given community, no school or agency has the resources to address all the needs of youth. Social-service agencies can furnish insights and data that can contribute greatly to academic achievement.

Government agencies. Government affects education, whether it is an agency providing federal money, a regulation that requires excessive paperwork, or a state action that facilitates providing quality education. Either way—curse or blessing—government relations have become a top priority for administrators.

Community organizations. Traditional groups dedicated to youth—such as the scouts and YMCA/YWCA—have a long history of helping students and bring a wealth of information to a community-relations effort.

Funders. For obvious reasons, it is important to include private foundations and government agencies that can provide funding for programs.

Senior citizens. In many communities, senior citizens are active and organized. They have the time and experience and often want to give back to their community. Among their ranks are retired administrators, teachers, and business leaders.

The media. The local media are essential participants in the public-engagement process. (More on working with the media later in this chapter.)

Assessing the Community's Needs

Now that the leadership team or governing board is in place and it has targeted the key players it wants to engage, the next task of the board is to find out what the community, as well as the school, needs. There are three easy and inexpensive ways to gauge and engage the community.

E-mail. E-mail is a powerful low-cost tool for connecting the leadership team with other members of the community. Delivering news and inviting opinions can be easily accomplished through e-mail. Although e-mail responses on issues cannot be considered a representative sample of opinions, they are a convenient way to communicate with diverse audiences.

Focus groups. These are groups of 10 to 15 people who meet only once to discuss a specific topic. Focus groups can help school leaders understand community perceptions of the school and test ideas for the community-relations program. Leaders also gain a personal understanding of the pressures and attitudes at home and in the community that affect student achievement. Finally, focus groups are an ideal format to identify issues to address at larger public meetings.

Study circles. Although similar to focus groups, study circles differ somewhat. They consist of 8 to 12 people who meet several times and focus on one question or problem. Participants may receive information about enrollment, achievement levels, teacher qualifications, and other school topics to help inform their discussion. Whereas school staff members would not participate in focus groups, they may participate in study circles to clarify issues or explain data and to provide context.

CREATING A COMMUNITY-RELATIONS PLAN

Once the cast is assembled and the needs of the schools and community are known, the next step is to create a plan for engaging the public. Planning in school-community relations is no different from planning in other educational areas, says Fiore. A plan is essential. It helps set the goals for the overall community-relations program.

A plan also creates safeguards. With the public demanding greater accountability from and having greater access to schools, there are more opportunities for interaction between school leaders and the public than there were before. One faulty decision or insensitive comment can be damaging to school leaders and programs.

This section discusses the benefits and key elements of a plan for engaging the public. It also touches on creating a vision statement as part of that plan. (The vision process is covered in more detail in Chapter 7, "Visionary Leadership.")

Benefits of a Plan

Working from a plan has clear advantages. Monica Solomon and Maria Voles Ferguson note the following. A plan

- ties school improvement efforts to the public's priorities;
- keeps school leaders focused and helps them see how each component of the plan moves the community-relations program closer to its goals;
- provides a coherent picture of the overall work, not a fragmented collection of programs and activities;
- enables a school or district to match the work to available human and financial resources and to identify where to go for additional help; and
- permits more control over events and less communication by crisis, so work that should be routine and predictable actually becomes routine and predictable.

Making a Statement

The first step in developing a community-relations plan is to create the vision statement. The vision statement projects the best possible future, given the best possible circumstances. The vision statement, explain Wall and Luther, establishes the framework for decisions and for evaluating progress over time. It is built on information about the needs of the school and the community, an understanding of trends that will influence the future, and the realistic hopes of the participants in the process.

A vision statement is not the same as a mission statement. As Wall and Luther define it, a *vision statement* is "a shared image of the preferred future of the school and community that guides long-term development towards that future." They offer this sample vision statement:

> In the preferred future, our community will serve as the connecting, sheltering support for our schools. Business and social services along with law enforcement and churches will be actively involved in the lives of students and families through school-community programs. Regular Town Hall meetings will engage citizens and students together to identify community assets and opportunities. Through all types of school and community activities, the generations will connect and welcome one another.

A *mission statement* is "a statement of operational focus that guides day-to-day operations of the school organization." Here is a sample mission statement:

> Our school-community relations will be marked by a continuous process of authentic public engagement to consider the best ways to serve the community and its youth and to build a lasting and productive relationship between the school and its various constituencies. (Wall and Luther)

Communication is the key to establishing a shared vision and building support for it. An administrator's ability to lead and motivate depends to a large degree on communicating the vision to staff and the larger community.

Planning the Plan

When developing the community-relations plan, school leaders need to keep in mind several characteristics of an effective planning process suggested by Fiore.

Simplicity. Time and budget constraints will require a planning process that is straightforward, simple, and easily managed.

Visibility. Though school leaders can communicate a great deal of information without ever being seen by the community, being visible demonstrates a high level of commitment.

Accountability. Outcomes of the community-relations plan must be discernible and measurable.

Brevity. The plan should be succinct and in language understood by a wide audience.

When creating the actual plan, Resnick suggests the following steps: Listen to what people want, set specific goals, pinpoint your target audiences, be clear about what you want to say, use plain language, identify the most effective communicators, create opportunities to communicate, get the resources right, and set priorities.

Refining the Plan

The plan should include strategies to engage potential partners. Jeanne Jehl, Martin Blank, and Barbara McCloud advise school leaders to approach potential partners on their own turf with specific offers of assistance. Be specific about the purpose and terms of joint efforts, they add, and put in writing who will do what by when. Be prepared to work out problems as they arise, and change your approach when necessary.

Make sure the final plan includes the following elements:

- Two-way communication aimed at listening to community perspectives
- The goal of mutual understanding and developing common meaning and vision with community partners
- The special skills and knowledge of the community for guidance
- The use of community volunteers
- Educational results, not just a "feel-good" process
- Positive outcomes, not defense of the system

For guidance in creating a plan, school leaders can consult Fiore's useful checklist in Table 17.1.

Creating the Message

One of the key components of the plan is the message: what to communicate, what story to tell. Your message must be credible and consistent. Solomon and Ferguson suggest communicating what they call "a data story," a profile of a school's or district's data. It includes demographic information, statewide and standardized test scores, student attendance rates, graduation rates, number of students in honors programs, teacher quality and qualifications, safety and school climate, scholarships and academic awards won by students, number of Merit Scholarships, percentage of students going on to college, and job placement rates after high school graduation.

Data are powerful engagement tools. A data profile provides a clear starting point for stakeholders to agree on the need for improved student achievement. Guided by the data, educators, parents, and community members can identify strengths and weaknesses and

Table 17.1   Checklist for a Community-Relations Plan

- The plan makes use of appropriate and varied communication channels for the various audiences involved.
- All individuals with responsibility in the community-relations plan know what the goals and objectives are.
- The plan contains strategies for involving all stakeholder groups whenever possible.
- The goals, objectives, and desired outcomes of the plan are consistent with school philosophy and state law.
- The goals, objectives, and desired outcomes are stated in measurable terms to the extent possible.
- The plan's design takes into consideration the available human resources, funds, and facilities.
- The plan distinguishes between long-term and short-term goals and objectives.
- There are provisions in the plan for future audits of effectiveness and results.
- The plan is tailored to the specific needs of the school and its community.
- The plan takes into account the need for in-service education of the staff.

Source: Adapted from Douglas J. Fiore (2002).

set targets for improvement. The data also provide a solid basis for making local, state, and national comparisons of student achievement. The profile should include a process and a format for reporting results to the public. Once a baseline profile is assembled, it will help in monitoring progress over time.

The final piece of the plan is the action component. It assigns the ways to deliver the school's or district's message to the community.

DELIVERING THE MESSAGE

Numerous channels exist for delivering the message to the community. Skillful administrators know how to work the various channels to achieve their goals.

School leaders in Milwaukee, Wisconsin, for example, launched a marketing campaign in 2002 that used mass media to recruit students to the public schools. The district had been losing students to a state-adopted voucher program and to an influx of charter schools. The district spent $95,000 to spread its message through radio and TV advertising, signs on 75 city buses, 100 outdoor billboards, 177,000 tray liners in fast-food restaurants, and 246,000 postcards to families. Some of the district's business partners donated radio and TV airtime and newspaper space. The campaign was successful; enrollment increased.

Not all districts or schools, of course, have the same community-relations goals. And certainly few have large marketing budgets or partners with deep pockets.

This section outlines some of the most common forms, or channels, of communication available to school leaders. It also provides details on how to work with the news media.

Choosing the right channel to reach the right public is an important strategy in a community-relations program. Each channel has its own characteristics. Some are one-way channels that restrict feedback; others are two-way and highly interactive. No particular channel is best. In fact, communication channels are most effective when plied conjointly in a marketing mix.

Printed newsletter: Is personal as well as informative; tells the school's story in a few pages; has credibility; is good way to cite excellence of staff or students; is an excellent vehicle for parent education; becomes a permanent record; requires good design, writing, and editing; should be free of jargon; should be sent regularly to be effective; and should be mailed, not brought home by students.

Electronic newsletter: Is personal and can be targeted by creating separate messages for diverse audiences such as parents, business leaders, and policymakers; requires good writing and editing; should be free of jargon; requires routine maintenance of an address list; requires technical support; may be considered invasive by some receivers; and excludes people without home computers or e-mail accounts.

School bulletin: Is traditional and well accepted; is an excellent vehicle for focusing on one topic; is easy to create and inexpensive to produce; becomes a permanent record; requires good design, writing, and editing; should be free of jargon; and should be mailed or sent electronically, not brought home by students.

School events: Include back-to-school nights, open houses, tours, breakfast programs, parent-teacher conferences, principal-teacher conferences, and town-hall meetings; are informal, friendly ways to reach out to parents; serve as excellent two-way channels for acquiring feedback and information from parents and the community; are excellent ways to educate parents and the community on standards and school culture; require extra work from professional and support staffs; require extensive student involvement; and should have a specific purpose and be well planned and orchestrated so as not to waste anyone's time.

Superintendent's TV show: Puts a face on education; can be videotaped for future presentations; requires a time commitment of superintendent and staff; requires an engaging on-air personality who can speak plainly to the community; may be considered a waste of money by some constituents; can be expensive to produce; and is more cost-effective on cable-access channels, but seen by fewer people.

District or school guide or annual report: Serves as a channel for reaching policymakers and opinion leaders as well as parents and other community members; becomes a permanent record; requires first-rate (but not lavish) design, writing, and editing; should be free of jargon; should be mailed, not brought home by students; can be costly to produce; may be considered a waste of money by some constituents; has a short shelf life; and needs to be updated annually.

Program brochures and fact sheets: Are excellent channels for one topic such as an event; are quick, easy, and inexpensive to produce in house; can be mailed alone or with other pieces, handed out, or displayed in a rack; require good design and copywriting; should be free of jargon; and have a short shelf life.

School Web site: Allows people to visit at their convenience; requires technical support; must be updated daily; must be interactive; requires ability to respond to any inquiries within one day; needs compelling graphics and stories about the school; and must be user friendly, easy to navigate, and quick to load.

Phone calls: Facilitate highly personal one-to-one interaction; can convey good news or bad news in a short time; require good phone techniques, including "smiling" with the voice and active listening; should be brief and to the point; and may require evening or weekend work.

E-mail messages: Are an effective one-to-one channel; are a quick and easy way to broadcast news or updates; require routine maintenance of an address list; require technical support; may be considered invasive by some receivers; and exclude people without home computers or e-mail accounts.

School information videos: Can be a compelling way to tell the school's story to large groups; are highly credible and acceptable; can be produced by a school or district that has the talent and technical capabilities; must be of the highest quality; and may be considered a waste of money by some constituents.

Executive (superintendent) bulletins or letters: Are an excellent channel for communicating with all stakeholders; are also useful for goodwill and good-news messages and for updating and explaining policy and educational issues; can be delivered on an irregular schedule; become a permanent record; require skillful writing and editing; should be free of jargon; and should be mailed, not brought home by students.

Personal notes: Are an outstanding tool, with a highly personal touch, for communicating goodwill to staff, colleagues, parents, and members of the community; require skillful writing and editing; and are most compelling when handwritten.

Radio and TV spots: Reach a broad audience; are an excellent way to announce events; are most effective when combined with other channels; can be expensive to produce; are effective only when heard or seen frequently; and may be considered a waste of money by some constituents.

Print ads: Reach a broad audience in a highly acceptable manner; are an excellent way to announce events; are effective only when seen frequently; and are most effective when combined with other channels.

Billboards and signs: Are a cost-effective method seen often by many people and are most effective when combined with other channels.

Public-service announcements: Are a good but limited way to announce events; incur only the cost of staff time; require skillful writing because they are spoken; can be abused if schools create too many, too often; have no guarantee of being run; and are usually run late at night when there are fewer listeners or viewers.

WORKING WITH THE NEWS MEDIA

For small-town weekly newspapers and national news magazines alike, education issues are perennial hot topics. Editors continually search for stories on education. This fact of publishing life offers school leaders an opportunity for a most beneficial partnership. Schools and districts can have their stories told in a credible, cost-effective way. News outlets can receive the raw material they need to fill their pages or airtime. The keys to this important relationship are trust and professionalism from both partners.

A Working Relationship

Any job is easier when you know the people with whom you work. Get to know key personnel in the local media, if not personally, at least professionally. Know the names of editors at the publications and of assignment editors or news directors at the radio and TV stations you are targeting. Send news releases to that person, not to "city editor" or "news director."

Get to know "beat" reporters also. Most large newspapers assign the education beat to one or two reporters. At smaller papers, reporters generally cover all the beats. A general beat reporter may not know very much about education issues; you may have to educate that person.

Periodically invite reporters, editors, and news directors to your school without trying to pitch them a story. Acquaint them with the school scene and education issues. Be very careful, however, about offering gifts, even lunch, to reporters and editors; you may compromise their code of ethics. When talking with reporters, avoid education jargon. You can give them story ideas and information, but, ultimately, editors and news directors decide what will be covered.

In some small communities, an administrator may be able to call an editor with an item. But, generally, the favored method of getting a story to the media is to issue a news release. (The modern term, by the way, is *news release*, not *press release*.) The news release is the foundation of an effective public-affairs program. It is the most reliable way for the media to learn about your school. Except for the exploits of its sports teams, the media don't know much about a school's activities. It may fall to you as superintendent, principal, vice principal, or director of institutional advancement to keep the media informed.

News and Newsworthiness

Be certain that every news release contains news. What makes news? People and events make news. Editors generally consider the following five elements to have news value:

Proximity. People are interested in local names and events. Your school's Standard Aptitude Test scores are of little interest in the next town.

Surprise. Novel and unusual items make news—the old man-bites-dog angle. Innovative programs, new uses for educational technology, and unique teaching practices make good copy.

Progress. Many education stories fall into this category. Stories about adequate yearly progress and more efficient use of funds interest readers.

Drama. At first glance, a story about a teacher shortage or an outbreak of lice may seem disastrous to a school. But newspaper readers identify, and often sympathize, with a school's struggles.

Human interest. These are the good-news stories about people. Readers respond emotionally to the individual. Staff or students overcoming personal challenges or volunteering their time to help others succeed is newsworthy.

Before issuing news releases, study your target publications to determine their editorial content. Local daily and weekly newspapers are good outlets; semiweekly business journals or monthly trade magazines are not. Know the kind of stories your target publications print.

The Effective Release

Editors don't expect you to deliver a full-blown story. But they do like to receive a release they can easily work with. The following are 10 tips on writing news stories that you can use when writing your news release:

1. *Remember the five Ws and one H.* To help pull together facts for your release, answer who, what, where, when, why, and how: the foundation of most news stories.

2. *Use the inverted pyramid formula.* A picture of the standard news story would look like an upside down, or inverted, pyramid. At the top—that is, the base of the pyramid— are the most important points. Secondary aspects of the story occur in descending order of importance, with the least important appearing last. The most important ideas appear in the lead paragraph. The lead should grab the reader's attention and focus on the point of the story. The ensuing paragraphs complement the lead by documenting facts, revealing further details, recapping important points, or explaining what the event or situation means to the reader.

3. *Include a headline.* The headline "hooks" the readers, in this case, the editors and news directors. It should grab their interest and make them want to read the release. Write headlines in the present tense, using a noun-verb-object structure. For example: "Kennedy High School exceeds state standards"; "Madison math teacher receives national award."

4. *Attribute every quote.* Editors and readers want to know who actually said it. Quotes such as "A district spokesperson confirmed the report" or "A parent praised the program" sound contrived. Editors and readers trust quotes attributed to real people.

5. *Keep yourself out of the story.* As the author of a news release, you are, in effect, a news reporter. Reporters must be objective; they do not participate in the events they describe.

6. *Write tightly.* Try to keep your release to one or two pages. Be brief and specific. Avoid jargon. Make the paragraph the main element of your release. Introduce one idea per paragraph. Keep paragraphs short, from two to three sentences. Keep sentences short, from 17 to 26 words.

7. *Include artwork.* Photographs, drawings, and graphs add interesting detail to your story. They also land you more space in the paper. Always describe, on the back, what each

photograph, drawing, or graph represents. Pick photos that you think will appeal to the photo editor as well as the reader. Write captions for photos.

8. *Send your release to one person.* Don't try to cover all your bases by sending your release to the city editor, an education reporter, and a columnist. It is best to deal with only one person, the editor. If, however, out of courtesy, you want to send a copy of your release to a reporter with whom you have been working, let the editor and the reporter know that you are submitting multiple copies.

9. *End simply.* If you have used the inverted-pyramid formula, you have placed important facts at the beginning. End simply by stating the least important fact. Recaps, observations, catchy phrases, and well-known quotes are for feature articles, not news stories.

10. *Use the standard form.* Don't try to catch the editor's eye with brightly colored paper, fancy letterheads, or snappy mottos. You do not have to type across the top in big letters, "News Release"; editors recognize a release when they see one. Nor do you need to type "For Immediate Release"; the editor knows when a story is timely. Submit your release on plain white bond paper. You can use letterhead, if you wish.

If not using letterhead, type the name and address of your school in the top left corner. In the top right corner, type the name of a contact person the media can call for more information. Include an evening phone number. Skip down two lines, and type the name and phone number of the person who wrote the release. Tab over to the right, and type the date of the release. Skip down several lines, and type the headline, flush left. Indent first lines of paragraphs. Double-space the text.

If your release is more than one page long, type the word *more* at the bottom of each page except the last. Begin the second and subsequent pages by typing one or two words from the headline and numbering the pages "2-2-2," "3-3-3," and so forth until the last page. When you get to the end of the release, type the word *end*.

Table 17.2 shows the format of an effective news release.

The Professional Touch

You can cement your relationship with the local media by acting like a professional. The following is professional behavior that most media people appreciate:

- Cooperate with editors and reporters. Anticipate their needs and have background information available. Direct reporters to the most knowledgeable and well-spoken experts in your school or office.
- Honor deadlines. Newspapers run on strict deadlines for news stories and calendar items. Radio and TV stations' deadlines can be up to a half hour before airtime. Learn the deadlines and honor them.
- Do not call the editor to see if he or she is going to run your release. A news release is not an ad. The paper is not bound to print your story. Editors make editorial decisions based on factors such as space, timeliness, and importance of the story.
- Do not ask a reporter if you can approve the article before it is published. Such a request is insulting to a writer and hardly ever granted.
- Never hold a news conference without announcing something truly newsworthy.

Table 17.2   Sample News Release

Kennedy High School	CONTACT:
123 Main Street	Susan Avery, Principal
Filbert City, Oregon 97400	555-1234, ext. 1 (days)
	555-4321 (evenings)

Jack Wu, Vice Principal
555-1234, ext. 2 (days)
555-6789 (evenings)   May 3, 2006

Kennedy High School scholars win national competition

Filbert City, OR—A team of Kennedy High School juniors and seniors won first place in the National High School Scholastic Relays, an academic competition held May 1. The six-member Kennedy team scored a total of 995 points of a possible 1,000 to take top honors in the small-school category (20–200 students).

Kennedy team members were juniors Jason Collins, Brittany Howe, and Irene Ito, and seniors Michael Williams, Josephina Hernandez, and Alex Pivonka.

The Kennedy students competed against more than 3,000 of their peers from 600 high schools of similar size across the country. Using their classroom computers, the contestants answered 200 challenging questions in biology, physics, American history, and current events, earning points for the speed and accuracy of their answers.

"We at Kennedy High are extremely proud of our team of scholars and their academic coach, 12th-grade science teacher Don Mincks," said Kennedy Principal Susan Avery. "These folks gave up many evenings and Saturdays to prepare for the relays. It goes to prove that big things can come from small schools."

The National High School Scholastic Relays, designed to promote learning and recognize academic achievement, are conducted over the Internet to allow all students the opportunity to compete in a large academic event from their classroom computers. Presented each spring, the relays are sponsored by Scholastic Software Creations of St. Paul, Minnesota.

END

- Do not favor one outlet over another. If you have a story to tell, spread it around. Include all the papers and radio and TV stations in your market. If you send a picture to one outlet, send it to others. You gain nothing by being exclusive.
- With TV, follow up news releases that announce events with a brief fax message or phone call to the assignment editor the day before the event. Electronic media respond more quickly than print media to breaking events, known as "spot news." Don't be disappointed if the TV cameras don't show up for your new computer lab dedication because they are covering a major fire.

Meeting the Press

As an administrator, you may be the designated spokesperson for your school or district. This means you may be the one who speaks to reporters, who is quoted in the papers, and who is taped for the 6:00 news. As much as you can, prepare before meeting the media. Anticipate questions and rehearse your answers. Even though it is important to cooperate with the media, you do not have to drop everything when they ask you to. If you can, choose your time and place to meet. You will be more comfortable and appear more credible if you are on your own turf and prepared.

During interviews, focus on and be sure you understand each question before answering. Some reporters can be aggressive and self-serving. Ask for clarification, and pause to consider your answer if necessary, even on camera. Avoid "no comment" statements. Instead, say something such as, "We don't have all the facts yet." As much as possible, use your school's name. Instead of saying, for instance, "We are proud of our test scores," say, "We at Kennedy High are proud of our test scores."

On-camera interviews require additional focus and communication skills. TV is a visual medium; try to choose a visually interesting or highly recognizable setting for your taped interview. Remove clutter from the area, and designate someone to keep curious onlookers away. Keep your hands free to gesture; this makes you appear more natural and interesting. Don't lean against the back of your chair. Lean forward to show you are alert and competent. Maintain eye contact with the interviewer, not the camera.

There may come a time when you will have to respond to a crisis at your school. Careful planning can mitigate the situation. Here are points to consider:

1. Be prepared for trouble; appoint and train a response team.

2. Appoint one person as the "point person" to speak for the school; top administrators are the most credible.

3. Prepare one consistent message or response.

4. Try to take control. Be proactive; issue news releases or call a news conference.

5. Get the situation over with and out of the public eye.

6. Try to get all the information out immediately. If you don't, people will wonder what else you may be holding back.

7. Do not refuse to answer questions, be candid and truthful, and do not minimize the problem.

8. Do not blame anyone.

9. Accept responsibility if appropriate.

10. Involve all the local media; do not play favorites.

EVALUATING COMMUNITY-RELATIONS EFFORTS

Educational assessment is a well-established science. Nevertheless, assessing the multiple outcomes of a community-relations program is not as simple as measuring the results of a multiple-choice exam. The relationship between the school and the community is complex and difficult to quantify. Researchers are devising ways to capture the multifaceted nature of outcomes through research and evaluation measurements.

Research compiled by Catherine Jordan, Evangelina Orozco, and Amy Averett at the Southwest Educational Development Laboratory has shown that a range of results can be monitored and measured in school and community connections. Studies have shown, for instance, that school-reform efforts have been influenced by community involvement. Changes in school climate and school culture have also been affected by parent participation. Schools have benefited from partnerships with businesses and foundations by acquiring resources. Working with universities, schools have increased their instructional capacity. Community organizations have proven instrumental in developing and implementing curriculum. In many cases, the community has even furnished instructors in such subject areas as art and music.

Jordan and her colleagues caution, however, that many factors affect the relationship between the school and community and the many outcomes of that relationship. Measurements of school and community connections have not yet captured the full picture of these connections and their results.

Nevertheless, there are ways to track some of the efforts of a community-relations program. Keeping "clip files" is the most basic tracking technique. Collecting print and video clips helps you determine what kind of coverage you have been getting in the media. Staff or a commercial service can undertake the collecting.

Tracking costs is a given. Administrators can determine cost-effectiveness by calculating what it costs to produce promotional materials (per-copy cost) and what it costs to engage community members (per-reach cost). These numbers are arrived at by dividing the total expenditures by the number of copies printed or by the number of people in the audience.

Anne Meek believes it is important to make these figures public because costs draw the most scrutiny from the school board and public. If a director of institutional advancement can report that it costs, say, only 23 cents to contact each person in the district, it may be easier to justify future spending.

Just as they help form strategy for a community-relations plan, surveys and focus groups can help determine results of the plan. To measure qualitative results, questions to survey takers and focus group members should center on awareness rather than on perceptions. Is the name of the school or superintendent more recognizable now than it was before? Do parents understand school policy? Is the public more aware of education issues? If so, what is the most important issue facing local schools? The district office of research and evaluation or a commercial research firm can carry out the gathering of opinions.

Finally, partners can monitor, assess, and improve the quality of their collaborative efforts through a simple instrument such as the one that follows, adapted from a checklist by Martin J. Blank and Barbara Langford. Statements are rated on a scale of from 1 (*disagree*) to 5 (*agree*):

- Our partnership has developed a clear vision.
- Our partnership has developed a workable community-relations plan with clear goals.
- Our partnership has achieved those goals.
- Our partnership has successfully engaged a broad base of individuals and organizations representing the school and the community.
- Our partnership has established a clear organizational structure. Individuals understand and accept the responsibilities of their roles.

- All partners have an understanding of who the other partners are, what organizations they come from, and what those organizations do.
- Our partnership regularly communicates with all partners to keep them informed about its work.
- Our partnership engages in activities to create awareness about and increase support for the work of the partnership.
- Our partnership has identified and mobilized financial and human resources from partner organizations and other entities throughout the community.
- All things considered, our partnership has been successful.

CONCLUSION: ENGAGING FOR MUTUAL BENEFIT

In this era of increased accountability, many people in the community want a say in deciding how schools should be run. For professionals in education, this poses a dilemma: Will outsiders hinder or help efforts to improve student performance? When met with an open mind and a spirit of cooperation, school-community partnerships can benefit both the school and the community. School leaders have realized that individual stakeholders and stakeholder groups can be powerful allies in the effort to raise the academic achievement of all students.

School leaders must not, however, consider public engagement as the magic bullet in solving problems such as the achievement gap, high dropout rates, and school violence. Public engagement in merely one more tool to help our youth succeed in school and in life.

REFLECTIONS

1. As a school leader, have you made involvement in your community a priority? Do you volunteer with youth sports activities or community fundraising events? Do you belong to the local chapter of organizations such as Rotary or Toastmasters?

2. How, in your view, can engaging the community advance the educational mission of the school, particularly by contributing to students' academic achievement?

3. How would you rate the friendliness of the school or building you work in? Does it appear inviting to the public, or is it closed up like a prison? Are parking spaces designated for visitors? Reception areas? Are there signs that direct visitors?

4. What is your opinion of collaboration? Do you prefer to make all the decisions and take on all the responsibilities yourself? Can you work with others, even if it means compromising and sacrificing some of your ideas and ambitions?

5. What is your perception of the news media? Do you see the media as a watchdog? A community builder? A reliable source of information? A manipulator of public opinion and taste? An overly powerful estate? A business?

6. Do you believe it is the responsibility of a school leader to teach the public, not only students, the value and values of education?

18

Managing Data for Decision Making

Creating Knowledge From Information

Gerald Tindal, Luke Duesbery, and
Leanne R. Ketterlin-Geller

I n this chapter, we focus on academic measures that teachers and administrators can use to make decisions that should help students perform better. With the current emphasis on standards, proficiency seems to be the coin of the realm, and administrators need to be skilled at managing data for purposes of accountability. Use of data to guide school improvement is essential to satisfy the Adequate Yearly Progress provisions of the No Child Left Behind (NCLB) Act.

We use curriculum-based measures as our primary example, though other classroom assessment systems may be used. The U.S. Department of Education encourages use of these measures because they represent one form of progress monitoring that has a scientific basis.

The advantage of using curriculum-based measures is that we can show how various graphic displays of data illuminate curriculum-based decisions (screening, diagnosis, progress monitoring, and program evaluation). By highlighting the relationship between decision making and graphic displays, we can demonstrate how to convert achievement information into valued knowledge.

We begin by introducing three principles that govern the use of data to make decisions. Next, we describe the requisite infrastructure needed to interpret information effectively and accurately. *Graphicacy*, the ability to communicate and display information, is emphasized, because decisions are best made with appropriate displays of student information.

Then, we discuss technically adequate measures to provide reliable and valid estimates of performance. In describing the development of such measures, we emphasize universal designs for assessment that differentiate access skills from target skills. By including both types of skills, we make sure our data, graphic displays, and resulting decisions address the needs of all students (as required by federal legislation).

Finally, we illustrate how school leaders can improve their curricular decision making through the use of graphic displays. We highlight screening with a normative reference, diagnostics with a criterion-referenced approach, and progress monitoring with an individual-referenced approach. We use all three approaches to target summative program evaluations.

PRINCIPLES OF DATA-DRIVEN DECISION MAKING

A series of fundamental principles can guide us through the process of transforming data into information. These principles illuminate the path for creating the kind of information that can become the leverage for improvement. By its nature, this new knowledge is latent; that is, we do not know the effects of our decision until after we have made it. In this respect, these principles are not necessarily sequential, but rather are cyclical in nature. No decision is ever final, but is subject to revision once we generate new data about its effects.

In this section, we present three fundamental principles to guide educators in making decisions driven by data. Subsequent sections will elaborate on these principles.

First, an important prerequisite to managing any data system is the technical adequacy of measurement. High-quality measurement is at the heart of the decision-making process, and without it, decisions may be made inappropriately. Furthermore, measurement instruments need to be universal in design: Because we are responsible for all students, the information system has to be completely inclusive of and responsive to each individual student.

Second, decision making requires both a meaningful and appropriate referent and a graphic means of communication. A measure can reference the fit of individuals within groups (normatively), the skill being learned (criterion related), or change over time for students (individually).

Third, these three references can be displayed visually so the interpretation can be explicit. However, we consider data management from the viewpoint of infrastructure and communication to those both inside and outside the organization. Information must be aligned with both decisions and graphic displays to provide bridges of explanation. Transforming information into knowledge requires value-added meaning in which displays make sense of information graphically and visually. Displays can then both mirror the data and focus the audience so they can be useful in making different decisions.

In summary, the data-driven decision-making system is one in which student information conforms to three principles:

1. It is reliable in its construction and measurement as well as universally accessible.

2. It is integrated across various decisions made in a concerted manner to create validity.

3. It is visually compelling so that the graphic display not only presents but virtually interprets the data.

This system, however, requires a cycle of development and a commitment of resources that begins with a proper infrastructure and continues in an ongoing manner.

DEVELOPING AN INFRASTRUCTURE FOR MANAGING AND INTERPRETING DATA

The whole process of making data-driven decisions is a never-ending cycle that proceeds from the sources of data to the decisions based on the data (with the help of graphic displays). This cyclical process begins with creation of an infrastructure, resolves issues of measurement of students' performance, and leads to development of graphic displays of the measurement data that can facilitate sound decision making. As users gain experience with the system and identify the need for additional information on which to base decisions, their desire for additional data and more sophisticated displays drives further enhancements to the infrastructure.

The steps to this process are likely to be sequential as well as concurrent as the infrastructure interacts with new demands for information and new decisions to be made.

The two critical elements in this process—the measures and the graphic-display systems—require an infrastructure supportive of interpretation. Only by thoughtfully designing a data-management system to include appropriate methods for entering, storing, and retrieving data can this information be useful for making decisions. We discuss each component of designing an effective infrastructure and provide examples to illustrate how this process can be established in a district or school.

In the discussion that follows, we illustrate the importance of graphicacy in decision making by describing our work with a school district to develop a system for measuring students' progress in reading. We describe how we developed curriculum-based measures of reading, gathered and analyzed data on both the assessment tools and student performance, displayed and communicated information through graphs, and thereby enabled the district's personnel to make more informed decisions.

Infrastructure for Data Management

The development of an infrastructure for data management is a critical step in the process of using data to make decisions because it lays the foundation for what information will be collected and reported. In turn, this information dictates the questions that can be asked of and answered by the data.

The backbone of the infrastructure is the data file used to store information. The data file forms the basis for all reporting and interpreting; therefore, considerable thought must go into what information is collected, how the data are entered, and how people access the information once it is stored.

The first step in designing any data file is to decide which variables to include. Without various independent variables, sometimes referred to as *marker variables* (such as student demographics, teacher name, and school or district characteristics), it is simply not possible to analyze the data in any meaningful manner. Once the variables have been selected, care must be taken to collect information for each of the variables for each student so that no values are missing.

Cells without values will be reported as missing and therefore cannot enter the analysis. To illustrate this point, consider the data file in Table 18.1, which lists data under a number of marker variables. Some data are missing from this file, however, in the columns for teacher, gender, and status, thus making it impossible to include all students in an analysis of outcomes by those three variables. Note, also, that no analysis can be done by disability because it is not included as a variable. Any data that are missing may reflect a form of bias and weaken the applicability of the analysis to the population or the decision.

Were this data file complete (and contained data on more and different schools, districts, and so forth), we could make comparisons between scores (the dependent variable) by districts, schools, teachers, gender, ethnicity, and status (the marker or independent variables). With a sample that is large enough (roughly 15 students per group), it might even be possible to compare combined subgroups (for instance, students with disabilities having an individualized educational program [IEP] in Ms. Effect's rooms against students with IEPs in another teacher's room).

When establishing an infrastructure, it is also important to consider how the information will be imported into the data file and subsequently retrieved. As with many software programs, the infrastructure can be designed to suit the needs and technology capabilities of the users. Data can be entered by downloading files into a central database, via a Web-based access system, or by manually entering data into a spreadsheet. In addition, supports must be in place to store data securely and then efficiently retrieve information for decision making.

When designing the data input, storage, and retrieval systems, it is also important to consider how the infrastructure will interact with the existing data-management programs already in place in the school or district. To help personnel make decisions based on multiple variables, a fully integrated system is needed, one that includes information about student demographics, academic performance, behavioral supports, and any other relevant sources. The solutions to these issues need to be resolved within the context of the school or district.

Example of an Integrated System

To illustrate the process of designing an infrastructure to support decision making, we present an example of a districtwide effort to measure students' reading performance

Table 18.1 Data File for Storing and Reporting Outcomes

District Name	School Name	Teacher Name	Grade	Student Name	Student ID	Gender	Ethnicity	Status	Score
President	Washington	Effect	4	James	130330	Male	Black	ELL	23
President	Washington	Effect	4	Bette	130136		White	No IEP	13
President	Washington		4	Juan	130228	Male	Hispanic	No IEP	20
President	Washington	Effect	4	Michelle	130170	Female	White	IEP	10
President	Washington	Effect	4	Sevrina	130328	Female	White	White	15

Note: ELL = English-language learner; IEP = individualized educational program.

that included an integrated system for capturing and retrieving data. In this particular district, an infrastructure existed that allowed us to focus primarily on the measurement system. Eventually, though, we had to upgrade this infrastructure so principals in each of the buildings could have access for staff development.

To provide some context to the situation, we first describe the measurement system that was developed, and then we describe the data-management system. Both of these elements are being used to enhance the infrastructure, reflecting our earlier point that the system is cyclical and recurring.

In Pacific School District (name changed for confidentiality), we developed a reading-measurement system over the course of 3 years. In this work, we assisted the district in creating and implementing a process to assess students' reading skills prior to state-level standardized testing. The system was designed to identify students who might not meet state benchmarks, to monitor their progress, and to help district personnel evaluate their programs.

In cooperation with the district's leaders, we developed a series of curriculum-based measures to formally assess the reading progress of students twice each year. The three reading domains measured were vocabulary, oral reading fluency, and general reading comprehension (using multiple-choice comprehension tests). Great effort was made in this process to standardize the measures in their administration and scoring as well as to use multiple measures to ensure that the measures were technically adequate.

Following its creation, the measurement system gained acceptance and became institutionalized across the district. To help district personnel use the resulting data to make multiple decisions, the information the system was generating needed to be easily accessible. How to display the information thus was as important as the design for gathering data.

Various graphic displays were needed not only to help personnel manage the data but also to come to conclusions about student performance. The displays would play a critical role in the processes of screening students, making specific diagnostic assessments, and monitoring progress. Furthermore, both teachers and principals needed to be trained to interpret the graphic displays. Consequently, a Web-based data-input system with support needed to be developed concurrently with the graphical display of these outcomes.

Eventually, as teachers began to log onto the system, the technologies needed for storing and managing the data also increased. For example, the reading measures needed to fit into the total district's information system so that a student's record could include not only his or her performance but also many different demographic variables (such as school name, teacher name, student name, student ID, gender, ethnicity, and educational status). With this information, personnel could better analyze students' reading performance to target key groups, such as those highlighted by NCLB: race/ethnicity, English-language learners, special education students, and students in poverty.

To make possible this greater sophistication of data analysis, the infrastructure's method of delivering information had to change. Instead of a server that stored fixed graphs, a dynamic system controlled by the individual user had to be installed. Part of this process required movement of files from a central server to multiple servers distributed among buildings (in a controlled manner) so each school's principal and teachers could drive the analysis. The decision-making process was thus effectively decentralized and distributed to allow leadership at the most local level (even among grade-level teams within schools) to become part of the fabric of decision making.

Graphicacy for Interpretation

A good infrastructure allows the user to manipulate the data to make comparisons (using statistical analyses) and also to display the information in graphic form so that it can be interpreted to make decisions. This process of interpreting data and making decisions is made clearer by appropriately displaying data through graphs. Although we strive to communicate information clearly, individual users will, nonetheless, vary in their perception of our displays. Graphs set the stage for further discussion of data, but their usefulness depends on the graphicacy of the audience, that is, the users' level of skill in the interpretation of graphic displays.

Howard Wainer suggests that good graphics follow three general principles: Actual data are displayed, information is accurate, and data are presented in a clear format. In different situations, these data displays might take the shape of tables, graphs, diagrams, maps, and so forth, often dependent on the type of decision to be made.

In our own work with Pacific School District, we use a combination of images and tables to create meaningful information. We base our graphicacy on the work of three scholars in the field who offer insight into the creation of meaningful data displays: William S. Cleveland, Edward R. Tufte, and Wainer.

Cleveland holds that a critical link exists between the encoding of data and the visual decoding or perception of the information. No matter how well developed the data display is, without competent visual decoding, the display cannot function effectively. By understanding the human visual system, Cleveland believes we can address what is a best practice, and by creating displays that harness those skills present in our audience, we can communicate well.

Therefore, Cleveland recommends that we concentrate on creating displays that are simple to interpret but at the same time contain complex information. The first priority is data reduction in analysis, and then attention can be given to comparison of results. In this way, the data analysis serves to further our hypotheses and refine our questions.

In his book *The Visual Display of Quantitative Information*, Tufte describes data graphics as "instruments for reasoning about quantitative information." He sees them as a part of the recurring process described earlier, not simply as an end point in the decision-making process.

As Tufte explains, graphs reveal data; they do not simply present the data. To this end, he focuses on those graphicacy skills that can lead the developer to create clear data displays. Graphical excellence consists of both substance and design. *Substance* refers to the necessity for the data display to communicate something interesting, multivariate, and clear. In contrast, *design*, according to Tufte, has to do with clarity, precision, and efficiency, irrespective of content.

Tufte discusses the need to remove distracting and unimportant features of the display and to create a high ratio of data to ink. Most important, he calls for data displays to be efficient in their use of viewer time. Developers need to strive for displays that communicate the maximum amount of information in the least amount of time.

Finally, Wainer notes that the goal of displaying data to communicate information is a threefold endeavor: reduction of text, clarity of focus, and emphasis on a particular aspect. While achieving these goals, good data displays need to be efficient. In other words, displays should convey a complex and multivariate set of data, and they must do so in the simplest manner possible. His central point is that "revelation accompanies simplicity." Meaningful data display must be comprehensible and add value to the interpreter.

Wainer also notes that data displays require integrity. It is not our mission to manipulate the display of data to suit a particular purpose, though this is clearly possible. Our mission, instead, is to represent the data honestly, thereby allowing the user to draw inferences that might not have been arrived at without the display and thus informing decision making.

Summary

Schools currently do not suffer from a lack of data; rather, they typically lack coordinated efforts to understand and use the data. Over time, school data systems become so encumbered with superfluous data that they become virtually useless from the practitioner's perspective. Teachers and administrators cannot be expected to wade through pools of data, searching for relevant information about their students.

Accessibility of data begins with an infrastructure that allows interested parties to interact with the data to find answers to questions and make decisions. With access to information from a well-designed data-management system, teachers and administrators can make judgments based not only on intuition, but also on student performance data. Graphical displays help the users see trends and patterns in the data, so with these insights they can make better decisions.

GETTING ACCURATE DATA FROM ALL STUDENTS: TECHNICAL ADEQUACY AND UNIVERSAL DESIGN

Once the requisite infrastructure is in place to allow users to input, store, and retrieve data and the graphic display systems are designed, the next step in the data-driven decision-making cycle is to design measurement systems that lead to meaningful and accurate data about the performance of all students. To this end, measurement systems must be technically adequate.

Beginning assessment books, of which there are hundreds, uniformly address reliability and validity as the two primary components of technical adequacy. *Reliability* refers to the consistency of measurement (stability across time, judges, or forms), whereas *validity* addresses truthfulness of the measure and usability of the results for making decisions. See Chapter 14 ("Instructional Leadership: Progress Monitoring") for a more thorough explanation of these concepts.

Separating the Access Skills From the Target Skills

This traditional description of assessment lacks an important consideration: Even within educational measurement, skills are rarely uniform in their definition, seldom reflect a single behavior, and often inadvertently include unintended facets in their measurement. Indeed, many skills can influence measurement of student performance. Some skills are targeted by the test, and some serve as access skills that students must employ to demonstrate proficiency on the target skills.

For measurement to be accurate, access skills not targeted by the test need to be separated from the target skills and not influence either performance or subsequent decisions. For the knowledge and skills that are targeted by the test, accurate measurement relies on the accumulation of evidence that supports the appropriate uses and interpretations of the data.

For example, most math problem-solving tasks require students to read the task to gain access to the problem. Reading, according to its most essential definition, requires students to decode and interpret written text, process words, and make sense of the information. In addition, many problem-solving tasks require some kind of motor skill either to complete a multiple-choice response or to write an answer. As another example, the target skill for a test of students' knowledge of science vocabulary is the recall of definitions for scientific vocabulary words, whereas access skills may include the ability to read the words or write the definitions.

Access skills pose a significant problem for accurate measurement of student knowledge and skills in any targeted area. If a student has a deficiency in the access skills needed to understand the material or to express his or her knowledge, performance on the targeted skills may suffer, resulting in inaccurate inferences about the student's level of proficiency. Judging a student's level of proficiency in the target skill without considering the influence of access-skill proficiency may result in inappropriate decisions that can have significant consequences for the student.

To reduce the negative effects of a student's limited access skills on the interpretations of his or her proficiency on the targeted skills, educators typically provide accommodations that change the way in which the material is delivered or the student is expected to respond. These accommodations consist of alterations to the setting, timing, presentation mode, or response set, but they do not alter the underlying construct of the test.

These kinds of accommodations still may not successfully support a student with limited access skills. To be most helpful, the accommodations must go two steps further. They must be tailored to fit the student's specific deficiencies, and they must be administered on a consistent basis. Yet within a classroom setting, teachers are frequently unable to meet these requirements. What typically follows is the delivery of inappropriate accommodations that may jeopardize the interpretation of students' knowledge and skills in the targeted domain.

Universal Design for Assessment

Universal design for assessment, an emerging aspect in measurement design, proposes a seamless and a priori integration of accommodations into materials during the development stages so the materials are maximally accessible to the largest number of students. For those students who need supplemental support, universally designed assessments evaluate deficiencies in access skills through a series of basic-skills tests and tailor-made assessments to alleviate the negative outcomes of limited access skills (Leanne R. Ketterlin-Geller).

Once the barriers caused by limited access skills are removed, proficiencies in the targeted skills can then be evaluated. Target skills for any one assessment, however, may involve multiple access skills.

Consider the following mathematics problem, for example: Carlos has six blue marbles, three green marbles, and five red marbles. Lee has half as many blue marbles, twice as many green marbles, and four times as many red marbles as Carlos. Carlos and Lee add all the marbles to a jar. If Carlos picks out a marble without looking, what is the probability that the marble he chooses will be red?

At first glance, this may appear to be a simple statistics problem, but it is much more than that. As teachers of statistics, mathematics, or algebra will readily see, the student must also perform several other calculations. To appropriately classify this problem, the teacher must reference the target skills, which include addition, division, and multiplication, in addition to statistics. An incorrect score on this problem may not necessarily lead to information about the student's proficiencies in statistics, but must be referenced to the suite of other skills, not the least of which also is reading. This example illustrates the importance of clearly defining the target skills to make appropriate decisions about proficiencies.

Evaluating the Measurement System

Let's assume that information about all students has been included in the measurement system by applying the principles of universal design to assessments. Now, the trustworthiness and accuracy of the interpretations and uses of the results must be evaluated before making educational decisions. Evidence from a variety of sources is needed to determine if the test is appropriate in format and content and provides reliable information about performance in the tested area. Only then can educators determine if it accurately represents the target skills or construct being measured.

The accumulated evidence still must be judged in light of the consequences of the decisions being made. For example, significant evidence is needed to support the trustworthiness and accuracy of the results to place a student in special education or award a high school diploma on the basis of an exit exam. In contrast, if the measure is designed for classroom monitoring of progress from one unit to the next, the stakes are much lower and require less evidence to support the decision.

In sum, we described the rationale behind collecting student performance information that appropriately assesses the target skill or construct. Offering universally designed assessments can be a daunting task, but it helps ensure that access skills do not jeopardize our interpretation of test results. Now we will focus on how the results of universally designed assessments can be interpreted. Accurate interpretation requires making three types of decisions that rely heavily on graphic displays of information to clearly communicate results and support conclusions.

REFERENCE FOR INTERPRETING RESULTS: USING GRAPHIC DISPLAYS TO EVALUATE PERFORMANCE

At the core of the processes of interpreting student performance data and making data-driven decisions lies one of three decision-making references: normative, criterion, and individual (Gerald Tindal and Douglas Marston). Without a reference, it is not possible to make an interpretation. Measurement alone provides no value for understanding. With a reference, a value can be affixed to a measure of behavior.

For example, to know that a student earned 10 points on a test or reads 20 words per minute is not particularly helpful. Rather, these numbers need to be contextualized for interpretation; it is with one of these three references that the performance is contextualized.

We illustrate each of these references in relation to the previously described project conducted with Pacific School District. As you may recall, we worked with the school district's leadership to design and implement a measurement system in reading. Not only did we help design the data-management infrastructure, but we also worked with curriculum and assessment personnel to create a curriculum-based measure system. The measures tested the domains of vocabulary, fluency, and comprehension and were evaluated for their technical adequacy.

Using the results of the administration of these measures, school personnel made decisions about screening, diagnostics, progress monitoring, and program evaluation. The three reference points drove these decisions: normative, criterion, and individual:

1. Norm-referenced decisions addressed the question of *who* (to focus on students at risk or needing accelerated programs).

2. Criterion-referenced decisions addressed the issue of *what* (to do instructionally).

3. Individual-referenced decisions focused on *why* (to identify the reason programs work or do not work to change student performance).

Norm-Referenced Decisions

Our first set of decisions rests on norm-referenced data, in which interpretation is relative to the standing of an individual within a group. A number of different scores are possible to report, but the critical decision involves relative performance. How low or high is a student's performance in relation to that of others? Interpreting results of an assessment system from a norm-referenced perspective is critical, because one of the major objectives is to identify students who are performing low (or high) on the target measures, when compared with the student's peer group.

Two central problems, both having to do with the reference group, plague most norm-referenced decisions. The group is either a distant group (a sample from a published test that has little real value for the students in a teacher's classroom) or a local group that is not well described and displayed. For example, the former (standardization sample) often excludes students with disabilities and students for whom English is a second language. The latter, local group is often very persuasively appropriate to a classroom teacher but difficult to describe normatively.

Consider the type of display in Table 18.2, which teachers commonly use to present data about students in their classroom. The display uses a grade-book format (in a tabular manner without graphs). In this example of a second-grade classroom, information is presented for a list of students (each row) based on gender (the only marker variable) for letter sounds (number identified correctly in one minute), words read in 40 seconds from three domains (Grades 1 and 2), words correctly read per minute from a passage, whether

Table 18.2   Typical Tabular Display of Students' Reading Performance
in a Classroom

Gender	Letter Sound	G1_2	G1_2	G2_2	Words Correct	Listen Comp	MC Total	OE Total
F			24	23	129	N	5	4
M			24	22	89	N	5	4
F			24	24	156	N	5	4
F			23	24	122	N	4	4
F	44	7	10		17	Y	5	4
F	26	2	1		5	Y	3	4
F	30	5	7		11	Y	4	4
M			22	21	73	N	5	4
M			23	23	67	N	5	3
M	28	3	4		6	Y	2	2
M			22	17	45	N	5	4
F	40					Y		0

Note: F = female; M = male; Listen Comp = listening comprehension; MC = multiple choice; OE = open-ended.

or not students had the comprehension passage read to them, the number of multiple-choice questions they answered correctly, and the value of their open-ended written response.

Take note of the incredible range in performance. This particular teacher has students who read as few as 5 and 6 words correctly per minute as well as those who read more than 100 words correctly per minute (to a maximum of 156). Notice that when the passage is read to the low-fluency students, they can actually answer some of the multiple-choice comprehension questions correctly (three and two items are answered correctly, respectively), though most students answer all of them correctly (and without having them read). The questions become: Who is at risk, what are the skills that they have and need, and why does a program work (or not work) to change student performance?

Transforming Raw Scales to Relative Scores

We begin the data-driven decision making by asking who is at risk, using a norm-referenced approach. However, to make norm-referenced interpretations, administrators need to understand scales and the ways that they can be transformed. We can, for example, transform the students' raw scores of words correct per minute to relative scores that provide information about how many students are below or above them in a hypothetical group of 100 students—a percentile rank (PR).

We used this procedure, with different data, to produce the box-and-whiskers plot in Figure 18.1. In this figure, depicting students in fourth grade, the box bottom represents the 25th PR, the box top is the 75th PR, and the middle line in the box is the 50th PR. The horizontal line above is the 90th PR, and the horizontal line below is the 10th PR. All values above and below these lines are individual students' scores.

Figure 18.1   Box-and-Whiskers Plot of Oral Reading Fluency for
Fourth-Grade Students

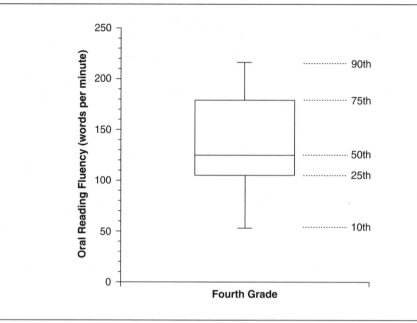

In this example, a score of 100 words correct per minute might be at the 25th PR: Only 25 students out of 100 are below this level; most (75 of 100) are above this level.

Because norm-referenced scores are designed to reflect relative standing, they rarely are used with raw scores. Instead, they are converted to reflect relative standing (much like the PR example). For example, administrators need to know students' relative standing that is not fixed to a particular unit. In our example, the student's grade level (fourth) limits the interpretation (for example, second-grade students simply read fewer words correctly per minute than do fifth-grade students).

Furthermore, it is not possible to compare different measures with each other because each measure has its own units (or scales). Finally, most published tests use some form of scaled score so, by converting curriculum-based measures to this metric, a more direct comparison can be made.

Plotting z Scores to Identify Low-Performing Students

To help identify students in need of intervention, we chose to plot student data with the familiar histogram using *z* scores (a form of scaled score), which is one of the most universal relative scales in measurement. In this scale, the distribution is changed using the mean (the sum of all scores divided by the number of scores) and the standard deviation (how much each score differs from the mean).

All distributions have a mean and a standard deviation, so the actual math is quite easy. A *z* score value is simply the standard deviation subtracted from or added to the mean. For example, in oral reading fluency, the standard deviation is often 35 words correct per minute; if the mean in fourth grade is 90 words correct per minute, the z score value of $+1$ would be $90 + 35 = 125$, and a z score of -1 would be $90 - 35 = 55$).

The z score simply describes how many standard deviations a student is from the mean and is not confined to the actual scale of the original measure. Remember, with a norm-referenced interpretation, we only care about differences from others, not absolute levels of performance.

In our work with Pacific School District, we rescale students' performance to z scores that range from -3 to $+3$. By plotting z scores, we are better able to determine the distribution of students. By definition, those students falling between $+/-1$ standard deviation represent about 67 percent of the sample. Below the -1 standard deviation mark, we see students in need of some intervention, and below the -2 standard deviation mark, we see students in need of significant intervention.

This distribution usually reveals a normal curve across a continuum of performance, with fewer students at either the low or high ends and most in the middle. An example of this type of histogram is displayed in Figure 18.2, which was derived from data comparable to the data used in the box-and-whiskers plot (oral reading fluency of fourth-grade students).

By examining the x axis of the histogram, we can see that our sample distributes quite normally. We also can see, however, that we have more students above $+2$ standard deviations than students below -2 standard deviations from the mean. Those students in our sample who are -2 standard deviations from the mean consequently need individual identification and intervention.

Figure 18.2 z Scores of Oral Reading Fluency, Distribution of Students
          in Fourth Grade

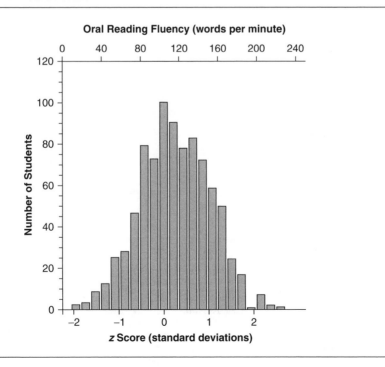

Displaying Multiple Measures

With only one measure, however, we always are in doubt about interpretation. What does it mean, for example, for a student to be low in oral reading fluency? How is this performance related to other measures of performance? When graphs contain multiple measures, we learn much more than when they contain only one measure. We learn how well measures are related to each other and how individual students perform concurrently.

As another example of norm-referenced decision making, we were interested in associating our local curriculum-based measures with the state standardized assessment. In keeping with principles of graphicacy, we created a norm-referenced display that communicated the maximum amount of information in the least amount of space.

In this case, we used a scatter plot (see Figure 18.3) that displays the concurrent performance for each student from two measures. On the *x* axis, students' oral reading fluency is scaled, whereas the *y* axis represents performance on the state assessment of reading using scaled scores. The cut score for the state test also is superimposed over the data (in this grade, students must achieve a level of 214 points on the state test to pass).

In addition, we calculated a district target for the oral reading fluency representing the average norm level of performance for the grade (132 words correct per minute). Each dot on the graph represents a single student in the Pacific School District in fourth grade: his or her state reading score and oral reading fluency score.

Below the state cut-score line, we see the group of students who did not meet the state benchmark in reading. To the left of the district oral reading fluency target line, we see the students who did not meet the district oral reading fluency target of 132 words per minute.

Figure 18.3   Oral Reading Fluency Versus State Reading Score in Fourth Grade

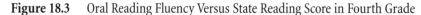

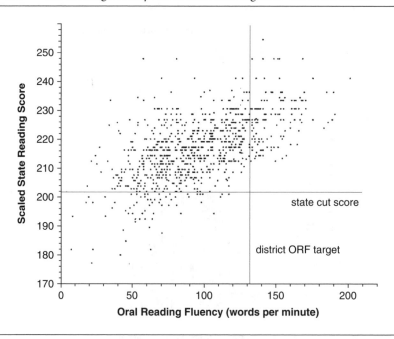

Thus, the bottom left quadrant represents those students in need of intervention because they did not pass the state test and they were below the district fluency averages.

Pacific School District uses this multivariate approach to identify students in need of extra support in reading. Furthermore, because the reading measures can be administered early in the year (with the state test taken later in the year), teachers have several months to provide additional instruction or design individual interventions. As such, the data are used to make decisions from a normative perspective.

Criterion-Referenced Decisions

Our second set of decisions rests on criterion-referenced data, which are usually demarcated by a very specific set of skills and a level of performance reflecting mastery. With the standards movement, this form of reference is prominent. Standards provide the reference by stating what students are expected to know and be able to do within a given subject by a specific grade level as well as how well students are expected to perform.

Most standards-based tests used for large-scale assessments reflect this decision-making system. It has the advantage of comparing students' actual level of performance with the expected level, and thus it can be used to make decisions about mastery of the standards.

For example, in Oregon, a general science standard is as follows: "Explain relationships among the Earth, sun, moon, and the solar system." In Grade 5, the benchmark for this standard states: "Describe the Earth's place in the solar system and the patterns of movement of objects within the solar system using pictorial models. Describe Earth's position and movement in the solar system. Recognize that the rotation of the Earth on its axis every 24 hours produces the night-and-day cycle."

To measure the level of mastery of this content, a test item might ask:

"Which statement best describes Earth's movement in relation to the sun?

1. The sun goes around the Earth.

2. The sun and Earth go around each other.

3. The Earth goes around the sun.

4. The sun and Earth go around other planets."

This example reflects the alignment between the state standards and the test items used to measure proficiency on the standards. Alignment is a critical component for criterion-referenced decisions.

Another critical feature of criterion-referenced decisions is the focus on specific skills. To better understand student performance on these specific skills, it is often helpful to examine the level of proficiency for a group of students on a set of items that represent a given skill or content area. This analysis allows educators (particularly teachers) to identify which skills or knowledge students have mastered and what information needs to be re-taught.

Often, educators informally look at patterns of student performance and make these types of conclusions. Although this informal approach represents a form of decision making, it is not rooted in data. To base these decisions on data, educators should examine student performance more systematically.

To illustrate how to use data to make judgments about proficiency in a given skill or content area, we present two different graphic displays that represent student performance at the item level. In our first graphic display of this approach, we have taken 15 items from Pacific School District's multiple-choice reading comprehension test.

In the stacked bar chart in Figure 18.4, we present each item's difficulty for each of the four options (three distractors and a correct option). The options are stacked from the most difficult distractor (on the left) to the easiest distractor, and finally the correct option is displayed last (light blue bar to the right). Notice that the length of this last option also displays the overall easiness or difficulty of the item.

In our example, the last two items (at the top of the graph) are the most difficult (have the shortest correct bar). This graphic display could be used to identify which items (and which corresponding skills or content areas) are challenging to students. The display thus provides a systematic approach to making instructional decisions.

In a second graphic display of this approach, we display in Figure 18.5 an item-response curve, also called the item-characteristic curve (ICC). This display is valuable for administrators because most standardized tests now use this kind of analysis. To interpret results from state tests, this kind of information is important to understand.

Typically, the ICC display presents the range of abilities for students (on the bottom x axis ranging from low to high ability) and the probability of answering the question

Figure 18.4   Stacked Bar Chart Reflecting Multiple-Choice Item Difficulties

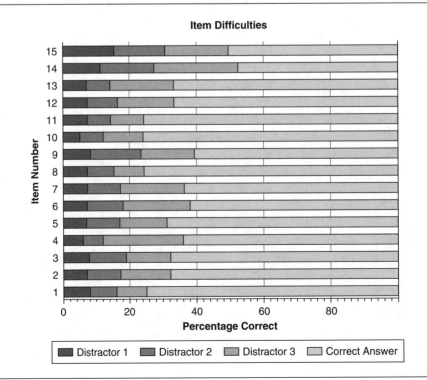

Figure 18.5   Item-Characteristic Curve for Question 6 on the Reading
Comprehension Measure

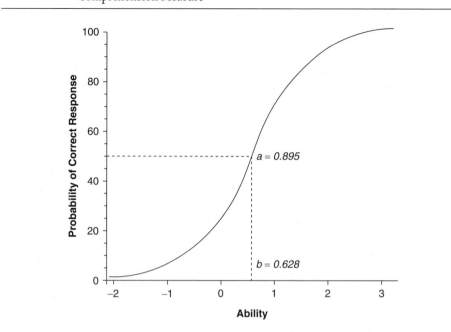

correctly (on the vertical y axis ranging from a 0 percent chance to a 100 percent chance). This curve depicts a tail (lower left part) in which low-ability students have a low percentage of answering correctly; it also reflects just the opposite with high-ability students who have a near-100-percent chance of answering the test item correctly (in the upper left section). In between, we have students of middle ability who have a 50-percent chance of answering the item correctly. Given the shape and location of the ICC, we can gauge the difficulty of each question and deem how it performs for different-ability test takers.

Figure 18.5 presents an ICC for a question on Pacific School District's reading comprehension test (all questions have their own curves and should distribute across the range of abilities). This display simply reflects a formal analysis of what most teachers do informally every day in their classroom.

The b value noted refers to the difficulty level at which there is a 50-percent chance that a student will answer the questions correctly. In this example, a student with an ability of 0.628 standard deviations above the average ability will have a 50-percent chance of answering the question correctly. Thus, it could be said that this question is relatively difficult. A student with the mean ability (0 on the x axis) has about a 20-percent chance of getting the question correct. See Ronald Hambleton for further explanation of ICCs in data display and communication.

Individually Referenced Decisions

Our third and last set of decisions rest on individually referenced data: those that involve a comparison of a student's performance with previous levels within a progress-monitoring framework. The essential decision focuses on why programs are working—whether it is acceptable to maintain the same instructional program given the current rate of improvement. Curriculum-based measure is the most prominent measurement system that provides results usable for these types of decisions.

Returning to our example of the Pacific School District, we examine how graphic displays can help make individually referenced decisions. Based on Figure 18.3, in which oral reading fluency performance is plotted with the state test results, the district transitions students who fall into the lower left quadrant into tiered intervention programs. Once low-performing students are identified, the district moves to bimonthly oral reading fluency measurement of these students for progress monitoring.

Student trajectories in reading are plotted individually (see Figure 18.6 for a specific student), and they are closely monitored so that the effectiveness of the current instructional strategy can be evaluated quickly and changes made when necessary. A trend line in the graph conveys expected growth toward target level during the intervention. In this particular example, reading growth is steadily moving toward the trend line, indicating a successful intervention for this student.

When several consecutive measures indicate movement beyond the district cut score in oral reading fluency, the student can move back into the mainstream reading program. In this type of evaluation, we usually are interested in noting the slope or rate of change, though variability also may be considered in developing optimal programs.

If the teacher in this example is interested in determining the progress this student is making relative to others' progress, the original materials from the norm-referenced assessments could be readministered and the student's performance plotted on the box-and-whiskers or histogram plots, as demonstrated earlier. This information would help determine if extra supports are still necessary.

Figure 18.6   Oral Reading Fluency Progress Monitoring

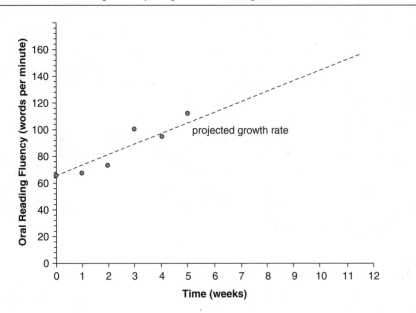

CONCLUSION: THE GOAL IS PROGRESS FOR ALL STUDENTS

Data-driven decisions must be made using technically adequate measures that are developed with the principles of universal design in mind. They also must have a reference point from which decisions can be made. Norm-referenced decisions allow us to look at group differences and allocate resources strategically. Criterion-referenced decisions focus on specific skills and mastery. Finally, individually referenced decisions allow students' progress to be tracked and growth trajectories inferred.

Our case example of Pacific School District highlights decisions from these references using data displays not only to illustrate key points but also to reinforce the cyclical nature of the process in which data are displayed and used to make decisions.

We summarize our views with the following five statements, which are sequential and recurring, in that the base issues address first an infrastructure, then a focus on measurement of performance, and finally systems for decision making using graphical displays. It is not possible to identify all the component parts without first identifying the process, measures, decisions, and graphical displays. In turn, the infrastructure is likely to change in development as a function of implementation, and the process begins again.

1. *An infrastructure is needed to support the entire process.* To provide an efficient and effective means for entering, storing, and retrieving data for decision making, a data-management infrastructure is essential. It must include a well-conceptualized data-file structure useful for making comparisons and graphically displaying results. For this system to become integrated into everyday practices, training becomes a paramount issue. The process of creating and implementing an infrastructure probably will never end, as increased use and sophistication drive the need for more infrastructure supports.

2. *Measures of performance must be technically adequate and considerate of all students.* The measures of performance that are administered within the classroom or by the school district need to be sensitive to classroom instruction and individual progress. Only with good measurement can appropriate decisions be made. Curriculum-based measures are likely to provide the best system to use in a total data-driven system in conjunction with state large-scale tests.

3. *Critical skills often include both targeted skills and access skills, which influence performance.* When the measures are being developed, teachers need to participate so they can ensure that the administration and scoring system is sensible and sensitive. Furthermore, the measurement system needs to reflect attention primarily to target skills that are not influenced unduly by access skills. By considering the needs of all students who will be taking the test, educators can increase the participation by students with disabilities, English-language learners, and students who need additional supports in the general education testing system.

4. *Decisions need a reference for making an interpretation.* Three different references are necessary for a complete data-management system that allows students to be screened (normative), diagnostic information to be documented (criterion mastery), progress to be monitored (individual change), and outcomes to be evaluated (all three).

5. *Student performance must be displayed appropriately to make decisions.* Tabular reference can assist in reducing the complexity of information, but graphs help communicate the information in the most transparent and simple manner. These graphs can display groups of students using percentile ranks and normative (z) scores as well as scatter plots that are multivariate. Furthermore, criterion-referenced views of specific skills can be displayed in a similar manner with single or multiple skills. Finally, growth or change can be displayed for an individual student over time.

REFLECTIONS

1. What infrastructure is in place for managing student performance information? Are data stored with directories, and are all the necessary variables present in the data file? Are the data complete (all variables have values), or are data missing? How accessible are these data (for transfer and manipulation)? What training is needed to make them accessible (in terms of technology use)? How can student performance information be entered, stored, and displayed?

2. Are classroom-based measures available for administrators to use with teachers? Are these measures technically adequate? Is performance on them sensitive to all students, and are they universally designed? What are the target skills versus the access skills? How can adjustments be made to ensure decisions are made on the basis of target skills? What kind of training is needed to develop this measurement system?

3. Are all three references available for interpreting student performance: norm referenced for allocating resources, criterion referenced for making instructional decisions, and individually referenced for reflecting change over time within individuals? Are these references appropriately displayed through graphs? Do the norm-referenced graphs appropriately display the distribution of students across the measures and use scales that are interpretable? Do the criterion-referenced displays reflect critical skills in the scope and sequence of the curriculum and instruction? Do the individually referenced displays reflect growth?

19

Allocating Human, Financial, and Physical Resources

Faith E. Crampton and Randall S. Vesely

This chapter explores resource-allocation issues of importance to educational leaders. We highlight best practices with the goal of assisting leaders in making sound decisions about resources as they seek to maximize student learning. Our focus is primarily on resource-allocation issues of concern to site-level administrators, such as principals and assistant principals. Much of the content is relevant as well to educational leaders at the program and even district levels.

As conceived in this chapter, student learning is much broader than the knowledge base covered on most government-mandated, high-stakes achievement tests, which often assess a narrow range of cognitive skills. Student learning also encompasses the affective domain, which includes appreciation of and participation in art, music, drama, and the humanities as part of the curricular or extracurricular programs of a school or district. Students also learn in meaningful ways from participation in other extracurricular activities, such as student clubs and associations, student government, and athletics.

In a departure from the current literature about site-level resource allocation, we espouse a resource-management framework that integrates educational planning with resource planning to maximize student learning. Other approaches in the professional literature tend to focus on fiscal issues, such as budgeting, in isolation from educational planning and student learning. Our framework includes the human, fiscal, and physical resources that play a critical role in student learning, recognizing that the first step toward sound resource allocation is a comprehensive educational plan.

HUMAN RESOURCES: CREATING AND SUSTAINING HUMAN AND SOCIAL CAPITAL

Elementary and secondary education is labor intensive; that is, much of the work of educating children and young adults requires direct contact with education employees, be they teachers, professional and support staff, or administrators. School district budgets reflect the labor-intensive nature of prekindergarten through twelfth-grade education. It is not uncommon for 80 percent of the typical district budget to be personnel costs, which include salaries, wages, and benefits of all district employees, as John R. Ray, Walter G. Hack, and I. Carl Candoli point out.

The labor intensiveness of education distinguishes it from many public-sector organizations and private-sector businesses, often leading to misunderstandings by the public and media about the real costs of education. For example, in the United States, over time, many businesses and industries have lowered expenses and raised productivity by reducing labor costs. This reduction has taken place, at least in part, by finding ways to provide the same products and services with fewer employees or lower-cost employees.

Critics of public education often point to these examples and ask why public education cannot be more efficient, defined as lowering costs while providing the same level of output, often narrowly defined as student achievement. The research literature refers to this approach to fiscal analysis as "production function" analysis. It is based on an economic-efficiency model grounded conceptually in the process of manufacturing or a "production line." The application of this model to educating children has many critics. (See, for example, Richard A. King, Austin D. Swanson, and Scott R. Sweetland's recent book, *School Finance: Achieving High Standards With Equity and Efficiency*.)

Public schools should always be mindful of efficiency given their dependence on local, state, and federal taxpayer dollars. Critics fail to understand that in most cases, schools and districts cannot reduce personnel costs and provide the same quality of education to students. In fact, the opposite may be true. Schools and districts with large class sizes, particularly in the early elementary grades, may become more productive by decreasing class size to 15 to maximize student achievement, as Barbara Nye, Larry V. Hedges, and Spyros Kostantopoulos contend. Class-size reduction is particularly effective for low-income and ethnic-minority students, groups who typically score lower than more affluent, white peers on standardized achievement tests and so are at greater risk of academic failure and dropping out of school, according to Deborah Land and Nettie Legters.

Nor can school districts, in most instances, reasonably use lower-cost employees to reduce expenditures. All states have licensure requirements for public school employees, such as teachers and administrators. School districts may not lower costs, for example, by hiring an aide to teach fourth grade, even though that individual would cost only a fraction of a licensed teacher. In addition, most communities want their children taught by someone with the appropriate education and experience that a teaching license represents.

The Challenge of Developing Human and Social Capital

Creating and sustaining the human and social capital represented by school employees represents a critical task for educational leaders. In this context, *human capital development* refers to the recruitment and retention of high-quality, diverse faculty, other professional staff, and support staff, as well as their compensation and deployment. *Social capital* refers to the creation and maintenance of professional networks, both formal and informal, as well as collegial relations that support student learning (James P. Spillane and Charles L. Thompson).

Educational leaders build and nurture social capital by facilitating the development of collaborative relationships among faculty and staff within a school or district and with other school districts, local universities, state departments of education, and professional organizations. These relationships assist all education employees in growing professionally in their careers, deriving greater satisfaction from their work, and learning new strategies to enhance student learning.

Human capital in education consists of personnel who serve in diverse categories and have a range of responsibilities. Schools and districts employ a wide range of administrators, faculty, other professional staff, and support staff (R. Craig Wood and colleagues). At the school level, administrators generally include principals and assistant principals. At the secondary level, there may be additional full-time and part-time administrative positions, such as department chairs, program directors, and coordinators.

Faculty members include classroom teachers and resource teachers in areas such as special education, gifted and talented education, and bilingual education, who may or may not be classroom based. Other professional staffs include guidance counselors, librarians, technology coordinators, psychologists, and school nurses.

Support staff may be divided into instructional and noninstructional employees, though it is important to remember that all support staff contribute to student learning. Instructional support staffs include aides and assistants who work directly with teachers, and other professional staff, such as librarians and technology coordinators. Noninstructional staffs include secretarial and clerical employees, food-service workers, custodians, maintenance workers, and bus drivers.

How can school-based educational leaders successfully recruit and retain high-quality employees and address the human and social capital development of these diverse groups? In this section, our focus will be mostly on classroom teachers, but we'll also consider other professional staff and instructional and noninstructional support employees.

Teacher Development

Recent research indicates that the single most important factor in student achievement is the classroom teacher (Linda Darling-Hammond and Jon Snyder). Hence, their recruitment, retention, professional development, compensation, and deployment are central to optimizing student learning. Depending on the degree of authority districts delegate to site-based educational leaders, their involvement in teachers' human and social capital development will vary. In addition, the site leader must be knowledgeable about and sensitive to the provisions of a collective-bargaining agreement.

Recruitment

Recruitment of quality teachers is the first step to maximizing student learning. What are the qualities that schools and districts should search for in the recruitment process? Research, such as that reviewed by Jennifer Rice King, points to the following characteristics:

- Academic ability
- Scores on teacher licensure examinations
- Certification status
- Degrees
- Background in content and pedagogy
- Teaching experience

Academic ability refers to measures such as grade point averages for academic coursework. Many states now require teacher licensure examinations, so schools and districts may want to request reports of scores from applicants. Certification status refers to the teacher's having the proper licensure for the position—both grade level and content area—as required by the particular state. Research on degree levels indicates that teachers with advanced degrees specific to their area are more effective than those, for example, with only an undergraduate degree. Effective teachers tend to be those with greater years of experience as well.

From a budgetary point of view, teachers with advanced degrees and greater years of experience generally will be more costly to the district than will beginning teachers with an undergraduate degree because most district salary schedules provide financial incentives for years of experience and advanced degrees. Therefore, schools and districts need to make prudent choices about resource allocation, investing their resources in teachers who are going to be the most effective.

If initial recruitment strategies are unsuccessful in shortage areas, such as special education, bilingual education, science, and mathematics, educational leaders may be tempted to hire noncertified teachers using state provisions for temporary licenses. However, given the research evidence and requirements of newer laws such as the No Child Left Behind Act of 2001, educational leaders must be aggressive in recruiting qualified teachers in hard-to-staff areas.

Across the country, schools and districts have adopted creative strategies, such as offering signing bonuses, moving expenses, and low-interest home mortgages in conjunction with local lenders to increase their applicant pool. In addition to the usual advertising, some schools and districts go directly to potential applicants, setting up "recruiting fairs" across the region and country to woo applicants (Catherine A. Lugg and colleagues). If all recruiting efforts have failed, and the only choice is to hire a teacher with an emergency licensure, the new teacher should be encouraged to obtain licensure as soon as possible and then provided with support and incentives, such as tuition reimbursement and release time to attend courses leading to licensure.

Finally, educational leaders may want to investigate a "grow your own" approach to filling hard-to-staff teacher positions. They may encourage talented classroom aides to pursue a teaching degree and licensure, and then they may match them with mentors. This is a strategy for the long term, but it has the advantage of developing teachers who are familiar with the district and students and who may adapt more quickly than an outside candidate. This strategy can be particularly helpful in large urban school districts and isolated rural areas, which face some of the most acute teacher shortages.

Retention

Once high-quality teachers have been hired, how do site-based leaders retain them? In many school districts, particularly in urban and isolated rural areas, teacher turnover is a significant issue, according to Richard Ingersoll. Research indicates that induction of new teachers is critical to their success and retention.

Induction and mentoring activities that build the human and social capital of new teachers take many forms. Some schools pair new teachers with veteran teachers who are available on a formal or an informal basis to assist them in adapting to a new school. Other schools and districts reverse the traditional practice of giving new, inexperienced teachers some of the most challenging classes. In addition, new teachers may be given a reduced teaching load the first year. This allows them more time to adapt and to interact with veteran teachers and mentors.

Finally, the site leader needs to work with the new teacher to develop a professional development plan that engages the new teacher from the start in developing collaborative networks of colleagues within and outside the school. Effective retention strategies are critical in the first 5 years of a teacher's career, where research indicates turnover is 50 percent (Ingersoll).

Retention strategies are not limited to new teachers. Across their career span, teachers need to feel that their work with students is valued. Educational leaders also know that one way to maximize student success is to make it possible for teachers to engage in lifelong learning.

Professional Development as a Retention Strategy

Professional development plans can serve as an important retention tool if they meet several conditions. They should be tailored to teachers' needs, rather than follow the traditional "one size fits all" approach, according to Mark A. Smylie and Debra Miretzky. Plans for teachers' development should align with school and district educational plans to maximize student learning. Also, by developing the plans jointly with individuals or groups of veteran teachers, the site leader can enhance social capital through the development and nurturing of collaborative relationships within and outside the school.

To free time for teachers to develop and utilize these collaborative networks, leaders at both school and district levels may need to restructure the school day and schedule. Time is an important resource-allocation issue. The site-based leader may need to lobby central administration for funding for substitute teachers, for example, to free up time for teachers to engage in collaborative curriculum development. In elementary schools, one creative solution is to schedule special classes such as music and art in ways that allow groups of teachers the opportunity to engage in collaborative work.

Also, it is important for teachers to develop professional networks with local universities and relevant professional associations. University-based professional development schools that connect teachers with content-area specialists and teachers from surrounding districts are one option, according to Van Dempsey. Veteran teachers may also be encouraged to take additional coursework to update their content knowledge and pedagogical methods. By supporting such activities through tuition reimbursement policies, school districts invest in both the human and social capital of teachers.

Finally, schools and districts might want to encourage teachers to join and participate in relevant local, regional, and national professional associations. Underwriting teachers' membership dues is one option. At the site level, educational leaders may be able to use discretionary funds for this purpose. Most of these organizations charge modest dues, and even districts that are closely watching their bottom line can often afford to subsidize, for example, membership in one professional organization per teacher per year.

In larger districts where a number of teachers have an interest in the same professional organization, an institutional membership may be more cost-effective. These organizations often make available to teachers the latest research in convenient formats, such as online newsletters and e-mail updates. In addition, they generally hold national and regional conferences that allow teachers face-to-face networking opportunities. Even if the school or district budget can only allow teachers to attend such conferences on a rotating basis, for example, every 3 years, these are still an important networking opportunity. The networking is enhanced when the returning teacher shares with colleagues information and research presented at the conference.

Teacher Compensation and Rewards

Site-level leaders may have little or no control over teacher compensation, because it is centralized in many districts and governed by collective bargaining. Yet as a group, teachers remain undercompensated when compared with similar professions, according to Sylvia A. Allegretto, Sean P. Corcoran, and Lawrence Mishel. However, educational leaders can maintain and build teacher morale, motivation, and job satisfaction through the professional development activities previously mentioned, most of which are low cost, and through nonmonetary rewards.

Teachers are motivated by nonmonetary rewards such as recognition and appreciation of their accomplishments. Here the site leader plays a pivotal role in developing vehicles to spotlight teachers' accomplishments in the school, district, community, and beyond. For example, a teacher who receives an award from a professional or community organization may receive recognition in the school or district newsletter. A teacher who has recently received an advanced degree might be honored with a reception hosted by the principal or Parent Teacher Association to which the local media have been invited. If the degree work involved a research project, thesis, or dissertation, the teacher could give a brief presentation. Such activities can effectively boost teacher motivation, and they reward activities that research indicates are important in effective teaching and student learning.

Deployment of Teachers

Site leaders need to be cognizant of the most effective methods of teacher deployment. Research provides evidence that those students who are the most challenging to educate benefit from small class sizes of 15 students to one teacher and from being taught by the most qualified teachers—those with the most experience and advanced degrees in their area of expertise (Nye and colleagues).

Unfortunately, some schools and districts still follow a philosophy of giving the most challenging classes to novice teachers, those least well equipped to maximize student learning in tough situations. Site leaders may want to provide veteran teachers with incentives to teach these classes, such as a reduced teaching load, in effect giving these teachers extra preparation time.

In exchange, the veteran teacher may be expected to serve as mentor of a new teacher. Hence, veteran teachers enjoy a reduced teaching load while at the same time preparing new teachers to take on more challenging students in the future. At the same time, mentoring programs serve to improve the school's retention rate of new teachers.

Development of Other School Employees

Many of the strategies mentioned previously, which enhance the human and social capital of teachers, are also applicable to other school employees. Other professional staff—for example, librarians, school psychologists, guidance counselors, and nurses—will benefit from individualized professional development plans. They, too, are motivated by nonmonetary rewards such as recognition of professional accomplishments and appreciation for years of service.

Instructional support employees, such as aides and assistants, often have little time to interact with and learn from their counterparts within the school or district. The site leader can facilitate their professional growth by arranging time for them to meet and network; even small amounts of time can be beneficial. Local universities may offer formal and informal opportunities for aides and assistants to develop professionally through low-cost workshops and formal coursework. Turnover may be a serious issue for education aides and assistants because their wages are low and fringe benefits modest.

Noninstructional support staff members, such as custodians, bus drivers, and cafeteria workers, are often neglected with regard to human and social capital development. Recruitment, retention, compensation, and deployment issues exist for these groups as well. In larger districts, some or all of these employee groups may have collective-bargaining agreements. In such cases, site-level leaders need to be familiar with the provisions of several collectively bargained master contracts as they work with different support staff.

Staff development opportunities exist for noninstructional support staff as well. For example, the Wisconsin Association of School Business Officials, a state affiliate of the Association of School Business Officials International, holds an annual workshop for custodians to keep them current on cost-effective and safe methods of cleaning. The workshops include education about hazardous and toxic materials as well as ecological methods of cleaning and grounds maintenance. Other organizations provide safety updates for school bus drivers. Food-service workers need to remain current on federal nutritional requirements and reimbursement guidelines so that the school cafeteria serves nutritious, appealing lunches and breakfasts at affordable prices while the food-service program operates in a fiscally responsible manner.

Members of the noninstructional support staff are often taken for granted, so recognition and appreciation of their service by educational leaders can strengthen their retention, motivation, and job satisfaction. For example, a site leader might institute an employee-of-the-month program to recognize outstanding service on a regular basis. Students, teachers, or other staff members might nominate an individual for consideration by the school site council, which then makes the final decision and presents an award certificate to the employee at a monthly luncheon held in his or her honor.

FISCAL RESOURCES: MAKING THE BEST USE OF EXISTING FINANCIAL RESOURCES

Educational leaders often find themselves stretching financial resources to achieve multiple educational goals and mandates. Recent reform legislation, such as the No Child Left Behind Act, which comes with limited funding and increasing demands for improvement in student achievement, has placed additional pressures on local education resources. Even schools and districts blessed with adequate funding often realize that with additional resources they could accomplish even more.

Two major means are used to ensure that educational leaders optimize existing resources: budgeting and fiscal accountability. In this section, we discuss several approaches to budgeting, but our focus is on a comprehensive, planning-based model called the Planning, Programming, Budgeting, and Evaluation System (PPBES), which represents best practice. With regard to fiscal accountability, we also present relevant accounting and auditing measures. Recognizing that educational leaders are increasingly turning to alternative revenue sources to supplement current revenues, we also discuss the educational leader as entrepreneur. We explore several methods of securing additional revenues while pointing out the pros and cons of such activities.

Budgeting

According to Ray and colleagues, a budget is "a plan of financial operation incorporating an estimate of proposed expenditures for a given period or purpose, and the proposed means of financing them." Budgets represent both an expenditure and a revenue plan. This subsection focuses more on the expenditure side, because it has greater relevance to site-level educational leaders.

Schools and districts typically operate on a fiscal year that begins July 1 and ends June 30. Fiscal Year 2007 would begin July 1, 2006, and end June 30, 2007. Fiscal planning, however, should extend several years into the future. Most school districts function under a budget calendar that is in large part dictated by state requirements. For example, some states require that the school board vote and approve the next fiscal year's budget prior to its beginning on July 1. This date then requires school districts to work backward in setting a calendar of budget activities that will allow them to have a final budget for school board approval no later than June. Table 19.1 displays a sample budget calendar.

By becoming familiar with their district's budget, school leaders can better understand how the funds allocated to their schools fit into the broader district context of resource allocation. Table 19.2 ("Components of an Ideal Budget Checklist") shows school leaders how to identify major components of the district budget and relate them to the school site.

Schools and districts typically follow one of five major methods of budgeting, sometimes combining more than one method:

Table 19.1   Sample Budget Calendar

Month	Activities
Month 1	Budget year begins
Month 3	Quarterly revision—to incorporate accurate revenue and enrollment figures
Month 4	Population (enrollment) projections Staff needs projections Program changes and addition projections Facilities needs projection
Month 5	Staff requisitions—supplies Capital outlay preliminary requests
Month 6	Budget revisions (present budget) Central staff sessions on needs Maintenance and operations requests
Month 7	Rough draft of needs budget
Month 8	Meetings with staffs and principals to establish priorities Citizen committees' reports and reviews Central staff and board of education budget sessions
Month 9	Budget revision (present budget)
Month 10	Working budget draft Meetings with staff and community groups to revise working budget
Month 11	Final draft of working budget
Month 12	Budget hearings and adoptions of working budget

Source: Ray, John R., Walter G. Hack, and I. Carl Candoli. 2005. *School Business Administration: A Planning Approach*, 8th ed. Published by Allyn & Bacon, Boston, MA. Copyright © 2005 by Pearson Education. Reprinted by permission of the publisher.

1. Line-item budgeting

2. Program-based budgeting

3. Site-based budgeting

4. Zero-based budgeting

5. PPBES

Line-Item Budgeting

Line-item budgeting is the simplest method and serves as a building block for the others, according to William T. Hartman. A line-item budget consists of the following three lines:

Table 19.2   Components of an Ideal Budget Checklist

Background Information

_____ 1. Title page and/or cover
_____ 2. Table of contents or index
_____ 3. Letter of transmittal, legislative request, budget message, or executive request
_____ 4. Table of organization and/or program structure
_____ 5. Budget calendar
_____ 6. Explanation of budget terms, codes, and procedures (glossary)

Executive Summary

_____ 7. District goals of education
_____ 8. Explanation of budgeting approach or philosophy
_____ 9. Budget assumptions, priorities, and guidelines
_____10. Budget highlights
_____11. Revenue summary
_____12. Expenditure summary
_____13. Summary of the budget by funds
_____14. Summary of the budget by function/object
_____15. Program budget summary
_____16. Summary of the budget by location (school or other cost center)
_____17. Analysis of budget increase or decrease
_____18. Comparison of budget with previous year (5-year comparison recommended)

Budget Detail

_____19. Program profiles for each program
_____20. Program budgets for each program
_____21. School or other cost center profiles by location
_____22. School or other cost center budgets by location
_____23. Bonded indebtedness

Supplementary Information

_____24. Profile of the school district and of the town, county, or city
_____25. Enrollment projections and forecasting methodology (5-year minimum)
_____26. Salary schedules, staffing profiles, and employee benefits
_____27. Inflation impact statement
_____28. Statement of impact of state/local revenue or expenditure limitations
_____29. Statement of tax levy
_____30. Comparisons with other districts in geographical area/state/nationwide
_____31. Examples of cost reduction
_____32. Web address for access to budget online

Source: Crampton, Faith E. 2004. "Components of an Ideal Budget Checklist." Milwaukee: University of Wisconsin.

1. Personnel

2. Maintenance and operations

3. Supplies and equipment

Personnel expenditures include salaries, wages, and benefits of all employees, including professional, clerical, and support staff, both full-time and part-time. Salaries and wages alone do not represent the full cost of compensation. To calculate the total cost of an employee, districts must include paid benefits, such as health care and retirement contributions, which add as much as 30 to 40 percent of salary and wage costs. For example, a teacher whose annual salary is $30,000 actually costs the school district an additional $9,000 to $12,000, given these percentages, for a total compensation cost of $39,000 to $42,000. In addition, expenditures for substitute teachers and consultants go in the personnel line.

The *maintenance and operations* line refers to costs associated with the upkeep of school facilities and grounds on the maintenance side and utility costs on the operations side. Upkeep of facilities and grounds involves costs for cleaning or custodial services and for minor repairs needed to keep the equipment associated with a school building, for example, a furnace, in good working order. Major utility costs include those for gas, electricity, water, and sewer services. Even in a site-based budgeting environment, utility costs are often centralized so that site leaders may not be aware of their magnitude.

The third line, *supplies and equipment*, includes the vast array of materials and equipment items found in schools and districts. Schools and districts purchase everything from construction paper for teachers to cleaning chemicals for custodians. Educational supplies, such as textbooks, which are often associated with school supplies in the public's mind, are only one of the many items schools purchase. Staying aware of the most cost-effective approaches to purchasing so many kinds of educational and noneducational supplies can be a challenge, which represents another way public school districts differ from many public-sector organizations and private businesses. Schools and districts also lease or purchase a broad array of equipment, from classroom computers to cooking equipment for the school cafeteria.

In districts that delegate purchasing of supplies to the school site, educational leaders can feel overwhelmed by the array of supplies to be purchased with a limited budget. Often, the district's business administrator can provide cost-saving suggestions such as bulk or cooperative purchases across schools or districts. In cases where the school district has negotiated lower prices with particular suppliers, site leaders can take advantage of discounts from the preferred-vendor list. In addition, school districts may have policies on purchases of supplies and equipment—particularly higher-cost equipment such as computers, printers, and photocopiers—that site leaders must follow even though they have been given purchasing authority.

Program-Based Budgeting

Program budgeting builds on line-item budgeting by partitioning expenditures by program. These programs may be school based, district based, or both. For example, a school may have a program budget for special-education expenditures. With a program budget, the site leader would know exactly what his or her school is spending on special-education services. At the same time, the district may also have an overall special-education program budget that captures, in addition to all the school-based expenditures, districtwide costs for administration and support of special-education services. Other examples of program budgets include bilingual education and gifted and talented education. At the secondary school level, academic departments, such as English or biology, may be designated as programs for budgeting purposes. Program budgets can also be constructed for support services, such as transportation and food services. Program budgeting is more complex and time consuming than a simple line-item budget, but it provides educational leaders with greater information and data on which to base educational and fiscal decisions.

School-Based Budgeting

Site-based budgets, often referred to as school-based budgets, build on line-item and program budgeting. At the simplest level, a school-based budget may be a line-item budget that summarizes school expenditures on personnel, maintenance and operations, and supplies and equipment. A school budget can also be developed as a group of program budgets. For example, an elementary school may want to develop a program budget for each grade level. A middle school may want to develop program budgets not only by grade level, but also by content area, such that there is a school-based budget for English or mathematics.

Zero-Based Budgeting

When schools or districts face declining revenues and must make significant spending cuts, some turn to zero-based budgeting, a method to be considered only after all reasonable efficiencies have been achieved. In zero-based budgeting, the budget is built from the ground up each fiscal year; that is, there is no assumption that the educational leader will be able to start with the same level of funding allocated the previous year. The intention is to force those in charge of building budgets to fully justify every expenditure, with the expectation that this exercise will yield some expenditures that cannot be justified and hence can be eliminated, reducing the district's overall budget. Zero-based budgeting also requires participants to examine less costly methods of providing current levels of services. In the direst circumstances, participants are asked to consider the consequences of not funding particular services or programs. This is a budget method for desperate fiscal times and may be warranted as a one-time exercise when there is a sudden, unexpected, and substantial reduction in anticipated revenues.

PPBES

Whereas zero-based budgeting is a reactive and short-term approach, PPBES is a proactive and long-term approach that views budgeting as part of a holistic approach to resource allocation. PPBES represents best practice with regard to resource allocation because (a) it bases the budget on an educational plan, and (b) it builds into the system an evaluation component so schools and districts can assess whether they have met stated objectives. Educational leaders design and implement PPBES by means of a 10-step process:

1. Assess educational needs and problems.

2. Formulate goals and objectives.

3. Develop measurable objectives.

4. Design program structure and format.

5. Formulate alternative approaches to meet objectives.

6. Analyze and project costs of alternatives.

7. Select and adopt optimum alternatives.

8. Prepare budgets for the adopted programs.

9. Implement and monitor programs and budgets.

10. Evaluate educational and fiscal outcomes.

Actual budget preparation does not take place until Step 8. The first three steps explicitly address educational planning, beginning with a self-assessment, followed by formulation of comprehensive educational goals and objectives. Some schools or districts will prefer to develop a mission and vision statement before developing goals and objectives.

Objectives must be stated in measurable terms so they may be evaluated in Step 10. Stating objectives in measurable terms does not mean that objectives are limited to cognitive skills. Schools or districts may also develop measurable objectives in the affective domain, such as appreciation of art or music or the responsibilities of citizens in a democratic society. For example, an elementary school may specify an objective around raising reading scores by a certain amount for the next academic year.

Program structures, formats, and delivery systems follow from measurable objectives. In prekindergarten through twelfth-grade school districts, program structures, such as elementary, middle, and high school configurations, may be taken for granted as the only acceptable structure. PPBES allows educators and staff to think outside the box. Related to specifying program structure and format are the analysis and costing out of alternative approaches to meet objectives. For example, participants might brainstorm a number of strategies to improve students' reading skills, such as smaller class sizes, the addition of education aides, afterschool tutoring, or summer enrichment programs. Participants would analyze these alternatives for their track record of success in research and then estimate their costs so those charged with making the final decisions in Step 7 do so based on solid research evidence and fiscal data.

Implementation and monitoring of educational programs and budgets go hand in hand in Step 8. The normal academic year and fiscal year generally coincide sufficiently for a school or district to monitor implementation at least quarterly. A formal evaluation of educational and fiscal outcomes should be done annually (Step 10) to allow planners the opportunity to modify, add, or delete, as needed, goals or objectives and to make adjustments to budgets. By doing so, participants have begun the PPBES cycle anew, as indicated in Figure 19.1 ("Ten-Step Cycle of the Planning, Programming, Budgeting, and Evaluation System"). The result is continuous improvement of educational outcomes and resource allocation.

A frequent question posed about the process of PPBES is, who should participate? The answer is simple: everyone. The PPBES process should involve not only educational leaders, but also teachers, staff, and school-site councils (where applicable). *Staff members* are broadly defined to encompass all employees who support the educational process.

Figure 19.1   Ten-Step Cycle of the Planning, Programming, Budgeting, and Evaluation System

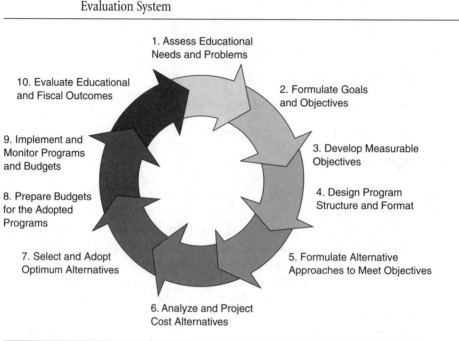

These include secretaries, food-service workers, custodians, and bus drivers, who are often overlooked in planning and budgeting processes. All these groups should be represented if a school or district is to maximize student learning and stretch existing fiscal resources as far as possible.

Fiscal Accountability

Educational leaders not only need to use fiscal resources well, but they also need to demonstrate in a tangible manner that they have done so. Fiscal accountability is demonstrated through accounting and auditing activities.

Accounting

Accounting involves the systematic coding and tracking of revenues and expenditures, generally using a state-mandated system of coding. For instance, in Wisconsin, schools and districts are required to follow the coding system laid out in the *Wisconsin Uniform Financial Accounting Requirements* manual, developed by the Wisconsin Department of Public Instruction (2004b). Accounting encompasses all financial transactions and involves the following activities:

- Recording of financial transactions
- Classifying (coding) of financial transactions
- Tracking of financial transactions
- Analysis of financial transactions

The amount of time site leaders need to spend overseeing accounting activities will depend on the level of fiscal authority the school district delegates to them. In many instances, districts use a modified approach to site-based budgeting and accounting that limits the school's expenditure authority to supplies and equipment, approximately 10 to 15 percent of the actual budget. Regardless of the degree of expenditure authority, all financial transactions must be recorded at the school level, using either accounting software specific to the school district or a commercial software package such as Excel. Most states mandate proper accounting records. Complete and accurate accounting records assist schools and districts in making the best use of fiscal resources because they provide (a) a consistent framework for reporting financial data, (b) a system for monitoring revenues and expenditures, and (c) historical data for planning and budgeting.

Auditing

Auditing involves the study and evaluation of an accounting system to determine its accuracy and completeness. Schools and districts generally engage in two types of auditing: external and internal.

In many states, school districts are required to submit an annual external audit to the state department of education. External audits are independently conducted by professional auditors or accountants who are not employees of the school district and have no relationship with the district that could be interpreted as a conflict of interest.

Internal audits are conducted within the school district, often by the office of the school business administrator. Individual schools and programs should be subject to regular internal audits to ensure use of proper accounting procedures. The consequences of infrequent audits can be very serious in that unintentional as well as intentional mismanagement of funds may occur, leaving the school district as well as individual administrators liable. Site leaders often are responsible for assembling and organizing their schools' financial and accounting records for internal auditors. Although many educational leaders approach audits as stressful events, their anxiety is unnecessary if they have maintained complete and accurate records.

Student Activity Funds

A special case that deserves mention is the accounting for and auditing of student activity funds. Site leaders often oversee these funds. Student activity funds are generated by extracurricular activities at the school level, such as student clubs and associations, student governments, and athletics. For example, students may pay dues to belong to the French club, or the student council may engage in fundraising, such as bake sales, to support some of its activities. Admission fees may be charged for sporting events, concerts, and plays, which in turn provide support for new uniforms or equipment.

Because these activities usually generate small amounts of revenue individually, school leaders may not oversee these accounting practices with the same rigor they apply to those for curricular needs. Most states require, however, that the same accounting procedures be followed for student activity accounts. In addition, though the revenue generated by a single student activity may be small, the total revenues of all the activities are often substantial. Site leaders can exercise sound fiscal stewardship of student activities by following these guidelines:

- Documentation of student activity purpose
- Determination or supervision regarding student activity
- Written policies and procedures
- All people involved with student activity funds have read and understand policies
- External audit performed annually
- Internal audits performed regularly
- Controls over the exchange of funds consisting of:
  - Monthly bank statement reconciliations prepared by someone independent of person making deposit
  - Issuance of receipts for funds collected
  - Timely bank deposits
  - Check requisitions are used
  - Expenditures are approved by proper authority
  - Documentation retained for all expenses
  - All purchases made by check
  - Dual signatures on all checks written
  - No signed checks in advance or checks written for cash
  - Voided checks are retained
  - Monthly reports of activity transactions prepared and beginning fund balances reconciled to ending fund balances
  - Accounting records open to inspection
  - Review of financial reports by the school district business office
  - No deficit balances reported at year end unless a policy allows them (Wisconsin Department of Public Instruction 2004a)

Site leaders who underestimate the importance of appropriate stewardship of student activity funds do so at their peril. Failure in this responsibility can lead to charges of mismanagement of funds with consequences as serious as termination of employment.

Educational Entrepreneurship

Educational entrepreneurship is not new. For decades, schools and districts have generated money outside state and local tax revenues, largely through extracurricular activities. What appears new, according to a report by the U.S. General Accounting Office, is the increased sophistication and aggressiveness with which educational leaders are pursuing entrepreneurial revenues. Media accounts point to an increase in entrepreneurial revenue raising by schools and districts through activities such as parent fundraising, commercial advertising, corporate sponsorships, and recruitment of tuition-paying students, according to Faith E. Crampton and Paul Bauman. Entrepreneurship in education has different goals from commercialization and privatization. *Commercialization* refers to the introduction of profit-oriented, private-sector activities in schools and districts, such as the use of free or low-cost educational materials from a company or business that contain frequent references to their products (Alex Molnar). Many educators view commercialization as exploitative of children. Entrepreneurship, in contrast, has a proactive connotation, because it describes a conscious decision by a school or district to raise additional funds for educational activities.

Privatization in education has come to refer to two classes of activities: (a) contracting or outsourcing of school or district services to for-profit businesses, and (b) management of public schools by private-sector firms. Paul Bauman explains that privatization is generally viewed as an efficiency or cost-reduction measure rather than a revenue-raising activity.

Crampton and Bauman divide entrepreneurial activities into two categories: traditional and new. Traditional activities include school and parent fundraising, local education foundations, business-education partnerships, and student fees. Newer forms of entrepreneurship include advertising, corporate sponsorships and merchandising, and recruitment of tuition-paying students. The following sections briefly describe these entrepreneurial activities.

School and Parent Fundraising

For many years, school fundraisers such as bake sales, carnivals, raffles, bingo, and the collection of grocery coupons have provided discretionary funds, usually targeted for specific educational or extracurricular purposes. Schools and districts also have realized profits from ongoing enterprises, such as supply stores and vending machines. These efforts remain important for raising funds for extracurricular activities. Parent involvement in fundraising takes several forms—from individual parent activities to organized parent-teacher groups and special task forces.

Local Education Foundations

Nonprofit foundations formed to assist local school districts are another means of augmenting revenues. Because most states consider school districts quasi-governmental units, the school district and foundation usually must be separate entities with independent governance structures. The role of school district officials is limited to an advisory capacity. Local education foundations raise funds in a number of ways in addition to soliciting direct monetary donations from individuals, organizations, and businesses.

Business-Education Partnerships

The most common example of local business-education partnerships is the adopt-a-school program. These partnerships range from volunteering time to donating goods and services. Often these are in-kind partnerships that do not involve direct financial assistance. For example, a business may release employees to speak to a classroom on careers or to serve on a school or district committee. A computer company may donate used equipment to a school, or a grocery store may provide soft drinks and snacks for a school-related event. In cases of donated equipment, maintenance and repair costs are normally the ongoing responsibility of the school district. Sometimes local businesses approach schools and districts to engage in such partnerships. Ultimately, educational leaders need to evaluate carefully whether these partnerships are of value to them in reaching school and district educational goals.

Student Fees

Public schools cannot charge resident students a true user fee, that is, tuition, for general education because of state constitutional provisions providing free public schools. Fees, however, are widely used by schools and districts for both curricular and extracurricular activities. Some school districts charge a yearly textbook rental or supply fee as well as fees for elective courses, such as art, music, and advanced-placement courses. More recently, some school districts have sought to expand that traditional base to include services, such as student transportation. Extracurricular fees are assessed on activities in which students engage voluntarily and for which they do not earn credit for graduation, such as athletics and drama. Student fees are a potential burden for low-income families and may be a disincentive for poor students to pursue educational and extracurricular activities.

Advertising

A study by the U.S. General Accounting Office in 2000 confirmed that school-related advertising has been on the rise for the past several years. Examples include advertising of commercial products on school-hall walls, athletic uniforms, stadium walls, and buses, and in school or district newsletters and district reports. Advertisers have included soft-drink companies, fast-food restaurants, and local grocery-store chains.

Before schools or districts enter into contractual agreements for advertising, they should check state statutes for any guidelines for or limitations on such activities. Also, as with all legally binding documents, schools and districts should have their own legal counsel review the contracts to ensure they are in the best interests of all involved.

Corporate Sponsorships and Merchandising

In the past, securing corporate sponsors for state high school athletic tournaments was not unusual, but school districts in several states now seek corporate sponsorships for academic and extracurricular activities as well. Some school districts have copied the fundraising activities of colleges and universities in branding or marketing products bearing school or district logos. These efforts include direct marketing of products, such as coffee mugs and clothing, as well as royalties from the use of logos. In addition, school districts have issued affinity credit cards with their respective logos. If contractual agreements with third parties are part of corporate sponsorship or merchandising activities, school district attorneys should review these documents.

Recruitment of Tuition-Paying Students

Some school districts, particularly those with available space in classrooms, have recruited tuition-paying students from outside their boundaries. Until recently, this revenue-generating activity was found predominantly in metropolitan areas where students do not need to travel long distances to attend a school in a neighboring district. In addition, for older students, metropolitan areas offer public transportation as a means of convenient, low-cost transportation to a school outside their home district.

In many states, such interdistrict transfers are permissible because no state statutory or regulatory language forbids or limits them. In fact, states such as Wisconsin have formal interdistrict choice programs whereby the state provides additional funding to the sending and receiving districts, according to Merry Larsen and Dave Loppnow.

Policies providing state funding of interdistrict transfers have also given rise to *virtual schools*—online distance-education programs. School districts in several states can recruit students from across the state—and in some instances, even from outside the state—to enroll in their virtual schools. Transportation is not an issue with these schools, as they require no buses or buildings. Depending on state law, districts hosting a virtual school may receive some or all of the state funding that would have gone to the home school district; in practice, this funding is similar to tuition.

In Pennsylvania, for example, virtual schools set up as charter schools are entitled to the state aid that would have gone to the students' home districts. Pennsylvania's law set off a controversy among the state's school districts, Robert Tomsho reported, when one small district's virtual school began to siphon students—and the state funds that accompany them—from other districts.

Other Forms of Entrepreneurship

In addition, some researchers consider volunteers as an in-kind contribution to school revenues (Ron Zimmer and colleagues). Parents and community members who volunteer time for school-related activities do make important contributions. The time they contribute, however, should be considered a value-added activity rather than a revenue source, because volunteers cannot realistically substitute for school employees.

A final form of entrepreneurship worth mentioning is grantwriting. Schools and districts are increasingly looking to raise additional revenues through grants from state and federal sources as well as philanthropic organizations. Grants can be important sources of additional revenues. They range in size from mini-grants of about a thousand dollars to large federal grants, such as those under the Comprehensive School Reform Demonstration program, worth millions of dollars. The writing of grant applications, however, requires a substantial investment of staff time unless a school district has grantwriters.

PHYSICAL RESOURCES: MAINTAINING AND ENHANCING THE PHYSICAL ENVIRONMENT OF SCHOOLS

The contribution the physical environment of schools makes to student learning is often overlooked. The *physical environment* refers to all aspects of the interior and exterior of the school facility as well as the grounds, which include spaces as varied as parking lots, playgrounds, and athletic fields. According to David C. Thompson and R. Craig Wood, the physical environment of schools is also referred to as *school infrastructure*.

From a fiscal perspective, school infrastructure represents all the physical assets in a school district. These assets are a multimillion-dollar investment that must be protected and maintained. With the average new high school costing $20 million, the combined value of buildings and grounds in even a small school district is a huge investment of taxpayer dollars. From an educational perspective, school infrastructure represents physical capital that works in tandem with human and social capital to maximize student learning.

To establish the importance of the role of school infrastructure as an investment in physical capital, this section opens with recent research linking school infrastructure to student achievement. We then discuss the role of site-based educational leaders with regard to maintenance and operations; risk management, safety, and security; and school construction.

Research on School Infrastructure and Student Achievement

The five studies described in the following paragraphs are representative of research over the last decade on the relationship between the physical environment of schools and student achievement. They reflect the importance of school infrastructure in all types of school settings: urban; rural; and elementary, middle, and high schools.

The first two studies are dissertations on Virginia schools. In her 1993 study, Carol S. Cash examined the relationship between building condition and student achievement in small, rural high schools in Virginia. She rated buildings as substandard, standard, or above standard, based on the results of a survey she developed. Cash then compared those ratings with mean student achievement scores on the Virginia Test of Academic Proficiency. The achievement scores had been adjusted for socioeconomic status. Cash found that test scores rose with the improvement of building condition. She concluded, "Building condition is more than a static condition. It is a physical representation of a public message about the value of education. . . . Schools should reflect the environment of success."

In 1996, Eric Hines studied a sample of urban high schools in Virginia using methods similar to those of Cash and found that the physical environment of the school affected student achievement. Students in substandard school buildings scored, on average, at the 52nd percentile, whereas their counterparts in above-standard facilities scored dramatically higher, at the 66th percentile, on the Virginia Test of Academic Proficiency.

The third and fourth studies examined the relationship between infrastructure and students' success in urban schools in Washington, DC, and Milwaukee, Wisconsin. Maureen M. Berner hypothesized in her 1993 study that the condition of public school buildings in Washington, DC, was affected by parental involvement and that the condition of school buildings, in turn, would affect student achievement. She defined *parental involvement* as the size of a school's PTA budget per student. The sample included elementary, middle, and high schools. Socioeconomic variables, such as family income and racial composition of the student body in individual schools, were added as control variables.

Berner's results confirmed that the PTA budget per student had a positive, statistically significant effect on school building condition. She reasoned that this relationship existed because the school-based PTA would likely invest resources in maintaining and improving the physical environment. The study's findings also supported the second hypothesis, regarding the relationship between building condition and student achievement. The condition of the school had a strong impact on scores on the district-developed Comprehensive Test of Basic Skills.

In a 2001 study of the Milwaukee Public Schools, Morgan Lewis analyzed the relationship between the condition of school facilities and student achievement, using a sample of elementary, middle, and high schools. To determine school condition, trained school district staff members administered a survey that used a five-point rating scale (poor, marginal, average, good, and excellent). Student achievement scores came from the 1996 Wisconsin Student Assessment System, a statewide battery of tests.

Lewis used an analytic method that factored in building condition along with a number of student characteristics—such as attendance, mobility, truancy, suspensions, poverty, and race—added as control variables. The results were statistically significant, and Lewis concluded that building condition contributed significantly to student achievement in mathematics and reading.

The final study, based on 2,860 Texas elementary schools, represented a slightly different research method than the studies cited previously. In 1999, Elizabeth A. Harter analyzed the amount spent on school upkeep in relationship to student achievement for the 1992–1993 academic year and found evidence of the importance of maintaining school facilities. Student achievement data came from the Texas Assessment of Academic Skills in fourth-grade mathematics and reading. Student characteristics, such as academic potential and socioeconomic status, were control variables. Also included were geographic variables relating to school location, school size, and expenditure variables, broken out by spending categories, one of which was school upkeep or maintenance.

Harter compared mean per-pupil expenditures by spending categories for low-achieving and high-achieving elementary schools. On average, low-achieving schools spent substantially less on maintenance per pupil than did high-achieving schools. Harter concluded, "Spending for regular school upkeep . . . relates positively to student outcomes."

Maintenance and Operations

The research described previously points to the critical importance of the physical environment for students in all kinds of schools and communities. Results provide strong evidence that educational leaders must ensure that their schools and grounds are well maintained, as their condition plays an important role in student success.

Ray and colleagues define *maintenance* as the repair, replacement, and upkeep of school facilities and associated equipment, whereas *operations* refers to keeping facilities open or ready to be used. Operations involve mostly day-to-day activities, such as cleaning and grounds care. These activities include keeping proper temperature and lighting in the school, with an eye toward energy conservation, as Timothy Smith, William Fowler, and Bernard Greene explain. Operations tasks are usually the responsibility of school custodians, whereas maintenance tasks may require multiple employees with differing sets of skills. For example, a building custodian would generally replace a light bulb, but a district maintenance worker with specialized training or an electrician would replace a light fixture and wiring.

Site leaders are ultimately responsible for the appearance and condition of their schools. Faith E. Crampton, David C. Thompson, and Randall S. Vesely argue that site leaders need to become familiar with maintenance and operations policies and procedures so they can make sure the school environment is conducive to student learning.

Maintenance activities fit into two broad categories: routine or emergency. Emergency maintenance, like a boiler breakdown in the middle of winter, is to be avoided not only because of the expense involved, but also for its potential disruption of teaching and learning. In such a situation, a school may have to close for one or more days for emergency repairs, resulting in lost learning time. Most emergency maintenance, except that due to natural disasters such as hurricanes and tornadoes, can be avoided with attention to routine maintenance. For example, heating and cooling systems should be checked seasonally to keep them in proper working order, just as responsible homeowners have their furnaces checked in the fall and air conditioners in the spring.

Other types of equipment, such as photocopiers, which are used constantly in a school and undergo a great deal of wear and tear, should be inspected by the appropriate technicians at regular intervals so that they continue to run smoothly, and when technicians find that the equipment is no longer cost-effective to repair, it should be replaced. In a school with only one photocopier, a breakdown affects many staff and can impede the learning process.

Depending on the size of the school district and the presence or absence of collective-bargaining agreements, the responsibilities of the site leader with regard to maintenance and operations and associated employees can vary greatly. In smaller school districts, site leaders may be directly involved in the hiring, supervision, and evaluation of custodians. If so, they may want to look at model job descriptions and evaluation forms found in resources such as the *Planning Guide for Maintaining School Facilities*, a joint publication developed by the U.S. Department of Education and the Association of School Business Officials (Tom Szuba and Roger Young).

In larger school districts where the custodial staff are more likely to be organized under a collective-bargaining agreement, hiring, supervision, and evaluation may be centralized. In this case, site leaders will want to familiarize themselves with the content of collectively bargained contracts. In almost all school districts, the deployment of maintenance workers is centralized. Site leaders still need to be aware of relevant district policies for their utilization and the content of collective-bargaining agreements, if present.

Most school districts use a request system or work order to be submitted centrally either on a paper form or online. The site leader should encourage all building staff to make him or her aware of maintenance and repair issues immediately. Then the proper form should be submitted along with any needed follow-up to ensure the work is completed in a timely manner. By handling requests in this way, the site leader demonstrates to teachers and staff that the condition of their school is an important factor in the learning environment, according to Crampton, Thompson, and Vesely.

Site leaders can use simple, ready-made checklists, like the "School Building/Campus Curbside Critique" in Table 19.3, to make sure that the school building exterior and grounds are attractive, well maintained, and safe. More detailed lists for the interior, exterior, and grounds of a school facility are available in the *Planning Guide for Maintaining School Facilities* (Szuba and Young).

If the district outsources any maintenance or operations functions to private contractors, site leaders will need to familiarize themselves with district policies. Custodians and maintenance workers of private contractors are not district employees. If, for example, a school custodian is not doing a thorough job of cleaning, the site leader may

Table 19.3   School Building/Campus Curbside Critique

School/Campus _____ Date_____

	Yes	No
1. Is the parking lot clean and free of debris?	——	——
2. Are windows clean (devoid of dried-up tape)?	——	——
3. Are the grounds and sidewalk free of weeds, cigarette butts, scattered trash?	——	——
4. Is the front door clean (devoid of fingerprints, freshly painted)?	——	——
5. Are the items displayed in the windows and on doors current with the season?	——	——
6. Is the trash area clean (without overflowing dumpsters)?	——	——
7. Are the gutters and downspouts in good condition?	——	——
8. Are the draperies/blinds neat and organized looking?	——	——
9. Are the flower beds free of weeds?	——	——
10. Is the lawn mowed and well manicured?	——	——
11. Are the walls properly maintained with no graffiti?	——	——
12. Is the playground equipment safe?	——	——
13. Are entrances attractively landscaped?	——	——
14. Are all exterior lights burning at night?	——	——
15. Are parking lots and playgrounds free of puddles?	——	——
16. Is exterior paint adhering properly?	——	——

Comments for Maintenance: Record any condition that threatens safety (a broken step, pothole, faulty railing, etc.)

_____

_____

_____

_____

_____

_____
                                                           Signature

cc: Maintenance Director

Source: Strickland, Jessie Shields, and T. C. Chan. 2002. "Curbside Critique: A Technique to Maintain a Positive School Yard Image." *School Business Affairs* 68 (May): 24–27. Reprinted with permission of the Association of School Business Officials International (ASBO). Use does not imply any endorsement or recognition by ASBO International and its officers or affiliates.

need to report the problem to a district administrator, who in turn reports it to the private contractor. The private contractor is then responsible for correcting the problem.

Risk Management, Safety, and Security

Although risk management is often associated with legal liability and insurance, with responsibility residing primarily at the central-office level (Thompson and Wood), this chapter approaches risk management from a safety and security viewpoint. Many of the activities school districts undertake to reduce liability and hence potential fiscal loss begin with a concern about the safety and security of employees who work in the school district, students who attend district schools, students' family members who visit schools and attend school events, and other community members involved with the schools. When risk management is viewed in this manner, site leaders must assume a proactive stance in maximizing safety and security. Although this chapter does not deal with reduction of violence, the management and maintenance of a school to enhance safety and security will reduce the risk of violence to students, staff, and visitors.

Some of the measures are straightforward. Educational leaders can significantly enhance their schools' safety by following the practices outlined under maintenance and operations. For example, installing sufficient exterior lighting of the school grounds, parking lots, and other areas, such as athletic fields used for night events, is an effective, low-cost deterrent to crime. Keeping exterior and interior door locks in good working order so they cannot be easily compromised helps ensure the safety of people and property. Trimming hedges or bushes near doors and windows will maximize visibility and deter their use as a cover by vandals and criminals.

Some school districts have proactive policies in place to guide site-based leaders, but if not, they can use simple assessment tools, such as those found in *Safe School Design: A Handbook for Educational Leaders,* by Tod Schneider, Hill Walker, and Jeffrey Sprague. In addition, attention to items on the "Curbside Critique" is helpful. For example, cracked, uneven sidewalks and parking-lot potholes place students and adults at risk of falling or being injured. Prompt removal of graffiti discourages gang activity and vandalism. Attention to these kinds of routine maintenance issues can reduce injuries and absences that impede learning while improving the overall learning environment.

School Construction and Modernization

Increasingly, site-based leaders are expected to take a leadership role in school construction and modernization, according to Brian O. Brent and Marie Cianca. Faith E. Crampton, David C. Thompson, and Janis M. Hagey note that school construction activities refer not only to the construction of new facilities but also to additions to existing facilities, renovations, retrofitting, deferred maintenance, and major improvements to school grounds.

Depending on the degree of decentralization in the school district, site leaders will have varying levels of responsibility for infrastructure projects. In all cases, leaders have an affirmative responsibility to safeguard employees and students from dangerous or hazardous situations that might arise in the construction process. In addition, they must prevent the construction processes from having a negative impact on learning. Some examples follow.

Renovations can include modernizing the school to make it technology ready. Activities might include upgrading electrical and communications wiring within a portion of the school facility or the entire facility. Site leaders need to apprise themselves of the construction schedule to move students and staff from areas under construction. Even in nonclassroom areas, leaders need to see that areas with exposed electrical wiring are cordoned off for safety.

Retrofitting may involve infrastructure projects such as window replacement and insulation to achieve greater energy efficiency or removal of hazardous substances such as asbestos. As with renovations, leaders must attend to issues of scheduling and safety.

Deferred-maintenance projects, such as the replacement of a leaky roof, often require interior work to replace water-damaged ceiling tiles. Exterior roof work can be noisy; to avoid disturbance of classroom learning, temporary room changes may be necessary. Consultation with central-office administrators may be desirable to see if noisy or hazardous work can be conducted outside school hours.

In the happy event that staff and students move into a newly constructed school, site leaders will need to deal with issues of transition and new occupancy. Soon after moving in, they should conduct a post-occupancy survey in cooperation with the district's facilities office to get feedback on what is working and what isn't in the new facility, as Glen I. Earthman recommends. On a day-to-day basis during the first weeks and months of occupancy, site leaders will need to deal with minor problems, such as an electrical switch not working. To address these issues, the site leader needs to find out whether the district has a policy for reporting post-occupancy problems. Reports may need to go to the central office, which in turn will notify the contractor to correct the problem. For small problems, school districts may utilize their maintenance workers.

CONCLUSION: COMPREHENSIVE PLANNING IS BEST PRACTICE

This chapter has presented the range of responsibilities site-based educational leaders face with regard to allocation of the human, fiscal, and physical resources needed to maximize student learning. Particular emphasis was placed on discussion of best practices described in professional and research literature. Best practices are based on research or evidence that permits educational leaders to make sound decisions regarding resource allocation.

Allocation of human resources requires the site leader to develop the human and social capital of the faculty and staff. Human capital involves the recruitment, retention, compensation, and deployment of high-quality faculty as well as other professional and support staff:

- Educational leaders support the development of social capital by nurturing collaborative relationships among faculty and staff within their schools and districts.
- They provide opportunities for networking with local universities, state departments of education, and professional organizations.
- Professional and staff development, along with peer networking, are powerful tools for all education employees that contribute to employee motivation and job satisfaction while at the same time increasing their knowledge and expertise. Together, these strategies translate into higher student achievement.

Fiscal resources lie at the heart of educational leaders' allocation decisions. Leaders often must stretch existing financial resources to meet mandates and maximize student learning. Sound budgeting practices and fiscal accountability measures ensure the best use of limited resources:

- Although several methods of budgeting exist, PPBES represents best practice, because it requires development of the budget in the context of the school or district educational plan. As such, the budget becomes a means to an end—achievement of educational goals and objectives—rather than an end in itself.
- PPBES strengthens educational and fiscal accountability by including an evaluation component, which also serves as a feedback loop for continuous improvement of educational outcomes and fiscal management.
- Educational leaders further demonstrate fiscal accountability through the consistent use of generally accepted accounting and auditing practices that extend to all revenues and expenditures of schools and districts, including those generated from extracurricular activities.
- At the same time, educational leaders are becoming entrepreneurs who seek out additional revenues for their schools and districts through traditional and new approaches to fundraising.

Site leaders have major responsibility for maintaining and enhancing the physical environment of their schools. Research now indicates that the condition of schools can affect student learning:

- Educational leaders need to be knowledgeable about school maintenance and operations, making sure the school is clean, attractive, and in good repair.
- Sound maintenance and operations practices also improve the safety and security of employees, students, parents, and community members who are involved with the school throughout the day as well as at nights and on weekends.
- As school infrastructure ages and student enrollments increase, site leaders have increasingly become involved with school construction and modernization projects. Here, too, the leader's central responsibility is to ensure the well-being of employees and students.
- With new school construction, site leaders play an important role in helping faculty and staff make the transition to a new facility.

The effective allocation of human, fiscal, and physical resources rests on comprehensive educational planning with the focus on maximizing student learning. Particularly in an environment of site-based management, school leaders are the chief executive officers of their schools. They lead by example. In today's environment of high-stakes testing and sanctions, educational leaders must use every tool at their disposal to enhance student learning. Every fiscal resource must be put to full use in the name of student academic performance. Every element of the school environment counts, from teacher quality and class size to the physical environment in which students learn.

REFLECTIONS

1. How do your school and district develop and enhance human and social capital to maximize student learning? Are these mechanisms effective? What do they cost?

2. What other means of developing human capital and social capital might your school or district want to consider? Discuss their cost and effectiveness and contrast them with current practices.

3. What type of budgeting does your school use? How does it link to the school and district educational plans?

4. Describe your school district's budget calendar and its relationship to your school's budget process.

5. Who has input into the development of your school budget? Is it an inclusive process? If not, how could the development process be changed to make it more inclusive?

6. Do the interior and exterior of your school offer an attractive and inviting learning environment for students and staff? If yes, what makes it so? If not, what could be done to improve the physical environment of your school?

References

INTRODUCTION: LEADERSHIP FOR EXCELLENCE IN LEARNING

Bennis, Warren, and Burt Nanus. 1985. *Leaders: The Strategies for Taking Charge.* New York: Harper and Row.

Bolman, Lee G., and Terrence E. Deal. 1994. "Looking for Leadership: Another Search Party's Report." *Educational Administration Quarterly* 30, 1 (February): 77–96.

Bredeson, Paul V. 1993. "Letting Go of Outlived Professional Identities: A Study of Role Transition and Role Strain for Principals in Restructured Schools." *Educational Administration Quarterly* 29, 1 (February): 34–68.

Brubaker, Dale L. 1995. "How the Principalship Has Changed: Lessons From Principals' Life Stories." *NASSP Bulletin* 79, 574 (November): 88–95.

Clark, Kenneth E., and Miriam B. Clark. 1992. "Introduction." In *Impact of Leadership*, edited by Kenneth E. Clark, Mariam B. Clark, and David P. Campbell. 1–10. Greensboro, NC: Center for Creative Leadership.

Collins, Jim. 2001. *Good to Great: Why Some Companies Make the Leap...and Others Don't.* New York: Harper-Collins.

Conley, David T., and Paul Goldman. 1994. *Facilitative Leadership: How Principals Lead Without Dominating.* Eugene: Oregon School Study Council, University of Oregon, August. OSSC Bulletin Series.

Copland, Michael A. 2001. "The Myth of the Superprincipal." *Phi Delta Kappan* 82 (March): 528–32.

Council of Chief State School Officers. 1996. *Interstate School Leaders Licensure Consortium: Standards for School Leaders.* Washington, DC: Author.

Edmonds, Ronald. 1979. "A Discussion of the Literature and Issues Related to Effective Schooling." Unpublished paper.

Ferrandino, Vincent L., and Gerald N. Tirrozi. 2004. "Principals' Perspective." *Education Week* 23 (June 9): 31.

Fiedler, Fred E., Martin M. Chemers, and Linda Mahar. 1976. *Improving Leadership Effectiveness: The Leader Match Concept.* New York: John Wiley & Sons.

Hallinger, Philip, and Ronald H. Heck. 1996. "Reassessing the Principal's Role in School Effectiveness: A Review of Empirical Research, 1980–1995." *Educational Administration Quarterly* 32, 1 (February): 5–44.

Hanson, E. Mark. 2003. *Educational Administration and Organizational Behavior.* 5th ed. Boston: Allyn & Bacon.

Johnson, Marlene M. 1993. *Leadership: Review of Selected Research*. Urbana, IL: The National Center for School Leadership.

Kanungo, Rabindra N., and Manuel Mendonca. 1996. *Ethical Dimensions of Leadership*. Thousand Oaks, CA: Sage Publications.

Krug, Samuel E. 1993. "Leadership Craft and the Crafting of School Leadership." *Phi Delta Kappan* 75, 3 (November): 240–44.

Leithwood, Kenneth A., and Carolyn Riehl. 2003. *What We Know About Successful School Leadership*. Philadelphia: Laboratory for Student Success, Temple University.

Mast, Carlotta. 2003. "Q & A With Jim Collins." *The School Administrator* 60 (December): 29–33.

Murphy, Joseph. 2005. "Unpacking the Foundations of ISLLC *Standards* and Addressing Concerns in the Academic Community." *Educational Administration Quarterly* 41, 1 (February): 154–91.

National Association of Elementary School Principals. 2001. *Leading Learning Communities: Standards for What Principals Should Know and Be Able to Do*. Alexandria, VA: Author.

National Association of Secondary School Principals. 2004. *Breaking Ranks II: Strategies for Leading High School Reform*. Reston, VA: Author.

National Institute on Educational Governance, Finance, Policymaking, and Management. 1999. *Effective Leaders for Today's Schools: Synthesis of a Policy Forum on Educational Leadership*. Washington, DC: Office of Educational Research and Improvement, U.S. Department of Education.

Pejza, John P. 1985. "The Catholic School Principal: A Different Kind of Leader." Paper presented at annual meeting of the National Catholic Educational Association, St. Louis, MO, April.

Portin, Bradley, with Paul Schneider, Michael DeArmond, and Lauren Gundlach. 2003. *Making Sense of Leading Schools: A Study of the School Principalship*. Seattle, WA: Center on Reinventing Public Education.

Richmon, Malcolm J., and Derek J. Allison. 2003. "Toward a Conceptual Framework for Leadership Inquiry." *Educational Management & Administration* 31, 1: 31–50.

Sashkin, Marshall, and Molly G. Sashkin. 2003. *Leadership That Matters: The Critical Factors for Making a Difference in People's Lives and Organizations' Success*. San Francisco: Berrett-Koehler.

Sergiovanni, Thomas J. 1992. *Moral Leadership: Getting to the Heart of School Improvement*. San Francisco: Jossey-Bass.

Skrla, Linda, David A. Erlandson, Eileen M. Reed, and Alfred P. Wilson. 2001. *The Emerging Principalship*. Larchmont, NY: Eye on Education.

Terry, George R. 1960. *Principles of Management*. 3rd ed. Homewood, IL: Richard D. Irwin.

Thomson, Scott D. 1980. "Editorial: Effective Leadership." *NASSP Newsletter* 27, 8 (April): 2.

Truman, Harry S. 1988. *More Plain Speaking*, edited by Margaret Truman and Scott Meredith. New York: Warner Books.

U.S. Department of Education, Office of Secondary and Elementary Education. 2002. *No Child Left Behind: A Desktop Reference*. Washington, DC: Author.

Welte, Carl E. 1978. "Management and Leadership: Concepts With an Important Difference." *Personnel Journal* 57, 11 (November): 630–32, 642.

1. THE LANDSCAPE OF SCHOOL LEADERSHIP

Archer, Jeff. 2002. "Fla's New Code Drops Requirement for Principal Licenses." *Education Week*, May 15.

Beck, Lynn, and Joseph Murphy. 1993. *Understanding the Principalship: Metaphorical Themes 1920s–1990s*. New York: Teachers College Press.

Brown, Robert J., and Jeffrey R. Cornwall. 2000. *The Entrepreneurial Educator*. Lanham, MD: Scarecrow Press.

Chan, Tak Cheung, and Harbison Pool. 2002. "Principals' Priorities Versus Their Realities: Reducing the Gap." Unpublished paper.

Chirichello, Michael. 2003. "Co-Principals: A Double Dose of Leadership." *Principal* 82, 4 (March/April): 40–43.

Cooley, Van, and Jianping Shen. 1999. "Who Will Lead? The Top 10 Factors That Influence Teachers Moving Into Administration." *NASSP Bulletin* 83, 606: 75–80.

———. 2003. "School Accountability and Professional Job Responsibilities: A Perspective From Secondary Principals." *NASSP Bulletin* 87, 634: 10–25.

Council of Chief State School Officers. 1996. *Interstate School Leaders Licensure Consortium (ISLLC) Standards for School Leaders*. Washington, DC: Author. www.ccsso.org

Cuban, Larry. 1988. *The Managerial Imperative and the Practice of Leadership in Schools*. Albany: The State University of New York Press.

Deal, Terrence E., and Kent D. Peterson. 1994. *The Leadership Paradox: Balancing Logic and Artistry in Schools*. San Francisco: Jossey-Bass.

DiPaola, Michael, and Megan Tschannen-Moran. 2003. "The Principalship at a Crossroads: A Study of the Conditions and Concerns of Principals." *NASSP Bulletin* 87, 634 (March): 43–66.

Doud, James L., and Edward P. Keller. 1998. *The K-8 Principal in 1998*. Alexandria, VA: National Association of Elementary School Principals.

Educational Research Service. 1998. *Is There a Shortage of Qualified Candidates for Openings in the Principalship? An Exploratory Study*. Arlington, VA: National Association of Elementary School Principals and National Association of Secondary School Principals.

Educational Research Service. 2000. *The Principal, Keystone of a High-Achieving School: Attracting and Keeping the Leaders We Need*. Arlington, VA: National Association of Elementary School Principals and National Association of Secondary School Principals.

Elmore, Richard F. 2000. *Building a New Structure for School Leadership*. Washington, DC: The Albert Shanker Institute. 40 pages. www.shankerinstitute.org/education.html

Farkas, Steve, Jean Johnson, Ann Duffett, and Tony Foleno, with Patrick Foley. 2001. *Trying to Stay Ahead of the Game: Superintendents and Principals Talk About School Leadership*. New York: Public Agenda.

Feistritzer, C. Emily. 2003. *School Administrator Certification in the United States, State-by-State 2003*. Washington, DC: National Center for Educational Information.

Gates, Susan M., and others. 2003. *Who Is Leading Our Schools? An Overview of School Administrators and Their Careers*. Santa Monica, CA: RAND.

Goodwin, Rebecca H., Michael L. Cunningham, and Ronald Childress. 2003. "The Changing Role of the Secondary Principal." *NASSP Bulletin* 87, 634: 26–42.

Hall, Robert F., and Max E. Pierson. 2002. "Supply, Demand, Push Salaries Higher." *Illinois School Board Journal* (January/February).

Hallinger, Philip, and Kamontip Snidvongs. 2005. *Adding Value to School Leadership and Management: A Review of Trends in the Development of Managers in the Education and Business Sectors*. Nottingham, England: National College for School Leadership.

Hess, Frederick. 2003. *A License to Lead? A New Leadership Agenda for America's Schools*. Washington, DC: Progressive Policy Institute.

Hoyle, John. 2001. "I've Got Standards, You've Got Standards, All God's Children Got Standards." *AASA Professor* 24, 2: 27–32.

Hurley, J. Casey. 2001. "The Principalship: Less May Be More." *Education Week* 20 (May 23).

Institute for Educational Leadership. 2000. *Leadership for Student Learning: Reinventing the Principalship.* Washington, DC: Author.

Lashway, Larry. 2003. *Leaders for America's Schools: Training, Recruiting, & Selecting Principals for Success.* Eugene, OR: ERIC Clearinghouse on Educational Management, Electronic Edition, 2003.

Leithwood, Kenneth, and Carolyn Riehl. 2003. *What Do We Already Know About Successful School Leadership?* Washington, DC: American Educational Research Association.

Leithwood, Kenneth, and Daniel Duke. 1999. "A Century's Quest to Understand School Leadership." In *Handbook of Research on Educational Administration*, 2nd ed., edited by Joseph Murphy and Karen Seashore Louis. 45–72. San Francisco: Jossey-Bass.

Leithwood, Kenneth, and Doris Jantzi. 1999. "Transformational Leadership Effects: A Replication." *School Effectiveness and School Improvement* 10, 4: 451–79.

Leithwood, Kenneth, and others. 2004. *How Leadership Influences Student Learning.* Minneapolis, MN: Center for Applied Research and Educational Improvement and the Ontario Institute for Studies in Education.

Levine, Arthur. 2005. *Educating School Leaders.* New York: The Education Schools Project.

McEwan, Elaine K. 2003. *10 Traits of Highly Effective Principals.* Thousand Oaks, CA: Corwin Press.

MetLife. 2004. *The MetLife Survey of the American Teacher: An Examination of School Leadership.* New York: Author.

Murphy, Joseph. 2002. "Reculturing the Profession of Educational Leadership: New Blueprints." *Educational Administration Quarterly* 38, 2: 171–91.

———. 2003. "Reculturing Educational Leadership: The ISLLC Standards Ten Years Out." Washington, DC: National Policy Board for Educational Administration. www.npbea .org/Resources/catalog.html

Murphy, Joseph, and Amanda Datnow. 2003. "Leadership Lessons From Comprehensive School Reform Designs." In *Leadership Lessons From Comprehensive School Reforms*, edited by Joseph Murphy and Amanda Datnow. 263–78. Thousand Oaks, CA: Corwin Press.

National Association of Elementary School Principals. 2001. *Leading Learning Communities: Standards for What Principals Should Know and Be Able to Do.* Alexandria, VA: Author.

National Association of Secondary School Principals. 2001. *Priorities and Barriers in High School Leadership: A Survey of Principals.* Reston, VA: Author.

National Association of State Boards of Education. 1999. *Principals of Change: What Principals Need to Lead Schools to Excellence.* Alexandria, VA: Author.

Portin, Bradley, Paul Schneider, Michael DeArmond, and Lauren Gundlach. 2003. *Making Sense of Leading Schools: A Study of the School Principalship.* Seattle, WA: Center on Reinventing Public Education.

Pounder, Diana G., and Randall J. Merrill. 2001. "Job Desirability of the High School Principalship: A Job Choice Theory Perspective." *Educational Administration Quarterly* 37, 1: 27–57.

Prince, Cynthia. 2002. *The Challenge of Attracting Good Teachers and Principals to Struggling Schools.* Arlington, VA: American Association of School Administrators.

Reyes, Pedro, Lonnie H. Wagstaff, and Lance D. Fusarelli. 1999. "Delta Forces: The Changing Fabric of American Society and Education." In *The Handbook of Research on Educational Administration*, 2nd ed., edited by Joseph Murphy and Karen Seashore Louis. 183–202. San Francisco: Jossey-Bass.

Ricciardi, Diane, and Joseph Petrosko. 2001. "A Role Paradox for New Administrators: Challenges of Daily Practice and Demands for Reform." *Planning and Changing* 32, 1/2: 24–45.

Roza, Marguerite, Mary Beth Celio, James Harvey, and Susan Wishon. 2003. *A Matter of Definition: Is There Truly a Shortage of School Principals?* Seattle, WA: Center on Reinventing Public Education.

Sergiovanni, Thomas J. 2000. *The Lifeworld of Leadership: Creating Culture, Community, and Personal Meaning in Our Schools.* San Francisco: Jossey-Bass.

Sheldon, Timothy D., and Lee W. Munnich Jr. 1999. *Administrative Autumn: A Study of Minnesota's Aging Educational Leaders and the Difficulty in Finding Their Replacements.* Minneapolis, MN: Hubert H. Humphrey Institute of Public Affairs.

Sherer, Jennifer Z. 2004. "Distributed Leadership Practice: The Subject Matters." Preliminary draft prepared for the symposium "Recent Research in Distributed Leadership" at the annual meeting of the American Educational Research Association, San Diego, CA, April 15. http://www.sesp.northwestern.edu/ docs/distpracticesubjectSHE.pdf

Southern Regional Education Board. 2002. *Are SREB States Making Progress? Tapping, Preparing, and Licensing School Leaders Who Can Influence Student Achievement.* Atlanta, GA: Author. www.sreb.org

Spillane, James P., Richard Halverson, and John B. Diamond. 2000. *Toward a Theory of Leadership Practice: A Distributed Perspective.* Evanston, IL: Institute for Policy Research.

Stein, Mary Kay, and Barbara S. Nelson. 2003. "Leadership Content Knowledge." *Educational Evaluation and Policy Analysis* 25, 4: 423–48.

Thomas B. Fordham Foundation. 2003. *Better Leaders for America's Schools: A Manifesto.* Washington, DC: Author.

Tirozzi, Gerald N. 2001. "The Artistry of Leadership: The Evolving Role of the Secondary School Principal." *Phi Delta Kappan* 82, 6: 434–39.

Triant, Bill. 2003. *Autonomy and Innovation: How Do Massachusetts Charter School Principals Use Their Freedom?* Washington, DC: Thomas B. Fordham Foundation.

Waters, Tim, and Sally Grubb. 2004. *Leading Schools: Distinguishing the Essential From the Important.* Aurora, CO: Mid-Continent Research for Education and Learning.

Whitaker, Kathryn. 2001. "Where Are the Principal Candidates? Perceptions of Superintendents." *NASSP Bulletin* 85, 625: 82–92.

Williams, Alicia R., Nancy Protheroe, and Michael C. Parks. 2003. *Salaries and Wages Paid Professional and Support Personnel in Public Schools, 2002–2003.* Arlington, VA: Educational Research Service.

Winter, Paul A., James S. Rinehart, and Marco A. Munoz. 2001. "Principal Certified Personnel: Do They Want the Job?" Paper presented at the annual meeting of the University Council for Educational Administration, Cincinnati, OH, November 2–4.

Wolcott, Harry. 1973. *The Man in the Principal's Office: An Ethnography.* Austin, TX: Holt, Rinehart and Winston.

Young, Michelle D., and others. 2005. "An Educative Look at 'Educating School Leaders.'" Paper prepared for the University Council for Educational Administration, the National Council of Professors of Educational Administration, and the American Educational Research Association. *School Leadership News* (AERA Division A Newsletter), 11 Addendum.

Zeitoun, Peter, and Rose Mary Newton. 2002. "Strategies for Reinventing the Principalship." Unpublished paper.

2. THE EFFECTS OF LEADERSHIP

Cotton, Kathleen. 2003. *Principals and Student Achievement: What the Research Says.* Alexandria, VA: Association for Supervision and Curriculum Development.

Fouts, Jeffrey T. 2003. *A Decade of Reform: A Summary of Research Findings on Classroom, School, and District Effectiveness in Washington State.* Seattle: Washington School Research Center.

Goldring, Ellen, and William Greenfield. 2002. "Understanding the Evolving Concept of Leadership in Education: Roles, Expectations, and Dilemmas." In *The Educational Leadership Challenge:*

Redefining Leadership for the 21st Century, One Hundred-First Yearbook of the National Society for the Study of Education. Part I, edited by Joseph Murphy. 1–19. Chicago: National Society for the Study of Education.

Hallinger, Philip, and Ronald H. Heck. 1998. "Exploring the Principal's Contribution to School Effectiveness: 1980–1995." *School Effectiveness and School Improvement* 9, 2: 157–91.

Heck, Ronald H., and Philip Hallinger. 1998. "Next Generation Methods for the Study of Leadership and School Improvement." In *Handbook of Research on Educational Administration,* 2nd ed., edited by Joseph Murphy and Karen Seashore Louis. 141–62. San Francisco: Jossey-Bass.

Leithwood, Kenneth A., and Carolyn Riehl. 2003. *What Do We Already Know About Successful School Leadership?* Paper prepared for the American Educational Research Association Division A Task Force on Developing Research in Educational Leadership. Philadelphia: Laboratory for Student Success, Temple University.

Leithwood, Kenneth A., Karen Seashore Louis, Stephen Anderson, and Kyla Wahlstrom. 2004. *How Leadership Influences Student Learning.* Minneapolis, MN, and Toronto, Canada: Center for Applied Research and Educational Improvement, and Ontario Institute for Studies in Education, September. www.wallacefoundation.org

Scheurich, James J. 1998. "Highly Successful and Loving Public Elementary Schools Populated Mainly by Low-SES Children of Color: Core Beliefs and Cultural Characteristics." *Urban Education* 33, 4: 451–91.

Waters, Tim, Robert J. Marzano, and Brian McNulty. 2003. *Balanced Leadership: What 30 Years of Research Tells Us About the Effects of Leadership on Student Achievement.* Aurora, CO: Mid-Continent Research for Education and Learning.

3. PORTRAIT OF A LEADER

Ahnee-Benham, Maenette K. P., and L. A. Napier. 2001. "An Alternative Perspective of Educational Leadership for Change: Reflections on Native/Indigenous Ways of Knowing." In *Second International Handbook of Educational Leadership and Administration,* edited by Kenneth Leithwood and Philip Hallinger. Dordrecht, The Netherlands: Kluwer Academic Publishers.

Allison, Derek J., and Patricia A. Allison. 1993. "Trees and Forests: Details, Abstraction, and Experience in Problem Solving." In *Cognitive Perspectives on Educational Leadership,* edited by Philip Hallinger, Kenneth Leithwood, and Joseph Murphy. 130–45. New York: Teachers College Press.

Armstrong, Colleen. 1992. "How's Your Story Arsenal?" *Principal* 71, 3: 40–41.

Autry, James A. 1994. *Life and Work: A Manager's Search for Meaning.* New York: William Morrow.

Bass, Bernard M. 1990. *Bass & Stogdill's Handbook of Leadership: Theory, Research, and Managerial Applications.* 3rd ed. New York: The Free Press.

Bennis, Warren. 1984. "Transformative Power and Leadership." In *Leadership and Organizational Culture: New Perspectives on Administrative Theory and Practice,* edited by Thomas J. Sergiovanni and John E. Corbally. 64–71. Urbana: University of Illinois Press.

———. 2003. *On Becoming a Leader.* New York: Basic Books.

Bennis, Warren, and Burt Nanus. 1985. *Leaders: The Strategies for Taking Charge.* New York: Harper & Row.

Blase, Joseph, and Jo Roberts Blase. 2000. *Empowering Teachers: What Successful Principals Do.* 2nd ed. Thousand Oaks, CA: Corwin Press.

———. 2003. *Breaking the Silence: Overcoming the Problem of Principal Mistreatment of Teachers.* Thousand Oaks, CA: Corwin Press.

Blumberg, Arthur. 1989. *School Administration as a Craft: Foundations of Practice.* Boston: Allyn & Bacon.

Blumberg, Arthur, and William Greenfield. 1986. *The Effective Principal: Perspectives on School Leadership*. 2nd ed. Newton, MA: Allyn & Bacon.

Brown, Robert J., and Jeffrey R. Cornwall. 2000. *The Entrepreneurial Educator*. Lanham, MD: Scarecrow Press.

Burns, James MacGregor. 1978. *Leadership*. New York: HarperCollins.

———. 2003. *Transforming Leadership*. New York: Atlantic Monthly Press.

Carlyle, Thomas. *On Heroes and Hero Worship and the Heroic in History*. www.gutenberg.org/etext/1091

Clark, Kenneth E., and Miriam B. Clark, eds. 1990. *Measures of Leadership*. West Orange, NJ: Leadership Library of America.

Collins, Jim. 2001. *Good to Great: Why Some Companies Make the Leap . . . and Others Don't*. New York: HarperCollins.

Dillard, Cynthia B. 1995. "Leading With Her Life: An African American Feminist (Re)Interpretation of Leadership at an Urban High School." *Educational Administration Quarterly* 31, 4: 539–63.

Duke, Daniel L. 1986. "The Aesthetics of Leadership." *Educational Administration Quarterly* 22, 1: 7–27.

Eagly, Alice H., Stephen J. Karau, and Blair T. Johnson. 1992. "Gender and Leadership Style Among School Principals: A Meta-Analysis." *Educational Administration Quarterly* 28, 1: 76–102.

Evans, Robert. 1996. *The Human Side of School Change: Reform, Resistance, and the Real-Life Problems of Innovation*. San Francisco: Jossey-Bass.

Feistritzer, C. Emily. 1986. *Profile of Teachers in the U.S.* Washington, DC: National Center for Education Information.

Follett, Mary Parker. 1995. *Mary Parker Follett—Prophet of Management*, edited by Pauline Graham. Boston: Harvard Business School Press.

Foster, William. 1985. "Leadership as a Critical Practice." *The Australian Administrator* 6, 2.

Funk, Carole, Barbara Polnick, Anita Pancake, and Gwen Schroth. 2004. "Profiles of Outstanding Female and Male Superintendents: A Comparative Study of Leadership Dimensions." In *Educational Leadership: Knowing the Way, Showing the Way, Going the Way*, edited by Carolyn S. Carr and Connie L. Fulmer. 331–45. Lanham, MD: Scarecrow Education.

Gardner, Howard. 1995. *Leading Minds: An Anatomy of Leadership*. New York: Basic Books.

Goble, Frank. 1970. *The Third Force: The Psychology of Abraham Maslow*. New York: Grossman.

Goleman, Daniel, Richard Boyatzis, and Annie McKee. 2003. *Primal Leadership: Learning to Lead With Emotional Intelligence*. Boston: Harvard Business School Press.

Gough, Harrison G. 1990. "Testing for Leadership With the California Psychological Inventory." In *Measures of Leadership*, edited by Kenneth Clark and Miriam Clark. 355–79. West Orange, NJ: Leadership Library of America.

Heifetz, Ronald A., and Marty Linsky. 2002. *Leadership on the Line: Staying Alive Through the Dangers of Leading*. Boston: Harvard Business School Press.

Hord, Shirley M., and Gene E. Hall. 1984. "Principals Use Research-Based Techniques for Facilitating School Effectiveness." Paper presented at annual meeting of the American Educational Research Association, New Orleans, LA.

Hughes, Richard L., Robert C. Ginnett, and Gordon J. Curphy. 1993. *Leadership: Enhancing the Lessons of Experience*. Homewood, IL: Irwin.

Ingersoll, Richard M. 2003. *Who Controls Teachers' Work? Power and Accountability in America's Schools*. Cambridge, MA: Harvard University Press.

Jaques, Elliott. 1989. *Requisite Organization: The CEO's Guide to Creative Structure and Leadership*. Arlington, VA: Cason Hall.

Kaplan, Robert E. 1991. *The Expansive Executive*. 2nd ed. Greensboro, NC: Center for Creative Leadership.

Kouzes, James M., and Barry Z. Posner. 1987. *The Leadership Challenge: How to Get Extraordinary Things Done in Organizations.* San Francisco: Jossey-Bass.

———. 1993. *Credibility: How Leaders Gain and Lose It. Why People Demand It.* San Francisco: Jossey-Bass.

Krug, Samuel E. 1992. "Instructional Leadership: A Constructivist Perspective." *Educational Administration Quarterly* 28, 3: 430–43.

Lortie, Dan C. 1975. *Schoolteacher: A Sociological Study.* Chicago: University of Chicago Press.

Marshall, Catherine. 1992. "School Administrators' Values: A Focus on Atypicals." *Educational Administration Quarterly* 28, 3: 368–86.

McCaulley, Mary H. 1990. "The Myers-Briggs Type Indicator and Leadership." In *Measures of Leadership,* edited by Kenneth Clark and Miriam Clark. 381–418. West Orange, NJ: Leadership Library of America.

Meadows, B. J. 1992. "Nurturing Cooperation and Responsibility in a School Community." *Phi Delta Kappan* 73, 6: 480–81.

Mendez-Morse, Sylvia. 1992. *Leadership Characteristics That Facilitate School Change.* Austin, TX: Southwest Educational Development Laboratory.

Morris, Edmund. 1979. *The Rise of Theodore Roosevelt.* New York: Coward, McCann and Geoghegan.

Moxley, Russ S. 1999. *Leadership and Spirit: Breathing New Vitality and Energy Into Individuals and Organizations.* San Francisco: Jossey-Bass.

Northouse, Peter G. 2001. *Leadership: Theory and Practice.* 2nd ed. Thousand Oaks, CA: Sage Publications.

Palus, Charles J., William Nasby, and Randolph Easton. 1991. *Understanding Executive Performance: Life-Story Perspective. An Exploration of the Foundations of Leadership in Terms of Personal Identity.* Greensboro, NC: Center for Creative Leadership.

Portin, Bradley, with Paul Schneider, Michael DeArmond, and Lauren Gundlach. 2003. *Making Sense of Leading Schools: A Study of the School Principalship.* Seattle, WA: Center on Reinventing Public Education.

Prestine, Nona A. 1993. "Extending the Essential Schools Metaphor: Principal as Enabler." *Journal of School Leadership* 3, 4: 356–79.

Richardson, Michael D., and others. 1992. "Teacher Perception of Principal Behaviors: A Research Study." Paper presented at the annual meeting of the Mid-South Educational Research Association, Knoxville, TN, November.

Sashkin, Marshall, and Molly G. Sashkin. 2003. *Leadership That Matters: The Critical Factors for Making a Difference in People's Lives and Organizations' Success.* San Francisco: Berrett-Koehler.

Sergiovanni, Thomas. 1992. *Moral Leadership: Getting to the Heart of School Improvement.* San Francisco: Jossey-Bass.

Sternberg, Robert J., and Elena L. Grigorenko. 2001. *Practical Intelligence and the Principal.* Philadelphia: Center for Research in Human Development and Education.

Wright, Peter L., and David S. Taylor. 1994. *Improving Leadership Performance: Interpersonal Skills for Effective Leadership.* 2nd ed. London: Prentice Hall.

4. LEADERSHIP STYLES AND STRATEGIES

Bass, Bernard M. 1990. *Bass & Stogdill's Handbook of Leadership: Theory, Research, and Managerial Applications.* 3rd ed. New York: The Free Press.

Bass, Bernard M., and Bruce J. Avolio. 1994. "Introduction." In *Improving Organizational Effectiveness Through Transformational Leadership,* edited by Bernard M. Bass and Bruce J. Avolio. 1–9. Thousand Oaks, CA: Sage Publications.

Beck, Lynn G., and Joseph Murphy. 1993. *Understanding the Principalship: Metaphorical Themes 1920s–1990s*. New York: Teachers College Press.

Benfari, Robert. 1991. *Understanding Your Management Style: Beyond the Myers-Briggs Type Indicators*. Lexington, MA: Lexington Books.

Blake, Robert R., and Jane S. Mouton. 1985. *The Managerial Grid III: The Key to Leadership Excellence*. Houston: Gulf Publishing Company.

Blase, Joseph, Jo Blase, Gary L. Anderson, and Sherry Dungan. 1995. *Democratic Principals in Action: Eight Pioneers*. Thousand Oaks, CA: Corwin Press.

Blase, Joseph, and Jo Roberts Blase. 2000. *Empowering Teachers: What Successful Principals Do*. 2nd ed. Thousand Oaks, CA: Corwin Press.

Blumberg, Arthur. 1989. *School Administration as a Craft: Foundations of Practice*. Boston: Allyn & Bacon.

Bolman, Lee, and Terry Deal. 1992. "Reframing Leadership: The Effects of Leaders' Images of Leadership." In *Impact of Leadership,* edited by Kenneth E. Clark, Miriam B. Clark, and David P. Campbell. 269–80. Greensboro, NC: Center for Creative Leadership.

———. 1997. *Reframing Organizations: Artistry, Choice and Leadership*. 2nd ed. San Francisco: Jossey-Bass.

Bridges, Edwin. 1992. *The Incompetent Teacher: Managerial Responses*. Washington, DC: Falmer Press.

Burns, James MacGregor. 1978. *Leadership*. New York: Harper and Row.

Callahan, Raymond E. 1962. *Education and the Cult of Efficiency*. Chicago: University of Chicago Press.

Conger, Jay A. 1989. *The Charismatic Leader: Behind the Mystique of Exceptional Leadership*. San Francisco: Jossey-Bass.

Conley, David T., and Paul Goldman. 1994. *Facilitative Leadership: How Principals Lead Without Dominating*. OSSC Bulletin Series. Eugene: Oregon School Study Council.

Deal, Terrence E., and Kent D. Peterson. 1994. *The Leadership Paradox: Balancing Logic and Artistry in Schools*. San Francisco: Jossey-Bass.

De Pree, Max. 1989. *Leadership Is an Art*. New York: Doubleday.

Dunlap, Diane, and Paul Goldman. 1990. "Power as a System of Authority vs. Power as a System of Facilitation." Unpublished paper.

Farkas, Steve, Jean Johnson, Ann Duffett, and Tony Foleno, with Patrick Foley. 2001. *Trying to Stay Ahead of the Game: Superintendents and Principals Talk About School Leadership*. New York: Public Agenda.

Fiedler, Fred E. 1967. *A Theory of Leadership Effectiveness*. New York: McGraw-Hill Book Company.

Fiedler, Fred E., Martin M. Chemers, and Linda Mahar. 1976. *Improving Leadership Effectiveness: The Leader Match Concept*. New York: John Wiley and Sons.

Hall, Gene, William L. Rutherford, Shirley M. Hord, and Leslie L. Huling. 1984. "Effects of Three Principal Styles on School Improvement." *Educational Leadership* 41, 5: 22–29.

Hanson, E. Mark. 2003. *Educational Administration and Organizational Behavior*. 5th ed. Boston: Allyn & Bacon.

Heifetz, Ronald A. 1994. *Leadership Without Easy Answers*. Cambridge, MA: Belknap Press.

Hersey, Paul, and Kenneth Blanchard. 1993. *Management of Organizational Behavior: Utilizing Human Resources*. 6th ed. Englewood Cliffs, NJ: Prentice Hall.

Hord, Shirley M. 1992. *Facilitative Leadership: The Imperative for Change*. Austin, TX: Southwest Educational Development Laboratory.

Ingersoll, Richard M. 2003. *Who Controls Teachers' Work? Power and Accountability in America's Schools*. Cambridge, MA: Harvard University Press.

Kirby, Peggy C., Louis V. Paradise, and Margaret I. King. 1992. "Extraordinary Leaders in Education: Understanding Transformational Leadership." *Journal of Educational Research* 85, 5: 303–11.

Leithwood, Kenneth. 1993. "Contributions of Transformational Leadership to School Restructuring." Paper presented at the convention of the University Council for Educational Administration, Houston, TX, October.

Leithwood, Kenneth, and Carolyn Riehl. 2003. *What Do We Already Know About Successful School Leadership?* Washington, DC: American Educational Research Association.

Leithwood, Kenneth, and Daniel L. Duke. 1999. "A Century's Quest to Understand School Leadership." In *Handbook of Research on Educational Administration,* 2nd ed., edited by Joseph Murphy and Karen Seashore Louis. 45–72. San Francisco: Jossey-Bass.

Liontos, Lynn Balster. 1993. *Transformational Leadership: Profile of a High School Principal.* Eugene: Oregon School Study Council, University of Oregon.

Locke, Edwin A. 2003. "Leadership: Starting at the Top." In *Shared Leadership: Reframing the Hows and Whys of Leadership,* edited by Craig L. Pearce and Jay A. Conger. 271–84. Thousand Oaks, CA: Sage Publications.

Lortie, Dan. 1975. *Schoolteacher: A Sociological Study.* Chicago: University of Chicago Press.

McMurry, Robert N. 1958. "The Case for Benevolent Autocracy." *Harvard Business Review* 36, 1: 82–90.

McNeil, Linda. 1986. *Contradictions of Control: School Structure and School Knowledge.* New York: Routledge and Kegan Paul.

Murphy, Joseph, and Amanda Datnow. 2003. "Leadership Lessons from Comprehensive School Reform Designs." In *Leadership Lessons From Comprehensive School Reforms,* edited by Joseph Murphy and Amanda Datnow. 263–78. Thousand Oaks, CA: Corwin Press.

Myers, Isabel Briggs, and Peter B. Myers. 1980. *Gifts Differing.* Palo Alto, CA: Consulting Psychologists Press.

Northouse, Peter G. 2001. *Leadership: Theory and Practice.* 2nd ed. Thousand Oaks, CA: Sage Publications.

Patterson, Jerry L., Stewart C. Purkey, and Jackson V. Parker. 1986. *Productive School Systems for a Nonrational World.* Alexandria, VA: Association for Supervision and Curriculum Development.

Pittenger, David J. 1993. "The Utility of the Myers-Briggs Type Indicator." *Review of Educational Research* 63, 4: 467–88.

Prestine, Nona. 1993. "Extending the Essential Schools' Metaphor: Principal as Enabler." *Journal of School Leadership* 3: 356–79.

Roberts, Nancy. 1985. "Transforming Leadership: A Process of Collective Action." *Human Relations* 38, 11: 1023–46.

Sashkin, Marshall, and Molly G. Sashkin. 2003. *Leadership That Matters: The Critical Factors for Making a Difference in People's Lives and Organizations' Success.* San Francisco: Berrett-Koehler.

Sergiovanni, Thomas J. 1992. *Moral Leadership: Getting to the Heart of School Improvement.* San Francisco: Jossey-Bass.

———. 1994. *Building Community in Schools.* San Francisco: Jossey-Bass.

Shedd, Joseph B., and Samuel Bacharach. 1991. *Tangled Hierarchies: Teachers as Professionals and the Management of Schools.* San Francisco: Jossey-Bass.

Stoll, Louise, Raymond Bolam, and Pat Collarbone. 2002. "Leading for Change: Building Capacity for Change." In *The Second International Handbook of Educational Leadership and Administration,* edited by Kenneth Leithwood and Philip Hallinger. 41–73. Dordrecht, The Netherlands: Kluwer Academic Publishers.

Tannenbaum, Robert, and Warren H. Schmidt. 1958. "How to Choose a Leadership Pattern." *Harvard Business Review* 36, 2: 95–101.

Tyack, David, and Elizabeth Hansot. 1982. *Managers of Virtue: Public School Leadership in America, 1820–1980.* New York: Basic Books.

Vroom, Victor H., and Arthur G. Jago. 1988. *The New Leadership: Managing Participation in Organizations.* Englewood Cliffs, NJ: Prentice Hall.

Waters, Tim, Robert J. Marzano, and Brian McNulty. 2003. *Balanced Leadership: What 30 Years of Research Tells Us About the Effects of Leadership on Student Achievement.* Aurora, CO: Mid-Continent Research for Education and Learning.

Weber, Max. 1958. *From Max Weber: Essays in Sociology.* Translated, edited, and with an introduction by H. H. Gerth and C. Wright Mills. New York: Oxford University Press.

5. DEVELOPING SCHOOL LEADERS

Ackerman, Richard, Laura Ventimiglia, and Melissa Juchniewicz. 2002. "The Meaning of Mentoring: Notes of a Context for Learning." In *Second International Handbook of Educational Leadership and Administration*, edited by Kenneth Leithwood and Philip Hallinger. 1133–161. Dordrecht, The Netherlands: Kluwer Academic Publishers.

Aiken, Judith. 2002. "The Socialization of New Principals: Another Perspective on Principal Retention." *Educational Leadership Review* 3, 1: 32–40. www.ncpea.net/

Anderson, Mark. 1989. "Inducting Principals: A Study of the Job-Specific Information and Assistance Needs of Beginning Principals in Oregon and Washington." Unpublished doctoral dissertation. Eugene: University of Oregon. *Dissertation Abstracts International* 50: 3421A.

Baltzell, Catherine, and Robert A. Dentler. 1983. *Selecting American School Principals: A Sourcebook for Educators.* Cambridge, MA: Abt Associates.

Barnett, Bruce G., Margaret R. Basom, Diane M. Yerkes, and Cynthia J. Norris. 2000. "Cohorts in Educational Leadership Programs: Benefits, Difficulties, and the Potential for Developing School Leaders." *Educational Administration Quarterly* 36, 2: 255–82.

Barth, Roland S. 2001. *Learning by Heart.* San Francisco: Jossey-Bass.

Bloom, Gary. 1999. "One-on-One Support for New Principals: Sink or Swim No More." *Thrust for Educational Leadership* 29, 1: 14–17. www.acsa.org.

Blumberg, Arthur. 1989. *School Administration as a Craft: Foundations of Practice.* Boston: Allyn & Bacon.

Bridges, Edwin M., and Philip Hallinger. 1995. *Implementing Problem-Based Learning in Leadership Development.* Eugene: ERIC Clearinghouse on Educational Management, University of Oregon.

Browne-Ferrigno, Tricia. 2003. "Becoming a Principal: Role Conception, Initial Socialization, Role-Identity Transformation, Purposeful Engagement." *Educational Administration Quarterly* 39, 4: 468–503.

Browne-Ferrigno, Tricia, and Rodney Muth. 2004. "Leadership Mentoring in Clinical Practice: Role Socialization, Professional Development, and Capacity Building." *Educational Administration Quarterly* 40, 4: 468–94.

Capasso, Ronald L., and John C. Daresh. 2001. *The School Administrator Internship Handbook.* Thousand Oaks, CA: Corwin Press.

Chan, T. C., Linda Webb, and Charles Bowen. 2003. "Are Assistant Principals Prepared for Principalship? How DO Assistant Principals Perceive?" Paper presented at the Annual Meeting of the Sino-American Education Consortium, Kennesaw, GA, October 10–11.

Chappelow, Craig. 1998. "360-Degree Feedback." In *The Center for Creative Leadership Handbook of Leadership Development*, edited by Cynthia McCauley and others. 58–84. Greensboro, NC: Center for Creative Leadership.

Clark, Kenneth E., and Miriam B. Clark. 1996. *Choosing to Lead*. 2nd ed. Greensboro, NC: Center for Creative Leadership.

Creighton, Theodore, and Gary Jones. 2001. "Selection or Self-Selection? How Rigorous Are Our Selection Criteria for Education Administration Programs?" Paper presented at the 2001 Conference of the National Council of Professors of Educational Administration, Houston, TX, August 7–11.

Crow, Gary M., and L. Joseph Matthews. 1998. *Finding One's Way: How Mentoring Can Lead to Dynamic Leadership*. Thousand Oaks, CA: Corwin Press.

Daresh, John. 2001. "Building Leaders for the Future: The Socorro Independent School District Assistant Principals Academy." Paper presented at the Annual Meeting of the National Council of Professors of Educational Administration, Houston, TX, August 7–11.

———. 2002. *What It Means to Be a Principal: Your Guide to Leadership*. Thousand Oaks, CA: Corwin Press.

———. 2004. "Mentoring School Leaders: Professional Promise or Predictable Problems?" *Educational Administration Quarterly* 40, 4: 495–517.

Dempster, Neil. 2001. *The Professional Development of School Principals: A Fine Balance*. Brisbane, Australia: Centre for Leadership & Management, Griffith University.

Doud, James L., and Edward P. Keller. 1998. *The K-8 Principal in 1998*. Alexandria, VA: National Association of Elementary School Principals.

Duke, Daniel L. 1987. *School Leadership and Instructional Improvement*. New York: Random House.

Dukess, Laura F. 2001. *Meeting the Leadership Challenge: Designing Effective Principal Mentor Programs: The Experiences of Six New York City Community School Districts*. New York: New Visions for Public Schools.

Educational Testing Service. 2003. *Guide to the Use of Scores: Graduate Record Examinations 2003–2004*. Princeton, NJ: Author. www.ets.org

Ehrich, Lisa C., Brian Hansford, and Lee Tennent. 2004. "Formal Mentoring Programs in Education and Other Professions: A Review of the Literature." *Educational Administration Quarterly* 40, 4: 518–40.

Elmore, Richard F., and Deanna Burney. 2000. *Leadership and Learning: Principal Recruitment, Induction and Instructional Leadership in Community School District #2, New York City*. Pittsburgh, PA: Learning Research and Development Center, University of Pittsburgh. www.lrdc.pitt.edu/hplc

Erikson, Erik H. 1963. *Childhood and Society*. 2nd ed. New York: W.W. Norton and Company.

Farkas, Steve, Jean Johnson, Ann Duffett, and Tony Foleno, with Patrick Foley. 2001. *Trying to Stay Ahead of the Game: Superintendents and Principals Talk About School Leadership*. New York: Public Agenda.

Feistritzer, C. Emily. 2003. *Certification of Principals and Superintendents in the U.S.* Washington, DC: National Center for Education Information. www.ncei.com

Fink, Elaine, and Lauren B. Resnick. 1999. *Developing Principals as Instructional Leaders*. Pittsburgh, PA: High Performance Learning Communities Project, Learning Research and Development Center, University of Pittsburgh. www.lrdc.pitt.edu/hplc

Gardiner, Mary E., Ernestine Enomoto, and Margaret Grogan. 2000. *Coloring Outside the Lines: Mentoring Women Into School Leadership*. Albany: State University of New York Press.

Gronn, Peter, and Kathy Lacey. 2005. "Positioning Among Aspirant School Principals." *School Management and Leadership* 24, 4: 405–24.

Harburg, E. Y. 1965. *Rhymes for the Irreverent*. New York: Grossman.

Hart, Ann Weaver. 1993. "A Design Studio for Reflective Practice." In *Cognitive Perspectives on Educational Leadership,* edited by Philip Hallinger, Kenneth Leithwood, and Joseph Murphy. 213–30. New York: Teachers College Press.

Hartzell, Gary N., Richard C. Williams, and Kathleen T. Nelson. 1995. *New Voices in the Field: The Work Lives of First-Year Assistant Principals.* Thousand Oaks, CA: Corwin Press. ED 385 914.

Heifetz, Ronald A., and Marty Linsky. 2002. *Leadership on the Line: Staying Alive Through the Dangers of Leading.* Boston: Harvard Business School Press.

Kelley, Carolyn, and Kent D. Peterson. 2002. "The Work of Principals and Their Preparation: Addressing Critical Needs for the Twenty-First Century." In *The Principal Challenge: Leading and Managing Schools in an Era of Accountability*, edited by Marc S. Tucker and Judy B. Codding. 247–312. San Francisco: Jossey-Bass.

Killion, Joellen. 2002. "Online Learning in Educational Leadership: Promise or Peril." *The AASA Professor* 25, 2: 3–9.

Lashway, Larry. 1999. *Measuring Leadership: A Guide to Assessment for Development of School Executives.* Eugene: ERIC Clearinghouse on Educational Management, University of Oregon.

Lepsinger, Richard, and Antoinette D. Lucia. 1997. *The Art and Science of 360° Feedback.* San Francisco: Jossey-Bass.

Levine, Arthur. 2005. *Educating School Leaders.* New York: The Education Schools Project.

Marshall, Catherine, and Katherine L. Kasten. 1994. *The Administrative Career: A Casebook on Entry, Equity, and Endurance.* Thousand Oaks, CA: Corwin Press.

Matthews, L. Joseph, and Gary M. Crow. 2003. *Being and Becoming a Principal: Role Conceptions for Contemporary Principals and Assistant Principals.* Boston: Allyn & Bacon.

Milstein, Mike. 1993. "Learnings Across the Terrain." In *Changing the Way We Prepare Educational Leaders: The Danforth Experience,* edited by Mike Milstein and others. 178–218. Newbury Park, CA: Corwin Press.

Morford, Linda M. 2002. "Learning the Ropes or Being Hung: Organizational Socialization Influence on New Rural High School Principals." Paper presented at the Annual Meeting of the American Educational Research Association, New Orleans, LA, April 2.

Moxley, Russ S. 1999. *Leadership and Spirit: Breathing New Vitality and Energy Into Individuals and Organizations.* San Francisco: Jossey-Bass.

Murphy, Joseph. 1992. *The Landscape of Leadership Preparation: Reframing the Education of School Leaders.* Newbury Park, CA: Corwin Press.

National Association of Elementary School Principals. 2001. *Leading Learning Communities: Standards for What Principals Should Know and Be Able to Do.* Alexandria, VA: Author.

National Association of State Boards of Education. 1999. *Principals of Change: What Principals Need to Lead Schools to Excellence.* Alexandria, VA: Author.

Norris, Cynthia J., Bruce G. Barnett, Margaret R. Basom, and Diane M. Yerkes. 2002. *Developing Educational Leaders: A Working Model: The Learning Community in Action.* New York: Teachers College Press.

Osterman, Karen F., and Robert B. Kottkamp. 1993. *Reflective Practice for Educators: Improving Schooling Through Professional Development.* Thousand Oaks, CA: Corwin Press.

Palmer, Parker. 2000. *Let Your Life Speak: Listening for the Voice of Vocation.* San Francisco: Jossey-Bass.

Parkay, Forrest W., Gaylon G. Currie, and John W. Rhodes. 1992. "Professional Socialization: A Longitudinal Study of First-Time High School Principals." *Educational Administration Quarterly* 28, 1: 43–75.

Peterson, Kent D. 2001. "The Professional Development of Principals: Innovations and Opportunities." Paper commissioned for the first meeting of the National Commission for the Advancement of Educational Leadership Preparation, Racine, WI, September.

Portin, Bradley, Paul Schneider, Michael DeArmond, and Lauren Gundlach. 2003. *Making Sense of Leading Schools: A Study of the School Principalship.* Seattle, WA: Center on Reinventing Public Education.

Pounder, Diana G., and Randall J. Merrill. 2001. "Job Desirability of the High School Principalship: A Job Choice Theory Perspective." *Educational Administration Quarterly* 37, 1: 27–57.

Prestine, Nona A. 1993. "Apprenticeship in Problem-Solving: Extending the Cognitive Apprenticeship Model." In *Cognitive Perspectives on Educational Leadership,* edited by Philip Hallinger, Kenneth Leithwood, and Joseph Murphy. 192–212. New York: Teachers College Press.

Restine, L. Nan. 1997. "Experience, Meaning, and Principal Development." *Journal of Educational Administration* 35, 3: 253–67.

Schmidt, Michèle. 2002. "Emotions in Educational Administration: An Unorthodox Examination of Teachers' Career Decisions." In *Second International Handbook of Educational Leadership and Administration,* edited by Kenneth Leithwood and Philip Hallinger. 1103–131. Dordrecht, The Netherlands: Kluwer Academic Publishers.

Scribner, Jay Paredes, and Joe F. Donaldson. 2001. "The Dynamics of Group Learning in a Cohort: From Nonlearning to Transformative Learning." *Educational Administration Quarterly* 37, 5: 605–36.

Southern Regional Education Board. 2002. *Are SREB States Making Progress? Tapping, Preparing, and Licensing School Leaders Who Can Influence Student Achievement.* Atlanta, GA: Author. www.sreb.org

———. 2003. *Academies in the Lead: Redesigning Leadership Academies for Student Achievement.* Atlanta, GA: Author. www.sreb.org

———. 2005. *The Principal Internship: How Can We Get It Right?* Atlanta, GA: Author. www.sreb.org

Starratt, Robert J. 2004. *Ethical Leadership.* San Francisco: Jossey-Bass.

Sternberg, Robert J., and Elena L. Grigorenko. 2001. *Practical Intelligence and the Principal.* Philadelphia: Laboratory for Student Success.

U.S. Department of Education. 2004. *Innovative Pathways to School Leadership.* Washington, DC: Author.

Weller, L. David, and Sylvia J. Weller. 2001. *The Assistant Principal: Essentials for Effective School Leadership.* Thousand Oaks, CA: Corwin Press.

WestEd. 2003. *Moving Leadership Standards Into Everyday Work: Descriptions of Practice.* San Francisco: Author.

Williamson, Ronald, and Martha Hudson. 2001. "The Good, the Bad, the Ugly: Internships in Principal Preparation." Paper presented at the Annual Conference of the National Council of Professors of Educational Administration, Houston, TX, August.

Winter, Paul A., James S. Rinehart, and Marco A. Munoz. 2001. "Principal Certified Personnel: Do They Want the Job?" Paper presented at the annual meeting of the University Council for Educational Administration, Cincinnati, OH, November 2–4.

6. ETHICAL LEADERSHIP

Apple, Michael. 1979. *Ideology and Curriculum.* London: Routledge & Kegan Paul.

Barber, Benjamin R. 1997. "Public Schooling: Education for Democracy." In *The Public Purpose of Education and Schooling,* edited by John I. Goodlad and Timothy J. McMannon. 21–33. San Francisco: Jossey-Bass.

Barton, Paul E. 2003. *Parsing the Achievement Gap: Baselines for Tracking Progress.* Princeton, NJ: Educational Testing Service.

Beck, Lynn G. 1994. *Reclaiming Educational Administration as a Caring Profession.* New York: Teachers College Press.

Beck, Lynn G., and Joseph Murphy. 1994. *Ethics in Educational Leadership Programs: An Expanding Role.* Thousand Oaks, CA: Corwin Press.

Blase, Joseph, Jo Blase, Gary L. Anderson, and Sherry Dungan. 1995. *Democratic Principals in Action: Eight Pioneers.* Thousand Oaks, CA: Corwin Press.

Block, Peter. 1987. *The Empowered Manager: Positive Political Skills at Work.* San Francisco: Jossey-Bass.

———. 1993. *Stewardship: Choosing Service Over Self-Interest.* San Francisco: Berrett-Koehler.

Blumberg, Arthur, and William Greenfield. 1986. *The Effective Principal: Perspectives on School Leadership.* Boston: Allyn & Bacon.

Bridges, William. 1994. *JobShift: How to Prosper in a Workplace Without Jobs.* Reading, MA: Addison-Wesley.

Bull, Barry L., and Martha M. McCarthy. 1995. "Reflections of the Knowledge Base in Law and Ethics for Educational Leaders." *Educational Administration Quarterly* 31, 4: 613–31.

Callahan, Raymond E. 1962. *Education and the Cult of Efficiency.* Chicago: University of Chicago Press.

Campbell, Carol, Anne Gold, and Ingrid Lunt. 2003. "Articulating Leadership Values in Action: Conversations With School Leaders." *International Journal of Leadership in Education* 6, 3: 203–21.

Carey, Kevin. 2004. *The Funding Gap 2004: Many States Still Shortchange Low Income and Minority Students.* Washington, DC: The Education Trust.

Chaleff, Ira. 1995. *The Courageous Follower: Standing Up to and for Leaders.* San Francisco: Berrett-Koehler.

Colby, Anne, and William Damon. 1992. *Some Do Care: Contemporary Lives of Moral Commitment.* New York: The Free Press.

Council of Chief State School Officers. 1996. *Interstate School Leaders Licensure Consortium Standards for School Leaders.* Washington, DC: Author. www.ccsso.org

Counts, George S. 1932. *Dare the School Build a New Social Order?* New York: John Day Company.

Dempster, Neil, and Pat Mahony. 1998. "Ethical Challenges in School Leadership." In *Effective School Leadership: Responding to Change,* edited by John MacBeath. 125–39. London: Paul Chapman Publishing, Ltd.

Dewey, John. 1956. *The Child and the Curriculum and The School and Society.* Chicago: University of Chicago Press.

English, Fenwick. 2002. *About Standardization and the Policing Function of ELCC. NCATE: A Position Paper.* Huntsville, TX: National Council of Professors of Educational Administration.

Fauske, Janice R., and Bob L. Johnson Jr. 2003. "Principals Respond to the School Environment With Fluidity, Alignment, Vigilance, and Fear." In *Studies in Leading and Organizing Schools,* edited by Wayne Hoy and Cecil Miskel. 91–119. Greenwich, CT: Information Age Publishing.

Flintham, Alan. 2003. *Reservoirs of Hope: Spiritual and Moral Leadership in Headteachers.* Nottingham, England: National College for School Leadership.

Fullan, Michael. 2003. *The Moral Imperative of School Leadership.* Thousand Oaks, CA: Corwin Press.

Gallagher, Maggie. 1995. "Which Way for Education: Process or Performance?" *Seattle Times,* November 7.

Gardner, Howard. 1995. *Leading Minds: An Anatomy of Leadership.* New York: Basic Books.

Glickman, Carl D. 2003. *Holding Sacred Ground: Essays on Leadership, Courage, and Endurance in Our Schools.* San Francisco: Jossey-Bass.

Goodlad, John I., Corrine Mantle-Bromley, and Stephen John Goodlad. 2004. *Education for Everyone: Agenda for Education in a Democracy*. San Francisco: Jossey-Bass.

Greenfield, William D., Jr. 1991. "Rationale and Methods to Articulate Ethics and Administrator Training." Paper presented at the annual meeting of the American Educational Research Association, Chicago, April.

Greenleaf, Robert K. 1977. *Servant Leadership: A Journey Into the Nature of Legitimate Power and Greatness*. New York: Paulist Press.

Gutmann, Amy. 1999. *Democratic Education*. Princeton, NJ: Princeton University Press.

Hodgkinson, Christopher. 1991. *Educational Leadership: The Moral Art*. Albany: State University of New York Press.

Holt, John. 1964. *How Children Fail*. New York: Pitman.

Hostetler, Karl. 1986. "Ethics and Power: Implications for the Principal's Leadership." *NASSP Bulletin* 70, 488: 31–16.

Jackson, Philip W. 1986. *The Practice of Teaching*. New York: Teachers College Press.

Jeald, Craig D. 2002. *All Talk, No Action: Putting an End to Out-of-Field Teaching*. Washington, DC: The Education Trust.

Kanungo, Rabindra N., and Manuel Mendonca. 1996. *Ethical Dimensions of Leadership*. Thousand Oaks, CA: Sage Publications.

Kasten, Katherine L., and Carl R. Ashbaugh. 1988. "A Comparative Study of Values in Administrative Decision Making." *Journal of Research and Development in Education* 21, 3: 16–23.

Kidder, Rushworth M. 1995. *How Good People Make Tough Choices*. New York: William Morrow.

Kirby, Peggy C., Louis V. Pardise, and Russell Protti. 1990. "The Ethical Reasoning of School Administrator: The Principled Principal." Paper presented at the annual meeting of the American Educational Research Association, Boston, April.

Kouzes, James M., and Barry Z. Posner. 1993. *Credibility: How Leaders Gain and Lose It, Why People Demand It*. San Francisco: Jossey-Bass.

———. 1995. *The Leadership Challenge: How to Keep Getting Extraordinary Things Done in Organizations*. San Francisco: Jossey-Bass.

Kozol, Jonathan. 1991. *Savage Inequalities: Children in America*. New York: Crown Publishing.

MacIntyre, Alasdair. 1981. *After Virtue: A Study in Moral Theory*. Notre Dame, IN: Notre Dame Press.

Macmillan, C. J. B. 1993. "Ethics and Teacher Professionalization." In *Ethics for Professionals in Education: Perspectives for Preparation and Practice*, edited by Kenneth Strike and P. Lance Ternasky. 189–201. New York: Teachers College Press.

Marshall, Catherine, and Michael Ward. 2004. "'Yes, but…': Education Leaders Discuss Social Justice." *Journal of School Leadership* 14, 5: 530–63.

Matthews, L. Joseph, and Gary M. Crow. 2002. *Being and Becoming a Principal: Role Conceptions for Contemporary Principals and Assistant Principals*. Boston: Allyn & Bacon.

Noddings, Nel. 1992. *The Challenge to Care in Schools: An Alternative Approach to Education*. New York: Teachers College Press.

———. 2002. *Educating Moral People: A Caring Alternative to Character Education*. New York: Teachers College Press.

Norton, David. 1988. "'Character Ethics and Organizational Life.'" In *Papers on the Ethics of Administration*, edited by N. Dale Wright. 47–66. Provo, UT: Brigham Young University.

Osterman, Karen F., and Kottkamp, Robert B. 1993. *Reflective Practice for Educators: Improving Schooling Through Professional Development*. Thousand Oaks, CA: Corwin Press.

Palmer, Parker. 1998. *The Courage to Teach: Exploring the Inner Landscape of a Teacher's Life*. San Francisco: Jossey-Bass.

Purpel, David E., and Svi Shapiro. 1995. *Beyond Liberation and Excellence: Reconstructing the Public Discourse on Education.* Westport, CT: Bergin & Garvey.

Reed, Cynthia J., Joe L. Ross, Dorothy Dolasky, and Teresa Irvin. 1999. "Breaking Boundaries: Preparing Educational Leaders to Be Policy Advocates." Paper prepared for Mid-South Educational Research Association, Mississippi State University, Auburn, AL.

Richmon, Malcom J. 2003. "Persistent Difficulties With Values." In *The Ethical Dimensions of School Leadership,* edited by Paul T. Begley and Olof Johannsson. 33–47. Dordrecht, The Netherlands: Kluwer Academic Publishers.

Rishel, Kenn C., and Suzanne Tingley. 1995. "Lessons in Grace." *Executive Educator* 17, 4: 25–26.

Rocha, René A. 2003. *Spare the Rod, Suspend the Child? Discipline Policy and High School Dropouts.* College Station, TX: Texas Educational Excellence Project.

Schrader, Dawn E. 1993. "Lawrence Kohlberg's Approach and the Moral Education of Education Professionals." In *Ethics for Professionals in Education: Perspectives for Preparation and Practice,* edited by Kenneth Strike and P. Lance Ternasky. 84–101. New York: Teachers College Press.

Sergiovanni, Thomas J. 1992. *Moral Leadership: Getting to the Heart of School Improvement.* San Francisco: Jossey-Bass.

———. 2005. *Strengthening the Heartbeat: Leading and Learning Together in Schools.* San Francisco: Jossey-Bass.

Shields, Carolyn M. 2003. *Good Intentions Are Not Enough: Transformative Leadership for Communities of Difference.* Lanham, MD: Scarecrow Press.

Sichel, Betty A. 1993. "Ethics Committees and Teacher Ethics." In *Ethics for Professionals in Education: Perspectives for Preparation and Practice,* edited by Kenneth Strike and P. Lance Ternasky. 162–75. New York: Teachers College Press.

Sirotnik, Kenneth A. 2004. "Accountability for Promoting Democracy." *School Administrator* (May).

Sizer, Theodore R., and Nancy Faust Sizer. 1999. *The Students Are Watching: Schools and the Moral Contract.* Boston: Beacon Press.

Smith, Arthur E., Paul D. Travers, and George J. Yard. 1990. "Codes of Ethics for Selected Fields of Professional Education." St. Louis, MO.

Sockett, Hugh. 1993. *The Moral Base for Teacher Professionalism.* New York: Teachers College Press.

Solomon, Robert C. 1990. *A Passion for Justice: Emotions and the Origin of the Social Contract.* Reading, MA: Addison-Wesley.

Starratt, Robert J. 1994. "Afterword." In *Ethics in Educational Leadership Programs: An Expanding Role,* edited by Lynn Beck and Joseph Murphy. 100–03. Thousand Oaks CA: Corwin Press.

———. 2004. *Ethical Leadership.* San Francisco: Jossey-Bass.

Strike, Kenneth A., Emil J. Haller, and Jonas F. Soltis. 2005. *The Ethics of School Administration.* 3rd ed. New York: Teachers College Press.

Thomas, M. Donald. 1984. "How Can School Leaders Be Courageous?" *NASSP Bulletin* 68, 476: 36–40.

Tyack, David. 2003. *Seeking Common Ground: Public Schools in a Diverse Society.* Cambridge, MA: Harvard University Press.

Tyack, David, and Elizabeth Hansot. 1982. *Managers of Virtue: Public School Leadership in America, 1820-1980.* New York: Basic Books.

Wilson, James Q. 1993. *The Moral Sense.* New York: The Free Press.

Wirth, Arthur G. 1989. "The Violation of People at Work in Schools." *Teachers College Record* 90, 4: 535–49.

7. VISIONARY LEADERSHIP

Barth, Roland S. 1990. *Improving Schools From Within: Teachers, Parents, and Principals Can Make the Difference.* San Francisco: Jossey-Bass.

Beach, Robert H., and Ron Lindahl. 2004. "A Critical Review of Strategic Planning: Panacea for Public Education?" *Journal of School Leadership* 14, 2: 211–34.

Bennis, Warren, Jagdish Parikh, and Ronnie Lessem. 1994. *Beyond Leadership: Balancing Economics, Ethics, and Ecology.* Cambridge, MA: Blackwell Publishers.

Blase, Joseph, and Jo Roberts Blase. 2000. *Empowering Teachers: What Successful Principals Do.* 2nd ed. Thousand Oaks, CA: Corwin Press.

Block, Peter. 1987. *The Empowered Manager: Positive Political Skills at Work.* San Francisco: Jossey-Bass.

Blumberg, Arthur, and William Greenfield. 1986. *The Effective Principal: Perspectives on School Leadership.* Newton, MA: Allyn & Bacon.

Bridges, William. 1991. *Managing Transitions: Making the Most of Change.* Reading, MA: Addison-Wesley.

Burns, James MacGregor. 1978. *Leadership.* New York: HarperCollins.

Chance, Edward W., and Marilyn L. Grady. 1990. "Creating and Implementing a Vision for the School." *NASSP Bulletin* 74, 529: 12–18.

Collins, James C., and Jerry I. Porras. 2002. *Built to Last: Successful Habits of Visionary Companies.* New York: Harper Business.

Conley, David T., Diane M. Dunlap, and Paul Goldman. 1992. "The 'Vision Thing' and School Restructuring." *OSSC Report* 3, 2: 1–8. Eugene: Oregon School Study Council.

Conley, David T., and Paul Goldman. 1994. *Facilitative Leadership: How Principals Lead Without Dominating.* OSSC Bulletin Series. Eugene: Oregon School Study Council.

Covey, Stephen R. 2004. *The 8th Habit: From Effectiveness to Greatness.* New York: Free Press.

Cunningham, William G., and Donn W. Gresso. 1993. *Cultural Leadership: The Culture of Excellence in Education.* Boston: Allyn & Bacon.

Deal, Terry. 1995. "Symbols and Symbolic Activity." In *Images of Schools: Structures and Roles in Organizational Behavior,* edited by Samuel B. Bacharach and Bryan Mundell. 108–36. Thousand Oaks, CA: Corwin Press.

Dolan, W. Patrick. 1994. *Restructuring Our Schools: A Primer on Systemic Change,* edited by Lilot Moorman. Kansas City, KS: Systems and Organization.

Drucker, Peter F. 1994. "The Age of Social Transformation." *Atlantic Monthly* 274, 5: 53–80.

Evans, Robert. 1996. *The Human Side of School Change: Reform, Resistance, and the Real-Life Problems of Innovation.* San Francisco: Jossey-Bass.

Fullan, Michael. 1997. *What's Worth Fighting for in the Principalship.* New York: Teachers College Press.

Gardner, Howard. 1995. *Leading Minds: An Anatomy of Leadership.* New York: Basic Books.

Gitlin, Andrew, and Frank Margonis. 1995. "The Political Aspect of Reform: Teacher Resistance as Good Sense." *American Journal of Education* 103: 377–405.

Hallinger, Philip, and Ronald H. Heck. 2001. "What Do You Call People With Visions?" In *Second International Handbook of Educational Leadership and Administration,* edited by Kenneth Leithwood and Philip Hallinger. 9–40. Dordrecht, The Netherlands: Kluwer Academic Publishers.

Hammer, Michael, and Steven A. Stanton. 1995. *The Reengineering Revolution: A Handbook.* New York: Harper Collins Publishers.

Herman, Jerry J. 1990. "Action Plans to Make Your Vision a Reality." *NASSP Bulletin* 74, 523: 14–17.

Holcomb, Edie L. 2004. *Getting Excited About Data: Combining People, Passion, and Proof to Maximize Student Achievement.* 2nd ed. Thousand Oaks, CA: Corwin Press.

Hoyle, John R. 2006. *Leadership and Futuring: Making Visions Happen.* 2nd ed. Thousand Oaks, CA: Corwin Press.

Hurst, David K. 1995. *Crisis & Renewal: Meeting the Challenge of Organizational Change.* Boston: Harvard Business School Press.

Kaufman, Roger. 1995. *Mapping Educational Success: Strategic Thinking and Planning for School Administrators.* Thousand Oaks, CA: Corwin Press.

Kouzes, James M., and Barry Z. Posner. 1995. *The Leadership Challenge: How to Keep Getting Extraordinary Things Done in Organizations.* San Francisco: Jossey-Bass.

Leithwood, Kenneth, Doris Jantzi, and Rosanne Steinbach. 1999. *Changing Leadership for Changing Times.* Buckingham, England: Open University Press.

Leithwood, Kenneth A., and Carolyn Riehl. 2003. *What We Know About Successful School Leadership.* Philadelphia: Laboratory for Student Success, Temple University.

Licata, Joseph W., and Gerald W. Harper. 2001. "Organizational Health and Robust School Vision." *Educational Administration Quarterly* 37, 1: 5–26.

Louis, Karen Seashore, and Matthew Miles. 1990. *Improving the Urban High School: What Works and Why.* New York: Teachers College Press.

Mann, Horace. [1848] 1957. *The Republic and the School: On the Education of Free Men,* edited by Lawrence A. Cremin. New York: Teachers College Bureau of Publications.

Nanus, Burt. 1992. *Visionary Leadership: Creating a Compelling Sense of Direction for Your Organization.* San Francisco: Jossey-Bass.

Quinn, Robert E. 2004. *Building the Bridge as You Walk on It: A Guide for Leading Change.* San Francisco: Jossey-Bass.

Reeves, Douglas B. 2002. *The Daily Disciplines of Leadership: How to Improve Student Achievement, Staff Motivation, and Personal Organization.* San Francisco: Jossey-Bass.

Sashkin, Marshall, and Molly G. Sashkin. 2003. *Leadership That Matters: The Critical Factors for Making a Difference in People's Lives and Organizations' Success.* San Francisco: Berrett-Koehler.

Schwartz, Peter. 1991. *The Art of the Long View.* New York: Doubleday.

Senge, Peter M. 1990. *The Fifth Discipline: The Art and Practice of the Learning Organization.* New York: Doubleday.

Senge, Peter M., and others. 2000. *Schools That Learn: A Fifth Discipline Fieldbook for Educators, Parents, and Everyone Who Cares About Education.* New York: Doubleday.

Sergiovanni, Thomas J. 1992. *Moral Leadership: Getting to the Heart of School Improvement.* San Francisco: Jossey-Bass.

Sheive, Linda Tinelli, and Marian Beauchamp Schoenheit. 1987. "Vision and the Work Life of Educational Leaders." In *Leadership: Examining the Elusive,* edited by Linda Sheive and Marian Schoenheit. 16–29. Alexandria, VA: Association for Supervision and Curriculum Development.

Siskin, Leslie Santee. 1997. "The Challenge of Leadership in Comprehensive High Schools: School Vision and Departmental Divisions." *Educational Administration Quarterly* 33 (Supplement): 604–23.

Starratt, Robert J. 1995. *Leaders With Vision: The Quest for School Renewal.* Thousand Oaks, CA: Corwin Press.

Tyack, David, and Larry Cuban. 1995. *Tinkering Toward Utopia: A Century of Public School Reform.* Cambridge, MA: Harvard University Press.

Wagner, Tony. 1995. "Seeking Common Ground: Goal-Setting with All Constituencies." *Educational Leadership* 53, 4: 40–44.

Waters, Tim, Robert J. Marzano, and Brian McNulty. 2003. *Balanced Leadership: What 30 Years of Research Tells Us About the Effect of Leadership on Student Achievement.* Aurora, CO: Mid-Continent Research for Education and Learning.

8. CULTURAL LEADERSHIP

Bishop, John H., and others. 2003. "Nerds and Freaks: A Theory of Student Culture and Norms." In *Brookings Papers on Education Policy*, edited by Diane Ravitch. 141–213. Sponsored by the Brown Center on Education Policy. Washington, DC: Brookings Institution.

Burnham, Joan, and Shirley Hord, eds. 1993. *Toward Quality in Education: The Leader's Odyssey.* Washington, DC: National LEADership Network Study Group on Restructuring Schools, May.

Collins, Jim. 2001. *Good to Great: Why Some Companies Make the Leap . . . and Others Don't.* New York: Harper-Collins.

Deal, Terrence E., and Kent D. Peterson. 1999. *Shaping School Culture: The Heart of Leadership.* San Francisco: Jossey-Bass.

Fullan, Michael. 2003. "The Change Leader." *Educational Leadership* 60, 8 (May): 16–20.

Glickman, Carl D., Stephen P. Gordon, and Jovita M. Ross-Gordon. 2004. *Supervision and Instructional Leadership: A Developmental Approach.* 6th ed. Boston: Allyn & Bacon.

Hoy, Anita Woolfolk, and Wayne Kolter Hoy. 2003. *Instructional Leadership: A Learning-Centered Guide.* Boston: Allyn & Bacon.

Leithwood, Kenneth, Karen Seashore Louis, Stephen Anderson, and Kyla Wahlstrom. 2004. *How Leadership Influences Student Learning. Executive Summary.* Minneapolis: Center for Applied Research and Educational Improvement, University of Minnesota; Toronto, Canada: Ontario Institute for Education.

Leithwood, Kenneth A., and Carolyn Riehl. 2003. *What We Know About Successful School Leadership.* Philadelphia: Laboratory for Student Success, Temple University.

Maehr, Martin L., and Rachel M. Buck. 1993. "Transforming School Culture." In *Educational Leadership and School Culture*, edited by Marshall Sashkin and Herbert J. Walberg. 40–60. Berkeley, CA: McCutchan Publishing.

Mast, Carlotta. 2003. "Q & A With Jim Collins." *The School Administrator* 60 (December): 29–33.

National Association of Secondary School Principals. 2004. *Breaking Ranks II: Strategies for Leading High School Reform.* Reston, VA: Author.

Olson, Lynn. 2004. "Q&A: Educator Reflects on Romance with Schooling." *Education Week* 23 (May 12).

Patterson, Jerry, Janice Patterson, and Loucrecia Collins. 2002. *Bouncing Back: How Your School Can Succeed in the Face of Adversity.* Larchmont, NY: Eye on Education.

Royal, Mark A., and Robert J. Rossi. 1997. "Schools as Communities." *ERIC Digest* (March): 111. Eugene: ERIC Clearinghouse on Educational Management, University of Oregon.

Sashkin, Marshall, and Molly G. Sashkin. 2003. *Leadership That Matters: The Critical Factors for Making a Difference in People's Lives and Organizations' Success.* San Francisco: Berrett-Koehler.

Schein, Edgar H. 1992. *Organizational Culture and Leadership.* 2nd ed. San Francisco: Jossey-Bass.

———. 1999. *The Corporate Culture Survival Guide: Sense and Nonsense About Culture Change.* San Francisco: Jossey-Bass.

Sergiovanni, Thomas J. 1992. *Moral Leadership: Getting to the Heart of School Improvement.* San Francisco: Jossey-Bass.

———. 2001. *The Principalship: A Reflective Practice Perspective*. 4th ed. Boston: Allyn & Bacon.

Stine, Deborah E. 2000. "The Opening of a New High School: The Emergence of a Culture." Summary of a paper presented at the Annual Meeting of the American Educational Research Association, New Orleans, LA, April 23–28.

Sullivan, Anna M. 2002. "Enhancing Peer Culture in a Primary School Classroom." Paper presented at the Australian Association for Research in Education International Education Research Conference, Brisbane, Australia.

9. ACCOUNTABLE LEADERSHIP

Abe, Debby. 2004. "Parents Want Fourth 'R': Recess." *Tacoma News-Tribune*, December 5.

Abelmann, Charles, and Richard Elmore. 1999. *When Accountability Knocks, Will Anyone Answer?* Philadelphia: Consortium for Policy Research in Education.

Adams, Jacob E., Jr., and Michael W. Kirst. 1999. "New Demands and Concepts for Accountability: Striving for Results in an Era of Excellence." In *Handbook of Research on Educational Administration*, 2nd ed., edited by Joseph Murphy and Karen Seashore Louis. 463–89. San Francisco: Jossey-Bass.

Black, Paul, and others. 2004. "Working Inside the Black Box: Assessment for Learning in the Classroom." *Phi Delta Kappan* 86, 1: 8–21.

Boren, James. 1972. *When in Doubt, Mumble: A Bureaucrat's Handbook*. New York: Van Nostrand Reinhold.

Chubb, John E. 2003. "Ignoring the Market: *A Nation at Risk* and School Choice." *Education Next* 4, 3: 80–83. www.educationnext.org/20032/index.html

Crane, Eric W., Stanley Rabinowitz, and Joy Zimmerman. 2004. *Locally Tailored Accountability: Building on Your State System in the Era of NCLB*. San Francisco: WestEd.

Darling-Hammond, Linda. 1989. "Accountability for Professional Practice." *Teachers College Record* 91, 1: 59–80.

Elmore, Richard F. 2003. *Knowing the Right Thing to Do: School Improvement and Performance-Based Accountability*. Washington, DC: NGA Center for Best Practices, National Governors Association.

Evans, Robert. 1996. *The Human Side of School Change: Reform, Resistance, and the Real-Life Problems of Innovation*. San Francisco: Jossey-Bass.

Firestone, William A., and Dorothy Shipps. 2003. "How Do Educational Leaders Interpret the Multiple Accountabilities They Face?" Paper presented at the annual meeting of the American Educational Research Association, Chicago, April 22.

Fouts, Jeffrey T. 2003. *A Decade of Reform: A Summary of Research Findings on Classroom, School, and District Effectiveness in Washington State*. Seattle: Washington School Research Center.

Goodlad, John. 1984. *A Place Called School: Prospects for the Future*. New York: McGraw-Hill.

Hargreaves, Andy. 2004. "Inclusive and Exclusive Educational Change: Emotional Responses of Teachers and Implications for Leadership." *School Leadership and Management* 24, 2: 287–309.

Haynes, Eddy A., and Joseph Licata. 1995. "Creative Insubordination of School Principals and the Legitimacy of the Justifiable." *Journal of Educational Administration* 33, 4: 21–35.

Helfand, Duke, and Joel Rubin. 2004. "Few Parents Move Their Children out of Failing Schools." *Los Angeles Times*, November 8.

Hendrie, Caroline. 2005. "NAEP Study Fuels Debate Over Charter Schools." *Education Week*, January 5.

Jacob, Brian A., and Steven D. Levitt. 2004. "To Catch a Cheat." *Education Next* 4, 1: 68–75. www.educationnext.org.

Jones, Ken. 2004. "A Balanced School Accountability Model: An Alternative to High-Stakes Testing." *Phi Delta Kappan* 85, 8: 584–90.

Karp, Stan. 2004. "NCLB's Selective Vision of Equality: Some Gaps Count More Than Others." In *Many Children Left Behind: How the No Child Left Behind Act Is Damaging Our Children and Our Schools*, edited by Deborah Meier and George Wood. 53–65. Boston: Beacon Press.

Kelley, Carolyn, Herbert Heneman III, and Anthony Milanowski. 2002. "Teacher Motivation and School-Based Performance Awards." *Educational Administration Quarterly* 38, 3: 372–401.

Lake, Robin, Maria McCarthy, Sara Taggart, and Mary Beth Celio. 2000. *Making Standards Stick: A Follow-Up Look at Washington State's School Improvement Efforts in 1999–2000*. Seattle, WA: Center on Reinventing Public Education.

Lake, Robin J., Paul T. Hill, Lauren O'Toole, and Mary Beth Celio. 1999. *Making Standards Work: Active Voices, Focused Learning*. Seattle, WA: Center on Reinventing Public Education. www.crpe.org.

Lashway, Larry. 2001. *The New Standards and Accountability: Will Rewards and Sanctions Motivate America's Schools to Peak Performance?* Eugene: ERIC Clearinghouse on Educational Management, University of Oregon.

Leithwood, Kenneth A., and Carolyn Riehl. 2003. *What We Know About Successful School Leadership*. Philadelphia: Laboratory for Student Success, Temple University.

Marzano, Robert J., and John S. Kendall. 1998. *Awash in a Sea of Standards*. Aurora, CO: Mid-Continent Regional Educational Laboratory.

Mitchell, Ruth. 1996. *Front-End Alignment: Using Standards to Steer Educational Change*. Washington, DC: The Education Trust.

National Commission on Excellence in Education. 1983. *A Nation at Risk: The Imperative for Educational Reform*. Washington, DC: U.S. Department of Education.

Odden, Allan, and Marc Wallace. 2004. "Experimenting with Teacher Compensation." *School Administrator* 61 (October).

Reeves, Douglas. 2003. *Accountability for Learning: How Teachers and School Leaders Can Take Charge*. Alexandria, VA: Association for Supervision and Curriculum Development.

Sergiovanni, Thomas J. 2000. *The Lifeworld of Leadership*. San Francisco: Jossey-Bass.

Skrla, Linda. 2003. "Productive Campus Leadership Responses to Accountability: Principals as Policy Mediators." In *Studies in Leading and Organizing Schools*, edited by Wayne Hoy and Cecil Miskel. 27–50. Greenwich, CT: Information Age Publishing.

Stiggins, Rick. 2004. "New Assessment Beliefs for a New School Mission." *Phi Delta Kappan* 86, 1: 22–27.

Wagner, Robert B. 1989. *Accountability in Education: A Philosophical Inquiry*. New York: Routledge.

Waters, Tim, Robert J. Marzano, and Brian McNulty. 2003. *Balanced Leadership: What 30 Years of Research Tells Us About the Effect of Leadership on Student Achievement*. Aurora, CO: Mid-Continent Research for Education and Learning.

10. SITE-BASED MANAGEMENT

Beck, Lynn G., and Joseph Murphy. 1998. "Site-Based Management and School Success: Untangling the Variables." *School Effectiveness and School Improvement* 9, 4 (December): 358–85.

Blase, Joseph, and Jo Blase. 2000. "Effective Instructional Leadership: Teachers' Perspectives on How Principals Promote Teaching and Learning in Schools." *Journal of Educational Administration* 38, 2: 130–41.

Brown, Frank. 2001. "Site-Based Management: Is It Still Central to the School Reform Movement?" *School Business Affairs* 67, 4 (April): 5–6, 8–9.

Brown, Robert, and G. Robb Cooper. 2000. "School-Based Management: How Effective Is It?" *Bulletin of the National Association of Secondary School Principals* 84, 616 (May): 77–85.

Candoli, I. Carl. 1995. *Site-Based Management in Education: How to Make It Work in Your School.* Lancaster, PA: Technomic Publishing Company, Inc.

Dempster, Neil. 2000. "Guilty or Not: The Impact and Effects of Site-Based Management on Schools." *Journal of Educational Administration* 38, 1: 47–63.

Drury, Darrel W. 1999. *Reinventing School-Based Management: A School Board Guide to School-Based Improvement.* Alexandria, VA: National School Boards Association.

Goodman, Richard H., and William G. Zimmerman Jr. 2000. *Thinking Differently: Recommendations for 21st Century School Board/Superintendent Leadership, Governance, and Teamwork for High Student Achievement.* Arlington, VA: Educational Research Service.

Grissmer, David, and Ann Flanagan. 1998. *Exploring Rapid Achievement Gains in North Carolina and Texas.* Washington, DC: National Education Goals Panel.

Institute for Educational Leadership, Inc. 2001. *Leadership for Student Learning: Restructuring School District Leadership.* Washington, DC: Author.

Johnson, Patsy E., and Joyce Logan. 2000. "Efficacy and Productivity: The Future of School-Based Decision-Making Councils in Kentucky." *Journal of School Leadership* 10, 4 (July): 311–31.

Kowalski, Theodore. 2003. *Responses to Student Needs and Public Dissatisfaction in Contemporary School Administration.* Boston: Allyn & Bacon.

Krishnamoorthi, Raja S. 2000. "Making Local School Councils Work: The Implementation of Local School Councils in Chicago Public Elementary Schools." *Journal of Law & Education* 29, 3 (July): 285–314.

Leithwood, Kenneth A., and Carolyn Riehl. 2003. *What We Know About Successful School Leadership.* Philadelphia: Laboratory for Student Success, Temple University.

National Association of Secondary School Principals. 2004. *Breaking Ranks II: Strategies for Leading High School Reform.* Reston, VA: Author.

Oswald, Lori Jo. 1995. "School-Based Management." *ERIC Digest* 99 (July). Eugene: ERIC Clearinghouse on Educational Management, University of Oregon.

Robertson, Peter J., and Kerri L. Briggs. 1998. "Improving Schools Through School-Based Management: An Examination of the Process of Change." *School Effectiveness and School Improvement* 9, 1 (March): 28–57.

Sewal, Angela M. 1999. *Central Office and Site-Based Management: An Educator's Guide.* Lancaster, PA: Technomic Publishing Company, Inc.

Stiefel, Leanna, Amy Ellen Schwartz, Carole Portas, and Dae Yeop Kim. 2001. *School Budgeting and School Performance: The Impact of New York City's Performance Driven Budgeting Initiative.* New York: Institute for Education and Social Policy, New York University.

Warden, Christina. 2002. "Using Site-Based Budgeting to Improve Student Achievement." *School Business Affairs* 68, 9 (October): 16–22.

Wohlstetter, Patricia. 1995. "Getting School-Based Management Right: What Works and What Doesn't." *Phi Delta Kappan* 57, 1 (September): 22–26.

Wood, R. Craig, David C. Thompson, Lawrence O. Picus, and Don I. Tharpe. 1995. "Site-Based Management." In *Principles of School Business Management.* 2nd ed. Reston, VA: Association of School Business Officials International.

Woods, Deanna. 2002. *Moving Forward: From Where You Are to School Improvement That Lasts.* Portland, OR: Northwest Regional Educational Laboratory.

Wyman, Benjamin F. 2000. "Decentralization Continued: A Survey of Emerging Issues in Site-Based Decision Making." *Journal of Law & Education* 29, 2 (April): 255–63.

11. DISTRIBUTED LEADERSHIP

Barth, Roland. 2001. "The Teacher Leader." *Phi Delta Kappan* 82, 6: 443–49.

Bennis, Warren. 2001. "The End of Leadership: Exemplary Leadership Is Impossible Without Full Inclusion, Initiatives, and Cooperation of Followers." In *Contemporary Issues in Leadership*, 5th ed., edited by Robert L. Taylor and William E. Rosenbach. 247–60. Boulder, CO: Westview Press.

Carnegie Corporation of New York. 1986. *A Nation Prepared: Teachers for the 21st Century.* New York: Author.

Court, Marian. 2003. *Different Approaches to Sharing School Leadership.* Nottingham, England: National College for School Leadership. www.ncsl.org.uk.

Covey, Stephen R. 2004. *The 8th Habit: From Effectiveness to Greatness.* New York: Free Press.

Crow, Gary M. 1998. "Implications for Leadership in Collaborative Schools." In *Restructuring Schools for Collaboration: Promises and Pitfalls,* edited by Diana G. Pounder. 135–53. Albany: State University of New York Press.

Cunningham, William F., and Donn W. Gresso. 1993. *Cultural Leadership: The Culture of Excellence in Education.* Needham Heights, MA: Allyn & Bacon.

Cushing, Katherine S., Judith A. Kerrins, and Thomas Johnstone. 2004. "Work Worth Doing." *Leadership* 22, 3. www.acsa.org.

Drath, Wilfred H. 2001. *The Deep Blue Sea: Rethinking the Source of Leadership.* San Francisco: Jossey-Bass.

Elmore, Richard F. 2000. *Building a New Structure for School Leadership.* Washington, DC: The Albert Shanker Institute.

Fletcher, Joyce K., and Katrin Käufer. 2003. "Shared Leadership: Paradox and Possibility." In *Shared Leadership: Reframing the Hows and Whys of Leadership,* edited by Craig L. Pearce and Jay A. Conger. 21–47. Thousand Oaks, CA: Sage Publications.

Gronn, Peter. 2002. "Distributed Leadership." In *Second International Handbook of Educational Leadership and Administration,* edited by Kenneth Leithwood and Philip Hallinger. 653–96. The Netherlands: Kluwer Academic Publishers.

Gronn, Peter, and Andrew Hamilton. 2004. "'A Bit More Life in the Leadership': Co-Principalship as Distributed Leadership Practice." *Leadership and Policy in Schools* 3, 1: 3–36.

Helfand, Duke. 2003. "Co-Principals: Divvying up a Monster Job." *Los Angeles Times,* December 20.

Johnson, Bob L., Jr. 1998. "Organizing for Collaboration: A Reconsideration of Some Basic Organizing Principles." In *Restructuring Schools for Collaboration: Promises and Pitfalls,* edited by Diana G. Pounder. 9–25. Albany: State University of New York Press.

Katzenbach, Jon R., and Douglas K. Smith. 2003. *The Wisdom of Teams: Creating the High-Performance Organization.* New York: HarperBusiness.

Lambert, Linda. 1998. *Building Leadership Capacity in Schools.* Alexandria, VA: Association for Supervision and Curriculum Development.

———. 2003. *Leadership Capacity for Lasting School Improvement.* Alexandria, VA: Association for Supervision and Curriculum Development.

Locke, Edwin A. 2003. In *Shared Leadership: Reframing the Hows and Whys of Leadership,* edited by Craig L. Pearce and Jay A. Conger. 271–84. Thousand Oaks, CA: Sage Publications.

Murphy, Joseph. 2005. *Connecting Teacher Leadership and School Improvement.* Thousand Oaks, CA: Corwin Press.

Murphy, Joseph, and Amanda Datnow. 2003. "Leadership Lessons From Comprehensive School Reform Designs." In *Leadership Lessons From Comprehensive School Reforms*, edited by Joseph Murphy and Amanda Datnow. 263–78. Thousand Oaks, CA: Corwin Press.

National College for School Leadership. 2004. *Co-headship: A Call for Consultation*. Nottingham, England: Author.

Ogawa, Rodney T., and Steven T. Bossert. 2000. "Leadership as an Organizational Quality." In *The Jossey-Bass Reader on Educational Leadership*. 38–58. San Francisco: Jossey-Bass.

O'Toole, James, Jay Galbraith, and Edward E. Lawler III. 2003. "The Promise and Pitfalls of Shared Leadership." In *Shared Leadership: Reframing the Hows and Whys of Leadership*, edited by Craig L. Pearce and Jay A. Conger. 250–67. Thousand Oaks, CA: Sage Publications.

Sergiovanni, Thomas J. 1992. *Moral Leadership: Getting to the Heart of School Improvement*. San Francisco: Jossey-Bass.

Siu-Runyan, Yvonne, and Sally Joy Heart. 1992. "Management Manifesto." *The Executive Educator* 14, 1: 23–26.

Snyder, Karolyn J., and Robert H. Anderson. 1986. *Managing Productive Schools: Toward an Ecology*. Chicago: Harcourt Brace Jovanovich.

Spillane, James P., and Jennifer Z. Sherer. 2004. "A Distributed Perspective on School Leadership: Leadership Practice as *Stretched Over* People and Place." Paper presented at the annual meeting of the American Educational Research Association, San Diego, CA, April.

Spillane, James P., Richard Halverson, and John B. Diamond. 2001. "Investigating School Leadership Practices: A Distributed Perspective." *Educational Researcher* 31: 23–28.

Storey, Anne. 2004. "The Problem of Distributed Leadership in Schools." *School Management and Leadership* 24, 3: 249–66.

Supowitz, Jonathan A. 2000. "Manage Less, Lead More." *Principal Leadership* 1, 3: 14–19.

Thomas B. Fordham Institute and The Broad Foundation. 2003. *Better Leaders for America's Schools: A Manifesto*. Washington, DC: Author.

Wasley, Patricia A. 1991. *Teachers Who Lead: The Rhetoric of Reform and Realities of Practice*. New York: Teachers College Press.

Weiss, Carol H. 1993. "Shared Decision-Making About What: A Comparison of Schools With and Without Teacher Participation." *Teachers College Press* 95, 1: 69–92.

York-Barr, Jennifer, and Karen Duke. 2004. "What Do We Know About Teacher Leadership? Findings From Two Decades of Scholarship." *Review of Educational Research* 74, 3: 255–316.

12. POLITICAL LEADERSHIP

Blase, Joseph, and Gary Anderson. 1995. *The Micropolitics of Educational Leadership: From Control to Empowerment*. New York: Teachers College Press.

Blase, Joseph, and Jo Blase. 2003. *Breaking the Silence: Overcoming the Problem of Principal Mistreatment of Teachers*. Thousand Oaks, CA: Corwin Press.

Block, Peter. 1987. *The Empowered Manager: Positive Political Skills at Work*. San Francisco: Jossey-Bass.

Bolman, Lee G., and Terrence E. Deal. 1997. *Reframing Organizations: Artistry, Choice, and Leadership*. San Francisco: Jossey-Bass.

Burns, James MacGregor. 1978. *Leadership*. New York: Harper and Row.

Conley, David T. 2003. *Who Governs Our Schools? Changing Roles and Responsibilities*. New York: Teachers College Press.

Copland, Michael Aaron. 2003. "The Bay Area School Reform Collaborative: Building the Capacity to Lead." In *Leadership Lessons From Comprehensive School Reforms*, edited by Joseph Murphy and Amanda Datnow. 159–83. Thousand Oaks, CA: Corwin Press.

Cuban, Larry. 1975. "Hobson vs. Hanson: A Study in Organizational Response." *Educational Administration Quarterly* 11, 2: 15–37.

———. 1988. *The Managerial Imperative and the Practice of Leadership in Schools*. Albany: State University of New York Press.

Cusick, Philip A. 1992. *The Educational System: Its Nature and Logic*. New York: McGraw-Hill.

Etzioni, Amitai. 1961. *A Comparative Analysis of Complex Organizations: On Power, Involvement, and Their Correlates*. New York: Free Press.

Farkas, Steve, Jean Johnson, Ann Duffett, and Tony Foleno, with Patrick Foley. 2001. *Trying to Stay Ahead of the Game: Superintendents and Principals Talk About School Leadership*. Washington, DC: Public Agenda. www.publicagenda.org

French, John P. R., Jr., and Bertram H. Raven. 1960. "The Bases of Social Power." In *Group Dynamics*, edited by Dorwin Cartwright and Alvin Zander. 607–23. New York: Harper and Row.

Gardner, Howard. 2004. *Changing Minds: The Art and Science of Changing Our Own and Other People's Minds*. Boston: Harvard Business School Press.

Glasman, Naftaly, and Mike Couch. 2001. "Balancing Desires and Responses: Private Contacts Between Individual Parents and the Principal." *Peabody Journal of Education* 76: 52–74.

Goldring, Ellen B. 1995. "Striking a Balance: Boundary Spanning and Environmental Management in Schools." In *Images of Schools: Structures and Roles in Organizational Behavior*, edited by Samuel B. Bacharach and Bryan Mundell. 283–314. Thousand Oaks, CA: Corwin Press.

Greene, Robert. 1998. *The 48 Laws of Power*. New York: Penguin Books.

Hanson, E. Mark. 2003. *Educational Administration and Organizational Behavior*. 5th ed. Boston: Allyn & Bacon.

Heifetz, Ronald A., and Marty Linsky. 2002. *Leadership on the Line: Staying Alive Through the Dangers of Leading*. Boston: Harvard Business School Press.

Ingersoll, Richard M. 2003. *Who Controls Teachers' Work? Power and Accountability in America's Schools*. Cambridge, MA: Harvard University Press.

Kirst, Michael. 1995. "Federal, State, and Local Control." In *Learning From the Past: What History Teaches Us About School Reform*, edited by Diane Ravitch and Maris A. Vinovskis. 25–56. Baltimore: Johns Hopkins University Press.

Lake, Robin, Maria McCarthy, Sara Taggart, and Mary Beth Celio. 2000. *Making Standards Stick: A Follow-up Look at Washington State's School Improvement Efforts in 1999–2000*. Seattle, WA: Center on Reinventing Public Education.

Lortie, Dan. 1975. *Schoolteacher: A Sociological Study*. Chicago: University of Chicago Press.

Morgan, Gareth. 1997. *Images of Organization*. 2nd ed. Thousand Oaks, CA: Sage Publications.

Neustadt, Richard E. 1960. *Presidential Power, the Politics of Leadership*. New York: Wiley.

Ravitch, Diane. 2003. *The Language Police: How Pressure Groups Restrict What Students Learn*. New York: Alfred A. Knopf.

Sergiovanni, Thomas J. 2000. *The Lifeworld of Leadership: Creating Culture, Community and Personal Meaning in Our Schools*. San Francisco: Jossey-Bass.

Sergiovanni, Thomas J., Paul Kelleher, Martha M. McCarthy, and Frederick M. Wirt. 2004. *Educational Governance and Administration*. 5th ed. Boston: Allyn & Bacon.

Spring, Joel. 1997. *Political Agendas for Education: From the Christian Coalition to the Green Party*. Mahwah, NJ: Lawrence Erlbaum.

Wise, Arthur E. 1979. *Legislated Learning: The Bureaucratization of the American Classroom*. Berkeley, CA: University of California Press.

13. INSTRUCTIONAL LEADERSHIP: SUPPORTING THE LEARNING PROCESS

Anderson, Lorin W., and others, eds. 2001. *A Taxonomy for Learning, Teaching, and Assessing: A Revision of Bloom's Taxonomy of Educational Objectives*. New York: Longman.

Beaudoin, Marie-Nathalie, and Maureen Taylor. 2004. *Breaking the Culture of Bullying and Disrespect, Grades K-8: Best Practices and Successful Strategies*. Thousand Oaks, CA: Corwin Press.

Black, Paul, and Dylan William. 1998. "Inside the Black Box: Raising Standards Through Classroom Assessment. *Phi Delta Kappan* 80, 2 (October): 139–44.

Cawelti, Gordon. 2004. *Handbook of Research on Improving Student Achievement*. 3rd ed. Arlington, VA: Educational Research Service.

Committee for Children. 2001. "Steps to Respect: A Bullying Prevention Program." Seattle, WA: Committee for Children.

Driscoll, Marcy. 2004. *Psychology of Learning for Instruction*. 3rd ed. Boston: Allyn & Bacon.

Good, Thomas, L., and Jere E. Brophy. 2003. *Looking in Classrooms*. 9th ed. Boston: Allyn & Bacon.

Gredler, Margaret E. 2001. *Learning and Instruction: Theory Into Practice*. 4th ed. New York: Prentice Hall.

No Child Left Behind Act of 2001, Pub. I, No. 107-110, 115 Stat. 1425 (2002).

Olweus, Dan. 1993. *Bullying at School: What We Know and What We Can Do*. Cambridge, MA: Blackwell.

Pintrich, Paul R., and Dale H. Schunk. 2002. *Motivation in Education: Theory, Research, and Applications*. 2nd ed. Columbus, OH: Merrill-Prentice Hall.

Pintrich, Paul R., Ronald W. Marx, and Robert A. Boyle. 1993. "Beyond Cold Conceptual Change: The Role of Motivational Beliefs and Classroom Contextual Factors in the Process of Conceptual Change." *Review of Educational Research* 63: 167–99.

Porch, Stephanie. 2002. "Schoolwide Approaches to Discipline." *ERS Informed Educator*. Arlington, VA: Educational Research Service.

Portin, Bradley, Paul Schneider, Michael DeArmond, and Lauren Gundlach. 2003. *Making Sense of Leading Schools: A Study of the School Principalship*. Seattle: Center on Reinventing Public Education, University of Washington.

Roberts, Walter B., Jr. 2006. "Bullying From Both Sides: Strategic Interventions for Working With Bullies and Victims." Thousand Oaks, CA: Corwin Press.

Stiggins, Richard J. 2001. *Student-Involved Classroom Assessment*. 3rd ed. Upper Saddle River, NJ: Merrill Prentice Hall.

Stipek, Deborah. 1998. *Motivation to Learn: From Theory to Practice*. 3rd ed. Boston: Allyn & Bacon.

Sullivan, Keith, Mark Cleary, and Ginny Sullivan. 2004. "Bullying in Secondary Schools: What It Looks Like and How to Manage It." Thousand Oaks, CA: Corwin Press.

Whitehurst, Grover J. 2002. "Statement of Grover J. Whitehurst, Assistant Secretary for Research and Improvement, Before the Senate Committee on Health, Education, Labor, and Pensions." Washington, DC: U.S. Department of Education, June.

14. INSTRUCTIONAL LEADERSHIP: PROGRESS MONITORING

Beghetto, Ronald A. 2004. "Toward a More Complete Picture of Student Learning: Assessing Students' Motivational Beliefs." *Practical Assessment, Research & Evaluation*, 9, 15 (August). http://PAREonline.net/getvn.asp?v=9&n=15

Bernhardt, Victoria, L. 2004. *Data Analysis for Continuous School Improvement*. 2nd ed. Larchmont, NY: Eye on Education.

Black, Paul, and Dylan William. 2004. "The Formative Purpose: Assessment Must First Promote Learning." In *Towards Coherence Between Classroom Assessment and Accountability*, edited by Mark Wilson. 20–50. Chicago: University of Chicago Press.

Gronlund, Norman E. 2003. *Assessment of Student Achievement*. 7th ed. Boston: Allyn & Bacon.

Joint Committee on Standards for Educational Evaluation. 2002. *The Student Evaluation Standards: How to Improve Evaluations of Students*. Thousand Oaks, CA: Corwin Press.

Leithwood, Kenneth, Doris Jantzi, and Rosanne Steinbach. 1998. "Leadership and Other Conditions Which Foster Organizational Learning in Schools." In *Organizational Learning in Schools,* edited by Kenneth Leithwood and Karen Seashore Louis. 67–90. Lisse, The Netherlands: Taylor & Francis The Netherlands.

Mengeling, Michelle. 2000. "Computer Software Products for Classroom Assessment Purposes." In *Research Review for School Leaders (Vol. III)*, edited by William G. Wraga and Peter S. Hlebowitsh. 277–300. Mahwah, NJ: Lawrence Erlbaum.

Mitchell, Coral, and Larry Sackney. 1998. "Learning About Organizational Learning." In *Organizational Learning in Schools,* edited by Kenneth Leithwood and Karen Seashore Louis. 177–99. Lisse, The Netherlands: Taylor & Francis The Netherlands.

Popham, James W. 2002. *Classroom Assessment: What Teachers Need to Know*. 3rd ed. Boston: Allyn & Bacon.

Schmoker, Mike. 2001. *The Results Fieldbook: Practical Strategies From Dramatically Improved Schools*. Alexandria, VA: Association for Supervision and Curriculum Development.

Stiggins, Richard J. 2000. "The Principal's Assessment Responsibilities." In *Research Review for School Leaders (Vol. III)*, edited by William G. Wraga and Peter S. Hlebowitsh. 201–36. Mahwah, NJ: Lawrence Erlbaum.

———. 2001. *Student-Involved Classroom Assessment*. 3rd ed. Upper Saddle River, NJ: Merrill Prentice Hall.

Worthen, Blaine R., James R. Sanders, and Jody L. Fitzpatrick. 1997. *Program Evaluation: Alternative Approaches and Practical Guidelines*. 2nd ed. New York: Longman.

15. INSTRUCTIONAL LEADERSHIP: CULTIVATING A LEARNING-FOCUSED COMMUNITY IN SCHOOLS

Ames, Carol. 1992. "Classrooms: Goals, Structures, and Student Motivation." *Journal of Educational Psychology* 84: 261–71.

Ames, Carol, and Jennifer Archer. 1988. "Achievement Goals in the Classroom: Students' Learning Strategies and Motivation Processes." *Journal of Educational Psychology* 80: 260–67.

Beghetto, Ronald A. 2001. "Virtually in the Middle: Alternative Avenues for Parental Involvement in Middle Schools." *The Clearing House* 75: 22–25.

———. 2004. "Toward a More Complete Picture of Student Learning: Assessing Students' Motivational Beliefs." *Practical Assessment, Research & Evaluation* 9, 15 (August). http://pareonline.net/getvn.asp?v=9&n=15

Chappuis, Steve, Richard Stiggins, Judy Arter, and Jan Chappuis. 2004. *Assessment FOR Learning: An Action Guide for School Leaders*. Portland, OR: Assessment Training Institute.

Fullan, Michael. 2000. *Change Forces: The Sequel*. London: Falmer Press.

Kaplan, Avi, Michael J. Middleton, Tim Urdan, and Carol Midgley. 2002. "Achievement Goals and Goal Structures." In *Goals, Goal Structures, and Patterns of Adaptive Learning*, edited by Carol Midgley. 21–54. Mahwah, NJ: Lawrence Erlbaum.

King, M. Bruce, Karen Seashore Louis, Helen M. Marks, and Kent D. Peterson. 1996. "Participatory Decision Making." In *Authentic Achievement: Restructuring Schools for Intellectual Quality*, edited by Fred M. Newmann and others. 245–63. San Francisco: Jossey-Bass.

Kumar, Revathy, Margaret H. Gheen, and Avi Kaplan. 2002. "Goal Structures in the Learning Environment and Students' Disaffection From Learning and Schooling." In *Goals, Goal Structures, and Patterns of Adaptive Learning*, edited by Carol Midgley. 143–74. Mahwah, NJ: Lawrence Erlbaum.

Lave, Jean, and Etienne Wenger. 1991. *Situated Learning: Legitimate Peripheral Participation*. Cambridge, England: Cambridge University Press.

Maehr, Martin, and Carol Midgley. 1996. *Transforming School Cultures*. Boulder, CO: Westview Press.

Midgley, Carol, ed. 2002. *Goals, Goal Structures, and Patterns of Adaptive Learning*. Mahwah, NJ: Lawrence Erlbaum.

National Conference of State Legislatures. 2002. *The Role of School Leadership in Improving Student Achievement*. Washington, DC: Author.

Ormrod, Jeanne E. 2002. *Educational Psychology: Developing Learners*. 4th ed. Upper Saddle River, NJ: Merrill Prentice Hall.

Pintrich, Paul R., and Dale H. Schunk. 2002. *Motivation in Education: Theory, Research, and Applications*. 2nd ed. Upper Saddle River, NJ: Merrill Prentice Hall.

Roeser, Robert W., Roxana Marachi, and Hunter Gehlbach. 2002. "A Goal Theory Perspective on Teachers' Professional Identities and the Contexts of Teaching. In *Goals, Goal Structures, and Patterns of Adaptive Learning*, edited by Carol Midgley. 205–42. Mahwah, NJ: Lawrence Erlbaum.

Stiggins, Richard J. 2001. *Student-Involved Classroom Assessment*. 3rd ed. Upper Saddle River, NJ: Merrill Prentice Hall.

Wenger, Etienne. 1999. *Communities of Practice: Learning, Meaning, and Identity*. Cambridge, England: Cambridge University Press.

Wenger, Etienne, Richard McDermott, and William M. Snyder. 2002. *Cultivating Communities of Practice*. Boston: Harvard Business School Press.

16. COMMUNICATING

Bovée, Courtland L., and John Thill. 2000. *Business Communication Today*. 6th ed. Upper Saddle River, NJ: Prentice Hall.

Chance, Patti L., and Edward W. Chance. 2002. "Communication: The Impact of Organizational Structure on Information Flow and Perceptions." In *Introduction to Educational Leadership and Organizational Behavior: Theory Into Practice*. 153–72. Larchmont, NY: Eye on Education.

Davis, Stephen H. 1997. "The Principal's Paradox: Remaining Secure in a Precarious Position." *NASSP Bulletin* 81, 592 (November): 73–80.

First, Patricia F., and David S. Carr. 1986. "Removing Barriers to Communication Between Principals and Teachers." *Catalyst for Change* 15, 3 (Spring): 5–7.

Geddes, Doreen S. 1995. *Keys to Communication: A Handbook for School Success*. Thousand Oaks, CA: Corwin Press.

Glaser, Susan R., and Anna Eblen. 1986. "Organizational Communication Effectiveness: The View of Corporate Administrators." *Journal of Applied Communication Research* 14, 2 (Fall): 119–32.

Guffey, Mary Ellen. 1997. *Business Communication: Process & Product.* 2nd ed. Cincinnati, OH: South-Western College Publishing.

Hanson, E. Mark. 2003. "Organizational Communication." In *Educational Administration and Organizational Behavior.* 5th ed. 217–33. Boston: Allyn & Bacon.

Hensley, Phyllis A., and LaVern Burmeister. 2004. "The Artistry of Communication." *Leadership* (March/April): 30–33.

Jung, Charles, and others. 1973. *Interpersonal Communications: Participant Materials and Leader's Manual.* Portland, OR: Northwest Regional Educational Laboratory.

Kowalski, Theodore J. 2003. "Important Aspects of Practice." In *Contemporary School Administration: An Introduction.* 2nd ed. 224–46. Boston: Allyn & Bacon.

Lee, Valerie E., and Robert G. Croninger. 1999. *Elements of Social Capital in the Context of Six High Schools.* Washington, DC: Office of Educational Research and Improvement, U.S. Department of Education.

Lehr, Arthur E. 2003. "Quality Writing, Quality Leadership." *The School Administrator* 60 (January): 35.

Leithwood, Kenneth A., and Carolyn Riehl. 2003. *What We Know About Successful School Leadership.* Philadelphia: Laboratory for Student Success, Temple University.

Marks, Helen. 1999. "Social Capital by Design: Normative Systems and Social Structures in Six High Schools." Paper presented at the annual meeting of the American Educational Research Association, Montreal, Canada, April 3.

Martinez, M. Cecilia. 2003. *One Principal Developing School Capacity Through Building Social Capital.* New Brunswick, NJ: Center for Educational Analysis, Rutgers University.

MetLife, Inc. 2003. *MetLife Survey of the American Teacher: An Examination of School Leadership.* New York: Harris Interactive Inc.

Parsons, Randall B. 2001. "Ten Principles for Principals." *Principal* 81 (March): 49–51.

Rebore, Ronald W. 2003. *A Human Relations Approach to the Practice of Educational Leadership.* Boston: Allyn & Bacon.

Scheflen, Albert E., and Alice Scheflen. 1972. *Body Language and Social Order.* Englewood Cliffs, NJ: Prentice Hall.

Tannen, Deborah. 1994. *Talking From 9 to 5.* New York: William Morrow and Company, Inc.

Villani, Christine J., and Linda L. Lyman. 2001. "Strengthening Communication Skills." *The AASA Professor* 24, 3 (Spring): 2–4.

17. ENGAGING THE PUBLIC

Bartusek, Lisa. 2003. "Governance: Engaging the Community Around School Improvement Starts With the Board." *American School Board Journal* 190 (January/February): 38–40.

Blank, Martin J., and Barbara Langford. 2000. *Strengthening Partnerships: Community School Assessment Checklist.* Washington, DC: Coalition for Community Schools.

Brown, L. Joan. 2001. "Networking With the Community." *School Business Affairs* 67, 5 (May): 23–26.

Cunningham, Chris. 2002. "Engaging the Community to Support Student Achievement." *ERIC Digest* 157. Eugene: ERIC Clearinghouse on Educational Management, University of Oregon.

Davis, Patricia W., and P. J. Karr-Kidwell. N.d. *School Leaders and Community: Research and a Plan for Collaboration.*

Fiore, Douglas J. 2002. *School Community Relations.* Larchmont, NY: Eye on Education.

Jehl, Jeanne, Martin Blank, and Barbara McCloud. 2001. *Education and Community Building: Connecting Two Worlds.* Washington, DC: Institute for Educational Leadership.

Jordan, Catherine, Evangelina Orozco, and Amy Averett. 2001. *Emerging Issues in School, Family, & Community Connections: Annual Synthesis 2001.* Austin, TX: Southwest Educational Development Laboratory.

Leithwood, Kenneth A., and Carolyn Riehl. 2003. *What We Know About Successful School Leadership.* Philadelphia: Laboratory for Student Success, Temple University.

Martinez, M. Cecilia. 2003. *One Principal Developing School Capacity Through Building Social Capital.* New Brunswick, NJ: Center for Educational Analysis, Rutgers University.

Meek, Anne. 1999. *Communicating With the Public: A Guide for School Leaders.* Alexandria, VA: Association for Supervision and Curriculum Development.

MetLife, Inc. 2003. *The MetLife Survey of the American Teacher, 2003: An Examination of School Leadership. A Survey of Teachers, Principals, Parents and Students.* New York: Author.

National Association of Elementary School Principals. 2001. *Standards for What Principals Should Know and Be Able to Do.* Alexandria, VA: Author.

National Conference of State Legislatures. 2001. *Improving Student Achievement: Linking State Policy to Effective Practice.* Washington, DC: Author.

Resnick, Michael A. 2000. *Communities Count: A School Board Guide to Public Engagement.* Alexandria, VA: National School Boards Association.

Solomon, Monica, and Maria Voles Ferguson. 1999. *How to Build Local Support for Comprehensive School Reform.* Getting Better by Design Series, Vol. 7. Arlington, VA: New American Schools.

Wall, Milan, and Vicki Luther. 2000. *Better Schools Through Public Engagement.* Lincoln, NE: Heartland Center for Leadership Development.

18. MANAGING DATA FOR DECISION MAKING: CREATING KNOWLEDGE FROM INFORMATION

Cleveland, William S. 1994. *Elements of Graphing Data.* 2nd ed. Monterey, CA: Wadsworth.

Hambleton, Ronald. 1994. "Using Performance Standards to Report National and State Assessment Data: Are the Reports Understandable and How Can They Be Improved?" Paper presented at the Joint Conference on Standard Setting for Large-Scale Assessments, Washington, DC, October 5–7.

Ketterlin-Geller, Leanne R. 2003. "Establishing a Validity Argument for Universally Designed Assessments." Unpublished doctoral dissertation. Eugene: University of Oregon.

Tindal, Gerald, and Douglas Marston. 1991. *Classroom-Based Assessment.* Columbus, OH: Charles Merrill.

Tufte, Edward R. 1983. *The Visual Display of Quantitative Information.* Cheshire, CT: Graphics Press.

U.S. Department of Education. 2002. *Strategies for Making Annual Yearly Progress—Using Curriculum-Based Measurement for Progress Monitoring.* Presented at the Student Achievement and School Accountability Conference, October. www.ed.gov/admins/lead/account/sasa conference02.html#handouts

Wainer, Howard. 1997. *Visual Revelations: Graphical Tales of Fate and Deception from Napoleon Bonaparte to Ross Perot.* New York: Copernicus.

19. ALLOCATING HUMAN, FINANCIAL, AND PHYSICAL RESOURCES

Allegretto, Sylvia A., Sean P. Corcoran, and Lawrence Mishel. 2004. *How Does Teacher Pay Compare?* Washington, DC: Economic Policy Institute.

Bauman, Paul. 1996. *Governing Education: Public Sector Reform or Privatization?* Needham Heights, MA: Allyn & Bacon.

Berner, Maureen M. 1993. "Building Conditions, Parental Involvement, and Student Achievement in the District of Columbia Public School System." *Urban Education* 28 (April): 11: 6–29.

Brent, Brian O., and Marie Cianca. 2003. "Should Principals Be Involved in School Renovations?" In *Saving America's School Infrastructure*, edited by Faith E. Crampton and David C. Thompson. 215–31. Research in Education Fiscal Policy and Practice: Local, National, and Global Perspectives Series, Vol. II. Greenwich, CT: Information Age Publishing.

Cash, Carol S. 1993. "Building Conditions and Student Achievement and Behavior." Unpublished doctoral dissertation. Blacksburg: Virginia Polytechnic Institute and State University.

Crampton, Faith E. 2004. "Components of an Ideal Budget Checklist." Milwaukee: University of Wisconsin.

Crampton, Faith E., David C. Thompson, and Janis M. Hagey. 2001. "Creating and Sustaining School Capacity in the Twenty-First Century: Funding a Physical Environment Conducive to Student Learning." *Journal of Education Finance* 27 (Fall): 633–52.

Crampton, Faith E., David C. Thompson, and Randall S. Vesely. 2004. "The Forgotten Side of School Finance Equity: The Role of School Infrastructure Funding in Student Success." *NASSP Bulletin* 88 (September): 12–28.

Crampton, Faith E., and Paul Bauman. 2000. "A New Challenge to Fiscal Equity: Educational Entrepreneurship and Its Implications for Schools, Districts, and States." *Educational Considerations* 28 (Fall): 53–61.

Darling-Hammond, Linda, and Jon Snyder. 2003. "Organizing Schools for Student and Teacher Learning: An Examination of Resource Allocation Choices in Reforming Schools." In *School Finance and Teacher Quality: Exploring the Connections*, edited by Margaret L. Plecki and David H. Monk. 179–206. Larchmont, NY: Eye on Education.

Dempsey, Van. 2003. "If We Don't Watch Where We're Going, We Might Not Like Where We Go: School Reform at the Turn of the Twenty-First Century." *Educational Considerations* 30 (Spring): 4–9.

Earthman, Glen I. 2000. *Planning Educational Facilities for the Next Century*. Reston, VA: Association of School Business Officials International.

Harter, Elizabeth A. 1999. "How Educational Expenditures Relate to Student Achievement: Insights from Texas Elementary Schools." *Journal of Education Finance* 24 (Winter): 281–302.

Hartman, William T. 1999. *School District Budgeting*. Latham, MD: Scarecrow Press.

Hines, Eric. 1996. "Building Condition and Student Achievement and Behavior." Unpublished doctoral dissertation. Blacksburg: Virginia Polytechnic Institute and State University.

Ingersoll, Richard. 2004. "Understanding the Problem of Teacher Quality in American Schools." *Education Statistics Quarterly* 1, 1. http://nces.ed.gov/programs/quarterly/vol_1/1_1/2-esq11-c.asp

King, Jennifer Rice. 2004. "A Best Fit Approach to Effective Teacher Policy." *Insights on Education Policy, Practice, and Research* 17 (September). www.sedl.org.

King, Richard A., Austin D. Swanson, and Scott R. Sweetland. 2003. *School Finance: Achieving High Standards With Equity and Efficiency*. Boston: Allyn & Bacon.

Land, Deborah, and Nettie Legters. 2002. "The Extent and Consequences of Risk in U.S. Education." In *Educating At-Risk Children, One Hundred-First Yearbook of the National Society for the Study of Education, Part II,* edited by Sam Stringfield and Deborah Land. 1–28. Chicago: University of Chicago Press.

Larsen, Merry, and Dave Loppnow. 2001. "Wisconsin." In *Public School Finance Programs of the United States and Canada: 1998–1999,* edited by Catherine C. Sielke, John Dayton, C. Thomas Holmes, and Anne Jefferson. Washington, DC: National Center for Education Statistics, Office of Educational Research and Improvement, U.S. Department of Education. http://nces.ed .gov/edfin/pdf/StFinance/Wisconsi.pdf.

Lewis, Morgan. 2001. *Facility Conditions and Student Test Performance in the Milwaukee Schools.* Scottsdale, AZ: Council of Educational Facilities Planners International.

Lugg, Catherine A., Katrina Buckley, William Firestone, and William Garner. 2001. "The Contextual Terrain Facing Educational Leaders." In *The Educational Leadership Challenge: Redefining Leadership for the 21st Century, One Hundred-First Yearbook of the National Society for the Study of Education, Part I,* edited by Joe Murphy. 20–41. Chicago: University of Chicago Press.

Molnar, Alex. 1996. *Giving Kids the Business: The Commercialization of America's Schools.* Boulder, CO: Westview Press.

No Child Left Behind Act of 2001, Pub. I, No. 107-110, 115 Stat. 1425 (2002). http://frwebgate.access .gpo.gov/cgi-bin/getdoc.cgi?dbname=107_cong_ public_laws&docid=f:publ110.107.pdf.

Nye, Barbara, Larry V. Hedges, and Spyros Konstantopoulos. 2000. "The Effects of Small Classes on Academic Achievement: The Results of the Tennessee Class Size Experiment." *American Educational Research Journal* 37 (Spring): 123–51.

Ray, John R., Walter G. Hack, and I. Carl Candoli. 2005. *School Business Administration: A Planning Approach.* 8th ed. Boston: Allyn & Bacon.

Schneider, Tod, Hill Walker, and Jeffrey Sprague. 2000. *Safe School Design: A Handbook for Educational Leaders.* Eugene: ERIC Clearinghouse on Educational Management, College of Education, University of Oregon.

Smith, Timothy, William Fowler, and Bernard Greene. 2003. *Effects of Energy Needs and Expenditures on U.S. Public Schools.* Washington, DC: U.S. Department of Education, National Center for Education Statistics. http://nces.ed.gov/pubs2003/2003018.pdf.

Smylie, Mark A., and Debra Miretzky. 2004. *Developing the Teacher Workforce. One Hundred-Third Yearbook of the National Society for the Study of Education. Part I.* Chicago: University of Chicago Press.

Spillane, James P., and Charles L. Thompson. 1997. "Reconstructing Conceptions of Local Capacity: The Local Education Agency's Capacity for Ambitious Instructional Reform." *Educational Evaluation and Policy Analysis* 19 (Summer): 185–203.

Strickland, Jessie Shields, and T. C. Chan. 2002. "Curbside Critique: A Technique to Maintain a Positive School Yard Image." *School Business Affairs* 68 (May): 24–27.

Szuba, Tom, and Roger Young. 2003. *Planning Guide for Maintaining School Facilities.* Washington, DC: Facilities Maintenance Task Force, National Center for Education Statistics, U.S. Department of Education.

Thompson, David C., and R. Craig Wood. 2001. *Money & Schools.* 2nd ed. Larchmont, NY: Eye on Education.

Tomsho, Robert. 2002. "Controversy Flares Over Public Funding of 'Cyber Schools.'" *Wall Street Journal,* April 5.

U.S. General Accounting Office. 2000. *Public Education: Commercial Activities in Schools.* Washington, DC: Author.

Wisconsin Department of Public Instruction. 2004a. "Student Activity Accounting." In *Wisconsin Uniform Financial Accounting Requirements*. Madison, WI: Author. www.dpi.state.wi .us/dpi/dfm/sfms/doc/stud_acct.doc.

———. 2004b. *Wisconsin Uniform Financial Accounting Requirements*. Madison, WI: Author. www.dpi.state.wi.us/dpi/dfm/sfms/pdf/wufar_final_rev3.pdf.

Wood, R. Craig, David C. Thompson, Lawrence O. Picus, and Don I. Tharpe. 1995. *Principles of School Business Management*. 2nd ed. Reston, VA: Association of School Business Officials International.

Zimmer, Ron, and others. 2001. *Private Giving to Public Schools and Districts in Los Angeles County: A Pilot Study*. Santa Monica, CA: RAND.

Index

CORWIN PRESS

The Corwin Press logo—a raven striding across an open book—represents the union of courage and learning. Corwin Press is committed to improving education for all learners by publishing books and other professional development resources for those serving the field of PreK–12 education. By providing practical, hands-on materials, Corwin Press continues to carry out the promise of its motto: **"Helping Educators Do Their Work Better."**